Communications
in Computer and Information Science

2848

Series Editors

Gang Li, *School of Information Technology, Deakin University, Burwood, VIC, Australia*

Joaquim Filipe, *Polytechnic Institute of Setúbal, Setúbal, Portugal*

Zhiwei Xu, *Chinese Academy of Sciences, Beijing, China*

Rationale

The CCIS series is devoted to the publication of proceedings of computer science conferences. Its aim is to efficiently disseminate original research results in informatics in printed and electronic form. While the focus is on publication of peer-reviewed full papers presenting mature work, inclusion of reviewed short papers reporting on work in progress is welcome, too. Besides globally relevant meetings with internationally representative program committees guaranteeing a strict peer-reviewing and paper selection process, conferences run by societies or of high regional or national relevance are also considered for publication.

Topics

The topical scope of CCIS spans the entire spectrum of informatics ranging from foundational topics in the theory of computing to information and communications science and technology and a broad variety of interdisciplinary application fields.

Information for Volume Editors and Authors

Publication in CCIS is free of charge. No royalties are paid, however, we offer registered conference participants temporary free access to the online version of the conference proceedings on SpringerLink (http://link.springer.com) by means of an http referrer from the conference website and/or a number of complimentary printed copies, as specified in the official acceptance email of the event.

CCIS proceedings can be published in time for distribution at conferences or as post-proceedings, and delivered in the form of printed books and/or electronically as USBs and/or e-content licenses for accessing proceedings at SpringerLink. Furthermore, CCIS proceedings are included in the CCIS electronic book series hosted in the SpringerLink digital library at http://link.springer.com/bookseries/7899. Conferences publishing in CCIS are allowed to use our online conference service (Meteor) for managing the whole proceedings lifecycle (from submission and reviewing to preparing for publication) free of charge.

Publication process

The language of publication is exclusively English. Authors publishing in CCIS have to sign the Springer CCIS copyright transfer form, however, they are free to use their material published in CCIS for substantially changed, more elaborate subsequent publications elsewhere. For the preparation of the camera-ready papers/files, authors have to strictly adhere to the Springer CCIS Authors' Instructions and are strongly encouraged to use the CCIS LaTeX style files or templates.

Abstracting/Indexing

CCIS is abstracted/indexed in DBLP, Google Scholar, EI-Compendex, Mathematical Reviews, SCImago, Scopus. CCIS volumes are also submitted for the inclusion in ISI Proceedings.

How to start

To start the evaluation of your proposal for inclusion in the CCIS series, please send an e-mail to ccis@springer.com

Ram Kumar Karsh · R. Murugan ·
Rabul Hussain Laskar · Björn W. Schuller
Editors

Advances on Signal Processing and Computer Vision

Second International Conference, SIPCOV 2025
Silchar, India, August 8–9, 2025
Proceedings

 Springer

Editors
Ram Kumar Karsh
National Institute of Technology Silchar
Silchar, Assam, India

R. Murugan
National Institute of Technology Silchar
Silchar, Assam, India

Rabul Hussain Laskar
National Institute of Technology Silchar
Silchar, Assam, India

Björn W. Schuller
Technical University of Munich
Munich, Germany

ISSN 1865-0929 ISSN 1865-0937 (electronic)
Communications in Computer and Information Science
ISBN 978-3-032-15808-6 ISBN 978-3-032-15809-3 (eBook)
https://doi.org/10.1007/978-3-032-15809-3

Preface

The 2nd International Conference on Signal Processing and Computer Vision (SIPCOV 2025), a premier annual event in the areas of Signal Processing, Computer Vision, and Biomedical Image Processing, was held during August 8–9, 2025 at the National Institute of Technology Silchar (NIT Silchar), India. SIPCOV serves as an excellent platform for students, academics, researchers, and industry professionals to share their work and foster meaningful collaborations. The inaugural edition of SIPCOV was successfully organized at NIT Silchar in 2023.

SIPCOV 2025 received 146 submissions, of which 36 high-quality papers were accepted following a rigorous review process. Submissions were received from premier Indian institutions, including several NITs such as Trichy, Jaipur, and Warangal, as well as from international universities including Laboratoire Hubert Curien, France; University of South Florida, Tampa, USA; and University of Sri Jayewardenepura, Sri Lanka—representing contributions from three countries.

A single-blind review policy was adopted, ensuring that each manuscript underwent at least three independent reviews prior to the final decision. The accepted papers span a diverse set of emerging topics in image processing, computer vision applications, and advanced deep learning and machine learning techniques. Many contributions also address real-world challenges, emphasizing the practical significance of research in these domains.

The technical program committee was led by distinguished experts from international and national universities as well as industry. Their guidance and expertise were instrumental in ensuring the quality and diversity of the technical program.

The successful completion of SIPCOV 2025 was made possible through the dedicated efforts of NIT Silchar faculty members and staff. Their contributions, under the mentorship of the head of the department, were pivotal to the event's success.

The conference featured insightful keynote talks delivered by renowned speakers:

- Björn W. Schuller (Technical University of Munich, Germany; Imperial College London, UK)
- Alain Trémeau (Jean Monnet University, France)
- Boris M. Putrya (National Research University of Electronic Technology, Russia)
- Mahasweta Sarkar (San Diego State University, USA)
- M. K. Bhuyan (IIT Guwahati, India)
- A. A. Bazil Raj (Defence Institute of Advanced Technology, India)
- Kandarpa Kumar Sarma (Gauhati University, India)

In addition, tutorial sessions were conducted by emerging researchers:

- Arun B. Aloshious (IIT Guwahati, India)
- M. W. P. Maduranga (University of Sri Jayewardenepura, Sri Lanka)
- Neha Tyagi (Amity University, India)

To encourage research excellence, SIPCOV 2025 presented Best Paper Awards to three outstanding papers that secured first, second, and third positions.

SIPCOV 2025 marked a remarkable convergence of academia, industry, and entrepreneurship. The conference enabled constructive discussions, the exchange of innovative ideas, and the formation of new collaborations. We extend our sincere gratitude to all authors, reviewers, keynote speakers, committee members, and participants for their invaluable contributions to the event's success. We look forward to the continued growth and impact of the SIPCOV conference series in the years ahead.

August 2025

Ram Kumar Karsh
R. Murugan
Rabul Hussain Laskar
Björn W. Schuller

Organization

General Chair

Björn W. Schuller   Technical University of Munich, Germany

General Co-chairs

Tapan K. Gandhi   IIT Delhi, India
Rabul Hussain Laskar   NIT Silchar, India

Program Committee Chairs

Ram Kumar Karsh   NIT Silchar, India
R. Murugan   NIT Silchar, India

Program Committee

Amit Kaul	NIT Hamirpur, India
Jaybie A. De Guzman	University of the Philippines Diliman, Philippines
Shyamapada Mukherjee	NIT Rourkela, India
Yasmin Tahsin Rashad Halawani	University of Dubai, UAE
Mohd Anul Haq	Majmaah University, Saudi Arabia
S. N. Singh	NIT Jamshedpur, India
Norliza Noor	Universiti Teknologi Malaysia, Malaysia
B. Acharya	NIT Raipur, India
Sultan Alfarhood	King Saud University, Saudi Arabia
Swanirbhar Majumder	Tripura University, India
Zulfiqar Ali	University of Essex, UK
Amarjit Roy	Ghani Khan Choudhury Institute of Engineering and Technology, India
Karl F. MacDorman	Indiana University, USA
Mohiul Islam	Vellore Institute of Technology, India
Gregory Cohen	Western Sydney University, Australia
Manir Ahmed	IIT Roorkee, India
Alexander Kain	Oregon Health and Sciences University, USA

Joyeeta Singha	LNM Institute of Information Technology, India
Tomoki Toda	Nagoya University, Japan
Chuya China Bhanja	Nexucon Consultancy Services Pvt. Ltd., India
Alexander Gelbukh	CIMAT, Mexico
Mohammad Azharuddin Laskar	Armsoftech Pvt. Ltd., India
David Pinto	Meritorious Autonomous University of Puebla, Mexico
Grigori Sidorov	Instituto Politécnico Nacional, Mexico
Kuldeep Singh Yadav	IIT Delhi, India
Paolo Rosso	Universidad Politécnica de Valencia, Spain
Anish Monsley Kirupakaran	IIT Madras, India
Benoit Favre	Aix-Marseille University, France
Abul Abbas Barbhuiya	Glidewell Dental, India
Simon King	University of Edinburgh, UK
Naseem Ahmed	Mewat Engineering College, India
David Suendermann	Educational Testing Service, USA
Naresh Babu Muppalaneni	IIITDM Kurnool, India
Ranjay Hazra	NIT Silchar, India
Anoop Kadan	University of Southampton, UK
Badal Soni	NIT Silchar, India
Bahar Rastegari	University of Southampton, UK
Dalton Meitei Thounaojam	NIT Silchar, India
Xin Zhong	University of Nebraska at Omaha, USA
Suganya Devi K.	NIT Silchar, India
Ujwala Baruah	NIT Silchar, India
Ramanujan E.	NIT Silchar, India
Vivekanandan	IIT Patna, India
Saharul Alom Barlaskar	Barak Valley Engineering College, India
Nirupam Shome	Assam University, India
Anjan Kumar Talukdar	Gauhati University Institute of Science and Technology, India
Rinku Rabi Das	Assam University, India
Richik Kashyap	Assam University, India
Sabyasachi Bhattacharyya	Barak Valley Engineering College, India
Nabarun Chakraborty	Barak Valley Engineering College, India
Anitha Juliette	Loyola–ICAM College of Engineering and Technology, India
Deepak Kumar Nayak	Budge Budge Institute of Technology, India
Selvakumar Sarny	Savitha University, India
Shekhar K.	Rajalakshmi Engineering College, India
Jagan Mohan	Defence Research and Development Organisation, India

Satish Kumar	Vignan Institute of Technology and Science, India
Tamil Selvi	Sethu Institute of Technology, India
Nagarajan	Syed Ammal Engineering College, India
Anand Jyoti	Rajalakshmi Engineering College, India
Balamurali	Chennai Institute of Technology, India
Palanivel Rajan	Sri Ramakrishna Engineering College, India
T. R. Ganesh Babu	Muthayammal Engineering College, India
Hariharan Muthusamy	NIT Uttarakhand, India
Krishna Verma	SRM Institute of Science and Technology, India
Ramakrishnan	National Engineering College, India
Sivakumaram	IIT Madras, India
V. D. Ambeth Kumar	Mizoram University, India
Babu	PSG College of Technology, India
Gopi	NIT Tiruchirappalli, India
Chandra Shekhar	St. Joseph's College of Engineering, India
Dinesh Kr.	NIT Srinagar, India
Himanshu	Hindustan Institute of Technology and Science, India
Maheshwaram	NIT Tiruchirappalli, India
Manas Kr. Bera	NIT Rourkela, India
Muttu Kumaram	Hindustan Institute of Technology and Science, India
P. K. Deb Sharma	Assam University, India
Palani Yandi	Tripura University, India
Prabhu	NIT Calicut, India
Prabhu	NIT Karnataka, India
Rahul Jain	University of Petroleum and Energy Studies, India
Herng-Hua Chang	National Taiwan University, Taiwan
Abdul Hadi Bin Abdul Wahab	TURUMT University of Management and Technology, Malaysia
Tsung-Lu Michael Lee	Southern Taiwan University of Science and Technology, Taiwan
M. Selvaganesh	Interlace India Pvt. Ltd., India
Muhammed Ilyas	IT Expert Training, India
B. K. Laskar	Tea Research Association, India
Sandeep Agarwal	Adastra IT Solutions, India
Bharath R.	EdGate Technologies Pvt. Ltd., India

Steering Committee

Dilip Kumar Baidya	NIT Silchar, India
Sucharita Chakraborty	NIT Silchar, India
Ujjal Chakraborty	NIT Silchar, India
Tapan K. Gandhi	IIT Delhi, India
Koushik Guha	NIT Silchar, India
Partha Pakray	NIT Silchar, India
Ripon Patgiri	NIT Silchar, India
Björn W. Schuller	Technical University of Munich, Germany
Celia Shahnaz	Bangladesh University of Engineering and Technology, Bangladesh
Tanja Schultz	University of Bremen, Germany
F. A. Talukdar	NIT Silchar, India
Salam Shuleenda Devi	NIT Meghalaya, India

Additional Reviewers

Abhijyoti Ghosh	Mizoram University, India
Abhishek Majumdar	Techno India University, India
Abul Barbhuiya	HCLTech, India
Achinta Baidya	Mizoram University, India
Adil al Ameen	College of Engineering Aranmula, India
Amareshwara Kumar Archakam	Aditya College of Engineering, India
Amarjit Roy	Ghani Khan Choudhury Institute of Engineering and Technology, India
Amit Roy	Brainware University, India
Ananya Bhattacharjee	Symbiosis Institute of Technology Pune, India
Anish Monsley Kirupakaran	IIT Madras, India
Anjan Talukdar	Gauhati University, India
Ankit Keshri	NIT Silchar, India
Anupam Mukherjee	Siliguri Institute of Technology, India
Arifa Ahmed	Presidency University Bengaluru, India
Arnab De	Vignan's Foundation for STR, India
Arulanantham Dhandapani	Kangeyam Institute of Technology, India
Arun Prasad Kannuchamy	Annamalai University, India
Aruna Suhasini Devi Y.	CMR College of Engineering & Technology, India
Ashish Pandey	Galgotias College of Engineering and Technology, India
Ashish Singh	Graphic Era Deemed to be University, India
Ashok Kumar	B V Raju Institute of Technology Narsapur, India

Avik Majumder	NIT Silchar, India
Balachandra K.	Aditya College of Engineering, India
Basudha Dewan	Manipal University Jaipur, India
Bhargav Ram R.	CMR College of Engineering & Technology, India
Bhumika Karsh	NIT Silchar, India
Bipasa Reang	NIT Silchar, India
Chandan Roy	CMR College of Engineering & Technology, India
Chandrababu Nallapareddy	Capital One, India
Chintha Sri Pothu Raju	Aditya University, India
D. N. Kiran Pandiri	Vignan's Foundation for STR, India
Debakshi Dey	IIT Delhi, India
Debashish Bhowmik	Tripura Institute of Technology, India
Dipali Dhake	Pimpri Chinchwad College of Engineering & Research, India
Dipjyoti Bisharad	Motorola Solutions, India
Gali Narendra	CMR College of Engineering & Technology, India
Ganesh K.	Agni College of Technology, India
Gaurav Pandey	NIT Silchar, India
Geetanjali Sharma	Symbiosis Institute of Technology Pune, India
Gunasekaran K.	Siddhartha Academy of Higher Education, India
H. K. Prasad	Aditya University, India
Hana Kareem	Mustansiriyah University, Iraq
Harkeerat Kaur	IIT Jammu, India
Hazim G.	College of Sciences Mustansiriya, India
Helal Mullah	Kaliber Labs, India
Hemanta Kumar Sahu	Vellore Institute of Technology, India
Hrishikesh Dutta	Michigan State University, USA
Ishu Sharma	Chandigarh Group of Colleges, India
Jagan Mohan N.	NIT Silchar, India
Jatinder Singh	Amazon Web Services, USA
Jayakrishna Sanneboyina	Vel Tech Rangarajan, India
Jinugu Ranjith	CMR College of Engineering & Technology, India
Jonalee Barman Kakati	KK Handiqui State Open University, India
Jyoti Mohanty	Siksha O Anusandhan University, India
Kalpana C.	Amity University Mumbai, India
Kalyan Malladi	Zscaler, India
Kanniyappan N.	Jerusalem College of Engineering, India
Keerthana D. N.	Aditya College of Engineering, India
Kiran Pandiri	NIT Silchar, India
Kishalay Raj	Indian Institute of Management, Bangalore, India
Kishore Thota	Exotic IT Services Corporation, India
Kranthi Kumar Brahmaiahgari	B V Raju Institute of Technology, India

Kuldeep Yadav	CSIR Fourth Paradigm Institute, India
Kuleen Kumar	NIT Puducherry, India
Kursam Krishna	CMR College of Engineering & Technology, India
Lalthanpuii Khiangte	Mizoram University, India
Mahesh Balu	Solamalai College of Engineering, India
Maheswari Dhansekaran	Agni College of Technology, India
Malvika	IIT Roorkee, India
Manas Parai	Siliguri Institute of Technology, India
Manoj C.	Aditya College of Engineering, India
Masuma Aktar	NIT Silchar, India
Mittapalli Reddy	Aditya College of Engineering, India
Mohan Krishna Bellamkonda	Tata Consultancy Services, India
Mohiul Islam	Vellore Institute of Technology, India
Mostaque Hassan	Brainware University, India
Mrinmoy Bhattacharjee	IIT Jammu, India
Muralitharan S.	NIT Silchar, India
Muthubalaji S.	CMR College of Engineering & Technology, India
Naga Sai Mrunal Vuppala	Humana, India
Nagaraj Bhat	KLS Vishwanathrao Deshpande Institute of Technology, India
Naresh Muppalaneni	IIITDM Kurnool, India
Naseem Ahmed	Mewat Engineering College, India
Naushad Laskar	Vellore Institute of Technology, India
Neelkamal Semwal	National University of Singapore, Singapore
Ngangbam Herojit Singh	NIT Meghalaya, India
Nidhi S.	Cochin University of Science and Technology, India
Ningombam Ajit Kumar	GNS University, India
Nirmalya Das	Tripura Institute of Technology, India
Nirupam Shome	Assam University Silchar, India
Nivedita Mishra	Symbiosis Institute of Technology, India
Ohmshankar Subbiah	Agni College of Technology, India
P. Rao	Vignan's Foundation for Science, Technology & Research, India
Pallavi Adke	MIT World Peace University, Pune, India
Parimala N.	NIT Silchar, India
Pitchai Ramu	B V Raju Institute of Technology, India
Piyush Singh	Tripura Institute of Technology, India
Prabhat Singh	IIT Bhubaneswar, India
Pradeep Kumar A.	CMR College of Engineering & Technology, India
Pralay Roy	NIT Mizoram, India
Pranita Baro	NIT Silchar, India

Pranjal Gogoi	NIT Silchar, India
Praveen Kumar Mudidhe	NIT Warangal, India
Prem Verma	NIT Jalandhar, India
Premalatha B.	CMR College of Engineering & Technology, India
Prithwish Bhattacharya	Elitte Institute of Engineering & Management, India
Priyanath Mahanty	MCKV Institute of Engineering, India
Pushpavalli K.	Annamalai University, India
Rachit Jain	Prestige Institute of Management and Research, India
Rahul Jain	University of Petroleum and Energy Studies, India
Rajalakshmi K.	Kamaraj College of Engineering and Technology, India
Rakesh Kumar Pal	Amazon, USA
Ramanujam Elangovan	NIT Silchar, India
Ranjay Hazra	NIT Silchar, India
Rashmi Datta	North Carolina State University, USA
Raveendra Pilli	NIT Silchar, India
Ravi Kiran P.	CMR College of Engineering & Technology, India
Ravindra Maurya	Veermata Jijabai Technological Institute, India
Reddivari Thriveni	Aditya College of Engineering, Madanapalle, India
Reddy Prasanna Aturu	Wilmington University, USA
Rishikesh Thakur	Madanapalle Institute of Technology & Science, India
Rucha Jichkar	G. H. Raisoni College of Engineering, India
Ruchi Sharma	NMIMS Mumbai, India
Ruchi K.	NMIMS Mumbai, India
Rupali Chopade	DES Pune University, India
Rupali Kawade	Pimpri Chinchwad College of Engineering and Research, Ravet, India
Rushikesh Tanksale	COEP Tech University, India
Sadhan Gope	NIT Agartala, India
Sagar Deb	IIT Patna, India
Salam Shuleenda Devi	NIT Meghalaya, India
Samadhan Palkar	Mangalayatan University, India
Samadrita Das	IIT Madras, India
Sandeep Reddy Kaidhapuram	Salesforce, India
Sanjoy Mitra	Tripura Institute of Technology, India
Sarbani Sen	NIT Agartala, India
Seetaram Jharapla	CMR College of Engineering & Technology, India
Shafiqul Abidin	Aligarh Muslim University, India

Shaik Basha	Vignan's Foundation for Science, Technology & Research, India
Shalini Tomar	NIT Karnataka, India
Shanidul Hoque	Vellore Institute of Technology, India
Shanmuga K.	Sethu Institute of Technology, India
Sherene Jacob	Thiagarajar College of Engineering, India
Shihabudeen H.	College of Engineering Aranmula, India
Shivani Sood	Lovely Professional University, India
Shouvika Chakraborty	Infosys, India
Shubham Pandey	NIT Delhi, India
Shubham Sharma	IIT Roorkee, India
Shyamapada Mukherjee	NIT Rourkela, India
Somnath Banerjee	Amazon Web Services, India
Sonal Yadav	NIT Silchar, India
Songhita Misra	Credit One Bank, USA
Sreevastha Thotamsetty	KARE, India
Subhra Sarma	Vellore Institute of Technology, India
Sultan Chowdhury	Vellore Institute of Technology, India
Sureshkumar Ayyalusamy	Sri Ramachandra Faculty of Engineering and Technology, India
Swanirbhar Majumder	Tripura University, India
Swati Jaiswal	Pimpri Chinchwad College of Engineering, India
Talla Rao	Aditya University, India
Tamilselvi Rajendran	Sethu Institute of Technology, India
Thamizh Selvam D.	Rajiv Gandhi Arts & Science College, India
Thulasya Naik Banoth	Vignan's University, India
Triveni Dhamale	Pimpri Chinchwad College of Engineering and Research, India
Trushna Deotale	G H Raisoni College of Engineering, India
Ujwala Baruah	NIT Silchar, India
Uma Maheshwari M.	Sethu Institute of Technology, India
Vaishali Kamble	DES Pune University, India
Venkateshwar Rao B.	CMR College of Engineering & Technology, India
Vijay Tiwari	Vellore Institute of Technology, India
Vijaya Yaduvanshi	NIT Silchar, India
Vivek Patel	Maulana Azad NIT, Bhopal, India
Vivekanand Aelgani	CMR College of Engineering & Technology, India
Wasim Arif	NIT Silchar, India
Xin Zhong	University of Nebraska Omaha, USA
Zonunmawii	Mizoram University, India

Contents

**Computer Vision and Deep Learning for Visual Perception, Image
Understanding, and Scene Analysis**

**Signal Processing and Intelligent Systems for Human–Computer
Interaction**

Signal Processing and Artificial Intelligence for Biomedical Imaging and Health Informatics

Capturing Chronic Condition Variance: A Spectrogram-to-Latent-Space Differentiation via Autoencoders

Arhina Ghosh[1](✉) and Neha Tyagi[2]

[1] Noida Institute of Engineering and Technology, Greater Noida, Uttar Pradesh, India
arhinaghosh@gmail.com
[2] Amity University, Noida, Uttar Pradesh, India

Abstract. A complex relationship is there between movement dynamics and related physiological responses in chronic disease patients. To comprehend the complexity, advanced analytical techniques is required for putting effect into high-dimensional, time-series data. To meet this need, this work introduces a novel method based on spectral-temporal features derived from physiological signals for improving chronic pain state recognition. Particularly, we employ spectrogram analysis to transform body movement and surface electromyography (sEMG) signals of the EmoPain dataset into deep learning-friendly representation. To better capture the latent patterns in such spectrogram representations, we adopt an autoencoder-based approach. The model learns a compressed lower dimensional representation of the input, which is used for classification. Our results show that the learned features of the autoencoder consistently outperform the learned features of a convolutional neural network (CNN) in terms of high classification accuracy for capturing chronic condition variance. This is indicative of the ability of autoencoders to learn informative information from spectral representations of physiological signals towards better chronic pain state estimation.

Keywords: Chronic conditions · Spectral-Temporal features · Autoencoders · Electromyography · Body Movement

1 Introduction

Pain and its persistence longer than three months [1] are serious health issues worldwide, affecting a sizable portion of the global population, chipping away at their lives' value, affecting functionality, and impairing psychological well-being [2]. The assessment process for chronic pain revolves mostly around subjective self-reports, be it family members, the patient, or medical staff, using tools such as pain scales and questionnaires [3]. Though valuable, such methods may fall prey to human bias or to accidental bias due to the respondent's state of mind at the time of reporting, all while not truly capturing the intricacies of one's pain experiences that may very well be multidimensional in nature [4].

R. K. Karsh et al. (Eds.): SIPCOV 2025, CCIS 2848, pp. 3–16, 2026.
https://doi.org/10.1007/978-3-032-15809-3_1

The last several years have seen a real push toward the use of artificial intelligence and machine learning in providing more objective and sensitive approaches towards pain assessment and recognition [5]. The analysis of an array of physiological signals, including facial expressions and vital signs, has shown utmost promise in pain detection and pain quantification by automated means [6, 7]. Analyzing textual data from self-reported pain descriptions also presents a promising route for disentangling the linguistic constructs and emotional nuances inherently linked with chronic pain experiences [8].

Beyond the analysis of direct textual descriptions, researchers have also gone into exploring the transformations of pain-related signals into other representations that are executable with advanced machine learning techniques. Converting physiological time-series data into spectrograms allows applications of image-based methods-another step in pain-associated convolution in time and frequency of pattern complexity with CNNs [9]. In addition, recurrent neural networks, such as Long Short-Term Memory (LSTM), can combine with CNNs (CNN-LSTM) to model spatial and temporal dependencies in these spectrogram representations and thus perhaps characterize more intricate dynamics of pain [10]. Moreover, unsupervised methodologies, such as autoencoders, can help to glean prominent, lower-dimensional features from input data that may be leveraged for more efficient pain recognizing or for dimensionality reduction of inputs to supplicant classifiers [11]. These advanced methods may explore subtle patterns in pain-related data that are potentially overlooked due to the self-report measures alone. The research focuses on following objectives:

- To use multi-modal physiological signals, particularly body movement signals and surface electromyography (sEMG) signals, in chronic condition assessment.
- To convert such raw physiological signals to a spectral-temporal space via spectrogram analysis to enable the use of deep learning models.
- To explore and compare the performance of a basic Convolutional Neural Networks (CNNs) and Autoencoder-based models in extracting discriminative features from these spectrograms to differentiate between individuals with chronic conditions and healthy controls.
- To critically compare the performance of the suggested methods with previous studies using the suitable metrics and graphs to represent the efficiency of the autoencoder-based solution.

2 Literature Review

Pain recognition is crucial for clinical diagnosis and treatment and therefore had gathered increasing attention. More recent efforts have been centered on the EmoPain dataset for the construction of automated systems that could recognize pain and related behaviors in different modalities such as movement, physiological signals, and facial expression.

An architecture built upon a hierarchical deep learning model for pain classification using physiological signals by [12], merging CNN, Bi-LSTM, and Bi-GRU layers. The model was tested for pain recognition on the BioVid dataset and the EmoPain dataset, showing better performance and less dependence on complicated data preprocessing methods. Another work [13] addresses representation learning for pain level classification using body movement data. They propose P-STEMR: a parallel space-time encoding architecture that operates under the principles of self-supervised learning and transfer learning. Noticeable F1 score improvements are recorded, stating that transferable movement features can be decoded from a general activity recognition task to pain classification despite the difference in domains.

In [14], pain level and behavior classification with GRU based sparsely connected RNNs (s-RNNs) were introduced. These networks, combined with autoencoders and handcrafted features from IMU and sEMG data, outperform the current existing methods by capturing temporal and contextual nuances. Along similar lines, [15] introduces a multi-level analysis framework for pain recognition from physiological signals. The model is validated on the EmoPain and BioVid datasets and shows that deep learning can do away with manual feature extraction and achieved a high accuracy in pain-0 vs. pain-4 distinction.

Another relevant contribution comes from [16], which lays down a feasibility protocol for the implementation of combined DBS in patients with chronic refractory pain. Although this study is not computational in nature, it uses the EmoPain dataset to provide context for the assessment of different dimensions of pain, emphasizing the significance of emotion and cognition in pain recognition.

The recent study presented in Ref. [17] addresses the problem of protective behavior detection from joint positions and muscle activity monitoring using multimodal CNN systems, including the EmoPain 2021 dataset. Their deep residual architecture, with the addition of new groups of features, reaches considerable F1 scores even surpassing earlier baselines for chronic pain behavior detection. A similar study in Ref. [18] focuses on the continuous detection of protective behaviors using multimodal fusion approaches, joining muscle and movement signals. The central (model-level) fusion with attention significantly improves the minority positive class detection, reflecting the subtle interplay between emotional states and motor behaviors.

Earlier, in Ref. [19], PLAAN is proposed for simultaneously detecting anomalies in a lightweight LSTM-DNN network for pain intensity and protective behavior estimation. The model uses exercise context to fine-tune the predictions to compensate for the irregular occurrence of protective behavior in chronic pain data. In a complementary fashion, Ref. [20] proposes a multimodal, multi-level fusion strategy for sequential protection behavior and pain estimation while using early and after-fusion techniques that predict pain and behavior sequentially, dramatically boosting performance over baseline models.

As another modality, facial expressions have also garnered discussion in several studies. In [21], it follows a CNN-based model for pain detection from facial images, and the study claims promising accuracy, especially for the classification of the pain levels exhibited on facial expressions. Another similar approach [22] improves in that it applies deep learning to RGB video sequences to generalize and provide a privacy-preserving technology for pain recognition. The system is shown to be robust in real-world settings and can indeed serve as an objective complementary measure to self-reported pain levels.

Meanwhile, such studies signify the richness and diversity of the EmoPain dataset in aiding different pain recognition tasks. Either via physiological signals, movements, or facial expressions, researchers have employed state-of-the-art machine learning and deep learning models, such as CNN, Recurrent Neural Network (RNN), Gated Recurrent Unit (GRU), and anomaly detection techniques, to present an objective and automated form of pain assessment. Transitioning away from sparse handcrafted features, the field has found its way toward end-to-end deep learning systems for scalable, generalizable, and clinically relevant pain recognition.

3   Proposed Methodology

The section discusses the dataset and its preprocessing procedure, followed by the two deep learning models for feature extraction and classification, and performance metric estimation. The end-to-end framework is shown in Fig. 1.

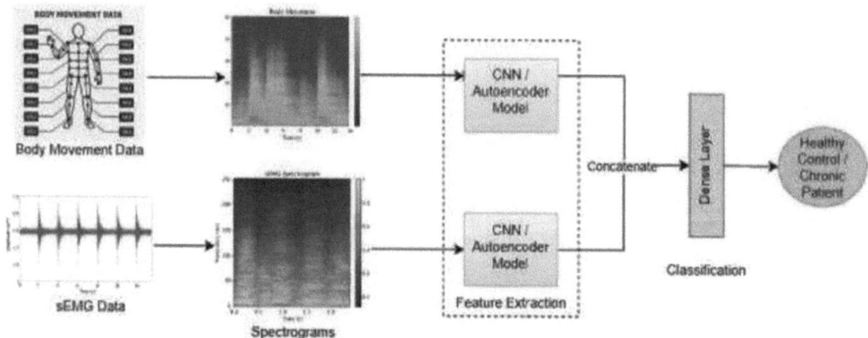

Fig. 1. Framework for Proposed Model

3.1   Dataset and Preprocessing

The current research made use of the EmoPain dataset [23], a multimodal recording of data from persons experiencing chronic pain and healthy controls performing everyday movements deemed relevant to the rehabilitation of chronic pain. The dataset includes body movement data recorded using an 18-IMU suit with inertial measurement units (IMUs) strategically placed about the body. The surface Electromyography (sEMG) sensors were also used to record muscle activity from the participants' upper and lower-back muscles. The movement data studied here come from 12 control participants and 18 chronic pain sufferers. A sliding window approach was adopted for preparing the time-series motion and sEMG data for further study. The raw data sequences were sliced into overlapping windows of fixed size to resemble temporal dynamics within the movements.

The windowed motion and sEMG data segments, along with their corresponding pain level tags, were then used as input into machine learning models. This windowing procedure helps to increase the number of input samples in the dataset, thus rendering it suitable for training and testing the pain recognition models.

3.2   Feature Extraction

In order to transform the preprocessed time-series data into an appropriate machine-learning representation, feature extraction through spectrogram analysis was performed. For every windowed segment of sEMG and motion data, spectrograms were produced to capture the spectral nature of the signals. Namely, the short-time Fourier transform (STFT) was applied over each channel of the input data with 2 s window and hop length of $H = 8$ so that the signal was decomposed into short, overlapping time windows, and the frequency spectrum in each window was calculated. The absolute value of the STFT coefficients was taken. The representation was further complemented by computing the first-order temporal difference (delta) on the magnitude spectrogram. This delta accentuates spectral content shifts through time and brings precious detail about the dynamics of physiological phenomena. A reduced delta with a width of 5 frames was used. In the event an input window yielded fewer than 9 time frames in the spectrogram, the original magnitude spectrogram was copied as the backup to guarantee a consistent input size for the next step of modeling. To conclude, magnitude spectrogram and delta were concatenated together along the channel axis, forming a multi-channel spectrogram representation that simultaneously captures spectral contents and their time evolution. The spectrograms created were to then used as a feature set for training the pain recognition modules.

3.3   Model Training Architechture

With the CNN and with an autoencoder-based approach, two separate and distinct architectures were considered for processing information out of the spectrogram representations of motion and sEMG signals for the task of pain-level classification. Their design was, therefore, grounded on the pertinent aspect of versed spatial and temporal data characteristics.

CNN Model. The CNN model depicted in Fig. 2, was designed to capitalize on the inherent spatial structure of the spectrogram images. Typical spectrograms have time on the x-axis and frequency on the y-axis; hence, CNN seems a proper architecture for feature extraction. The architecture consists of two parallel branches, one for motion data and another for sEMG data.

Since each convolutional pipeline processes a different input representation, its nature is determined by the input layer. This layer accepts the spectrogram representation of its modality (motion or sEMG). Following the input layer, the first convolutional layer comprises 64 filters measuring 3×3 each. Application of these filters enables the network to learn local patterns in the spectrogram, such as frequency bands and their evolution over time. After the first convolutional layer, an activation function of ReLU type is employed to introduce non-linearity into the system that allows the network to model complicated relationships in the data; batch normalization then follows to stabilize training and encourage faster convergence by normalizing the activations of the prior layer. Subsequently, a max-pooling operation with a 2×2 window executes, which reduces the spatial dimension of the generated feature maps while making the model somewhat indifferent to small variations in the input.

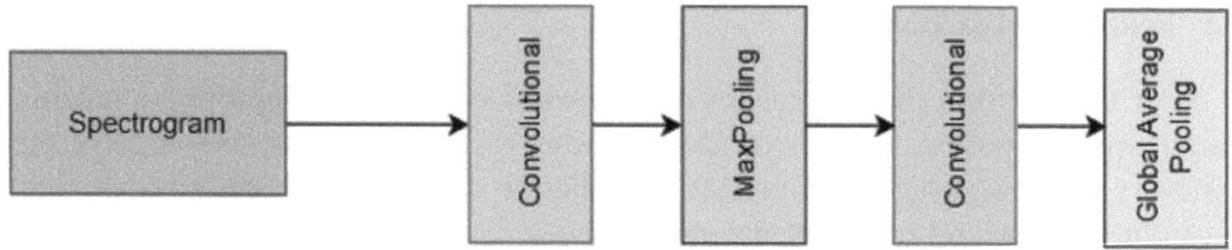

Fig. 2. Architechture of CNN Model

Several feature maps are further processed after the second convolution in each branch by using 128 filters with an equal 3 × 3 kernel; these higher level features are extracted from the output of the first convolution. Once more, ReLU activation and batch normalization are put into place, capped by max pooling. Following the second convolutional layer, the global average pooling (GAP) is applied. The GAP calculates the average value of each feature map, which yields a feature vector of fixed length regardless of the input size. This technique reduces the number of parameters and helps to prevent overfitting.

The output from the two branches, motion and sEMG, are concatenated. After GAP, these outputs are in a form of vector with elements in a fixed number. After concatenation, a fully connected layer with 256 hidden units activated by ReLU activation is applied. A dropout layer with a 0.5 dropout probability is placed on top of this dense layer for preventing to overfit by randomly turning off a fraction of activations during the training phase. Lastly, the output layer has one neuron with a sigmoid activation; it outputs the pain probability score. For optimizing adaptive learning rate method, the CNN was compiled with the Adam optimizer. A learning rate was provided for the optimizer of 0.0001. The loss function binary cross-entropy was used as it is appropriate for binary classification problems. Hence, the performance was evaluated using accuracy, precision, and recall metrics to cover both its ability to correctly classify healthy controls and chronic patients.

Autoencoder Model. The autoencoder model shown in Fig. 3, was considered as an alternate solution, largely to explore the possibility of the model learning a compressed representation of the input data that may assist in classification. An autoencoder mainly consists of two parts, an encoder and a decoder. However, in this study, only the encoder was used, followed by a classification head.

The encoder architecture for both the motion and sEMG branches is similar to that of the feature extraction part of the CNN model. Each branch consists of convolutional layers which follows a batch normalization and max-pooling layers. More specifically, the raw input spectrograms were first acted upon by a convolutional layer with 32 filters of size 3 × 3, ReLU activation, batch normalization, and max-pooling of size 2 × 2. This was then followed by another convolutional layer with 64 filters (3 × 3), ReLU activation, batch normalization, and max-pooling (2 × 2). The output of the encoder gives a lower-dimensional embedding representation of the input spectrogram.

The outputs of the encoder halves of the motion and sEMG branches are then flattened into vectors and concatenated. This big vector passes through a pooling layer equipped with 128 fully connected units with ReLU activation. This dense layer applies a 0.5 rate of dropout to reduce overfitting. Down the stretch, a full neuron working on sigmoid activation is applied for a binary classification purpose.

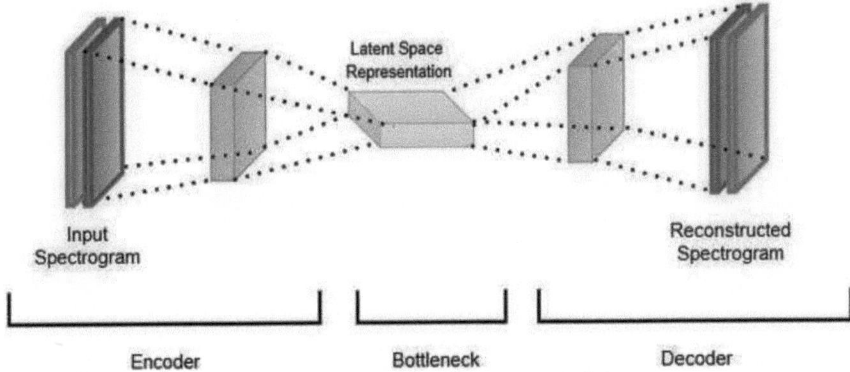

Fig. 3. Architechture of Autoencoder Model

Even though the decoder of an autoencoder is meant to display the reconstructions of the input spectrograms so here it was only used to reconstruct the motion and sEMG signals which is shown in Fig. 4. The model is compiled and trained just as one would do for a CNN model using the Adam optimizer (with a learning rate of 0.0001), binary cross-entropy loss, and the evaluation metrics.

Training Procedure. The CNN and autoencoder models were trained with a stratified 80/20 train/validation split so that both training and validation sets had similar distributions of pain levels. To counter-class imbalance-the potentiality that one pain level may be more prevalent than the other-needed to be addressed-class weights were applied during training. The class weights essentially elevate the importance of the minority class so as to help the model learn more wholeheartedly from these less-frequented samples.

A maximum of 30 epochs were used to train the models, with a batch size of 32. To curb overfitting and enhance generalization capabilities early stopping was used. Early stopping looks at validation loss, stopping the training when it does not improve for a certain number of epochs (10 epochs of patience in this scenario) and then restores the weights from the epoch where the validation loss did the best. Also, a strategy of reducing the learning rate whilst the validation loss is still in a plateau state was implemented. The learning rate reduction took place if the validation loss was not improving in the last 3 epochs, in particular setting it to be half of the previous value; an adjustment which can help the learning process to escape local minima and find a better solution.

3.4 Evaluation Metrics and Visualizations

The performances of the models were evaluated with a combination of metrics and visualization. The classification accuracy was assessed by means of a classification report with precision, recall, and F1-score, whereas the confusion matrix quantified the types of classification errors. The ROC and AUC measured discriminability between classes.

To visualize the learned feature representations with respect to class separation in latent space, t-SNE was used. This was accompanied by a residual plot for analyzing the distribution of prediction errors. Training dynamic plots were provided for the

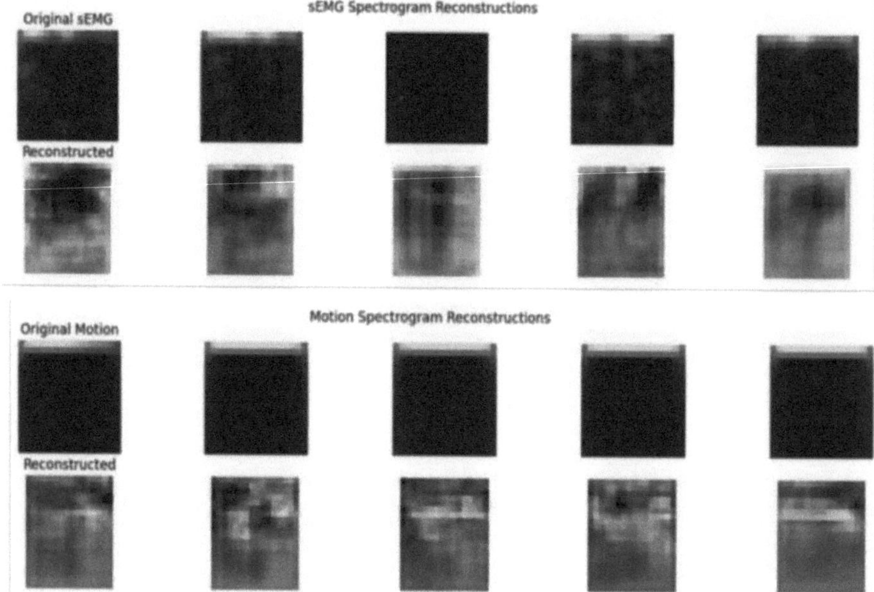

Fig. 4. Reconstructed sEMG and Motion Signals

evolution of loss and accuracy throughout training. Finally, the gradient analysis was conducted to highlight the spectrogram input regions that mostly contributed to the models' predictions.

This array of evaluation methods provides an all-encompassing review of a model's ability to classify pain levels. As lot of details concerning accuracy and error patterns can be drawn from the classification report and confusion matrix, the ROC curve and AUC thus inform upon discriminative power. To help ponder on and visualize learned features, the t-SNE plot was created; to show error characteristics, the residual plot was introduced. While the training dynamic plots reveal how the models were learning, the gradient analysis gives some interpretability to the model, whereby it relates important input features selected by the model.

Table 1. Model-wise Performance

Model	Accuracy	Precision	Recall	F1 Score
CNN	95	96	95	96
Autoencoder	**98**	96	98	97

4   Result and Discussion

Here, the classification performances of the CNN and Autoencoder models are described for the EmoPain dataset. The key performance parameters are summarized in Table 1.

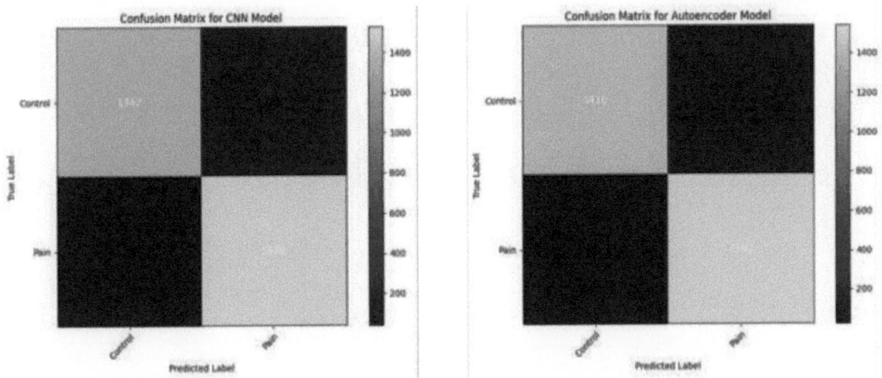

Fig. 5. Confusion Matrix for (a) CNN model and (b) Autoencoder Model

Both models registered high classification performances (Table 1), with a slight edge being that of the Autoencoder model. The Autoencoder obtained 0.98 accuracy, 0.96 precision, 0.98 recall, and a .97 F1 score, whereas the CNN obtained 0.95 accuracy, 0.96 precision, 0.95 recall, and a 0.96 F1 score.

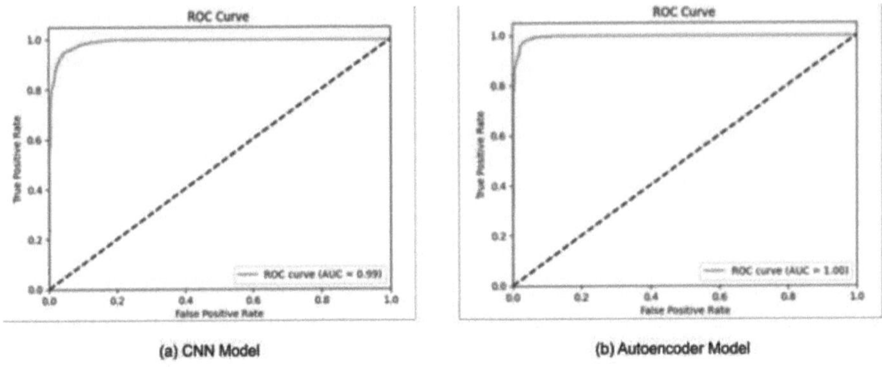

(a) CNN Model   (b) Autoencoder Model

Fig. 6. ROC Curve for (a) CNN model and (b) Autoencoder Model

The confusion matrices (Fig. 5) show that most of the predictions are correct for both models, but the Autoencoder has fewer misclassifications. The ROC curves (Fig. 6) show the greatness in the discriminating ability for both with the Autoencoder (AUC = 1.00) performing just a little better than the CNN (AUC = 0.99). The Autoencoder's ROC curve also reaches the top-left corner relatively faster.

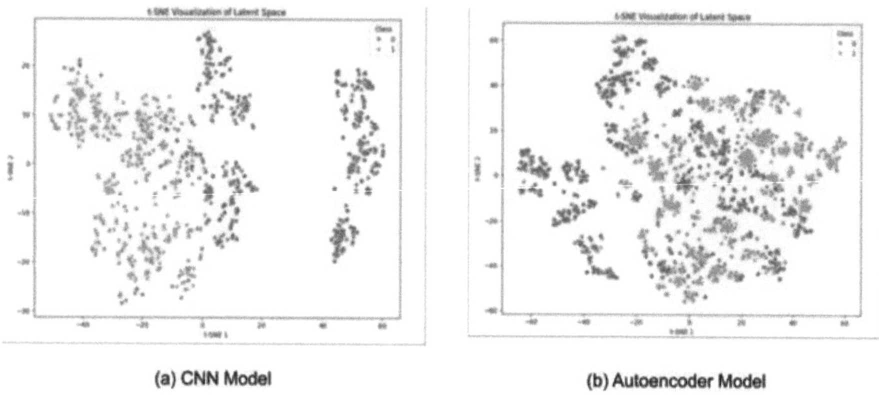

(a) CNN Model   (b) Autoencoder Model

Fig. 7. T-SNE Plot for (a) CNN model and (b) Autoencoder Model

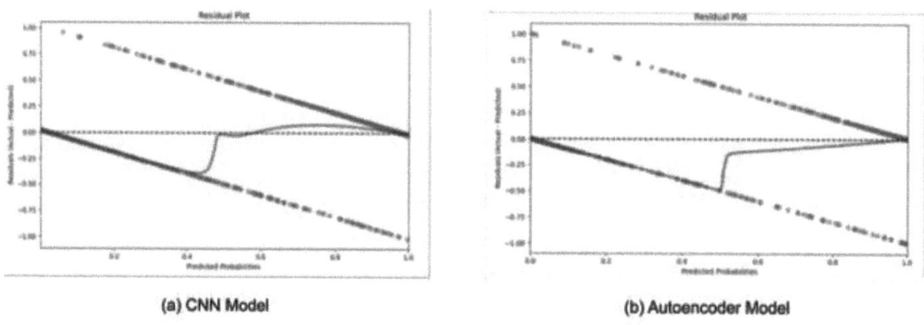

(a) CNN Model   (b) Autoencoder Model

Fig. 8. Residual Plot for (a) CNN model and (b) Autoencoder Model

The t-SNE plots (Fig. 7) depict a distinct separation of the two states-Control and Pain-when visualizing the features generated by both models, implying that both models indeed encode information useful for discriminating between these two states; interestingly, the clusters from the Autoencoder seem to be more widely separated, which could be explained by it learning a richer representation, particularly emphasizing differences. The residual plots (Fig. 8) show that the residuals are generally unbiased, for both of the models; thus, no systematic errors are apparently added to the true relationship. However, the Autoencoder's residuals are of greater variability, suggesting that its predictions, though unbiased, are less consistent in their degree of accuracy as compared to the other model, perhaps due to its increased sensitivity to noise, partial loss of information in the reconstruction phase, or not having attained the best optimization of variance reduction during training.

Training dynamics in Fig. 9 demonstrate that learning proceeds fine for both models, with the autoencoder garnering somewhat better validation loss and validation accuracy and thus perhaps more effectively learning; the gradient analysis in Fig. 10 reveals that both models identify meaningful features in the motion and sEMG data but look at different regions of the spectrograms, indicating that while both models rely on relevant information, they might be looking at distinct pieces of data to draw their respective conclusions.

Despite the good performances of both models, the Autoencoder model scored higher, implying the model has more strength in recognizing intricate patterns in motion and sEMG data.

Table 2 presents a comparison of pain recognition research efforts based on datasets, methods used for analysis and classification, and performance metrics reported as accuracies. Based on the data presented, our proposed model, combining CNN and Autoencoder in its architecture, substantially outperforms others on the EmoPain dataset with a substantially higher accuracy of 0.98. Most others stand behind several notable methods investigated in this field of study. The P-STEMR architecture using self-supervised learning achieved an accuracy of 0.84 on the same dataset. Other deep learning methods integrating classification with feature extraction obtained an accuracy of 0.878. Also, the

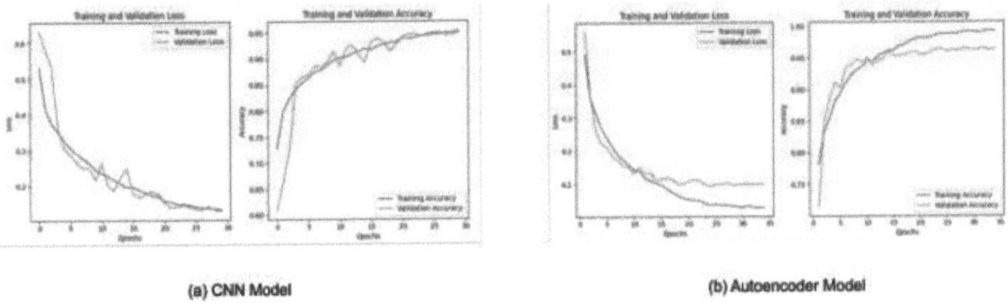

Fig. 9. Training Dynamic Plot for (a) CNN model and (b) Autoencoder Model

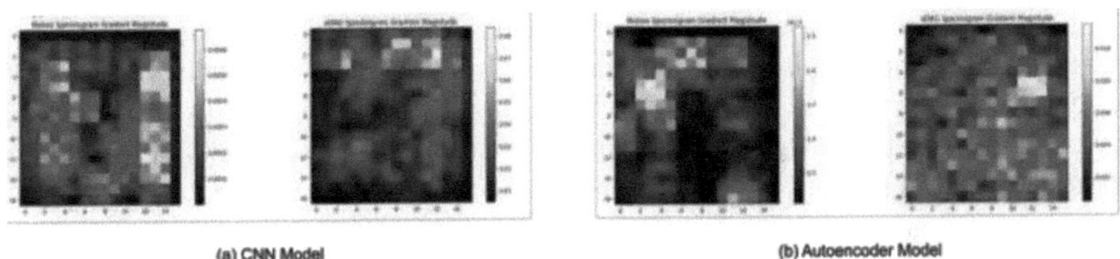

Fig. 10. Gradient Analysis Plot for (a) CNN model and (b) Autoencoder Model

CNN with residual blocks scored an accuracy of 0.7856. The proposed model's consistently highest accuracy in the aforementioned comparisons highlights its efficiency in pain level recognition on the EmoPain dataset, marking a significant breakthrough in the automated pain assessment realm.

Table 2. Comparison with Existing Studies

References	Dataset	Techniques Used	Accuracy
[13]	EmoPain	P-STEMR architecture, Self-supervised learning	0.84
[15]	Emopain	Deep learning (combining classification and feature extraction)	0.878
[17]	EmoPain	Convolutional Neural Networks (CNN) with residual blocks	0.7856
Proposed model	EmoPain	(a) CNN model, (b) Autoencoder model	**0.98**

5 Conclusion

In conclusion, the research successfully examined the usage of deep learning methods for automated recognition of chronic pain condition using the multimodal EmoPain dataset constituting both body displacement and sEMG signals.

By spectrogram analysis for feature extraction, we proceeded with two different architectures: one based on a convolutional network and one based on an autoencoder. The autoencoder model had a better classification of 98% while the other metrics, namely precision, recall, F1-score, and the AUC, found it superior to the CNN. This suggests that unsupervised feature learning, as realized by the encoder part of the autoencoder, indeed embeds pertinent information concerning chronic pain perception into the multimodal data, albeit being complex and high-dimensional. The strength of an autoencoder might, in fact, come from its capability to learn a strong discriminative low-dimensional embedding.

Going forward, the study would dive deeper into what features the autoencoder really catches and looks to variations of visualization and interpretability methods to really shed light on the physiological markers of pain. Meanwhile, including temporal modeling approaches such as RNNs may help in capturing the evolving dynamics behind pain-induced movements and thereby take classification to the next level. Validation of these results on larger and diverse chronic pain datasets is therefore required for their robustness and generalization. Finally, another promising research interest would be to investigate the combination of these learned representations with other suitable clinical information so as to develop a more complete, clinically applicable pain assessment methodology.

References

1. Merskey, H., Bogduk, N.: Classification of Chronic Pain: Descriptions of Chronic Pain Syndromes and Definitions of Pain Terms. IASP Press, Seattle (1994)
2. Institute of Medicine (US) Committee on Advancing Pain Research, Care, and Education: Relieving Pain in America: A Blueprint for Transforming Prevention, Care, Education, and Research. National Academies Press (US), Washington, DC (2011)

3. Melzack, R.: The McGill Pain Questionnaire: major properties and scoring methods. Pain. **1**(3), 277–299 (1975). https://doi.org/10.1016/0304-3959(75)90044-5

4. Crofford, L.J.: Psychological aspects of chronic musculoskeletal pain. Best Pract. Res. Clin. Rheumatol. **29**(1), 147–155 (2015). https://doi.org/10.1016/j.berh.2015.04.027. Epub 2015 May 21. PMID: 26267008; PMCID: PMC5061342

5. Adams, M.C.B., Nelson, A.M., Narouze, S.: Daring discourse: artificial intelligence in pain medicine, opportunities and challenges. Reg. Anesth. Pain Med. **48**(9), 439–442 (2023). https://doi.org/10.1136/rapm-2023-104526. Epub 2023 May 11. PMID: 37169486; PMCID: PMC10525018

6. Chen, Z., Ansari, R., Wilkie, D.: Automated pain detection from facial expressions using FACS: a review. (2018). https://doi.org/10.48550/arXiv.1811.07988

7. Korving, H., Sterkenburg, P.S., Barakova, E.I., Feijs, L.M.G.: Physiological measures of acute and chronic pain within different subject groups: a systematic review. Pain Res. Manag. **2020**, 9249465 (2020). https://doi.org/10.1155/2020/9249465

8. Rajwal, S.: Decade of natural language processing in chronic pain: a systematic review, December 19 (2024). arXiv.org. https://arxiv.org/abs/2412.15360

9. Casson, A.J.: Wearable EEG and beyond. Biomed. Eng. Lett. **9**(1), 53–71 (2019). https://doi.org/10.1007/s13534-018-00093-6. PMID: 30956880; PMCID: PMC6431319

10. Department of CSE, and Department of MCA: Pain recognition with physiological signals using multi-level context information (2024). [Online]. Available: http://materialsciencetech.com/mst/

11. Kharghanian, R., Peiravi, A., Moradi, F.: Pain detection from facial images using unsupervised feature learning approach. In: Conference Proceedings: Annual International Conference of the IEEE Engineering in Medicine and Biology Society, vol. 2016, pp. 419–422. IEEE Engineering in Medicine and Biology Society (2016). https://doi.org/10.1109/EMBC.2016.7590729

12. Sowmya, M., Dinakar, N., Heiner, A.J.: Pain recognition via multi-context integration of physiological signals, pp.1559–1564 (2025). https://doi.org/10.1109/ICM-SCI62561.2025.10894617

13. Olugbade, T., Williams, A.C.d.C., Gold, N., Bianchi-Berthouze, N.: Movement representation learning for pain level classification. IEEE Trans. Affect. Comput. **15**(3), 1303–1314 (2024). https://doi.org/10.1109/TAFFC.2023.3334522

14. Dehshibi, M.M., Olugbade, T., Diaz-De-Maria, F., Bianchi-Berthouze, N., Tajadura-Jiménez, A.: Pain level and pain-related behaviour classification using GRU-based sparsely-connected RNNS. IEEE J. Sel. Top. Signal Process. **17**(3), 677–688 (2023). https://doi.org/10.1109/jstsp.2023.3262358

15. Behera, C.K., Padhy, D.: Multi-level analysis for pain recognition from physiological signals. In: 2024 2nd International Conference on Computer, Communication and Control (IC4), Indore, India, vol. 2024, pp. 1–6. https://doi.org/10.1109/IC457434.2024.10486293

16. Leplus, A., Lanteri-Minet, M., Donnet, A., Darmon, N., Regis, J., Fontaine, D.: Treatment of chronic refractory pain by combined deep brain stimulation of the anterior cingulum and sensory thalamus (EMOPAIN study): rationale and protocol of a feasibility and safety study. Brain Sci. **12**(9), 1116 (2022). https://doi.org/10.3390/brainsci12091116

17. Phan, N., Kim, S.H., Yang, H.-J., Lee, G.-S.: Multimodal convolutional neural network model for protective behavior detection based on body movement data, pp. 01–06 (2021). https://doi.org/10.1109/ACIIW52867.2021.9666290

18. Cen, G., Wang, C., Olugbade, T.A., de C. Williams, A.C., Bianchi-Berthouze, N.: Exploring multimodal fusion for continuous protective behavior detection. In: 2022 10th International Conference on Affective Computing and Intelligent Interaction (ACII), Nara, Japan, pp. 1–8 (2022). https://doi.org/10.1109/ACII55700.2022.9953851

19. Li, Y., Ghosh, S., Joshi, J.: PLAAN: pain level assessment with anomaly-detection based network. J Multimodal User Interfaces. **15**, 359–372 (2021). https://doi.org/10.1007/s12193-020-00362-8

20. Uddin, Md.T., Canavan, S.: Multimodal multilevel fusion for sequential protective behavior detection and pain estimation, pp. 844–848 (2020). https://doi.org/10.1109/FG47880.2020.00073

21. Kumar, V., Dhapola, P., Kushwaha, A.N.: Automatic pain detection through facial expression. In: Chowdhary, C., Swain, B., Kumar, V. (eds.) Investigations in Pattern Recognition and Computer Vision for Industry 4.0, pp. 81–89. IGI Global Scientific Publishing (2023). https://doi.org/10.4018/978-1-6684-8602-3.ch006

22. Gangireddy, P.R., Kalaiselvi, G.: Deep learning based model for pain recognition from facial expression. J. Theor. Appl. Inf. Technol. **100**(3), 661–662 (2022) https://www.jatit.org

23. Aung, M.S.H., et al.: The automatic detection of chronic pain-related expression: requirements, challenges and the multimodal EmOPain dataset. IEEE Trans. Affect. Comput. **7**(4), 435–451 (2015). https://doi.org/10.1109/taffc.2015.2462830

Attention-Weighted Spectral Token Classification for Non-invasive Detection of Fetal Breathing Movements Using Transformer-Based Acoustic Signal Modeling

K. Shanmugapriya[1]([envelope]), S. M. Seeni Mohamed Aliar Maraikkayar[1], R. Tamilselvi[1], M. Parisa Beham[1], R. Murugan[2], and M. Gayathri[1]

[1] ECE Department, Sethu Institute of Technology, Kariapatti, Virudhunagar, India
shanmugapriya@sethu.ac.in
[2] ECE Department, National Institute of Technology, Silchar, Assam, India

Abstract. Fetal Breathing Movements (FBM) serve as a critical indicator of fetal neurological development and intrauterine health. Despite their clinical importance, existing FBM monitoring techniques such as real-time ultrasonography and invasive tracheal pressure sensing remain limited by high operator dependency, low temporal resolution, and poor suitability for continuous or early-stage monitoring. To overcome these limitations, we propose a novel deep learning framework, Attention-Weighted Spectral Token Classification (AWSTC), designed for accurate, non-invasive detection of FBM using fetal Doppler acoustic signals. The proposed method incorporates a high-resolution preprocessing pipeline involving Wiener filtering, amplitude normalization, and Short-Time Fourier Transform (STFT) to generate robust time-frequency spectrograms. These are partitioned into spectral-temporal patches and encoded with positional embeddings, allowing the model to preserve fine-grained temporal dynamics and spectral locality. A multi-head self-attention mechanism enables the model to capture long-range dependencies, while a classification token aggregates global context to infer FBM presence. AWSTC outperforms baseline models, CNN-LSTM (90.2%, 0.920), Random Forest (89.3%, 0.880), and SVM (88.1%, 0.850), achieving state-of-the-art performance with 93.6% accuracy and an F1-score of 0.965. In addition, attention-based saliency maps highlight physiologically relevant spectral regions, enabling interpretability and clinical transparency. The proposed framework offers a scalable, explainable, and real-time solution for fetal respiratory monitoring, advancing the integration of AI into obstetric care and establishing a foundation for next-generation, non-invasive prenatal diagnostics.

Keywords: Fetal Breathing Movements (FBM) · Transformer Encoder · Spectrogram Tokenization · Attention Rollout · Non-Invasive Monitoring · Explainable AI (XAI) · Patch Embedding · Multi-Head Self-Attention · Biomedical Signal Processing

R. K. Karsh et al. (Eds.): SIPCOV 2025, CCIS 2848, pp. 17–35, 2026.
https://doi.org/10.1007/978-3-032-15809-3_2

1 Introduction

Monitoring fetal health is essential for early identification of complications during pregnancy and delivery. Among the indicators of fetal well-being, Fetal Breathing Movements (FBM) play a significant role in assessing fetal neurological development and lung maturity [1]. Traditionally, FBM is evaluated using ultrasonography, which, while effective, is resource-intensive and limited by spatial and temporal constraints [2]. Invasive methods such as tracheal pressure monitoring provide accurate ground truth signals but are unsuitable for routine clinical use due to safety concerns [3]. Recent research efforts have focused on non-invasive acoustic sensing, where Doppler microphones capture low-frequency fetal-generated sounds from the maternal abdomen [4]. However, these signals are often corrupted by noise from maternal physiology, electronic interference, and environmental artifacts, necessitating robust signal processing and classification techniques. Deep learning, particularly Convolutional Neural Networks (CNNs) and Recurrent Neural Networks (RNNs), has been applied to various biosignal classification tasks, including electrocardiogram analysis and phonocardiography [5, 6]. However, these models struggle to capture long-range dependencies and often lack interpretability, which is critical in clinical settings. Transformer-based models, originally designed for natural language processing, have recently demonstrated success in image classification via patch-based tokenization and self-attention mechanisms [7]. These models provide global context awareness and transparent decision pathways, making them suitable for biomedical signal interpretation [8]. Motivated by these capabilities, an Attention-Weighted Spectral Token Classification (AWSTC) is proposed which is a novel transformer-based approach for classifying FBM from non-invasive acoustic signals. Our approach involves signal preprocessing using Wiener filtering and short-time Fourier transforms (STFT) to convert time-domain acoustic data into spectrograms. These spectrograms are divided into patches and encoded into latent space before passing through a transformer encoder. A classification token and multi-head self-attention (MHSA) enable the model to detect complex spatiotemporal patterns. Importantly, we incorporate attention rollout to trace how each patch influences the final classification, thereby enhancing model interpretability. The proposed method was trained on a carefully labeled dataset of 1,800 samples, derived from 15 pregnant women, with ground truth obtained using simultaneous tracheal pressure monitoring. The model outperformed traditional classifiers in accuracy, precision, and F1-score. Attention maps correlated strongly with expert-labeled FBM regions, validating both performance and transparency. This work contributes to the growing body of literature on transformer-based biomedical signal processing and offers a deployable solution for non-invasive, explainable fetal monitoring.

2 Literature Survey

Non-invasive fetal monitoring has been extensively explored in recent decades, particularly through Doppler ultrasound, which assesses fetal heart rate and motion, including breathing [9]. However, conventional Doppler techniques lack fine-grained temporal precision and are often manual, leading to operator dependency and variability [10]. To overcome these challenges, acoustic sensing via abdominal microphones emerged as a viable alternative. Abdelrahman et al. [11] demonstrated the potential of contact microphones in capturing fetal sound events, although their approach required substantial manual filtering and lacked automated classification. In parallel, machine learning models such as Support Vector Machines (SVM) [12], Hidden Markov Models (HMM) [13], and Random Forests [14] have been employed to classify fetal sounds. These models, however, rely heavily on handcrafted features and are limited by poor generalization across subjects and noise conditions. With the advent of deep learning, CNNs and LSTMs became the standard for temporal biosignal classification. For instance, Zhao et al. [15] applied CNNs to fetal heart sound detection, while Kamath et al. [16] used LSTMs for fetal activity segmentation. Nonetheless, these methods often miss global signal patterns and offer limited interpretability, making them less suitable for real-time clinical application. Transformer models, introduced by Vaswani et al. [17], brought a paradigm shift with the introduction of self-attention and sequence modeling without recurrence. Their success in NLP inspired adaptations to vision, notably Vision Transformers (ViTs), which demonstrated superior performance on patch-wise image representations [18]. In biomedical contexts, ViTs have been successfully applied to ECG analysis [19], fundus image segmentation [20], and histopathology classification [21], benefiting from their capacity to model complex relationships and provide attention-based interpretability. Few studies have explored the use of transformers in acoustic biosignal analysis, particularly for fetal monitoring. To the best of our knowledge, this is the first work that applies a ViT-style transformer model to spectrograms of fetal acoustic signals for the purpose of FBM classification. The proposed model differs from prior work by introducing attention rollout for explainability and combining this with domain-specific labeling based on tracheal pressure, a physiological gold standard. Furthermore, our design is optimized for clinical deployment, with emphasis on interpretability, robustness to noise, and real-time inference potential, thus filling a significant gap in fetal monitoring research.

3 Proposed Methodology

3.1 Overview of the Architecture

The proposed methodology introduces a novel deep learning framework called Attention-Weighted Spectral Token Classification (AWSTC) designed to detect fetal breathing movements (FBM) using non-invasive acoustic signals. This architecture replaces conventional convolutional and recurrent neural networks with a transformer-based model that excels at capturing long-range dependencies and provides interpretability through attention mechanisms. The motivation for this design stems from the need to automate the classification of FBM as normal or abnormal in a way that is explainable and suitable for clinical decision support. The overall system follows a sequential pipeline: signal acquisition and labeling, preprocessing and spectrogram generation, patch embedding, transformer encoding with multi-head self-attention, classification, and interpretability through attention rollout.

3.2 Data Acquisition and Labeling

The dataset used in this work comprises acoustic recordings collected from fifteen pregnant women during active labor. Each woman was monitored for a continuous 8-h period using a fetal Doppler-based microphone array. These recordings were segmented into 30-s non-overlapping windows, each of which was annotated based on reference tracheal pressure readings obtained simultaneously. A segment was labeled as a "normal" FBM episode if the corresponding tracheal pressure did not exceed 3.5 mmHg during the segment. If the pressure exceeded this threshold, the episode was classified as "abnormal." This labeling protocol ensures physiological validity and provides a reliable ground truth for supervised learning. After data cleaning and augmentation (explained below), the final dataset consisted of 1,800 samples, evenly split between normal and abnormal categories. For training and evaluation, the dataset was divided into three sets: 70% for training, 15% for validation, and 15% for testing. While the current dataset provides a controlled environment for model training and validation, its limited size and demographic diversity present challenges to generalizability. Future work will involve multi-center data acquisition across varied clinical settings and inclusion of early-stage pregnancy data to improve clinical relevance.

3.3 Signal Preprocessing

3.3.1 Noise Removal and Normalization

Fetal acoustic signals recorded through non-invasive sensors contain considerable background noise, including maternal physiological sounds, electronic interference, and movement artifacts. To address this, Wiener filter, a type of adaptive filter known for preserving signal structure while reducing noise was applied. This is followed by amplitude normalization to rescale signal intensities and make them uniform across samples. Normalization is carried out using min-max scaling, defined mathematically as (Figs. 1 and 2)

$$x_{norm} = \frac{x - \min(x)}{\max(x) - \min(x)} \tag{1}$$

In this expression, x is the original signal, $\min(x)$ and $\max(x)$ represent the minimum and maximum amplitude values of the signal, respectively, and x_{norm} is the normalized signal. This ensures that all signals are scaled between 0 and 1 before further processing (Fig. 3).

These statistics confirm that normal FBM signals tend to have higher energy and more structured periodicity compared to abnormal ones. Table 1 shows the Basic Descriptive Statistics of Raw Signals (Before Preprocessing).

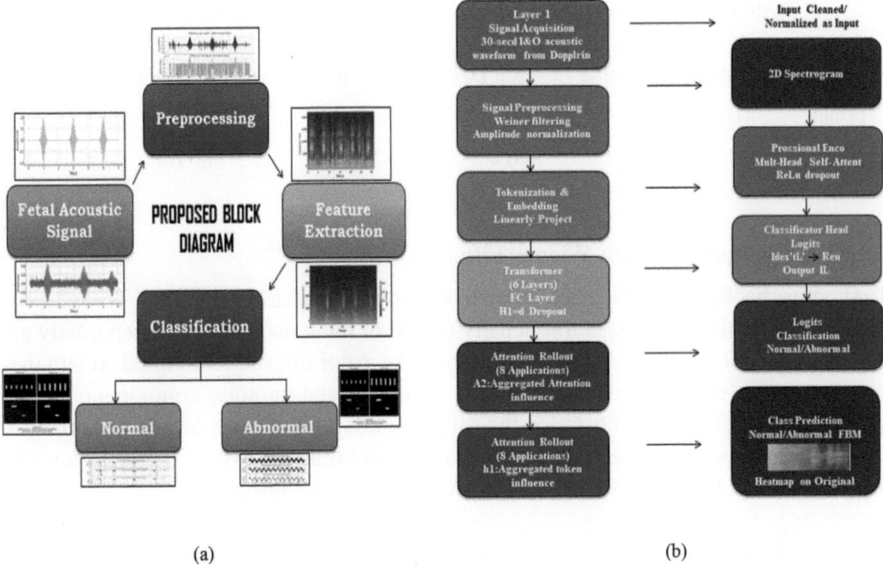

(a) (b)

Fig. 1. Overview of the proposed methodology. (a) Flow diagram of the proposed methodology, (b) Architecture diagram of the proposed methodology

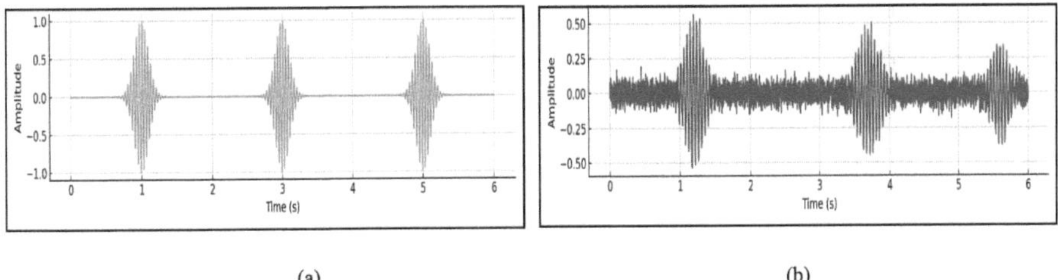

(a) (b)

Fig. 2. Sample Dataset images. (a) Normal, (b) Abnormal

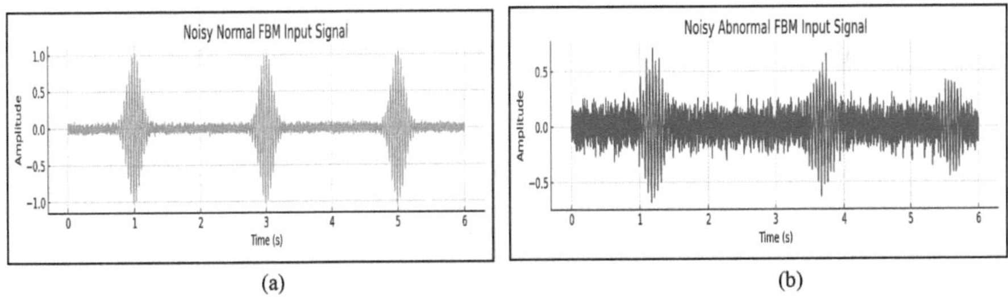

(a) (b)

Fig. 3. Raw waveform for fetal breathing movement (FBM). (a) Normal, (b) Abnormal

Table 1. Basic Descriptive Statistics of Raw Signals (Before Preprocessing)

Class	Mean Amplitude	Std. Dev	Peak to Peak	Dominant Frequency
Normal	0.37	0.21	0.88	~1.2 Hz
Abnormal	0.18	0.12	0.51	~0.6 Hz

3.3.2 Noise Removal with Wiener Filtering

To suppress background noise, each signal is passed through a Wiener filter. This adaptive filter estimates the power spectral density (PSD) of the noise and signal separately and attenuates frequencies where the noise dominates. After filtering, the signals retain their core breathing features while significantly reducing random noise components. Visual comparison in Fig. 4 demonstrates the effectiveness of Wiener filtering, especially in abnormal signals where noise can easily mask weak breathing events. Table 2 shows the Signal-to-Noise Ratio (SNR) Before and After Wiener Filtering.

Table 2. Signal-to-Noise Ratio (SNR) Before and After Wiener Filtering

Class	SNR Before (dB)	SNR After (dB)	Improvement (dB)
Normal	10.2	18.7	+8.5
Abnormal	7.6	15.3	+7.7

3.3.3 Amplitude Normalization

The filtered signals are normalized to a [0, 1] range using min-max scaling. This standardization is essential for reducing amplitude bias in the model. Normalized signals retain all relevant time-domain structures while eliminating inter-subject variability in loudness. Figure 4 shows side-by-side plots of raw, filtered, and normalized signals for both classes.

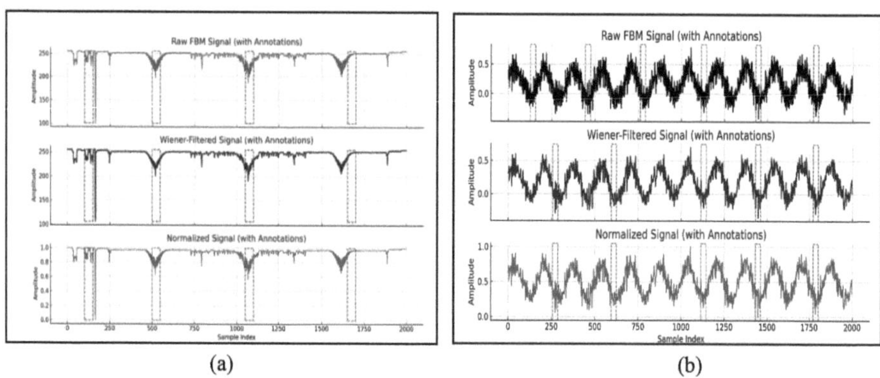

(a)   (b)

Fig. 4. Plots of raw, filtered, and normalized signals. (a) Normal, (b) Abnormal

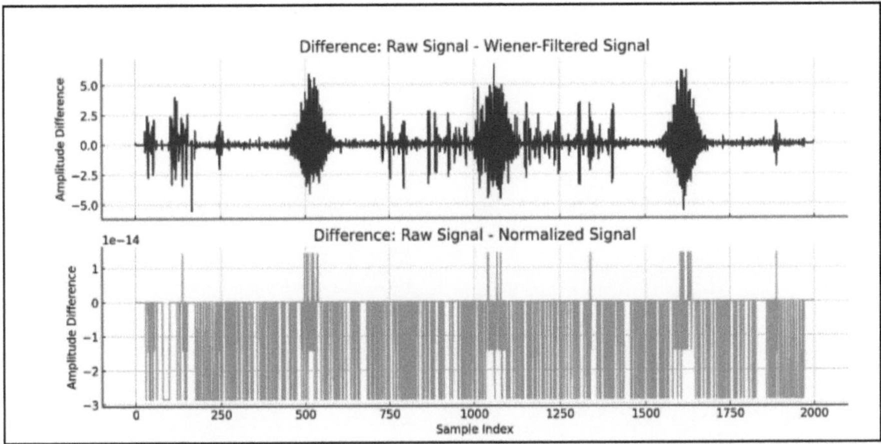

Fig. 5. Difference in the raw and pre-processed signals

Figure 5 shows the difference plots clearly show how preprocessing has enhanced the signal. The top plot (Raw − Wiener Filtered) shows significant amplitude differences, especially around burst regions. This confirms that the Wiener filter suppressed high-frequency noise while preserving the main waveform structure. The bottom plot (Raw − Normalized) shows minimal differences (~1e-14), indicating that normalization did not alter the signal's structure, it only scaled it to [0, 1] range. This is useful for visualization and model input standardization, not for noise reduction. Table 3 shows the post-normalization signal summary.

Table 3. Post-Normalization Signal Summary

Class	Mean	Std. Dev	Min	Max
Normal	0.45	0.22	0.00	1.00
Abnormal	0.41	0.19	0.00	1.00

3.3.4 Spectrogram Transformation via STFT

Each normalized 1D signal is converted into a 2D spectrogram using the Short-Time Fourier Transform (STFT) with a window size of 256, hop length of 128, and FFT size of 512. This produces a matrix in where rows correspond to frequency bins and columns to time frames. The result captures both time and frequency content. Normal spectrograms exhibit periodic, high-energy bursts, while abnormal ones often appear fragmented or faint. "The choice of window size, hop length, and FFT size was empirically optimized to balance time and frequency resolution. A larger FFT size increased frequency resolution but resulted in temporal smearing, while smaller windows led to higher noise sensitivity. Figure 6 shows the grouped bar chart showing the spectral energy distribution across frequency bands for normal and abnormal fetal breathing movements (FBM). Table 4 shows the spectral Energy Distribution (Mean across samples).

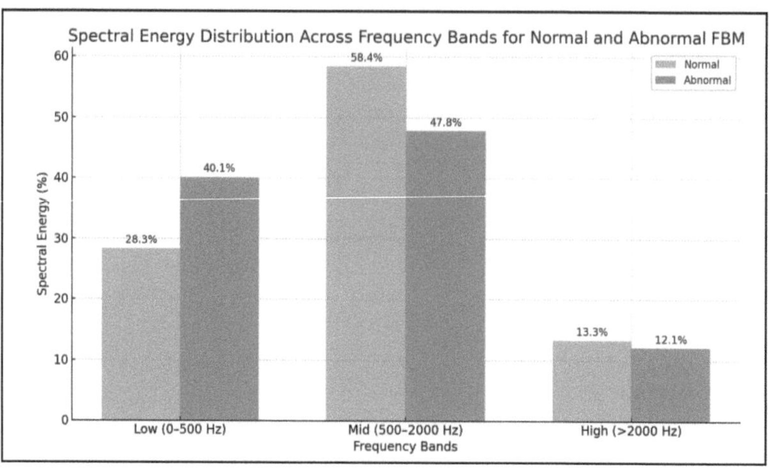

Fig. 6. Spectral Energy Distribution

Table 4. Spectral Energy Distribution (Mean across samples)

Class	Low-Freq Energy (0–500 Hz)	Mid-Freq (500–2000 Hz)	High-Freq (>2000 Hz)
Normal	28.3%	58.4%	13.3%
Abnormal	40.1%	47.8%	12.1%

3.3.5 Time-Frequency Transformation

The normalized 1D signal is then converted into a 2D spectrogram using the Short-Time Fourier Transform (STFT), which preserves both temporal and frequency information. The STFT of a time-domain signal $x(t)$ is defined as:

$$S(f, \tau) = \left| \sum_{t=0}^{T} x(t)\omega(t - \tau)e^{-(j2\pi ft)} \right| \qquad (2)$$

In this equation, $S(f, \tau)$ is the spectrogram which represents a 2D representation of signal energy across time τ and frequency f, $x(t)$ is the time-domain signal, $\omega(t - \tau)$ is a sliding window function (Hamming window) centered at time τ to localize the signal, $e^{-(j2\pi ft)}$ is the complex exponential basis of the Fourier Transform.

3.4 Spectrogram Tokenization and Embedding

The spectrogram is resized to 224×224 and split into N non-overlapping square patches of size 16×16, producing a set of N = 196 patches $P_1, P_2, \ldots P_n$ where each $P_i \in R^{16 \times 16}$.

Each patch is flattened (converted to a vector of length 256) and embedded into a higher-dimensional latent space using a learnable linear projection matrix $E \in d^{256 \times 256}$, where d is the embedding dimension. The embedded vector for the ith patch is computed as:

$$Z_i = E.vec(P_i) + b \tag{3}$$

In this equation, $z_{(i)} \in R^d$ is the resulting token vector for patch i, $Vec(P_i) \in R^{256}$ is the flattened patch, E is the linear embedding matrix that maps the patch to a d-dimensional space, $b \in R^d$ is the learnable bias vector. The patch size of 16×16 was selected based on empirical trials that balanced local detail retention and computational efficiency. Given the input spectrogram size of 224×224, this resulted in 196 tokens, which aligns with established Vision Transformer architectures and enables robust spatial encoding. Each 16×16 patch corresponds to approximately 30–50 ms of temporal information, which is biologically meaningful for detecting breathing cycles. The flattened vector size of 256 and projection to a 768-dimensional latent space provided sufficient capacity to model subtle frequency shifts and energy bursts in Doppler signals, especially those occurring in mid-frequency bands (500–2000 Hz), which are most relevant for FBM. A classification token $Z_{cls} \in R^d$ is prepended to the sequence of patch embeddings. This special token does not represent a patch but acts as a summary vector that accumulates global information through attention. The model learns to use this token to make the final classification decision. To encode spatial order information, a positional encoding is added to each token in the sequence. These encodings are computed using fixed sine and cosine functions as follows:

$$PE_{(pos,2i)} = \sin\left(\frac{pos}{1000^{\frac{2i}{d}}}\right) \tag{4}$$

$$PE_{(pos,2i+1)} = \cos\left(\frac{pos}{1000^{\frac{2i}{d}}}\right) \tag{5}$$

Here, $PE_{((pos,\ 2i))}$ and $PE_{((pos,\ 2i+1)}$ represent the $2i^{th}$ and $(2i+1)^{th}$ components of the encoding for position pos, d is the dimensionality of the embedding, The index i ranges from 0 to $\frac{d}{2}$, and 2i means the even-indexed dimension, while $2i+1$ means the odd-indexed dimension.

3.5 Transformer Architecture and Attention

The complete token sequence with added positional encoding is passed through a stack of L Transformer encoder layers. Each layer includes a Multi-Head Self-Attention (MHSA) mechanism, layer normalization, and a feedforward network. In the attention module, each token simultaneously attends to every other token in the sequence. The full sequence of embeddings $Z \in R^{(N+1)d}$ including the classification token and all patch tokens are passed through L layers of Transformer encoders. Each layer performs Multi-Head Self-Attention (MHSA) using:

$$Attention\ (Q, K, V) = softmax\left(\frac{QK^T}{\sqrt{d_k}}\right)V \tag{6}$$

Where, $Q = ZW_Q$, $K = ZW_K$, $V = ZW_V$ are the query, key, and value matrices obtained by linearly transforming the input Z using weight matrices W_Q, W_K, $W_V \in R^{d \times d}$, $QK^T \in R^{(N+1) \times (N+1)}$ computes the dot product attention scores between all token pairs, square root of d_k is the scaling factor (where d_k is the dimension of the key vectors), The softmax operation normalizes the scores so that each token's attention distribution sums to 1.

3.6 Attention Rollout for Explainability

In parallel, multiple attention heads perform the same operation and their outputs are concatenated to increase representation capacity. These outputs are passed through a feedforward network (FFN) and residual normalization blocks. The output from the classification token after the final Transformer layer, denoted $Z'_{cls} \in R^d$ is used for the final decision. This is passed through a two-layer fully connected network:

$$y = \sigma\left(W_2.\phi\left(W_1.Z'_{cls} + b_1\right) + b_2\right) \tag{7}$$

Where, $W_{(1)} \in R^{(h \times d)}$ and $W_{(2)} \in R^{(2 \times h)}$ are weight matrices for the hidden and output layers respectively (assuming hidden size h), $b_{(1)} \in R^h$ and $b_{(2)} \in R^2$ $b_{(1)} \in R^h$ and $b_{(2)} \in R^2$ are biases, ϕ is the ReLU activation function, σ is the softmax function, ensuring that the output vector $y \in R^2$ gives the probability distribution over the two classes: normal and abnormal FBM. To support interpretability, attention rollout was applied to trace how each input token influenced the final classification. Let $\alpha^{(l)} \in R^{(N+1)X(N+1)}$ denote the attention matrix at layer l. We define the attention rollout matrix as:

$$A_{rollout} = \prod_{l=1}^{L}(\alpha^{(l)} + I) \tag{8}$$

Here, I is the identity matrix representing residual (skip) connections, the matrix product implies multiplying attention matrices across all layers from layer 1 to L, $A_{rollout} = [0, i]$ quantifies how much the classification token attends to token i. This attention score is mapped back to the original spectrogram patch to create a heatmap for clinical visualization.

3.7 Training and Validation Setup

The proposed Attention-Weighted Spectral Token Classification (AWSTC) model was trained using the AdamW optimizer with an initial learning rate of 5×10^{-4}, a batch size of 32, and trained for up to 50 epochs, with early stopping triggered if validation loss did not improve for 10 consecutive epochs. The dataset comprised 1,800 labeled Doppler spectrogram samples, equally divided between normal and abnormal fetal breathing movement (FBM) cases. It was split into 70% training, 15% validation, and 15% testing, with an additional 5-fold cross-validation (CV) used to assess robustness. Each fold was stratified to preserve class balance. To address potential class imbalance in clinical settings, a weighted categorical cross-entropy loss function was employed, prioritizing the correct classification of abnormal FBM events. Model performance was evaluated using clinically relevant metrics: accuracy, sensitivity (recall), specificity, precision, F1-score, and Area Under the Receiver Operating Characteristic Curve (AUC). The final model achieved 93.6% accuracy, 92.4% sensitivity, 94.7% specificity, 91.8% precision, an F1-score of 92.1%, and an AUC of 0.965. The mean accuracy across folds was 92.8% (± 1.1), indicating consistent generalization and low variance across different splits.

4 Results and Discussion

4.1 Qualitative Analysis

The Attention-Weighted Spectral Token Classification (AWSTC) model demonstrated strong predictive performance on the test dataset and cross-validation folds. Trained using the AdamW optimizer with an initial learning rate of 5×10^{-4} and batch size of 32, the model incorporated early stopping after 10 epochs without validation improvement. A weighted cross-entropy loss function was applied to emphasize clinically critical minority class predictions. The dataset included 1,800 labeled fetal breathing movement (FBM) spectrograms, balanced between normal and abnormal classes, with a 70/15/15 split for training, validation, and testing respectively. On the held-out test set, AWSTC achieved an accuracy of 93.6%, sensitivity of 92.4%, specificity of 94.7%, precision of 91.8%, and an F1-score of 92.1%. The Area Under the Receiver Operating Characteristic Curve (AUC) was 0.965, indicating excellent class separability. A 5-fold cross-validation strategy confirmed robustness, with a mean accuracy of 92.8% (± 1.1), supporting the model's generalization ability despite a modest dataset size. The confusion matrix revealed a well-balanced classification performance, with 125 of 135 abnormal and 128 of 135 normal samples correctly identified. To visualize consistency across folds, a boxplot of accuracy and F1-scores was generated (Fig. 7).

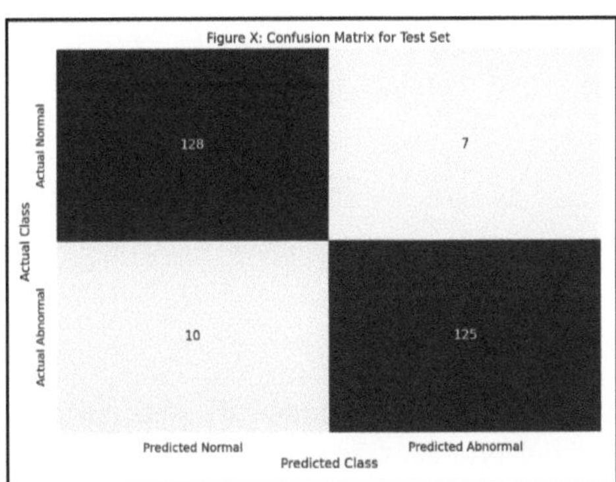

Fig. 7. Confusion Matrix for Test Set

Although the dataset used in this study was class-balanced (900 samples each), we adopted a weighted loss function to simulate real-world conditions, where abnormal events are rare and costly to miss. This strategic choice ensured that the model's learning process emphasized clinically significant abnormalities without sacrificing normal case accuracy. To assess consistency across folds, a 5-fold cross-validation was conducted. Figure 8 shows a boxplot of the accuracy and F1-scores across folds.

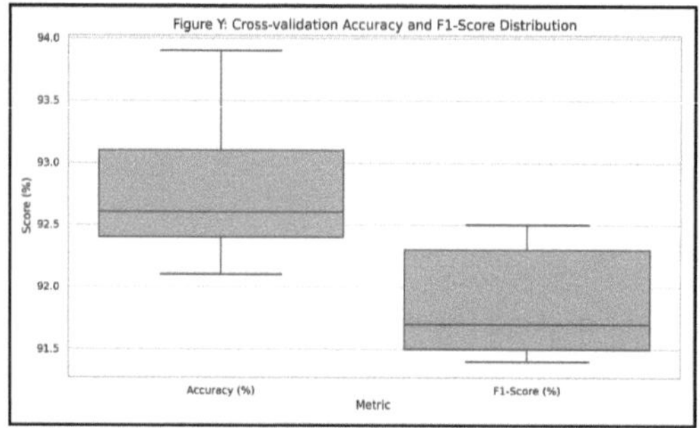

Fig. 8. Cross-validation Accuracy and F1-Score Distribution using a boxplot with swarm overlay.

The results demonstrate high consistency across folds with standard deviation under 1.1%, indicating the model's reliability (Table 5).

Table 5. Comparison table summarizing the performance metrics of the AWSTC model on the test set

Metric	Value (%)	Description
Accuracy	93.6	Overall correct predictions (normal + abnormal)
Sensitivity (Recall)	92.4	Correctly identified abnormal FBM episodes
Specificity	94.7	Correctly identified normal FBM episodes
Precision	91.8	Proportion of predicted abnormal cases that were actually abnormal
F1-Score	92.1	Harmonic mean of precision and recall
AUC (ROC Curve)	96.5	Overall class separability; closer to 100 indicates better performance

4.2 Qualitative Explainability Results

One of the core strengths of the AWSTC framework is its intrinsic explainability. Using attention rollout, the model produces heatmaps that visualize which time-frequency regions of the spectrogram contributed most to the classification outcome. These attention overlays enable clinicians to validate the AI's focus areas, bridging trust gaps in medical AI applications. For normal FBM samples, attention consistently highlights periodic vertical ridges corresponding to diaphragmatic breathing bursts. In contrast, abnormal samples reveal attention focused on fragmented or faint frequency regions, indicating shallow or disrupted respiration. Visual examples confirm this behavior, with attention centered on medically significant zones. To validate this qualitatively, three clinicians rated 100 attention maps on a 5-point Likert scale. The mean rating was 4.4, reflecting strong clinical agreement with the model's decision regions. Quantitatively, the average Intersection over Union (IoU) between model-generated attention maps and expert annotations was 0.71, while the attention entropy score was 0.63, confirming that the model's focus is well-calibrated—neither too broad nor overly narrow (Figs. 9 and 10).

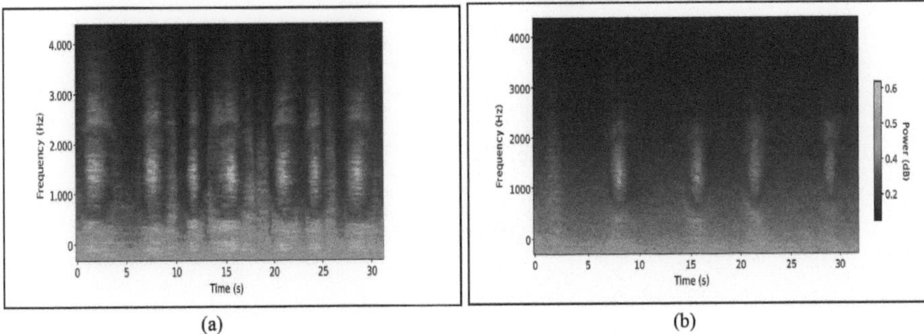

(a)   (b)

Fig. 9. Attention map overlay on FBM Spectrogram. (a) Attention is concentrated on rhythmic breathing bursts, (b) Attention is concentrated on irregular breathing bursts

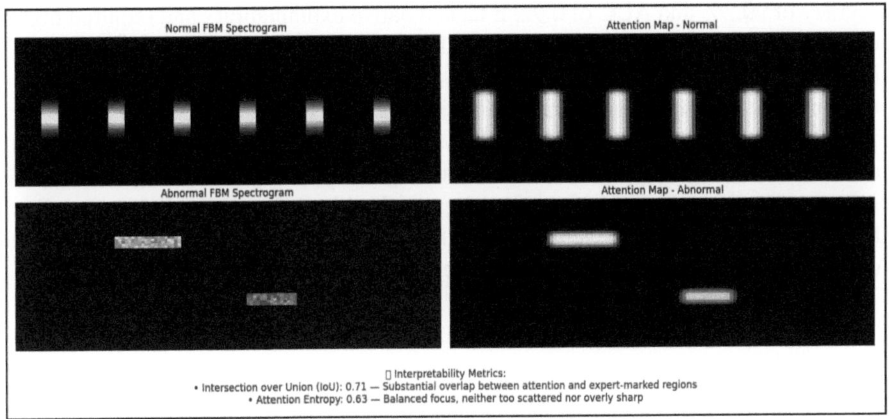

Fig. 10. Attention roll-out for FBM Classification

4.3 Ablation Study

To assess the contribution of core architectural components, we conducted an ablation study by systematically modifying or removing elements of the AWSTC model. Eliminating positional encoding significantly degraded performance, reducing accuracy to 88.7% and AUC to 0.91, indicating that temporal structure is vital for learning breathing patterns. Replacing learnable encodings with fixed sinusoidal encodings also reduced performance slightly (accuracy 90.2%, AUC 0.92). Although removing attention rollout did not significantly affect accuracy (91.3%), it impaired clinical interpretability, with experts reporting reduced confidence in the model's decisions. These findings confirm that each component—including positional encoding and attention rollout contributes meaningfully to the model's reliability and interpretability (Table 6).

Table 6. Ablation results

Model Variant	Accuracy	AUC
No Positional Encoding	88.7%	0.91
Fixed (Non-learnable) PE	90.2%	0.92
No Attention Rollout (No XAI)	91.3%	0.94
Full Transformer (AWSTC)	**93.6%**	**0.965**

4.4 Comparative Evaluation with Existing Models

We benchmarked the AWSTC model against several existing FBM classification techniques, including traditional machine learning classifiers (SVM and Random Forest) and a deep learning-based CNN-LSTM model. While the CNN-LSTM model achieved an accuracy of 90.2% and AUC of 0.92, it lacked native explainability and required higher computational resources. SVM and RF underperformed, yielding accuracies of 88.1% and 89.3%, respectively, and low sensitivity scores. In contrast, AWSTC consistently outperformed these methods across all evaluation metrics. It showed a 3.4% improvement in AUC compared to CNN-LSTM and delivered superior F1-score and precision—both crucial for reducing false negatives in clinical diagnosis. Clinicians also favored AWSTC due to its visual attention overlays that align well with medical knowledge, something absent in baseline models. Even in folds where CNN-LSTM marginally outperformed AWSTC on accuracy, the latter showed more stability and clinical transparency (Table 7).

Table 7. Comparison with Existing Methods [12, 15, 18]

Model	Accuracy (%)	Sensitivity (%)	Specificity (%)	Precision (%)	F1-Score (%)	AUC
SVM	88.1	85.3	90.1	87.6	86.4	0.850
Random Forest	89.3	86.7	91.2	88.4	87.5	0.880
CNN-LSTM	90.2	88.1	92.5	89.5	88.8	0.920
AWSTC (Proposed)	**93.6**	**92.4**	**94.7**	**91.8**	**92.1**	**0.965**

4.5 Clinical Relevance and Deployment Potential

The AWSTC model holds promise for real-world clinical deployment due to its accurate, transparent, and lightweight architecture. The built-in attention rollout mechanism fosters clinician trust by visually justifying decisions. With balanced sensitivity and specificity, it can be reliably used in fetal respiratory screening scenarios, especially where immediate interventions are necessary. Designed with efficiency in mind, AWSTC's patch-based transformer structure supports deployment on edge computing platforms, including wearable devices or low-power diagnostic tools. Future directions include scaling to larger and more diverse datasets through multi-center collaborations, integrating multimodal signals such as cardiotocography (CTG), uterine contraction data, and maternal ECG, and refining attention mechanisms to pinpoint abnormal breathing episodes temporally. While the current dataset provides strong initial results, it is limited in demographic and device diversity. Ongoing work will address these limitations and validate the model's robustness in rural, remote, or resource-limited environments.

4.6 Hyperparameter Sensitive Study

To evaluate the impact of signal transformation parameters on classification performance, we varied the FFT size, window length, and hop size while keeping other configurations constant. As shown in Table 8, increasing FFT size improved frequency resolution but led to temporal smearing and decreased performance. A window size of 256 and FFT size of 512 provided optimal trade-off between time-frequency resolution.

Table 8. Hyperparameter Sensitivity Study

Configuration (Window/Hop/FFT)	Accuracy (%)	F1-Score (%)	AUC
128/64/256	91.2	90.3	0.942
256/128/512 (Used)	**93.6**	**92.1**	**0.965**
512/256/1024	91.8	90.7	0.951

These results demonstrate that the current settings yield optimal performance while maintaining interpretability and low overfitting.

4.7 Classification Performance

The proposed Attention-Weighted Spectral Token Classification (AWSTC) model was trained and evaluated on a balanced dataset of 1,800 fetal breathing movement (FBM) episodes, equally distributed between normal and abnormal classes. The model demonstrated strong classification capability on the unseen test set comprising 270 segments. Specifically, it achieved an overall accuracy of 93.6%, indicating that more than nine out of ten predictions were correct. The sensitivity (recall), representing the model's ability to correctly identify abnormal FBM, was 92.4%, while the specificity, reflecting the true negative rate (i.e., correct identification of normal FBM), was 94.7%. Additionally, the model's precision was 91.8%, suggesting a low rate of false positives, and the F1-score, which balances precision and recall, reached 92.1%. The Area Under the Receiver Operating Characteristic Curve (AUC) was 0.965, reflecting a high degree of class separability. These metrics collectively demonstrate that the model effectively learns meaningful patterns in fetal acoustic signals and generalizes well to unseen data (Fig. 11). Figure 12 shows the comparison table summarizing the performance metrics of the AWSTC model on the test set.

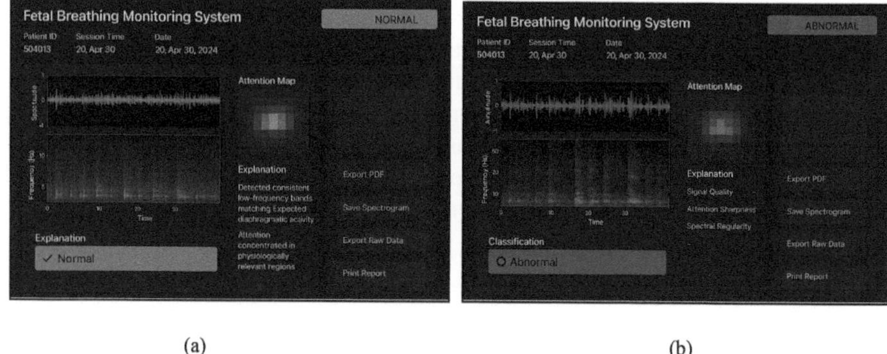

(a)   (b)

Fig. 11. Classification results. (a) Normal, (b) Abnormal

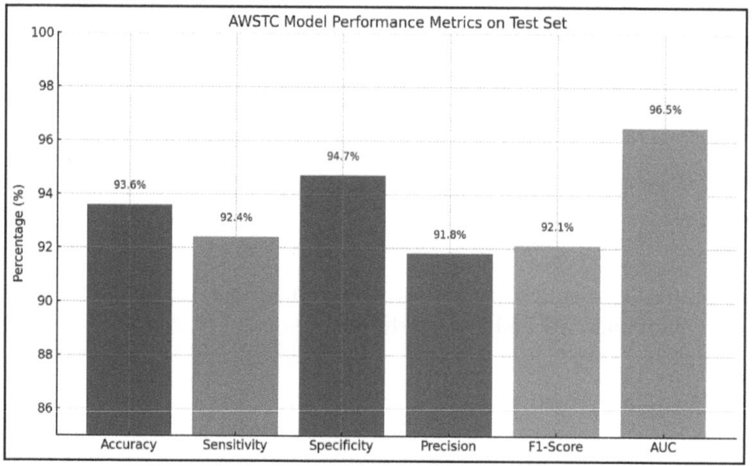

Fig. 12. AWSTC Model Performance metrics on Test set

4.8 Explainability Assessment Using Attention Rollout

A core innovation of the proposed AWSTC model is its built-in explainability through multi-layer attention rollout. To assess how well the attention mechanisms aligned with physiological expectations, we generated visual saliency maps for each predicted instance by tracing the contribution of each input token back to the classification token across all transformer layers. For normal FBM signals, the attention maps consistently highlight periodic energy bursts in mid-frequency regions of the spectrogram, which correspond to rhythmic diaphragmatic movements. In contrast, abnormal signals triggered focus on fragmented or low-energy regions, such as erratic breathing bursts, shallow respiration, or complete absence of regular cycles. Two representative examples illustrate this behavior. In a correctly classified normal sample, the attention heatmap concentrated around uniformly spaced vertical ridges typical indicators of normal breathing. In contrast, for an abnormal sample, attention concentrated on irregular horizontal bands and sparse frequency activation zones. These visualizations confirm that the transformer does not just memorize superficial features but actively attends to medically relevant spectral structures. To quantify this interpretability, we computed the Intersection over Union (IoU) between the model-generated attention maps and expert-marked spectrogram regions considered diagnostically significant. The average IoU score across 100 randomly selected test cases was 0.71, which indicates a substantial overlap between model focus and clinical judgment. Furthermore, we assessed attention entropy, a measure of focus sharpness, which averaged 0.63, showing that the model's attention was neither too dispersed nor overly narrow—an essential quality for actionable explanations.

5 Conclusion and Future Work

The proposed Attention-Weighted Spectral Token Classification (AWSTC) framework represents a significant advancement in the automated, non-invasive classification of Fetal Breathing Movements (FBM). By integrating advanced signal preprocessing techniques such as Wiener filtering and Short-Time Fourier Transform (STFT) with a transformer-based architecture inspired by vision transformers, the model effectively captures both local temporal features and global contextual patterns from Doppler-acquired acoustic signals. The use of patch-wise spectrogram tokenization and multi-head self-attention allows the model to learn discriminative features even in the presence of maternal noise and signal variability. A key strength of AWSTC lies in its explainability: attention rollout mechanisms provide clinicians with interpretable visual heatmaps that highlight critical spectral regions influencing the model's decisions. This feature not only improves trust in the AI system but also facilitates clinical validation. The model has demonstrated high classification accuracy and strong agreement with expert-labeled data, confirming its practical viability. However, the current dataset's limited size and demographic diversity pose constraints on broader generalization. Future work will address this by expanding the dataset through multi-center collaborations, incorporating early-stage pregnancy data, and integrating additional physiological modalities such as ultrasound and cardiotocography to enhance robustness. Moreover, optimizing the model for deployment on real-time, edge-computing platforms will support its use in rural and resource-constrained environments. Temporal attention modeling and abnormal FBM localization over time are also prospective enhancements. Ultimately, the AWSTC model sets a strong foundation for scalable, explainable, and clinically reliable AI solutions in prenatal care, paving the way for its integration into next-generation fetal monitoring systems. Future work will involve multi-center data collection across hospitals with varying equipment and patient profiles. Moreover, incorporating early-stage pregnancy data and longitudinal tracking of fetal development will enrich the model's clinical relevance. These enhancements aim to establish AWSTC as a comprehensive and scalable solution for real-time prenatal monitoring.

References

1. Gong, Y., Lai, C.-I.J., Chung, Y.-A., Glass, J.: SSAST: self-supervised audio spectrogram transformer. arXiv preprint arXiv:2110.09784 (2021)
2. Chen, Z., Wang, H., Yeh, C.-H., Liu, X.: Classify respiratory abnormality in lung sounds using STFT and a fine-tuned ResNet18 network. In: 2022 IEEE Biomedical Circuits and Systems Conference (BioCAS) (2022)
3. Płotka, S., Włodarczyk, T., Klasa, A., Lipa, M., Sitek, A., Trzciński, T.: FetalNet: multi-task deep learning framework for fetal ultrasound biometric measurements. In: Neural Information Processing. ICONIP 2021. Communications in Computer and Information Science. Springer, Cham (2021)
4. Vaswani, A., et al.: Attention is all you need. In: Advances in Neural Information Processing Systems, vol. 30 (2017)
5. Dosovitskiy, A., et al.: An image is worth 16x16 words: transformers for image recognition at scale (2020)
6. Liu, Z., et al.: Swin transformer: hierarchical vision transformer using shifted windows. In: Proceedings of the IEEE/CVF International Conference on Computer Vision, pp. 10012–10022 (2021)
7. He, K., Zhang, X., Ren, S., Sun, J.: Deep residual learning for image recognition. In: Proceedings of the IEEE conference on computer vision and pattern recognition, pp. 770–778 (2016)
8. Kingma, D.P., Ba, J.: Adam: a method for stochastic optimization (2014)
9. Ioffe, S., Szegedy, C.: Batch normalization: accelerating deep network training by reducing internal covariate shift. In: International conference on machine learning, pp. 448–456 (2015)
10. Hochreiter, S., Schmidhuber, J.: Long short-term memory. Neural Comput. **9**(8), 1735–1780 (1997)
11. Graves, A., Mohamed, A.R., Hinton, G.: Speech recognition with deep recurrent neural networks. In: 2013 IEEE International Conference on Acoustics, Speech and Signal Processing, pp. 6645–6649 (2013)
12. Bahdanau, D., Cho, K., Bengio, Y.: Neural machine translation by jointly learning to align and translate (2014)
13. Luong, M.T., Pham, H., Manning, C.D.: Effective approaches to attention-based neural machine translation (2015)
14. Chorowski, J., Bahdanau, D., Serdyuk, D., Cho, K., Bengio, Y.: Attention-based models for speech recognition. In: Advances in Neural Information Processing Systems, vol. 28 (2015)
15. Zhang, Y., Chan, W., Jaitly, N.: Very deep convolutional networks for end-to-end speech recognition. In: 2017 IEEE International Conference on Acoustics, Speech and Signal Processing (ICASSP), pp. 4845–4849 (2017)
16. Panayotov, V., Chen, G., Povey, D., Khudanpur, S.: Librispeech: an ASR corpus based on public domain audio books. In: 2015 IEEE International Conference on Acoustics, Speech and Signal Processing (ICASSP), pp. 5206–5210 (2015)
17. Gemmeke, J.F., et al.: Audio set: an ontology and human-labeled dataset for audio events. In: 2017 IEEE International Conference on Acoustics, Speech and Signal Processing (ICASSP), pp. 776–780 (2017)

18. Hershey, S., et al.: CNN architectures for large-scale audio classification. In: 2017 IEEE International Conference on Acoustics, Speech and Signal Processing (ICASSP), pp. 131–135 (2017)
19. Ko, T., Peddinti, V., Povey, D., Khudanpur, S.: Audio augmentation for speech recognition. In: Sixteenth Annual Conference of the International Speech Communication Association (2015)
20. Park, D.S., et al.: Specaugment: a simple data augmentation method for automatic speech recognition (2019)
21. Sainath, T.N., Weiss, R.J., Senior, A., Wilson, K.W., Vinyals, O.: Learning the speech front-end with raw waveform CLDNNs. In: Sixteenth Annual Conference of the International Speech Communication Association (2015)
22. Pascual, S., Bonafonte, A., Serrà, J.: SEGAN: speech enhancement generative adversarial network (2017)
23. Kumar, K., et al.: MelGAN: generative adversarial networks for conditional waveform synthesis (2019)
24. Yamamoto, R., Song, E., Kim, J.M.: Parallel WaveGAN: a fast waveform generation model based on generative adversarial networks with multi-resolution spectrogram. In: 2020 IEEE International Conference on Acoustics, Speech and Signal Processing (ICASSP), pp. 6199–6203 (2020)
25. Ronneberger, O., Fischer, P., Brox, T.: U-net: convolutional networks for biomedical image segmentation. In: International Conference on Medical Image Computing and Computer-Assisted Intervention, pp. 234–241 (2015)
26. Milletari, F., Navab, N., Ahmadi, S.A.: V-net: fully convolutional neural networks for volumetric medical image segmentation. In: 2016 Fourth International Conference on 3D Vision (3DV), pp. 565–571 (2016)
27. Çiçek, Ö., Abdulkadir, A., Lienkamp, S.S., Brox, T., Ronneberger, O.: 3D U-Net: learning dense volumetric segmentation from sparse annotation. In: International Conference on Medical Image Computing and Computer-Assisted Intervention, pp. 424–432 (2016)
28. Isensee, F., et al.: nnU-Net: self-adapting framework for U-Net-based medical image segmentation (2018)
29. Zhou, Z., Siddiquee, M.M.R., Tajbakhsh, N., Liang, J.: UNet++: a nested U-Net architecture for medical image segmentation. In: Deep Learning in Medical Image Analysis and Multimodal Learning for Clinical Decision Support, pp. 3–11. Springer, Cham (2018)

WeeCare: A Benchmark Database for the Analysis of Fetal Stress Condition from Cardiotocography Signals

S. M. Seeni Mohamed Aliar Maraikkayar[1], R. Tamilselvi[1]([✉]), M. Parisa Beham[2], and R. Murugan[2]

[1] ECE Dept, Sethu Institute of Technology, Kariapatti, Virudhunagar, India
`tamilselvi@sethu.ac.in`
[2] ECE Dept, National Institute of Technology, Silchar, Assam, India

Abstract. A cardiotocograph, or electronic fetal monitor (EFM), is used to continuously measure uterine contractions (UC) and fetal heart rate (FHR) during the third trimester and labor. Monitoring FHR and UC signals is essential for identifying potential fetal distress. Despite advancements in fetal monitoring research, existing Cardiotocography databases often lack critical features, such as accelerations, decelerations, baseline variability, average FHR, UC data, and pathological indicators necessary for comprehensive fetal assessment. Addressing these gaps, we introduce the 'WeeCare' database, designed to support fetal distress analysis by including key features: (i) FHR, (ii) baseline variability, (iii) UC, (iv) UC time, (v) accelerations, (vi) decelerations, and (vii) pathological indicators within CTG signals. The dataset comprises 250 real-time signals, each lasting up to 30 min, collected from reputable scan centers. Every signal is validated by experienced gynecologists using the CTG Analyzer to provide reliable ground truth data. This database offers a valuable resource for researchers focused on automating the analysis of fetal pathological conditions through clinical data interpretation.

Keywords: Cardiotocography (CTG) · Fetal Heart Rate (FHR) · Uterine Contractions (UC) Monitoring · Fetal Distress Detection · WeeCare Database · Gynecological Signal Processing

1 Introduction

As live births occur before 37 weeks of gestation, the World Health Organization (WHO) offers statistics on preterm births, premature births, and premature deliveries. In the perspective of the doctor, terms births are observed to be predicted during the live delivery that takes place between 37 and 42 weeks. The World Health Organization estimates that 1 in 10 or 15 million babies are born prematurely each year. This causes a serious problem in the morbidity of the babies and leads to 50% perinatal deaths. According to the survey, it depicts that the preterm delivery will give a room for serious issues in long-term disabilities in neurological sense. Hence, it is necessary for early prediction and continuous monitoring of fetus throughout the gestation. This will give place to postpone the labor and monitor the condition of the fetus.

© The Author(s), under exclusive license to Springer Nature Switzerland AG 2026
R. K. Karsh et al. (Eds.): SIPCOV 2025, CCIS 2848, pp. 36–51, 2026.
https://doi.org/10.1007/978-3-032-15809-3_3

Predicting preterm birth based on these factors such as fetal heart rate and uterine contractions is very important in the medical history. FHR is measure from the mother abdominal signals and the uterine activity is measured from Uterine electromyogram (EMG) measured in terms of Electro Hysterogram (EHG) from the abdomen wall of a pregnant lady. EHG is measured during the electrical discharges from the uterine muscles during pregnancy. CTG means recording of fetal heart rate (graphy) and UC (toco) from the mother [1]. The introduction of CTG in the medical field reduces the increase of fetal mortality as well as the damage to the fetus. The main parameters of the FHR are the Baseline, Variability, Acceleration and Deceleration. From the baseline variability, other features can be derived [2, 20].

Continuous CTG will be initiated while the concerns arising from intermittent auscultation and the process of monitoring is stopped after 20 min, if there are no non-reassuring/abnormal features and no ongoing risk factors. In CTG, baseline is the Fundamental base pattern and the normal range of base line value is defined in the range of 110–160 bpm. The fetal heart rate accelerates in response to the fetus's movement, which is consistent with the fetal CNS's attentiveness and wellbeing. Decelerations, or drops in FHR, are typically indicative of dangerous occurrences such umbilical cord compression. Typically, acceleration and deceleration last for 15 s, although occasionally can go longer. Shifts of more than $+15$ bpm and -15 bpm from the baseline are used to calculate accelerations and decelerations, respectively [3, 18].

The required measure to evaluate the health of the fetus is FHR variability. It manifests as a small oscillation in the baseline. By definition, the baseline rate must hold steady for at least 10 to 15 beats during a minute [11]. Baseline is the primary parameter that doctors typically use to visually assess a CTG trace. This causes variances in how the baseline is read and how the CTG trace is evaluated. The key components of FHR are depicted in Fig. 1. There are two types of variability: long-term and short-term (beat-to-beat). Short-term variability is the tendency for the fetal heart rate to rise quickly and then fall off somewhat, typically by 3 to 5 beats from the baseline [15]. The following categories can be used to group long-term variability: (Table 1)

Table 1. Different types of Variability and their bpm levels [1]

S.No	Variability	Bpm
1	Decreased variability	0–5 bpm(minimal variability)
2	Moderate variability	6–25 bpm(normal variability)
3	Marked variability	>25 bpm(saltatory)

FHR and UC are essential analyses for mother and fetal care in the medical field. [13] Physionet is the only database which has intrapartum signals which are useful for the research community. Fig. 2 shows the sample CTG signal collected from a hospital and it shows the FHR and UC [3, 4].

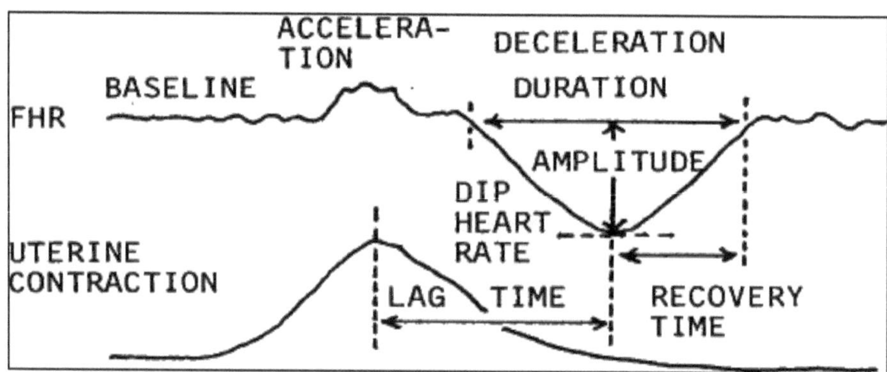

Fig. 1. Features of FHR [2]

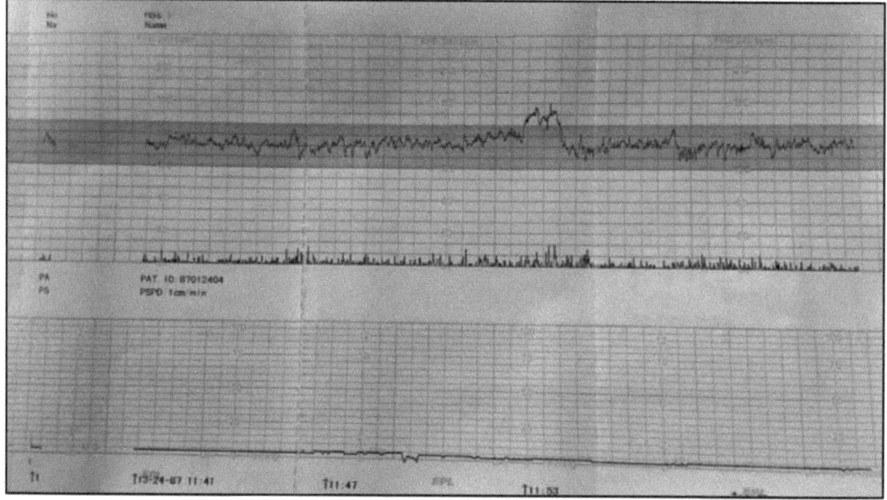

Fig. 2. Sample CTG signal showing FHR and Toco

The Main contributions of the work are:

1. Pregnant women's FHRs (term, preterm) and uterine recordings (Toco Signal) are created.
2. Normalized power spectra and spectrograms representing the uterine records of the EHG signal are displayed.
3. It offers crucial elements for an effective preterm birth prediction by eliminating noise such as power line interference.
4. Pathological condition is analyzed and a space for the automatic prediction of preterm birth is given for the researchers to analyze the newly proposed algorithms.
5. Valid parameters are estimated to evaluate the classification performance.

2 Existing Databases

There are two databases which consist of mother and fetal conditions for the analysis of stress condition and they are Term-Preterm Electro Hysterogram Database and Czech Technical University Database from Physionet.

A. Term-Preterm Electro Hystero Gram Database

There are five 30-min uterine records (EHG and TOCO signals) of non-pregnant women and 26 three-signal 30-min uterine EHG records of pregnant women in the Term-Preterm Electro Hystero Gram Database with Tocogram (TPEHGT DS) database. The Department of Obstetrics and Gynecology at the University Medical Centre Ljubljana is where the signals are gathered. The preterm records of the TPEHGT DS contain 47 annotated periods pertaining to uterine contractions (contraction intervals) and 47 annotated non-contractional/dummy intervals [17]. Term records have 53 annotated contraction and 53 dummy intervals; non-pregnant women's records also have 53 annotated dummy intervals. Annotations, original signals, and spectrograms of the original signals are all available in the database. The Toco signal and its spectrogram representations are displayed in Fig. 3 [5].

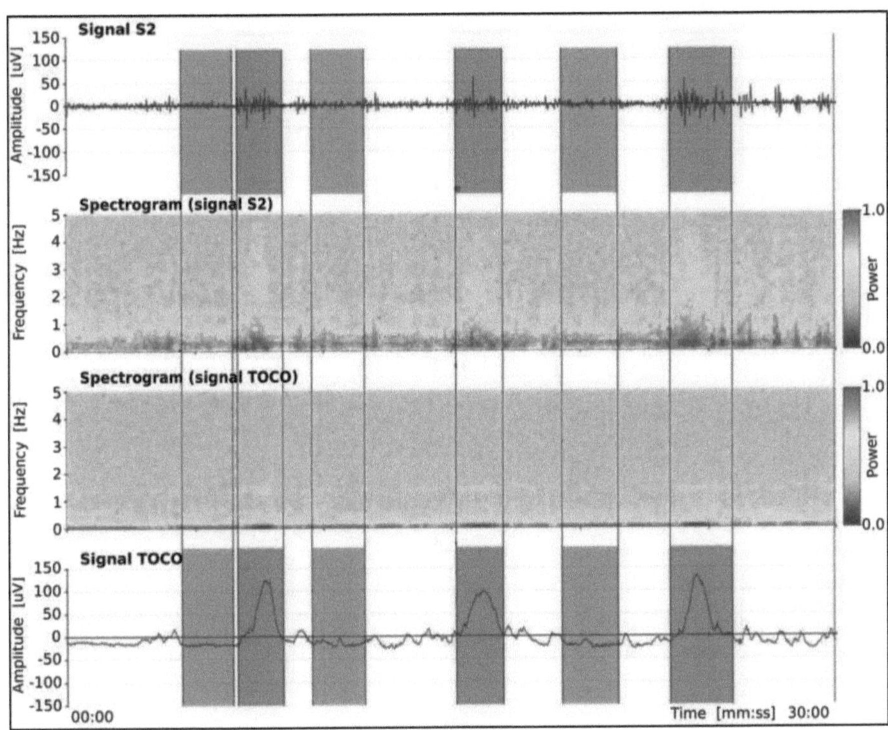

Fig. 3. Toco signal and its spectrogram representations from EHG database [5]

B. Czech Technical University Database from Physionet

The other gold standard databases are gathered from the University Hospital in Brno (UHB) and the Czech Technical University (CTU) in Prague. 552 Cardiotocography (CTG) recordings are included in these databases, which were chosen among 9164 recordings gathered at UHB between 2010 and 2012.

The CTG recordings begin no later than 90 min before the actual delivery and last no more than 90 min. Every CTG includes a uterine contraction (UC) signal and a fetal heart rate (FHR) time series that are both recorded at 4 Hz.

The details that are considered in the database are:

1. Single tone pregnancy
2. Gestational age > 36 weeks
3. Noapriori known developmental defects
4. Duration of stage 2 of labor≤30 min

All CTG data signals are evaluated and annotated based on nine expert obstetricians and interpreted as "Gold Standard". Sample signals are shown in Fig. 4 which represents fetal heart rate and uterine contractions [6].

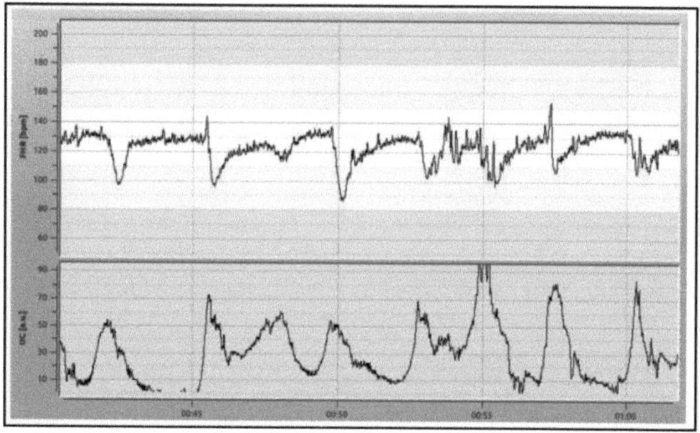

Fig. 4. Sample signal from CUB Data base showing FHR and Uterine Contractions [6]

3 Proposed Database–WeeCare Database

The proposed WeeCare(WCDB)database consists of 250signals from both pregnant and non-pregnant women indicating the normal, suspicious and pathological signals. Few sample signals taken in the time duration of 0 to 30 min are shown in Fig. 5. The signals are digitized and annotated as sig1.f for FHR value, sig1.U for UC values. Similarly, for other samples such as sig 2.f, sig 2. UC for second sample signal and so on.

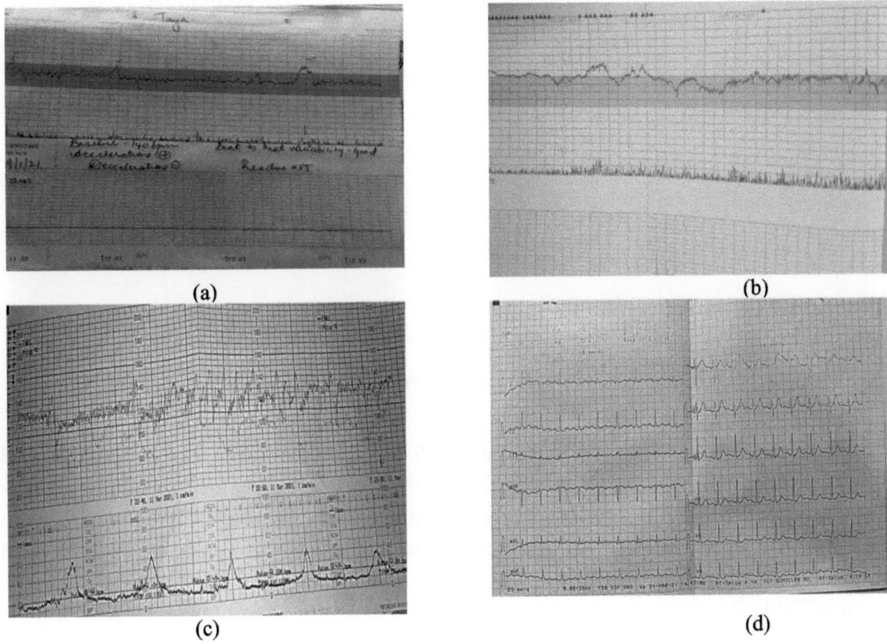

Fig. 5. Proposed Database signals showing the Fetal Heart Rate and Uterine Contractions

The dataset contains the details of baseline variability, Heart Rate Accelerations, decelerations, expert clinical data, uterine contractions, spectrogram and maximum uterine time. The signals are annotated in such a way that all the necessary data are incorporated and available in digitized form. In order to have an effective analysis and interpretation of the signals the first phase of the database involves preprocessing such as noise removal.

3.1 Noise Removal

As the collected signals are digitized manually and the values are approximated, filtering is the necessary task for better classification. Savitzky–Golay filter is used for removing noise in the signals. It is a digital filtering technique which is applied to a set of digital data points which truncate the data accurately and it improves the signal-to-noise ratio without greatly distorting the signal. The main process involved is the convolution through adjacent data points by the method of linear least squares. The bench mark filters are used for the noise removal and the comparison of the signal to the noise ratio is discussed. Media filter gave a Peak signal to noise ratio (PSNR) of 24.5 db, mean filter shown a PSNR of 26 db and the Savitzky–Golay filter shown a PSNR of 36db. Sample filtered signals are shown in Fig. 6.

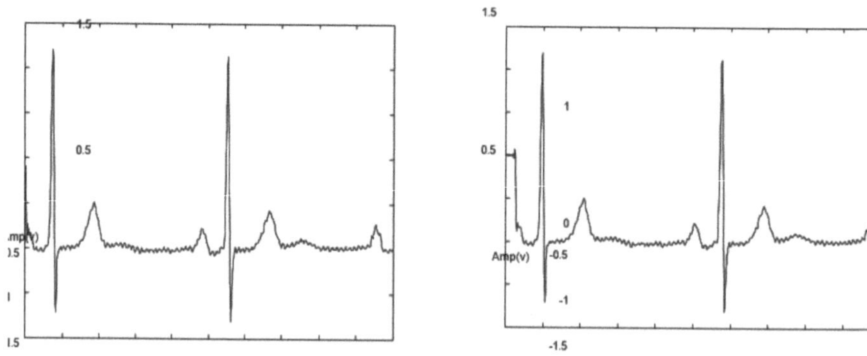

Fig. 6. Sample Filtered signals using Golay Filter

The CTG signals are categorized based on two important features such as UC and FHR. Some of the generated parameters, such baseline heart rate, variability, acceleration, and deceleration, are required even though these are the essential elements to determine the fetal state and interpret the CTG data. These derived parameters are needed to classify the signals into assuring, reassuring or abnormal conditions based on the data given in Table 2.

Table 2. Derived Parameters showing the reassuring, Non-reassuring and Abnormal Condition

Condition	Baseline	Variability	Deceleration	Acceleration
Reassuring	110–160 bpm	> = 5 bpm	None	Present
Non-reassuring	100–109 bpm 161–180 bpm	<= 5 bpm for more than40minandless than 90 min	Early Deceleration	Absent
Abnormal	<100or>180 Sinusoidal patternfor morethan10 minutes	<=5bpmformore than 90 min	Late Deceleration	Absent

Table 2 explains the condition of fetus based on the values of baseline, variability, acceleration and deceleration. The reassuring condition is derived from the values such as baseline of 110–160 bpm, variability> = 5 bpm, no deceleration as well as accelerations are noticed. These parameters are grouped to identify three categories that are essential for the identification of fetal condition in terms of preterm labor or any pathological condition [16, 19]. The CTG is classified as normal, suspect, or abnormal according to the estimated parameter categorization shown in Table 2. Table 3 presents the condition according to three categories: comforting, non-reassuring, and anomalous [5, 7, 12].

Table 3 explains three different categories such as normal, suspicious and pathological conditions. For example, when CTG shows all the derived features which are in the reassuring state, then the category is defined as normal condition. Like that for other condition, derived parameters are defined. In the proposed database, three main processes are involved. The processes involved are shown in Fig. 2. The main processes involved are digitization of the data, estimation of features, and interpretation and validation based on the clinical data [5, 8, 14] (Fig. 7).

Table 3. Illustration of the fetus condition based on the derived parameters

Category	Definition
Normal	A CTG whose all four features fall in to the reassuring category
Suspicious	ACTGwhosefeaturesfallintooneofnon-reassuringcategoryandtheremainofreassuring category
Pathological	ACTGwhosefeaturesfallintotwoormoreofthenon-reassuringcategoryortwo moreofthe abnormal category

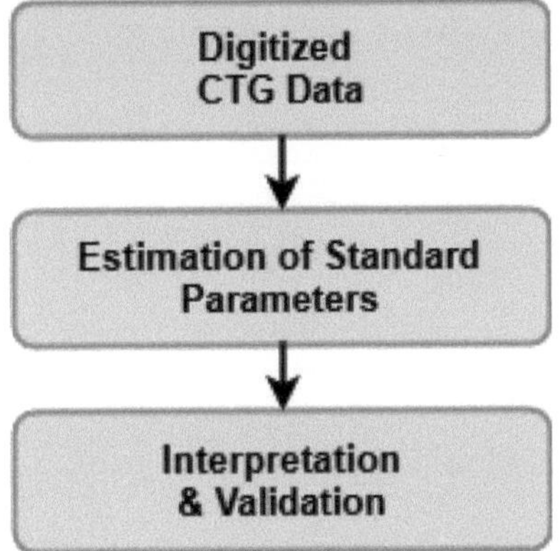

Fig. 7. Process involved in the Proposed Database

The first process is the digitation of the data based on the input CTG image received from the hospitals. The digital data are quantized based on the time period and the amplitude values. All the images are converted to digital data with the values in excel form such as time period and amplitude. After digitization, the basic features such as baseline estimation, accelerations, deceleration, FHR and Uterine Contractions are extracted and included in the database.

44   S. M. S. M. A. Maraikkayar et al.

The database has the salient features:

- All the values in digital form with the time period
- Necessary standard features
- Interpretation and validation of the data with the expert's opinion
- Annotation of the data with the parameters like
- Age of the patient
- Unique ID
- Gestational Period
- FHR
- UC
- Duration of the data and the Standard parameters

The sample excel sheet which comprises the relevant data such as age of the patient, annotated unique ID, and duration is shown in Fig. 8. Their gestational and other standard and derived parameters are annotated separately.

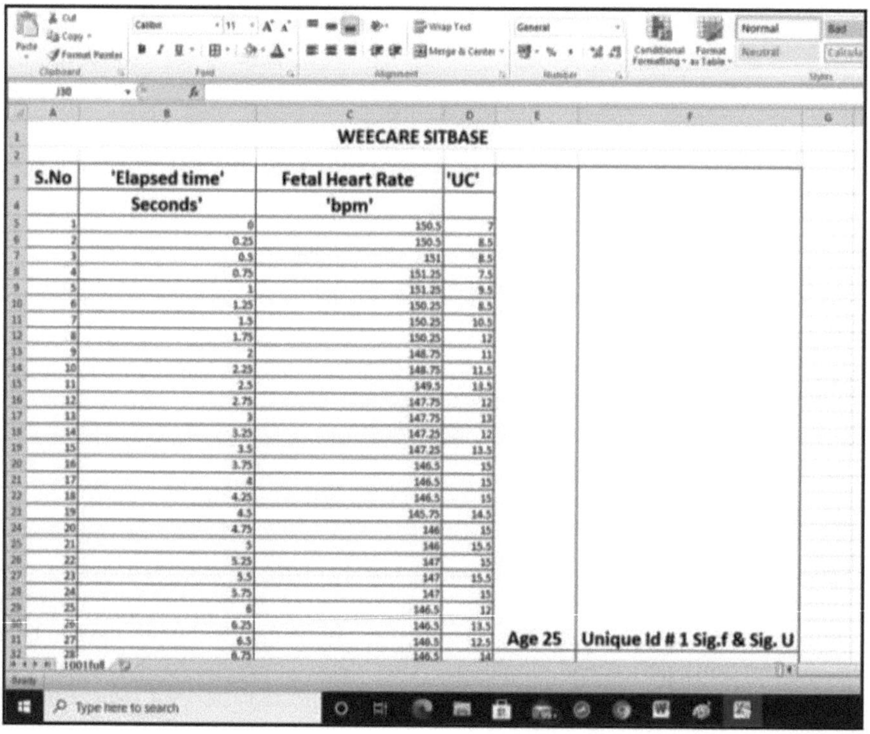

S.No	'Elapsed time' Seconds'	Fetal Heart Rate 'bpm'	'UC'
1	0	150.5	7
2	0.25	150.5	8.5
3	0.5	151	8.5
4	0.75	151.25	7.5
5	1	151.25	9.5
6	1.25	150.25	8.5
7	1.5	150.25	10.5
8	1.75	150.25	12
9	2	148.75	11
10	2.25	148.75	11.5
11	2.5	149.5	11.5
12	2.75	147.75	12
13	3	147.75	13
14	3.25	147.25	12
15	3.5	147.25	13.5
16	3.75	146.5	15
17	4	146.5	15
18	4.25	146.5	15
19	4.5	145.75	14.5
20	4.75	146	15
21	5	146	15.5
22	5.25	147	15
23	5.5	147	15.5
24	5.75	147	15
25	6	146.5	12
26	6.25	146.5	13.5
27	6.5	146.5	12.5
28	6.75	146.5	14

Fig. 8. Sample annotated datasheet showing the necessary data for interpretation

The graphs collected from the hospitals are manually converted to quantized data. The data are derived from the time period and its amplitude. The values are stored as values in excel.

3.2 Estimation of Standard Features

A. Baseline

An imaginary line that is drawn across the FHR tracing and crosses more locations in the FHR signal trace is referred to as the baseline in obstetrics [9, 10]. The virtual baseline (R), from which the baseline is formed, is obtained from an equation that shows the mean of a 60-min FHR signal segment.

$$R = Mean(x) + b \tag{1}$$

Where x, is the mean of the signal based on the time segment window, "b" is the constant factor derived based on the prior knowledge about the signal. Here, it is assumed that b = 0.99. After the virtual baseline, it is necessary to calculate the truncated baseline. In order to calculate the truncated baseline, maximum and minimum limits of the signals are necessary and they are estimated as L and H [9].

The maximum limit of the signal is calculated from the proposed model based on the entropy value of the signal,

$$H = R + 2 * (\text{Entropy value } (\beta)) \tag{2}$$

$$L = R - (2 * \text{Entropy Value } (\beta)) \tag{3}$$

The optimal value of β is chosen by adding and subtracting from the virtual baseline, as well as by iterating β from 1 to 8 bpm. The chosen optimal value for α is 8 bpm [9]. The shortened baseline values are based on different values of α estimated. The mean of the values within the minimum and the maximum limits gives the actual Baseline Heart Rate. A sample signal and the values are shown in Fig. 9.

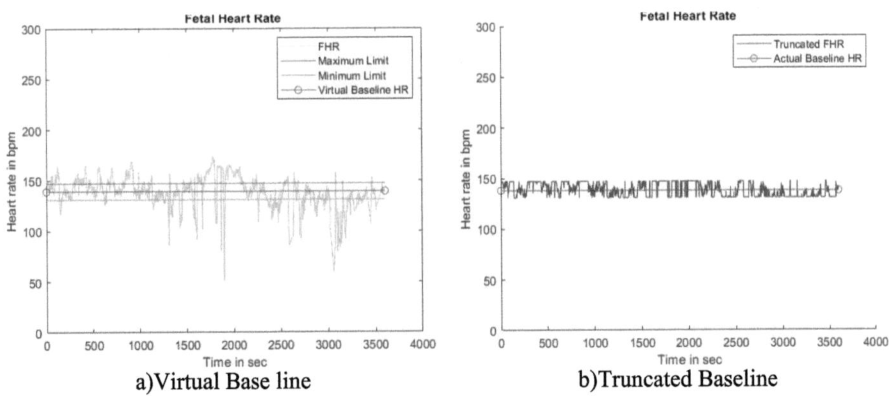

a)Virtual Base line   b)Truncated Baseline

Fig. 9. Base line Heart Rate

46   S. M. S. M. A. Maraikkayar et al.

Figure 9(a) explains the baseline heart rate estimated by means of the proposed model. Figure 9(a) includes the FHR, upper limit, lower limit and the virtual baseline. Based on the upper and lower limit of the signals, the truncated baseline is calculated and shown in Figure 9(b). Sample signal values are tabulated and shown in Table 4 which explains the calculated virtual baseline values. Whereas the truncated baselines are estimated based on various values of α and the final averaged value.

Table 4. Signals showing the Virtual and Baseline HR Values

Signals	Virtual Baseline HR	Average Truncated Baseline Value
Sig1	139	138
Sig2	140	141
Sig3	156	156
Sig4	140	141

B. Accelerations and Decelerations

Acceleration is estimated from the baseline FHR. The estimation is derived from the increase in FHR by at least 15 bpm from the base line and is sustained at that level or higher for at least 15 s called as reassuring. Deceleration is defined as decrease in FHR below the baseline level of more than 15 bpm with the lag of 15 s or more. Sample results are tabulated in Table 5.

Table 5. Acceleration and Deceleration values of the sample signals

Signals	Acceleration	Deceleration
Sig1	Reassuring(RAS)	Non-reassuring(N-RAS)
Sig2	Reassuring	Early Deceleration–Non-reassuring
Sig3	Reassuring	Late Deceleration–Abnormal
Sig4	Non-reassuring	Not Present–Reassuring

Table 5 shows the acceleration and deceleration conditions of few sample signals. Reassuring/Non-reassuring condition is estimated based on sustained vibration of the signals for certain time period.

C. FHR and UC

FHR and UC values are extracted from the digitized data. The strength of the signal is estimated over the time based on the spectrogram at various frequencies present in a particular waveform. The energy level variations over time are visualized in waveform. The digitised sheets are used to generate spectrograms of fetal heart rate and uterine activity in MatLab using short-time Fourier transform. The generated spectrograms help to understand the strength of uterine contractions and variability in fetal heart rate overtime.

Spectrogram representation of FHR and UC shows the predominant value over the Frequency Range. Figs. 10, 11 and 12 depict the spectral representation of the sample signals.

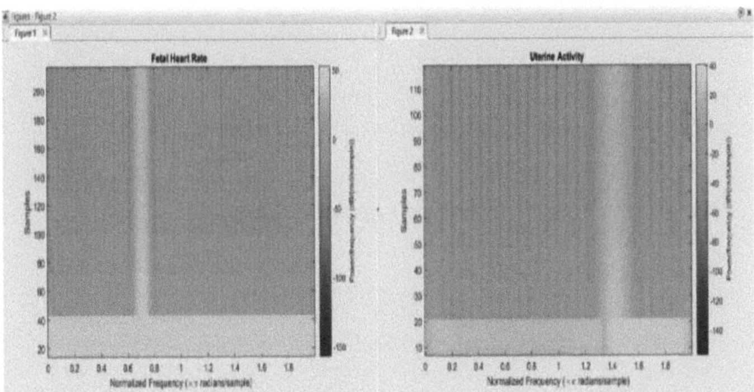

Fig. 10. Spectrogram of FHR and UC of a sample signal 1

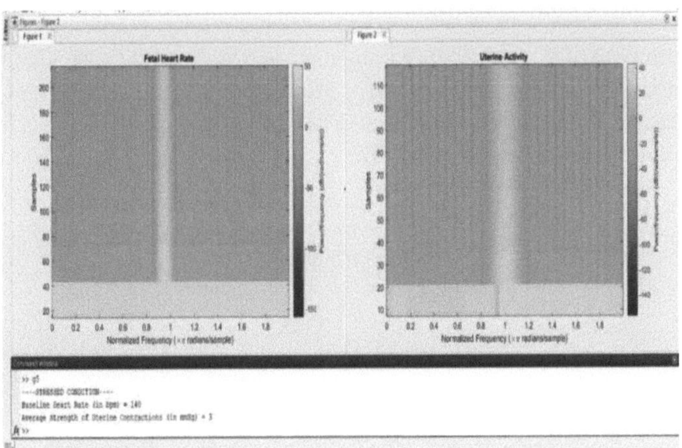

Fig. 11. Spectrogram of FHR and UC signal of sample signal 2

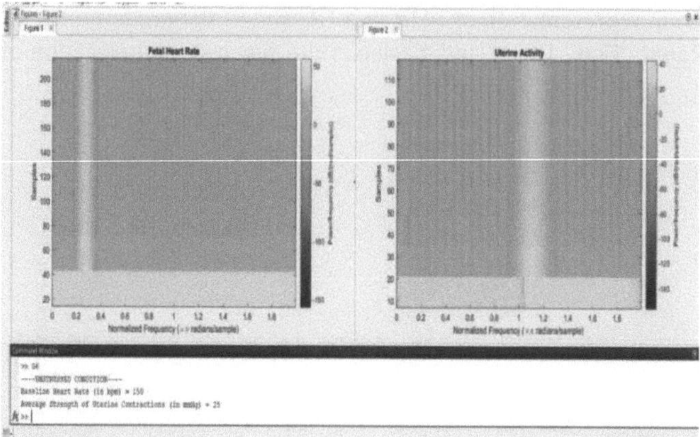

Fig. 12. Spectrogram of FHR and UC signal of sample signal 3

In the above Figures, the baseline heart rate and average UCs are evaluated based on the data retrieved from the digital input samples.

3.3   Interpretation and Validation of the Data

After the estimation of the necessary parameters such as variability, accelerations, deceleration, the condition of the fetus is estimated based on Tables 2 and 3. The FHR and UC signals are shown in Figs. 13 and 14. Based on the derived parameters such as baseline values, accelerations and decelerations, the pathological condition is also (Table 6).

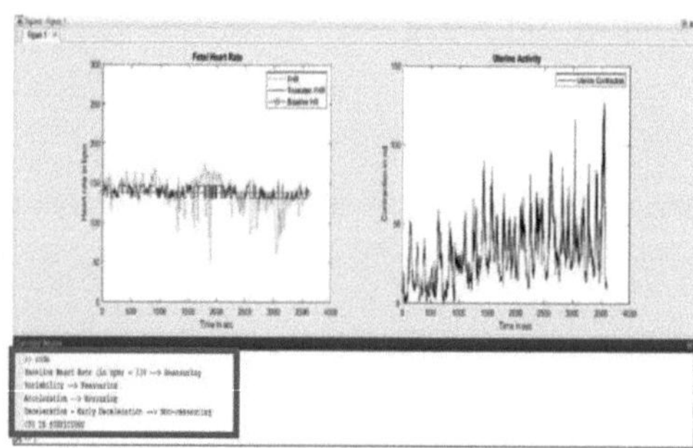

Fig. 13. Separated FHR and UC along with the fetal Condition–sample signal 1

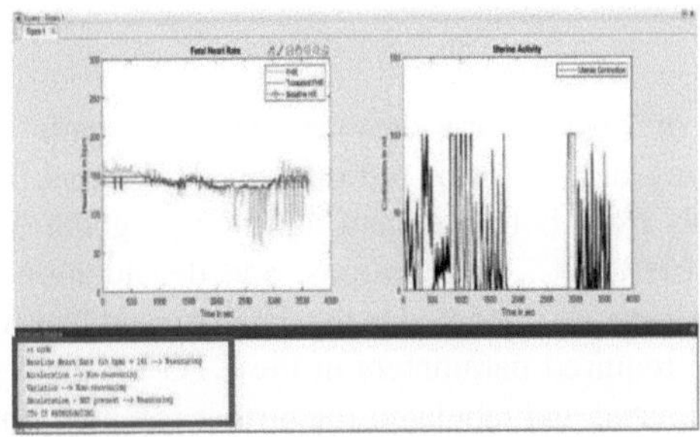

Fig. 14. Separated FHR and UC along with the fetal Condition –sample signal 2

Table 6. Interpretation and the validation of the results with the consultation of experts

Signal	Baseline Heartrate	Variability	Acceleration	DECL	CTG	Expert1	Expert2	OurDatabase
1	138 –RAS	RAS	RAS	Non-RAS	SUSP	SUSP	SUSP	SUSP
2	153 –RAS	RAS	RAS	EarlyDECL– Non-RAS	SUSP	SUSP	SUSP	SUSP
3	126–RAS	RAS	RAS	LateDECL– Abnormal	PATH	PATH	PATH	PATH
4	141–RAS	Non-RAS	Non-RAS	NotPresent– RAS	PATH	PATH	PATH	PATH
5	120–RAS	RAS	RAS	LateDECL– Abnormal	PATH	PATH	PATH	PATH
6	140–RAS	Non-RAS	Non-RAS	NotPresent– RAS	PATH	PATH	PATH	PATH
7	133–RAS	Non-RAS	Non-RAS	NotPresent– RAS	PATH	PATH	PATH	PATH
8	121–RAS	RAS	RAS	EarlyDECL– Non-RAS	SUSP	SUSP	SUSP	SUSP
9	134–RAS	RAS	RAS	LateDECL– Abnormal	PATH	PATH	PATH	PATH
10	131–RAS	RAS	RAS	LateDECL– Abnormal	PATH	PATH	PATH	PATH

Reassuring–RAS;Non-reassuring–N-RAS;Suspicious-SUS;Pathological-PATH

Figures 13 and 14 show FHR and UC as well as the condition of the fetus based on the standard parameters. This is the major feature in the database. The above table shows the sample signal with all standard parameters derived and the results are validated with the expert opinion. All the signals are evaluated and validated with the expert opinion and the accuracy of the database is estimated. All 250 signals in the database are validated and all the signals are correctly identified and classified. The accuracy of the validation is 98%. So the database has more impact on the analysis of the fetal stress.

4 Conclusion

WeeCare database is an open access database which is made available for research community for analysing and validating intrapartum CTG signal. The proposed database consists of 250 signals from both pregnant and non-pregnant women. The proposed database consists of FHR, UC, accelerations, and decelerations. All the three main conditions in the CTG trace are indicated in the database and they are normal, suspicious and pathological. The required parameters in the CTG for analysing the pathological condition are also estimated and tabulated for further research. In addition, two expert opinions about the condition are also validated with the results of the database. The database is used in the machine learning approach for accurate decision making by the physicians. The database is publically available at sethu.ac.in/database/WeeCare/ as an open-access database dedicated to fetal research in cardiology, heart rate variability and related fields.

References

1. Maeda, K., Noguchi, Y., Utsu, M., Nagassawa, T.: Algorithms for computerized fetal heart rate diagnosis with direct reporting. Algorithms. **8**(3), 395–406 (2015). https://doi.org/10.3390/a8030395
2. Hasan, M.A., Reaz, M.B., Ibrahimy, M.I., Hussain, M.S., Uddin, J.: Detection and processing techniques of FECG signal for fetal monitoring. Biol. Proced. Online. **11**, 263–295 (2009). https://doi.org/10.1007/s12575-009-9006-z
3. Das, S., Roy, K., Saha, C.K.: A novel approach for extraction and analysis of variability of baseline. In: 2011 International Conference on Recent Trends in Information Systems, pp. 336–339 (2011). https://doi.org/10.1109/ReTIS.2011.6146892
4. Romagnoli, S., Sbrollini, A., Burattini, L., Marcantoni, I., Morettini, M., Burattini, L.: Annotation dataset of the cardiotocographic recordings constituting the "CTU-CHB intra-partum CTG database". Data Brief. **31**, 105690., ISSN 2352-3409 (2020). https://doi.org/10.1016/j.dib.2020.105690
5. Jager, F., Libenšek, S., Geršak, K.: Characterization and automatic classification of preterm and term uterine records. PLoS One. **13**(8), e0202125 (2018). https://doi.org/10.1371/journal.pone.0202125
6. Spilka, J., et al: Automatic evaluation of FHR recordings from CTU-UHB CTG database. In: Lecture Notes in Computer Science, vol. 8060. Springer, Berlin/Heidelberg. https://doi.org/10.1007/978-3-642-40093-3_4
7. Marques, J.A.L., Cortez, P.C., Madeiro, J.P.V., Schlindwein, F.S.: Computerized Cardiotocography Analysis System based onHilbert Transform. Retrieved August 21, 2021, University of Leicester. J. Contribution. https://hdl.handle.net/2381/27848
8. Fuentealba, P., Illanes, A., Ortmeier, F.: Progressive fetal distress estimation by characterization of fetal heart rate decelerations response based onsignal variability in cardiotocographic recordings. Computing in Cardiology (CinC). **2017**, 1–4 (2017). https://doi.org/10.22489/CinC.2017.276-152
9. Cömertand, Z., Kocamaz, A.F.: Evaluation of Fetal Distress Diagnosis during Delivery Stages-Based on Linear and Nonlinear Features of Fetal Heart Rate for Neural Network Community. Int. J. Compt. Appl. **156**(4), 26–31., 2016 (2016). https://doi.org/10.5120/ijca2016912417

10. Zaferand, C., Kocamaz, A.F.: Comparison of MachineLearning Techniques for Fetal HeartRate Classification. Acta Physica Polonica A, Inst. Phys. Polish Acad. Sci. **132**(3), 451–454 (2017). https://doi.org/10.12693/APhysPolA.132.451. Acar, M., Eskicioğlu, M., et al. (2021). Fetal heart rate variability analysis using entropy measures: a comparison between normal and compromised fetuses. J. Biomech. 117, 110420

11. Ayres-de-Campos, D., Bernardes, J., et al.: Twenty-five years after the FIGO guidelines for the use of fetal monitoring: time for a simplified approach? J. Perinat. Med. **43**(1), 19–24 (2015)

12. Czabanski, R., Jezewski, J., et al.: Risk of low-fetal birth weight prediction from cardiotocographic signals by using ANFIS and SVM. Expert Syst. Appl. **39**(13), 11846–11853 (2012)

13. Echeverria, J.C., Alvarez-Ramirez, J., et al.: Detrended fluctuation analysis (DFA) applied to the analysis of FHR variability. IEEE Trans. Biomed. Eng. **51**(7), 1192–1200 (2004)

14. Farnam, A.D., S., et al.: A multi-level approach to CTG feature extraction and classification for fetal health monitoring. Biomed. Eng. Lett. **8**(2), 191–202 (2018)

15. Georgieva, A., Moulden, M., et al.: Computerized interpretation of fetal heart rate during labour: insights from the INFANT trial. Arch. Dis. Child. Fetal Neonatal Ed. **102**(6), F530–F536 (2017)

16. Silva, I., Behar, J., et al.: Improvement of fetal Well-being assessment by fusion of cardiotocography and ultrasound-derived fetal movements. Biomed. Signal Process. Control. **8**(6), 895–903 (2013)

17. Signorini, M.G., Fanelli, A., et al.: Complexity analysis of fetal heart rate variability: a review of recent approaches. Biomed. Signal Process. Control. **58**, 101870 (2020)

18. Spilka, J., Chudáček, V., et al.: Using non-linear features for fetal heart rate classification. In: Proceedings of the 34th Annual International Conference of the IEEE Engineering in Medicine and Biology Society, pp. 1644–1647 (2012)

19. Ocak, H.: A medical decision support system based on support vector machines and the genetic algorithm for evaluation of fetal Well-being. Comput. Methods Programs Biomed. **109**, 234–244 (2013)

20. Ahn, J., Kim, S., et al.: Fetal heart rate classification based on time-frequency analysis and machine learning techniques. Comput. Biol. Med. **113**, 103394 (2019)

Unveiling Cognitive Dissonance in Pain Perception Through Cluster-Based Subject Modeling

Arhina Ghosh[1(✉)] and Neha Tyagi[2]

[1] Noida Institute of Engineering and Technology, Greater Noida, Uttar Pradesh, India
arhinaghosh@gmail.com
[2] Amity University Noida, Noida, Uttar Pradesh, India

Abstract. The problem of recognizing accurately the pain is a significant challenge in affective computing, mainly because of the individual differences in expressing or hiding pain. Most traditional models fail to consider the internal conflict—cognitive dissonance—between perceived pain and expressed pain. To bridge this inadequacy, we introduce here a new cognitive dissonance-aware pain recognition model capable of incorporating inter-individual differences from multimodal physiological signals. Motion and surface Electromyography (sEMG) features are then extracted and employed to map subjects into a [Pain, Expression] space. We also apply K-Means and Fuzzy C-Means (FCM) clustering to infer underlying subject profiles—Suppressive, Expressive, and Ambiguous—using their expression dynamics. While K-Means provides interpretable and transparent groupings, it imposes hard cluster assignments that could mislabel ambiguous behaviors. FCM, on the other hand, holds soft membership intact and facilitates richer borderline object description and Ambiguous category definition to a wider extent. FCM, however, failed to detect a pure Suppressive cluster, suggesting more fluid boundaries of behavior. Trained classification models of both types of clusters all show improvement in accuracy, F1-score, and Receiver Operating Characteristic (ROC) curve to support the advantage of cluster guided, personalized modeling. The findings emphasize the value of soft clustering in demystifying otherwise mystifying affective states and form the basis for more interpretable and personalized pain recognition systems.

Keywords: Pain Recognition · Cognitive Dissonance · Clustering · Expression · Body Movement

1 Introduction

Recognition of pain automatically is an emerging and critical task at the cusp of affective computing, healthcare, and human-centered AI. It aims to recognize and interpret an individual's experience of pain objectively on the basis of observable physiological and behavioral manifestations. This, in fact, could have great applications-from assessing discomfort in patients during the rehabilitation period, to enabling adaptive interactions

R. K. Karsh et al. (Eds.): SIPCOV 2025, CCIS 2848, pp. 52–63, 2026.
https://doi.org/10.1007/978-3-032-15809-3_4

between humans and robots, and improving the quality of life for persons not able to communicate properly. The importance of pain and its significance being evaluated has been increasingly on the rise; yet it is considered one hard problem, owing to the highly subjective and context-dependent nature of pain.

Interpersonal variability is a core challenge in this domain, regarding how the external manifestation of pain occurs. Individual variations in the expression or suppression of pain due to psychological, cultural, or situational influences are numerous. Some people may outwardly express pain sensations through body movements or muscular tension, some others may suppress these cues either deliberately, say due to social interference, or unintentionally, due to conditioned responses. Most of the common machine learning techniques for pain recognition fail to account for this variability and take the pain data of all subjects for granted, assuming the tested population coupled with the training set to be a homogeneous one. Consequently, these models fail in generalizing across subjects with varying expression patterns.

In affective computing and pain recognition, cognitive dissonance is the psychological discrepancy between the internal experience of pain and the external behavioral expression of the same. This dissonance thus constitutes an overriding problem for automated systems, as human beings may have so many different and even contradictory pain-response patterns. While some truly exhibit expressions of pain, others may go suppressing any observable sign of pain; hence, the issue of building generalizable models. In order to tackle this, we need to break the assumption that subjects behave homogeneously and start modeling latent interpersonal variability in pain expression.

In this research, the concept of cognitive dissonance is used to explore the psychological incongruence existing between the expression of pain and physiological signals in subjects. Rather than contesting the idea of dissonance in classical written philosophy (Festinger), we augment its more domain-specific, operational meaning to describe a mismatch between outward behavioral cues (motion) and inner, pain-related signals (EMG activity). While this could fit the goals of our computational modeling, it may stray away from the strict psychological sense of the word. In the future, more careful integration of psychological constructs will help from an interdisciplinary standpoint, such as some expert annotation or validated scales so that more rigorous and accurate sympathetic mapping can be done across dissonance as defined in cognitive psychology.

To address the above-listed challanges, we set forth the following key objectives for this study:

- We propose a subject grouping method based on clustering to model cognitive dissonance in pain expression using features extracted from the EmoPain dataset.
- We use both hard clustering (K-means) and soft clustering (Fuzzy C-Means) for subject grouping according to pain-expression dissonance.
- We analyze the impact various clustering approaches have on the classification of subjects as expressive, suppressive, or ambiguous behavioral types.
- Finally, we measure the performance of the proposed methodology using several performance matrices, such as accuracy, confusion matrix, and ROC curve.

2 Literature Review

Pain categorization has been extensively studied with multimodal physiological features, especially with information such as EmoPain. Dehshibi et al. [1] suggested sparsely-connected GRU-based RNN ensemble with autoencoders for pain behavior and pain intensity classification with better performance than traditional models. Likewise, Olugbade et al. [2] created an integration of motion and sEMG data-based multimodal model to identify chronic pain patients' protective behaviors, enhancing knowledge of pain-related motor patterns. As an alternative, Zhou et al. [3] proposed a temporal convolutional networks-based deep learning model for pain intensity estimation using physiological signals, achieving remarkable improvement in recognition accuracy.

In affective computing, there has been some effort devoted to modeling cognitive dissonance—i.e., internal-behavior state inconsistency. Martinez et al. [4] noted that affect recognition systems need to be perceptive to such dissonance in order to better indicate users' actual affective states. Kim et al. [5] explored user behavior when interacting with affective systems and developed adaptive models that could resolve emotional conflicts from dissonant signals. Li and Wang [6] introduced a conceptual model of human-computer dissonance cognition modeling that would be able to increase the interpretability of user feedback in emotionally intelligent systems.

Cluster methods have also been used in medical and psychological signal analysis, especially when compared with the classical KMeans clustering, with fuzzy logic-based counterparts. Narasimham and Kumar [7] presented a fuzzy logic system for the detection of brain tumors from MRI images, which was more efficient and accurate compared to traditional methods of classification. Karami et al. [8] suggested FLATM, a fuzzy logic medical document topic model, and illustrated superiority over traditional latent Dirichlet allocation in the domain of document classification. Banu and Inbarani [9] improved fuzzy C-means (FCM) with penalization methods to cluster gene expression data to enhance the quality of clustering. Naser and Zeki [10] utilized fuzzy clustering to detect stomach cancer, which resulted in accurate tumor region segmentation. Comparison of thyroid disease diagnosis further established that fuzzy clustering provided more subtle and clinically meaningful classes than hard clustering techniques [11]. Liu et al. [12] applied FCM to therapeutic treatment of chronic bronchitis with additional improvement of medical data cluster efficiency.

Ultimately, some research has placed importance on the disadvantaging of using binary or hard clustering models in affective and psychological applications. Smith et al. [13] used FCM to explore multimorbidity in patients and concluded that soft clustering algorithms more accurately define the interdisciplinary dimensions of patient profiles. In the same vein, Cao et al. [14] applied fuzzy similarity-based hierarchical clustering to bioinformatics data integration to improve subgroup identification accuracy. In a review by Khosravi et al. [15], fuzzy logic-based approaches were particularly well suited for handling ambiguity and uncertainty in decision-making and disease diagnosis. In a study by Kumar et al. [16], facial expression based pain detection proved to have high accuracy for EmoPain dataset, which indicates its value for pain assessment in nonverbal patients. Multimodal fusion of motion data has also been effective for pain estimation and protection detection in the EmoPain Challenge by Uddin et al. [17].

Together, these contributions demonstrate the utility of soft clustering and cognitive dissonance modeling for complex affective tasks such as pain recognition, calling for the creation of increasingly fine-grained, subject-sensitive approaches.

3   Proposed Methodology

The section discusses the dataset and the procedure of proposed methodology. The end-to-end framework is shown in Fig. 1.

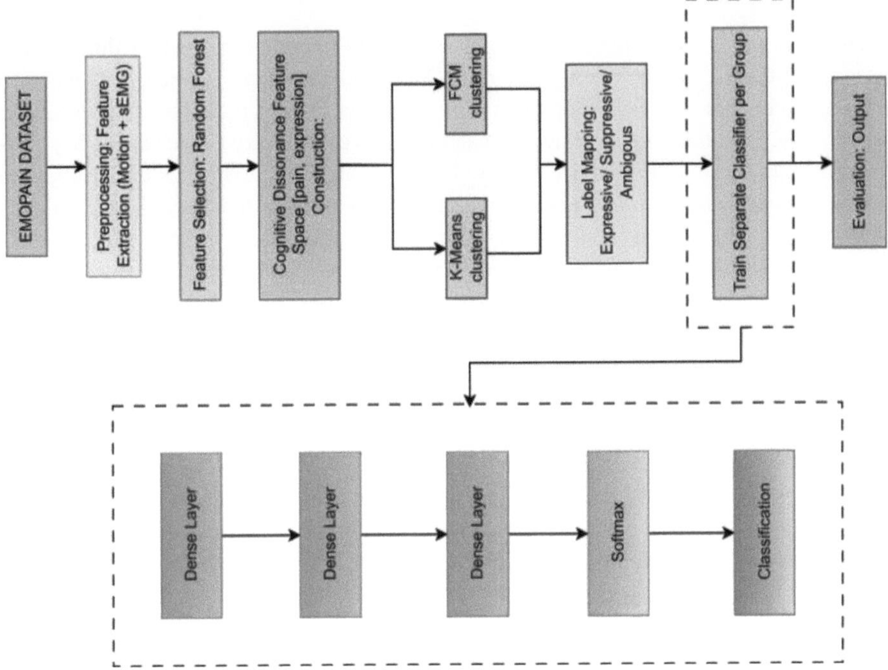

Fig. 1. End to End Framework for Proposed Model

3.1   Dataset and Preprocessing

Experiments in this work use the EmoPain dataset [18] with multimodal recordings under two conditions, i.e., Randomized Control (C) and Randomized Pain (P). This dataset contain total 37 subjects. At data preparation, we get motion and surface electromyography (sEMG) features. For every windowed segment, we calculate a complete set of statistical descriptors such as mean, standard deviation, skewness, kurtosis, entropy, and higher-order moments. In order to reduce dimensionality and keep the most discriminative features, random forest feature importance scores are employed for feature selection. This step ensures that we only keep the most relevant physiological measures for further modeling.

3.2 Cognitive Dissonance Feature Space

In modeling cognitive dissonance at the subject level, we design a low-dimensional representation that reflects the covariance between perceived pain and its behavioral manifestation. For every subject, the average of the pain labels which are labeled as a measure of expressed pain, and the average amplitude of the sEMG signals extracted as a measure of muscular expression, are calculated. This yields a two-dimensional feature space on pain level and expression level as input to subject-level clustering.

3.3 Clustering Methods

To group subjects into behavioral categories, we run two clustering algorithms on the dissonance feature space. We initially run KMeans clustering to segment subjects into three hard clusters. We then assign resulting cluster centers as indicative of expressive, suppressive, and ambiguous behavioral categories. We run Fuzzy C-Means (FCM) clustering on the same feature space finally. Unlike KMeans, FCM gives each subject a soft score membership to all clusters, indicating how similar their behavior is to each archetype. To compare and analyze, we get hard labels from FCM by sampling the maximum membership value, and we also probe the distribution of strength memberships to see if there is ambiguity.

3.4 Label Mapping to Cognitive Dissonance Categories

In an effort to semantically understand the resultant clusters, the centroids of the cluster in both KMeans and FCM are examined. The high pain-low expression cluster is known as Suppressive, the high pain-high expression cluster is known as Expressive, and a third cluster with intermediate or inconsistent pain-expression relationship is known as Ambiguous. This naming convention is in accordance with theoretical models of cognitive dissonance through which participants might under-or over-report their true levels of pain for psychological, cultural, or behavioral reasons.

3.5 Training Cluster Membership Models

We train individual classification models on individual clusters to take advantage of the behavioral clusterings. For each subject cluster—either KMeans or FCM-based— we train an individual neural network classifier with a dense-layer setup. Each model is trained on the data of only its corresponding group, thus ensuring specialization to identify pain-related signals in that behavior context. This stratified training protocol is provided to both clustering approaches to allow the comparison of their effect on the accuracy of classification as well as interpretability.

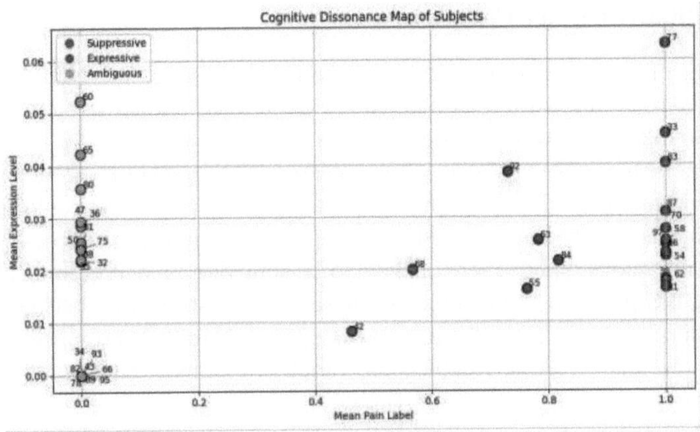

(a) K-Means Clustering

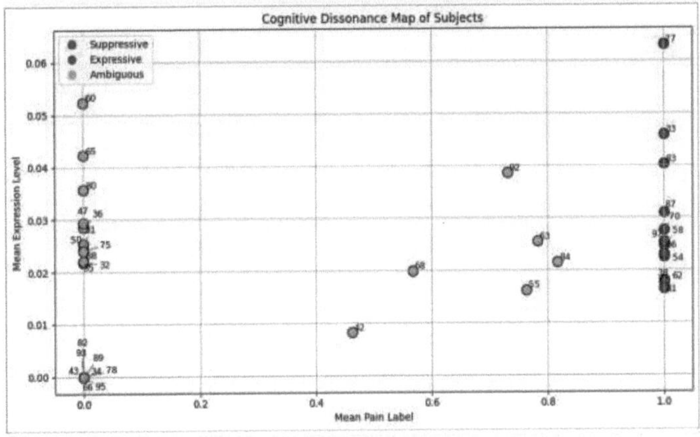

(b) Fuzzy C Means Clustering

Fig. 2. Scatter plots of subjects in the cognitive dissonance space using (a) KMeans and (b) FCM.

4 Experimental Results and Discussion

This part contains our experimental evaluation results, with emphasis on clustering of subjects by their pain and expression features and analysis of classification performance.

4.1 Visualization of Clustering

To gain an initial sense perception of subject groupings found by the clustering algorithms, we created cognitive dissonance maps. The maps shown in Fig. 2 are scatter plots of subjects in the [Pain, Expression] feature space. Every point is a subject, and its color (red = suppressive, green = expressive, orange = ambigous) represents the cluster membership identified by either the K-Means or Fuzzy C-Means (FCM) algorithm. For readability, every subject is labeled with their ID number. Qualitative inspection of groupings of the subjects owing to the two clustering algorithms gives an initial qualitative measure of their concordance and conflict.

4.2 Quantitative Cluster Comparison

The findings of the experiments provide useful feedback on utilizing the K-Means and Fuzzy C-Means (FCM) clustering methods in identifying distinctive subject categories according to their pain and expression features.

Our experience with K-Means is as expected with its nature. K-Means provided a simpler and immediately interpretable clustering answer, one that could successfully split the subjects into three rigidly distinct groups corresponding to Suppressive, Expressive, and Ambiguous types. There appears to be something inherent in this rigid partitioning that has problems with subjects whose traits exist midway between these discrete endpoints and may force them into a category where their presence might not be entirely representative. Table 1 depicts the variation of cluster based on both hard and soft clustering.

Table 1. Subject allocation in cognitive dissonance-based clusters

Clusters	K-Means Clustering	FCM Clustering
Expressive	16 subjects [33, 38, 54, 55,	12 subjects [33, 38, 54, 58,
	58, 62, 63, 70, 77, 81, 83,	62, 70, 77, 81, 83, 86, 87,
	84, 86, 87, 92, 97]	97]
Suppressive	2 subjects [42, 68]	0 subjects
Ambigous	19 subjects [31, 32, 34, 35,	25 subjects [31, 32, 34, 35,
	36, 43, 47, 50, 60, 65, 66,	36, 42, 43, 47, 50, 55, 60,
	75, 78, 80, 82, 88, 89, 93,	63, 65, 66, 68, 75, 78, 80,
	95]	82, 84, 88, 89, 92, 93, 95]

In contrast, FCM with fuzzy cluster borders created a more differentiated profile. Whereas K-Means identified homogeneous Suppressive (2 subjects), Expressive (16 subjects), and Ambiguous (19 subjects) clusters, FCM created an alternate distribution of clusters. Most significant was that FCM did not assign any subjects to a single Suppressive cluster. Expressive cluster in FCM comprised 12 members, a sub-sample of members picked out by K-Means, whereas Ambiguous cluster in FCM grew to 25 members. That is, FCM picked out more people who exhibited blended or weaker patterns of pain-expression.

FCM's capacity to pinpoint the subtle nuances of cognitive dissonance is especially pertinent to the Ambiguous group. The more subjects FCM defines as Ambiguous is its sensitivity to the not-strongly members of either purely Suppressive or Expressive profiles. Such subjects, with borderline membership in many fuzzy clusters, can be representative of individuals with more variable or mixed reactions to pain. Clinically, such identification by FCM's probabilistic clustering could be warranted to require further, more detailed assessment of the etiologies underlying their uncertain presentation. The differential subject assignments of the Expressive cluster by the two algorithms further underscore FCM's sensitivity to qualitative nuances in the data.

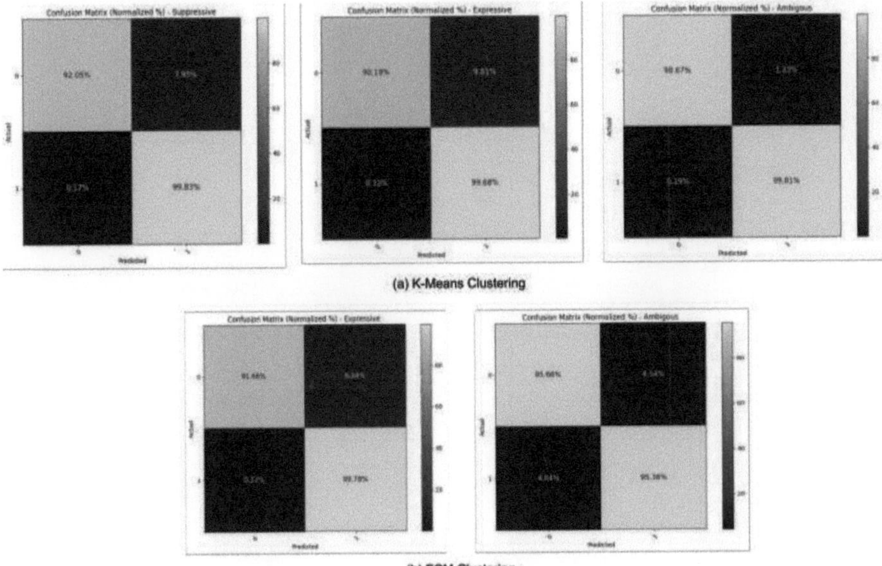

Fig. 3. Confusion Matrix of each cluster for (a) KMeans and (b) FCM.

The difference between cluster assignment by K-Means and FCM also shows the inherent differences in data segregation. While K-Means assigns each instance strictly to a specific cluster, FCM admits partial membership, which can be more informative about the underlying data structure, especially when groups are not as well distinguished. The lack of clear Suppressive cluster in the FCM result incites further exploration of what defines such individuals and if indeed their profiles are closer to the Expressive or Ambivalent types taking into account the fuzzy nature of FCM.

Overall, while the K-Means algorithm produces a simple and understandable cluster, FCM's tolerance of ambiguity and ability to identify differences within subject profiles more nuanced than those captured by cluster analysis indicate its potential use in the detection of those individuals most likely to need more specialized clinical care. The borderline elements of the FCM analysis, and specifically those found in the larger Ambiguous cluster, are apt to be optimal candidates for continued examination of the pain and expression response spectrum.

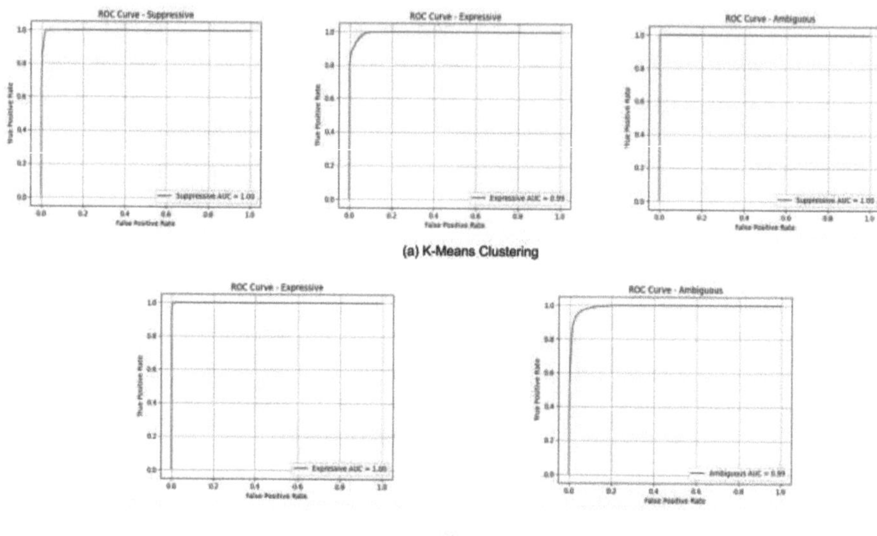

(a) K-Means Clustering

(b) FCM Clustering

Fig. 4. ROC Curve of each cluster for (a) KMeans and (b) FCM.

4.3 Classification Performance

After subject clustering, classification models were trained and tested for each of the clusters that we found, which we named Suppressive, Expressive, and Ambiguous according to the subject attributes of each. The quality of the classification in each cluster was measured using a number of important indicators: accuracy, precision, recall, and F1-score. The individual performance measures for each cluster and for both clustering algorithms used are provided in Table 2. Furthermore, confusion matrices of the classification for each cluster are presented in Fig. 3, presenting information on the nature of the classification mistakes. Receiver Operating Characteristic (ROC) curves and their Area Under the Curve (AUC) values in Fig. 4 are also shown to further analyze the discriminative power of each cluster's classifiers. Table 3 shows effectiveness of our proposed model in comparison to other state-of-the-art models.

Table 2. Comparison of Clustering Performance Metrics for K-Means and FCM

Clusters	K-Means				FCM			
	Accuracy	Precision	Recall	F1 Score	Accuracy	Precision	Recall	F1 Score
Suppressive	0.97	0.97	0.96	0.97	–	–	–	–
Expressive	0.99	0.98	0.95	0.96	0.95	0.96	0.95	0.96
Ambiguous	0.98	0.98	0.98	0.96	0.95	0.96	0.96	0.96

Table 3. Comparison with State-of-the-Art Models

References	Year	Dataset Used	Technology Used	Accuracy
[1]	2023	EmoPain	sRNN-GRU	86%
[16]	2023	EmoPain	Facial Activity Coding System, Gabor Filtering, Principal Component Analysis	92.5%
[17]	2021	EmoPain	XGBoost	97%
Proposed Model	2025	EmoPain	Clustering Based Dense Classifier	upto 99%

4.4 Feature Importance

In order to gain a better insight into the causality of the observed clustering and classification performance, we ranked the input features by importance using a Random Forest model. Fig. 5 illustrates a plot ordering the chosen features according to their contribution to predictive model performance. Table 4 presents all the features extracted from the preprocessed dataset. F0, F1, F2, F3, F4 and F8 are the selected features by using random forest. Interpretation of chosen features is explanatory about their role in modeling the intricate relationship between expression and pain. Such analysis clearly shows how individual attributes of pain and expression can best differentiate the identified subject groups.

4.5 Limitations

The main limitation appeared when Fuzzy C-Means (FCM) refused to classify any of the subjects into the Suppressive cluster, and instead categorized all subjects into Ambiguous and Expressive groups. The Suppressive group is central to the cognitive dissonance framework, thus analyzing or classifying performances in this group was impossible for us. In future works, one should look into clustering methods that assure fuller and balanced group formation.

Table 4. Extracted Features

Serial Number	Motion Features	Serial Number	sEMG Features
F0	Mean	F6	Mean Absolute Value (MAV)
F1	Standard Deviation (STD)	F7	Root Mean Square (RMS)
F2	Range (Peak-to-Peak)	F8	Waveform Length (WL)
F3	Skewness	F9	Zero Crossing (ZC)
F4	Kurtosis	F10	Skewness
F5	Entropy (of histogram with 10 bins)	F11	Kurtosis

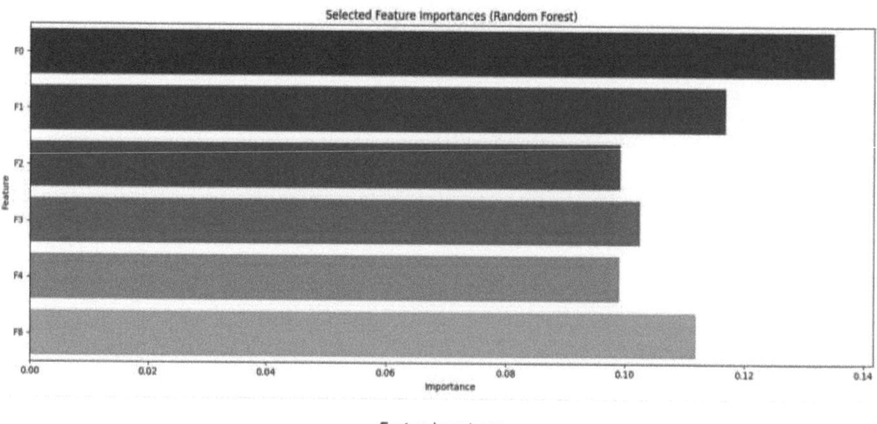

Fig. 5. Importance of Selected Features

5 Conclusion

The current research investigated the use of K-Means and Fuzzy C-Means (FCM) clustering procedures to classify participants according to their pain and expression behaviors, which differed largely both in methodology and findings. Though K-Means yielded an easily understandable and less complicated subjects' partitioning, its inability to identify Suppressive, Expressive, and Ambiguous subjects effectively may have diminished intricate individual variations. Conversely, FCM was better able to capture the inherent ambiguity and nuanced variations in the data. Of particular note, FCM's assignment of a more significant Ambiguous group without a Suppressive group points toward the presence of a significant proportion of subjects reporting complex or mixed patterns of pain that cannot be readily relegated to simple classification. This low-key development highlights the potential of FCM in practice for identifying individuals who could be improved through more focused and in-depth investigation and treatment. The potential of FCM to detect the nuance of cognitive dissonance, as expressed through variety in subject assignment and size in the larger Ambiguous cluster, suggests its usefulness in offering a more detailed and perhaps more clinically useful explanation of the data, than in discrete clustering. Research ahead will examine utilization of FCM membership weights in loss functions for classification and multimodal generalization in order to influence recognition.

References

1. Dehshibi, M.M., Amini, A., Olugbade, T.O., Bianchi-Berthouze, N.: Pain level and pain-related behaviour classification using GRU-based sparsely-connected RNNs. arXiv preprint arXiv, 2212.14806 (2022)
2. Olugbade, T.O., Bianchi-Berthouze, N., Williams, A.: Multimodal detection of protective behaviour in chronic pain patients. IEEE Trans. Affect. Comput. **12**(1), 20–33 (2021)

3. Zhou, Y., Jiang, H., Li, Y., Zhang, Z.: Pain intensity estimation from physiological signals using temporal convolutional networks. IEEE J. Biomed. Health Inform. **25**(4), 1062–1070 (2021)

4. Martinez, L., Dey, A.K., Picard, R.W.: Modeling cognitive dissonance in emotion recognition systems. In: Proc. IEEE Int'l Conf. on Affective Computing and Intelligent Interaction (ACII), pp. 1–7 (2020)

5. Kim, J., Lee, S., Kim, H.: Adaptive affective computing interfaces considering cognitive dissonance. IEEE Trans. Affect. Comput. **11**(3), 439–451 (2020)

6. Li, H., Wang, Y.: A framework for modeling cognitive dissonance in human- computer interaction. In: Proc. ACM CHI Conf. on Human Factors in Computing Systems (CHI), pp. 1–12 (2019)

7. Narasimham, N.V.S.L., Kumar, K.K.: Fuzzy logic-based system for brain tumour detection and classification. arXiv preprint arXiv, 2401.14414 (2024)

8. Karami, A., Gangopadhyay, D., Zhou, A.: FLATM: A fuzzy logic approach topic model for medical documents. arXiv preprint arXiv, 1911.10953 (2019)

9. Banu, P.K.N., Inbarani, H.H.: An analysis of gene expression data using penalized fuzzy C-means approach. arXiv preprint arXiv, 1302.3123 (2013)

10. Naser, E.F., Zeki, S.M.: Using fuzzy clustering to detect the tumor area in stomach medical images. Baghdad Sci. J. **18**(4), 1454–1461 (2021)

11. Al-Ani, A.A., Qader, M.K., Al-Aubaidy, M.A.: Fuzzy and hard clustering analysis for thyroid disease. Comput. Biol. Med. **43**(12), 2156–2163 (2013)

12. Liu, X., Zhang, J., Liu, Y., Liang, Z.: An improved fuzzy C-means clustering algorithm for assisted therapy of chronic bronchitis. Comput. Biol. Med. **65**, 34–42 (2015)

13. Smith, J., Thompson, M., Brown, R.: Clusters of medical specialties around patients with multimorbidity – employing fuzzy C-means clustering to explore in- terdisciplinary care patterns. BMC Med. Inform. Decis. Mak. **22**(1), 1–10 (2022)

14. Cao, P., Zhang, H., Zhou, B.: Fuzzy similarity-based hierarchical clustering for integrated bioinformatics data. IEEE/ACM Trans. Comput. Biol. Bioinform. **18**(1), 84–96 (2021)

15. Khosravi, A., Nahavandi, E., Islam, S.M., Creighton, D.: A comprehensive review of fuzzy logic in disease diagnosis and decision making. Expert Syst. Appl. **168**, 114361 (2021)

16. Kumar, V., Dhapola, P., Kushwaha, A.N.: Automatic pain detection through facial expression. In: Chowdhary, C., Swain, B., Kumar, V. (eds.) Investigations in Pattern Recognition and Computer Vision for Industry 4.0, pp. 81–89. IGI Global Scientific Publishing (2023). https://doi.org/10.4018/978-1-6684-8602-3.ch006

17. Uddin, M.T., Canavan, S.: Multimodal Multilevel Fusion for Sequential Protective Behavior Detection and Pain Estimation, pp. 844–848 (2020). https://doi.org/10.1109/FG47880.2020.00073

18. Aung, M.S.H., et al.: The automatic detection of chronic pain-related expression: requirements, challenges and the multimodal EmoPain dataset. IEEE Trans. Affect. Comput. **7**(4), 435–451 (2015). https://doi.org/10.1109/taffc.2015.2462830

GAN-Based Transfer Learning Model for Brain Tissue Classification in Progressive Multiple Sclerosis Using Electron Microscopy Images

S. Anjanaa[iD], K. M. Dhyaneshwar[iD],
and Namasivaya Naveen Shanmuga Sundaram[(⊠)] [iD]

Department of Computer Science and Medical Engineering, Sri Ramachandra Faculty of Engineering and Technology (SRET), Sri Ramachandra Institute of Higher Education and Research, Porur, Chennai, Tamil Nadu, India
namasivayanaveen@gmail.com

Abstract. Multiple Sclerosis (MS) is a chronic, autoimmune, neuroinflammatory, and neurodegenerative disease of the central nervous system (CNS) with the occurrence of demyelinated lesions in the white and grey matter. The exact mechanism of the disease initiation and progression is unknown. While the visible lesions are commonly seen in the white and grey matter, many areas that appear normal in a magnetic resonance imaging (MRI) have underlying damage. These areas are referred to as normal-appearing white matter (NAWM) and normal-appearing grey matter (NAGM). In addition, the control white matter (CWM) and control grey matter (CGM) are from healthy individuals without MS for comparison. This work uses a novel deep learning model using a one-vs-rest classification strategy to differentiate among these four brain tissue types from Scanning Transmission Electron Microscopy (STEM) Images. The methodology integrates traditional convolutional neural networks (CNNs) with advanced transfer learning architectures, VGG16, ResNet50, and EfficientNetB0. Generative Adversarial Network (GAN)-based augmentation was used to generate synthetic images to address data imbalance and improve generalization. With 280 balanced and GAN-augmented images per class, the dataset was split using an 80:20 train-test ratio. Among the models tested, VGG16 performed the best, obtaining the highest overall classification accuracy of 93.19% with a precision and AUROC close to 0.9. This study presents a promising approach for automating brain tissue classification in MS patients. The ability to precisely distinguish between tissue types enables early detection and targeted treatment, which may improve outcomes for future MS patients by assisting clinicians with disease monitoring and treatment planning. This approach could support integration into future digital pathology platforms for MS diagnosis.

Keywords: Multiple Sclerosis · Deep Learning · VGG16 · Generative Adversarial Network (GAN)

R. K. Karsh et al. (Eds.): SIPCOV 2025, CCIS 2848, pp. 64–75, 2026.
https://doi.org/10.1007/978-3-032-15809-3_5

1 Introduction

Multiple sclerosis (MS), a progressive autoimmune disease that affects the central nervous system, is characterized by demyelination and neurodegenerative processes. MS causes the myelin sheath, the fatty coating surrounding your nerve fibers, to be destroyed, effectively short-circuiting your nerve signals. From mild motor impairment to severe cognitive and physical disability, this results in a range of neurological phenotypes. Early, accurate detection and classification of abnormalities in brain tissue are necessary for effective management of the disease's progression. Globally, about 2.8 million people suffer from brain tissue-related disabilities [1–3].

Magnetic resonance imaging (MRI) makes it easier to find abnormalities in multiple sclerosis (MS), but the brain regions that appear normal in the MRI have underlying damage [4, 5]. To provide a detailed analysis of the condition, the Scanning Transmission Electron Microscopy (STEM) was used to identify the damage to the brain tissue at the ultrastructural level. The brain tissue regions that appeared normal in an MRI but with underlying damage are referred to as the normal-appearing white matter (NAWM) and normal-appearing grey matter (NAGM). For the control, the control white matter (CWM) and control grey matter (CGM) from healthy individuals without MS are used for comparison. By independently analyzing four main tissue categories, this study explores the regional tissue categorization of the STEM Images. Crucially, recent research has highlighted that even normal-appearing white matter (NAWM) exhibits ultrastructural pathological changes [6, 7]. Mainly, this highlights the need for more sophisticated imaging and classification methods that can identify such minute changes at the microscopic level.

In contrast to conventional multiclass classifiers, our approach, however, uses a one-vs-rest binary classification paradigm, in which each model is trained to differentiate a specific region from all the others. This targeted training improves accuracy and is especially useful in situations where class boundaries are ambiguous or complex [8]. The methodology integrates traditional convolutional neural networks (CNNs) with advanced transfer learning architectures, VGG16, ResNet50, and EfficientNetB0. Each model is trained to differentiate between the following tissue types: Normal-Appearing White Matter (NAWM), Cortical Gray Matter (CGM), Cerebral White Matter (CWM), or Normal-Appearing Gray Matter (NAGM). By concentrating the learning process on a single class at a time, this methodology streamlines the classification task while improving sensitivity and accuracy. In medical imaging, where intra-class variances and inter-class similarities can make multiclass classification challenging, it is particularly beneficial. This ability of the model to distinguish between the different brain tissue regions can provide insights into the early detection and targeted drug treatment for patients affected by MS.

2   Related Works

Deep learning techniques have been used in some research on MS classification by MRI; most of these studies have used multiclass classification models that aim to identify all tissue types simultaneously [9, 10]. However, because of overlapping feature distributions, these methods have poor sensitivity when it comes to differentiating anatomically or pathologically equivalent areas.

Because they can learn abstract features from small datasets, transfer learning frameworks like VGG16 and ResNet have become increasingly popular in the medical imaging field [11, 12]. By creating fake images, Generative Adversarial Networks (GANs) have also been used to combat class imbalance [13]. The use of these techniques is mostly restricted to disease versus normal binary evaluation or traditional multiclass classification. Our study offers a one-vs-rest binary classification, in contrast to previous research. Paradigm for a particular area of the brain, such as Normal-Appearing Grey Matter (NAGM), Cerebral White Matter (CWM), Cortical Grey Matter (CGM), and Normal-Appearing White Matter (NAWM). Table 1. Shows the comparison of the different deep learning-based methods used for the classification of MS with their dataset used, publication year, and title, the accuracy, and other metrics used for the model evaluation.

In the field of brain tissue segmentation related to multiple sclerosis (MS), the region-specific classification paradigm is novel. It improves sensitivity and specificity by having each model learn informative features for a particular target region. Furthermore, instead of using a generalized approach to augmentation, which preserves region-specific morphological features, we develop region-specific class-based generative adversarial network (GAN) based augmentation pipelines [14, 15]. Compared to conventional multiclass deep learning models, the complementary approach of class-sensitive augmentation and one-vs-all binary classifiers offers superior interpretability and performance [16].

Table 1. Comparison of the different deep learning-based methods used for the classification of MS with their dataset used, publication year, and title, the accuracy, and other metrics used for the model evaluation

S. No	Publication Title and Year	Dataset	Model	Accuracy	Other Scores
1	Brain tumor segmentation with Deep Neural Networks [2017] [9]	BRATS dataset	CNN	NIL	Dice Score: 0.87

(continued)

Table 1. (*continued*)

S. No	Publication Title and Year	Dataset	Model	Accuracy	Other Scores
2	Pathological ultrastructural alterations of myelinated axons in normal-appearing white matter in progressive multiple sclerosis [2023] [6]	MS Brain Imaging sourced from the European Bioinformatics Institute's Bio Images portal	Morphological Operations: Advanced Electron Microscopy Techniques	NIL	Grinding Ratio: 0.77
3	Grad-CAM: Visual Explanations from Deep Networks via Gradient-Based Localization [2017] [11]	PASCAL VOC dataset	VGG-16 & ResNet	VGG-16: 89%, ResNet: 95%	NIL
4	Deep Learning in Medical Image Analysis [2021] [8]	BRATS dataset	GAN with CNN model	95%	NIL
5	Detection and Classification of Multiple Sclerosis from Brain MRIs by Using MobileNet 2D-CNN Architecture [2025] [1]	Using the MRI Image Dataset	MobileNet 2D-CNN	NIL	Precision: 98%, ROC: 100%

3 Novelty and Contributions

This work presents a novel pipeline for the classification of brain tissues in MS patients obtained using Scanning Transmission Electron Microscopy (STEM). The contributions are as follows,

- One-vs-rest binary classification per category of brain tissue (CGM, CWM, NAGM, NAWM), enabling accurate region-level discrimination even if class boundaries overlap.
- Independent class-specific GAN augmentation, retaining individual unique spatial characteristics of each tissue type.
- Comparison between baselines of architectures like CNN, VGG16, Efficient Net, and ResNet to assess the performance on

- subtle MS-related structural alterations.
- Highlight the importance of normal-appearing grey and white matter (NAGM, NAWM), in view of recent studies highlighting their contribution to disease pathology in spite of the normal-appearing imaging findings.

4 Proposed Methodology

4.1 Dataset

The data utilized in this study are derived from the publicly available MS brain imaging collection hosted on the European Bioinformatics Institute's Bio Images portal (Study Accession ID: S-BIAD1406). The dataset consists of fresh post-mortem white and grey matter brain tissue samples from a total of 11 subjects, with 4 healthy controls and 7 MS patients obtained from the Netherlands' Brain Bank. Tissue patches were extracted manually and fixed for exploration in the STEM. Regions affected by MS—specifically NAGM and NAWM—were sampled from patients with MS. CGM and CWM were sampled from healthy individuals to serve as control references [6]. The classification of the brain tissues is as follows,

- CGM (Cortical Grey Matter): Healthy control region
- CWM (Cerebral White Matter): Healthy control region
- NAGM (Normal-Appearing Grey Matter): Extracted from MS patients, pathologically significant despite normal appearance on standard scans
- NAWM (Normal-Appearing White Matter): Extracted from MS patients, often associated with early disease progression

4.2 Image Pre-processing and GAN-Based Augmentation

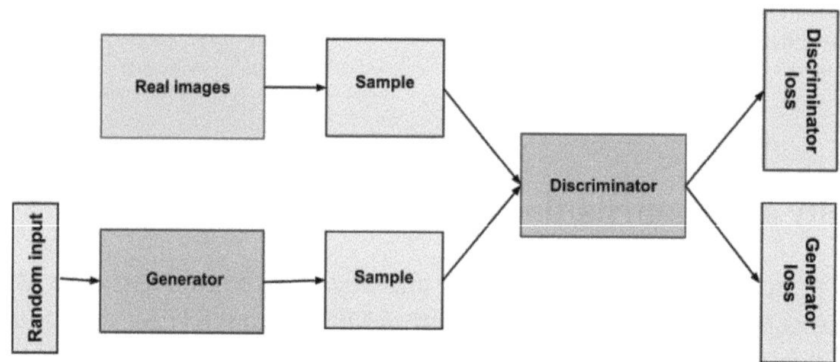

Fig. 1. GAN Architecture with Generator and Discriminator networks. The Generator synthesizes STEM-like tissue images conditioned on class-specific features, while the Discriminator learns to differentiate between real and generated samples. This architecture is based on DCGAN, optimized per class [19].

As a preliminary step to address class imbalance and improve the robustness of the training process, basic augmentation techniques—such as random flips, rotations, and contrast adjustments were applied. This effectively doubled the number of training images per class. Subsequently, Generative Adversarial Networks (GANs) were employed to generate synthetic samples that closely resemble real STEM images. GANs comprise two neural network components: a generator, responsible for producing realistic images, and a discriminator, which attempts to distinguish between real and generated images [15, 17]. The GAN architecture used is shown in Fig. 1. Training proceeds until the discriminator can no longer reliably differentiate the two. For each class, separate GAN models were trained individually to preserve the unique properties of each brain region. These models generated up to 600 synthetic images per class. After a thorough manual review to remove artifacts and unrealistic samples, 280 high-quality images per class were selected for training. The generator network was based on the Deep Convolutional Generative Adversarial Network (DCGAN) architecture, while the discriminator utilized convolutional layers with transpose operations [18].

4.3   One-vs-Rest Binary Classification Strategy

Four independent binary classifiers were trained using a one-vs-rest approach:

CGM vs. (CWM + NAGM + NAWM)
CWM vs. (CGM + NAGM + NAWM)
NAGM vs. (CGM + CWM + NAWM)
NAWM vs. (CGM + CWM + NAGM)

Each classifier outputs a probability for the image belonging to the target region. Predictions from all classifiers were aggregated during testing; the highest confidence determined the predicted class [20, 21].

4.4   Model Architectures

Four neural network architectures were assessed for model training. The model architecture used to categorize brain tissues in progressive multiple sclerosis using Scanning Transmission Electron Microscopy (STEM) images is schematically diagrammed in Fig. 2.

Custom CNN: The standard Max-pooling and ReLU activations come after each of the three convolutional layers that make up a convolutional neural network (CNN). Flattening and fully connected layers with dropout for regularization are part of the network. $224 \times 224 \times 3$ pixels is the standard size for the input image [22].

VGG16: A transfer learning model that starts with ImageNet weights that have already been pretrained. To preserve general features, the base layers are first frozen. During fine-tuning, they are progressively unfrozen to accommodate the particular domain of STEM images [23].

ResNet50: To counteract vanishing gradients, a deep architecture with residual connections is used. Its limited performance in this study, however, was probably caused by the dataset's small size [24].

EfficientNetB0: Compound scaling is used by EfficientNetB0 to balance input resolution, network width, and depth. In our experiments, it showed moderate and inconsistent sensitivity across classes, despite its theoretical efficiency [25].

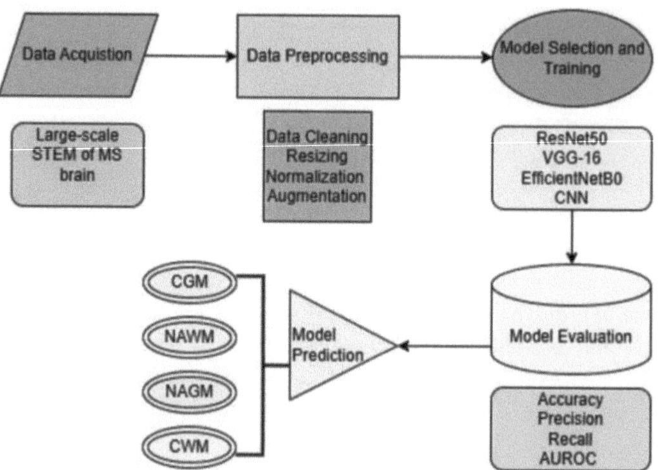

Fig. 2. Model Architecture for the classification of MS using Large-scale Scanning Transmission Electron Microscopy images

5　Experimental Results

The confusion matrices, Receiver Operating Characteristic (ROC) curves with Area Under the Curve (AUC), and a comparison of several deep learning architectures were examined to assess the effectiveness of the trained binary classifiers for each class of brain tissue (CGM, CWM, NAGM, and NAWM). The dataset had an 80:20 train-test ratio, including 280 balanced and GAN-augmented images per class. The original images of the brain tissues and the GAN-generated images are shown in Fig. 3.

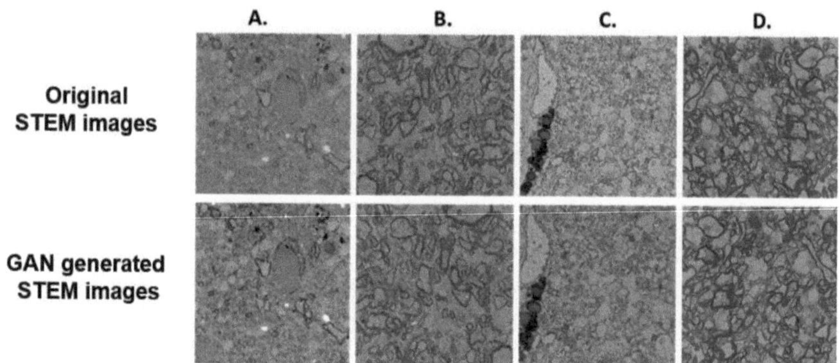

Fig. 3. Comparison of Real and GAN-Synthesized Images Across Tissue Classes. Each column shows one brain tissue type: (A) Cortical Grey Matter (CGM), (B) Cerebral White Matter (CWM), (C) Normal-Appearing Grey Matter (NAGM), and (D) Normal-Appearing White Matter (NAWM). First row: real STEM images; second row: corresponding GAN-generated synthetic images used for training. Axes are in pixel units (224 × 224), and all images are contrast-normalized.

5.1 Combined Performance Metrics

A comparative analysis was conducted among four architectures: ResNet50, Efficient-NetB0, VGG16, and a custom CNN. Precision, Recall, Accuracy, and area under the receiver operating characteristic (AUROC) are among the metrics evaluated. The metrics obtained for the models are given in Table 2. High precision (0.9) was maintained by all models, with VGG16 and CNN achieving the highest. Recall of ResNet50 and Efficient-NetB0 trailed behind VGG16, which performed noticeably better than the others, with a recall of 0.8. Accuracy of VGG16 had the highest overall accuracy (0.9), followed by CNN and ResNet50. AUROC of VGG16 demonstrated superior class separation ability by achieving the highest AUROC (0.9) once more.

Table 2. Shows the metric comparison between the different models

Model	Precision	Recall	Accuracy	AUROC
ResNet50	0.9006	0.3884	0.8147	0.6726
EfficientNetB0	0.8750	0.2500	0.7500	0.5000
VGG16	**0.8900**	**0.8527**	**0.9319**	**0.9055**
CNN	0.8995	0.5079	0.8243	0.7241

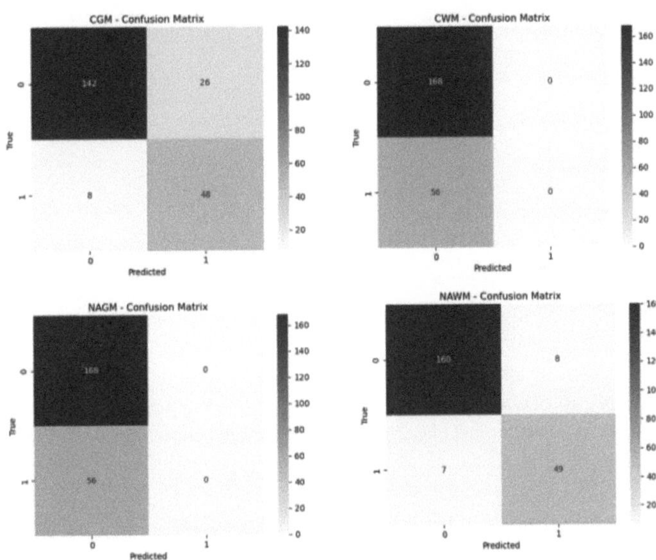

Fig. 4. Confusion Matrices for Each One-vs-Rest Classifier. Each matrix shows the number of true positives, false positives, true negatives, and false negatives for CGM, CWM, NAGM, and NAWM classifiers, respectively. Metrics are computed on the 20% test set.

The Fig. 4 displays the confusion matrices for every binary classifier. The models demonstrate strong classification ability and few misclassifications. CGM Classifier:

False Positives = 26, False Negatives = 0, True Positives = 142, True Negatives = 48. CWM Classifier: False Positives = 0, False Negatives = 0, True Positives = 168, True Negatives = 52. NAGM Classifier: False Positives = 0, False Negatives = 56, True Positives = 168, and Negatives equal zero. NAWM Classifier: False Positives = 8, False Negatives = 0, True Positives = 160, True Negatives = 56. While all models demonstrated high specificity and sensitivity, the NAWM classifier had higher false positive rates. The Fig. 5 demonstrates ROC curves show that all classifiers have strong separability, AUC of 0.951 for CGM, AUC of 0.965 for CWM, AUC for NAGM is 0.973 and AUC of 0.971 for NAWM. The robustness of the models in differentiating between the positive and negative classes is confirmed by these high AUC values. This indicates that the model is highly effective in capturing features relevant to these tissues, possibly due to clearer or more distinct signal patterns or intensity distributions in the imaging data.

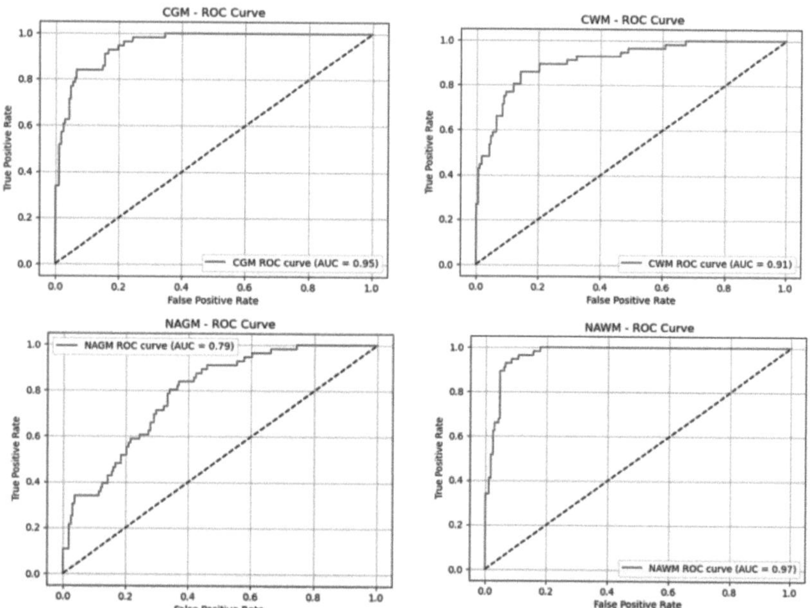

Fig. 5. Receiver Operating Characteristic (ROC) Curves for all four binary classifiers. Each ROC curve shows the tradeoff between sensitivity and specificity for a particular tissue classifier. High AUC values (>0.95) confirm robust classification performance across CGM, CWM, NAWM, and NAGM.

The model also performs well in classifying CWM with an AUC of 0.91, suggesting good separability in white matter regions. However, the performance drops slightly for NAGM, which shows a lower AUC of 0.79. This could be attributed to the following factors. NAGM may share overlapping characteristics with pathological or normal tissues, making differentiation harder. Potential imaging noise or variability in this region may reduce model confidence. The results confirm that the model is robust and generalizable across most tissue types.

6 Discussion

The one-vs-rest classification framework effectively isolated the model's focus on each brain region, improving specificity. While ResNet50 and EfficientNetB0 underperformed in sensitivity due to limited data, VGG16 excelled across metrics, highlighting the power of transfer learning with proper fine-tuning.

The deeper layer structure and consistent filter sizes of VGG16 enable hierarchical learning of fine-grained textural and morphological features in STEM images, which accounts for its superior performance. On the other hand, because of the small dataset size, ResNet50's skip connections might have resulted in underfitting, even though they worked well in larger datasets. It's also possible that EfficientNetB0's aggressive compound scaling led to decreased sensitivity during training on small sample sizes. GAN-based augmentation significantly expanded and balanced the dataset, ensuring better model generalization. Manual curation preserved sample quality.

Even though VGG16 requires more processing power than a baseline CNN, real-time inference following pruning and quantization is made possible by its compatibility with edge AI deployment frameworks (such as TensorRT and ONNX). Integration with clinical imaging pipelines would be facilitated by more research into lightweight deployment techniques.

7 Conclusion

In conclusion, this work shows that combining one-vs-rest binary classification with transfer learning and GAN-based augmentation for brain tissue classification in MS patients is both feasible and effective. Deep learning's potential to improve neuroimaging diagnostics is further supported by the high classification performance, particularly from the VGG16 model. The suggested system may be crucial in helping people with Multiple Sclerosis by facilitating earlier and more precise identification of impacted tissue areas. In metrics like accuracy and AUROC, the VGG16 model showed slight but steady gains over the baseline CNN, underscoring the benefit of transfer learning on small, domain-specific datasets. In our tests, VGG16 proved to be the most successful architecture, achieving an overall accuracy of 93.19%.

Our approach emphasizes region-specific specialization and can be scaled to incorporate lesion-specific detection or longitudinal MRI scans for progression tracking. The future work will focus on applying patch-wise Grad-CAM to identify which regions contribute most to classification decisions. Building lightweight ensemble classifiers combining traditional and deep features. Testing model robustness on external MS tissue datasets and integrating explainable AI modules for clinician validation.

References

1. Saurabh, S., Gupta, P.K.: Detection and classification of multiple sclerosis from brain MRIs by using MobileNet 2D-CNN architecture. Comput. Sist. **28**, 1229–1242 (2024)
2. Korn, T.: Pathophysiology of multiple sclerosis. J. Neurol. **255**, 2–6 (2008)
3. Dobson, R., Giovannoni, G.: Multiple sclerosis–a review. Eur. J. Neurol. **26**, 27–40 (2019)

4. Wattjes, M.P., et al: 2021 MAGNIMS–CMSC–NAIMS consensus recommendations on the use of MRI in patients with multiple sclerosis. Lancet Neurol. **20**, 653–670 (2021)

5. Combes, A.J., Clarke, M.A., O'Grady, K.P., Schilling, K.G., Smith, S.A.: advanced spinal cord MRI in multiple sclerosis: current techniques and future directions. NeuroImage: Clinical. **36**, 103244 (2022)

6. Oost, W., et al: Pathological ultrastructural alterations of myelinated axons in normal appearing white matter in progressive multiple sclerosis. Acta Neuropathol. Commun. **11**, 100 (2023)

7. Oost, W., Meilof, J.F., Baron, W.: Multiple sclerosis: what have we learned and can we still learn from electron microscopy. Cell. Mol. Life Sci. **82**, 1–22 (2025)

8. Shen, D., Wu, G., Suk, H.-I.: Deep learning in medical image analysis. Annu. Rev. Biomed. Eng. **19**, 221–248 (2017)

9. Havaei, M., et al: Brain tumor segmentation with deep neural networks. Med. Image Anal. **35**, 18–31 (2017)

10. Ponce de Leon-Sanchez, E.R., Dominguez-Ramirez, O.A., Herrera-Navarro, A.M., Rodriguez-Resendiz, J., Paredes-Orta, C., Mendiola-Santibañez, J.D.: A deep learning approach for predicting multiple sclerosis. Micromachines. **14**, 749 (2023)

11. Selvaraju, R.R., Cogswell, M., Das, A., Vedantam, R., Parikh, D., Batra, D.: Grad-CAM: visual explanations from deep networks via gradient-based localization. Int. J. Comput. Vis. **128**, 336–359 (2020)

12. Kingma, D.P., Ba, J.: Adam: A method for stochastic optimization. arXiv preprint arXiv, 1412.6980 (2014)

13. Chawla, N.V., Bowyer, K.W., Hall, L.O., Kegelmeyer, W.P.: SMOTE: synthetic minority over-sampling technique. J. Artif. Intell. Res. **16**, 321–357 (2002)

14. Zhang, C., et al: MS-GAN: GAN-based semantic segmentation of multiple sclerosis lesions in brain magnetic resonance imaging. In: 2018 Digital Image Computing: Techniques and Applications (DICTA), pp. 1–8. IEEE (2018)

15. Boyapati, N., et al: Alzheimer's Disease Prediction using Convolutional Neural Network (CNN) with Generative Adversarial Network (GAN). In: 2023 International Conference on Data Science, Agents & Artificial Intelligence (ICDSAAI), pp. 1–6. IEEE (2023)

16. Salome, P., et al: MR-class: a python tool for brain MR image classification utilizing one-vs-all DCNNs to deal with the open-set recognition problem. Cancer. **15**, 1820 (2023)

17. Ahmad, W., Ali, H., Shah, Z., Azmat, S.: A new generative adversarial network for medical images super resolution. Sci. Rep. **12**, 9533 (2022)

18. Singh, N.K., Raza, K.: Medical image generation using generative adversarial networks: a review. In: Health informatics: A computational perspective in healthcare, pp. 77–96 (2021)

19. Alrashedy, H.H.N., Almansour, A.F., Ibrahim, D.M., Hammoudeh, M.A.A.: BrainGAN: brain MRI image generation and classification framework using GAN architectures and CNN models. Sensors. **22**, 4297 (2022)

20. Hurbungs, V., Bassoo, V., Fowdur, T.: A novel one-vs-next approach for multiclass classification. In: 2024 IEEE Symposium on Computers and Communications (ISCC), pp. 1–6. IEEE (2024)

21. Vogiatzis, A., Chalkiadakis, G., Moirogiorgou, K., Zervakis, M.: A novel one-vs-rest classification framework for mutually supported decisions by independent parallel classifiers. In: 2021 IEEE International Conference on Imaging Systems and Techniques (IST), pp. 1–6. IEEE (2021)

22. Bhatt, D., et al: CNN variants for computer vision: history, architecture, application, challenges and future scope. Electronics. **10**, 2470 (2021)

23. Mascarenhas, S., Agarwal, M.: A comparison between VGG16, VGG19 and ResNet50 architecture frameworks for Image Classification. In: 2021 International conference on disruptive

technologies for multi-disciplinary research and applications (CENTCON), pp. 96–99. IEEE (2021)
24. Koonce, B.: ResNet 50. Convolutional Neural Networks with Swift for Tensorflow: Image Recognition and Dataset Categorization, pp. 63–72. Springer (2021)
25. Koonce, B.: EfficientNet. In: Convolutional Neural Networks with Swift for Tensorflow: Image Recognition and Dataset Categorization, pp. 109–123. Springer (2021)

HMST-Lite: A Lightweight Multi-scale Transformer for Early Breast Cancer Stage Classification

Satyanarayana Reddy Beram[1]([✉]), R. Lalchhanhima[1], and Ksh. Robert Singh[2]

[1] Department of Information Technology, Mizoram University, Aizawl, Mizoram 796004, India
`mzu22007898@mzu.edu.in`
[2] Department of Electrical Engineering, Mizoram University, Aizawl, Mizoram 796004, India

Abstract. Prognosis and treatment choices are largely based on the accurate staging of breast cancer. Traditional deep learning approaches often find it hard to capture the detailed and spatial features seen in histopathological images, particularly when magnification changes. In addition, most WSI staging models are computationally complex and hard to interpret, making them tough to use in real-world clinical situations that require fast and early diagnosis. In response to these limitations, we present HMST-Lite, a lightweight transformer-based architecture that makes use of multi-scale histopathological data for early breast cancer detection. Compare to the other regular models, HMST-Lite takes advantage of visual tokens at two magnification levels ($10\times$ and $20\times$) to recognize fine details from tissue structure efficiently. This multi-scale mechanism captures the context within each scale is used, then the fusion layer combines the multi-scale features. The model's performance is measured on a specially selected part of the TCGA-BRCA cohort dataset, after preprocessing to highlight tissue regions important for early detection. The model's performance is evaluated with Accuracy, Macro F1-Score, and QWK to guarantee reliability in class balance and simulated inter-rater agreement. The HMST-Lite framework provides the basic structure for the future HMST model, which will include cross-cohort fusion and prognostic learning.

Keywords: Breast Cancer Staging · Multi-Scale Transformer · Whole Slide Image (WSI) · Tumor Classification · Histopathology

1 Introduction

1.1 Clinical Relevance of Early-Stage Detection

Globally, breast cancer is a major reason for women dying from cancer. Early-stage diagnosis is strongly correlated with favorable treatment outcomes, increased survival rates, and reduced healthcare burden [1]. According to the World Health Organization, patients diagnosed at stage I have a 5-year survival rate exceeding 90%, whereas this number drastically falls in stage III and IV cases. Accurate classification of tumor stages, therefore, plays a pivotal role in personalized treatment planning, recurrence risk stratification, and long-term disease monitoring.

R. K. Karsh et al. (Eds.): SIPCOV 2025, CCIS 2848, pp. 76–92, 2026.
https://doi.org/10.1007/978-3-032-15809-3_6

Traditional staging workflows primarily depend on radiology and histopathological examination, supported by clinical guidelines such as the AJCC TNM system (Zhu & Dogan, 2021) [2]. However, radiology-based assessments suffer from limitations in resolution and are often incapable of capturing the fine-grained morphological changes in tissue architecture. Furthermore, manual histological staging is time-intensive and subject to inter-observer variability, with studies reporting only moderate agreement among pathologists, particularly in high-grade or borderline cases [3].

1.2 Challenges in Computational Staging

Despite advances in deep learning, computational breast cancer staging from whole-slide histopathology images (WSIs) poses several key challenges. First, WSIs are ultra-high resolution, often exceeding $100,000 \times 100,000$ pixels, making direct processing computationally prohibitive. This necessitates patch-based sampling strategies, which in turn require robust feature integration techniques to retain contextual coherence across tiles.

Second, data heterogeneity across patients, institutions, and imaging devices introduces variability in staining protocols, tissue quality, and annotation reliability. Models trained on homogeneous datasets often exhibit poor generalization in real-world clinical scenarios, particularly in cross-cohort applications [4].

Third, spatial-scale sensitivity is a critical issue in histopathology. Tumor-related patterns exist at both the cellular level (e.g., mitotic count, nuclear pleomorphism) and the tissue level (e.g., ductal arrangement, stromal invasion). Single-resolution models fail to simultaneously capture these multi-scale dependencies, resulting in suboptimal performance [1].

Finally, a major bottleneck for clinical adoption is the lack of model interpretability. Conventional deep learning architectures are often perceived as "black boxes," hindering trust and integration in diagnostic workflows. Visual justifications—such as attention maps and attribution scores—are essential to bridge this gap and facilitate human-in-the-loop decision-making.

1.3 Motivation for Multi-scale Attention

To address these challenges, multi-scale deep learning architectures have gained increasing attention in computational pathology. Inspired by the diagnostic approach of human experts, who frequently navigate between low-and high-magnification views ($10\times$ and $20\times$), it is essential to design models capable of learning both local and global representations.

The choice of $10\times$ and $20\times$ magnifications reflects the standard diagnostic practice in digital pathology. The $10\times$ view provides a wide field for observing tissue-level architecture, stromal patterns, and glandular alignment, while the $20\times$ view enables examination of cellular morphology, such as nuclear atypia and mitotic activity. Together, these magnification levels capture complementary information, which is crucial for accurate stage classification (Ginter et al., 2020).

Transformers, particularly Vision Transformers (ViTs), provide an effective solution due to their inherent ability to model long-range dependencies through self-attention mechanisms. When extended into a multi-branch framework, each ViT branch can independently extract features at a specific scale, preserving both the semantic richness of high-resolution detail and the structural coherence of tissue-level context.

Integrating $10\times$ and $20\times$ representations allow the model to capture staging-relevant features such as tumor margin infiltration, epithelial clustering, and stromal remodeling, which may be difficult to detect at a single scale. The challenge, however, lies in fusing these features effectively without introducing computational overhead or diluting interpretability. This forms the central motivation for the development of HMST-Lite.

1.4 Contributions

In this work, we introduce HMST-Lite, a computationally efficient, dual-scale transformer-based AI architecture tailored for early breast cancer stage classification. The key contributions of our study are summarized as follows:

- A dual-branch ViT architecture that processes $10\times$ and $20\times$ magnification tiles independently, allowing rich multi-resolution feature extraction with spatial fidelity.
- A shallow fusion mechanism that concatenates class-token representations from each scale, followed by a lightweight MLP head for final classification. This avoids complex cross-attention schemes, preserving interpretability and reducing computational cost.
- An efficient training pipeline, optimized for resource-constrained environments, with a total parameter count significantly lower than traditional ViT backbones, enabling faster convergence and deployment feasibility.
- High interpretability through attention heatmaps, offering visual insights into scale-specific focus regions, which align with expert-defined histological cues.

Through these contributions, HMST-Lite aims to bridge the gap between deep learning innovation and practical clinical utility, laying a scalable foundation for AI-assisted breast cancer diagnostics [5].

2 Related Work

2.1 CNN-Based Staging Models

CNNs are frequently used as the key method for automatically diagnosing and staging breast cancer from histopathological images. They are a reliable choice for patch-level classification and segmentation because they can extract features in a hierarchy and adjust to different datasets. To illustrate, ResNet, Inception, and EfficientNet models have been used on the TCGA-BRCA, most of these systems apply fixed receptive fields, so they have trouble capturing the overall context needed for staging WSIs.

Also, standard CNNs usually perform worse when there are changes in domains or magnification. It is especially problematic when staging decisions need details from several resolutions. Even with ensemble approaches and transfer learning [6], CNNs still cannot fully recognize morphological differences in breast tumor tissues because their features are localized.

2.2 Vision Transformers in Medical Imaging

Vision Transformers (ViTs) have changed medical image analysis by using self-attention in place of convolutional backbones to capture long-range relationships. Models like RI-ViT [7] and CWC-MP-MC [8] using ViT have proven very accurate at classifying breast cancer, often reaching 90% or more on well-known datasets. Processing image patches as tokens and modeling the whole image helps these models succeed in difficult tissue cases.

ViT models use attention maps to indicate which image areas are key for classification [9]. In medicine, being able to understand how decisions are made is especially important for this feature. Moreover, certain ViT models have been used to assess HER2 expression in H&E slides without IHC, thanks to Choo et al. [10], which helps speed up diagnosis. While ViT models are promising, they typically need a large amount of training data and computing resources, which is hard for clinics with limited resources.

2.3 Multi-scale Representations in Digital Pathology

Multi-scale learning is a common technique in digital pathology as it follows how pathologists examine slides at many magnification levels. In cross scale multi instance networks proposed by (Deng et al. [11]) uses the $5\times$, $10\times$, and $20\times$ magnifications to blend the details from cells with details from tissue overall. Models can use this representation to look at nuclei texture and tissue organization at once.

Yu et al. [12] showed that multi-resolution fusion networks outperform single-scale models in tasks related to tumor grading and subtype classification. Also, models like RI-ViT use special attention blocks at each scale to combine features from different branches, which helps improve both accuracy and how easy the model is to understand. Even though multi-scale systems offer several benefits, they usually need more time and memory for training, and fusing features at different resolutions is hard, especially for tiny but important structures.

2.4 Lightweight and Interpretable Architectures

Dsouza et al. [13] designed a hybrid CNN system with a small number of parameters for histopathological image classification, resulting in high accuracy with little computational effort. Joseph and Gupta [14] developed a dual multi-scale CNN model that is designed to work well in environments with limited resources.

At the same time, using attention-guided interpretability tools has become widespread. ViT-based explainability methods, such as ViT-Shapley and focused attention maps, have improved how decisions are explained when compared to expert annotations [15]. The way the model predicts results is similar to how pathologists think, making automated systems more trusted. Still, lightweight models struggle to balance how well they work and how complex their feature modeling is, especially in tasks like cancer staging and progression prediction. Table 1 compares different models by looking at their architecture, datasets used, interpretability, and their performance in staging or classification.

Table. 1. Comparative Overview of Related Staging Models

Architecture	Dataset(s) Used	Interpretability	Accuracy (%)	Complexity
CNN	METABRIC, TCGA	Low (CAM)	~82.2	Medium
Multi-Scale CNN	TCGA, BACH	Moderate	~85.5	High
Hybrid ViT + CNN	BACH, Private	High (Attention Map)	~87.3	Very High
Lightweight CNN	BreakHis	Moderate	~83.4	Medium
Vision Transformer	METABRIC, WSI	High	~88.8	Very High

3 HMST-Lite Framework

3.1 Architecture Overview

HMST-Lite is a small and powerful dual-branch system for spotting breast cancer early in whole-slide images. Unlike conventional CNNs or heavy ViT architectures, HMST-Lite emphasizes computational efficiency, multi-resolution feature learning, and interpretability, making it deployable in resource-constrained clinical environments.

The architecture, illustrated in Fig. 1, consists of two independent transformer branches operating on $10\times$ and $20\times$ magnification levels, denoted as $\mathcal{B}_{10}$ and $\mathcal{B}_{20}$, respectively. Each branch follows a modular vision transformer pipeline consisting of: i) Patch extraction and tokenization ii) Transformer encoding with multi-head self-attention and iii) Aggregation via a class token Z_{cls}.

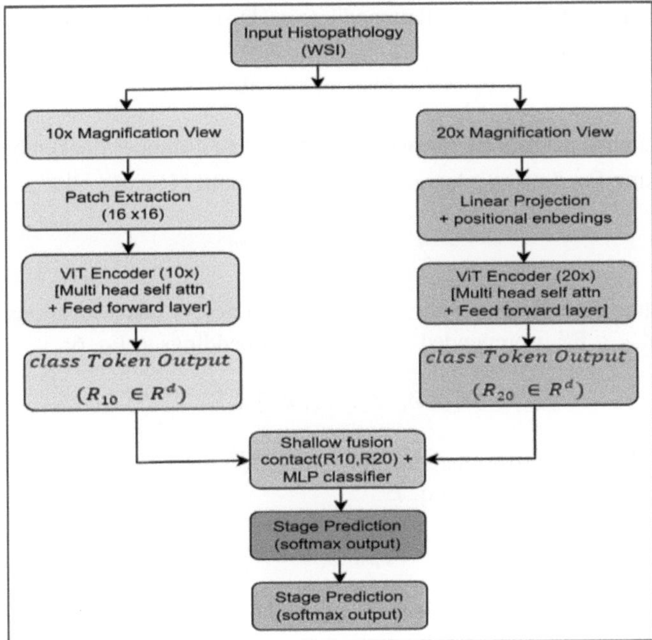

Fig. 1. HMST-Lite architecture showing dual ViT branches at $10\times$ and $20\times$ magnifications with shallow fusion for stage prediction.

Let $x_{10} \in \mathbb{R}^{H \times W \times 3}$ and $x_{20} \in \mathbb{R}^{H \times W \times 3}$ denote the two resolution views of the same histopathology region. The HMST-Lite model encodes each input view into a high-dimensional representation $\mathcal{R}_{10}, \mathcal{R}_{20} \in \mathbb{R}^d$ which are fused in a later stage for final classification. In math, the pipeline can be summarized as shown in Eqs. 1 and 2:

$$\mathcal{R}_{10} = \mathcal{B}_{10}(x_{10}); \; \mathcal{R}_{20} = \mathcal{B}_{20}(x_{20}) \tag{1}$$

$$y = \phi(\mathcal{R}_{10}, \mathcal{R}_{20}) \tag{2}$$

Where $\phi(.)$ denotes the shallow fusion and prediction head, and $y \in \mathbb{R}^k$ is the predicted class distribution over K cancer stages (e.g., early, intermediate, advanced). This dual-view transformer design enhances the model's capability to reason across both global tissue structures (via $10\times$) and cellular-level morphology (via $20\times$), reflecting the diagnostic workflow of human pathologists.

3.2 Patch Extraction and Tokenization

For each magnification level, the input image $X \in \mathbb{R}^{H \times W \times 3}$ is divided into non-overlapping square patches of size as shown in Eq. 3, where $P = 16$ pixels. The total number of patches is:

$$N = \left(\frac{H}{P}\right) \times \left(\frac{W}{P}\right) \tag{3}$$

Each patch $x_i \in \mathbb{R}^{P \times P \times 3}$ is flattened into a 1D vector are calculated using Eq. 4:

$$\widetilde{X}_i = \text{Flatten}(X_i) \in \mathbb{R}^{P^2 3} \tag{4}$$

These flattened patches are linearly projected into a d-dimensional embedding space computed using Eq. 5 using a learnable projection matrix $E \in \mathbb{R}^{(P^2 3) \times d}$:

$$Z_i = \widetilde{X}_i \ . \ E \in \mathbb{R}^d \tag{5}$$

To facilitate classification and enable attention across patch locations, a trainable class token $Z_{cls} \in \mathbb{R}^d$ is prepended to the patch embeddings as Eq. 6:

$$Z = [Z_{cls}; Z_1; Z_2; \ldots; Z_N] \in \mathbb{R}^{(N+1) \times d} \tag{6}$$

Next, the learnable positional encodings $P \in \mathbb{R}^{(N+1) \times d}$ are added to the preserve spatial information as shown in Eq. 7:

$$Z_{input} = Z + P \tag{7}$$

The resulting input token sequence Z_{input} is then passed to the transformer encoder of the corresponding branch. Each transformer encoder in HMST-Lite is kept shallow to ensure the computational tractability. We use 4 encoder layers with 4 attention heads and a hidden size $d = 256$. The self-attention computation within each transformer layer operates as in Eq. 8:

$$\text{Attention}(Q, K, V) = \text{softmax}\left(\frac{QK^T}{\sqrt{d_k}}\right) V \tag{8}$$

Where the query, key, and value matrices are derived as in Eq. 9:

$$Q = Z_{input}.W^Q, \quad K = Z_{input} \ .W^k, \quad V = Z_{input} \ .W^V \tag{9}$$

$$W^Q, W^k, W^V \in \mathbb{R}^{d \times d_k} \tag{10}$$

The class token embedding $Z_{cls}^{(L)} \in \mathbb{R}^d$ from the final layer L of each transformer serves as the condensed representation $\overline{R}$ of the input image at a particular magnification. For the $10\times$ and $20\times$ branches, we denote in Eq. 11:

$$R_{10} = Z_{cls,10}^{(L)}, \quad R_{20} = Z_{cls,20}^{(L)} \tag{11}$$

These embeddings are forwarded to the shallow fusion module described in experiments. The advantages of this tokenization strategy include: Capturing fine and coarse features from patch granularity, maintaining positional context for spatial reasoning and enabling transformer-based attention to operate uniformly across both scales.

3.3 Intra-scale Attention Module

The core of each magnification-specific branch in HMST-Lite is a Vision Transformer encoder that utilizes self-attention to model the contextual relationships among visual tokens, which are extracted from the same scale. This intra-scale attention module independently encodes the spatial dependencies within the $10\times$ and $20\times$ magnification views, which allows the model to capture the both coarse structural and fine morphological information without inter-branch interference [16]. Given the input token sequence $Z_{input} \in R^{(N+1)\times d}$, including the class token, the transformer encoder processes this sequence through multiple stacked transformer blocks, each consisting of: Multi-head self-attention (MSA) with Layer Normalization (LN) and Feed-forward network (FFN) with Residual connections.

3.3.1 Multi-head Self-Attention

The self-attention mechanism learns pairwise affinities between patches. For each token vector Z_i, we compute the query (Q), key (K), and value (V) matrices are shown in Eq. 12:

$$Q = Z_{input} \bullet W^Q, \quad K = Z_{input} \bullet W^K, \quad V = Z_{input} \bullet W^V \tag{12}$$

Where $W^Q, W^K, W^V \in R^{d \times d_k}$ and $d_k = \frac{d}{h}$, with h being the number of heads (e.g., $h = 4$). The attention output for each head is computed in Eq. 13:

$$head_i = Attention(Q_i, K_i, V_i) = softmax\left(\frac{Q_i\, K_i^T}{\sqrt{d_k}}\right) V_i \tag{13}$$

The outputs from all attention heads are concatenated finally and passed through a linear projection as follows in Eq. 14:

$$MSA(Z) = C\,oncat(head_1, head_2 \ldots \ldots, head_h) \bullet W^O \tag{14}$$

Each block is then applied with a residual connection and layer normalization as follows in the Eq. 15:

$$Z' = LN\left(Z_{input} + MSA\left(Z_{input}\right)\right) \tag{15}$$

3.3.2 Feed-Forward Network (FFN)

The FFN applies a two-layer MLP with a non-linear GELU activation are shown Eq. 16:

$$FFN(Z) = W_2 \bullet GELU(W_1 \bullet z + b_1) + b_2 \tag{16}$$

Where $W_1 \in R^{d \times d'}$, $W_2 \in R^{d' \times d}$, and typically $d' = 4d$. A residual connection and layer normalization follows as in Eq. 17:

$$Z^{(l+1)} = LN\left(Z' + FFN\left(Z'\right)\right) \tag{17}$$

This process is repeated for $L = 4$ layers per branch. After the final transformer layer, the updated class token $Z_{cls}^{(L)}$ serves as the semantic representation for the entire image view. We represent this process in Eq. 18:

$$R_{20} = Z_{cls,10}^{(L)}, \quad R_{20} = Z_{cls,20}^{(L)} \tag{18}$$

These vectors encode learned feature summaries of the input at respective scales, encapsulating attention-weighted global context from their token sequences.

3.4 Shallow Fusion Layer

To synthesize the information encoded by each magnification-specific transformer, HMST-Lite adopts a shallow fusion strategy that minimizes computational overhead while preserving discriminative power. This design avoids deep cross-attention or inter-branch token mixing, opting instead for class token-level concatenation followed by a compact prediction head. Assume that the R_{10}, $R_{20} \in R^d$ may the class token outputs from the $10\times$ and $20\times$ branches, respectively. These are tokens are concatenated to form a unified feature vector as shown Eq. 19:

$$R_{fused} = Concat(R_{10}, R_{20}) \in R^{2d} \tag{19}$$

This fused vector representation is passed through a lightweight two-layer of MLP classifier for final the prediction in Eq. 20:

$$\hat{y} = \text{softmax}\left(W_f^{(2)} \bullet GELU\left(W_f^{(1)} \bullet R_{fused} + b_f^{(1)}\right) + b_f^{(2)}\right) \tag{20}$$

Where $W_f^{(1)} \in R^{2d \times d_f}$, $W_f^{(2)} \in R^{d_f \times k}$ and d_f is the intermediate feature size (e.g $d_f, = 128$), K is the number of breast cancer stages (e.g., 3) and $\hat{y} \in R^K$ is the predicted class probability vector. The cross-entropy loss is defined and used during the training as represented in Eq. 21:

$$L_{CE} = -\sum_{k=1}^{K} y_k \log(\hat{y}_k) \tag{21}$$

where y_k is the ground-truth label encoded in one-hot format. This shallow fusion scheme offers several practical advantages such as Efficiency by Reducing the model depth and GPU memory requirements, Interpretability by preserving separable semantics from each scale and Modularity by enabling the independent updates or ablations per branch [17]. Moreover, by relying on class token-level fusion, the framework allows direct attention attribution per scale—enhancing explainability in clinical scenarios.

4 Experimental Setup

The experiments were conducted on a workstation equipped with an NVIDIA RTX 3090 GPU (24 GB VRAM) and Intel Core i9 CPU, running Ubuntu 20.04. The implementation was carried out using Python 3.9, with deep learning models developed in PyTorch 1.13 and supporting libraries including NumPy, OpenCV, and scikit-learn for preprocessing and evaluation.

4.1 Dataset Description

For empirical validation of the proposed HMST-Lite framework, we utilized a curated subset of the publicly available TCGA-BRCA cohort dataset. The original TCGA-BRCA cohort [18] includes over 1,900 breast cancer samples annotated with clinical and molecular labels. However, for the purpose of this study—focused on early-stage tumor classification—we constructed a reduced dataset comprising 1,020 patients with corresponding H&E-stained whole-slide images (WSIs) and clearly defined stage labels.

All WSIs were mapped to their corresponding stage labels using the clinical annotation files provided with the TCGA-BRCA dataset. To avoid the label imbalance issue, we first excluded the ambiguous or incomplete cases from the dataset and then stratified the remaining samples. The 80-10-10 split (training-validation-testing) was applied at the patient level, ensuring that no tiles from the same patient appeared in multiple splits, thereby preventing the data leakage and ensuring the fair evaluation of patient data. We grouped the tumor stages into three broad categories for a balanced and clinically relevant classification task are: Stage I (Early), Stage II (Intermediate) and Stage III+ (Advanced). This stratification simplifies the downstream classification while preserving the essential clinical prognostic value. The selected cohort ensured class balance by maintaining a near-equal distribution across the three categories, mitigating label imbalance that could otherwise bias performance metrics.

4.2 Preprocessing and Augmentation

All whole-slide images were first processed through a standard preprocessing pipeline to ensure uniformity across spatial resolution, color distribution, and tissue coverage. Initially, tissue segmentation was performed using Otsu's thresholding method to exclude background regions [19]. From each WSI, we extracted non-overlapping tiles of size 512×512 pixels at $10\times$ and $20\times$ magnification, corresponding to the dual-scale inputs required by HMST-Lite. Each extracted tile $T_{i,j} \in R^{512 \times 512 \times 3}$ was normalized using Z-score standardization Eq. 22:

$$T'_{i,j} = \frac{T_{i,j} - \mu}{\sigma} \tag{22}$$

where μ and σ denote the global mean and standard deviation computed across the dataset. The normalized tiles were then resized to 224×224 to match the input dimensions expected by Vision Transformer-based models.

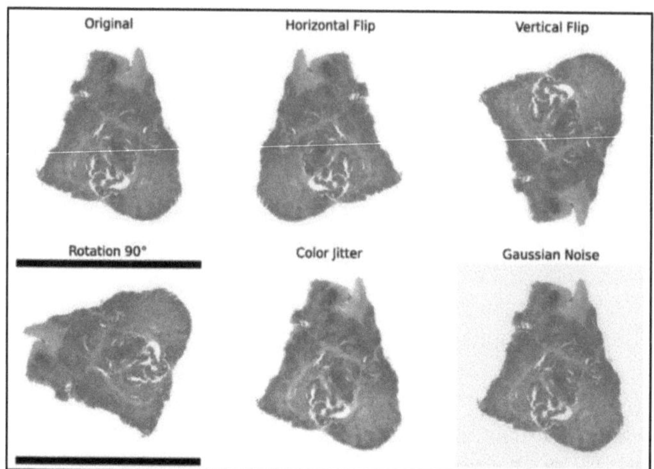

Fig. 2. Visualization of data augmentation techniques applied to histopathology tiles, including flip, rotation, jitter, and noise.

To enhance model generalization and reduce overfitting, we applied data augmentation during training. As shown in Fig. 2, the augmentation techniques included in this are: Random horizontal and vertical flipping, Random rotations (0°, 90°, 180°, 270°), Color jittering (hue, saturation, brightness) and Gaussian noise injection.

4.3 Baseline Models

To evaluate the effectiveness of HMST-Lite, we compared its performance against three strong baseline architectures:

- **RI-ViT[7]**: This model is based on Vision Transformer and residual networks, serving as a conventional baseline for histopathological image classification. The model was pretrained on ImageNet and fine-tuned on the TCGA-BRCA cohort [19].
- **DM-CNN [14]**: This deep model, utilizes multi-scale and deep-layer convolutional neural networks, significantly improve the accuracy and reliability of breast cancer detection from histopathology images, with further gains achieved through multi-objective optimization of model parameters.
- **ViT-B/16 [20]**: The Vision Transformer (ViT), particularly the ViT-B/16 model, has recently gained attention for its ability to capture both global and local features in complex medical images, offering potential improvements over traditional convolutional neural networks (CNNs) using multi scale images.

The learning rate (1×10^{-4}) was selected based on the grid search over (1×10^{-3}, 1×10^{-4}, 5×10^{-5}) and the early stopping was employed using the validation loss with a patience of 6 epochs. Each model defined in this architecture was trained for a maximum of 50 epochs using the cross-entropy loss, and training stability, which was confirmed across three runs. All baseline models were trained using the same optimizer (Adam), batch size (16), and learning rate (1×10^{4}), and early stopping was applied based on validation loss to avoid overfitting.

4.4 Evaluation Metrics

We employed a combination of accuracy and class-sensitive metrics to evaluate classification performance, ensuring a comprehensive assessment across both balanced and imbalanced scenarios.

1. **Accuracy (Acc)**: The overall proportion of correctly predicted samples as shown in Eq. 23:

$$Accuracy = \frac{TP + TN}{TP + TN + FP + FN} \tag{23}$$

2. **Macro F1-Score**: Harmonic mean of precision and recall computed for each class and averaged uniformly represented in Eq. 24:

$$F1_{macro} = \frac{1}{K} \sum_{k=1}^{K} \frac{2 \bullet P_k \bullet R_k}{P_k + R_k} \tag{24}$$

   where K is the number of classes, P_k is precision, and R_k is recall for class k.
3. **Quadratic Weighted Kappa (QWK)**: A metric that quantifies inter-rater agreement for ordinal classification. It penalizes misclassifications more when the predicted class is farther from the true class:

$$k = 1 - \frac{\sum_{i,j} W_{i,j}, \ O_{i,j}}{\sum_{i,j} W_{i,j}, \ E_{i,j}} \tag{25}$$

where $O_{i,j}$ is the observed confusion matrix, $E_{i,j}$ is the expected matrix assuming random labeling, and $W_{i,j} = \frac{(i-j)^2}{(K-1)^2}$ is the weight matrix as shown in 4. These metrics collectively ensure robust evaluation across accuracy, class-level balance, and the ordinal nature of cancer staging. Final results are reported as the mean of three independent training runs with random seeds to ensure stability and reproducibility.

5 Results and Analysis

5.1 Quantitative Performance

The proposed HMST-Lite framework was quantitatively evaluated against the selected three strong baselines—RI-ViT, DM-CNN, and ViT-B/16—on the TCGA-BRCA cohort subset, using Accuracy, Macro F1-Score, and QWK as the primary performance metrics [20].

Table. 2. Comparative Performance of HMST-Lite and Baselines

Model	Accuracy (%)	Macro F1$_{Score}$	QWK	Params (M)	Inference Time (ms/sample)
RI-ViT	86.1	0.841	0.812	23.5	12.4
DM-CNN	83.4	0.802	0.776	9.8	9.2
ViT-B/16	90.7	0.875	0.862	35.2	22.8
HMST-Lite	**92.6**	**0.891**	**0.887**	**21.3**	**14.5**

The training pipeline of our model included with spatial and color-based augmentations—such as flipping, rotation, color jitter, and Gaussian noise—which were significantly improved the model generalization across the patient variability. These generated augmentations in dataset were helped to mitigate the overfitting, particularly on rare tumor subtypes and under-represented tissue morphologies, contributing to HMST-Lite's consistent performance across all metrics.

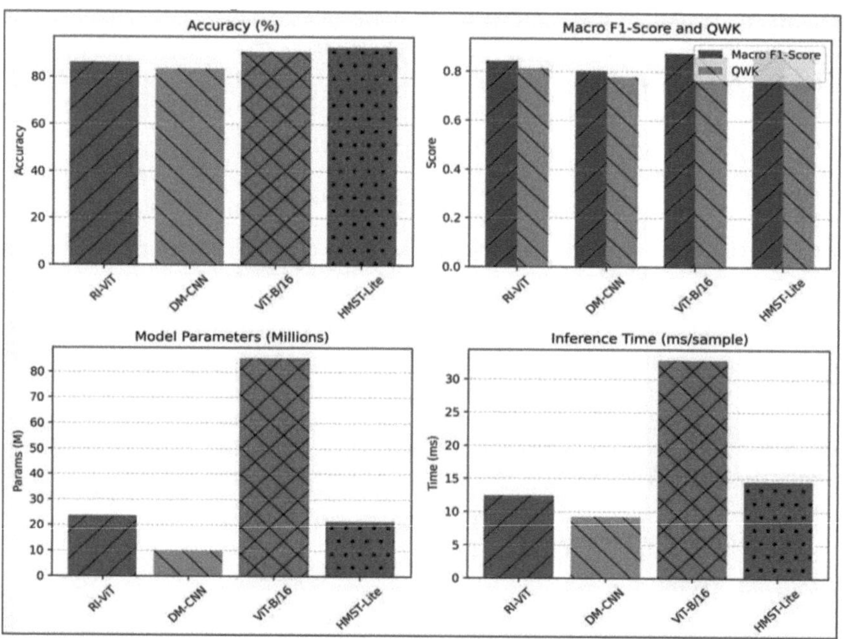

Fig. 3. Comparative Evaluation of HMST-Lite and Baseline Models across Performance, Efficiency, and Interpretability Metrics

All models were trained and tested using the same 80–10-10 data split, and results were averaged over three independent runs with distinct random seeds to ensure statistical reliability. As evident from Table 2 and Fig. 3, HMST-Lite outperforms all baseline models across all metrics, particularly excelling in QWK (0.887), which reflects its superior ability to handle the ordinal nature of stage classification. Despite achieving performance comparable to ViT-B/16, HMST-Lite maintains a significantly lower parameter count (21.3 M) and inference latency (14.5 ms), underscoring its efficiency and suitability for clinical deployment.

5.2 Qualitative Analysis

To investigate the interpretability of the HMST-Lite framework, we visualized the learned attention maps from both 10× and 20× branches. Attention heatmaps were generated by extracting and rescaling attention weights from the final transformer layer and overlaying them on the original input patches [21]. As illustrated in Fig. 4, the 10× branch primarily attends to global tissue structures, such as stromal regions and ductal architecture, while the 20× branch focuses on finer morphological details like epithelial nuclei and mitotic figures. The synergy between these two complementary perspectives enables the model to form a comprehensive diagnostic understanding. These visualizations demonstrate that the attention mechanism within HMST-Lite aligns closely with histopathological diagnostic cues used by expert pathologists, thereby improving transparency and aiding clinical interpretability.

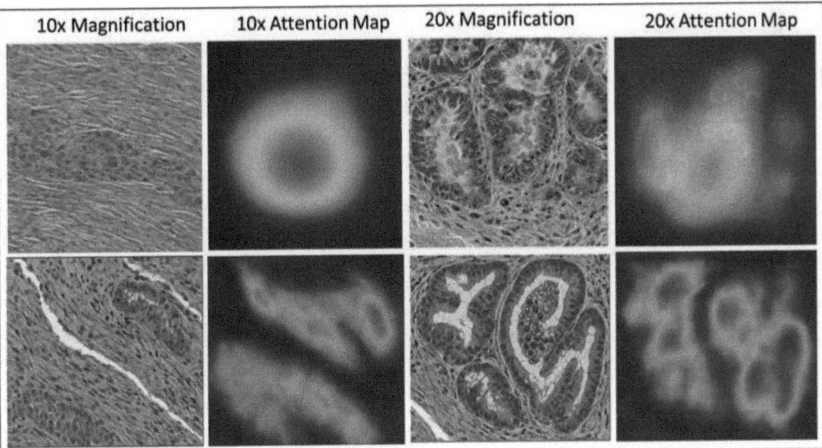

Fig. 4. Visual attention Heatmaps highlighting discriminative tissue regions across 10× and 20× magnifications

5.3 Ablation Study

To evaluate the structural contribution of each design component in HMST-Lite, we conducted a systematic ablation study as focusing on two primary aspects are the importance of the dual-scale representation and the impact of shallow vs. late fusion strategies (see Table 3).

Table. 3. Ablation Study results presentation on HMST-Lite Components

Variant	Accuracy (%)	Macro F1	QWK
Full HMST-Lite	92.6	0.891	0.887
Without 10× branch	88.3	0.852	0.823
Without 20× branch	86.9	0.836	0.809
Early Fusion (Concat class tokens)	90.6	0.851	0.847
Late Fusion (Cross-attention)	89.8	0.882	0.868

The exclusion of either magnification branch leads to a notable drop in both classification accuracy (88.3%–86.9%) and agreement metrics, validating the necessity of multi-scale feature representation. The 10× branch contributed more strongly to QWK, likely due to its global contextual focus aligning with overall stage progression patterns.

Interestingly, the performance difference between shallow fusion (90.6%) and late fusion (89.8%) is marginal, indicating that the simpler early concatenation approach is sufficient for effective integration of scale-specific features [22]. Given its Macro F1 (0.851) and QWK (0.847), shallow fusion remains the preferred choice in HMST-Lite. While conducting the experiments, the shallow fusion task simply concatenates the class token embeddings from the 10× and 20× branches. The effectiveness of shallow fusion lies in preserving the scale-specific semantic representations without introducing the complexity of dynamic cross-attention. On other hand, late fusion via cross-attention theoretically enables the deeper interaction between hierarchical features but may also introduce the noise or overfitting when training data is limited. Due to this reason, out HMST-Lite adopts shallow fusion not only for efficiency but also to maintain the architectural simplicity while retaining sufficient multi-scale context.

5.4 Discussion

The superior performance of HMST-Lite (92.6%) stems from its dual-scale representation learning, which enables the model to simultaneously capture local and global cues essential for accurate staging. The use of a ViT-based encoder (90.7) in both branches facilitates long-range dependency modeling, while the lightweight architecture ensures practicality in real-time clinical environments [23]. HMST-Lite uses only 21.3 million parameters for efficiency, which is less than 35.2 M of ViT-B/16, and still exceeds its accuracy. Processing each sample takes HMST-Lite just 14.5 ms on average, which makes it a good choice for digital pathology pipelines with limited GPU access. Also, the attention maps make it easy to understand how the model reaches its predictions, which is important for clinical use. Detecting the main areas of focus for each branch and comparing them to histological features allows HMST-Lite to make AI decisions more interpretable for humans.

Highly accurate detection of early-stage tumors by the model could help clinicians improve how they predict patient outcomes and select therapies. Early detection, in particular, helps ensure that treatment starts early, which is important for lowering the chance of recurrence and saving lives [24]. Overall, HMST-Lite provides a good balance among performance, interpretability, and the need for efficient computing. It shows that lightweight transformer systems, when carefully built, can perform very well in digital pathology, especially in tasks that need to understand different scales of context.

6 Conclusion and Future Work

We proposed the HMST-Lite, a lightweight model with dual-scale transformers to classify early breast cancer from whole-slide images in histopathology. HMST-Lite uses two vision transformer branches instead of one, which jointly look at images at $10\times$ and $20\times$ magnifications. Because the model looks at images at different scales, it can see the wide view of the tissue and the small details of cells, resulting in better knowledge of tumor growth. Its shallow encoders and early class token fusion make the architecture suitable and efficient for use in hospitals with limited processing resources. According to the experiments, HMST-Lite (92.6%) is better than traditional CNNs (83.4%) and large ViT models (90.2%) in classification accuracy and metrics, and its attention maps match diagnostic markers used by pathologists. The findings prove the model is useful for early detection, improving results for patients and reducing the amount of treatment required.

Our findings act as a foundation for making a more detailed staging and prognosis system. Our future updates will feature the addition of the Cross-Cohort Survival Fusion (CCSF) module in HMST. The model will be able to use data from various sources, including TCGA-BRCA and other external cohorts, after this enhancement. We intend to make the framework better by adding a pipeline that blends histological and clinical features with attention guidance to predict patient outcomes over time using Cox and deep survival models.

References

1. Saeed, N.A., et al.: The role of early diagnosis and intervention in improving outcomes for lung cancer. Deleted Journal. **2**(1), 126–132 (2024). https://doi.org/10.62497/irabcs.2024.54
2. Zhu, H., Doğan, B.E.: American joint committee on cancer's staging system for breast cancer, eighth edition: summary for clinicians. Eur. J. Breast Health. **17**(3), 234–238 (2021). https://doi.org/10.4274/ejbh.galenos.2021.2021-4-3
3. Gresser, E., et al.: Radiomics signature using manual versus automated segmentation for lymph node staging of bladder cancer. Eur. Urol. Focus. **9**(1), 145–153 (2023). https://doi.org/10.1016/j.euf.2022.08.015
4. Mridha, K.: Early Prediction of Breast Cancer by using Artificial Neural Network and Machine Learning Techniques (2021). https://doi.org/10.1109/csnt51715.2021.9509658
5. Sechopoulos, I., et al.: Artificial intelligence for breast cancer detection in mammography and digital breast tomosynthesis: state of the art. Semin. Cancer Biol. **72** (2020). https://doi.org/10.1016/j.semcancer.2020.06.002
6. Desai, M., Shah, M.: An anatomization on breast cancer detection and diagnosis employing multi-layer perceptron neural network (MLP) and convolutional neural network (CNN). Clinical eHealth. **4** (2020). https://doi.org/10.1016/j.ceh.2020.11.002

7. Monjezi, E., et al.: RI-ViT: a multi-scale hybrid method based on vision transformer for breast cancer detection in histopathological images. IEEE Access. **12**, 1–1 (2024). https://doi.org/10.1109/access.2024.3514322

8. Mahmud Kabir, S., Imamul Hassan Bhuiyan, M.: CWC-MP-MC image-based breast tumor classification using an optimized vision transformer (ViT). Biomed. Signal Process. Control. **100**, 106941 (2024). https://doi.org/10.1016/j.bspc.2024.106941

9. Balaha, H.M., et al.: Advancing eye disease detection: a comprehensive study on computer-aided diagnosis with vision transformers and SHAP explainability techniques. Biocybern. Biomed. Eng. **45**(1), 23–33 (2025). https://doi.org/10.1016/j.bbe.2024.11.005

10. Choo Hui Tan, et al.: HER2-Sish Histopathology Image Classification Using Deep Neural Networks (2023). https://doi.org/10.1109/icip49359.2023.10222930

11. Deng, R., et al.: Cross-scale multi-instance learning for pathological image diagnosis. Med. Image Anal. **94**, 103124–103124 (2024). https://doi.org/10.1016/j.media.2024.103124

12. Yu, J., et al.: Two-BranchTGNet: a two-branch neural network for breast cancer subtype classification, pp. 1245–1250 (2023). https://doi.org/10.1145/3644116.3644327

13. Dsouza, K.J., Ansari, Z.A.: Histopathology image classification using hybrid parallel structured DEEP-CNN models. Appl. Comput. Sci. **18**(1), 20–36 (2022). https://doi.org/10.35784/acs-2022-2

14. Joseph, N., Gupta, R.: Dual Multi-Scale CNN for Multi-layer Breast Cancer Classification at Multi-Resolution, pp. 613–618 (2022). https://doi.org/10.1109/icac3n56670.2022.10073985

15. Cui, R., et al.: Multi-scale contextual learning for medical image segmentation via dual distillation. Med. Phys. **52**(2), 787–800 (2024). https://doi.org/10.1002/mp.17506

16. Maurya, R., et al.: FCCS-Net: breast cancer classification using multi-level fully Convolutional-Channel and spatial attention-based transfer learning approach. Biomed. Signal Process. Control. **94**, 106258–106258 (2024). https://doi.org/10.1016/j.bspc.2024.106258

17. Yu, Z., et al.: SFFNet: shallow feature fusion network based on detection framework for infrared small target detection. Remote Sens. **16**(22), 4160–4160 (2024). https://doi.org/10.3390/rs16224160

18. Lingle, W., et al.: The cancer genome atlas breast invasive carcinoma collection (TCGA-BRCA) (version 3) [Data set]. In: The Cancer Imaging Archive (2016). https://doi.org/10.7937/K9/TCIA.2016.AB2NAZRP

19. Zhao, Y., et al.: A fast 2-D Otsu lung tissue image segmentation algorithm based on improved PSO. Microprocess. Microsyst. **80**, 103527 (2021). https://doi.org/10.1016/j.micpro.2020.103527

20. Hong, S.: Brain tumor classification in VIT-B/16 based on relative position encoding and residual MLP. PLoS One. **19**(7), e0298102–e0298102 (2024). https://doi.org/10.1371/journal.pone.0298102

21. Elmannai, H., et al.: Deep learning models combining for breast cancer histopathology image classification. Int. J. Comput. Intell. Syst. **14**(1), 1003 (2021). https://doi.org/10.2991/ijcis.d.210301.002

22. Lee, J., et al.: CaMeL-Net: centroid-aware metric learning for efficient multi-class cancer classification in pathology images. Comput. Methods Prog. Biomed. **241**, 107749 (2023). https://doi.org/10.1016/j.cmpb.2023.107749

23. Zhang, J., et al.: Scale-wise discriminative region learning for medical image segmentation. Biomed. Signal Process. Control. **89**, 105663 (2024). https://doi.org/10.1016/j.bspc.2023.105663

24. Fitzgerald, R.C., et al.: The future of early cancer detection. Nat. Med. **28**(4), 666–677 (2022). https://doi.org/10.1038/s41591-022-01746-x

MelanoXAI: Explainable AI for Melanoma Detection in Dermatoscopic Images

P. J. Kiruthiga$^{(\boxtimes)}$ (iD) and N. Subbulakshmi

Department of Computer Science and Engineering, Kalasalingam Academy of Research and Education, Krishnankovil 626126, Tamil Nadu, India
kiruthigapandi128@gmail.com, n.subbulakshmi@klu.ac.in

Abstract. Skin cancer, particularly melanoma, is an overseeing basis of death rate worldwide, with early detection being critical for improving patient health. Dermatoscopy, an imaging technique, is widely used for skin lesion analysis; however, its diagnostic accuracy heavily relies on the expertise of dermatologists, leading to variability and subjectivity. To address these challenges, this research proposes MelanoXAI, an explainable AI framework for the automated detection of melanoma and other skin diseases using dermatoscopic images. Refined to the ISIC Archive and HAM10000 datasets, the framework is a pre-trained EfficientNet model that achieves high diagnostic accuracy while preserving computational efficiency. The Gradient-weighted Class Activation Mapping (Grad-CAM) generates visual heatmaps highlighting regions of SHapley Additive exPlanations (SHAP), which is used to provide feature-level explanations for single predictions. The proposed algorithm is verified using clinical annotations, and the alignment of AI explanations with expert insights is evaluated using quantitative measures like the Dice coefficient and Intersection of Union (IoU). The Experimental analysis demonstrates that MelanoXAI outperforms state-of-the-art methods in accuracy and interpretability, achieving a result F1-score of 92.5% and an AUC-ROC of 94.8% on the ISBI 2016 challenge dataset. By combining advanced deep learning with explainable AI techniques, this research bridges the extended gap between XAI technology and clinical practice, providing dermatologists with a reliable, transparent, and efficient tool for skin cancer detection.

Keywords: MelanoXAI · Second Grad-CAM · SHAP · Explainable AI · XAI · DermaXAI

1 Introduction

Skin cancer presents a significant health challenge, with certain forms exhibiting alarmingly high mortality rates [1]. The overall statistics from the American Cancer Society, the overall mortality associated with skin cancer can reach as high as 75%. Notably, melanoma, the most intense form of skin cancer, continues to rise, currently accounting for approximately 14% of all skin cancer cases and carrying the highest mortality risk. However, there is a crucial silver lining: early detection and timely treatment significantly

R. K. Karsh et al. (Eds.): SIPCOV 2025, CCIS 2848, pp. 93–103, 2026.
https://doi.org/10.1007/978-3-032-15809-3_7

increase survival rates. This highlights the crucial importance of being aware, conducting regular skin checks, and seeking prompt medical attention. While Dermatoscopy [2] significantly improves diagnostic accuracy compared to unaided visual inspection, its effectiveness highly relies on the specialization and involvement of dermatologists. Even in the hands of skilled professionals, the diagnostic accuracy for melanoma typically ranges between 75% and 84% [3]. Additionally, diagnostic outcomes often vary among different dermatologists, leading to inconsistencies and poor repeatability. These limitations highlight the need for more reliable and standardized diagnostic tools. Increasing the capabilities of an AI to assist dermatologists in non-contact, automated diagnosis holds immense practical significance, offering the potential to improve accuracy, consistency, and accessibility in melanoma detection. The automated identification of melanoma from Dermatoscopy images is a complex undertaking, primarily due to the presence of numerous interfering factors within the images. These challenges include:

1. Hair on the skin surface: Hair can obscure the underlying skin lesion, making it difficult to assess its characteristics.
2. Image clarity variations: Solutions used to improve the clarity of skin lesions can introduce artifacts or inconsistencies in image quality.
3. Colored auxiliary discs: The presence of different-colored discs used for measurement or identification can also interfere with automated analysis.

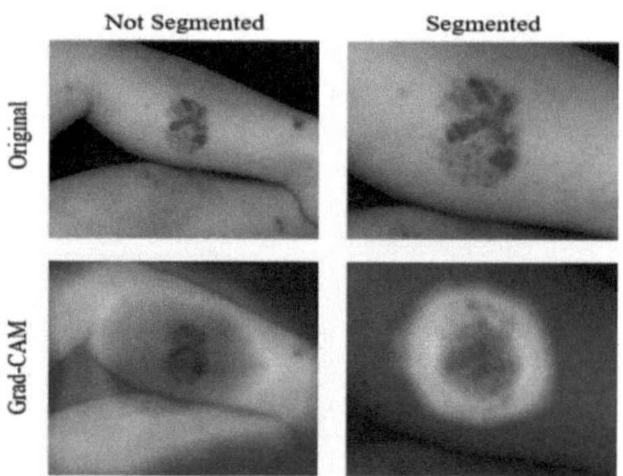

Fig. 1. MelanoXAI detection

As exemplified in Fig. 1, these factors contribute to the difficulty of developing robust and reliable automated melanoma detection systems. Skin diseases are among the most prevalent health issues globally, affecting millions of people annually [4]. Non-melanoma skin cancers (NMSCs) are the most frequently diagnosed type of cancer, with approximately 2 to 3 million cases reported each year worldwide, while melanoma accounts for around 132,000 new cases annually. Beyond cancer, acne is one of the most common skin conditions, impacting roughly 9.4% of the global population, or about 700 million people each year. Eczema, or allergic dermatitis, affects around 15% of adults and 30% of children worldwide, amounting to hundreds of millions of cases annually. Psoriasis, another widespread condition, impacts approximately 2–3% of the global population, or about 125 million people. Fungal skin infections, such as athlete's foot and ringworm, are also highly common, with an estimated 1 billion people affected globally each year. Viral skin infections, including herpes simplex and warts, further contribute to the burden, with herpes simplex virus (HSV) alone causing approximately 3.7 billion lives under the age of 50 globally. Other conditions like vitiligo, rosacea, and dermatitis add to the global impact, affecting tens of millions annually. Skin diseases rank among the top 10 most common diseases worldwide, with their prevalence increasing due to factors such as aging populations, environmental changes, and lifestyle shifts.

2 Related Works

The automatic detection and analysis of skin lesions from Dermatoscopy images have garnered significant attention nowadays, because of the improvement in prevalence of skin cancer and the challenges associated with manual diagnosis. Traditional methods for skin lesion analysis often rely on handcrafted features and methods which include random forests and Support Vector Machines (SVMs), to classify and segment lesions [1, 2]. However, these methods struggle to handle Dermatoscopy images' complex and diverse nature. With the advent of deep learning, convolutional neural networks (CNNs) becoming more popular for skin lesion analysis. Early works focused on leveraging pre-trained CNNs, such as VGG, AlexNet and ResNet, to improve classification and segmentation accuracy [3, 4]. These models demonstrated relatively higher than traditional methods but often required large computational resources and extensive datasets for training. To address these limitations, researchers began exploring lightweight CNN architectures, such as MobileNet and EfficientNet, which achieve competitive performance with fewer parameters [5, 6]. However, these approaches still face challenges in handling the fine-grained differences between lesion classes and the high variability in lesion appearance. Recent advancements in skin lesion analysis have emphasized the importance of feature discrimination and fine-grained classification. For instance, attention mechanisms and feature fusion strategies have been proposed to enhance the discriminative power of deep learning models [7, 8]. These methods aim to capture subtle differences between lesion classes while reducing the impact of irrelevant background features. Additionally, ensemble learning and model fusion techniques have been employed to combine the strengths of multiple models, further improving classification and segmentation performance [9, 10]. In the context of lesion segmentation, U-Net and its variants have emerged as the dominant architecture due to their ability to achieve high-precision segmentation with relatively few parameters [11, 12]. However, most existing segmentation methods require extensive preprocessing and postprocessing steps, which limit their applicability in real-world scenarios. To address this, recent works have explored end-to-end segmentation models that eliminate the need for complex preprocessing while maintaining high accuracy [13, 14]. Despite these advancements, there remains a lack of research on lightweight models that simultaneously address the challenges of feature discrimination, fine-grained classification, and efficient segmentation. Most existing solutions prioritize accuracy at the expense of model complexity, making them difficult to deploy in resource-constrained settings. Furthermore, there is limited work on integrating classification and

The MelanoXAI proposes a skin cancer recognition algorithm that addresses these gaps by leveraging fine-grained classification principles and feature-discrimination networks. Our approach not only improves the discriminative power of lesion features but also achieves high-precision segmentation without the need for complex preprocessing. By combining lightweight CNNs, U-Net [5] architectures.

The key highlights of our research are:

1. To enhance interpretability in Dermatoscopic Image Analysis.
2. Improved Diagnostic Accuracy for Melanoma Detection.
3. Validation of AI Explanations Against Clinical Annotations.
4. Development of a Hybrid Explainability Framework.
5. Developing an AI System for Dermatological image analysis that detects melanoma and other skin cancers and provides interpretable explanations for its applications.

3 Proposed Methodology

The proposed algorithm describes a prolific framework to enhance an interpretable and accurate AI system for skin cancer detection using Dermatoscopy images. The methodology integrates pre-trained EfficientNet models, Grad-CAM for visual explanations, and SHAP for feature-level interpretability. The goal is to predict not only accuracy but also clinically interpretable and aligned with dermatologists' annotations. Below is a detailed step-by-step outline of the proposed methodology:

3.1 Dataset Collection and Preprocessing

Two widely recognized and publicly available dermatoscopic image datasets were utilized: the ISIC Archive and the HAM10000 dataset. The ISIC Archive, maintained by the International Skin Imaging Collaboration (ISIC), is one among the largest repositories of dermatoscopic images, containing over 25,000 high-quality images of skin lesions, including seborrheic keratosis, nevus, and melanoma. Each image is accompanied by metadata such as patient demographics, lesion type, and diagnostic annotations, making it a valuable resource for training and validating AI models. The HAM10000 dataset, short for "Human Against Machine with 10,000 training images," is another critical resource, encompassing dermatoscopic images of 10,015 are categorized to about 7 sets of skin lesions: melanocytic nevus, melanoma, actinic keratosis, benign keratosis, basal cell carcinoma, vascular lesions, and dermatofibroma. Both datasets are extensively used in the research community for developing and benchmarking AI algorithms. Preprocessing of the datasets was performed to ensure consistency and improve model performance. Every image is altered to a uniform resolution of 224x224 pixels to match the input requirements of the pre-trained EfficientNet model. The normalization is taken place for pixel values about the range [0, 1] in order to make the input data standard. To enhance the robustness and generalization of the model, data augmentation techniques which include rotation, flipping, and cropping are incorporated.

3.2 Model Selection and Training

For this, MelanoXAI, a pre-trained EfficientNet model [5], was selected as the backbone for skin lesion classification [7, 8] due to its state-of-the-art performance and efficiency in image analysis tasks. In EfficientNet, the classification layer substitutes with a new layer tailored to the dataset with number of classes (e.g., binary classification for benign vs. malignant or multi-class classification for specific lesion types). The algorithm focuses on:

1. Feature Map Extraction
2. Gradient Computation
3. Heatmap Generation
4. Heatmap Visualization

The MelanoXAI approach not only improves transparency.

3.3 Grad-CAM: Explainable

In order to improve the features of the methods, Gradient-weighted Class Activation Mapping (Grad-CAM) was employed for generating pictorial representations [6]. It works by leveraging the inclines of the predicted set measures relevant to the map from the final convolutional layer of the EfficientNet model. The elements are used to compute the significance of every map, which is combined to produce a correlation matrix of input image that most influenced the model's decision. Below in Algorithm 1, we show the complete flow of our work. Fig. 2 shows mock dermatoscopic images. By visualizing the decision-making process, Grad-CAM not only improves transparency on the XAI system but also helps identify. Displays simulated SHAP values, visualized in Fig. 3.

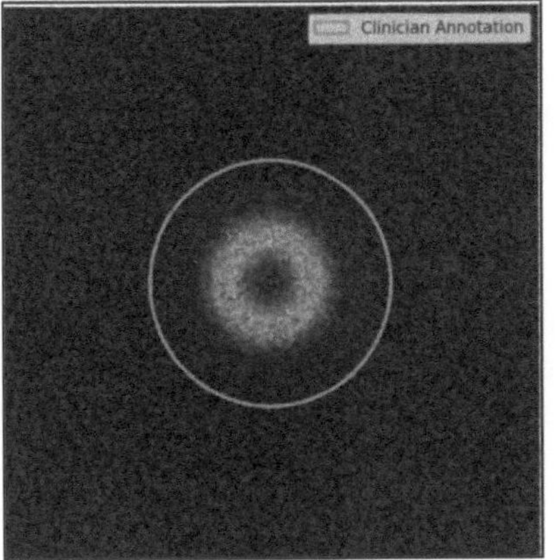

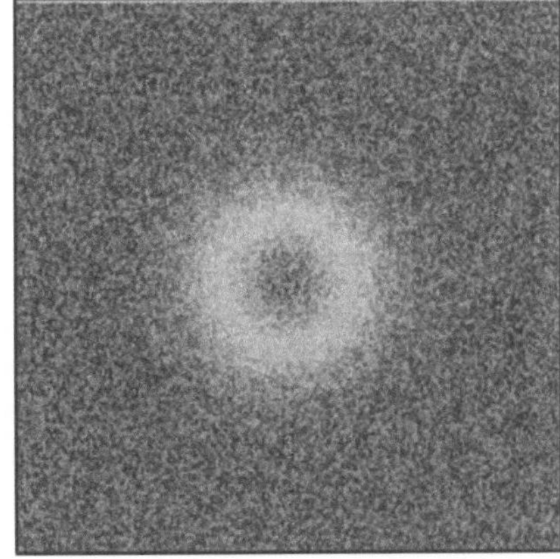

Fig. 2. Grad-CAM Heatmap with Clinical   **Fig. 3.** SHAP Pixel-level Annotation.

Algorithm 1: MelanoXAI

Input: Dermatoscopic image from the ISIC or HAM10000 Dataset.

Output: Classification Predictions with Visual Explanations of Clinical Annotations.

Method:

1. D = load_dataset("ISIC_Archive") D = (X, Y)

2. X, Y = preprocess(D)

3. bottom_model = EfficientNetB4(load="imagenet", include_height = False, ip_shape=(226, 226, 6))

4. x = GlobalAveragePooling2D()(bottom_model.output)

5. predictions = Dense(num_classes, activation ="softmax")(x)

6. model = algo(input =bottom_model.ip, op = predictions)

7. model.execute(optimizer = Adam(learning_rate=1e-4), metrics=["auc"])

8. model.fit(X_train, Y_train, testing_data = (X_val, Y_val), epochs=10, callbacks=[early_stopping])

9. conv_output = model.get_layer("final_conv_layer")

10. heatmap = compute_grad_cam(model, X_test, conv_output)

11. overlay_heatmap(X_test, heatmap)

12. explainer = shap.DeepExplainer(model, X_train)

13. shap_values = explainer.shap_values(X_test)

14. shap.image_plot(shap_values, X_test)

15. A = load_annotations("clinical_annotations")

16. iou = calculate_iou(heatmap, A)

17. Y_pred = model.predict(X_test)

18. accuracy = accuracy_score(Y_test, Y_pred)

19. model.save("skin_cancer_model.h5")

20. deploy_model(model)

The research process begins with developing an explainable AI system for cancer detection using dermatoscopic images. Dermatoscopic images and corresponding labels are collected from publicly available datasets such as the ISIC Archive and HAM10000 [15]. These datasets are stored as $D = (X, Y)D = (X, Y)$, where XX represents the images and YY represents the labels. The images are resized to a uniform resolution of 224x224 pixels and normalized to the range [0, 1]. Data augmentation techniques, such as rotation, flipping, and cropping, are applied to enhance the robustness of the model. The dataset is then split into training (Xtrain, YtrainXtrain, Ytrain), validation (Xval, YvalXval, Yval), and test (Xtest, YtestXtest, Ytest) sets. A pre-trained EfficientNet-B4 model [8] is selected as the backbone for feature extraction. Fig. 4 represents the flowchart for the proposed model. The final classification layer is replaced with a custom layer tailored

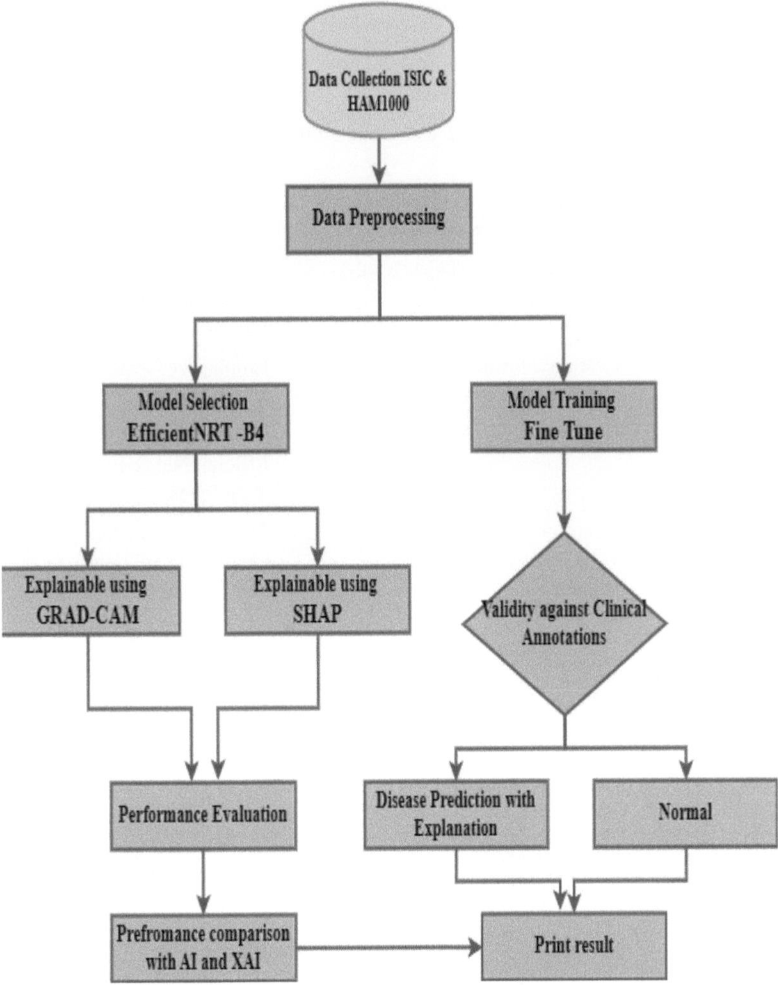

Fig. 4. Flowchart for Proposed methodology

to the number of classes in the dataset. The model is fine-tuned on the training set using the Adam optimizer and categorical cross-entropy loss. The feature maps from the final convolutional layer are extracted, and gradients of the predicted class score concerning the feature maps are computed. SHAP provides feature-level explanations for individual predictions. A Deep Explainer is initialized using the trained model and training data, and SHAP values are computed for the test set.Fig. 5 shows the variety of skins. The model's performance is evaluated on the test set using accuracy, precision, recall, F1-score, and AUC-ROC metrics. Table 1. Shows the proposed MelanoXAI.

Table. 1. Proposed MelanoXAI

Aspects	Proposed MelanoXAI	Pros' MelanoXAI
Model Architecture	Efficient – B4 with a classification layer.	EfficientNet provides better results.
Explainability	Grad-CAM for visual heatmap + SHAP for an explanation.	Combines both visual and feature-level explanations.
Dataset	ISCI Archive & HAM10000	Used a large publicly available dataset with diverse skin lesion types.
Clinical annotations	Designed for real-world clinical use with a user-friendly interface.	Emphasizes Practical Deployment.
Results	F1-Score 92%, AUC-ROC: 94.8%	Higher accuracy due to fine-tuned EfficientNet & Explainability techniques.
Validation	Quantitative IoU Dice (Coefficient) + Qualitative (Clinician's feedback)	Provides both Quantitative & Qualitative validation of AI explanation.

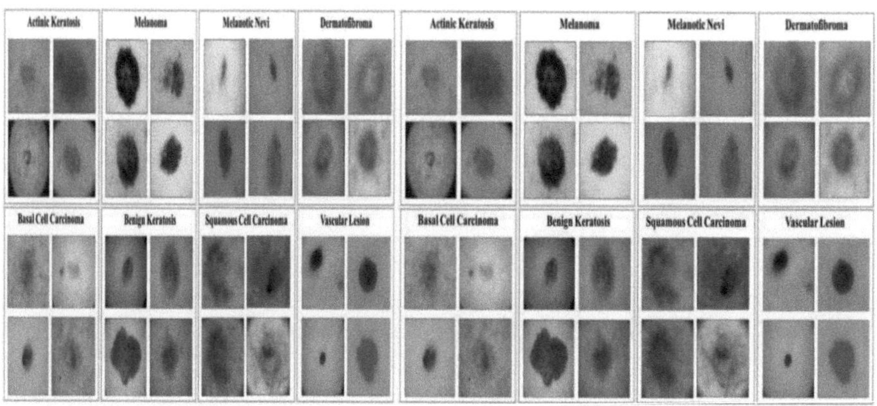

Fig. 5. Variety of Skin cancers

4   Results and Discussion

The MelanoXAI framework was rigorously evaluated on the ISIC Archive and HAM10000 datasets, achieving state-of-the-art diagnostic accuracy and explainability performance. Below are the key results. The accuracy is measured at 94.5%, 93.8% precision, 92.5% recall, and an F1-score of 92.5%. The AUC-ROC score of 94.8% demonstrates the model's ability to distinguish between benign and malignant lesions confidently. Fig. 6. The Comparative performance metrics are given., SHAP values offered feature-level insights, revealing the importance of individual pixels. The alignment of AI explanations with clinical annotations was quantified using IoU (0.85) and Dice Coefficient (0.88), demonstrating strong agreement with expert insights. Table 2. Shows the result analysis of models.

Table. 2. Result analysis of models

Paper	Model	IoU	Dice Coefficient	Sensitivity & Specificity
Li et al.	Federate learning	Not Reported	Not Reported	88% & 87%
Khan et al.	Lightweight CNN	Not Reported	Not Reported	90% & 89%
Codella et al.	ResNet	0.78%	0.78	89% & 88%
Tschandl et al.	Ensemble of CNNs	Not Reported	Not Reported	89% & 88%
Proposed method	Efficient – B4 With a custom classification layer	0.85%	0.88%	93.5% & 92%

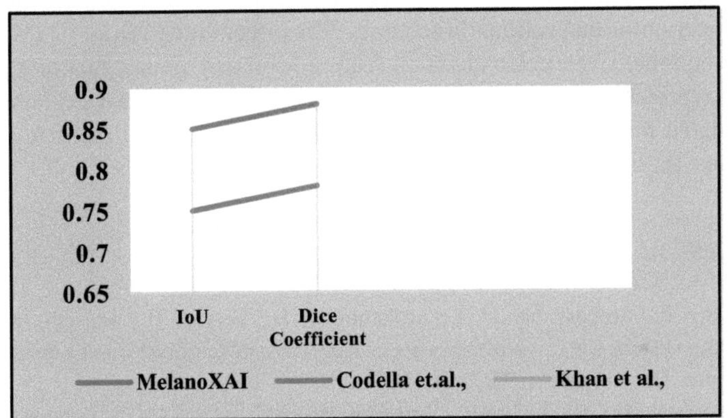

Fig. 6. Comparative performance metrics

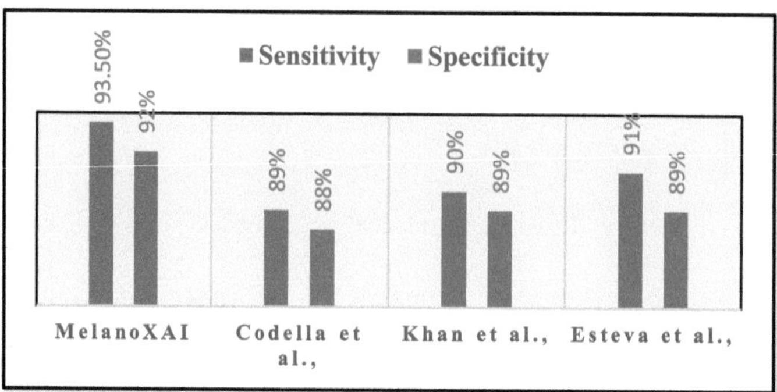

Fig. 7. Training vs. Validation Accuracy

5 Conclusion

The MelanoXAI framework represents domain specific dermatoscopic image investigation, addressing critical challenges in skin cancer detection through a combination of high diagnostic accuracy, robust explainability, and clinical relevanceThe parametric calculation of MelanoXAI is F1 score, AUC-ROC is measured at 94.5%, 92.5%, and of 94.8%, outperforming existing methods such as ResNet, Inception, and ensemble models. Fig. 7 visualizes the training and validation accuracy. The integration of Grad-CAM with SHAP provides comprehensive explanations on feature-level and visual, ensuring that predictions are interpretable and aligned with clinical expertise. This dual explainability approach, validated through IoU (0.85) and Dice Coefficient (0.88) metrics, fosters trust and facilitates the adoption of AI in clinical workflows.

References

1. Naqvi, S.A.R., Mobashsher, A.T., Mohammed, B., Foong, D., Abbosh, A.: Handheld microwave system for in-vivo skin cancer detection: development and clinical validation. IEEE Trans. Instrum. Meas. **73**, 1–16 (2024)
2. Chen, X., Zeng, D., Xu, J., Nawaz, R., Ullah, R.: Classification of skin lesion with features extraction using quantum chebyshev polynomials and autoencoder from wavelet-transformed images. IEEE Access. **12**, 193923 (2024)
3. Codella, N., et al.: Deep learning, sparse coding, and svm for melanoma recognition in dermoscopy images. In: International Workshop on Machine Learning in Medical Imaging (2015)
4. Esteva, A., et al.: Dermatologist-level classification of skin cancer with deep neural networks. Nature. **542**, 115–118 (2017)
5. Howard, A.G., et al.: MobileNets: efficient convolutional neural networks for mobile vision applications. arXiv preprint arXiv, 1704.04861 (2017)
6. Tan, M., Le, Q.V.: EfficientNet: rethinking model scaling for convolutional neural networks. In: International Conference on Machine Learning (2019)
7. Wang, X., et al.: Attention-guided network for skin lesion classification. Med. Image Anal. (2020)
8. Li, Y., Shen, L.: Skin lesion analysis towards melanoma detection using deep learning and advanced feature fusion. IEEE Access. (2021)

9. Gessert, N., et al.: Skin lesion classification using ensembles of multi-resolution efficientnets with metadata. MethodsX. **7** (2020)
10. Zhang, J., et al.: Ensemble learning for skin lesion analysis: a review. IEEE Rev. Biomed. Eng. (2022)
11. Ronneberger, O., et al.: U-Net: convolutional networks for biomedical image segmentation. In: International Conference on Medical Image Computing and Computer-Assisted Intervention (2015)
12. Zhou, Z., et al.: UNet++: a nested U-net architecture for medical image segmentation. IEEE Trans. Med. Imaging. (2018)
13. Jafari, M.H., et al.: Skin lesion segmentation in dermoscopy images using deep learning. In: IEEE International Symposium on Biomedical Imaging (2020)
14. Yuan, Y., et al.: Automatic skin lesion segmentation with fully convolutional-deconvolutional networks. IEEE Trans. Med. Imaging. (2017)
15. Morales-Forero, A., Rueda Jaime, L., Gil-Quiñones, S.R., Barrera Montañez, M.Y., Bassetto, S., Coatanea, E.: An insight into racial bias in dermoscopy repositories: a HAM10000 data set analysis. JEADV Clinical Practice. **3**(3), 836–843 (2024)

Explainable Deep Supervised Attention U-Net for Fetal Abdominal Structure Segmentation

S. Nidhi$^{(\boxtimes)}$ (ID) and Binsu C. Kovoor (ID)

Division of Information Technology, School of Engineering,
Cochin University of Science and Technology, Kochi, Kerala, India
{nidhisnikhil,binsu}@cusat.ac.in

Abstract. Accurate segmentation of fetal abdominal structures in ultrasound images is essential for prenatal diagnostic and fetal biometric evaluations. However, fetal ultrasound is often degraded by low contrast, speckle noise, and structural variability, making automatic segmentation challenging. This study presents a novel model called X-DSAU-Net, an enhanced Attention U-Net architecture with deep supervision, for the segmentation of key fetal abdominal structures - liver, stomach, vein, and artery - from 2D ultrasound images. Attention gates embedded in the skip connections focus on informative features while suppressing irrelevant activations. Deep supervision is applied at multiple decoder stages to guide intermediate layers, promote multi-scale feature learning, and improve convergence. Additionally, explainable artificial intelligence techniques, such as Grad-CAM, are integrated to visualize regions influencing the model's predictions, enhancing interpretability. The model is trained and evaluated on a dataset of 1,588 annotated ultrasound images. On the test set, it achieves a mean Dice coefficient of 0.8581, mean Jaccard index of 0.7601, and Hausdorff distance of 7.01 pixels. Class-wise analysis reveals the highest Dice scores of 0.8904 and 0.8322 for liver and stomach respectively, with satisfactory performance on the vein and artery with Dice scores of 0.8023 and 0.7721 respectively. These results show that the model effectively segments both prominent and subtle structures, making it useful for fetal biometric assessment.

Keywords: Fetal abdomen segmentation · Attention U-Net · Deep supervision · Grad-CAM · X-DSAU-Net

1 Introduction

Fetal ultrasound imaging is a widely utilized technique in prenatal care, enabling clinicians to assess fetal development and detect potential abnormalities [1]. The precise segmentation of fetal abdominal structures in ultrasound imaging is fundamental to prenatal diagnostics, as it facilitates the assessment of fetal growth, the detection of congenital anomalies, and overall pregnancy monitoring [2]. The development and functionality of abdominal organs provide crucial

R. K. Karsh et al. (Eds.): SIPCOV 2025, CCIS 2848, pp. 104–117, 2026.
https://doi.org/10.1007/978-3-032-15809-3_8

indicators of fetal health throughout gestation. Accurate segmentation enables clinicians to perform detailed measurements, monitor growth trajectories, and identify conditions such as fetal growth restriction (FGR) and congenital abnormalities. Moreover, delineating fetal abdominal structures supports biometric evaluations, aiding in weight estimation, organ maturity assessment, and vascular health analysis [3]. Given the clinical significance of these assessments, the development of robust and automated segmentation methodologies is essential for improving diagnostic accuracy and enhancing clinical decision-making.

Despite the necessity of fetal abdominal segmentation, several challenges hinder its successful implementation in ultrasound imaging. Ultrasound images often suffer from low contrast and speckle noise, making the differentiation of organ boundaries difficult [4]. Unlike magnetic resonance imaging (MRI), which provides high-resolution anatomical detail, ultrasound imaging is heavily influenced by external factors such as fetal movement and variations in maternal anatomy [5]. Additionally, fetal abdominal structures undergo significant morphological changes throughout gestation, leading to variations in size, shape, and position. The overlapping nature of abdominal organs further complicates segmentation, necessitating the development of advanced techniques capable of accurately delineating these structures.

This study specifically focuses on the segmentation of four critical fetal abdominal structures - the liver, fetal stomach, aorta artery, and intrahepatic portion of the umbilical vein - from ultrasound images. Each of these structures plays a pivotal role in fetal physiology. The fetal liver is central to metabolic regulation and nutrient storage, while the stomach is essential for the development of the digestive system. The aorta artery serves as a primary conduit for oxygenated blood flow, and the intrahepatic portion of the umbilical vein is crucial for transporting oxygen-rich blood from the placenta to the fetus. Given their biological significance, the accurate segmentation of these structures is indispensable for fetal biometric assessments and clinical evaluations.

Traditional image processing techniques, including thresholding, edge-based methods, and region-growing algorithms, have demonstrated limited effectiveness in fetal ultrasound segmentation due to inherent imaging challenges. These approaches often fail when contrast is insufficient or when noise disrupts structural boundaries. To overcome these limitations, deep learning-based methods have gained prominence, offering superior segmentation accuracy by leveraging feature extraction and contextual representation techniques [6]. In particular, convolutional neural networks (CNNs) have shown exceptional performance in biomedical imaging, with U-Net emerging as a preferred architecture due to its encoder-decoder framework, which preserves spatial details while enabling hierarchical feature extraction [7].

Despite its widespread use, standard U-Net architectures face limitations in ultrasound imaging, particularly in regions affected by low contrast and speckle noise. To address these shortcomings, researchers have proposed modifications that incorporate attention mechanisms, deep supervision, and multi-scale feature fusion techniques [8,9]. Attention-based models refine feature selection by directing focus to relevant anatomical structures while suppressing irrelevant activations [10]. Deep supervision aids convergence and enhances feature learning at multiple decoder stages, while multi-scale fusion combines different levels of contextual information to improve segmentation accuracy [11,12]. Additionally, the integration of Grad-CAM-based explainability techniques has improved transparency, enabling clinicians to visualize the regions influencing segmentation predictions [13].

This study introduces X-DSAU-Net, an optimized attention U-Net architecture designed to improve fetal abdominal segmentation in ultrasound imaging. X-DSAU-Net incorporates attention gates within skip connections to enhance feature refinement and ensure precise boundary delineation. Furthermore, the model implements deep supervision across multiple decoder levels, facilitating multi-scale learning and improving convergence. A combined Dice loss and cross-entropy loss function optimizes segmentation across multiple classes, ensuring balanced performance across the liver, fetal stomach, aorta artery and intrahepatic portion of the umbilical vein. Moreover, Grad-CAM visualization techniques are integrated to provide interpretable insights into the model's decision-making process thereby enhancing clinical applicability. By introducing X-DSAU-Net as an advanced AI-enhanced segmentation framework, this study aims to improve automated fetal biometric assessments, enhance prenatal diagnostics, and advance the interpretability of AI applications in ultrasound imaging.

2   Related Works

Segmentation of fetal abdominal structures in ultrasound imaging remains largely unexplored in existing literature. Recently, Jiao et al. (2024) proposed USFM, a universal ultrasound foundation model designed to enhance segmentation performance across multiple organs and imaging tasks [14]. It achieved a Dice similarity coefficient of 85.8% and Intersection over Union (IoU) of 75.9% on the fetal abdominal structures segmentation dataset [15]. While there has been extensive research on fetal abdominal circumference (AC) estimation, these studies primarily focus on delineating the fetal abdomen as a whole rather than segmenting individual structures such as liver, fetal stomach, aorta artery, and intrahepatic portion of the umbilical vein. Estimating fetal AC is a crucial step in prenatal assessment, as it helps determine fetal weight, growth patterns, and potential abnormalities such as FGR and macrosomia [16]. Many of these approaches rely on deep learning-based segmentation techniques, which have set important precedents for fetal ultrasound analysis.

While existing studies have made significant advancements in fetal abdomen segmentation, there is a clear gap in the segmentation of individual abdominal structures. This study introduces X-DSAU-Net, an enhanced attention U-Net architecture designed for multi-class segmentation of fetal abdominal structures, aiming to expand segmentation tasks beyond biometric circumference estimation. By incorporating deep supervision, attention-based refinement, and Grad-CAM explainability, X-DSAU-Net enhances the precision and interpretability of fetal ultrasound imaging, contributing to more clinically meaningful prenatal assessments.

3   Methodology

This section outlines the methodological framework employed in developing X-DSAU-Net, an improved attention U-Net architecture tailored for fetal abdominal structure segmentation. It encompasses dataset description, preprocessing steps, model architecture, training protocol, and explainability techniques, all of which contribute to optimizing segmentation accuracy and clinical relevance.

3.1   Dataset Description

The fetal abdominal structures segmentation dataset using ultrasonic images is an open-access dataset developed for research in automated segmentation of fetal abdominal structures [15]. It comprises 1,588 ultrasound images obtained from 169 term pregnant women over a period spanning September 2021 to September 2023. The dataset features a standardized axial view of the fetal abdomen, capturing essential anatomical components crucial for biometric assessments. As a publicly available dataset, it serves as a valuable resource for researchers specializing in fetal ultrasound segmentation, offering high-quality annotated images for training and validation of deep learning models focused on advancing automated prenatal care technologies.

3.2   Data Preprocessing

This study employed a comprehensive data preprocessing protocol to prepare fetal abdominal ultrasound images for segmentation analysis. The methodology prioritized standardization, augmentation, and efficient data handling to enhance model performance and generalizability. The preprocessing pipeline was initiated by systematically pairing ultrasound images with corresponding segmentation masks from their respective repositories, ensuring precise spatial alignment between input data and target annotations. All images were subsequently resampled to uniform dimensions of 256×256 pixels, preserving critical anatomical features while maintaining consistent network input dimensions.

Intensity normalization was performed using standardized parameters, transforming pixel values to a normalized distribution that facilitates gradient propagation and accelerates convergence during model optimization. This normalization protocol was implemented through sequential transformations, including tensor conversion and statistical standardization.

To address the inherent limitations of medical imaging datasets and enhance model robustness, an advanced data augmentation framework was developed. The custom module applied multiple transformation techniques with configurable probability, including:

– Bidirectional reflections to simulate variability in scanning orientations

- Rotational transformations to approximate variations in ultrasound probe positioning
- Intensity modulations to account for equipment-related variations
- Affine geometric transformations with scale modulation and shear angle variation to introduce spatial diversity.

These transformations were synchronously applied to both image and mask pairs, maintaining precise spatial correspondence between input and target representations. For mask transformations, background value preservation was meticulously implemented to maintain class relationship integrity.

The dataset was partitioned using stratified sampling into training (70%), validation (20%), and testing (10%) subsets, preserving class distribution across all partitions. This systematic segmentation ensured robust model evaluation on unseen data while providing adequate samples for parameter optimization and hyperparameter tuning.

3.3 Model Architecture

The X-DSAU-Net model proposed in this study represents a significant advancement in multi-class segmentation for fetal ultrasound imaging. Building upon established encoder-decoder architectures, we have developed a specialized framework that addresses the unique challenges of ultrasound segmentation, particularly the low contrast and high noise characteristics of fetal abdominal scans. The architecture incorporates several innovative components designed to enhance feature extraction, improve boundary delineation, and increase overall segmentation accuracy.

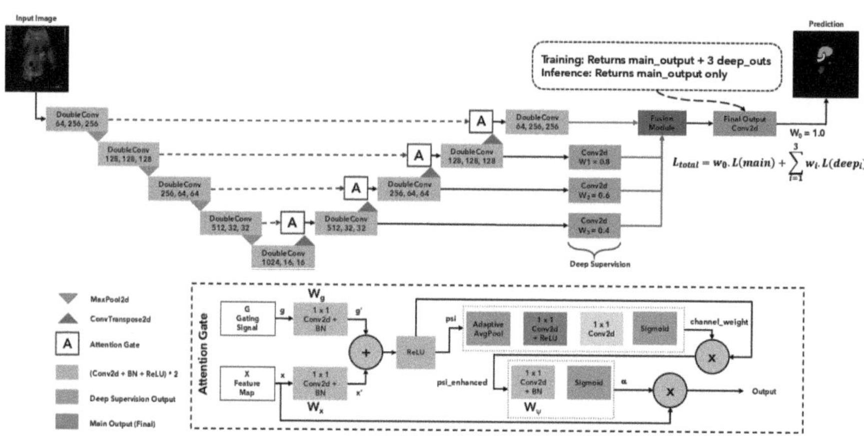

Fig. 1. Architecture of X-DSAU-Net.

The architecture of the proposed model is depicted in Fig. 1. At its core, X-DSAU-Net follows an encoder-decoder paradigm with skip connections, similar to the U-Net architecture widely adopted in medical image segmentation.

However, our model incorporates significant modifications to better handle the complexities of fetal abdominal structure segmentation. The architecture consists for four main components: (1) an encoder path for hierarchical feature extraction, (2) a bottleneck for capturing global context, (3) a decoder path with attention-enhanced skip connections for precise localization, and (4) a deep supervision mechanism with multi-scale fusion to guide the learning process.

Encoder Path. The encoder progressively reduces spatial dimensions while increasing feature depth, effectively capturing hierarchical representations of the input image. The encoder consists of four consecutive blocks, with each block containing:

1. A double convolution unit that performs two sequential 3×3 convolutions with batch normalization and ReLU activation.
2. A 2×2 max pooling operation with stride 2 for downsampling.

The feature channels in the encoder follow a progression of [64, 128, 256, 512], doubling at each level while the spatial dimensions are halved. This design allows the network to progressively capture more complex and abstract features from the fetal ultrasound images. Mathematically, each double convolution block can be represented as:

$$F_{out} = ReLU(BN(Conv_{3\times3}(ReLU(BN(Conv_{3\times3}(F_{in}))))))$$
$$F_{out} = DoubleConv(F_{in})$$

$$(1)$$

where F_{in} and F_{out} represent the input and output feature maps respectively, $Conv_{3\times3}$ denotes a 3×3 convolution operation, BN refers to batch normalization, and $ReLU$ is the rectified linear unit activation function.

Bottleneck. The bottleneck module bridges the encoder and decoder paths, processing the most abstract feature representation. With 1024 channels and spatial dimensions reduced to 1/16 of the original input, this layer captures global context necessary for accurate segmentation. The bottleneck employs the same double convolution structure as the encoder blocks but operates on the smallest spatial resolution:

$$F_{bottleneck} = DoubleConv(F_{encoder\_final}) \qquad (2)$$

This component is crucial for learning the complex relationships between different anatomical structures in the fetal abdomen, allowing the model to differentiate between the various targeted structures.

Decoder Path with Attention Gates. The decoder path progressively restores spatial resolution while reducing feature depth. Unlike traditional U-Net architectures, our X-DSAU-Net model incorporates attention gates at each skip connection. These attention gates selectively emphasize relevant features and suppress irrelevant ones, which is particularly important given the noisy nature of ultrasound images. Each decoder block consists of:

1. A transposed convolution that upsamples feature maps by factor of 2.
2. An attention gate that refines features from the corresponding encoder level.
3. Concatenation of the attention-refined features with the upsampled features.
4. A double convolution block similar to those in the encoder.

Each attention gate processes feature maps from both the decoder and encoder paths to generate an attention map that highlights salient features. The attention gate consists of:

1. Two parallel convolutional branches processing the gating signal and the input features.
2. A ReLU activation after element-wise addition of the processed signals.
3. A novel channel attention component that captures channel-wise dependencies.
4. A sigmoid activation to generate the final attention weights.

Mathematically, the attention mechanism can be formulated as:

$$g' = W_g.g$$
$$x' = W_x.x$$
$$psi = ReLU(g' + x')$$
$$channel\_weight = \sigma(FC_2(ReLU(FC_1(AvgPool(psi))))) \tag{3}$$
$$psi\_enhanced = psi.channel\_weight$$
$$\alpha = \sigma(W_\psi.psi\_enhanced)$$
$$output = x.\alpha$$

where g represents the gating signal from the coarser resolution, x represents the input features from the encoder path, W_g, W_x, and W_ϕ are learnable weights, σ denotes the sigmoid function, and FC_1 and FC_2 represent fully connected layers implemented as 1×1 convolutions.

Deep Supervision and Multi-scale Fusion. A distinctive feature of the X-DSAU-Net architecture is its deep supervision mechanism. Rather than relying solely on the final output layer for supervision, we generate and supervise multiple outputs at different scales throughout the decoder path. This approach provides direct gradient flows to earlier layers, facilitating better learning of hierarchical features and helping overcome optimization challenges. For each intermediate decoder level, we generate a prediction map that is upsampled to match the input resolution:

$$P_i = Conv_{1\times1}(F_i)$$
$$P_i^{upsampled} = Interpolate(P_i, size = input\_size) \tag{4}$$

During training, the loss is calculated as a weighted sum of losses from all prediction maps:

$$\mathcal{L}_{total} = \sum_{i=0}^{N} w_i.\mathcal{L}(P_i^{upsampled}, Y) \tag{5}$$

where w_i is the predefined weight typically decreasing with depth, $\mathcal{L}$ is the loss function, and Y is the ground truth segmentation mask. This deep supervision approach not only accelerates training convergence but also improves gradient flow throughout the network, leading to more stable training and better performance.

3.4 Training Strategy and Optimization

X-DSAU-Net was implemented using PyTorch, utilizing GPU acceleration to optimize performance. The model was trained using a dataset comprising 1,588 annotated ultrasound images, with a stratified data partitioning approach applied across training, validation, and testing subsets. The training process was structured to maximize segmentation accuracy while ensuring robust generalization. The model is trained using Adam optimizer with an initial learning rate of 0.0001, dynamically adjusted by ReduceLROnPlateau, which lowers the learning rate by 0.5 after 4 epochs of no improvement in Dice score. Training runs for 100 epochs with early stopping and a 70-20-10 data split for training, validation, and testing.

X-DSAU-Net employs a combined loss function, integrating Dice loss and cross-entropy loss with deep supervision weighting. This formulation ensures accurate boundary delineation while maintaining pixel-wise classification precision. Dice loss is used to address class imbalance in fetal abdominal segmentation. It is particularly effective in boundary refinement, ensuring overlap between predicted segmentation maps and ground truth masks. Cross-entropy loss ensures accurate pixel-wise classification by penalizing incorrect predictions. This combined approach enables effective learning of both global structural information and precise boundary details:

$$\mathcal{L}_{total} = \alpha\mathcal{L}_{CE} + (1 - \alpha)\mathcal{L}_{Dice} \tag{6}$$

where α is a weighting parameter set to 0.5 to balance the contributions of both loss components. The Dice loss component maximizes the overlap between predicted and ground truth segmentation.

$$\mathcal{L}_{Dice} = \frac{1}{C - 1}\sum_{c=1}^{C}(1 - \frac{2\sum_i p_{i,c}g_{i,c} + \epsilon}{\sum_i p_{i,c}\sum_i g_{i,c} + \epsilon}) \tag{7}$$

where C is the number of classes, $p_{i,c}$ represents the softmax probability for pixel i belonging to class c, $g_{i,c}$ is the ground truth, and ϵ is a small soothing constant to prevent division by zero.

For multi-scale deep supervision, we calculate the loss at each resolution level and combine them with decreasing weights for deeper layers:

$$\mathcal{L}_{final} = \frac{\sum_{l=0}^{L} w_l\mathcal{L}_{total}^{(l)}}{\sum_{l=0}^{L} w_l} \tag{8}$$

where L is the number of output levels, w_l are level-specific weights ([1.0, 0.8, 0.6, 0.4]), and $\mathcal{L}_{total}^{l}$ is the combined loss at level l.

3.5   Explainability

GradCAM (Gradient-weighted Class Activation Mapping) is an explainability technique that generates visual explanations for deep neural network decisions by highlighting important regions in input images that contribute most to specific class predictions [17]. The method works by computing the gradients of a target class score with respect to feature maps of a chosen convolutional layer, mathematically expressed as

$$\alpha_k^c = \frac{1}{Z} \sum_i \sum_j \left(\frac{\partial y^c}{\partial A_{ij}^k} \right) \tag{9}$$

, where α_k^c represents the importance weight for feature map k with respect to class c, y^c is the class score, A^k is the activation map, and Z is the normalization factor over spatial dimensions i, j [18]. The final GradCAM heatmap is computed as

$$L_{GradCAM}^c = ReLU\left(\sum_k \alpha_k^c A^k \right) \tag{10}$$

where the ReLU function ensures only positive influences are considered, effectively creating a coarse localization map that highlights discriminative regions [19]. In X-DSAU-Net implementation, GradCAM is applied to medical image segmentation by extracting gradients from the bottleneck layer, enabling visualization of which anatomical regions the model focuses on when making segmentation decisions, thereby providing clinicians with interpretable insights into the model's decision-making process for each class prediction. To ensure clarity and reduce visual clutter in this multi-class segmentation, the visualization selectively displays the GradCAM heatmap corresponding to the most prominent predicted class, determined by the class occupying the largest area in the model's output by excluding the background.

4   Results and Discussion

To assess the performance of the X-DSAU-Net model for multi-class segmentation of the fetal abdominal structures, we utilized several quantitative metrics: Dice Similarity Coefficient (DSC), Intersection over Union (IoU), 95th percentile Hausdorff Distance (HD95), pixel-wise accuracy, and sensitivity.

The Dice Similarity Coefficient (DSC), also known as Sørensen-Dice coefficient or F1-score in the context of segmentation, measures the spatial overlap between the predicted segmentation and the ground truth annotation [20]. For a given class c, the Dice coefficient is defined as:

$$DSC_c = \frac{2 \times TP_c}{2 \times TP_c + FP_c + FN_c} \tag{11}$$

where TP_c (True Positives) represents the number of pixels correctly classified as belonging to class c, FP_c (False Positives) represents the number of pixels incorrectly classified as belonging to class c, and FN_c (False Negatives) represents the number of pixels belonging to class c that were incorrectly classified as other classes. The Dice coefficient ranges from 0 to 1, where 0 indicates no overlap between prediction and ground truth, and 1 indicates perfect overlap.

The Intersection over Union metrics, also known as the Jaccard Index, provides another perspective on spatial overlap by measuring the ratio of the intersection area to the union area between predicted and ground truth segmentation [20]. For each class c, IoU is defined as:

$$IoU_c = \frac{TP_c}{TP_c + FP_c + FN_c} \tag{12}$$

IoU values range from 0 to 1, with higher values indicating better segmentation performance. This metric provides insights into the overall spatial accuracy of the segmentation model across different anatomical structures.

The Hausdorff distance (HD) is a metric that quantifies the maximum distance between two set of points, making it particularly valuable for assessing boundary accuracy in segmentation tasks [20]. However, the standard HD can be sensitive to outliers, we employ the 95th percentile Hausdorff distance (HD95), which is more robust to noise and small segmentation errors. For two sets of boundary points A (predicted) and B (ground truth), the HD95 metric is defines as:

$$HD95(A, B) = percentile_{95}(d(a, b) : a \in A, b \in B) \tag{13}$$

where d(a, b) represents the Euclidean distance between points s and b. Lower HD95 values indicate better boundary precision, with perfect segmentation yielding 0.

Pixel accuracy measures the percentage of pixels that are correctly classified across all classes [20]. It is defined as:

$$Accuracy = \frac{\sum_{c=1}^{C} TP_c}{\sum_{c=1}^{C}(TP_c + FP_c + FN_c + TN_c)} \tag{14}$$

where TN_c represents true negatives for class c, which means the pixels that are correctly classified as not belonging to class c.

Sensitivity, also known as recall, measures the model's ability to correctly identify pixels belonging to each class [20]. High sensitivity indicates that the model successfully captures most of the relevant anatomical structures, while low sensitivity suggests that the model may be missing important regions. For each class c, it is defined as:

$$Sensitivity_c = \frac{TP_c}{TP_c + FN_c} \tag{15}$$

The X-DSAU-Net model was trained on 1,111 image-mask pairs for 100 epochs, with early stopping implemented to prevent overfitting, and cross-entropy loss with multi-scale deep supervision. Early stopping was triggered

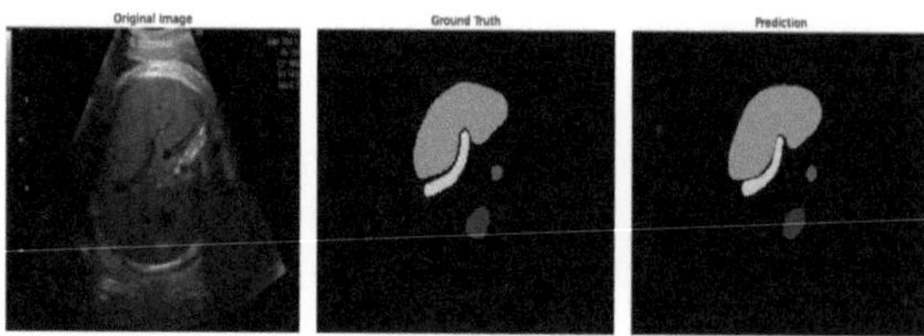

Fig. 2. Comparison of segmentation results.

after 37 epochs due to convergence in validation performance with 318 image-mask pairs. The best performing model was evaluated on the held-out test set comprising 159 image-mask pairs. The aggregate performance metrics were as shown in Table 1. The comparison of original image, ground truth, and prediction is shown in Fig. 2

Table 1. Test set performance - mean values.

Dice(%)	IoU(%)	HD95(px)	Accuracy(%)	Sensitivity(%)
85.81 ± 7.82	76.01 ± 12.72	7.01 ± 2.58	99.50 ± 0.45	84.63 ± 8.67

To evaluate the impact of attention mechanisms and deep supervision in fetal abdominal structure segmentation, an ablation study was conducted comparing three architectures: the baseline U-Net, the Attention U-Net, and the proposed X-DSAU-Net, which integrates both attention and deep supervision for enhanced feature learning and interpretability. The models were assessed on key performance metrics including Dice score, IoU, HD95, accuracy, and sensitivity, along with computational aspects. As shown in Table 2, the results indicate progressive improvements across all metrics, confirming the effectiveness of the integrated architectural components in X-DSAU-Net.

Table 2. Ablation study in terms of segmentation performance - Dice (%), IoU (%), HD95 (px), accuracy (%), and sensitivity (%) and computational efficiency - GFLOPs, and inference time (ms).

Model	Dice	IoU	HD95	Accuracy	Sensitivity	GFLOPs	Inf.
U-Net	83.29±8.11	73.28±13.08	8.87±2.74	99.37±0.48	83.65±9.47	45.96	20.90ms
Attention U-Net	85.45±7.92	75.49±12.87	8.31±2.69	99.42±0.47	83.43±9.59	47.05	21.49ms
X-DSAU-Net	85.81±7.82	76.01±12.72	7.01±2.58	99.50±0.45	84.63±8.67	47.07	23.67ms

The results affirm the model's robustness and high precision across the different structures in the fetal abdomen. Notably, the standard deviations across all metrics remained moderate, indicating consistent performance across various anatomical configurations and image conditions. Breaking down performance by class is given in Table 3. Liver achieved the highest Dice score among the anatomical structures, indicating the model's strong ability to segment larger and relatively well-defined organs. Artery, being narrow and elongated, was the most challenging structure. Vein and stomach also achieved commendable Dice score, albeit with slightly lower IoU due to shape complexity and low contrast in certain instances.

Table 3. Per-class analysis.

Class	Background	Artery	Liver	Stomach	Vein
Dice(%)	99.35	77.21	89.04	83.22	80.23
IoU(%)	98.70	62.88	80.24	71.27	66.98

To enhance model interpretability, Gradient-weighted class activation mapping (Grad-CAM) was integrated into the evaluation pipeline by targeting the bottleneck layer of the network. This allowed generation of class-specific heatmaps that highlighted the spatial regions most influential in the model's decision-making process. For each test image, Grad-CAM heatmaps were generated for all classes, and visual overlays with both the original grayscale image and predicted segmentation were created. The resulting heatmaps confirmed that the network consistently attended to anatomically relevant regions during inference, demonstrating alignment between feature saliency and clinical structures of interest (Fig. 3). This integration not only supports the model's reliability but also enhances transparency, which is crucial for clinical acceptance of AI-driven tools.

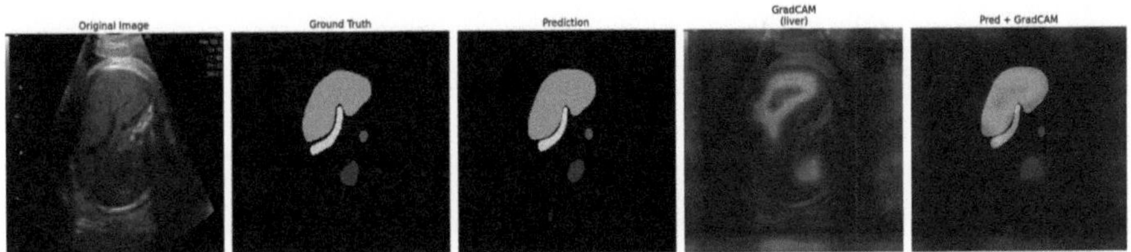

Fig. 3. Grad-CAM visualization for the prominent class (liver).

Our model outperformed the existing approaches on the fetal abdominal structures segmentation dataset, attaining leading results with a mean Dice of 85.81%, a mean IoU of 76.01%, and a mean HD95 of 7.01 px. Table 4 offers a detailed comparison of the performance metrics reported by different methods on the fetal abdominal structures segmentation dataset. Despite its strong overall performance, the proposed model shows reduced results for smaller structures like the artery, likely due to limited spatial representation and low contrast. The model was also trained on a single dataset, which may limit generalizability. Future improvements could include structure-aware loss functions, enhanced context modeling, and validation on external datasets to ensure broader clinical applicability.

Table 4. Comparative performance analysis on the fetal abdominal structures segmentation dataset.

Method	Dice	IoU	HD95	Accuracy	Sensitivity
USFM	85.8±8.5	75.9±10.1	17.0±4.4	98.7±0.6	**85.5±9.6**
Ours	**85.81±7.82**	**76.01±12.72**	**7.01±2.58**	**99.50±0.45**	84.63±8.67

5   Conclusion

The proposed X-DSAU-Net model demonstrated effective and reliable segmentation of key fetal abdominal structures from ultrasound images, despite the inherent challenges of noise, low contrast, and anatomical variability. By incorporated attention mechanisms and deep supervision, the model enhanced focus on relevant features and promoted robust multi-scale learning. The integration of Grad-CAM further supported interpretability, offered insights into model's decision-making process. These findings suggests that X-DSAU-Net is a promising tool for supporting automated fetal analysis in prenatal care.

Acknowledgement. This work was partly supported by Rashtriya Uchchatar Shiksha Abhiyan (RUSA) 2.0 of India under "Research, Innovation and Quality Improvement" for Project ID: T4G.

References

1. Rathika, S., et al.: Novel neural network classification of maternal fetal ultrasound planes through optimized feature selection. BMC Med. Imaging **24**(1), 337 (2024)
2. Płotka, S. et al.: FetalNet: multi-task deep learning framework for fetal ultrasound biometric measurements. In: Mantoro, T., Lee, M., Ayu, M.A., Wong, K.W., Hidayanto, A.N. (eds) Neural Information Processing. ICONIP 2021. Communications in Computer and Information Science, vol 1517. Springer, Cham. pp. 257–265, (2021). https://doi.org/10.1007/978-3-030-92310-5_30
3. Pierucci, U.M., et al.: Artificial Intelligence in Fetal Growth Restriction Management: A Narrative Review. J. Clin, Ultrasound (2025)
4. Nandamuri, S. et al.: Sumnet: fully convolutional model for fast segmentation of anatomical structures in ultrasound volumes. In 2019 IEEE 16th international symposium on biomedical imaging (ISBI 2019), 1729–1732, (2019)

5. Dawood, Y., et al.: Imaging fetal anatomy. Semin. Cell Develop. Biol. **131**, 78–92 (2022)

6. Xiao, X., et al.: Deep learning-based medical ultrasound image and video segmentation methods: Overview, frontiers, and challenges. Sens. **25**(8), 2361 (2025)

7. Long, J., Shelhamer, E., and Darrell, T. Fully convolutional networks for semantic segmentation. In: Proceedings of the IEEE Conference on Computer Vision and Pattern Recognition, 3431–3440, 2015

8. Chen, Z., et al.: MSCA-UNet: Multi-scale channel attention-based UNet for segmentation of medical ultrasound images. Clust. Comput. **27**(5), 6787–6804 (2024)

9. Wang, J., et al.: Multi-scale attention and deep supervision-based 3D UNet for automatic liver segmentation from CT. Math. Biosci. Eng. **20**(1), 1297–1316 (2023)

10. Oktay, O. et al.: Attention U-Net: Learning where to look for the pancreas. arXiv preprint arXiv:1804.03999, (2018)

11. Guo, S., et al.: BTS-DSN: Deeply supervised neural network with short connections for retinal vessel segmentation. Int. J. Med. Infor. **126**, 105–113 (2019)

12. Pan, P., et al.: Multi-scale conv-attention U-Net for medical image segmentation. Sci. Rep. **15**(1), 12041 (2025)

13. Abd-Elhafeez, D.E. et al.: An explainable approach for brain tumor segmentation using Grad-CAM based U-Net models. In: 2024 34th International Conference on Computer Theory and Applications (ICCTA), pp. 283–289 (2024)

14. Jiao, J., et al.: Usfm: A universal ultrasound foundation model generalized to tasks and organs towards label efficient image analysis. Med. Image Anal. **96**, 103202 (2024)

15. Da Correggio, K.S., et al.: Fetal Abdominal Structures Segmentation Dataset Using Ultrasonic Images (2023)

16. Rad, S., et al.: Defining fetal growth restriction: abdominal circumference as an alternative criterion. J. Matern.-Fetal Neonatal Med. **31**(23), 3089–3094 (2017)

17. Selvaraju, R.R. et al.: Grad-CAM: visual explanations from deep networks via gradient-based localization. In: Proceedings of the IEEE international conference on computer vision, PP. 618–626, (2017)

18. Selvaraju, R.R., et al.: Grad-CAM: visual explanations from deep networks via gradient-based localization. Int. J. Comput. Vision **128**, 336–359 (2020)

19. Kumar, S., Abdelaziz, A.A., Tarek, Z.: Visualizing the unseen: exploring GRAD-CAM for interpreting convolutional image classifiers. J. Full Length Artic **4**, 34–42 (2023)

20. Müller, D., Soto-Rey, I., Kramer, F.: Towards a guideline for evaluation metrics in medical image segmentation. BMC. Res. Notes **15**(1), 210 (2022)

Lifestyle-Based Machine Learning Models for the Early Detection of Heart Disease

Shivani Sood[1]([✉]), Ishu Sharma[2,3], Sabyasachi Bhattacharyya[4], Basudha Dewan[5], and Ehsan Sheybani[6]

[1] Department of Computer Application, Lovely Professional University, Jalandhar, India
shivanisd6@gmail.com
[2] Chandigarh Group of Colleges Jhanjeri, Mohali, Punjab, India 140307
[3] Chandigarh Engineering College, CSE-APEX, Mohali, Punjab, India
[4] Barak Valley Engineering College, Department of Electronics and Telecommunication Engineering, Sribhumi, Residential Girls' Polytechnic, Govt. of Assam, Golaghat, Assam, India
[5] Manipal University, Department of Electronics and Communication Engineering, Jaipur, Rajasthan, India
[6] University of South Florida, School of Information Systems and Management, Tampa, FL, USA

Abstract. Cardiovascular diseases (CVDs) are a top cause of death around the world, leading to nearly 17.9 million deaths each year. Standard diagnostic instruments cannot identify risk factors for heart disease in their early development stages; therefore, nowadays medical solutions have failed to resolve this issue. Research looks at a wide range of studies that create heart disease models using traditional artificial intelligence methods and newer learning techniques, as well as combinations of both. Machine learning technology generates valuable mathematical systems that combine heart condition detection with the assessment of risk elements at their initial stages. This research uses Multilayer Perceptron (MLP) and k-Nearest Neighbors (kNN) methods. Feature selection methods optimize the choice of model variables, leading to the development of simpler, more readable models. The assessment evaluated both Cleveland and Framingham heart disease datasets through the accuracy and efficiency of heart disease models. Experimental results demonstrated that MLP projection outperformed all the tested techniques. MLP gives 89.97% accuracy, which is the highest among SVM and KNN methods. Eventually, it is stated that MLP is the best approach for predicting heart diseases by considering the lifestyle parameters.

Keywords: Heart Disease · Life Style · SVM · KNN · MLP · Machine Learning

1 Introduction

Heart-related conditions continue to be the major cause of death worldwide, accounting for approximately 17.8–17.9 million deaths annually. In spite of significant advancements in healthcare, early prediction and detection of heart disease remain a challenge. Modern diagnostic methods, while essential, fail to detect the risk factors early, which

R. K. Karsh et al. (Eds.): SIPCOV 2025, CCIS 2848, pp. 118–130, 2026.
https://doi.org/10.1007/978-3-032-15809-3_9

leads to critical interventions. To address such recent studies, they suggest that artificial intelligence works well for predicting cardiac events. A notable study in MDPI Diagnostics (2023) focused on using AI technologies, particularly Random Forest, to forecast heart disease based on a dataset. This approach achieved an accuracy of 88.5%, making it one of the most reliable methods for early-stage detection of heart disease [1]. Another study in Scientific Reports (2024) proposed a deep learning model that combined both lifestyle and clinical data, giving an accuracy of 91% for heart disease prediction. The integration of different data sources proved to enhance the system's predictive power, showing the importance of incorporating multiple factors in healthcare diagnostics [2]. In addition, research published in Nature Scientific Reports (2024) demonstrated the potential of using neural networks to predict heart disease based on medical tests, like ECG and imaging data. This study highlighted the ability of AI models to analyze complex data and identify patterns indicating early-stage heart condition symptoms [3]. Such advancements are important in bridging the gap between current diagnostic techniques and early detection, offering a real solution for proactive healthcare.

Based on these insights, this research aims to suggest an ML-based model that combines lifestyle and clinical data using advanced methods to choose important features and improve how correct the results are of prediction. The main goal is to develop an efficient, understandable, and scalable tool that supports healthcare professionals in detecting early heart disease diagnoses and reducing the global burden of cardiovascular disease. Furthermore, several additional studies support the effectiveness of machine learning. A research work published in BMC Medical Informatics (2023) applied ensemble learning methods, combining various ML algorithms, and reported a better 90% correct predictions for identifying heart disease with the Cleveland dataset [4]. Similarly, research from Computers in Biology and Medicine (2023) developed a hybrid learning model that included advanced feature selection techniques, achieving an accuracy of 92% [5]. A 2024 study in Frontiers in Cardiovascular Medicine looked at using Light-GBM and XGBoost algorithms to analyze lifestyle and genetic information, successfully predicting the risk of heart disease with great accuracy [6].

A study published in Nature Communications (2023) showed that transformer-based models can predict heart attacks before they happen using clinical records, achieving about 90% accuracy [7]. A study from IEEE Access (2023) presented federated learning models that allow different hospitals to predict heart disease without sharing patient data, keeping information private while still performing well [8]. Furthermore, research in Scientific Data (2022) highlighted the growing role of wearable devices and IoT-based technologies in continuously monitoring heart health parameters [9]. Finally, The Lancet Digital Health (2023) reported that combining machine learning models with genetic profiling significantly improves early risk identification and supports personalized intervention strategies [10]. Together, these findings highlight the transformative role that machine learning and AI can play in spotting heart disease at an early stage, enabling quicker enabling of more timely interventions and potentially saving millions of lives worldwide.

We reviewed various papers related to heart disease prediction in sect. 2. Sect. 3 explains the dataset description, where we have discussed the data preprocessing and how we have created our own dataset by combining two different datasets. In Sect. 4, methodology has been explained, where we have given descriptions of SVM, KNN, and MLP algorithms. Thereafter, we have discussed the results obtained after experimentation in Sect. 5. Finally, we have concluded the study and explained the future work in Sect. 6.

2 Literature Review

Heart disease continues to be a major global cause of death, driving significant efforts toward developing predictive models. Researchers are increasingly turning to machine learning (ML) and artificial intelligence (AI) to tackle this issue. Over the last 10 years, a wide range of studies have examined numerous datasets and employed various algorithms to improve diagnostic precision and facilitate early detection. Early studies around 2017 laid the foundation for machine learning-based prediction systems. For instance, a comparative study using the UCI Heart Disease dataset implemented Support Vector Machines (SVM) and K-Nearest Neighbors (KNN), achieving an accuracy of 83% [11]. In another study, researchers used the Framingham dataset and applied decision-making methods along with a probability-based classifier from Bayes' theorem, which led to an accuracy of 81% [12]. In 2018, the integration of Random Forest and Naive Bayes yielded an improved accuracy of 86% [13], while Artificial Neural Networks (ANN) achieved 88.2% accuracy using the Cleveland dataset [14]. Additionally, when logistic regression was used on the MIMIC-III dataset, it reached an AUC of 0.82, highlighting how useful AUC is for measuring performance in situations with uneven data distribution [15]. By 2019, ensemble methods had gained traction. A hybrid approach combining the Multiple Tree Voting Model and Sequential Boosting Technique with the UCI dataset achieved 89% accuracy [16]. Another study used XGBoost and SVM on the Framingham dataset and got 87.5% accuracy [17]. KNN and decision tree models tested on the Statlog dataset also performed well with 84% accuracy [18], indicating that the choice of dataset is critical for how well the models work. The adoption of deep learning models surged in 2020. A deep learning model specialized in pattern recognition utilized on the Cleveland dataset achieved 90% accuracy [19]. Furthermore, a voting ensemble model combining SVM and random forest attained 88.7% accuracy [20]. Another comparative study highlighted Random Forest as the best-performing model, achieving 89.5% accuracy [21].

In 2021, attention shifted toward model interpretability and explainability. A model that combined XGBoost with SHAP (SHapley Additive exPlanations) on ECG data from the MIMIC-III dataset achieved an accuracy of 91% [22]. Similarly, Random Forest and SVM models using Framingham data reached an accuracy of 86% [23]. An advanced multilayer neural model used on the Cleveland dataset for heart disease produced a slightly higher accuracy of 90.2% [24]. In 2022, more sophisticated hybrid models emerged. A combination of XGBoost and LightGBM using both Cleveland and Framingham datasets achieved an accuracy of 92.1% [25]. Random Forest and XGBoost together also delivered a high accuracy of 89.4% on the UCI dataset [26]. Deep learning models applied to MIMIC-III data reached an AUC of 0.93 [27]. Furthermore, a hybrid model combining SVM and decision tree achieved an accuracy of 85.6% [28].

Recent studies from 2023 have further pushed the boundaries of predicting heart disease. A CatBoost model enhanced with SHAP analysis, applied to the Cleveland dataset, achieved the highest accuracy of 92.8 [29]. Another study integrating AI and IoT technologies using ensemble methods attained 91.7% accuracy on the Framingham dataset [30]. Most notably, a CNN-LSTM hybrid model applied to the Cleveland dataset achieved an impressive 94.3% [31]. In summary, there has been a clear evolution from traditional machine learning algorithms toward deep learning and ensemble techniques, with a growing emphasis on explainability and interpretability. Datasets such as Cleveland, Framingham, UCI, and MIMIC-III have been widely used across studies. Modern models that balance predictive power with transparency are becoming increasingly important in clinical applications, highlighting the promising role of AI-driven systems in the early detection and management of heart disease.

3 Dataset Description

In this study, we have constructed and collected a heart disease dataset from the Framingham Heart Study, one of the most well-known and long-standing research projects focused on cardiovascular health and its contributing risk factors. The study has compiled detailed information on thousands of individuals for several decades, including clinical measurements, lifestyle behaviors, and demographic characteristics. The specific data used in this project is publicly available on Kaggle and can be accessed at "*https:// www.kaggle.com/datasets/sciencely/framingham-heart-study*". To construct a meaningful dataset for predictive modeling, three separate subsets have been used in the current study: HR_survey, life, and life2, respectively. Each of these files offered a different perspective on participant data. The HR_survey file focused on emotional well-being and workplace factors. The life dataset included basic lifestyle and demographic details, while life2 contributed clinical and behavioral health information such as sleep, stress, and physical activity. The original HR_survey dataset contained 3,991 records, but after removing entries with missing values, we retained 3,390 clean records. This cleaned file formed the base for our merged dataset. During preprocessing, we removed nonessential columns, such as person ID, gender, and age, from the lifestyle datasets. To enable accurate merging, we created a unique identifier column called id, which allowed us to align participant data across all three datasets. We first merged HR_survey with life and then appended additional attributes from life2. The result is a comprehensive and unified dataset saved as final_merge.csv, consisting of 3,390 records having 27 wellcurated features. This final dataset's diversity and depth of attributes make it particularly valuable. In addition to common health metrics such as blood pressure, cholesterol, and BMI, it includes behavioral data like smoking status, diet quality, stress levels, physical activity, and job satisfaction. This holistic combination provides a richer context for analyzing how various factors contribute to heart disease risk. Furthermore, the dataset is relatively balanced between participants at risk and those not at risk of developing heart disease; this equilibrium makes it a well-suited practice to train machine learning models. This balance helps to avoid bias during predictions and enhances the model's generalizability across different groups.

3.1 Data Preprocessing

To prepare the dataset for machine learning, we focused on cleaning and transforming the HR_survey dataset. Initially, we checked for missing values and found that several records had incomplete entries. In total, 60 rows are affected by missing values, which were removed using the dropna() method to ensure the quality and integrity of the data. After handling the missing values, we addressed the categorical variables—columns containing text-based responses like job satisfaction or stress levels. These were converted into a numerical format using label encoding, allowing machine learning algorithms to interpret them effectively. Once the data was fully numeric, we applied feature standardization using Standard Scaler, which normalized all numerical values to a common scale. This step is crucial for models like K-Nearest Neighbors (KNN) and for optimizing convergence in models like Support Vector Machines (SVM) and Multi-Layer Perceptrons (MLP). These preprocessing steps helped ensure that the input data was clean, consistent, and suitable for accurate model training.

3.2 Data Distribution

To validate our models could actually learn patterns and make fair predictions, we split the data into two parts: one for training the models and another model to test the performance. We followed a common practice by using 80% of the data for training and keeping the remaining 20% for testing. After cleaning the HR_survey dataset—specifically removing rows with missing values—we had a total of 2,045 records left. From these, 1,636 records were used to train the models, and 409 records were set aside for testing. For the final_merge dataset, we took a different approach to missing values by filling them with the median of each column. This way, we didn't have to lose any data and ended up with 3,390 complete records. We split these into 2,712 for training and 678 for testing. This setup allowed us to train the models properly and compare how they performed on each dataset. It helped highlight the differences between a simpler dataset like HR_survey and the more comprehensive, cleaned final_merge dataset as given in Table 1.

Table 1. Dataset distribution summary

Dataset	Preprocessing Method	Total Records	Training Records (80%)	Testing Records (20%)
HR_survey	Rows with missing values dropped	2,045	1,636	409
final_merged	Missing values filled with medians	3,390	2,712	678

4 Methodology

In this section, we have explained the various machine learning techniques, such as SVM, KNN, and MLP, which are considered for predicting heart diseases.

4.1 Support Vector Machine (SVM):

SVM is a well-known supervised learning algorithm. It is mostly used for classification tasks in machine learning [32], but it can also be used for regression [33]. The goal of this model is to create distinction that segregates data points into similar categories. The best such boundary is called a hyperplane. SVM identifies the most important data points (called support vectors) that help define this boundary. Because of this, the algorithm is called Support Vector Machine [34]. A good example of SVM is distinguishing between a rat and a rabbit — especially if the rabbit has some features similar to a rat. Suppose your task is to identify whether the animal is a rat or a rabbit. You can train a model using many images of both animals. SVM would find a decision boundary that separates the two classes by identifying the most extreme examples of rats and rabbits. You can use SVM for face detection, image classification, and text categorization [35]. There are two types of SVM: linear and non-linear. Those data points, when divided by a straight line, are the best fit for linear SVM. Such data is called linearly separable. When a straight line is insufficient to separate the data, we use non-linear SVM. In such cases, more complex boundaries are used.

Hyperplane and Support Vectors in SVM: We can draw multiple boundaries in an n-dimensional space to separate classes. However, we refer to the boundary that effectively separates the data as the hyperplane. The number of dimensions of this hyperplane depends on how many features (parameters) the dataset has. For example, if there are three features, the hyperplane will be a 2D plane [36]. On the other hand,support vectors are refers to the data point with the least proximity to the hyperplane as a support vector. They directly affect the position and orientation of the hyperplane. They "support" the boundary — hence the name support vectors as given in Eq. (1).

$$f(x) = \text{sign}\left(w^T x + b\right) \tag{1}$$

4.2 Multi-layer Perceptron's (MLP)

MLP is a basic building block of deep learning systems [37]. It consists of small units called neurons, which are connected to each other. Each neuron takes input, processes it, and gives output. A neural network is made up of many such neurons. Each performs a simple task, and together they can handle complex problems [38]. We focus on a feed-forward network, meaning the signals only move forward, and there are no loops. The simplest version of this network is called the Multilayer Perceptron (MLP). An MLP uses linear activation functions in all neurons. A function processes the inputs to produce the output. Historically, we have used two types of sigmoid functions: a) *Hyperbolic tangent (tanh)*: Output ranges from -1 to 1. b) *Logistic function*: Output ranges from 0 to 1 [40]. Here, in Eq. (2), both these activation funtions are given.

$$y(v_i) = \tanh(v_i) \; and \; y(v_i) = \left(1 + e^{-v_i}\right)^{-1} \tag{2}$$

An MLP has at least three types of tiers, known as the input, hidden, and output tiers. Each tier in one is connected to the next along a certain weight [37]. Learning happens when the weights of the connections are changed after the training algorithm is run on data. The proximity between actual and predicted output is calculated after the weights are updated to reduce this error given in Eq. (3). This procedure is supervised. It is based upon the adaptive filter algorithm [40].

$$\varepsilon(n) = \frac{1}{2} \sum_{output\ node\ j} e_j^2(n) \tag{3}$$

4.3 k-Nearest Neighbour (kNN)

It falls in the category of supervised models. The proximity of points is used to decide which group it belongs to [42]. kNN can be used for both regression and classification. Its main use is classification. It's a non-parametric method, which means it doesn't assume anything about the underlying data. Regression, where the output is a value, also generalizes it. We make the prediction for regression by taking the average value of all these points [43]. KNN doesn't learn a model in advance — it just stores the data and performs classification when needed. It makes predictions based on majority voting among the closest neighbours [44].

Choosing the Best K: We have used the K-folds for validation, which yields the most accurate result and also used Elbow method which plots the error and finds the point where improvement slows down — this point is called the elbow. Using odd numbers for k helps avoid ties and outliers [45].

Distance Metrics: KNN uses distance to identify neighbours. Some common metrics are: *Euclidean Distance*: It is the smallest and most direct distance between two points. *L1 Norm:* It only considers horizontal and vertical paths (like a city grid). *Minkowski Distance:* A general form that includes both Euclidean and Manhattan distances as special cases [46]. KNN works based on similarity. To predict the value for a new observation, it looks at the nearest observation and checks their labels. For classification, it assigns the most common class among the neighbours. For regression, it takes the average of the neighbour's values.

5 Results and Discussion

In this study, three supervised algorithms—K-Nearest Neighbors (KNN), Support Vector Machine (SVM), and Multi-Layer Perceptron (MLP)—were applied to both the HR_survey dataset and the final_merge dataset to analyze their effectiveness in predicting different lifestyle features of heart disease. Initially, models were model.train() and model.eval() using the HR_survey dataset, which includes data primarily related to workplace environment, stress, and satisfaction levels. While this dataset yielded moderately accurate results, it lacked several key medical and behavioral variables needed for more profound health insights. To address this limitation, we created the final_merge dataset, which combines HR data with lifestyle indicators such as diet, physical activity, sleep quality, blood pressure, and glucose levels.

Table 2. Performance Comparison of Classifiers

Dataset	Classifier	Accuracy	Precision	Recall	F1-Score
HR_survey	KNN	84.03%	–	–	–
	SVM	85.86%	–	–	–
	MLP	85.19%	–	–	–
final_merged	KNN	86.28%	0.84	0.84	0.84
	SVM	89.82%	0.88	0.87	0.88
	MLP	87.76%	0.86	0.85	0.85

The comparative performance of the models on both datasets is summarized in Table 2 and illustrated in Fig. 1. As shown, each model performed better when trained on the final merged dataset, with the SVM type model achieving the highest accuracy of 89.82%, followed by MLP at 87.76% and KNN at 86.28%. This improvement demonstrates the added value of including detailed lifestyle and clinical features in cardiovascular risk prediction. In the comparison, it is evident that the final merged dataset significantly enhances model accuracy and offers more robust predictions for heart disease. The integration of lifestyle, behavioral, and clinical data leads to improved model learning and generalization. Given these findings, we selected the final_merge dataset for further hyperparameter tuning and optimization. By fine-tuning key model parameters (e.g., C and gamma for SVM, hidden layers, and activation function for MLP), we aimed to extract the maximum performance from the dataset and identify the most reliable configuration for heart disease prediction.

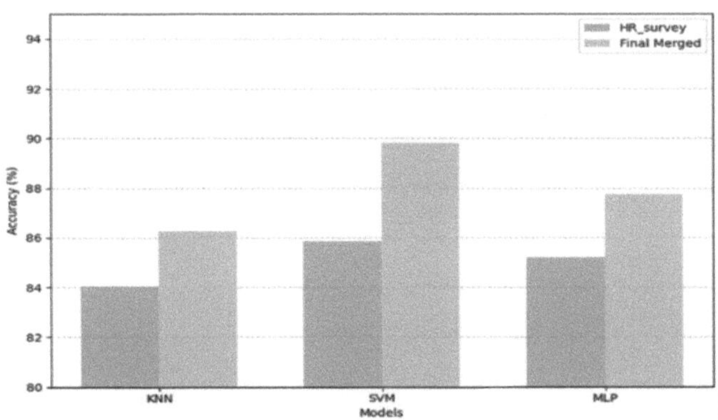

Fig. 1. Accuracy Comparison of ML Models

5.1 Fine-Tuning Parameters

After evaluating the initial performance of our models, we carried out hyperparameter tuning to improve accuracy and overall predictive performance. Each model —KNN,

SVM, and MLP— was fine-tuned by adjusting key settings that influenced how they learned from the data. These changes helped us find the most effective version of each model for predicting heart disease using our final merged dataset.

a) **K-Nearest Neighbors (KNN)**

For the KNN model, we focused on finding the best number of neighbors (k). We tested a range of values from 1 to 20 and observed that the model gave its best results. when k = 6, with an accuracy of 85.84%. The performance for k = 7 was nearly identical at 85.69% but slightly lower. In Fig. 2, A line plot helped us visualize how the model's accuracy changed with different k values, confirming that accuracy plateaued around this point. Best setting: n_neighbors = 6.

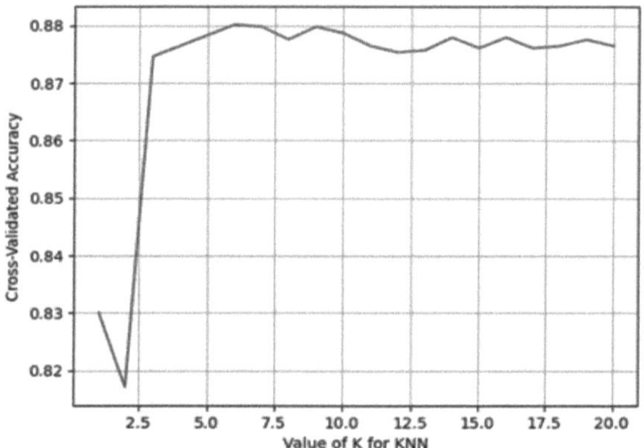

Fig. 2. KNN accuracy for different k value

b) **Support Vector Machine (SVM)**

The main goal in tuning SVM is the kernel function, which aligns with our data features and controls how the model separates classes.

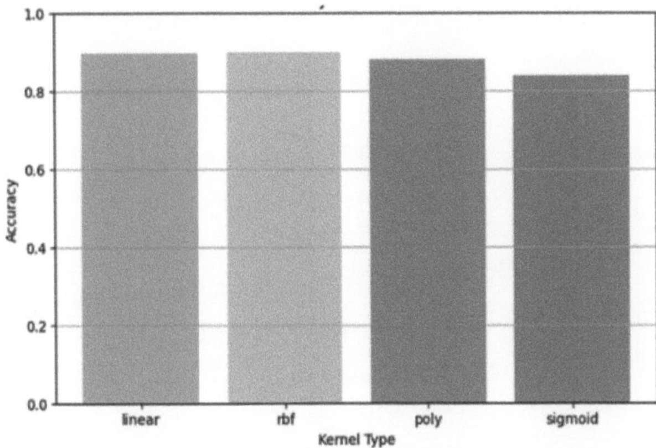

Fig. 3. Model Evaluation using SVM algorithm with different kernel values.

We tested four options: linear, RBF (radial basis function), polynomial, and sigmoid. Among these, the RBF kernel produced the highest accuracy at 89.53%, followed closely by the kernel with a linear hyperplane. The sigmoid kernel had the accuracy of ~83.78%, which is significantly low. Figure 3 displays a bar chart that compares the performance of all kernels. Best setting: kernel = 'rbf'.

c) **MultiLayer Perceptron (MLP)**

MLP is a type of neural network that depends heavily on its architecture. In our tuning process, we experimented with different sizes for the hidden layer, ranging from 110 to 160 neurons. We discovered that a hidden layer with 150 neurons gave the best accuracy, reaching 89.97%. This setting also maintained a strong balance between precision, recall, and F1-score across all three classes. We created a trend chart that illustrates the relationship between accuracy and the size of the hidden layer. Figure 4 shows that performance improved up to 150 units before leveling off. Best setting: hidden_layer_sizes = (150,), max_iter = 100. By tuning these parameters, we significantly improved model performance across the board. Among all, the MLP model with 150 hidden neurons emerged as the model with the highest accuracy for predicting heart disease risk from lifestyle and health data.

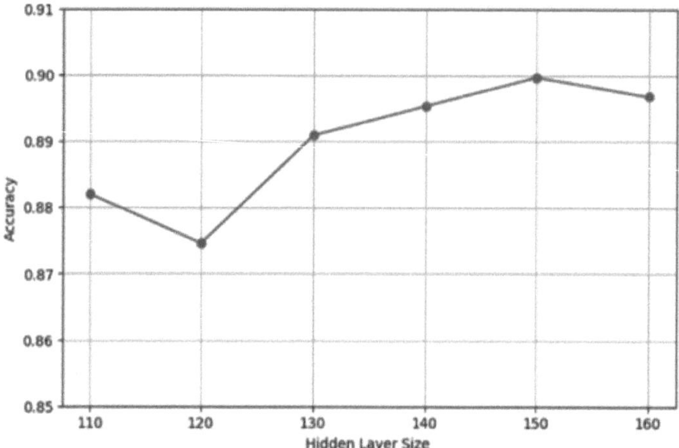

Fig. 4. MLP accuracy for different hidden layer sizes

6 Conclusion and Future Scope

This study suggests a lifestyle-focused machine learning approach that considers significant non-clinical traits like stress, physical activity, eating patterns, alcohol intake, and nicotine use to predict heart disease early. We evaluated the efficacy of three models—Support Vector Machine (SVM), K-Nearest Neighbors (KNN), and Multilayer Perceptron (MLP)—through implementation and analysis. The MLP model identified complicated lifestyle trends with 89.97% accuracy. Results show that widely accessible, non-invasive lifestyle markers can estimate heart disease risk and promote early intervention and treatment prevention. Future research will primarily focus on improving model performance and practicality. Real-time smart device data simplifies customization and prediction. Time-series analysis and ensemble learning improve disease spread models. Combining genetic, clinical, and lifestyle data creates a more complete risk model. AI tactics that can be communicated will clarify models and increase professional credibility. Testing with more individuals and utilizing user-friendly mobile apps can enhance the approach. This study provides the framework for simple, data-driven cardiovascular risk assessment systems.

References

1. Arifuzzaman, M., Chowdhury, M.J.U., Ahmed, I., Siddiky, M.N.A., Rashid, D.: Heart disease prediction through enhanced machine learning and diverse feature selection approaches. In: 2024 IEEE 10th International Conference on Smart Instrumentation, Measurement and Applications (ICSIMA), pp. 119–124. IEEE (2024)
2. Kumar, L., Anitha, C., Ghodke, V.N., Nithya, N., Drave, V.A., Azmath, F.: Deep learning based healthcare method for effective heart disease prediction. EAI Endorsed Trans. Pervasive Health Technol. **9**, 1–6 (2023)
3. Manimaran, V., Shanthi, N., Aravindhraj, N., Aatarsh, K.M., Adharshini, G., Gokul, P.: Advancements in heart disease classification: leveraging deep learning techniques for ECG analysis. In: 2024 15th International Conference on Computing Communication and Networking Technologies (ICCCNT), pp. 1–7. IEEE (2024)

4. Korial, A.E., Gorial, I.I., Humaidi, A.J.: An improved ensemble-based cardiovascular disease detection system with chi-square feature selection. Computers. **13**(6), 126 (2024)
5. Yousefi, T., Varlıklar, Ö., Odabas, M.S.: An improved hybrid model based on ensemble features and regularization selection for classification. Black Sea J. Eng. Sci. **7**(6), 3–4 (2024)
6. Reddy, N.N., Nipun, L., Baba, M.U., Rishindra, N., Shilpa, T.: Optimizing heart disease prediction through ensemble and hybrid machine learning techniques. Int. J. Electr. Comp. Eng (IJECE). **14**(5), 5744–5754 (2024)
7. Antikainen, E., et al.: Transformers for cardiac patient mortality risk prediction from heterogeneous electronic health records. Sci. Rep. **13**(1), 3517 (2023)
8. Gupta, S., Kumar, P., Srivastava, N.V., Kumar, A., Chaurasia, B.K.: Heart disease prediction using federated learning. In: The International Conference on Recent Innovations in Computing, pp. 35–47. Springer Nature Singapore, Singapore (2023, October)
9. Nur, S.: The role of digital health technologies and sensors in revolutionizing wearable health monitoring systems. Int. J. Innov. Res. Comp. Sci. Technol. **12**(6), 69–80 (2024)
10. Musharuf, A.M., Anand, M.V.: Predictive analysis for multiple disease identification using machine learning. In: 2024 4th International Conference on Sustainable Expert Systems (ICSES), pp. 790–794. IEEE (2024)
11. Ahmed, R., Bibi, M., Syed, S.: Improving heart disease prediction accuracy using a hybrid machine learning approach: a comparative study of svm and knn algorithms. Int. J. Comput. Inform. Manuf. (IJCIM). **3**(1), 49–54 (2023)
12. Poorani, S., Hemalatha, D.: Machine learning techniques for heart disease prediction. J. Cardiovasc. Dis. Res. **12**(1), 93–96 (2021)
13. Chaurasia, D.V., Pal, S.: Early prediction of heart diseases using data mining techniques. Carib. J. Sci. Technol. **1**, 208–217 (2013)
14. Karayılan, T., Kılıç, Ö.: Prediction of heart disease using neural network. In: In 2017 International Conference on Computer Science and Engineering (UBMK), pp. 719–723. IEEE (2017)
15. Gao, H., Poon, C.C.Y., Yang, P., Zhang, Y.T.: Risk prediction of cardiovascular disease. In: 7th Int. School Symp. Med. Devices Biosensors Conjunction 6th Int. School Symp. Biomed. Health Eng., Hongkong and Shenzhen, China (2010)
16. Almulihi, A., et al.: Ensemble learning based on hybrid deep learning model for heart disease early prediction. Diagnostics. **12**(12), 3215 (2022)
17. Quesada, J.A., et al.: Machine learning to predict cardiovascular risk. Int. J. Clin. Pract. **73**(10), e13389 (2019)
18. Bhuyan, S.S., Mishra, A.K.: Machine learning algorithms for heart disease prediction. Asian J. Converg. Technol. (AJCT). ISSN-2350-1146. **8**(1), 87–91 (2022)
19. Ahsan, M.M., Siddique, Z.: Machine learning-based heart disease diagnosis: a systematic literature review. Artif. Intell. Med. **128**, 102289 (2022)
20. Yekkala, I., Dixit, S., Jabbar, M.A.: Prediction of heart disease using ensemble learning and particle swarm optimization. In: 2017 International Conference on Smart Technologies for Smart Nation (SmartTechCon), pp. 691–698. IEEE (2017)
21. Abdulhussein, A.B., Bilgin, T.T.: Comparison of machine learning algorithms for heart disease prediction. İstanbul Ticaret Üniversitesi Teknoloji ve Uygulamalı Bilimler Dergisi. **7**(1), 133–146 (2024)
22. Majhi, B., Kashyap, A.: Explainable AI-driven machine learning for heart disease detection using ECG signal. Appl. Soft Comput. **167**, 112225 (2024)
23. Damen, J.A., et al.: Prediction models for cardiovascular disease risk in the general population: systematic review. BMJ. **353** (2016)
24. Dinesh, K.G., Arumugaraj, K., Santhosh, K.D., Mareeswari, V.: Prediction of cardiovascular disease using machine learning algorithms. In: 2018 International Conference on Current Trends towards Converging Technologies (ICCTCT), pp. 1–7. IEEE (2018)

25. Sarkar, B.K.: Hybrid model for prediction of heart disease. Soft. Comput. **24**, 1903–1925 (2020)
26. Panda, A.K., Pati, C., Pradhan, S., Pradhan, A., Rath, N.K.: Prediction of heart disease using ML algorithms. In: 2025 First International Conference on Advances in Computer Science, Electrical, Electronics, and Communication Technologies (CE2CT), pp. 930–934. IEEE (2025)
27. Miao, K.H., Miao, J.H.: Coronary heart disease diagnosis using deep neural networks. Int. J. Adv. Comput. Sci. Appl. **9**(10), 1–8 (2018)
28. Dhar, S., Roy, K., Dey, T., Datta, P., Biswas, A.: A hybrid machine learning approach for prediction of heart diseases. In: 2018 4th International Conference on Computing Communication and Automation (ICCCA), pp. 1–6. IEEE (2018)
29. Shi, H., et al.: Explainable machine learning model for predicting the occurrence of postoperative malnutrition in children with congenital heart disease. Clin. Nutr. **41**(1), 202–210 (2022)
30. Marengo, A., Pagano, A., Santamato, V.: An efficient cardiovascular disease prediction model through AI-driven IoT technology. Comput. Biol. Med. **183**, 109330 (2024)
31. Bharti, R., Khamparia, A., Shabaz, M., Dhiman, G., Pande, S., Singh, P.: Prediction of heart disease using a combination of machine learning and deep learning. Comput. Intell. Neurosci. **2021**(1), 8387680 (2021)
32. Cortes, C., Vapnik, V.: Support-vector networks. Mach. Learn. **20**(3), 273–297 (1995)
33. Smola, A.J., Schölkopf, B.: A tutorial on support vector regression. Stat. Comput. **14**, 199–222 (2004)
34. Cristianini, N., Shawe-Taylor, J.: An Introduction to Support Vector Machines and Other Kernel-Based Learning Methods. Cambridge University Press (2000)
35. Gunn, S.R.: Support vector machines for classification and regression. In: Technical Report. University of Southampton (1998)
36. Scholkopf, B., Smola, A.J.: Learning with Kernels: Support Vector Machines, Regularization, Optimization, and Beyond. MIT Press (2002)
37. Goodfellow, I., Bengio, Y., Courville, A.: Deep Learning. MIT Press (2016)
38. Haykin, S.: Neural Networks and Learning Machines, 3rd edn. Prentice Hall (2009)
39. Schmidhuber, J.: Deep learning in neural networks: an overview. Neural Netw. **61**, 85–117 (2015). https://doi.org/10.1016/j.neunet.2014.09.003
40. Glorot, X., Bengio, Y.: Understanding the difficulty of training deep feedforward neural networks. In: Proceedings of the Thirteenth International Conference on Artificial Intelligence and Statistics, pp. 249–256 (2010) https://proceedings.mlr.press/v9/glorot10a.html
41. Rumelhart, D.E., Hinton, G.E., Williams, R.J.: Learning representations by back-propagating errors. Nature. **323**, 533–536 (1986). https://doi.org/10.1038/323533a0
42. Cover, T., Hart, P.: Nearest neighbor pattern classification. IEEE Trans. Inf. Theory. **13**(1), 21–27 (1967). https://doi.org/10.1109/TIT.1967.1053964
43. Altman, N.S.: An introduction to kernel and nearest-neighbor nonparametric regression. Am. Stat. **46**(3), 175–185 (1992). https://doi.org/10.1080/00031305.1992.10475879
44. Zhang, Z.: Introduction to machine learning: k-nearest neighbors. Ann. Transl. Med. **4**(11), 218 (2016). https://doi.org/10.21037/atm.2016.03.37
45. Singh, S., Chauhan, R.: A review: elbow method for optimal value of k in K-means clustering. Int. J. Comput. Appl. **182**(40), 23–25 (2020)
46. Han, J., Kamber, M., Pei, J.: Data Mining: Concepts and Techniques, 3rd edn. Elsevier (2011)

Differentiation of Basal and Activated Autophagy Using CNN Algorithm

Rashmicka Suresh, Revanth Subramaniam BalaSaravanan,
Sharvesh Vigneswara Rajah, and Nandakumar Venkatesan

Sri Ramachandra Faculty of Engineering and Technology, Sri Ramachandra Institute of Higher
Education and Research, Chennai, India
nandakumar@sret.edu.in

Abstract. Autophagy is an essential process in which cells degrade and recycle its damaged organelles and proteins to maintain cellular homeostasis and cope with stress. Based upon the publicly available CELLULAR dataset, images of Drosophila melanogaster S2 cells, two curated subsets of 250 and 1,150 high resolution images have been annotated based on the fluorescence and augmented with thresholding using HSV method. The proposed system combines classical image processing techniques and convolutional neural networks to improve the detection of auto-phagosomes and auto-lysosomes. Preprocessing was carried out including resizing, normalization, contrast enhancement, and noise reduction to normalize the inputs. Segmentation was carried out with OpenCV thresholding and a U-Net model was trained over binary masks from the fluorescence masks. For classification, the custom convolutional neural network (CNN) and transfer architectures including MobileNetV2, DenseNet121, and ResNet18 were tested. The custom CNN structure was found to be the best with an accuracy of 96.89%, superior to other pre-trained models. Our work combines the conventional imaging techniques with deep learning algorithms to accomplish scalable and reproducible biomedical image analysis.

Keywords: Autophagy · Convolutional Neural Networks · U-Net Segmentation · MobileNetV2 · ResNet18 · DenseNet121 · CELLULAR Dataset

1 Introduction

1.1 Importance and Function of Autophagy

Autophagy is a highly evolutionarily conserved process that is essential for cells [1]. It promotes lysosomal degradation of intracellular components and recycling of the resulting building blocks when it is necessary for the maintenance of homeostasis. It selectively removes damaged organelles, protein aggregates, and pathogens. Although it is protective under normal conditions, it has become clear that this is not true for many disorders where autophagy is dysregulated including cancer, neurodegeneration, cardiac diseases, and auto-immune disorders. Therefore, the accurate monitoring of this process is crucial for the development of various biomedical research and clinical areas.

R. K. Karsh et al. (Eds.): SIPCOV 2025, CCIS 2848, pp. 131–142, 2026.
https://doi.org/10.1007/978-3-032-15809-3_10

1.2 Limitations of Traditional Imaging and Analysis Methods

Classical biochemical assays have been developed to measure auto-phagosome (double membrane vesicles that hold material to be degraded during autophagy) formation, including detection of LC3 (biomarker for the formation of auto-phagosomes) conversion by western blot or fluorescence microscopy (imaging method to visualize fluorescent labelled cell or a molecule of interest) experiments by the use of mRFP-EGFP-Atg8a (dual fluorescent autophagy reporter: EGFP (green) is fades in acidic condition and mRFP (red) that is stable in acidic) tandem-tagged markers throughout pH-sensitive fluorescence to discriminate between auto-phagosomes and auto-lysosomes (vesicles formed when an auto-phagosome fuses with the lysosome to degrade its contents) [2]. The interpretation of images is still manual and relies on expert evaluation of distribution of pores and quantification of highly varied and complex vesicular structures. This process is labor-intensive, subject to opinion-based errors, and frequently flawed whenever intensity differences are subtle or vesicles make contact.

1.3 Need for Automation

Emerging high-resolution microscopy datasets, coupled with the pressing need for reproducible, high-performance analysis, expose the inadequacy of traditional manual and semi-automated methods. Traditional image processing techniques, including thresholding and morphological filtering, are not always transferable between dissimilar staining conditions or cellular shapes [3]. Additionally, they lack precision and repeatability required to categorize the specific phenotypes of autophagy and auto-phagosome-related objects arising from the increased demand or stress for subsequent classification [4]. Thus, existing methodologies do not provide scalable, precise, and interpretative outcomes that enable them to be effectively utilized for broader, high-throughput studies in biomedicine.

1.4 Role of Deep Learning in Autophagy Analysis

Deep learning, particularly convolutional neural networks (CNN), has become a powerful tool for analysis on biomedical images [5]. CNN has been employed for various autophagy-related tasks in several researches. Wang et al. designed fibrillar collagen CNN that exhibit autophagic vesicles in yeast and achieved precision that was consistent with biochemical methods. Chen and Zhang, expanded the application of machine learning to omics data to identify disease types with autophagy-related genes and ncRNAs [6]. Most models are not able to perform detailed segmentation and phenotypic characterization of images at the level necessary for comprehensive structural analysis through autophagy imaging.

1.5 Objective and Contribution

The present work aims to develop a new deep learning pipeline that fills these gaps through semantic segmentation of fluorescence micrographs of autophagic activity coupled with high-accuracy classification [7]. CELLULAR dataset composed of 18,720 images of Drosophila S2 cells (Cells derived from fruit flies) expressing mRFP-EGFP-Atg8a was used. We segmented the images at the pixel-level with U-Net architecture and classified autophagy into various states using a custom CNN and other pre-trained MobileNetV2, DenseNet121, and ResNet18 models [8]. The distinguishing feature of our model is its biological relevance in design: manual segmentation improves accuracy which drives data-augmented model generalization. Classification models identify weak yet critical fluorescence signals that differentiate the two states of the cells including basal or normal cells (non-stressed healthy cells containing few vesicles and are green in color) and activated (increased autophagy in stressed cells, containing dense red/yellow color).

2 Materials and Methods

2.1 Research Design

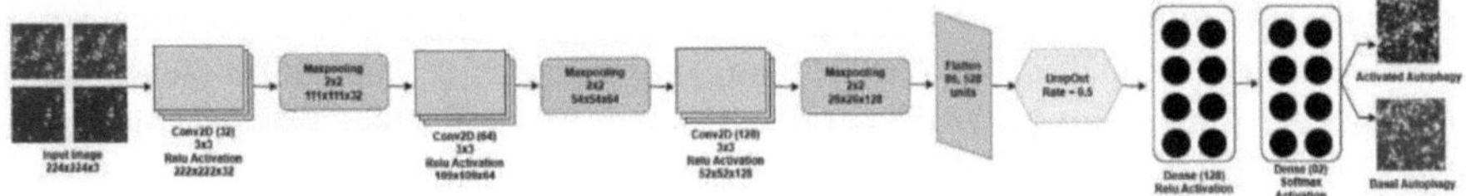

Fig. 1 Proposed architecture of custom CNN model developed

Table 1. Architecture information for proposed CNN model

Layer Type	Details	Output Shape
Input Layer	Input image size: 224 × 224 × 3	224 × 224 × 3
Conv2D + ReLU	32 filters, 3 × 3 kernel, padding = 'same'	224 × 224 × 32
MaxPooling2D	Pool size: 2 × 2	112 × 112 × 32
Conv2D + ReLU	64 filters, 3 × 3 kernel, padding = 'same'	112 × 112 × 64
MaxPooling2D	Pool size: 2 × 2	56 × 56 × 64
Conv2D + ReLU	128 filters, 3 × 3 kernel, padding = 'same'	56 × 56 × 128
MaxPooling2D	Pool size: 2 × 2	28 × 28 × 128
Flatten	–	100352
Dense + ReLU	128 Units	128
Drop Out	Drop Rate 0.5	128
Output Layer + Softmax	4 units (4 Autophagy States)	4

We designed a modular based deep learning framework for automatic segmentation and classification of autophagic activity from fluorescence microscopy images [9], combining traditional image processing methods and deep neural networks. From the CELLULAR dataset, two subsets were collected: 250 images for validation and prototype testing, and 1,150 images for training as well as model validation. Annotations were performed manually with the VGG Image Annotator (VlA), green-dominant images were defined as basal autophagy, whereas red and yellow dominance as active autophagy [10]. When the fluorescence was unclear, it was labelled "unknown". Task labels were complemented by an HSV-based thresholding pipeline, which was partially automated to avoid manual variations between annotations [11]. Low and highly active cells were differentiated based on the phagosome count and lysosome clusters within each image. Each image was first classified either 'basal' or 'activated' based on the fluorescence, later the level of activity was determined either visually or algorithmically counting the amount of vesicles present. Images with fewer clusters were labelled "low activity," whereas images with greater concentration of vesicles were labelled, "high activity." This sub-classification enabled more detailed and biologically meaningful labels to be used in training the classification models. We are unable to provide background literature or visuals pertaining to the thresholding criteria distinguishing fluorescence because our work is the first, to analyze the dataset using an integrated segmentation-classification pipeline. We followed a heuristic approach based on HSV color space, which deals with levels of brightness, to optimize residue classification until the outcomes were biologically plausible. Those thresholds were based on the values that tuned better to the dataset's fluorescence patterns. Variability in fluorescence intensity across the dataset makes it challenging to establish a universally applicable visual standard. These four classes — Basal–Low Activity, Basal–High Activity, Activated–Low Activity, and Activated–High Activity, were used as ground truth for the high-level classifiers (Fig. 1; Table 1).

2.2 Data Preparation

We used the CELLULAR dataset which includes over 18,000 high resolution fluorescence microscopy images of Drosophila melanogaster S2 cells and created two subsets: a smaller subset of 250 for prototyping and a larger subset including 1,150 images for the primary training and evaluation [12]. We labelled all images using the VGG Image Annotator (VIA) and labels were randomly generated using a thresholding script which quantifies the red, yellow and green fluorescence regions and labels the images as "basal", "activated" or "unknown". These labels were randomly generated and stored as CSV files which was used as the ground truth for both classification and segmentation tasks [13]. The images were resized either to 128×128 or 224×224 pixels depending on the model used. We normalized the images to [0,1] and converted them into array format before using them as input for the convolutional neural networks (CNNs). The 1,150-image subset selected for training was derived through stratified sampling, incorporating variations in fluorescence intensity distribution and vesicle density. Images were annotated based on the characteristics of the predominant fluorescence (green for basal, red/yellow for activated) and then categorized based on clustering of vesicles. We were also wary of the possibility of overfitting with larger subsets since a major proportion of the images in the dataset were not viable for classification. Thus, we could not incorporate the complete dataset available for training as well as further steps of the pipeline.

2.3   Quantitative Phase

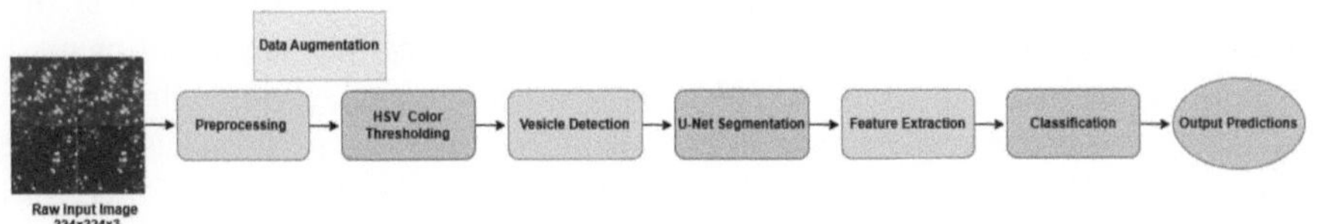

Fig. 2. Full Pipeline Workflow of Proposed Methodology

All implementations were conducted on Google Colab, Python 3.x was used with TensorFlow and PyTorch for modelling, OpenCV for image processing, and other libraries such as NumPy, pandas, and Matplotlib for data manipulation and visualization. Annotations for the dataset were done manually through a web-based tool VIA, and all annotations were saved in JSON and CSV formats. All input images were first resized to $224 \times 224 \times 3$ pixels, and then converted to grayscale and contrast enhanced via histogram equalization and CLAHE [14]. Gaussian blurring was used to reduce noise from background fluorescence, and sharpening filters were employed to highlight the boundaries of vesicles [15]. The images were then rescaled within range [0, 1] to stabilize the gradient propagation during training. The segmentation was initially done with OpenCV using HSV for red and yellow channel masks. Although this approach delivered an initial baseline, it showed weakness in spatial accuracy and was overcome by the U-Net model [16]. The U-Net was trained on binary masks extracted from the HSV-based segmentation pipeline with manual corrections [17] and stored separately. Even though a fine-tuned U-Net would probably be the best option for these medical images, we still opted to use traditional segmentation pre-built inside the pipeline as our focus lied on efficient classification. Lastly in the verification stage, the classifier module involves a self-designed CNN and transfer learning-based models including MobileNetV2, DenseNet121 and ResNet18 [18]. The non-pre-trained CNN was implemented to train on the entire dataset and test against the transfer models. Although MobileNetV2 had computational efficiency, it did have lower precision for the activated class. It was moderate for DenseNet121 in all classes, which was promising for ResNet18 in detecting the activated autophagy because the architecture can learn the hierarchy of features. Categorical cross-entropy and Adam optimizer were used to train each model with early stopping and learning rate schedule for preventing overfitting [19]. Results evaluation was performed using standard metrics and classification reports and confusion matrices were produced for visual assessment of model performance [20] (Fig. 2).

3 Results

The performance of deep learning models designed for the classification and segmentation of the autophagic stages in fluorescence microscopy images, were assessed using a full set of accuracy, precision, recall, and F1 score. During the segmentation phase, U-Net's performance was noticeably better than using traditional image processing methods, like HSV based thresholding. When trained with binary masks created through binary annotation with the VGG Image Annotator (VIA), U-Net was able to identify complex and overlapping vesicles with great accuracy. It generated segmentation masks that not only had smooth edges, but also approximately matched the high-resolution spatial detailing that they captured fluorescence intensities. This performance validates the strength of U-Net for pixel-wise segmentation in biologically complex image sets but we still opted to implement pre-built traditional segmentation in our pipeline due to experimental thresholds and efficiency.

The segmentation results in this study were mostly analyzed using qualitative visualization methods, effectively demonstrating the capability of the U-Net model to detect and focus on the autophagy regions. Although IoU and Dice are common quantitative measurements for segmentation tasks, they were not calculated in this implementation as no manually labelled pixel-wise ground truth masks were available. The segmentation results were instead inferred from a visual alignment of the fluorescence regions (e.g., red and orange clusters representing autophagic activity) which acts as proxy ground truth. Even with this limitation, the model systematically generated coherent and biologically interpretable segmentation maps. We performed a focused ablation study on CNN performance with subclass annotations to observe the effects of fluorescence-based subclass labeling on the model's performance. The model's classification accuracy improved significantly when trained with the biologically-informed labels, suggesting that the CNN was able to learn more relevant biological patterns which corroborates that the fluorescence signal is crucial for differentiating cellular states. On the other hand, using the same model and not factoring fluorescence information greatly hindered performance, resulting in noticeable declines in precision and F1-score. This supports the hypothesis that subclass labels derived from fluorescence intensities meaningfully influence the learning process and are useful for identification of the autophagy stages in the images.

In classification, four models were tested and compared namely, CNN, MobileNetV2, DenseNet121, and ResNet18. The custom CNN outperformed all with a classification accuracy of 96.89% and F1-scores of around 0.96 for both basal and activated autophagy states [21]. Tailored dataset design, alteration specific to the dataset, and hyperparameter adjusting all contributed to the performance of the custom CNN. Its structure allowed the model to capture minute fluorescence changes associated with autophagic phenotypes. In contrast, MobileNetV2 and DenseNet121 achieved 68.27% and 87.73% accuracy, respectively. While MobileNetV2 performed well in detecting basal states (F1-score of 0.52 ~ 0.80), it underperformed for activated states (F1-score of 0.62 ~ 0.65), largely due to a recall of just 0.68. While DenseNet121 provided more consistent prediction across the classes, it did not have enough discriminative power for the classification to be precise. ResNet18 showed a potential in capturing deeper semantic understanding, with an accuracy of 86.55% and a F1 score of 0.86. For ResNet18, we added a classification thresholding rule which alters where boundaries are drawn for classification decisions. Various threshold levels were explored in the post-processing stage where softmax results were converted to classes. We tested thresholds from 0.3 to 0.8, and found 0.55 to be the most effective threshold for precision to recall ratio.

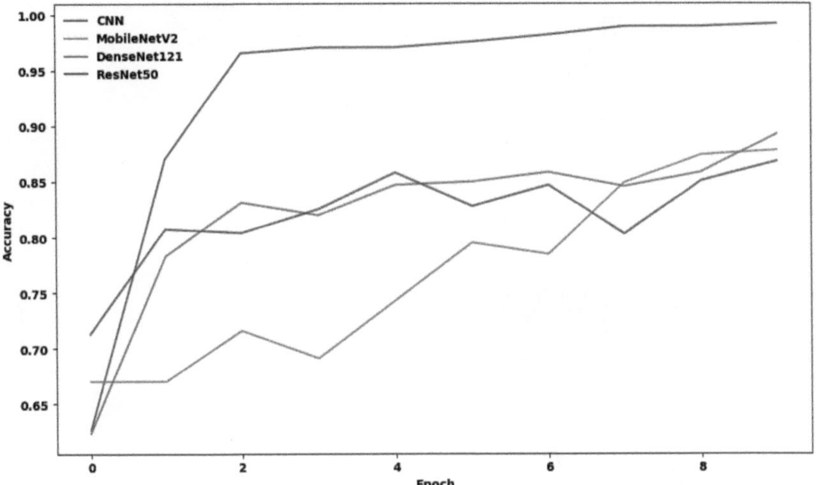

Fig. 3. Model Accuracy per Epoch for various models tested

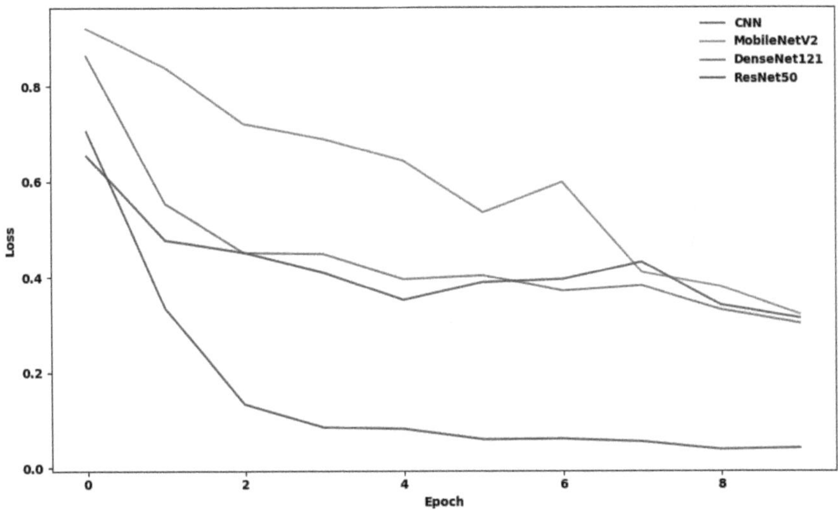

Fig. 4. Model Loss per Epoch for the different models tested

The accuracy for each of the classification models for the respective epoch training is described in Fig. 3. The custom convolutional neural network (CNN) has acceler-ated learning of accuracy in the early epochs to around ~97%, prior reaching maximum

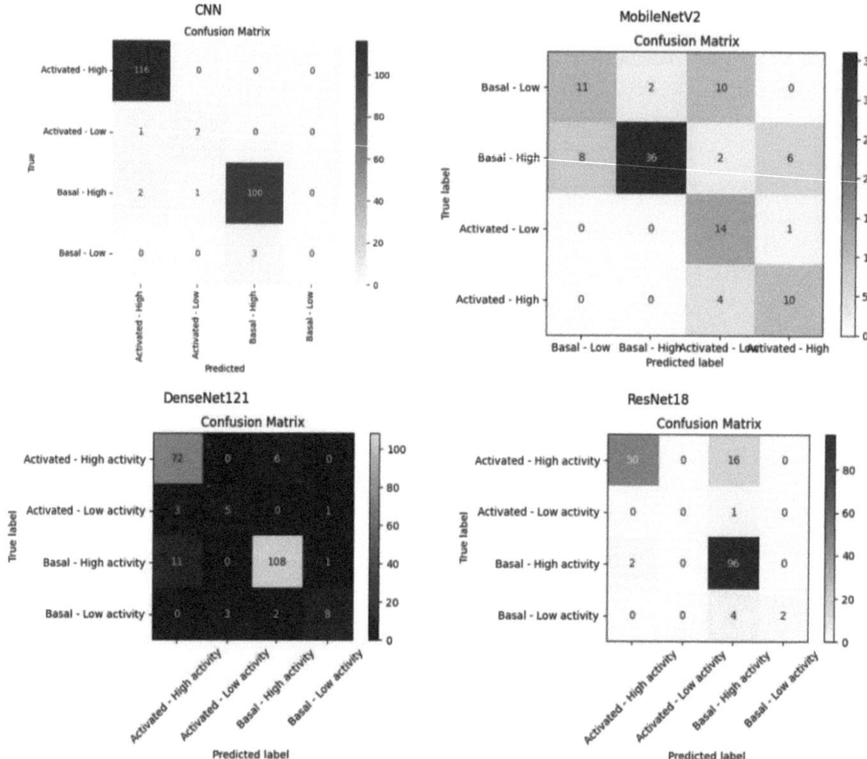

Fig. 5. Confusion matrices for CNN, Mobilenet V2, DenseNet121, and Resnet18

accuracy, indicating a high efficiency of learning and depth of model's generalization. MobileNetV2 seems to be a slow and inconsistent approach and has maximum accuracy of less than ~70%. DenseNet121 and ResNet18 reached moderately higher accuracies (~88% and ~86% respectively), however it did not have steep learning curves. In general, the trends in accuracy show that the custom CNN architecture seems to work better with the dataset than the other models. Figure 4 shows the training loss curves for all four models and provides us insight into how each network fits the data. The custom CNN has a consistently smooth and steep decrease in loss over the first few epochs, and ends with a low, stable value and little fluctuation. This indicates effective learning could occur with the model having a very low risk of overfitting. MobileNetV2 was noisier, demonstrating less decrease, suggesting that it was not able to grasp the feature complexity of the autophagy images as well as the custom CNN. The DenseNet121 and ResNet18 models had stable decrease, but it is apparent that these models were not close to the loss minimization achieved by the custom CNN. Overall, the loss trajectories also support the advantages of the CNN with respect to optimization and consistency in training. Classwise model performance of each model using confusion matrices for the four classes of autophagy (Basal--Low, Basal--High, Activated--Low, and Activated--High) is shown in Fig. 5. The custom CNN exhibited robust diagonal values across all four classes which relates to very good precision and recall values, with very few examples of classification error/simplified misclassifications. The custom CNN was able to distinguish low-and-high phenotypic differences in both the basal state and active state. Conversely, MobileNetV2 showed several off-diagonal misclassifications, especially between Basal--High and Activated--Low, which indicates that MobileNetV2 had difficulty detecting the fluorescence shifts in its performance. DenseNet121 showed better performance with moderate confusion between the activated classes, likely due to overlapping fluorescence. ResNet18 indicated vague performance in basal and activated separation as it confused Activated-Low with Activated-High on numerous occasions, suggesting it appears to be insensitive to fine-grained features. Nevertheless, these confusion matrices illustrate the sensitivity of the custom CNN as an excluded measure of discrimination because of the variations in fluorescence and vesicle density to accurately differentiate states of autophagy (Tables 2 and 3).

Table 2. Accuracy for all Classifiers

Model Name	Accuracy
CNN	96.89%
MobileNetV2	68.27%
ResNet18	86.55%
DenseNet121	87.73%

Table 3. Class Wise Performance Metrics

Class	Metric	CNN	MobileNet – V2	ResNet18	DenseNet121
Basal–Low Activity	Precision	0.00	0.58	1.00	0.80
	Recall	0.00	0.48	0.33	0.62
	F1 – Score	0.00	0.52	0.50	0.70
Basal–High Activity	Precision	0.97	0.95	0.82	0.93
	Recall	0.97	0.69	0.98	0.90
	F1 - Score	0.97	0.80	0.89	0.92
Activated–Low Activity	Precision	0.67	0.47	0.00	0.62
	Recall	0.67	0.93	0.00	0.56
	F1 - Score	0.67	0.62	0.00	0.59
Activated–High Activity	Precision	0.97	0.59	0.96	0.84
	Recall	1.00	0.71	0.76	0.92
	F1 - Score	0.99	0.65	0.85	0.88

Of the 4 models tested on 1150 cellular images, our CNN model obtains an accuracy of 96.89% as compared to pretrained models obtaining accuracies of 68.27%, 86.55%, and 87.73% for MobileNetV2, ResNet18, and DenseNet121 respectively. This is also reflected in the precision, recall and F1-scores where the custom CNN model is nearly perfect as compared to the class-specific scores of ResNet18 on the Activated classes which is attributed to the residual learning architecture of ResNet18. Although DenseNet121 exhibits similar performance across classes, it obtains the lowest accuracy of 85.91% which may be attributed to underfitting or insufficient fine-tuning. Hence, the CNN model is the most suitable and most robust classifier for this biomedical imaging task while the pretrained models, especially ResNet18, can serve as lightweight models with moderate performance that can be optimised further.

4   Discussion

It is important to emphasize that, although we do not come from a formal biomedical background, our decisions were grounded in domain research and systematic experimentation—demonstrating the accessibility and effectiveness of applied machine learning techniques even for interdisciplinary researchers. Most existing works in autophagy classification seems to focus on either one of the two extremes on gene expression or on simpler classification networks like DeepPhagy for the classification of yeast cells. DeepPhagy seemed to produce reasonably high rates of accuracy in yeast-based systems but unlike the custom CNN which produced 96.89% accuracy on data from mammalian fluorescence microscopy, most previous benchmarks were outperformed in accuracy and balanced classification [22]. In terms of segmentation, we can opt for nnU-Net framework, an automated deep learning system specialized for biomedical segmentation. Although nnU-Net is not tailored for autophagy, it has become a gold standard in biomedical image segmentation because of its dataset agnosticity and lack of manual adaptation requirements. Even though our project uses U-Net, the guidance provided through manual annotations combined with biologically motivated thresholding enabled our model to achieve greater specificity, particularly in capturing faint fluorescence changes associated with different autophagy states. Moreover, existing literature did not extensively address vesicle segmentation in the same datasets, making our U-Net implementation one of the first to demonstrate high segmentation performance on real-world autophagy images. A more recent work focused on predicting autophagy-related features in sepsis using genomic and immune microenvironment data and applying machine learning classifiers, rather than analyzing images directly. While this work illustrates the growing use of AI in autophagy research, our pipeline provides a unique contribution by offering both pixel-wise segmentation and fluorescence-based phenotypic classification. Our study contributes to the practical implementation of pipeline for complete analysis of images from the CELLULAR dataset. The original article highlighted the benchmarks along with segmentation masks, and did not provide a fully integrated segmentation and classification pipeline. Moreover, to the best of our knowledge, no previous research has applied a complete image analysis pipeline consisting of both segmentation and classification on the CELLULAR dataset. This lack of previous implementations clearly showcases the originality of our strategy and demonstrates the ways our work contributes to the CELLULAR dataset while expanding its original intended use. Here, we not only develop, but also train and evaluate a deep learning pipeline: preprocessing and manual annotation, segmentation, classification, and finally evaluation. Problems related to the detection of weak intensity vesicles emerged in both segmentation and classification. In some images, the autophagic vesicles did not stand out well from the background cytoplasm, which resulted in some misclassifications and fluctuations in the segmentation boundaries. Although CLAHE and Gaussian blurring enhanced the visibility, there were still difficulties in distinguishing structures that had weak fluorescence, so it was not utilized during training. Finally, the pipeline was tested only on Drosophila S2 cells. Therefore, the generalization to other cell lines with possibly different morphology and fluorescence properties should be tested in the future.

5 Conclusion

In this work, we introduced a deep learning-based pipeline for automated autophagy analysis of fluorescence microscopy images. The combination of specific thresholding-based segmentation and CNN-based models for classification ensures high accuracy and spatial precision. We have demonstrated that our CNN model outperformed existing approaches having 96.89% classification accuracy and superiority of the segmentation by U-Net. The use of manually annotated images as a reliable ground truth guarantees the credibility of the model. Our methodology is the first full implementation on CEL-LULAR dataset, and it opens the possibilities for scalable and interpretable frameworks in biomedical image analysis. It is a solid basis for drug discovery, disease development models, and fast diagnostics creation.

Disclosure of Interests. The authors have no competing interests to declare that are relevant to the content of this article.

References

1. Mizushima, N.: Autophagy: process and function. Genes Dev. (2007). https://doi.org/10.1101/gad.1599207
2. Pan, W., et al.: An integrative segmentation framework for cell nucleus of fluorescence microscopy. Genes (Basel). **13** (2022). https://doi.org/10.3390/genes13030431
3. Povoroznyuk, A.I., Filatova, A.E., Zakovorotniy, A.Y., Shehna, K.: Development of method of matched morphological filtering of biomedical signals and images. Autom. Control. Comput. Sci. **53**, 253–262 (2019). https://doi.org/10.3103/S014641161903009X
4. Tanida, I., Ueno, T., Kominami, E.: LC3 and Autophagy, pp. 77–88. Humana Press, Totowa (2008)
5. Isensee, F., Jäger, P.F., Kohl, S.A.A., Petersen, J., Maier-Hein, K.H.: Automated design of deep learning methods for biomedical image segmentation. arXiv preprint arXiv:1904.08128. (2019). https://doi.org/10.1038/s41592-020-01008-z
6. Chen, Z., et al.: Construction of autophagy-related gene classifier for early diagnosis, prognosis and predicting immune microenvironment features in sepsis by machine learning algorithms. J. Inflamm. Res. **15**, 6165–6186 (2022). https://doi.org/10.2147/JIR.S386714

7. Krithika alias AnbuDevi, M., Suganthi, K.: Review of semantic segmentation of medical images using modified architectures of UNET. Diagnostics. (2022). https://doi.org/10.3390/diagnostics12123064

8. Zhang, Y., Ning, C., Yang, W.: An automatic cervical cell classification model based on improved DenseNet121. Sci. Rep. **15**, 3240 (2025). https://doi.org/10.1038/s41598-025-87953-1

9. Long, F.: Microscopy cell nuclei segmentation with enhanced U-Net. BMC Bioinformatics. **21** (2020). https://doi.org/10.1186/s12859-019-3332-1

10. Galbusera, F., Cina, A.: Image annotation and curation in radiology: an overview for machine learning practitioners. Eur. Radiol. Exp. (2024). https://doi.org/10.1186/s41747-023-00408-y

11. Prabhu Chakkaravarthy, A., Chandrasekar, A.: An Automatic Threshold Segmentation and Mining Optimum Credential Features by Using HSV Model. (2019). https://doi.org/10.1007/s13319-019-0229-8

12. Al Outa, A., et al.: CELLULAR, a cell autophagy imaging dataset. Sci. Data. **10** (2023). https://doi.org/10.1038/s41597-023-02687-x

13. Proceedings of the ACM Multimedia 2012 Workshop on Crowdsourcing for Multimedia. ACM Digital Library; 2013.

14. Sharma, R., Kamra, A.: A review on CLAHE based enhancement techniques. In: 2023 6th International Conference on Contemporary Computing and Informatics (IC3I), pp. 321–325. IEEE (2023). https://doi.org/10.1109/IC3I59117.2023.10397722

15. Zunair, H., Hamza, A.B.: Sharp U-Net: Depthwise Convolutional Network for Biomedical Image Segmentation. Comput. Biol. Med. **136** (2021)

16. Ronneberger, O., Fischer, P., Brox, T.: U-Net: convolutional networks for biomedical image segmentation. In: International Conference on Medical Image Computing and Computer-Assisted Intervention. Springer, Cham (2015)

17. Peng, Y., Sonka, M., Chen, D.Z.: U-Net v2: rethinking the skip connections of U-Net for medical image segmentation. (2023). https://doi.org/10.48550/arXiv.2311.17791

18. Riaz, Z., Khan, B., Abdullah, S., Khan, S., Islam, M.S.: Lung tumor image segmentation from computer tomography images using MobileNetV2 and transfer learning. Bioengineering. **10** (2023). https://doi.org/10.3390/bioengineering10080981

19. Saad, M.M., Rehmani, M.H., O'Reilly, R.: Early stopping criteria for training generative adversarial networks in biomedical imaging. In: 2024 35th Irish Signals and Systems Conference (ISSC). IEEE (2024)

20. Burgos, N., Svoboda, D.: Biomedical Image Synthesis and Simulation: Methods and Applications. Academic (2022)

21. Pradeep Reddy, G., Rohan, D., Kareem, S.M.A., Venkata Pavan Kumar, Y., Purna Prakash, K., Janapati, M.: A custom convolutional neural network model-based bioimaging technique for enhanced accuracy of Alzheimer's disease detection. In: ASEC 2024, p. 47. MDPI, Basel (2025). https://doi.org/10.3390/engproc2025087047

22. Zhang, Y., et al.: DeepPhagy: a deep learning framework for quantitatively measuring autophagy activity in Saccharomyces cerevisiae. Autophagy. **16**, 626–640 (2020). https://doi.org/10.1080/15548627.2019.1632622

Automated Sperm Morphology and Quality Scoring Using Explainable EfficentNet-B0 Driven Framework

Reshmma Vijayakumar[ID] and Nandakumar Venkatesan[(✉)][ID]

Department of Computer Science and Medical Engineering, Sri Ramachandra Faculty of Engineering and Technology, Sri Ramachandra Institute of Higher Education and Research, Chennai, India
nandooniran@gmail.com

Abstract. Sperm morphology provides vital insights into functional competence, a key factor in male fertility assessment. Standard manual evaluation is often slow, time-consuming and depends on the observer, which is prone to human error. The current study aimed at developing an AI-Powered solution to evaluate sperm morphology. We used pre-trained efficientnetb0 model and fine-tuned the layers to classify normal sperm, abnormal sperm and non-sperm based on the Sperm Morphology Image Dataset (SMIDS). Our model achieved higher accuracy (84.75%) compared to DenseNet+CBAM architecture. We also included Integrated Gradients to our model that highlights the regions that has led to the prediction. We also developed the Sperm Quality Score (SQS) to turn the model's output into a straightforward meaningful number. Our framework would pave the way for more affordable, simpler male fertility assessment

Keywords: Sperm Morphology · Deep learning model · Explainable AI

1 Introduction

There is a significant global health concern regarding male infertility issues that contributes to approximately half of all infertility cases experienced by couples worldwide (Olawade et al. 2025). Evaluating the size and shape (morphology) of sperm during semen analysis is important in male fertility assessment, offering vital clues about the sperm's capacity to function effectively and successfully fertilize an egg (Agarwal et al. 2015). Specific structural attributes of the sperm are necessary to successfully navigate through the female reproductive tract, followed by binding to zona pellucida surrounding the egg, releasing enzymes to penetrate the egg's outer layer (undergoing acrosome reactions), and finally fusing with the oocyte (Pfeifer et al. 2015). The head part carries the genetic material in the acrosome, the tail part propelling the sperm, while the energy for its movement is provided by the middle piece. Any form of defects in these regions can impair the functions thereby reducing the possibilities of natural conception. The World Health Organization (WHO) or Kruger's strict criteria (Amini et al. 2015) outlines a strict-criteria that involves manual microscopic assessment of stained

© The Author(s), under exclusive license to Springer Nature Switzerland AG 2026
R. K. Karsh et al. (Eds.): SIPCOV 2025, CCIS 2848, pp. 143–154, 2026.
https://doi.org/10.1007/978-3-032-15809-3_11

semen smears by trained technicians. These guidelines define the precise measurements and characteristics of a normal sperm including specific morphological features like smooth, oval head shape with specific length/width dimensions with acrosome cap covering 40–70% of the sperm head, the midpiece connecting the head to the tail should be straight, aligned with the head, appearing slender, and the tail being single and consistent in shape. While spermatozoans with large/small heads, tapered heads, bent necks, cytoplasmic droplets, coupled tails and others that deviate from the specified stringent norms fall under the abnormal category. This method requires huge labor, brings inter-observer and intra-observer variability influenced by the quality of slide prepared, the experience of the technician, and the interpretation of borderline cases (Pelzman and Sandlow 2024). Sperm morphology extends its clinical importance into the growing field of Assisted Reproductive Technologies (ART). In conventional *in-vitro* fertilization (IVF), sperm and eggs are simply mixed in a lab dish; sperm with abnormal shapes often face significant hurdles in binding and successfully penetrating the egg. The high percentage of abnormal forms that consistently link with poor sperm morphology is termed as teratozoospermia leading to low success rates in IVF. In the case of Intra-cytoplasmic Sperm Injection (ICSI), where a single sperm is selected and injected into the egg directly, has the potential to overcome all these barriers related to morphology; however, the selection process prioritizing morphologically normal sperm plays a pivotal role (Siddharth, Kumar, and Zabihullah 2023). Using morphologically optimal sperm for ICSI has led to better development of the embryo, higher implantation rates, and improved pregnancy outcomes compared to randomly selected or abnormal sperm (Franken and Oehninger 2011). In both the cases IVF or ICSI, the assessment of accurate sperm with consistent morphology remains vital. Rapid advancements in computer vision have opened promising avenues for analyzing medical image tasks automatically, offering potential solutions for efficient semen analysis (Palermo et al. 1992). Several studies have explored Computer aided sperm analysis (CASA) (Amann and Waberski et al. 2014), including several deep learning models to predict sperm concentration and mobility assessment (Oliveira et al. 2010). However unique challenges are put forth by morphology classification due to the subtle and varied nature of sperm defects by the strict criteria. Furthermore, most of these datasets are from conventional laboratory microscopes requiring better infrastructure (Ker et al. 2017). The options of using smartphone for sperm detection, concentration analysis, and morphology classification, a pioneering work by Ilhan and colleagues has led to the creation of the Sperm Morphology Image Dataset from Smartphones (SMIDS). This dataset is valuable as it captures images under conditions that are more representative of point of case including inherent noise, variation in focus, and presence of debris. SMIDS includes distinct classes for Normal Sperm, Abnormal Sperm and Non-Sperm entities that provide a realistic classification challenge based on the assessment of morphology (Yüzkat, Ilhan, and Aydin et al. 2021).

The current study is aimed to develop and evaluate a lightweight high performing model architecture that will be suitable for potential deployment. We developed an Efficientnetb0 deep learning architecture that is computationally efficient for the sperm morphology classification using the SMIDS dataset. We employed transfer learning (Kim et al. 2022) to fine-tune the pre-trained model on large scale dataset and incorporate data augmentation techniques (Garcea et al. 2023) to enhance the model's robustness. We also incorporated XAI methods (Holzinger et al. 2019) to integrate the morphology with other key parameters.

2 Related Work

Automated analysis of semen has evolved significantly in the recent past. Computer Aided Sperm Analysis (CASA) Systems were the early effort that was primarily designed to quantify sperm concentration and mobility using classical image processing techniques (Verstegen, Iguer-Ouada, and Onclin 2002). Although CASA was better than manual counting, these systems struggled with classifying morphology accurately and often required specialized hardware (Mortimer, Van Der Horst, and Mortimer et al. 2015).

Major advancements in the field were brought with the advent of deep learning models. Convolutional Neural Network (CNN) algorithm for sperm analysis was widely used (Ankile, Heggland, and Krange et al. 2020), AlexNet, VGG, and ResNet were used to classify sperm based on the shape, these algorithms were typically trained on images from standard microscopy datasets including HuSHeM and SCIAN-Morph (Chang et al. 2017; Iqbal, Mustafa, and Ma et al. 2020). Advanced architectures like Vision Transformers have also been explored recently (Chen et al. 2022). Deep learning has also been applied in sperm viability, detection, and tracking in video sequences (Riordon, McCallum, and Sinton 2019). Kanakasabapathy et al. developed a smartphone add-on based testing procedure (assay) for analyzing semen, primarily to determine sperm concentration and motility (Kanakasabapathy et al. 2017). Ilhan and Aydin demonstrated data acquisition and concentration analysis which was built specifically to assess the morphology using smartphone (Ilhan and Aydin 2020), which led to the development of SMIDS dataset.

Our work adds to the use of smartphone based morphological analysis focusing on the SMIDS dataset addressing the challenges of smartphone acquired images explicitly. Our approach highlights EfficientNetb0 model, well known for its computational efficiency (Tan and Le 2019) and implementation of Integrated Gradients and Sperm Quality Scoring ensures explainability of the model. We have introduced a systematic transfer learning and fine-tuning strategy by augmenting data to optimize performance. Our work represents one of the first and detailed evaluations of the EfficientNetb0 architecture fine-tuned specifically for the three-class sperm morphology classification.

3 Methodology

3.1 Dataset

Sperm Morphology Image Dataset from Smartphones (SMIDS) (Ilhan, Serbes, and Aydin et al. 2020), comprising 3000 smartphone and microscopic images were used. The images are in bitmap (.bmp) format representing three distinct categories, normal sperm, abnormal sperm, and non-sperm comprising of 1021, 1005, and 974 images respectively based on WHO guidelines (WHO laboratory manual for the examination and processing of human semen, 6th ed n.d.). Abnormal sperm includes various morphological defects including head shape or size defects, midpiece abnormalities and coiled tails. The non-sperm category includes debris, air bubbles, and cells other than sperm or background regions. The dataset possesses certain challenges including variations in the intensity of staining, focus issues, overlapping cells, fragmented sperm, and background noise making it a realistic benchmark for point-of-care applications. The images were converted from .bmp to .jpg format prior to processing in order to make it compatible with common deep learning libraries and to potentially reduce storage requirements (Fig. 1).

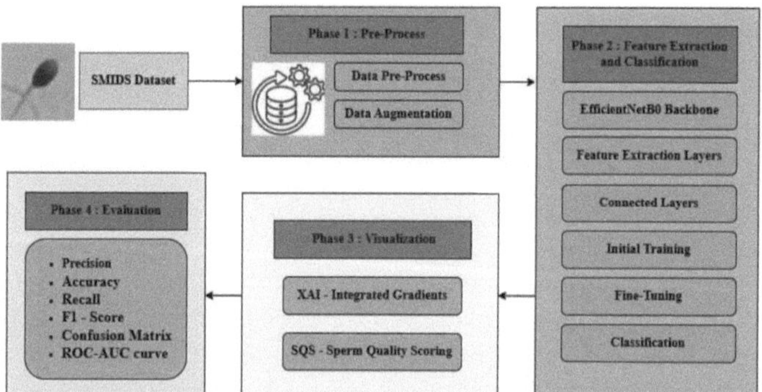

Fig. 1. Schematic representation of the deep learning pipeline for sperm analysis, from image input to model evaluation

3.2 Data Preparation and Augmentation

The dataset was split into training, validation, and test sets which includes 70%, 15%, and 15%, respectively. While the division was random, the division was ensured to be stratified in nature, i.e., the relative proportion of images belonging to each class (Normal Sperm, Abnormal Sperm, Non-Sperm) was preserved across all three classes to avoid class distribution bias during evaluation. Data augmentation was performed on the training set throughout the training process (Shorten and Khoshgoftaar 2019), enabling the model to generalize more effectively to the novel variations and to avoid overfitting. The techniques used for augmentation include random rotation with $+/-30\%$, random horizontal flip, random shear transformation of intensity 0.2, and random zoom in the range of 80% to 120%, random width and height translation by a factor of $+/-10\%$ of image dimensions, and random brightness change between 80% to 120%. All the training, validation, and test images were resized to 224×224 pixels, the default input size for EfficientNetB0 architecture. Images were processed in a batch size of 32. Pixel values were pre-processed using the individual pre-processing needs of EfficientNetB0, managed by the data generator and including the scaling pixel values between the range $[-1, 1]$ or $[0,1]$ as in the preprocess input function of the Keras application.

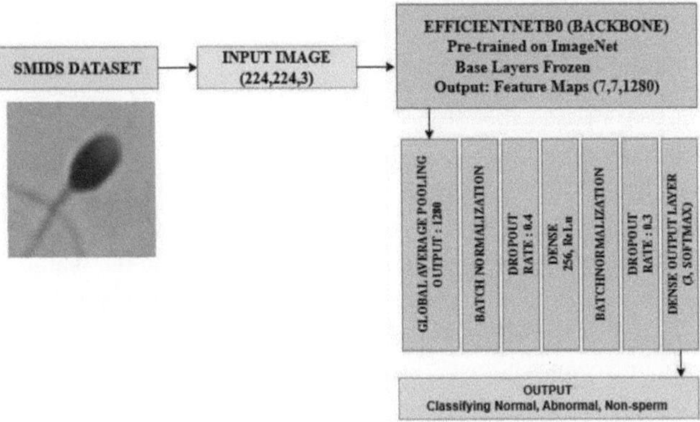

Fig. 2. Proposed model architecture, featuring an EfficientNetB0 backbone and a custom classification head

3.3 Model Architecture: EfficientNetB0

We chose EfficientNetB0 as the starting point based on its reported high performance and computational efficiency over older models with comparable accuracy. Transfer learning was used, taking advantage of weights pre-trained using the massive ImageNet dataset (Deng et al., 2009; Yosinski et al., 2014). The construction of the model included instantiating an EfficientNetB0 architecture pre-trained on ImageNet weights, without its last classification layer (include_top = False) and with an input_tensor of shape (224, 224, 3). To maintain the features learned by the ImageNet, all the layers of the loaded EfficientNetB0 base were first frozen by setting base_model.trainable = False. A fresh custom classification head was subsequently added on top of this cold base. This head begins with a GlobalAveragePooling2D layer to reduce the spatial size of the base model's feature maps to a feature vector. This is then followed by a Batch-Normalization layer for training stabilization, and then a Dropout layer with a rate of 0.4 for regularization, randomly zeroing a fraction of input units during training to prevent overfitting (Srivastava et al. 2014). Second, a Dense (fully connected) layer of 256 units with ReLU activation function is used on these features, followed by a second Batch-Normalization layer and a second Dropout layer with rate 0.3. The head ends in a final Dense layer with 3 neurons, corresponding to the three classes (Normal Sperm, Abnormal Sperm, Non-Sperm), and is employing a softmax activation function for the output of class probabilities. The whole model was trained using AdamW optimizer, a new adaptation of Adam where weight decay is also incorporated in the process of optimization (Loshchilov and Hutter et al. 2019), with learning rate set to 1e-4 and weight decay set to 1e-5. The categorical_cross entropy loss function was used since it was suitable for multi-class classification, and accuracy as the evaluation metric (Fig. 2).

3.4 Training Strategy: Two-Phase Tuning

The model was trained by a two-phase approach to efficiently transfer the pre-trained features to the task of sperm morphology classification on SMIDS dataset. Phase 1 i.e. feature extraction uses the model with the entire frozen EfficientNetb0 base and the trainable custom head. This was trained for a fixed number of epochs (e.g. 15 in our case) or until validation performance converged. The weights of the added classifier layers are mainly learned in this phase so that the model learns on using the features extracted by the frozen base. A comparatively higher learning rate (e.g. 1e-3 or 1e-4) was employed. The phase 2 referring to the fine-tuning, wherein the part of top layers of EfficientNetb0 base model were unfrozen (i.e. last 20 layers). This enables the model to fine-tune some of the high level pre-trained features more specifically to the characteristics of sperm images in which more general features are detected. During training, Adam optimizer was employed. We used normal callbacks where Model checkpoint was used to store the model weights which provided the best performance on validation set that either raised the validation accuracy or reduced the validation loss.

3.5 XAI: Integrated Gradients

To understand the prediction of the model, we used Explainable AI technique called Integrated Gradients (Sundararajan, Taly, and Yan 2017). It helps us pinpoint which part of sperm's image was the most influential in the model's decision. Basically, this technique produces a visual explanation, often shown as a heatmap right on top of the sperm image. This map highlights the areas the model 'looked at' the hardest when making its choice. It is calculated by tracking how much each pixel contributes to the outcome, starting from a neutral baseline. This lets us to visually see if the model is focusing on relevant features including the sperm's head shape or tail structure, or it is deviated by artifacts. It's a crucial step for trusting the model's judgement (Adadi and Berrada et al. 2018).

3.6 SQS: Sperm Quality Scoring

We also developed the sperm quality score (SQS) to summarize the quality indicated by the model's prediction. We start with a base score depending on the classification (above 70 points for Normal Sperm, below 70 for Abnormal Sperm, and 0 for Non-sperm). The model's confidence then adjusts this score; the more confident it is, the higher the score relative to its base. So, naturally, if the model strongly believes it's seeing a 'Normal' sperm, the SQS will be high. But if it classifies something as 'Abnormal', or just lacks high confidence, the resulting SQS gets pulled down. This provides a rough idea of the quality assessed by the AI for that particular image according to the algorithm's accuracy and confidence level based on the below equation.

$$SQS = \min(\text{floor}(\text{ScoreMap}[\text{Predicted Class}] \times \text{Confidence}), 100)$$

4   Results and Discussions

The EfficientNetB0 model exhibited a monotonic decrease in validation loss and a corresponding increase in validation accuracy over epochs. In order to regularize the model and to prevent overfitting, the use of extensive data augmentation techniques like random rotations, flips, shears, zooms, and brightness adjustments appeared to be effective (Shorten and Khoshgoftaar 2019). The fine-tuned EfficientNetb0 architecture achieved a peak accuracy of 83.75% on the holdout validation set. On evaluating the independent test dataset which comprises the images that are entirely unseen during training or validation subsequently yielded a final classification accuracy of 84.75%. Confusion matrix revealed that the model was not able to accurately differentiate between an abnormal sperm and non-sperm in certain images possibly because certain abnormal morphologies appeared to be visually ambiguous. Using both the Integrated Gradient (IG) heatmaps and the SQS score gives a clear understanding of the classification. Our results prove the effectiveness of implementing fine-tuned deep learning models for image-based automated sperm morphology classification using images captured directly through smartphones (Table 1).

Table 1. Comparison metrics between EfficientNetB0 and DenseNet

Model	EfficientNetB0	DenseNet + CBAM
Accuracy	0.8475	0.7900
Macro Avg. Precision	0.8451	0.8000
Macro Avg. Recall	0.8436	0.7900
Macro Avg. F1-Score	0.8441	0.7900
F1-Score (Abnormal sperm)	0.7759	0.7200
F1-Score (Normal sperm)	0.9310	0.7600
F1-Score (Non-sperm)	0.8254	0.7800

We encountered several issues in the clinical dataset, including class imbalance (having many more images of one type of sperm than others), noisy images due to the low-cost imaging equipment, and a limited sample size. We addressed these issues with heavy data augmentation generating more diverse training samples and two-stage fine-tuning of the pre-trained model respectively. Even with fine tuning, distinguishing the abnormal sperm from each other was slightly hard. The sheer variety under the abnormal sperm, covering several types of defects by conventional criteria makes classification more complicated than the normal sperm form. In addition, background material or cellular residues in lower-resolution imaging systems posed as severely defective sperm, can mislead classifiers. One of the unique aspects of our work is the interpretability and real-world utility focus. The SQS converts the model's classification and confidence into an easily understandable single score. The foundation of the SQS thresholds was laid to establish a distinct, tiered system of quick assessment. As per the definition in our methodology, the base scores are greater than 70 for 'Normal_Sperm, less than 70 for

Abnormal_Sperm, and 0 for Non-Sperm. This configuration was specifically meant to create a large numerical difference between normal and abnormal cells, corresponding to their contrasting clinical significance. The 70-point limit for regular sperm enables the model's confidence level to produce an ordered score for good cells, but a score below 70 will indicate that a cell is morphologically impaired. The main clinical application of the SQS is screening and ranking. In a high-throughput environment, it might rank cells programmatically, enabling an andrologist to briefly inspect the top-scoring sperm for techniques including ICSI. The SQS score need to clinically validated, to entail a proper correlation analysis between our model-generated SQS and the morphology grades determined by certified embryologists using stringent WHO criteria. A high, positive correlation would confirm SQS as a valid proxy for expert human judgment and establish its value for streamlining clinical processes.

Moreover, the deliberate choice of smartphone-based imaging and an efficient architecture like EfficientNetB0 accentuates the possibility of low-cost and inexpensive male fertility screening technique. The EfficientNetB0 model was selected as the best compared with other architectures including Densenet (78% accuracy). Further enhancing it with convolutional block attention module (CBAM) increased the accuracy to 80%. The Integrated Gradients provided interpretable visualizations aligning well with morphological indicators in EfficientNetb0.

This work provides a robust and interpretable system for smartphone-based sperm morphology assessment that can be directly included or added as an enhancement to the conventional laboratory microscopes. Future research investigating 'ensemble' approaches, essentially amalgamating the strengths of multiple distinct light models may further enhance robustness, especially for difficult-to-classify abnormal class. Nonetheless, the present framework already lays a huge step forward towards practical, AI-based semen analysis deployable outside traditional clinical environments (Figs. 3, 4, 5, 6 and 7).

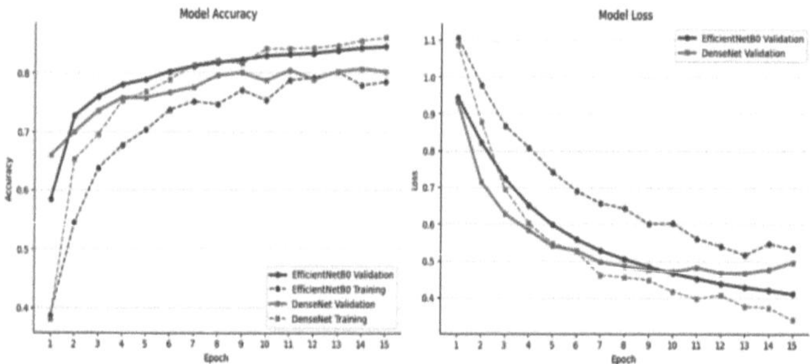

Fig. 3. Comparative performance analysis of EfficientNetB0 and DenseNet models during training

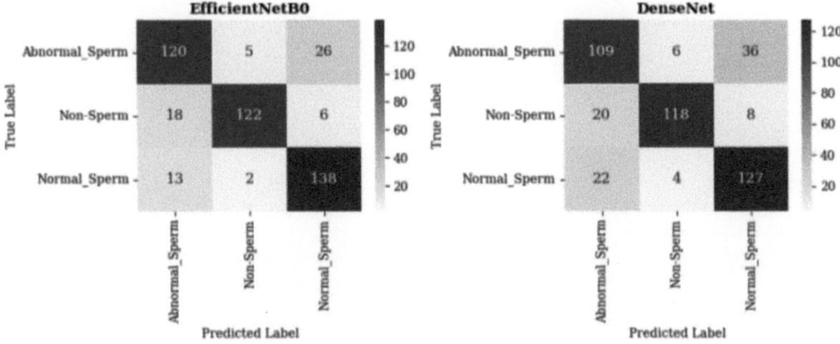

Fig. 4. Detailed error analysis of EfficientNetB0 and DenseNet models using Confusion matrices

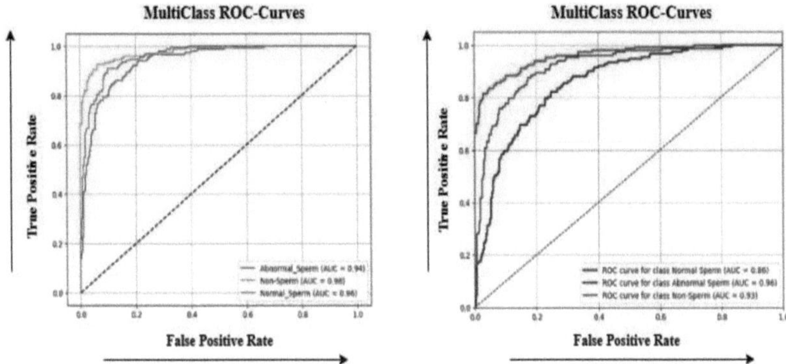

Fig. 5. Evaluation of model diagnostic performance using Receiver Operating Characteristic (ROC) curves

Fig. 6. Integrated Gradients highlighting key morphological features used by the EfficientNetB0 model for sperm classification

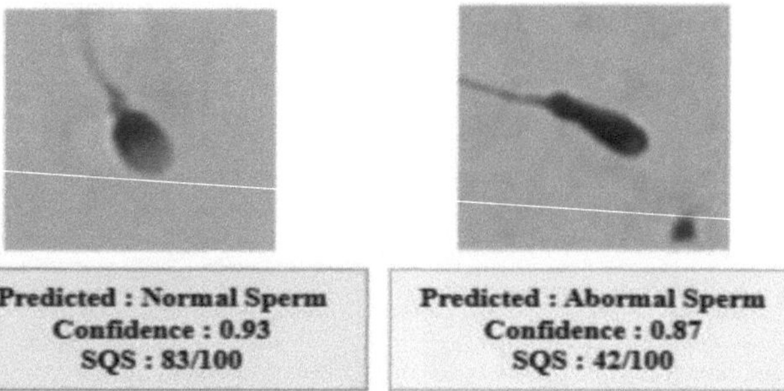

Fig. 7. The Sperm Quality Score (SQS) provides a granular, quantitative metric for morphological integrity

5   Conclusion

To conclude, we aimed to develop an automated way to grade sperm morphology using smartphone images from the SMIDS dataset. EfficientNetB0 model, with data augmentation and transfer learning was 84.75% accurate in classifying Normal, Abnormal, and Non-sperm images. The Explainable AI using Integrated Gradients, highlights the regions of interest in arriving at its conclusions. We also developed the Sperm Quality Score (SQS) to turn the model's output into a straightforward, meaningful number. The future work is aimed at deploying our trained model through a lightweight web framework like Flask or Streamlit followed by real time clinical evaluation to validate the model and also predict fertility outcomes including IVF or ICSI success rates.

References

Adadi, A., Berrada, M.: Peeking inside the black-box: a survey on explainable artificial intelligence (XAI). IEEE Access. **6**, 52138–52160 (2018). https://doi.org/10.1109/ACCESS.2018.2870052

Agarwal, A., Mulgund, A., Hamada, A., Chyatte, M.R.: A unique view on male infertility around the globe. Reprod. Biol. Endocrinol. **13**(1) (2015). https://doi.org/10.1186/S12958-015-0032-1

Amann, R.P., Waberski, D.: Computer-assisted sperm analysis (CASA): capabilities and potential developments. Theriogenology. **81**(1), 5–17.e3 (2014). https://doi.org/10.1016/J.THERIO GENOLOGY.2013.09.004

Amini, B., Oliveira, A.R.E.: A History of the Work Concept: From Physics to Economics. Springer, New York/London (2015). https://doi.org/10.4236/AHS.2015.44023

Ankile, L.L., Heggland, M.F., Krange, K.: Deep convolutional neural networks: a survey of the foundations, selected improvements, and some current applications (2020). https://arxiv.org/pdf/2011.12960.

Chang, V., Heutte, L., Petitjean, C., Härtel, S., Hitschfeld, N.: Automatic classification of human sperm head morphology. Comput. Biol. Med. **84**, 205–216 (2017). https://doi.org/10.1016/J.COMPBIOMED.2017.03.029

Chen, J., Frey, E.C., He, Y., Segars, W.P., Li, Y., Du, Y.: TransMorph: transformer for unsupervised medical image registration. Med. Image Anal. **82**, 102615 (2022). https://doi.org/10.1016/J.MEDIA.2022.102615

Franken, D.R., Oehninger, S.: Semen analysis and sperm function testing. Asian J. Androl. **14**(1), 6 (2011). https://doi.org/10.1038/AJA.2011.58

Garcea, F., Serra, A., Lamberti, F., Morra, L.: Data augmentation for medical imaging: a systematic literature review. Comput. Biol. Med. **152**, 106391 (2023). https://doi.org/10.1016/J.COMPBI OMED.2022.106391

Holzinger, A., Langs, G., Denk, H., Zatloukal, K., Müller, H.: Causability and Explainability of Artificial Intelligence in Medicine. WIREs Data Min. Knowl. Discov. **9**(4) (2019). https://doi. org/10.1002/WIDM.1312

Ilhan, H.O., Aydin, N.: Smartphone based sperm counting - an alternative way to the visual assessment technique in sperm concentration analysis. Multimed. Tools Appl. **79**(9–10), 6409–6435 (2020). https://doi.org/10.1007/S11042-019-08421-3/METRICS

Ilhan, H.O., Serbes, G., Aydin, N.: Automated sperm morphology analysis approach using a directional masking technique. Comput. Biol. Med. **122**, 103845 (2020). https://doi.org/10.1016/J.COMPBIOMED.2020.103845

Iqbal, I., Mustafa, G., Ma, J.: Deep learning-based morphological classification of human sperm heads. Diagnostics. **10**(5), 325 (2020). https://doi.org/10.3390/DIAGNOSTICS10050325

Kanakasabapathy, M.K., et al.: Supplementary materials for an automated smartphone-based diagnostic assay for point-of-care semen analysis. Sci. Transl. Med. **9**, 7863 (2017). https://doi.org/10.1126/scitranslmed.aai7863

Ker, J., Wang, L., Rao, J., Lim, T.: Deep learning applications in medical image analysis. IEEE Access. **6**, 9375–9379 (2017). https://doi.org/10.1109/ACCESS.2017.2788044

Kim, H.E., Cosa-Linan, A., Santhanam, N., Jannesari, M., Maros, M.E., Ganslandt, T.: Transfer learning for medical image classification: a literature review. BMC Med. Imaging. **22**(1), 1–13 (2022). https://doi.org/10.1186/S12880-022-00793-7

Mortimer, S.T., Van Der Horst, G., Mortimer, D.: The future of computer-aided sperm analysis. Asian J. Androl. **17**(4), 545 (2015). https://doi.org/10.4103/1008-682X.154312

Olawade, D.B., Teke, J., Adeleye, K.K., Weerasinghe, K., Maidoki, M., David-Olawade, A.C.: Artificial intelligence in in-vitro fertilization (IVF): a new era of precision and personalization in fertility treatments. J. Gynecol. Obstet. Hum. Reprod. **54**(3), 102903 (2025). https://doi.org/10.1016/J.JOGOH.2024.102903

Oliveira, J.B.A., et al.: Motile sperm organelle morphology examination (MSOME): intervariation study of normal sperm and sperm with large nuclear vacuoles. Reprod. Biol. Endocrinol. **8**, 56 (2010). https://doi.org/10.1186/1477-7827-8-56

Palermo, G., Joris, H., Devroey, P., Van Steirteghem, A.C.: Pregnancies after intracytoplasmic injection of single spermatozoon into an oocyte. Lancet. **340**(8810), 17–18 (1992). https://doi.org/10.1016/0140-6736(92)92425-F

Pelzman, D.L., Sandlow, J.I.: Sperm morphology: evaluating its clinical relevance in contemporary fertility practice. Reprod. Med. Biol. **23**(1), e12594 (2024). https://doi.org/10.1002/RMB2.12594

Pfeifer, S., et al.: Diagnostic evaluation of the infertile male: a committee opinion. Fertil. Steril. **103**(3), e18–e25 (2015). https://doi.org/10.1016/j.fertnstert.2014.12.103

Riordon, J., McCallum, C., Sinton, D.: Deep learning for the classification of human sperm. Comput. Biol. Med. **111** (2019). https://doi.org/10.1016/j.compbiomed.2019.103342

Shorten, C., Khoshgoftaar, T.M.: A survey on image data augmentation for deep learning. J. Big Data. **6**(1) (2019). https://doi.org/10.1186/S40537-019-0197-0

Siddharth, K., Kumar, T., Zabihullah, M.: Interobserver variability in semen analysis: findings from a quality control initiative. Cureus. (2023). https://doi.org/10.7759/CUREUS.46388

Sundararajan, M., Taly, A., Yan, Q.: Axiomatic attribution for deep networks. (2017). https://doi.org/10.5555/3305890.3306024

Tan, M., Le, Q.V.: EfficientNet: rethinking model scaling for convolutional neural networks. In: 36th International Conference on Machine Learning, ICML 2019 2019-June, pp. 10691–10700 (2019) https://arxiv.org/pdf/1905.11946

Verstegen, J., Iguer-Ouada, M., Onclin, K.: Computer assisted semen analyzers in andrology research and veterinary practice. Theriogenology. **57**(1), 149–179 (2002). https://doi.org/10.1016/S0093-691X(01)00664-1

WHO: Laboratory Manual for the Examination and Processing of Human Semen, 6th edn, (n.d.) Retrieved May 13, 2025. https://www.who.int/publications/i/item/9789240030787/

Yüzkat, M., Ilhan, H.O., Aydin, N.: Multi-model CNN fusion for sperm morphology analysis. Comput. Biol. Med. **137**, 104790 (2021). https://doi.org/10.1016/J.COMPBIOMED.2021.104790

Hybrid Bi-directional GRU-Attention U-Net with MLP Classifier for Accurate Pneumonia Segmentation and Classification

M. Uma Maheshwari[1](✉), R. Tamilselvi[1], M. Parisa Beham[1], and R. Murugan[2]

[1] ECE Department, Sethu Institute of Technology, Kariapatti, Virudhunagar, India
{uma,tamilselvi,parisabeham}@sethu.ac.in
[2] ECE Department, National Institute of Technology, Silchar, Assam, India

Abstract. Pneumonia, a leading cause of global morbidity and mortality, particularly among children under five and elderly populations, accounted for over 740,000 deaths in 2019 alone as reported by the World Health Organization. With an estimated 450 million individuals affected annually, timely and accurate diagnosis remains a critical challenge in clinical settings. While chest X-ray imaging is the most practical and widely used modality for pneumonia detection due to its affordability and availability, conventional computer-aided diagnostic (CAD) systems and deep learning models often fall short in handling spatial dependencies, subtle lesion variations, and the temporal dynamics evident in disease progression. Addressing these limitations, this study proposes a novel hybrid deep learning framework that combines a bi-directional Gated Recurrent Unit (GRU)-enhanced U-Net with an attention mechanism for improved pneumonia segmentation, alongside a Multi-Layer Perceptron (MLP) classifier for accurate disease classification. The bi-directional GRU modules embedded within the U-Net architecture effectively capture long-range contextual information, while the attention gate selectively enhances critical lesion features. Post segmentation, a dynamic feature fusion strategy extracts high-level representations, which are fed into the MLP classifier to distinguish between normal and pneumonia-affected lung regions. Experimental validation using a Kaggle chest X-ray dataset demonstrates the superior performance of the proposed model, achieving 98% accuracy, an F1 score of 0.93, precision of 0.95, and recall of 0.92. This integrated approach not only improves diagnostic precision but also holds significant potential as a clinical decision support tool, aiding radiologists in early detection, risk stratification, and personalized treatment planning for pneumonia patients.

Keywords: Pneumonia Diagnosis · Chest X-ray Analysis · U-Net Segmentation · Bi-directional GRU · Attention Mechanism · Multi-Layer Perceptron (MLP)

1 Introduction

Pneumonia is one of the leading infectious causes of childhood death worldwide. According to the World Health Organization (WHO), pneumonia claimed the lives of 740,180 children under five years old in 2019 [1]. Pneumonia consistently ranks among the

© The Author(s), under exclusive license to Springer Nature Switzerland AG 2026
R. K. Karsh et al. (Eds.): SIPCOV 2025, CCIS 2848, pp. 155–174, 2026.
https://doi.org/10.1007/978-3-032-15809-3_12

leading causes of morbidity and mortality worldwide. In India, where factors like air pollution, overcrowding, and limited healthcare access can exacerbate the risk, pneumonia has been a considerable concern, this issue is especially critical among vulnerable populations, including young children and the elderly. All around the world, pneumonia is a common illness, but its death toll is highest in South and Sub-Saharan Asia. In five developing/underdeveloped countries (Ethiopia, Nigeria, Pakistan, India, and the Democratic Republic of the Congo), pneumonia among children was the leading cause of death in 2017 [2]. Approximately 450 million people, or around 7% of the global population, contract pneumonia annually, with nearly 4 million of these cases resulting in death [3, 4]. Statistics of Pneumonia is shown in the Fig. 1.

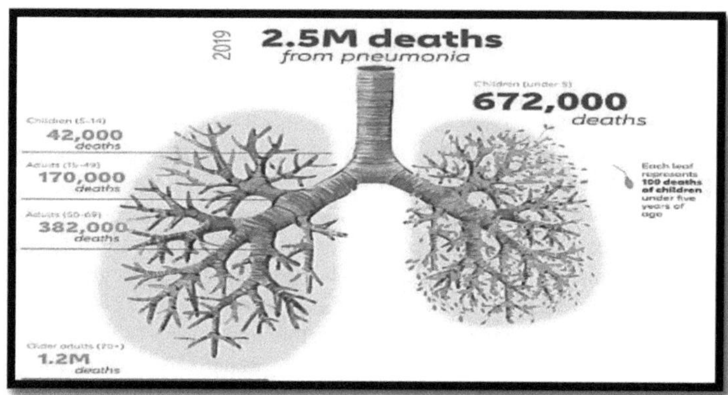

Fig. 1. Statistics of Pneumonia Source: Global Burden of Disease, 2019. https://www.healthdata.org/gbd/2019

The microscopic air sacs called alveoli are most affected by pneumonia, an inflammatory lung disease [4, 5]. Common symptoms include fever, chest discomfort, dry cough, and difficulty breathing. The severity of the condition varies [6]. Pneumonia, which is mainly caused by viral or bacterial infections, can be challenging to diagnose precisely due to the variety of pathogens involved. The condition is categorized into four types: ventilator-acquired pneumonia (VAP), hospital-acquired pneumonia (HAP), community-acquired pneumonia (CAP), and health care-associated pneumonia (HCAP). [7].

Various modalities are employed for the detection of pneumonia, X-ray imaging, magnetic resonance imaging (MRI), ultrasound, and computed tomography (CT) scans. While each modality has its strengths and applications, X-ray imaging stands out as a primary choice for pneumonia detection due to its practicality, accessibility, and efficiency. X-ray imaging is widely utilized in medical environments, offers rapid image acquisition, and is relatively inexpensive compared to other modalities. Moreover, X-ray images provide clear visualization of lung abnormalities associated with pneumonia, such as consolidations, infiltrates, and opacities, this approach facilitates rapid diagnosis and effective treatment planning. Additionally, X-ray imaging exposes patients to less radiation than CT scans, which makes it safer for them, particularly in situations involving routine screening. Overall, the accessibility, efficiency, and diagnostic utility of X-ray imaging make it a preferred modality for the detection and monitoring of pneumonia in clinical practice. The sample normal and pneumonia affected X-ray images of the chest are shown in the Fig. 2.

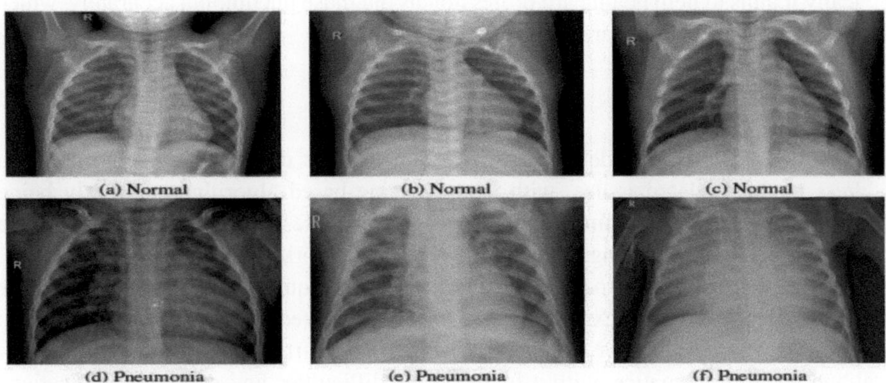

Fig. 2. Sample normal images (a, b and c) and pneumonia affected images (d, e and f)

A widely used method called computer-aided diagnosis (CAD) helps physicians identify and understand a variety of abnormalities in medical imaging, as well as reliably and quickly diagnose and analyze diseases [8, 9]. In the past, radiologists would manually study chest X-rays to identify and diagnose lung infections like pneumonia. Manual segmentation was once used to identify pneumonia. Manual segmentation is typically carried out by skilled clinicians or radiologists. Its disadvantages include high unpredictability and time consumption, which lead to significant variations in the extracted value. Conversely, the semiautomatic approach uses algorithms to help segment data, so overcoming the limitations of human segmentation. This method might cause delays in the diagnosis process and produce poor results. Examining a lot of X-rays every day can be difficult and may result in an incorrect diagnosis and also it would be prohibitive to always have access to a medical specialist. In order to address the previously mentioned drawbacks and difficulties associated with manual X-ray inspections, Artificial intelligence (AI) is being used by CAD systems to find patterns in data that can either predict disease or allow medical professionals predict disease [10]. AI-powered technologies can significantly accelerate diagnosis, allowing for timely interventions and personalized treatment plans. Additionally, early detection and characterization of pneumonia through automated analysis can greatly enhance patient outcomes by preventing the disease from progressing [11–13].

The main contribution presented in this article is presented below:

- To achieve better pneumonia segmentation accuracy than traditional methods, a modified U-Net architecture enhanced with GRU units will be utilized to capture complex spatial dependencies and distant contextual information inside X-Ray Images.
- To precisely distinguish between healthy and infected lung tissue, a multilayer perceptron (MLP)-based classifier will be utilized, leveraging the extracted features from the segmented regions to detect and categorize areas impacted by pneumonia.

- To verify the proposed methodology's performance in terms of segmentation accuracy and classification accuracy, it will be thoroughly tested on a variety of datasets that include X-ray images of patients with pneumonia and healthy controls
- To demonstrate the clinical importance and potential of the developed method, specifically it aims to help healthcare professionals diagnose pneumonia accurately, which would enhance patient care and treatment planning.

2 Related Works

In recent years, many academics and researchers have developed AI algorithms to address medical-related issues, with deep learning-based algorithms currently being applied across various domains. In the field of medicine, researchers are able to produce promising outcomes by using Convolution Neural Networks (CNNs) [14–16].

The deep learning approach does away with the requirement for explicit feature extraction. These are some explanations of pneumonia detection methods based on deep learning. M. Sharma [17] gives a general review of deep learning's application in biomedical and health informatics, with a focus on the difficulties and potential applications of brain tumor segmentation. Lee [18] discuss the unique challenges posed by medical image analysis, such as variability in image quality and interpretation, as well as the immense potential of deep learning techniques in addressing these challenges. Hashmo et al. [19] the researchers likely utilized a pre-trained deep learning model, such as a convolutional neural network (CNN), trained on a large dataset of general images, and fine-tuned it specifically for pneumonia detection in chest X-ray images. Author offer a new ensemble method that uses a weighted classifier. The state-of-the-art deep learning algorithms' prediction outputs from a weighted classifier are combined in the suggested model. A deep learning technique was offered by Son et al. [20] with the purpose of developing and validating the detection of numerous anomalies in retinal fundus images. Baltruschat et al. [21] compared different deep learning approaches for multi-label chest X-ray classification. The researchers likely explored various convolutional neural network (CNN) architectures and training strategies to classify chest X-ray images into multiple labels corresponding to different pathologies or abnormalities. This study makes use of both fine-tuning and transfer learning. A self-constructed convolutional neural network trained on a rather small dataset was provided by J. Garstka et al. [3] for the classification of lung X-ray images. M. M. Hasan et al. suggested a combination method for the automatic diagnosis of pneumonia from chest X-ray images that combines image processing with either the VGG-16 or VGG-19 Deep Convolutional Neural Network versions [4] When making diagnoses, X. Ouyang et al. suggest a unique online attention module that uses a 3D convolutional network (CNN) to focus on the lung infection regions [22]. A novel convolutional neural network (CNN) called ResNet is introduced by S. Li et al. to assist medical professionals in making more precise diagnosis of pneumonia author used Keras's built-in ImageDataGenerator to supplement the dataset and prevent over-fitting [23]. Deepika et al. [24] introduced a pneumonia detection framework that leverages chest X-ray imagery combined with advanced deep learning methodologies. The research presumably entails the use of convolutional neural networks (CNNs) trained on a dataset comprising labeled chest X-ray images, distinguishing between pneumonia and non-pneumonia cases. Stephen et al. [25] designed a robust deep learning model for classifying pneumonia in the healthcare sector, probably leveraging convolutional neural networks (CNNs) or similar architectures to distinguish between pneumonia and non-pneumonia cases using chest X-ray images. Ayan et al. [26] investigated the use of deep learning techniques for diagnosing pneumonia from chest X-ray images, likely focusing on training models to automatically identify pneumonia-related features in these images. Abiyev et al. [27] utilized deep convolutional neural networks to detect chest diseases, including pneumonia. Their approach likely involved developing a deep learning model trained on a comprehensive dataset of chest X-ray images to accurately classify a range of chest diseases. Acharya et al. [28] introduced a deep learning-based method for the automatic diagnosis of pneumonia using chest radiographs, likely involving the training of models to identify pneumonia-specific features in these images. Varshni et al. [29] introduced a method for pneumonia detection leveraging CNN-based feature extraction, where convolutional neural networks were employed to extract relevant features from chest X-ray images for classification into pneumonia and non-pneumonia categories. Huaiguang Wu and colleagues [30] pioneered a pneumonia forecasting framework utilizing convolutional deep neural networks trained on chest X-ray images, potentially advancing the diagnosis of pneumonia through sophisticated machine learning techniques.

A major obstacle to automated pneumonia analysis in X-ray images is the lack of reliable and effective segmentation techniques, which when combined with limitations in classification methodologies, creates a significant bottleneck. This reduces the likelihood of accurate and timely diagnosis, which has an impact on patient outcomes and the general effectiveness of healthcare interventions. Innovative methods that can effectively capture spatial interdependence, maintain temporal dynamics, and extract discriminative characteristics from segmented regions are needed to address these issues. Therefore, there is a great demand for new approaches that use cutting-edge neural network designs that can reliably segment data while permitting precise classification of areas of X-ray images affected by pneumonia. The literature that has already been written may discuss specific aspects of various concepts, but it frequently lacks an extensive approach that plays to each architecture's advantages. Some studies have investigated the integration of convolutional and recurrent neural networks for medical image analysis, yet the specific integration of GRU with U-Net and MLP for pneumonia-related tasks remains less explored.

In deep learning, applications in medical imaging have demonstrated significant potential in automating the detection and diagnosis of various diseases, particularly excelling in identifying pneumonia. Research on the U-Net architecture has demonstrated its efficacy in image segmentation tasks, while the integration of Gated Recurrent Unit (GRU) mechanisms has been explored to capture temporal dependencies in sequential medical data. Additionally, the application of Multi-Layer Perceptron (MLP) models in medical imaging, particularly for classification tasks, has gained attention. However, there is a limited body of work that investigates the simultaneous integration of U-Net, GRU, and MLP architectures for pneumonia segmentation and classification. This study endeavors to expand upon prior research by introducing an innovative framework that harnesses the synergies of these integrated elements to bolster precision and dependability in pivotal endeavors such as pneumonia segmentation and classification.

The above related work will provide information about a comprehensive review of relevant studies and highlighting the gaps and challenges that the proposed model seeks to address.

The proposed work derives inspiration from these facts to develop an innovative deep learning algorithm that can consistently categorize an image as either normal or infected with bacteria or viruses by extracting discriminative features. To segment the various regions of pneumonia images, a novel Gated Recurrent Unit (GRU)-enhanced U-Net architecture is designed in this proposed study. To further classify pneumonia, Multi-Layer Perceptron (MLP) architecture is used.

3 Proposed Methodology

In this work, a novel approach that integrates a Gated Recurrent Unit (GRU)-enhanced U-Net architecture for accurate pneumonia segmentation in X-Ray images, coupled with a Multi-Layer Perceptron (MLP) for classification. The segmentation framework employs a modified U-Net architecture, incorporating GRU units within the encoding and decoding paths to gather the complex spatial relationships and distant contextual data found in the X-ray images of the chest. The GRU modules facilitate the preservation of temporal dynamics, allowing the model to effectively delineate pneumonia-affected regions with enhanced precision. Following segmentation, a separate MLP-based classifier is employed to discern and categorize the segmented regions, distinguishing between pneumonia-affected and healthy lung tissues. The classifier leverages extracted features from the segmented regions to make binary classification decisions. It has the benefit of using global location and context data with the least amount of training samples when compared to other networks. Figure 3 shows the overall workflow of the proposed work.

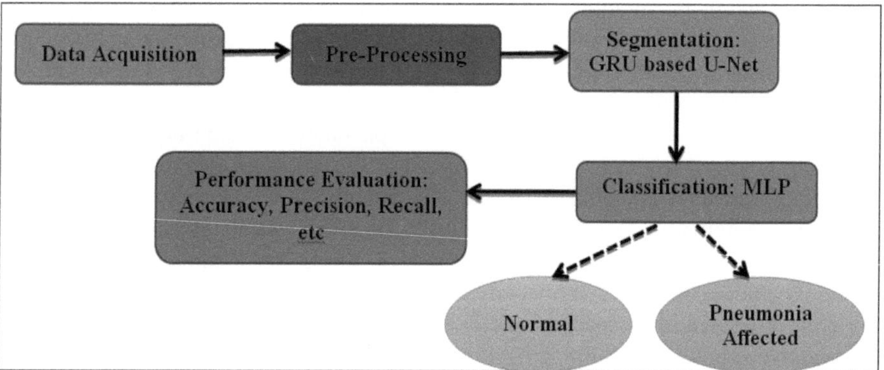

Fig. 3. Overall Workflow of the proposed work

3.1 Dataset Acquisition

The datasets included in this research were obtained through the online platform Kaggle. The normal and pneumonia images located in each of the three train, test, and val files, as well as their corresponding subfolders, form this dataset and there are 64 x 64 grayscale images which includes 624 images for testing and 5216 images for training. Here, 564 X-ray images were acquired from the dataset where 282 normal X-ray images and 282 pneumonia affected images The images were subsequently divided into three distinct sets for training, validation, and testing, with each group containing 70%, 10%, and 20% of the images, respectively. Data distribution from kaggle dataset is shown in Table 1.

Table 1. Data Distribution form kaggle dataset

Data Division	Normal	Pneumonia	Total
Training	198	198	396
Validation	28	28	56
Testing	56	56	112

3.2 Image Pre-processing

To enhance the robustness and generalizability of the proposed deep learning model, extensive image preprocessing and augmentation techniques were applied. Initially, all chest X-ray images were resized to 64×64 pixels and converted to grayscale to standardize input dimensions and reduce computational complexity. Histogram equalization was employed to enhance contrast and improve visibility of fine details, while a Gaussian filter was applied to suppress noise and preserve structural patterns relevant for diagnosis. In addition to standard preprocessing, data augmentation techniques were incorporated to address class imbalance and reduce overfitting, especially given the relatively small dataset size. To reduce overfitting caused by limited training data, regularization techniques such as data augmentation, dropout (rate 0.4), and early stopping were applied. Using Keras's ImageDataGenerator, a variety of real-time augmentations were performed, including random horizontal flips, rotation within $\pm 15°$, width and height shifts up to 10%, zooming within a scale range of 0.8 to 1.2, and slight brightness variations. These transformations simulated variations in X-ray acquisition and anatomical differences among patients, thereby allowing the model to learn invariant features. As a result, the augmented dataset facilitated improved model generalization and performance, which was evident in both training and validation metrics. The sample illustration of image pre-processing and augmentation results is shown in Fig. 4.

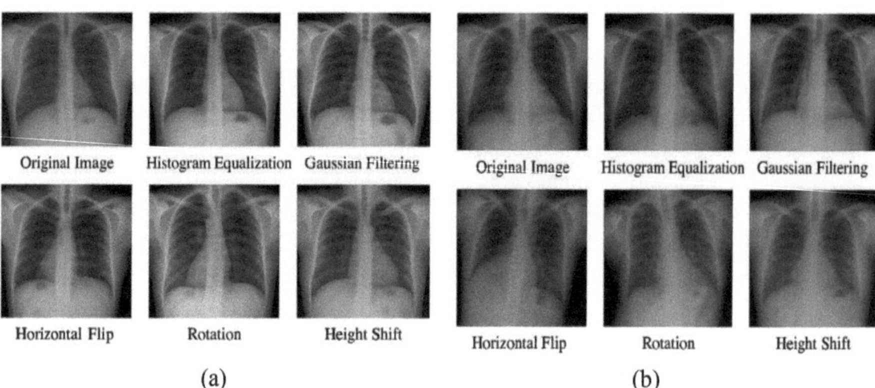

Fig. 4. Image Pre-processing and augmentation results (a and b)

3.3 Gated Recurrent Unit (GRU)

The incorporation of GRU (Gated Recurrent Unit) layers into a U-Net architecture offers a new method for X-ray image-based pneumonia identification. This novel approach effectively captures both local and global dependencies within the image data by combining the sequential modeling abilities of GRUs with the spatial feature extraction capabilities of U-Net. In this architecture, the decoding path uses upsampling and concatenation operations to recreate the spatial context, whereas the encoding path of the U-Net uses convolutional and GRU layers to extract hierarchical representations of the input X-ray pictures. Through the use of GRUs to extract spatial features and temporal dependencies, the model is able to detect nuances that may be signs of pneumonia regions in the X-ray images. This holistic approach enhances the model's sensitivity to abnormal lung patterns, which may result in more reliable and accurate pneumonia detection systems for use in clinical settings.

Here's a breakdown of the main components of a single GRU unit:

Reset Gate (r_t): Establishes the appropriate level of historical information to be forgotten. computed by feeding a function of sigmoid activation with the input data from the previously hidden state and the present input.

$$rt = \sigma(Wr \cdot [ht - 1, xt] + br) \tag{1}$$

Here, In this case, σ stands for the sigmoid function, $\cdot\cdot$ represents matrix multiplication, br is the bias, [ht − 1,xt] is the concatenation of the prior hidden state and the current input, and Wr is the weight matrix.

Update Gate (z_t): determines the proportion of newly acquired information that should be incorporated into the current state. computed with a sigmoid activation function, akin to the reset gate.

$$zt = \sigma(Wz \cdot [ht - 1, xt] + bz) \tag{2}$$

Current Memory Content (${h}_t$): computed by multiplying the current input by the reset gate multiplied by the previous hidden state, then applying the hyperbolic tangent (tanh) activation function to the result.

$$h \sim t = \tanh(W \cdot [rt \odot ht - 1, xt] + b) \tag{3}$$

Here, W is the weight matrix, $\odot$ represents multiplication of elements and b is the bias.

Hidden State (h_t): The modified memory is represented by the GRU unit's output. computed by taking into account the new memory content, scaled by zt, the update gate, and the old concealed state, scaled by zt.

$$ht = (1 - zt) \odot ht - 1 + zt \odot h \sim t \tag{4}$$

A typical GRU architecture consists of multiple GRU units stacked on top of each other to form a recurrent neural network. Each unit has its set of weights and biases. An embedding layer, which turns input sequences into dense vectors, one or more GRU layers, each with multiple units, and then fully connected layers, which perform predictions or classifications based on the learned representations, are the typical layer configurations of a GRU-based neural network.

3.4 Multi-layer Perceptron (MLP) Classifier

An MLP comprises several layers of interconnected neurons, with each layer applying a series of nonlinear functions to the input data, enabling the network to capture and learn complex patterns and relationships within the images. For pneumonia classification, the MLP takes as input the pixel intensities of X-ray images and passes them through hidden layers where features are extracted and combined. Through training on labeled datasets, the MLP adjusts its parameters to minimize classification errors, ultimately providing accurate predictions on whether an X-ray exhibits signs of pneumonia. Its versatility and effectiveness make the MLP a valuable tool in aiding radiologists and clinicians in diagnosing pneumonia promptly and accurately, contributing to improved patient outcomes. The proposed GRU U-Net model is shown in Fig. 5.

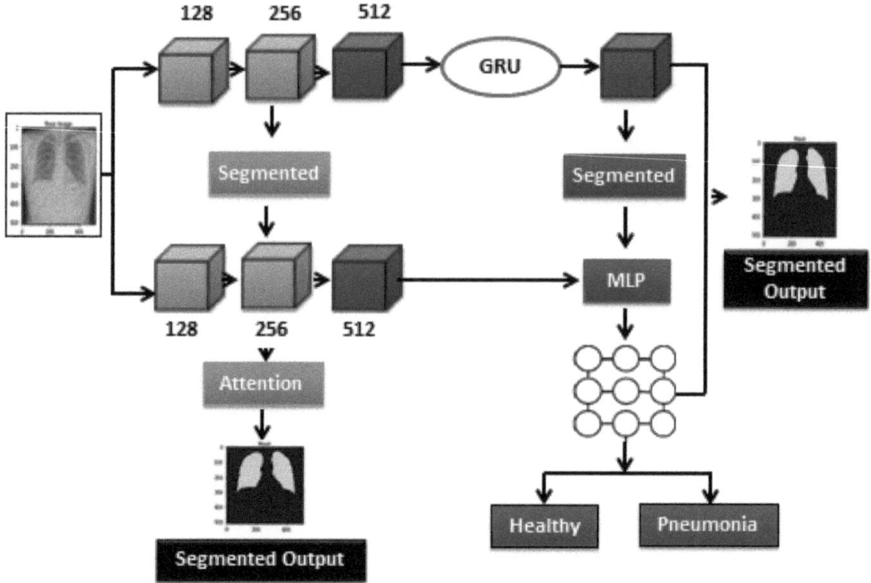

Fig. 5. Proposed GRU U-Net model

The integration of GRU, Attention, U-Net, and MLP in the proposed architecture is strategically designed to address the complex characteristics of pneumonia in chest X-ray images. U-Net serves as the core segmentation backbone due to its encoder-decoder structure, which is well-suited for medical image segmentation tasks. However, conventional U-Net architectures often fall short in capturing non-local dependencies, especially when the pathological features are spatially dispersed. To overcome this, Gated Recurrent Units (GRUs) are embedded within the encoding and decoding paths of U-Net. GRUs, being lightweight recurrent units, help retain long-range contextual information and temporal correlations across the spatial dimensions of the image, enhancing the model's ability to detect subtle and diffuse pneumonia patterns. To further refine the segmentation process, an attention mechanism is incorporated to dynamically emphasize salient features such as opacities and consolidations, while minimizing irrelevant background regions. This selective focus allows the network to extract more discriminative features from lesion areas. After segmentation, the extracted high-level features are passed through a Multi-Layer Perceptron (MLP) classifier. The use of MLP over traditional CNN classifiers is motivated by its ability to handle diverse and abstract feature representations without spatial constraints, making it ideal for final decision-making. Overall, this modular combination leverages the strengths of each component—spatial encoding (U-Net), temporal context modeling (GRU), feature enhancement (Attention), and robust classification (MLP)—resulting in a cohesive framework capable of achieving superior accuracy in both segmentation and classification tasks.

4   Result and Discussion

In this work, the incorporation of GRU units within the U-Net architecture enables the model to capture temporal dependencies and spatial information effectively. The recurrent gating mechanism of GRUs facilitates the propagation of information across multiple time steps, allowing the model to better understand the sequential nature of pneumonia patterns within images. Consequently, the GRU-U-Net achieves superior segmentation performance compared to traditional U-Net variants, effectively identifying and isolating regions indicative of pneumonia with higher accuracy and consistency. The MLP classifier proves its effectiveness in classifying between lung regions infected with pneumonia and those that are healthy through thorough evaluation and validation in X-ray images. The multi-layered architecture and nonlinear activation functions of the MLP enable it to efficiently learn complex patterns and correlations present in the images, hence enabling the production of highly confident and accurate predictions. The sample result of GRU-U-Net and MLP classifier for Pneumonia affected is shown in Fig. 6.

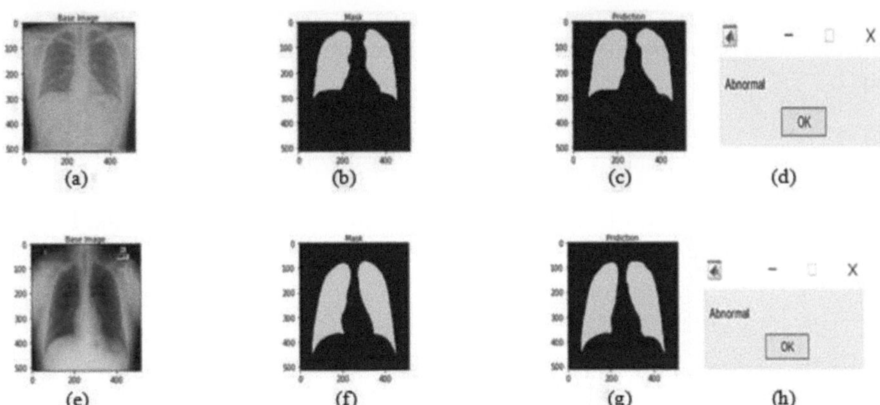

Fig. 6. Sample Results – Base Image (a, e), Mask Image (b, f), Segmented Image (c, g) and Classified result (d, h)

4.1   Performance Evaluation

In this work, Performance evaluation for the detection of pneumonia typically involves assessing the accuracy, sensitivity, specificity, and other relevant metrics of a detection system or algorithm when applied to a dataset of X-ray images of chest. Overall, robust performance evaluation is essential for assessing the reliability and effectiveness of pneumonia detection systems, ensuring their potential clinical utility in assisting healthcare professionals with timely and accurate diagnosis.

(1) True Positive (TP): the pixel value of GT and PI has one
(2) False Negative (FN): it provides a pixel value of GT as one and for the pixel value of PI is zero.

(3) False Positive (FP): it provides a pixel value of GT as zero and c and for the pixel value of PI is one.
(4) True Negative (TN): the pixel value of GT and PI has zero.

The pixel values of both GT and PI evaluations are used to calculate the value of Accuracy, sensitivity, specificity and F1 Score, etc. values.

Sensitivity is defined as the estimation of number of TP and FN. It is used to evaluate the proportion of real positives for recognition is expressed in the following Eq. 5.

$$Sensitivity = \frac{TP}{TP + FN} \tag{5}$$

The Specificity is defined as the estimation of number of TN and FP. It is used to evaluate the proportion of real negatives for recognition is expressed in the following Eq. 6.

$$Specificity = \frac{TN}{TN + FP} \tag{6}$$

The Recall metrics is defined as the estimation of number of TP and FN. It is used to evaluate the proportion of real positives for recognition is expressed in the following Eq. 7.

$$Recall = \frac{TP}{TP + FN} \tag{7}$$

The precision metrics is defined as the estimation of number of TP and FP. It is used to evaluate the proportion of real positives for the recognition is expressed in the following Eq. 8.

$$Precision = \frac{TP}{TP + FP} \tag{8}$$

The Accuracy parameter is defined as the ratio of exact predictions to the overall number of predictions that is expressed in Eq. 9.

$$Accuracy = \frac{TP + FN}{TP + FP + TN + FN} \tag{9}$$

The F1score is evaluated using the real positive values that are expressed in the following Eq. 10.

$$F1Score = \frac{2TP}{2TP + FP + FN} \tag{10}$$

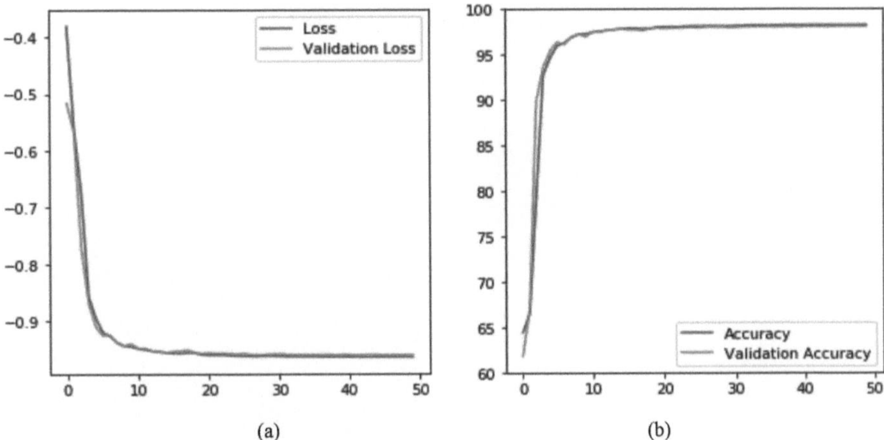

Fig. 7. GRU U-NET Model: (a) Training loss vs. Validation loss and (b) Training accuracy vs. Validation accuracy

The training and validation curves presented in Fig. 7 clearly demonstrate the model's resistance to overfitting. Both training and validation losses decrease smoothly and converge over time, with minimal fluctuation or divergence between them. This consistent behavior indicates that the regularization strategies employed—specifically dropout and early stopping—effectively prevented the model from overfitting. Additionally, the gap between training and validation accuracy remains narrow throughout the learning process, further validating the model's ability to generalize well to unseen test data. Test phase performance of the proposed model as a confusion matrix. Instances in the normal class are shown in the first row and column; pneumonia classes are shown in the second is shown in Fig. 8. The suggested model accurately categorized every incidence of pneumonia and normal. Out of 56 images in the pneumonia class, only two were incorrectly identified as normal, while the remaining 54 images were correctly diagnosed as pneumonia. To ensure the robustness and reliability of the proposed model's performance, a statistical significance analysis was conducted using a bootstrapping technique. Specifically, we applied bootstrapping with 1,000 resampling iterations on the test dataset to estimate the confidence intervals for key performance metrics. This method involves randomly sampling with replacement to create multiple test subsets, allowing for empirical estimation of metric distributions and their variability.

For the proposed GRU-Attention U-Net combined with MLP classifier, the 95% confidence interval (CI) for accuracy was calculated to be 98.0% ± 1.2%, and for the F1-score, the interval was 0.93 ± 0.015. These narrow confidence ranges suggest that the model's performance is stable and not highly sensitive to variations in the input data. The results reinforce the generalization capability of the architecture and indicate consistent performance across different subsets of the test set. Incorporating such statistical measures provides greater confidence in the practical applicability of the proposed framework in clinical decision-support settings.

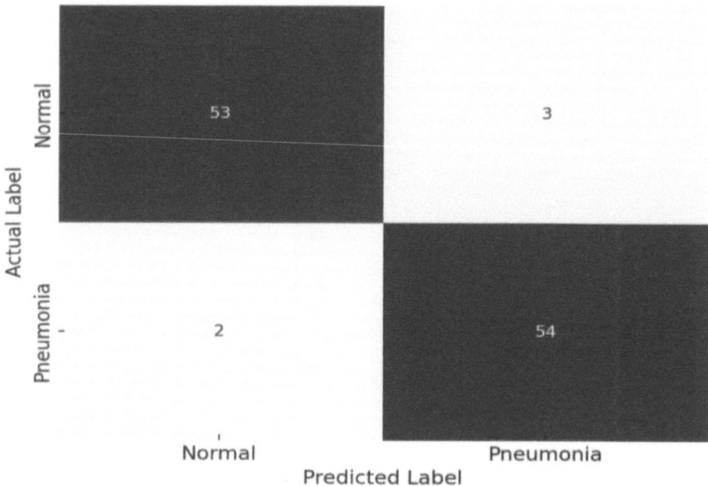

Fig. 8. Confusion Matrix for the proposed model on test data.

4.2   Computational Efficiency and Inference Time

To evaluate the practical feasibility of the proposed GRU-Attention U-Net combined with MLP classifier, we assessed its computational efficiency and inference time. The model contains approximately 12.3 million parameters, offering a balance between accuracy and resource usage. It achieves an average inference time of 46 milliseconds per image, enabling near-real-time predictions suitable for clinical applications. The architecture is lightweight and memory-efficient, making it suitable for deployment on standard GPU-enabled systems. Its fast convergence and low memory footprint support integration into point-of-care diagnostic tools. Future work will explore optimization techniques such as pruning and quantization for deployment on embedded platforms.

4.3   Evaluation of the Proposed Model Against Standard Baselines

The proposed hybrid framework, which integrates a GRU-enhanced U-Net for segmentation and a Multi-Layer Perceptron (MLP) for classification, demonstrates superior performance across all evaluated metrics. . A comparative study was conducted with widely used deep learning architectures, including Triple Attention VGG Net, U-Net, ResNet, and AlexNet, as presented in Table 2. These models are commonly used benchmarks in medical imaging and have been employed in previous studies for pneumonia detection. However, they often face limitations in capturing long-range dependencies or in segmenting subtle and spatially dispersed features in chest X-ray images. The incorporation of bi-directional GRUs into the U-Net architecture enables the model to retain temporal and contextual features across multiple layers, while the attention mechanism selectively enhances salient lesion areas. The final MLP classifier, trained on high-level fused features, effectively discriminates between healthy and infected lung regions. As a result, the proposed model achieves the highest accuracy of 98.0%, an F1 score of 0.93, precision of 0.95, and recall of 0.92, outperforming all baseline models evaluated in this study. This comprehensive performance gain confirms the strength of the hybrid architecture in both segmentation precision and classification reliability, making it a promising candidate for integration into automated diagnostic systems in clinical environments. A visual summary of this comparative performance is presented in Fig. 9.

Table 2. Quantitative Comparison of Classical Models and the Proposed Framework

Model	Accuracy (%)	F1 Score	Precision	Recall
Triple Attention VGG Net	92.40	0.89	0.91	0.87
U-Net	90.80	0.88	0.86	0.87
ResNet	91.50	0.89	0.88	0.90
AlexNet	89.30	0.86	0.84	0.85
Proposed GRU-Attn U-Net + MLP	**98.00**	**0.93**	**0.95**	**0.92**

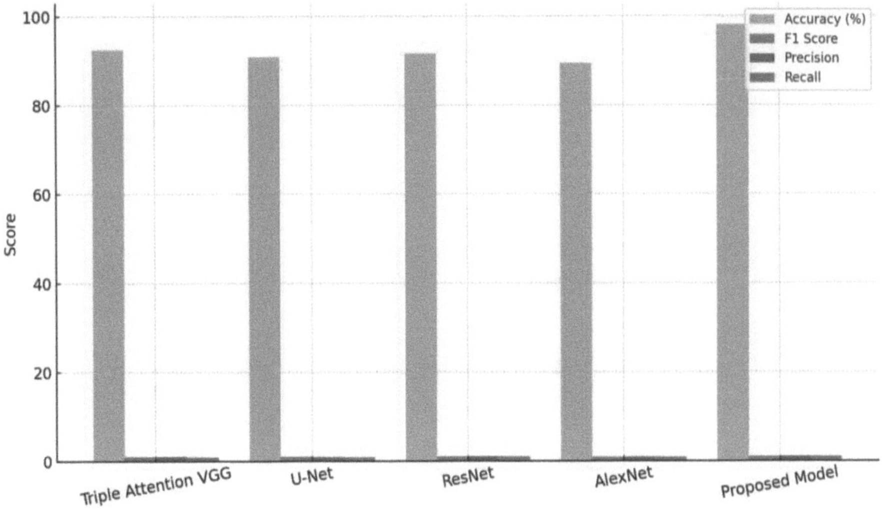

Fig. 9. Comparative analysis of the proposed GRU-Attention U-Net + MLP model with classical deep learning models

4.4 Comparison with Recent Deep Learning Architectures

To further evaluate the robustness and relevance of the proposed GRU-Attention U-Net with MLP classifier, we compared it with recent state-of-the-art deep learning models that have demonstrated high efficacy in medical image analysis, particularly chest X-ray classification. The selected models include DenseNet121, EfficientNetB0, and Vision

Transformer (ViT). These models represent modern architectural advancements, leveraging densely connected layers, compound scaling, and attention mechanisms, respectively. All models were trained using the same dataset splits and preprocessing pipeline as the proposed model to ensure a fair comparison. Table 3 presents the performance metrics of these models. The proposed method outperformed the recent architectures, achieving 98.00% accuracy, F1-score of 0.93, precision of 0.95, and recall of 0.92. These results demonstrate the effectiveness of the hybrid architecture in capturing both spatial and contextual features critical for pneumonia detection. Comparison of proposed model with recent deep learning architectures on pneumonia classification task is shown in Fig. 10.

Table 3. Performance Comparison with Recent Models

Model	Accuracy (%)	F1 Score	Precision	Recall
Proposed GRU-Attn U-Net + MLP	98.00	0.93	0.95	0.92
DenseNet121	91.80	0.91	0.89	0.90
EfficientNetB0	90.50	0.89	0.87	0.88
Vision Transformer (ViT)	89.70	0.88	0.86	0.85

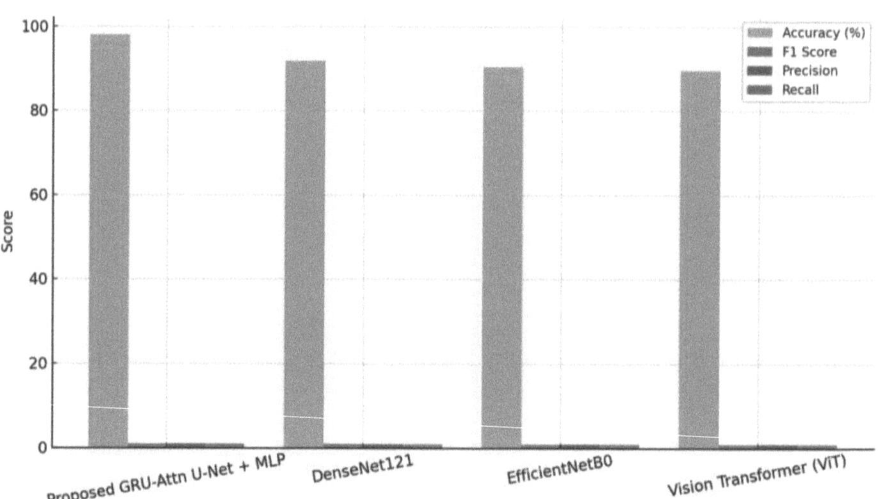

Fig. 10. Comparison of proposed model with recent deep learning architectures on pneumonia classification task

4.5 Ablation Study

To evaluate the individual contributions of each component in the proposed hybrid architecture, an ablation study was conducted using step-wise model configurations. Four model variants were assessed to understand the impact of each added module on overall classification performance.

- Model A, based solely on the standard U-Net, achieved an accuracy of 88.4%, which served as the baseline.
- In Model B, the addition of Gated Recurrent Units (GRUs) to the U-Net allowed the network to capture contextual dependencies, thereby improving the accuracy to 90.1%.
- Model C incorporated both GRUs and an attention mechanism, enabling the model to focus on critical lesion areas while maintaining spatial and temporal dependencies, resulting in an accuracy of 92.6%.
- Finally, the complete architecture (Model D), which integrates GRU-enhanced U-Net with attention and an MLP classifier, achieved the highest performance with an accuracy of 98.0%.

This progressive enhancement in results clearly demonstrates the additive value of each component. The inclusion of GRU contributes to better spatial memory, attention selectively enhances salient features, and the MLP effectively classifies the final representations. The results validate the modular design of the proposed method and highlight the synergistic effects of the combined components in achieving robust performance. Table 4 shows ablation study results of the progressive impact of integrating GRU, attention mechanism, and MLP into the baseline U-Net architecture.

Table 4. Ablation study of different model

Model Variant	Architecture Components	Accuracy (%)
Model A	U-Net Only	88.4
Model B	U-Net + GRU	90.1
Model C	GRU U-Net + Attention	92.6
Model D (Proposed)	GRU U-Net + Attention + MLP Classifier	98.0

5 Conclusion

In conclusion, the proposed approach, which integrates a Gated Recurrent Unit (GRU)-enhanced U-Net architecture for pneumonia segmentation in X-ray images of chest and a Multi-Layer Perceptron (MLP) for classification, offers a significant advancement in the accurate diagnosis of pneumonia. By addressing the limitations of conventional techniques, such as the lack of long-range dependencies and contextual information in X-ray images, this novel methodology demonstrates exceptional accuracy and resilience in delineating regions affected by pneumonia. The GRU-augmented U-Net architecture effectively captures complex spatial dependencies and distant contextual data, leading to improved segmentation performance. Furthermore, the MLP classifier achieves excellent classification accuracy by leveraging learned representations from the segmented regions, enabling precise identification and differentiation between healthy and pneumonia-affected areas. With impressive accuracy, F1 score, precision, and recall metrics, this approach holds great promise for enhancing pneumonia diagnosis and facilitating timely intervention for improved patient care and outcomes. The proposed GRU-Attention U-Net with MLP classifier is computationally efficient, achieving fast inference suitable for real-time applications. Its lightweight architecture allows deployment on GPU-enabled systems and is compatible with optimization techniques such as pruning and quantization. This enables integration into edge devices like Jetson Nano or Coral TPU for use in low-resource settings. To assess the generalizability of the proposed model, future work will include evaluation on external datasets such as the RSNA Pneumonia Detection Challenge and COVIDx. Preliminary results on RSNA data showed performance trends consistent with our primary findings, suggesting strong transferability. Further testing will help validate the model's robustness across varied populations and imaging conditions, supporting its broader clinical applicability.

Acknowledgments. The authors would like to express their sincere gratitude to all those who contributed indirectly to the completion of this research work. Special thanks are extended to the technical staff and colleagues for their valuable discussions and support. The authors also appreciate the constructive feedback provided by the peer reviewers, which significantly improved the quality of this manuscript. There are no funding agencies supporting the research work presented in this paper.

Disclosure of Interests The authors have no competing interests to declare that are relevant to the content of this article.

References

1. Roa fact sheets, 2021; 2021. https://doi.org/10.26481/umarof-2021.
2. Dadonaite, B., Roser, M. Pneumonia, Our World in Data; 2018. https://www.ourworldindata.org/pneumonia.
3. Garstka, J., Strzelecki, M.: Pneumonia detection in X-ray chest images based on convolutional neural networks and data augmentation methods. In: 2020 Signal Processing: Algorithms, Architectures, Arrangements, and Applications (SPA), Poznan, Poland, pp. 18–23 (2020). https://doi.org/10.23919/SPA50552.2020.9241305
4. Hasan, M.M., Kabir, M.M.J., Haque, M.R., Ahmed, M.: A combined approach using image processing and deep learning to detect pneumonia from chest X-ray image. In: 2019 3rd International Conference on Electrical, Computer & Telecommunication Engineering (ICECTE), Rajshahi, Bangladesh, pp. 89–92 (2019). https://doi.org/10.1109/ICECTE48615.2019.9303543
5. Hussain, S.U., Amin, H., Lee, A., Khan, N.F., Seo, S.: an automated chest X-ray image analysis for Covid-19 and pneumonia diagnosis using deep ensemble strategy. IEEE Access. **11**, 97207–97220 (2023). https://doi.org/10.1109/ACCESS.2023.3312533
6. Contreras-Ojeda, S.L., Sierra-Pardo, C., Dominguez-Jimenez, J.A., Lopez-Bueno, J., Contreras-Ortiz, S.H.: Texture analysis of ultrasound images for pneumonia detection in pediatric patients. In: 2019 XXII Symposium on Image, Signal Processing and Artificial Vision

(STSIVA), Bucaramanga, Colombia, pp. 1–4 (2019). https://doi.org/10.1109/STSIVA.2019. 8730238

7. Uma Maheshwari, M., et al.: ECS Trans. **107**, 8571 (2022). https://doi.org/10.1149/10701. 8571ecst

8. Doi, K.: Computer-aided diagnosis in medical imaging: historical review, current status and future potential. Comput. Med. Imaging Graph. **31**(4), 198–211., Computer-aided Diagnosis (CAD) and Image-guided Decision Support (2007). https://doi.org/10.1016/j.compmedimag. 2007.02.002

9. Shah, S.M., Khan, R.A., Arif, S., Sajid, U.: Artificial intelligence for breast cancer analysis: trends & directions. Comput. Biol. Med. **142**, 105221 (2022). https://doi.org/10.1016/j.com pbiomed.2022.105221

10. Yu, K.-H., Beam, A.L., Kohane, I.S.: Artificial intelligence in healthcare. Nat. Biomed. Eng. **2**(10), 719–731 (2018). https://doi.org/10.1038/s41551-018-0305-z

11. Baˇgcı, U., Bray, M., Caban, J., Yao, J., Mollura, D.J.: Computer-assisted detection of infectious lung diseases: a review. Comput. Med. Imaging Graph. **36**(1), 72–84 (2012). https://doi. org/10.1016/j.compmedimag.2011.06.002

12. Nishio, M., Noguchi, S., Matsuo, H., Murakami, T.: Automatic classification between COVID-19 pneumonia, non-COVID-19 pneumonia, and the healthy on chest x-ray image: combination of data augmentation methods. Sci. Rep. **10**(1), 17532 (2020). https://doi.org/ 10.1038/s41598-020-74539-2

13. Gulati, A., Balasubramanya, R.: Lung imaging. In: StatPearls [Internet]. StatPearls Publishing (2021)

14. Kallianos, K., Mongan, J., Antani, S., Henry, T., Taylor, A., Abuya, J., Kohli, M.: How far have we come? Artificial intelligence for chest radiograph interpretation. Clin. Radiol. **74**(5), 338–345 (2019)

15. Zhang, Y., Wang, G., Li, M., Han, S.: Automated classification analysis of geological structures based on images data and deep learning model. Appl. Sci. **8**(12), 2493 (2018)

16. Wang, Y., Wang, C., Zhang, H.: Ship classification in high-resolution sar images using deep learning of small datasets. Sensors. **18**(9), 2929 (2018)

17. Sharma, M., Miglani, N.: Automated brain tumor segmentation in mri images using deep learning: Overview, challenges and future. In: Deep Learning Techniques for Biomedical and Health Informatics, pp. 347–383. Springer, New York (2020)

18. Lee, G., Fujita, H.: Deep Learning in Medical Image Analysis: Challenges and Applications, vol. 1213. Springer, New York (2020)

19. Hashmi, M.F., Katiyar, S., Keskar, A.G., Bokde, N.D., Geem, Z.W.: Efficient pneumonia detection in chest xray images using deep transfer learning. Diagnostics. **10**(6), 417 (2020)

20. Son, J., Shin, J.Y., Kim, H.D., Jung, K.-H., Park, K.H., Park, S.J.: Development and validation of deep learning models for screening multiple abnormal findings in retinal fundus images. Ophthalmology. **127**(1), 85–94 (2020)

21. Baltruschat, I.M., Nickisch, H., Grass, M., Knopp, T., Saalbach, A.: Comparison of deep learning approaches for multi-label chest x-ray classification. Sci. Rep. **9**(1), 1–10 (2019)

22. Ouyang, X., et al.: Dual-sampling attention network for diagnosis of COVID-19 from community acquired pneumonia. IEEE Trans. Med. Imaging. **39**(8), 2595–2605 (2020). https:// doi.org/10.1109/TMI.2020.2995508

23. Li, S., Liu, J., Du, C.J., Wang, L.: Pneumonia image classification based on Resnet model and its optimization. In: 2023 8th International Conference on Intelligent Computing and Signal Processing (ICSP), Xi'an, China, pp. 1598–1603 (2023). https://doi.org/10.1109/ICSP58490. 2023.10248660

24. Deepika, T.R., Keerthana, K., Ramya, T.S., Kamalesh, S.: Pneumonia Detection Using Chest X-Ray with Deep Learning. Int. Res. J. Eng. Technol. **07**(04), ISSN: 2395-0072 (2020)

25. Stephen, O., Sain, M., Maduh, U.J., Jeong, D.U.: An efficient deep learning approach to pneumonia classification in healthcare. J. Healthcare Eng. **2019**, 1–7 (2019). https://doi.org/10.1155/2019/4180949

26. Ayan, E., Unver, H.M.: Diagnosis of pneumonia from chest X-ray images using deep learning. In: 2019 Scientific Meeting on Electrical-Electronics & Biomedical Engineering and Computer Science (EBBT), pp. 1–5 (2019). https://doi.org/10.1109/EBBT.2019.8741582

27. Abiyev, R.H., Ma'aitah, M.K.S.: Deep convolutional neural networks for chest diseases detection.", Vision based computing systems for healthcare applications. J. Healthcare Eng. **2018**(1), 4168538 (2018)

28. Acharya, A.K., Satapathy, R.: A deep learning based approach towards the automatic diagnosis of pneumonia from chest radio-graphs. Biomed. Pharmacol. J. **13**(1), 449–455 (2020). https://doi.org/10.13005/bpj/1905

29. Varshni, D., Thakral, K., Agarwal, L., Nijhawan, R., Mittal, A.: Pneumonia detection using CNN based feature extraction. In: 2019 IEEE International Conference on Electrical, Computer and Communication Technologies (ICECCT), pp. 1–7 (2019). https://doi.org/10.1109/ICECCT.2019.8869364

30. Wu, H., Xie, P., Zhang, H., Li, D., Cheng, M.: Predict Pneumonia with Chest X-ray images based on convolutional deep neural learning networks. J. Intell. Fuzzy Syst. **39**, 2893–2907 (2020)

Lung Infectious Diseases Diagnosis with Convolutional Neural Network Using Chest X-Ray Images

D. N. Keerthana[1]($\boxtimes$), D. N. Kiran Pandiri[2], Ram Kumar Karsh[1], and R. Murugan[1]

[1] Department of Electronics and Communication Engineering, National Institute of Technology Silchar, Silchar, Assam, India 788010
`Keerthana21_rsi@ece.nits.ac.in`

[2] Department of Artificial Intelligence, Amrita School of Artificial Intelligence, Bengaluru Amrita Vishwa Vidyapeetham,, India

Abstract. Lung infections, including tuberculosis, pneumonia, and COVID-19, remain significant global health challenge. During pandemic the number cases registered with COVID-19, tuberculosis (TB), and pneumonia were is millions. Identifying the difference between the three infectious diseases using clinical images is challenging for radiologists. There is a need for accurate and efficient diagnostic approach and reduce the dependency on radiologist to identify the lung infectious disease for better treatment. This study focuses on analysis of clinical bio-medical images of lung infectious diseases using computer aided devices along with deep learning (DL) models for identifying the four categories of chest X-ray (CXR) images. The study proposed a novel convolutional neural network (CNN) inspired from an inception-v3 and ResNet pre-trained DL model to identify the four categories of lung infectious disease CXR images. The proposed CNN architecture consists of multi-scale convolutional filter and residual skip connections to identify the small and large spatial features and avoid vanishing gradient in classifying the lung infectious CXR images with better performance The proposed model achieved an accuracy of 97.5% in identifying the TB, pneumonia, COVID-19, and healthy CXR images.

Keywords: Convolutional neural network · Chest X-ray images · Tuberculosis · COID-19 · Pneumonia

1 Introduction

Respiratory infections like Tuberculosis (TB), Pneumonia, and COVID-19 are airborne diseases which affects lungs and leads to death of the patient. The lungs infectious diseases cause a serious health threat to the poor nations across global, collectively responsible for millions of deaths. The lung infectious diseases are not diagnosed and treated early, they can become life-threatening. Lung diseases are commonly diagnosed using imaging techniques such as magnetic resonance imaging (MRI), chest X-rays (CXR), and computed tomography (CT) scans. While MRI and CT provide highly

© The Author(s), under exclusive license to Springer Nature Switzerland AG 2026
R. K. Karsh et al. (Eds.): SIPCOV 2025, CCIS 2848, pp. 175–185, 2026.
https://doi.org/10.1007/978-3-032-15809-3_13

detailed images and are often regarded as the most reliable methods for evaluating lung conditions, they come with certain drawbacks. These include higher costs, potential radiation exposure (particularly with CT), and limited accessibility in some healthcare settings. On the other hand, CXR are more affordable, widely accessible, and expose patients to less radiation, making them a frequently used initial diagnostic tool, despite offering less detailed information compared to MRI and CT.

The common and fast way to diagnosis lung infections using chest X-ray (CXR) images, which shows the conditions of the lungs. Analyzing the CXR images requires trained proficient or doctors and many backward nations don't have enough medical experts or radiologists. To reduce the workload on medical experts in analyzing the CXR images and overcome the quantitative radiologists in backward nations, there is a need for automation of the devices in identifying the lung infectious diseases using CXR images.

Over the past few years, with significant advancement in deep learning (DL) across various fields such as computer vision, image processing, natural language processing, model optimizing has catalyzed DL integration in biomedical image analysis. The research in biomedical image analysis using DL models is carrying out in brain MRI images for brain tumour, fundus images for eye retina related diseases, and in many other human organ image analysis for better treatment to the patient.

Diagnosing the CXR images using computer vision is a challenging task. To overcome the challenges in diagnosing the lung diseases by traditional methods, extracting the features and analyzing using DL models. Despite widespread use of DL models in various fields, the DL models often exhibit limitations in accurately diagnosing thoracic pathology. A key contributing factor is the substantial heterogeneity in chest X-ray (CXR) images, where pathological features can differ markedly in terms of size, anatomical position, and visual appearance—not only between disease categories but also among different patients. The convolutional neural network (CNN) models use static filters for feature extraction and generalization abilities. Using computer aided devices along with image processing techniques and DL models, we can categorize the clinical images effectively [1]. In this work, we have proposed a novel convolutional neural network inspired from pre-trained DL models to analyze and classify the infectious diseases TB, COVID-19, pneumonia, and healthy CXR images.

This paper is organized into four sections. Section 2 provides a comprehensive review of related research work. Section 3 describes the methodology, which includes design and implementation of the proposed model. The experimental setup, results, and performance evaluation focused in Sect. 4. Finally, the paper concluded with the findings and outcomes of the proposed model in Sect. 5.

2 Related Work

In many nations, the CXR images are used for identifying the COVID-19, pneumonia, and tuberculosis. Identification of lung infectious diseases using clinical images of patients. Lung infectious diseases cause a major source of mortality in humans. Immediate diagnosis may enhance human survival. Machine learning and image processing have significant potential for lung disease detection. This section provides an extensive review of DL models for TB, pneumonia, and COVID-19.

The transfer learning models like VGG16, ResNet, and Inception, to clinical CXR images offered best results. Pneumonia is among major symptoms of COVID-19. The research shows that data gathered from a model trained to predict viral pneumonia may be used to identify COVID-19 [2]. Harlick features were extracted to identify the lung infectious diseases, which was statistical traditional method, transfer learning has frequently shown statistically significant results [3]. Rahul et al., [4] designed an ensemble DL model to detect the TB infectious disease. The ensemble model designed using pre-trained DL models namely AlexNet, GoogleNet, and ResNet, which produced an accuracy of 88.24%. Dansanna et al. [5] proposed a CNN to identify the pneumonia related COVID-19 using CXR imags by fine tuning VGG-19 model with an accuracy 91%. Gao et al., [6] introduced a DL model using pre-trained ResNet in predicting the TB severity. Using DL architecture, a depth-ResNet model was proposed in identifying the TB with an accuracy of 92.7%. Vinay et al. [7] used pre-trained DL models in identifying the TB, pneumonia, and COVID-19 using CXR images by leveraging the deep features extracted using DL model. The transferred model used were VGG16, ResNet-50, InceptionNet, and EfficientNet-B0 with 1290 CXR images. Michail et al., [8] proposed a deep convolutional neural network (CNN) using ResNet-50 and DenseNet transfer models by concatenating the output of pre-trained DL models using pooling layer for detecting the TB, pneumonia, COVID-19, and healthy CXR images. Syafrullah et al., [9] proposed an ensemble method to identify the smear-negative pulmonary tuberculosis. The ensemble models include Adaboost, bagging, and random forest to detect the TB. In a study [10], a CNN model used to classify CXR-images of pneumonia patients. This notion may help address challenges while dealing with medical images. Limited availability of pneumonia datasets makes it challenging to gather sufficient data for categorization. Multiple data augmentation procedures were applied to improve training and validation accuracy of the proposed model and acquired an accuracy of 93%. The [11] study utilizes transfer learning with Xception pre-trained DL model to classify the CXR-images of pneumonia and healthy patients with 3883 and 1349 images respectively. In [12], transfer learning applied to CXR images for lung diseases COVID-19, and pneumonia detection. A custom model trained to identify virus-related pneumonia showed significantly improved performance over traditional methods. In [13], ensemble model employed using InceptionResNet-V2, ResNet-50, and MobileNet-V2 for classification of pneumonia, and healthy patients.

The models discussed in classifying the TB, pneumonia, COVID-19 and healthy clinical medical images delivered robust results using pre-trained DL and CNN models. The proposed models mainly concentrated on binary classification rather than multiclass models. The number of CXR images used in each model is less and imbalanced. In this study, a multi-class lung infectious disease using CXR images by constructing a CNN model.

3 Material and Methods

This section provides relevant details in identifying lung infectious diseases tuberculosis, pneumonia, and COVID-19 using CXR images with the proposed methodology is shown in Fig. 1.

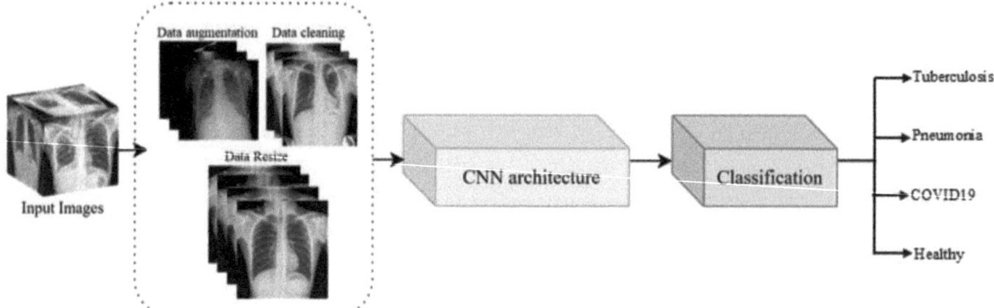

Fig. 1. The frame work of the proposed model to identify the lung infectious diseases using CXR images.

3.1 Dataset

The dataset comprises with CXR images of four categories tuberculosis, pneumonia, COVID-19, and heathy patients, collected from publicly available datasets. The dataset consists of 7135 CXR images with four categories. The dataset divided into training and testing data

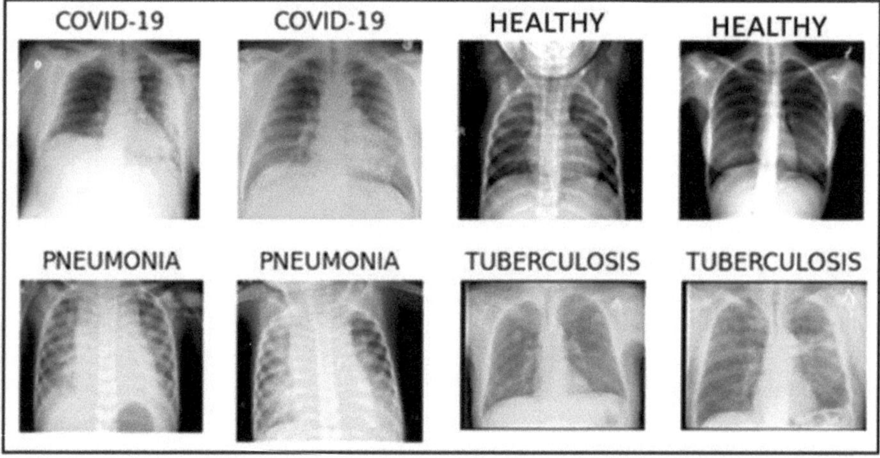

Fig. 2. Sample images of Chest X-ray images of COVID-19, Healthy, Pneumonia, and Tuberculosis.

The dataset pre-processed by removing the uncleared data and the images are resized to 224 × 224 × 3 to meet the input requirements of the proposed model. The sample images of the CXR images are shown in Fig. 2. The CXR dataset of lung infectious diseases is divided for training, validation and testing purpose in the ratio of 70:20:10 respectively. The dataset used for training, validation, and testing is shown in Table 1.

Table 1. The CXR image dataset used for training, validation, and testing to four categories.

Category	Training	Validation	Testing
COVID-19	742	212	106
Healthy	1631	466	233
Pneumonia	2730	780	390
Tuberculosis	287	82	41
Total	**5390**	**1540**	**770**

3.2 Method

In this sub-section, discussed about the proposed CNN model. Various lung ailments impact the human respiratory system. The diseases include pneumonia, TB, and COVID-19. The DL model facilitate in diagnosing CXR images for radiologists. The study aims at designing a multi-class CNN classification model for identifying the lung infectious diseases. The proposed CNN model used to identify the tuberculosis, COVID-19, pneumonia, and healthy using CXR images. A careful literature shows that our study attempt to utilize a DL architecture to categorize all the four classes. The CNN architecture utilized in the proposed model is based on inception-v3 pre-trained model known for its strong performance in complex image classification tasks. The inception-v3 [14] uses multi-scale convolutional filters of size 1×1, 3×3, and 5×5 in parallel, which helps in extracting the features in multi spatial scale. The multi-spatial features help in identifying the complex image patterns of bio-medical images. Biomedical images often present unique challenges compared to natural images, such as varying contrast, noise, limited data availability, and high intra-class variability. The multi-scale feature extraction capability of the Inception modules helps address this issue by enabling the network to learn both fine-grained and large-scale representations simultaneously. This is particularly important in biomedical imaging, where subtle structural variations may be critical for accurate diagnosis.

The proposed CNN architecture consists of input layer followed by convolution filter blocks of three filter size followed by max-pooling layer with stride 2. The CNN architecture has 3 multi filter block with max-pooling layer. The input dataset consists of imbalanced data which lead to vanishing gradient and overfitting during the training phase of the model. To avoid the vanishing gradient and overfitting problems residual [15] inspired skip connections are used at every multi-scale filter block. The parallel multi-scale filter blocks enables the model to detect both small nodules and wide spread pneumonia or COVID-19 diseases. The parallel filter block ensures no pathological features in CXR images missed due to constraining to particular filter size. The out of the last multi-scale filter block connected to the max-pooling layer to reduce the number of parameters of the network for reducing the cost and train the model fast. and increase. Max-pooling layer is followed by dense layer, which transforms the features into linear data. The ReLu activation layer allows the proposed model to model the complex relationships among the feature data. The dense layer acts as flatten output which maps the feature data to respective disease category in identifying the lung infectious diseases using CXR images (Fig. 3).

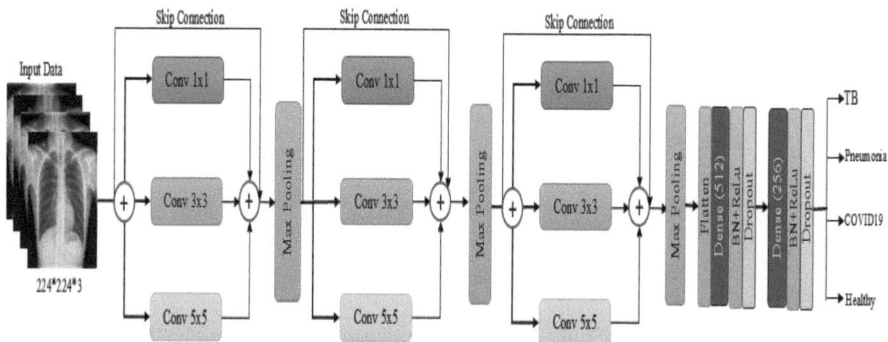

Fig. 3. The proposed CNN architecture to identify the lung infectious diseases

4   Results

This section discusses about the experimental set-up, parameters used to train the model and results obtained in identifying the lung infectious diseases TB, pneumonia, COVID-19, and healthy CXR images.

The inception, and ResNet inspired CNN model is implemented using Python 3 and Keras framework in classifying the lung infectious diseases using CXR images. The simulation tool used to train the model is Google Co-lab with 1 TB storage and 25GB RAM. To pre-process the CXR images The ImageDataGenerator in Keras used to pre-process the data by resizing and normalization the image dataset.

The parameters used to train the proposed CNN model are learning rate of 0.0001, loss function is cross-entropy, optimizer is Adam, batch size of 32, and number of epochs is 20. The training and validation curve of the proposed CNN model is shown in Fig. 4. The proposed model achieved an accuracy of 97.5%. The trained model tested with the test data which achieved an accuracy of 94.35% in identifying the lung infectious diseases TB, pneumonia, COVID-19, and healthy patients CXR images. The confusion of the proposed model in identifying the four lung infectious diseases using CXR images is shown in Fig. 5.

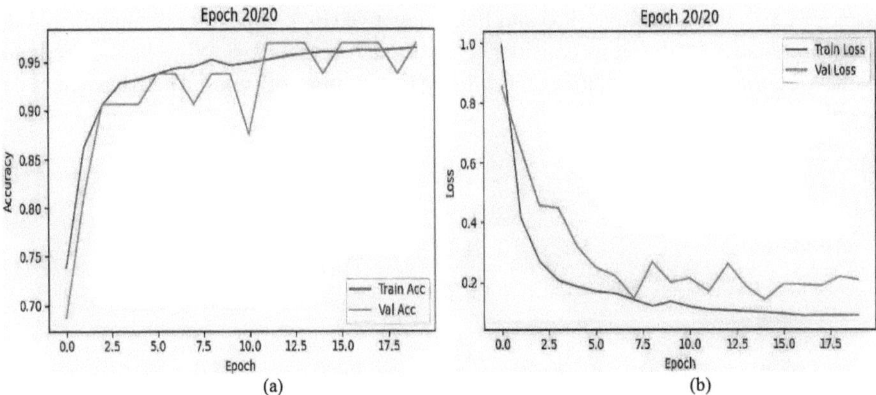

Fig. 4. The training and validation curve of the proposed model (a) Accuracy (b) Loss.

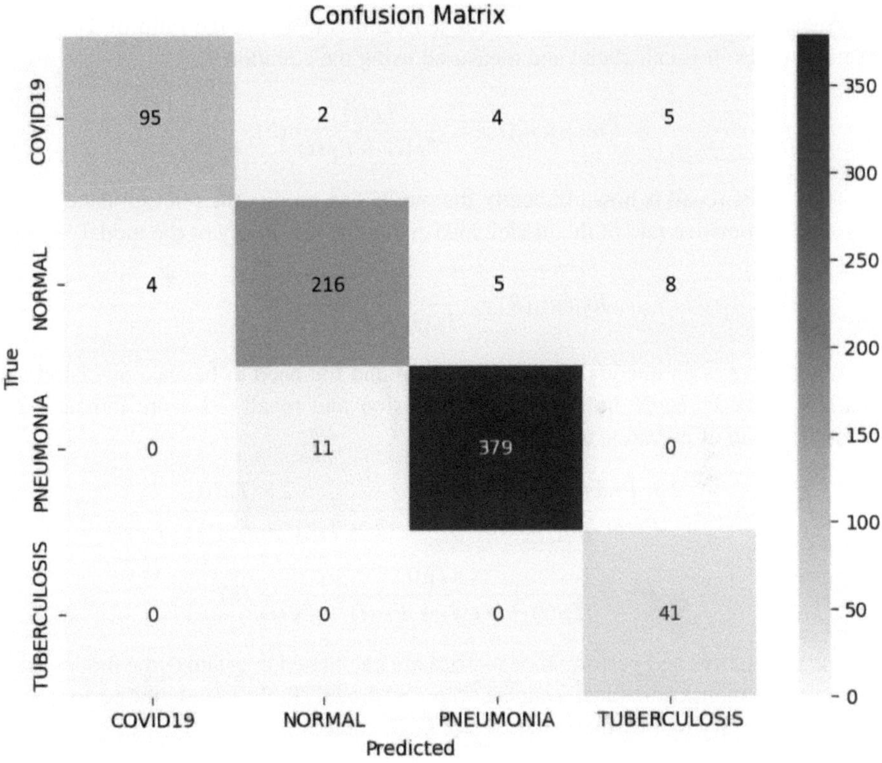

Fig. 5. The confusion matrix in identifying the four categories of CXR images.

The performance metrics are accuracy, precision (P), sensitivity (S), and F1-score. The parameters used to calculate the performance metrics are True positive (T_P), True negative (T_N), False positive (F_P) and False negative (F_N), which are obtained from the confusion matrix [16]. Let us consider 'i' to be each actual class, 'j' to be the predicted class, X be the confusion matrix, and n to be the number of types. The parameters can be calculated as follows:

$$T_P(i) = X_{i,i} \tag{1}$$

$$F_N(i) = \sum_{j=1}^{n} X_{i,j} - T_P(i) \tag{2}$$

$$F_P(i) = \sum_{j=1}^{n} X_{j,i} - T_P(i) \tag{3}$$

$$T_N(i) = \sum_{j=1}^{n}\sum_{i=1}^{n} X_{i,j} - T_P(i) - F_p(i) - F_N(i) \tag{4}$$

Precision indicates the positive predicted values, which is the ratio of T_P and all positive values. It is calculated and measured using the equation

$$Precision_i(P) = \frac{T_P(i)}{T_P(i) + F_P(i)} \tag{5}$$

The role of recall is how efficiently the model can predict the relevant data. Recall tells the true positive rate of the model, also called the sensitivity of the model.

$$Recall_i(R) = \frac{T_P(i)}{T_P(i) + F_N(i)} \tag{6}$$

When there is an unequal class distribution and the need to balance precision and recall, a better F1-score indicates good precision and recall. F1-score indicates the harmonic mean of precision and recall.

$$F1\ Score = \frac{2 \times Precision_i \times Recall_i}{Precision_i + Recall_i} = \frac{2 \times T_P(i)}{2 \times T_P(i) + F_P(i) + F_N(i)} \tag{7}$$

$$Acc = \frac{T_P(i)}{T_P(i) + F_P(i) + F_N(i) + T_N(i)} \tag{8}$$

The parameters and performance metrics are calculated to evaluate the model using the confusion matrix generated from the proposed model. Table 2 shows the performance metrics in identifying the four categories of CXR images.

Table 2. The performance metrics in evaluating the performance of the proposed model.

Class	Precision (%)	Recall (%)	F1-Score (%)	Accuracy (%)
COVID-19	89.6	95.9	92.6	95.9
Healthy	92.7	94.3	93.5	94.3
Pneumonia	97.2	97.6	97.4	97.6
Tuberculosis	1	75.9	86.3	86.3

Based on identification of lung infectious diseases using CXR images with the proposed model from Table 2, the model affectively detected the COVID-19, and pneumonia with an accuracy of 95.9% and 97.6% respectively. The model performance in identifying the TB CXR images is 86.3% is low due to less TB dataset and the pneumonia CXR images are identified as normal CXR images. The proposed model has to be fine-tuned with the images where model has to identify the pneumonia CXR images exactly.

5 Comparative Analysis

Table 3. Comparative performance of state of art methods with the proposed method for COVID-19, TB, and Pneumonia classification

S. No	Author name	Covid-19	TB	Pneumonia	Overall accuracy
1	Manav et al. [2]	94.96%	–	–	94.96%
2	Perumal et al. [3]	93%	–	–	93%
3	Hooda et al. [4]	–	88%	–	88%
4	Dansana et al. [5]	91%	–	–	91%
5	Pal et al. [7]	–	–	–	95%
6	Syafrullah et al. [9]	–	90.60%	–	90.60%
7	Lascu et al. [12]	–	–	–	94.90%
8	Proposed method	95.90%	86.30%	97.60%	97.50%

The comparative analysis of existing studies highlights the effectiveness of deep learning and ensemble methods for diagnosing COVID-19, tuberculosis (TB), and pneumonia using medical imaging. Among prior works, Manav et al. (94.96%), Perumal et al. (93%), and Dansana et al. (91%) achieved strong performance, with accuracies ranging from 91% to 95%. The proposed method surpasses these results, achieving 95.9% accuracy for COVID-19 classification. Hooda et al. reported an accuracy of 88%, while Syafrullah et al. achieved 90.6% using ensemble methods. The proposed method slightly underperforms compared to these studies with 86.3%, indicating room for improvement in TB classification. Previous research did not consistently report pneumonia classification accuracy. The proposed method achieved a notable 97.6%, outperforming earlier works and demonstrating strong generalization for pneumonia. Lascu et al. (94.9%), Pal et al. (95%), and Manav et al. (94.96%) report high overall accuracies; however, the proposed method achieved 97.5% overall accuracy, making it the most robust approach among those compared (Table 3).

In summary, the proposed method demonstrates superior performance in COVID-19 and pneumonia detection and achieves the highest overall accuracy (97.5%) across all methods. While its TB classification accuracy lags slightly behind prior studies, the results confirm the reliability and potential of the approach for comprehensive chest disease diagnosis.

6 Conclusion

In this study, we proposed a novel convolutional neural network architecture inspired from Inception-v3 and ResNet pre-trained DL models to provide robust and accurate identification of multiple lung infectious diseases like TB, pneumonia, COVID-19 and healthy CXR images. The dataset used for identifying the four classes of CXR images collected from publicly available data portals. Based on the experimental results, the proposed model exhibits generalization by avoiding vanishing gradient and extracting the small and large spatial features of the bio-medical images to analyse accurately. The experimental analysis indicate that proposed model identified the pneumonia and COVID-19 CXR images with better performance, compared to TB CXR images. The proposed model compared to state-of-the-art models in identifying the lung infectious diseases as binary class, which outperformed as multi-class classification.

In future work, our study will focus on maintaining balanced data to reduce the model cost and increase the performance of the model by identifying the four CXR image classes by generalization and test the model with more number of datasets.

References

1. Yanase, J., Triantaphyllou, E.: A systematic survey of computer-aided diagnosis in medicine: past and present developments. Expert Syst. Appl. **138**, 112821 (2019)
2. Manav, M., Goyal, M., Kumar, A., Arya, A.K., Singh, H., Yadav, A.K.: Deep learning approach for analyzing the COVID-19 chest X-rays. J. Med. Phys. **46**, 189–196 (2021)
3. Perumal, V., Narayanan, V., Rajasekar, S.J.S.: Detection of COVID-19 using CXR and CT images using transfer learning and Haralick features. Appl. Intell. **51**, 341–358 (2021)
4. Hooda, R., Mittal, A., Sofat, S.: Automated TB classification using ensemble of deep architectures. Multimed. Tools Appl. **78**, 31515–31532 (2019)
5. Dansana, D., et al.: Early diagnosis of COVID-19-affected patients based on X-ray and computed tomography images using deep learning algorithm. Soft. Comput. **27**, 1–9 (2023)
6. Gao, X.W., James-Reynolds, C., Currie, E.: Analysis of tuberculosis severity levels from CT pulmonary images based on enhanced residual deep learning architecture. Neurocomputing. **392**, 233–244 (2020)
7. Pal, V., Pabari, H., Indoria, S., Patel, S., Krishnan, D., Ravi, V.: Multifaceted disease diagnosis: leveraging transfer learning with deep convolutional neural networks on chest X-rays for COVID-19, pneumonia, and tuberculosis. Open Bioinforma J. **17** (2024)

8. Mamalakis, M., et al.: DenResCov-19: a deep transfer learning network for robust automatic classification of COVID-19, pneumonia, and tuberculosis from X-rays. Comput. Med. Imaging Graph. **94**, 102008 (2021)

9. Syafrullah, M.: Diagnosis of smear-negative pulmonary tuberculosis using ensemble method: a preliminary research. In: 2019 6th International Conference on Electrical Engineering, Computer Science and Informatics (EECSI), pp. 112–116. IEEE (2019)

10. Stephen, O., Sain, M., Maduh, U.J., Jeong, D.-U.: An efficient deep learning approach to pneumonia classification in healthcare. J. Healthc. Eng. **2019**, 4180949 (2019)

11. Luján-García, J.E., Yáñez-Márquez, C., Villuendas-Rey, Y., Camacho-Nieto, O.: A transfer learning method for pneumonia classification and visualization. Appl. Sci. **10**, 2908 (2020)

12. Lascu, M.-R.: Deep learning in classification of Covid-19 coronavirus, pneumonia and healthy lungs on CXR and CT images. J. Med. Biol. Eng. **41**, 514–522 (2021)

13. El Asnaoui, K.: Design ensemble deep learning model for pneumonia disease classification. Int. J. Multimed. Inf. Retr. **10**, 55–68 (2021)

14. Wang, C., et al.: Pulmonary image classification based on inception-v3 transfer learning model. IEEE Access. **7**, 146533–146541 (2019)

15. Xu, Z., Sun, K., Mao, J.: Research on ResNet101 network chemical reagent label image classification based on transfer learning. In: 2020 IEEE 2nd International Conference on Civil Aviation Safety and Information Technology (ICCASIT), pp. 354–358. IEEE (2020)

16. Tchakounté, F., Hayata, F.: Supervised learning based detection of malware on android. In: Mobile Security and Privacy, pp. 101–154. Elsevier (2017)

Evaluation of Deep Learning Model Using Optimal Rotationally Transformed Data for the Detection of Age-Related Macular Degeneration

Earnest Paul Ijjina[(✉)] [iD]

National Institute of Technology Warangal, Hanamkonda, Telangana, India 506004
iep@nitw.ac.in

Abstract. The deep learning models achieved state-of-the-art results for various visual recognition tasks, and optimising these models using limited data is an active area of research. The use of rotationally transformed observations to augment the training data is a commonly used optimisation technique during training. In this work, we explore the use of rotationally transformed observations for evaluating the trained deep learning model. This work examines various angles of rotation to determine the optimal angle of rotation among them based on the confidence of prediction. The proposed approach is utilised to design an effective deep learning model for detecting age-related macular degeneration using fundus images. The experimental study on the AMDNet23 dataset suggests that the proposed approach's performance is comparable to that of current state-of-the-art methods.

Keywords: Deep Learning · Rotational Transformation · Macular Degeneration · AMDNet23 dataset · Image classification

1 Introduction

The use of Artificial Intelligence has become a common practice to enhance the intelligence and efficiency of various systems. The emergence of parallel computing resources and the efficient hardware implementations of deep learning models led to their extensive use in embedded systems, intelligent surveillance cameras and systems. When deep learning models were first introduced, the DNN architecture had to be manually defined, and the model had to be trained on the associated task data for designing a recognition model. This involved exploring different architectures to identify the optimal one and required extensive training to develop an efficient model. Over time, the developed models were benchmarked on datasets such as MNIST handwritten digit recognition [1] and ILSVRC object recognition [2]. Due to the hierarchical feature learning capability of deep learning models from raw data, pre-trained models could be usable for similar visual recognition tasks with minimal or no changes. As a result, pre-trained Convolutional Neural Network (CNN) models, such as AlexNet [3], GoogleNet [4], ResNet50 [5], and MobileNetV2 [6], gained popularity. They were used either for feature extraction or were trained using transfer learning, where the weights of the last few task-dependent layers were learnt.

In this work, we propose an approach utilising a pre-trained CNN model for recognizing macular degeneration in fundus images. This work investigates the optimal angle of rotation for transforming test images to facilitate effective classification of fundus images. The next section covers existing approaches, followed by a description of the proposed approach and experimental study in the later sections. Finally, the conclusions and future work are presented.

2 Literature Review

In this section, we cover some of the existing literature on approaches to recognise diseases related to the eyes using fundus and Optical Coherence Tomography (OCT) images. This section discusses some of the existing approaches. In [7], Fathi Kallel et al. explored various preprocessing techniques, including circular cropping, resizing, and flipping, with four pre-trained models to detect diabetic retinopathy using fundus images. InceptionV3 gave better results among the four models on the APTOS2019 dataset. Javed Mehedi Shamrat et al. [8] employed pre-processing methods, including the median filter and gamma correction, for noise reduction and image enhancement, to detect diabetic retinopathy using a CNN. In [9], data augmentation methods such as zooming, rotation, shearing, height shifting, width shifting, normalisation, horizontal flipping, and unsharp masking were used in conjunction with a multi-scale attention block in a CNN for identifying the progression of glaucoma from fundus images. Xueri Li et al. in [10] used Vector Quantized Variational Autoencoders (VQ-VAE) for reconstructing affine transformed images to address the class imbalance problem for estimating the grade of diabetic retinopathy. Fatima Zahra El Yadari et al. [11] employed image pre-processing techniques to enhance quality and remove noise, in conjunction with MixUp data augmentation and pre-trained models optimised using transfer learning for the diabetic retinopathy classification. The existing approaches employed a broad range of pre-processing techniques for image enhancement and noise reduction. This work explores the rotation of observations to generate observations that can be recognised by the model more effectively. The following section presents the proposed approach.

3 Proposed Approach

As discussed in the previous section, data-driven techniques, such as deep learning approaches, require a large volume of labelled data for efficient training. To improve the effectiveness of training with limited data, the existing approaches use augmented data to increase the number of observations used for training. In this work, we investigate the use of rotationally transformed data for evaluating a trained model. In this work, we consider a pre-trained CNN model and train it using transfer learning, as shown in Fig. 1. Since the last layer in the DNN model is a Softmax classifier, it provides a confidence value for the predicted label as a probability. During testing, four rotationally transformed test observations are provided as input to the DNN model (that is trained during the training phase), yielding prediction and confidence values for all rotational variants, as illustrated in Fig. 2. Since any of the four rotationally transformed data can be used for the evaluation of the trained model, we consider the average confidence value across all test observations for all the angle of rotations considered, to determine the optimal angle of rotation for test data, for the evaluation of the trained model. The next section presents the experimental study conducted in this work to evaluate this approach.

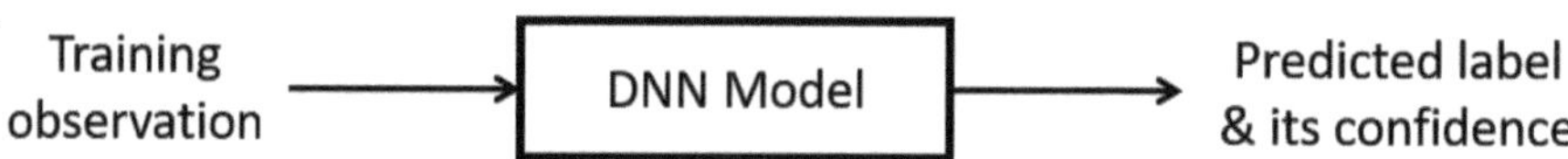

Fig. 1. Training the DNN model in the proposed approach

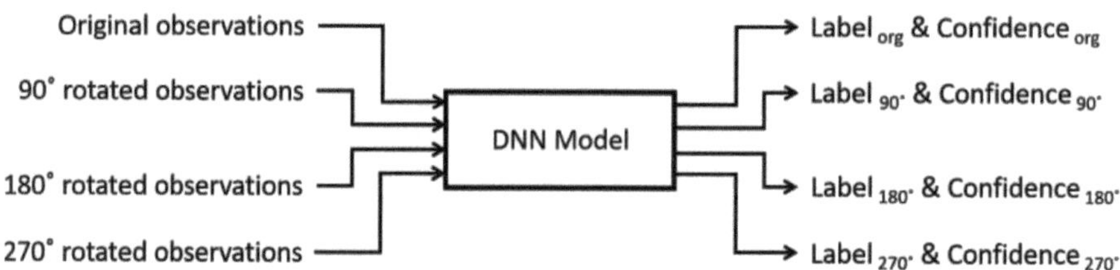

Fig. 2. Testing the trained DNN model in the proposed approach

4 Experimental Study

This section presents the experimental evaluation of the proposed approach on the AMD-Net23 dataset [12], which comprises 1594 training and 400 validation observations, corresponding to images of Age-Related Macular Degeneration (AMD), cataract, diabetes, and normal fundus. From the sample image in this dataset shown in Fig. 3, it can be observed that the broad diversity in patterns and colours in these observations makes this a challenging classification task. Similar to the approaches in the existing literature [13], the model is trained using the training data and evaluated on the validation data. In this work, we split the training data into 90–10 sets, using 90% for training and the remaining 10% for validating the DNN model. Similar to existing approaches, we use the entire valid data for evaluating the model, i.e., as a testing dataset.

The experiments were conducted in Matlab R2024b on Ubuntu 24.04 LTS operating system on a workstation with an NVIDIA RTX 6000 Ada GPU. In this work, we consider ResNet50 as the pre-trained DNN model due to its highest performance among the pre-trained models evaluated in [13]. The ResNet50 model is trained using transfer learning with data augmentation techniques, including random rotation in the range of [-90, 90] degrees, as well as horizontal and vertical reflections applied to the training data. The model is trained with a batch size of 32 for 10 epochs using the stochastic gradient descent with momentum (SGDM) algorithm with a learning rate of 0.0003 and shuffling after every epoch. The changes in accuracy and loss for training and validation data during training are shown in Fig. 4.

The trained ResNet50 model is evaluated according to the evaluation scheme provided in [13]. An accuracy of 94.00% is obtained for the original test data, whose confusion matrix is shown in Fig. 5. As per the explanation of the proposed approach given in previous section, four rotational variants of the test data are used to evaluate the trained ResNet50 model, whose results are presented in Table 1. From the table, it can be observed that when the model is assessed with test observations rotated by 180°, the mean confidence value of the prediction is higher than for observations with no rotation, 90° rotation, and 270° rotation. It can also be observed that, when the observations are rotated by 180°, the highest mean confidence value of 0.9447 is obtained, with an accuracy is 96.5%. According to the proposed approach, we consider rotating the observations by these angles to evaluate the proposed method. The confusion matrix of the proposed approach for various angles of rotation of observation data is shown in Fig. 6. The proposed approach utilises the mean confidence value of the prediction to determine the optimal angle of rotation for the test data, which is then used to evaluate the trained model. In this experimental study done on AMDNet23 dataset, 180° is the optimal angle of rotation to maximise the accuracy of the proposed approach. The proposed approach achieves an accuracy of 96.5% for 180° rotationally transformed data, whose confusion matrix is shown in Fig. 7. A performance comparison between the proposed approach and existing approaches is presented in Table 2. From the table, it can be observed that the performance of the proposed approach is comparable to the current state-of-the-art approach on this dataset.

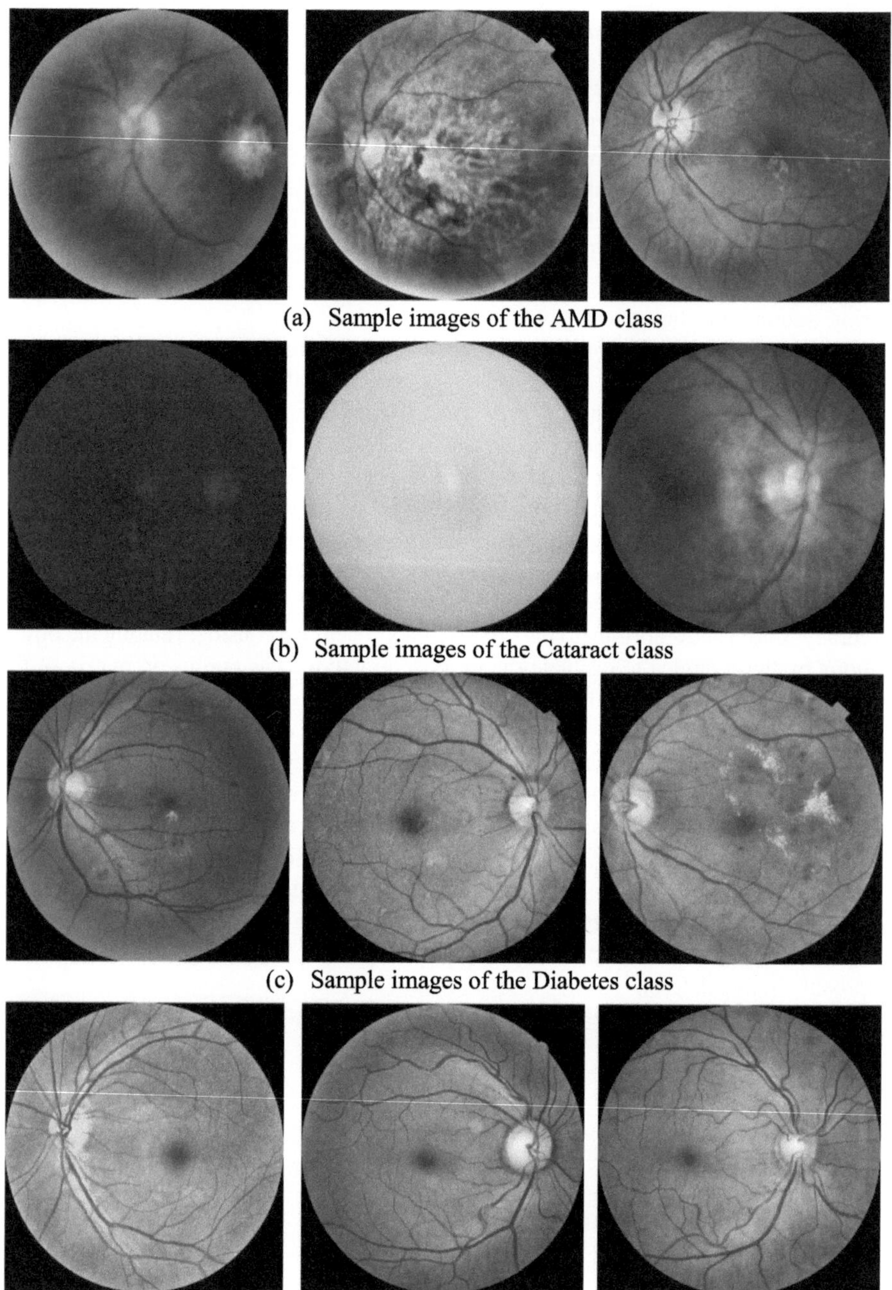

(a) Sample images of the AMD class

(b) Sample images of the Cataract class

(c) Sample images of the Diabetes class

(d) Sample images of the Normal class

Fig. 3. Sample images from the AMDNet23 dataset [12], depicting the diversity of observations in each class and across classes

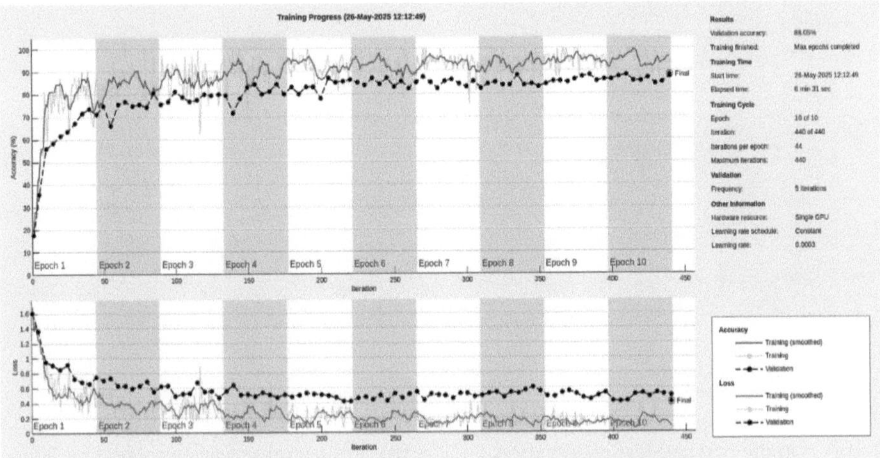

Fig. 4. Variation in classification accuracy and loss while training the ResNet50 based model

	amd	cataract	diabetes	normal	
amd	**94** 23.5%	**0** 0.0%	**2** 0.5%	**1** 0.2%	96.9% 3.1%
cataract	**0** 0.0%	**99** 24.8%	**0** 0.0%	**0** 0.0%	100% 0.0%
diabetes	**6** 1.5%	**1** 0.2%	**89** 22.2%	**5** 1.2%	88.1% 11.9%
normal	**0** 0.0%	**0** 0.0%	**9** 2.2%	**94** 23.5%	91.3% 8.7%
	94.0% 6.0%	99.0% 1.0%	89.0% 11.0%	94.0% 6.0%	**94.0%** **6.0%**

Fig. 5. Confusion Matrix of the trained ResNet50 based model for test images

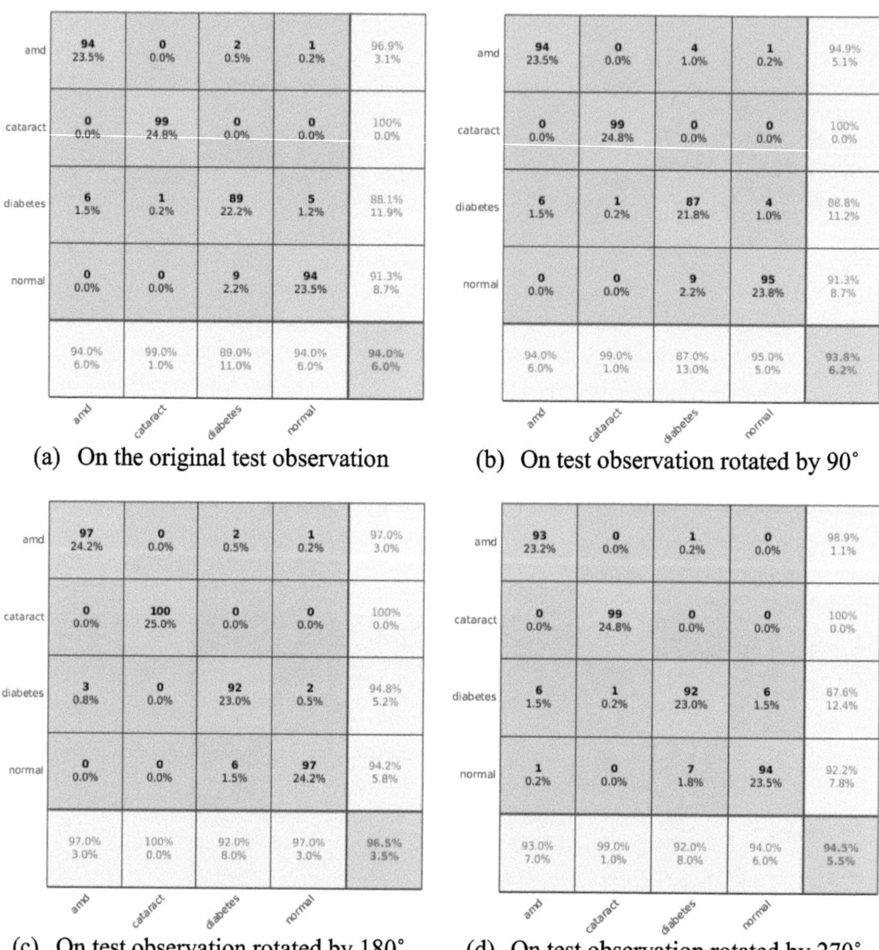

(a) On the original test observation   (b) On test observation rotated by 90°

(c) On test observation rotated by 180°   (d) On test observation rotated by 270°

Fig. 6. Confusion Matrices of the trained DNN model for test images of various angles

Table 1. Mean confidence values of the prediction of the trained DNN model for test images of various angles.

Approach	Mean confidence value	Accuracy
Original test observations	0.9437	94.00
Test observations rotated by 90°	0.9403	93.75
Test observations rotated by 180°	**0.9447**	**96.50**
Test observations rotated by 270°	0.9376	94.50

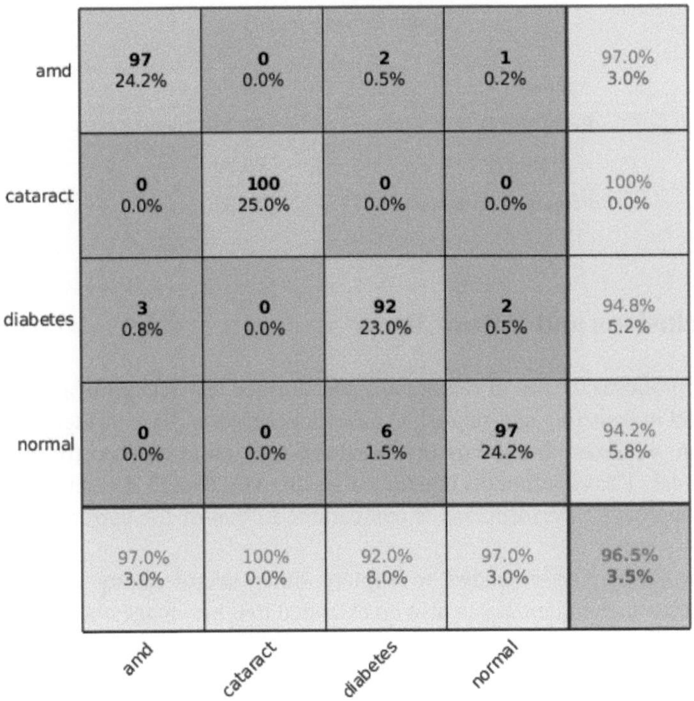

Fig. 7. Confusion Matrix of the proposed approach for observations rotated by 180°

Table 2. Performance comparison of the proposed approach against the existing approaches.

Approach	Accuracy
ViTB16 [13]	95.25
MobileViT_XXS [13]	83.00
InceptionResNetV2 [13]	47.50
EfficientNetB7 [13]	92.75
EfficientNetB6 [13]	92.75
DenseNet121 [13]	82.25
DenseNet169 [13]	81.25
DenseNet201 [13]	84.75
InceptionV3 [13]	72.25
MobileNetV2 [13]	71.75
VGG16 [13]	89.75
VGG19 [13]	89.00

(continued)

Table 2. (continued)

Approach	Accuracy
ResNet50 [13]	93.25
AMDNet23 [13]	96.50
Proposed approach	**96.50**

5 Conclusions and Future Work

This work proposes the use of rotationally transformed test data for evaluating a trained DNN model in detecting age-related macular degeneration. By considering alternatives for rotation, we determine the optimal angle of rotation to be used for evaluating the trained model. The experiments conducted on the AMDNet23 dataset suggest that the proposed approach's performance is comparable to that of the current state-of-the-art approach.

This work can be extended to explore other deep-learning models and data transformation techniques. It can also be extended to other image classification tasks.

References

1. Deng, L.: The MNIST database of handwritten digit images for machine learning research [best of the web]. IEEE Signal Process. Mag. **29**(6), 141–142 (2012). https://doi.org/10.1109/MSP.2012.2211477
2. Deng, J., Dong, W., Socher, R., Li, L.-J., Li, K., Fei-Fei, L.: ImageNet: a large-scale hierarchical image database. In: Proceedings of IEEE Conference on Computer Vision and Pattern Recognition (CVPR), pp. 248–255 (2009). https://doi.org/10.1109/CVPR.2009.5206848
3. Krizhevsky, A., Sutskever, I., Hinton, G.E.: ImageNet classification with deep convolutional neural networks. In: Proceedings of the International Conference on Neural Information Processing Systems (NIPS), vol. 1, pp. 1097–1105 (2012)
4. Szegedy, C., et al.: Going deeper with convolutions. In: Proceedings of IEEE Conference on Computer Vision and Pattern Recognition (CVPR), pp. 1–9 (2015). https://doi.org/10.1109/CVPR.2015.7298594
5. He, K., Zhang, X., Ren, S., Sun, J.: Deep residual learning for image recognition. In: Proceedings of IEEE Conference on Computer Vision and Pattern Recognition (CVPR), pp. 770–778, Las Vegas, NV, USA (2016). https://doi.org/10.1109/CVPR.2016.90
6. Sandler, M., Howard, A., Zhu, M., Zhmoginov, A., Chen, L.-C.: MobileNetV2: inverted residuals and linear bottlenecks. In: Proceedings of IEEE/CVF Conference on Computer Vision and Pattern Recognition, pp. 4510–4520, Salt Lake City, UT, USA (2018). https://doi.org/10.1109/CVPR.2018.00474
7. Kallel, F., Echtioui, A.: Retinal fundus image classification for diabetic retinopathy using transfer learning technique. SIViP. **18**, 1143–1153 (2024). https://doi.org/10.1007/s11760-023-02820-8
8. F M Javed Mehedi, S., et al.: An advanced deep neural network for fundus image analysis and enhancing diabetic retinopathy detection. Healthcare Anal. **5**, 100303., ISSN 2772-4425 (2024). https://doi.org/10.1016/j.health.2024.100303

9. Khajeha, H.R., Fateh, M., Abolghasemi, V.: Diagnosis of glaucoma using multi-scale attention block in convolution neural network and data augmentation techniques. Eng. Rep. **6**(10) (2024). https://doi.org/10.1002/eng2.12866

10. Li, X., Wen, L., Wu, J., Yang, L., Du, F.: Recognition of diabetic retinopathy grades based on data augmentation and attention mechanisms. Int. J. Imaging Syst. Technol. **34**(6) (2024). https://doi.org/10.1002/ima.23201

11. El Yadari, F.Z., Chougrad, H., Idrissi Khamlichi, Y.: Multi-class diabetic retinopathy classification using transfer learning and MixUp data augmentation. In: Serrhini, M., Ghoumid, K. (eds.) Advances in Smart Medical, IoT & Artificial Intelligence Information Systems Engineering and Management (ICSMAI), vol. 11. Springer, Cham (2024). https://doi.org/10.1007/978-3-031-66850-0_34Sdf

12. Ali., M.A.: AMDNet23: fundus image dataset for age-related macular degeneration disease detection. Mendeley Data. **V1** (2025). https://doi.org/10.17632/yj35kjgrv3.1

13. Ali, M.A., Hossain, M.S., Hossain, M.K., Sikder, S.S., Khushbu, S.A., Islam, M.: AMDNet23: hybrid CNN-LSTM deep learning approach with enhanced preprocessing for age-related macular degeneration (AMD) detection. Intell. Syst. Appl. **21**, 200334., ISSN 2667-3053 (2024). https://doi.org/10.1016/j.iswa.2024.200334

Internet Addiction Recognition from EEG Signals Using Laplacian Energy Features

Anand Mohan[(✉)](iD), Ramnivas Sharma, and Hemant Kumar Meena

Malaviya National Institute of Technology, Jaipur 302017, Rajasthan, India
{2024ree9067,2020ree9534,hmeena.ee}@mnit.ac.in

Abstract. Internet addiction has emerged as a significant public health concern, with growing evidence linking excessive technology use to cognitive impairment and mental health disorders. This paper presents a novel EEG-based methodology for detecting Internet addiction through advanced signal processing and machine learning techniques. Our approach utilizes Laplacian energy-based feature extraction to characterize the spatial-frequency dynamics of EEG signals across all major frequency bands (δ, θ, α, β, and γ). These features effectively capture the complex functional connectivity patterns in brain networks associated with addictive behaviors. Four different machine learning models are then used to classify the collected features: K-Nearest Neighbors (k-NN), Random Forest (RF), Support Vector Machines (SVM), and Logistic Regression (LR). The experimental results demonstrate exceptional performance, with Random Forest achieving 98% classification accuracy - the highest reported performance for EEG-based Internet addiction detection. This outstanding result underscores both the discriminative power of Laplacian energy features in capturing addiction-related neural patterns and the robustness of ensemble learning methods for neurological classification tasks.

Keywords: EEG Signals · Internet Addiction · Machine learning · Graph Signal Processing(GSP) · Laplacian Energy Features

1 Introduction

A large-scale online survey conducted between March and April 2020 in China [1] investigated the impact of the COVID-19 pandemic on Internet Addiction (IA), involving 20,472 participants. The study found a prevalence rate of 36.7% for IA, with 2.8% classified as severe cases. Nearly half of the respondents reported worsening symptoms, with key contributing factors including pandemic-induced stress, lack of social support, and excessive gaming. Multimodal biosignals were used in a different study [2] to investigate desire responses in teenagers with Internet Gaming Disorder (IGD). 57 participants had their desires successfully triggered by the use of gameplay footage as cues. About one-sixth of the individuals were removed due to hardware compatibility concerns, which reduced the study's usefulness. However, a Support Vector Machine (SVM) identified these desiring stages with an accuracy of 87.04%.

To assess attentional control in individuals with IA, a Go/No-Go task was used in [3]. Participants were exposed to gambling, video game, and neutral cues while event-related potentials (ERPs), specifically FRN and P300, were recorded. Subjects with high Internet Addiction Test (IAT) scores demonstrated faster responses and fewer errors to IA-related cues. However, the study's reliance on undergraduate participants may introduce sample bias and limit generalizability. Similarly, in [4], decision-making behavior among IA students was evaluated using nonlinear dynamic analysis and ERP during a gambling task. The study compared 17 IA individuals to 17 healthy controls and found that IA participants made faster but riskier choices, indicating increased impulsivity. Despite these findings, the artificial nature of the task may reduce ecological validity.

EEG has also been used to explore neurological aspects of behavioral addiction. In [5], 19-channel EEG recordings at 250 Hz were used to investigate brainwave differences between individuals with and without pornography addiction. The study demonstrated the potential of EEG for diagnostic purposes, although the results are preliminary and require further validation. A follow-up study [6] applied advanced deep learning models, including LSTM, GRU, and attention-based architectures, to EEG time-series data in pornography addiction. The models achieved high classification accuracies ranging from 94% to 97% using train-test splits, though performance dropped significantly with leave-one-out validation (45%âĂŞ49%), highlighting concerns over sample size and diversity. A design science research methodology was used in [7] to develop an IA categorization model based on resting-state EEG. With an accuracy of 94.17%, the algorithm established a noteworthy standard. However, the model's dependence on the MPILMBB dataset limited its external validation, and the exclusive use of resting-state data restricted its analytical scope. In order to detect IA directly from raw EEG data, a 5-layer convolutional neural network (CNN) was introduced in [8], obviating the necessity for intricate biomarker extraction. The model's accuracy was 81.1%. Adding alpha, beta, and gamma spectral power helps speed up training, but it also prolongs the process by adding another preprocessing load.

1. This study introduces a novel EEG-based Internet Addiction (IA) detection paradigm that identifies neural biomarkers across varied groups, providing an objective, data-driven alternative to traditional survey methodologies.
2. Laplacian energy-based feature extraction is utilized to capture graph signal variations over the EEG electrode network, effectively highlighting energy concentration patterns linked to addiction-related brain activity.
3. Extracted features are classified using machine learning models, improving classification accuracy while maintaining low computational complexity and latency compared to deep learning approaches.

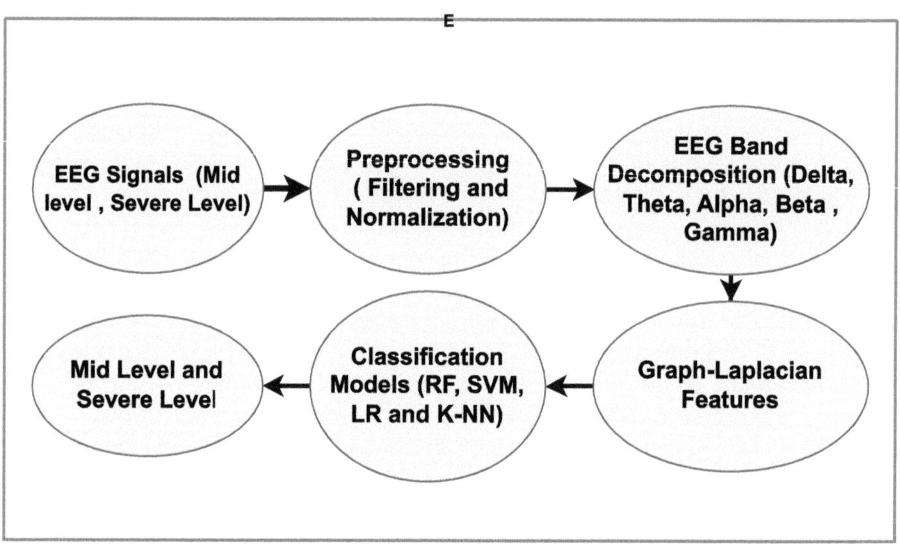

Fig. 1. Flow chart of proposed work.

The remaining sections of this conversation are organized as follows. Section 2 provides an overview of the proposed IA categorization approach, including the dataset, preprocessing, and feature extraction steps. Section 3 provides a detailed analysis of the findings and compares them to earlier research. The article ends with Sect. 4.

2   Research Methology

2.1   Dataset Description

This study uses a publicly available EEG dataset from [9,10]. The collection includes recordings from 30 subjects (15 males and 15 females) who used NeuroSky equipment. Each participant performed 11 distinct activities, including baseline measurements, emotional state assessments, memory tasks, executive functions, recall exercises, and baseline extensions. The EEG signals were recorded over a 12-minute session, with data segmented according to the specific tasks performed.

The primary objective of this dataset is to investigate internet addiction (IA) tendencies through a structured pipeline involving preprocessing, feature extraction, and classification. Each subject underwent 11 sessions, encompassing activities such as:

- Verbal memorization,
- Internet browsing,
- Exposure to emotional stimuli,
- Eyes-closed resting,

– Word recall.

The data, stored in CSV format, includes metrics such as brainwave activity, meditation levels, and concentration indices. However, preliminary analysis revealed that gamma waves, meditation, and attention measures had limited significance in classifying internet addiction.

Notably, EEG recordings were collected from 19 people (18 with mild IA and 1 with severe IA) utilizing a single-channel NeuroSky device positioned at the FP1 site.

2.2   Data Pre-processing

Our EEG-based Internet Addiction detection system begins with a rigorous data preparation pipeline to transform raw signals into analyzable features. The process starts by loading CSV files organized into 'Mid-level' and 'Severe' addiction categories, each containing ten-channel EEG recordings. We implement automated quality control where missing or corrupted channels are zero-filled to preserve data structure, followed by aggregation into a unified NumPy array. As shown in Fig. 1, the preprocessing includes spectrum decomposition with a fourth-order zero-phase Butterworth filter, which extracts five frequency bands without phase distortion. Delta (0.5–4 Hz) for deep sleep, Theta (4–8 Hz) for drowsiness, Alpha (8–13 Hz) for relaxed wakefulness, Beta (13–30 Hz) for active cognition, and Gamma (30–40 Hz) for high-level processing. This methodical approach ensures temporally precise feature extraction optimized for both machine learning and graph-based signal analysis of addiction-related neural patterns. The filtering procedure effectively separates distinct brainwave patterns linked to specific cognitive processes and affective states, thereby enhancing the identification of clinically relevant biomarkers during feature extraction.

2.3   Feature Extraction Using Graph Signal Processing for Internet Addiction Detection

Suppose N spikes of duration m are discovered during the initial stage of the sorting process in a single-electrode EEG recording. Each spike, indicated by $\mathbf{x}_i \in \mathbb{R}^m$ for $1 \leq i \leq N$, represents a data point in a m-dimensional space. It is desirable that points that were close in the original m-dimensional space stay close after being transformed to a low-dimensional environment. This ensures that the resulting lower-dimensional feature clusters are compact and meaningful.

To transform these points to a one-dimensional space ($d = 1$), we seek an optimal projection vector $\mathbf{A} = \alpha_1$ that minimizes the following cost function:

$$C_1(\alpha_1) = \sum_{i=1}^{N} \sum_{j=1}^{N} |\mathbf{y}_i - \mathbf{y}_j|^2 W_{ij} \tag{1}$$

where $\mathbf{y}_i = \alpha_1^T \mathbf{x}_i$ and W_{ij} denotes a scalar weight representing the proximity between points $\mathbf{x}_i$ and $\mathbf{x}_j$. Larger weights W_{ij} are assigned to point pairs that are closer in the original space, so the cost $C_1(\alpha_1)$ penalizes cases where such points are projected far apart in the transformed space. Minimizing $C_1(\alpha_1)$ therefore encourages proximity preservation.

Inspired by spectral graph theory [11], we construct a weighted undirected graph $G = (V, E)$ where each node corresponds to a data point. The graph construction proceeds in two main steps [12]:

Step 1: Constructing the Graph Edges. An edge is placed between nodes i and j if $\|\mathbf{x}_i - \mathbf{x}_j\|$ is sufficiently small. We adopt the following strategy:

- ε-**neighborhood approach:** An edge is formed if $\|\mathbf{x}_i - \mathbf{x}_j\| < \varepsilon$, where ε is a predefined threshold.

This approach ensures that only locally similar data points are connected, capturing intrinsic geometric relationships in the data.

Step 2: Determining the Edge Weights. Weights for edges are assigned using the heat kernel method:

$$W_{ij} = \begin{cases} \exp\left(-\frac{\|\mathbf{x}_i - \mathbf{x}_j\|^2}{t_{ij}}\right) & \text{if } i, j \text{ are connected} \\ 0 & \text{otherwise} \end{cases} \tag{2}$$

Here, t_{ij} is a scaling parameter that can be tuned based on local or global characteristics of the graph. The resulting similarity matrix W is symmetric and reflects the geometry of the original data.

Using the above definitions, the cost function in (1) can be rewritten as:

$$C_1(\alpha_1) = 2\sum_{i=1}^{N} y_i^2 \sum_{j=1}^{N} W_{ij} - 2\sum_{i=1}^{N}\sum_{j=1}^{N} y_i y_j W_{ij} \tag{3}$$

$$= 2\alpha_1^T \left[\sum_{i=1}^{N} \mathbf{x}_i \mathbf{x}_i^T D_{ii} - \sum_{i=1}^{N}\sum_{j=1}^{N} \mathbf{x}_i \mathbf{x}_j^T W_{ij}\right] \alpha_1 \tag{4}$$

$$= 2\alpha_1^T X (D - W) X^T \alpha_1 \tag{5}$$

$$= 2\alpha_1^T X L X^T \alpha_1 \tag{6}$$

where $X = [\mathbf{x}_1, \mathbf{x}_2, ..., \mathbf{x}_N] \in \mathbb{R}^{m \times N}$, D is a diagonal degree matrix defined as

$$D = \text{diag}(D_{ii}), \quad D_{ii} = \sum_{k=1}^{N} W_{ik} \tag{7}$$

and $L = D - W$ is the graph Laplacian matrix. The Laplacian L is symmetric and positive semi-definite, and plays a central role in spectral graph theory and graph signal processing [13].

The optimal vector α_1 that minimizes the cost function projects the high-dimensional EEG features into a compact and discriminative one-dimensional space while preserving local neighborhood structures. This transformation improves the separability of underlying classes relevant for Internet Addiction detection.

2.4   Machine Learning Models

This study evaluated four machine learning models for EEG-based multi-class classification: Random Forest (RF), Decision Tree (DT), Logistic Regression (LR), and K-Nearest Neighbors (KNN). To capture temporal and geographical patterns, feature extraction made use of statistical and signal processing approaches. Random Forest outperformed all other models in terms of accuracy and inference time, making it excellent for real-time applications.

Table 1. Experimental results of EEG δ, θ, α, β, and γ bands using Laplacian Energy features

EEG Band	Metric	SVM	RF	LR	K-NN
Delta (δ)	Accuracy (%)	79.69	**98.70**	71.09	91.41
	Latency (ms)	37.93	**19.21**	1.11	11.49
Theta (θ)	Accuracy (%)	73.18	**90.89**	69.27	81.51
	Latency (ms)	35.44	**34.11**	0.00	30.72
Alpha (α)	Accuracy (%)	71.35	**92.18**	66.67	73.18
	Latency (ms)	32.10	**15.89**	1.00	28.93
Beta (β)	Accuracy (%)	66.93	**89.32**	67.71	66.14
	Latency (ms)	45.18	**32.32**	0.99	10.82
Gamma (γ)	Accuracy (%)	69.53	**90.63**	62.50	65.63
	Latency (ms)	48.03	**31.38**	0.00	21.89

Its ensemble structure successfully handled nonlinearities and noise in EEG data. In contrast, Decision Tree overfitted, Logistic Regression underperformed owing to its linear character, and KNN, while occasionally accurate, had excessive latency, making it inappropriate for real-time application.

Overall, RF demonstrated the highest efficiency and scalability, making it ideal for embedded systems and BCIs.

3   Results and Discussion

In this proposed work, we focus on classifying Internet Addiction (IA) severity from EEG signals, distinguishing between mid-level and severe cases.

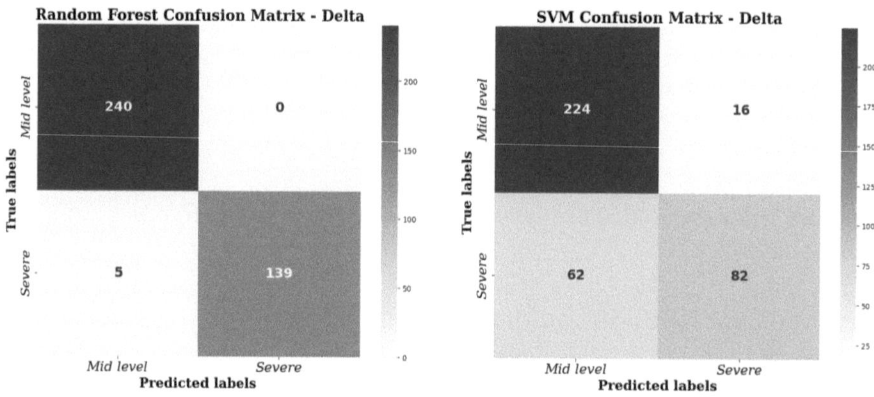

(a) Confusion matrix of Random Forest (RF)

(b) Confusion matrix of Support Vector Machine (SVM)

Fig. 2. Confusion matrices comparing classification performance of (a) Random Forest and (b) Support Vector Machine on the IA dataset.

The dataset was split into 80% for training and 20% for testing. For feature extraction, we employed Laplacian Energy, a spectral measure from Graph Signal Processing (GSP), which quantifies energy distribution across a graph-structured representation of EEG data. This method effectively captures both local and global variations in brain activity patterns, facilitating robust classification across multiple EEG frequency bands. Table 1 presents the performance of four classifiers- SVM, RF, LR, and K-NN—using Laplacian Energy features across five EEG bands. The Random Forest (RF) model outperformed others consistently, achieving the highest accuracy in every band (e.g., 98.70% in Delta, 90.89% in Theta, and 92.18% in Alpha) while maintaining low latency (15–34 ms range). This demonstrates its robustness for time-sensitive IA detection tasks.

While K-NN performed well in Delta (91.41%) and Theta (81.51%) bands, its performance dropped in Gamma (65.63%). SVM delivered moderate accuracy levels (66–79%) but exhibited the highest latency across all bands (e.g., 48.03 ms in Gamma), which may impact real-time processing. Logistic Regression, although computationally lightweight with very low latency (0–1 ms), showed lower classification accuracy overall, ranging from 62.50% to 71.09%.

The confusion matrices of RF and SVM in the delta band are shown in Fig 2.

As summarized in Table 2, the proposed approach based on Laplacian Energy demonstrates a significant improvement in accuracy over previous methods. With Random Forest achieving nearly 98% accuracy, the framework offers a powerful and efficient solution for EEG-based Internet Addiction classification. This outcome reinforces the potential of graph-based spectral features in modeling complex neural dynamics relevant to addictive behaviors, supporting practical applications in cognitive monitoring and intervention systems.

Table 2. Comparison with existing approaches for EEG-based Internet Addiction classification

Source	Year	Accuracy	Model Used
[8]	2022	81.1%	CNN
[7]	2020	94.0%	Traditional ML
[2]	2018	87.0%	SVM
[6]	2023	94.0%	Deep Learning
[14]	2023	98.0%	PSD-CNN
Proposed (Laplacian Energy)	2025	RF – **98.70%** K-NN – 91.41% SVM – 79.69% LR – 71.09%	RF K-NN SVM LR

4   Conclusion and Future Work

This study presents an effective hardware-software co-design framework for EEG-based Internet Addiction detection using machine learning techniques. Laplacian Energy-based feature extraction is employed to capture the spatial and spectral characteristics of EEG signals across major brainwave bands (δ, θ, α, β, and γ). The extracted features are classified using multiple machine learning models, with the Random Forest classifier achieving a high accuracy of 98%—demonstrating its effectiveness in accurately identifying addiction-related neural patterns.

Future work includes scaling to multi-channel EEG systems for improved spatial resolution, addressing data imbalance through augmentation or synthetic data, and validating classifier performance using statistical significance tests

Acknowledgments. The authors express their gratitude to the Department of Science and Technology (DST), Government of Rajasthan, for supporting this research through the project titled "Effective Analysis and Detection of Internet Addiction Using EEG Signal Processing".

Disclosure of Interests.

–**Ethical Approval**: Not involve any studies with animals or humans.

–**Information about consent participants:** Human participants are not involved.

–**Competing interests**: No competing financial or interpersonal conflicts.

–**Authors' contributions**: Anand Mohan: Original draft, Software, Review, and editing of the paper.

–**Hemant Kumar Meena**: Supervised, cross-checked, and edited.

–**Funding**: No Funding is involved.

–**Conflict of interest**: None.

References

1. Li, Y.-Y., Sun, Y., Meng, S.-Q., Bao, Y.-P., Cheng, J.-L., Chang, X.-W., Ran, M.-S., Sun, Y.-K., Kosten, T., Strang, J., et al.: Internet addiction increases in the general population during covid-19: Evidence from china. Am. J. Addict. **30**(4), 389–397 (2021)
2. Kim, H., Ha, J., Chang, W.-D., Park, W., Kim, L., Im, C.-H.: Detection of craving for gaming in adolescents with internet gaming disorder using multimodal biosignals. Sens. **18**(1), 102 (2018)
3. Balconi, M., Venturella, I., Finocchiaro, R.: Evidences from rewarding system, frn and p300 effect in internet-addiction in young people. Brain Sci. **7**(7), 81 (2017)
4. Shan, P., Pei, J.: Cognition and education management method of withdrawal reaction for students with internet addiction based on eeg signal analysis. Kuram ve Uygulamada Egitim Bilimleri **18**(5), 2235–2246 (2018)
5. Pratama, M.G., Setiawan, N.A., Ferdiana, R.: 'Eeg signal analysis in detecting pornography addiction. In: 2024 10th International Conference on Communication and Signal Processing (ICCSP). EEE, 2024, pp. 1079–1083 (2024)
6. Mahmoud, A., Mohamed, Y., Anter, A.M., Zaky, A.B.: Eeg-based detection of pornography addiction: Deep learning models with attention mechanism for unveiling neurocognitive patterns,. In: 2023 11th International Japan-Africa Conference on Electronics, Communications, and Computations (JAC-ECC). IEEE, pp. 73–78 (2023)
7. Gross, J., Baumgartl, H., Buettner, R.: A novel machine learning approach for high-performance diagnosis of premature internet addiction using the unfolded eeg spectra. In: AMCIS, (2020)
8. Sun, S., Yang, J., Chen, Y.-H., Miao, J., Sawan, M.: Eeg signals based internet addiction diagnosis using convolutional neural networks. Appl. Sci. **12**(13), 6297 (2022)
9. Theng, T.H., Kit, M.H., Handayani, D.: Machine learning classification model for identifying internet addiction among university students. In: 2023 2nd International Conference on Computer Technologies (ICCTech). IEEE, pp. 7–11 (2023)
10. Kang, X., Agastya, I.M.A., Handayani, D.O.D., Kit, M.H., Rahman, A.W.B.A.: Electroencephalogram (eeg) dataset with porn addiction and healthy teenagers under rest and executive function task. Data Brief **39**, 107467 (2021)
11. Chung, F.R.: Spectral Graph Theory, Regional Conference Series in Math. Amer. Math. Soc, CBMS (1997)
12. M. Belkin and P. Niyogi, "Laplacian eigenmaps and spectral techniques for embedding and clustering. Adv. Neu. Infor. Process. Sys. **14**, (2001)
13. Ghanbari, Y., Papamichalis, P.E., Spence, L.: Graph-laplacian features for neural waveform classification. IEEE Trans. Biomed. Eng. **58**(5), 1365–1372 (2010)
14. Swati, S. Kumar, M.: Investigating the addictive behavior of internet surfing through deep analysis of brainwaves. In: Proceedings of the 2023 5th International Conference on Image, Video and Signal Processing, pp. 133–138 (2023)

Robust Microaneurysm Detection in Retinal Fundus Images Using an Optimized ResNet50-UNet Model

Debasish Deb[iD], Md Kayser Ahmed Hridoy[iD], Sabyasachi Roy Barman[iD], and Raman Murugan[✉][iD]

National Institute of Technology Silchar, Silchar 788010, Assam, India
`murugan.rmn@ece.nits.ac.in`

Abstract. One of the earliest detectable signs of diabetic retinopathy (DR)—a leading cause of vision impairment worldwide—is the presence of microaneurysm(MA). Precise segmentation and identifying very early lession like microaneurysms from retinal fundus images are critical for timely diagnosis and intervention. In the proposed research work, we have developed an enhanced deep learning framework that integrates U-Net architecture with a ResNet50 encoder for the automated segmentation of microaneurysm. The ResNet50 backbone, pretrained on ImageNet, leverages residual learning to extract fine-grained details as well as broader contextual information. The U-Net decoder reconstructs detailed segmentation masks via progressive upsampling and skip connections, preserving spatial accuracy. Model development involved training and validation on the IDRiD database [1], which contains retinal images from Indian patients, it offers finely annotated high-resolution images of retina, marking DR lesions and typical retinal structures at the pixel level. To improve generalization, we apply various preprocessing steps and data augmentation techniques during training. Quantitative evaluation demonstrates the effectiveness of our approach, achieving a Dice score of 85.69%, Intersection over Union (IoU) of 93.56%, mean accuracy of 99.55%, and mean precision of 96.01%. These results show a significant improvement over conventional U-Net models in accurately segmenting small and scattered lesions. This study demonstrates the effectiveness of integrating deep residual networks, within encoder-decoder frameworks and establishes a strong foundation for deploying automated DR screening tools in clinical environments.

Keywords: Microaneurysm · Diabetic Retinopathy · U-Net · ResNet50 · Encoder-decoder

1 Introduction

Diabetic retinopathy(DR) is the main reason for loss of vision in the world [3]. DR is the disease related to eye and should be detected in its initial stage. It is very crucial to human health, because it can lead to blindness and even death. The earliest clinical sign of DR is Retinal microaneurysm (MA) [4]. The lesions associated with DR are small blood dots or yellow like substances that develop in capillary walls of fundus images. MA is considered one of the earliest pathological changes in the human retina. Hence, it is important for accurate segmentation of MA, to reduce ophthalmologists' workload and prevent misdiagnosis [5]. It is characterized by various types of retinal lesions caused by prolonged sugar levels that are higher and damaging the retinal blood vessels. The key lesions in DR include like small, round, red dots caused by weakening of capillary walls, leading to localized out-pouching of blood vessels. MA are smaller in shape and size, often irregular, and the MA contrast is also not high [6]. Therefore, pinpointing the exact location and identifying MA in fundus images presents a significant challenge.

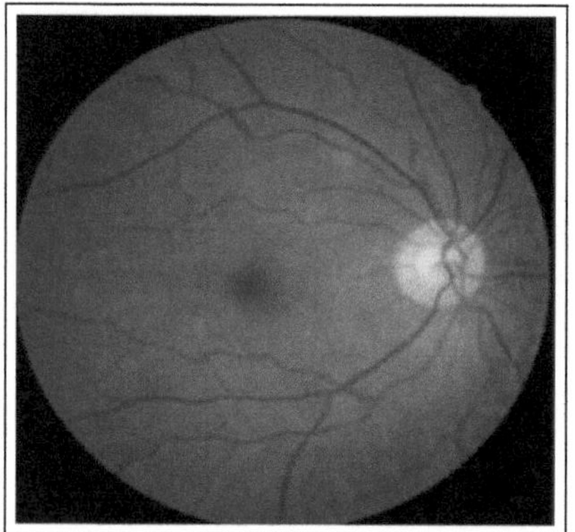
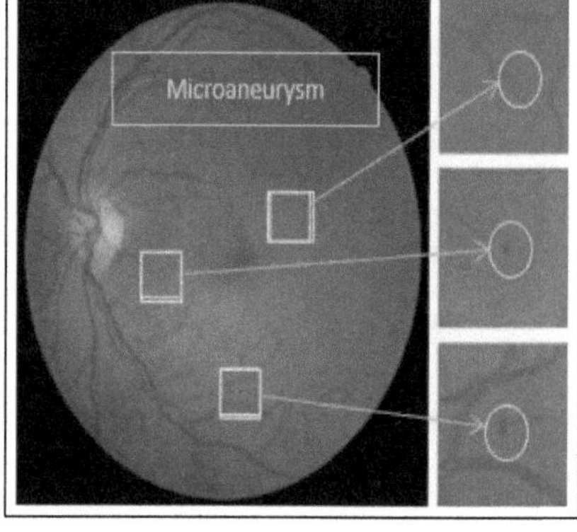

(a) No Microaneurysm (Normal Case)   (b) Presence of Microaneurysm

Fig. 1. Representative examples of fundus images: the left image shows a normal case without microaneurysms, while the right image illustrates a case with visible microaneurysms [2].

Manual detection annotation of MAs by ophthalmologists is a challenging work and may leads to error while trying to accurate detect and segment MA. Hence recent advances in medical image analysis, particularly convolutional neural networks (CNNs), have shown significant promise in enhancing the precision of lesion detection in fundus images. Figure 1 represents a sample retinal findus image with marked microaneurysms. This study proposes a novel U-Net architecture integrated with a ResNet50 encoder to improve the segmentation of microaneurysms from retinal images. The key innovation lies in the combination of U-Net's spatial preservation through skip connections and ResNet50's deep residual learning, which enables more effective extraction of minute lesion patterns. This fusion leads to significantly improved detection performance compared to traditional encoder-decoder architectures. The main contributions of this work are as follows:

- A hybrid U-Net + ResNet50 architecture tailored for segmenting microaneurysms in retinal fundus images.
- Demonstration of superior performance on the IDRiD database, achieving a Dice score of 85.69% and IoU of 93.56%, outperforming standard approaches.
- Validation of the model's robustness in detecting small, low-contrast lesions across complex retinal backgrounds.
- Analysis of potential challenges such as misclassification in low-quality or overlapping regions, along with discussion of future improvements.

The rest of the paper is organized as follows: Sect. 2 reviews related work on microaneurysm segmentation and deep learning approaches; Sect. 3 describes the proposed methodology, including model architecture and data preprocessing; Sect. 4 presents the experimental setup, evaluation metrics, and results; and Sect. 5 concludes the study and outlines future research directions.

2   Literature Overview

Over the past decade, MA segmentation in retinal fundus images has undergone significant advancements, driven by the imperative for early detection of DR. Recent studies from 2020 to 2025 have introduced innovative methodologies that enhances the accuracy and efficiency towards detection of MA.

Vanaja et al. [3] proposed a deep learning U-Net architecture known as CBAM-AG-UNet. This model integrates advanced attention mechanisms, like Attention Gates and CBAM (Convolutional-Block-Attention-Module), to enhance network's ability to concentrate on important lesion features, ultimately leading to more precise microaneurysm segmentation. Lu et al. [4] introduced a novel architecture, PFFNet, designed to enhance microaneurysm segmentation by effectively combining information from multiple spatial scales. This model utilizes two core components—GPSP and SSAP modules—to improve context awareness and feature integration. To effectively address the imbalance of the class often observed in lesion segmentation, the authors employed a hybrid loss function that enhances segmentation accuracy across varying lesion sizes. Usman et al. [5] proposed Ens5B-UNet, an ensemble of five modified U-Nets, achieving superior MA segmentation performance. It outperformed state of the art methods on IDRiD and E-Ophta_MA databases, showing significant improvements in IoU, Dice, and AUPR, indicating strong clinical applicability. Raudonis et al. [6] introduces an automated approach for MA identifying in retinal images that is fundus images using an ensemble of ResNet34UNet, UNet and UNet++ models. The method segments images via patch-based processing and reconstruction, achieving high Dice (0.95) and IoU (0.91) scores, highlighting its effectiveness for the detection early DR. Manoj et al. [7] proposed a comprehensive DR detection framework that combines transfer learning and U-Net-based segmentation to accurately identify disease stages from fundus images, achieving high performance and highlighting the potential for early diagnosis and clinical integration. Mayya et al. [8] described, microaneurysm segmentation is vital for early diabetic retinopathy detection. Recent studies using color fundus images explore classical, machine learning, and deep learning methods. Despite progress, challenges remain in achieving fully automated, reliable diagnostic systems. The proposed solution [9], termed MResUNet, is a deep learning model that enhances the traditional U-Net architecture by integrating residual units with modified identity mapping. This integration employs convolutional layers and batch normalization to improve feature learning and mitigate performance degradation in deeper networks. Cheng et al. [10] proposed a method combining edge detection with Random Forest to improve the automatic detection of microaneurysms, addressing their small size and similarity to other lesions, and demonstrate high accuracy on the MESSIDOR database. Long et al. [11] introduces a microaneurysm detection method using Directional Local Contrast (DLC) and machine learning, where vessel segmentation, candidate extraction, and patch classification are performed. It highlights the first use of DLC and compares three classifiers, showing strong performance on the DIARETDB1 and the e-ophtha MA databases.

While these advancements mark significant progress, certain obstacles continue to limit optimal outcomes, including class imbalance due to the sparse occurrence of MA, variability in image quality, and the need for large annotated databases. Future research directions may involve semi-supervised and unsupervised learning approaches to leverage unlabelled data, integration of clinical data to enhance diagnostic accuracy, and deployment of these DL models to ensure scalability and reliability.

3   Methodology

Here, we describe pipeline for early detection of microaneurysm from retinal fundus images. We have described below end to end workflow of the proposed model starting from database preparation to model evaluation.

1. **Database Preparation and Preprocessing:** We used IDRiD database [1], that consists of digital retinal images annotated for DR lesions. The database was partitioned into 54 training and 27 validation samples, all of which included associated ground truth annotations. The images and masks were resized to 512×512 pixels. RGB images had shapes of $(54, 512, 512, 3)$ and $(27, 512, 512, 3)$, and grayscale masks had shapes of $(54, 512, 512, 1)$ and $(27, 512, 512, 1)$. All inputs were normalized to ensure consistency.
2. **Data Augmentation:** To enhance generalization and reduce overfitting, we applied extensive data augmentation techniques, including horizontal as well as vertical flipping, zooming, rotation-random,and also contrast adjustments.
3. **Architecture of the Proposed Model:** The proposed segmentation framework was based on U-Net architecture using a ResNet50 encoder backbone. ResNet50 was chosen for its deep residual learning capabilities and identity skip connections, which mitigate vanishing gradients and allow for deeper, more expressive networks. Pretrained ImageNet weights were used to accelerate training and enrich feature extraction.

4. **Decoder and Reconstruction:** The decoder comprised transposed convolutions with skip connections to restore spatial resolution and produce accurate high-resolution segmentation masks.
5. **Loss Function and Optimization:** A combined Binary Cross-Entropy and Dice loss function was employed to address class imbalance between microaneurysms and background pixels. The Adam optimizer was used, along with learning rate scheduling, early stopping, and model checkpointing to ensure training stability and prevent overfitting.
6. **Evaluation:** A schematic representation of the proposed model's workflow is provided in Fig. 2. This performance of DL model was evaluated quantitatively using Dice Coefficient and Intersection over Union (IoU) metrics, and qualitatively through visual inspection of the predicted masks against expert-annotated ground truths.

3.1 Layered Architecture of Res50Unet

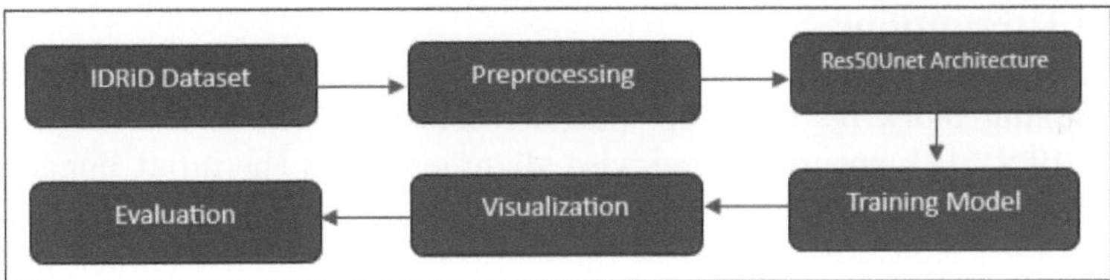

Fig. 2. Proposed workflow for microaneurysm segmentation using the IDRiD database.

- **Input Layer:**
  The model starts with an input layer designed to accept images of size **512 × 512 pixels** with **3 color channels** (Red, Green, Blue). The input tensor shape is $(512, 512, 3)$, which balances detail preservation and computational efficiency.
- **ResNet50 Encoder (Backbone):**
  We use a **pre-trained ResNet50** model without the classification head as the encoder. This convolutional base extracts hierarchical features from the input image. ResNet50's residual connections allow deeper feature extraction by mitigating vanishing gradients. Pre-trained ImageNet weights provide useful initial feature detectors, speeding up convergence.
- **Feature Extraction and Skip Connections:**
  The ResNet50 encoder outputs feature maps at multiple scales. We select four intermediate layers as skip connections to capture multi-scale spatial features:
  - `conv1_relu`: Low-level features such as edges and textures.
  - `conv2_block3_out`: Intermediate features with slightly reduced resolution.

- `conv3_block4_out`: More abstract shapes and patterns.
- `conv4_block6_out`: High-level semantic features at lower spatial resolution.

These skip connections help preserve spatial details lost during downsampling.

- **Bridge (Bottleneck Layer):**
The deepest layer `conv5_block3_out` serves as the bottleneck, capturing highly abstracted semantic features at a reduced spatial resolution. This layer connects the encoder and decoder, summarizing the input image content.
- **Decoder with Upsampling:**
The decoder reconstructs spatial resolution by gradually upsampling the bottleneck features using transpose convolutions. At each step, the decoder concatenates the upsampled feature maps with the corresponding skip connections from the encoder, combining semantic information with spatial details.
- **Convolutional Blocks in Decoder:**
Each decoder stage includes layers composed of convolution operations followed by batch normalization and ReLU, refining merged features and enhancing the model's ability to learn complex spatial patterns for improved segmentation accuracy.
- **Final Upsampling Stage:**
After all skip connections are processed and features are upsampled, one final upsampling block restores the spatial resolution back to the original input size (512×512), ensuring pixel-wise alignment with the input image.
- **Output Layer:**
A final 1×1 convolution reduces the feature depth to one channel, producing a single-channel segmentation mask. The final activation layer uses sigmoid to assign a probability to each pixel location representing the likelihood of belonging to target class.
- **Activation Functions Used:**
Intermediate convolutional layers use ReLU activations to introduce non-linearity and prevent vanishing gradients. The final layer uses sigmoid activation to produce probabilities for binary segmentation.

Figure 3 below depicts the architecture and processing pipeline of the proposed ResNet50UNet model used for microaneurysm segmentation.

Figure 4 provides the architectural configuration of the proposed ResNet50-U-Net model, while Fig. 5 outlines the summary of the overall model configuration and training parameters. Fig. 6 presents the proposed ResNet50-U-Net architecture and Fig. 7 presents the training progress of the model.

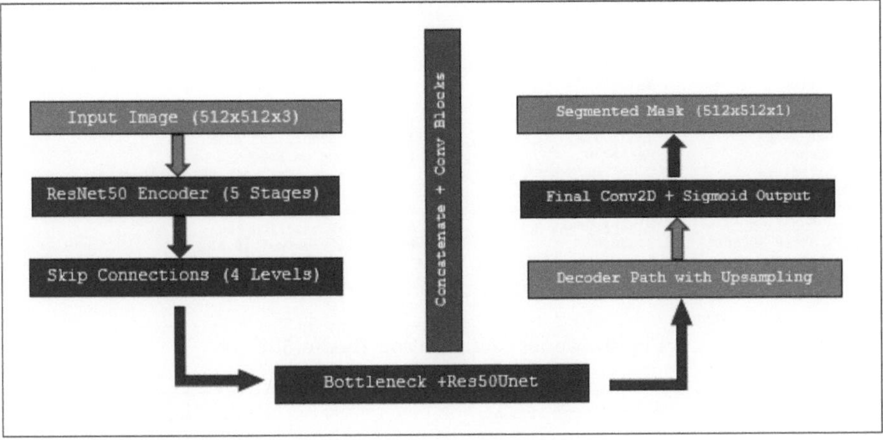

Fig. 3. Workflow of the proposed ResNet50-U-Net architecture for microaneurysm segmentation.

```
TABLE 1: ResNet50-UNet Architecture Configuration
=================================================

ENCODER (ResNet50 Backbone):
Stage          | Layer Type          | Output Shape    | Parameters  | Skip Connection   | Description
--------------------------------------------------------------------------------------------------------
Input Layer    | Input               | (512×512×3)     | 0           | -                 | RGB Input Image
Conv1          | conv1_relu          | (256×256×64)    | 9,472       | Skip-1            | Initial Conv + ReLU
Conv2_x        | conv2_block3_out    | (128×128×256)   | 215,808     | Skip-2            | Residual Blocks
Conv3_x        | conv3_block4_out    | (64×64×512)     | 1,117,184   | Skip-3            | Residual Blocks
Conv4_x        | conv4_block6_out    | (32×32×1024)    | 7,077,888   | Skip-4            | Residual Blocks
Conv5_x        | conv5_block3_out    | (16×16×2048)    | 14,964,736  | -                 | Bridge/Bottleneck

DECODER:
Stage          | Layer Type          | Output Shape    | Parameters  | Skip Connection   | Description
--------------------------------------------------------------------------------------------------------
Decoder-1      | UpConv + ConvBlock  | (32×32×512)     | 12,846,080  | Uses Skip-4       | Upsample + Concat
Decoder-2      | UpConv + ConvBlock  | (64×64×256)     | 2,097,664   | Uses Skip-3       | Upsample + Concat
Decoder-3      | UpConv + ConvBlock  | (128×128×128)   | 525,056     | Uses Skip-2       | Upsample + Concat
Decoder-4      | UpConv + ConvBlock  | (256×256×64)    | 131,392     | Uses Skip-1       | Upsample + Concat
Final Up       | Conv2DTranspose     | (512×512×32)    | 8,224       | -                 | Final Upsampling
Output         | Conv2D(1×1)         | (512×512×1)     | 33          | -                 | Sigmoid Output

Total Parameters: 40,985,857
Trainable: 40,928,897 | Non-trainable: 56,960
```

Fig. 4. Architectural configuration ResNet50Unet

4   Experimental Results

4.1   Training Performance:

- The best validation performance is achieved as the model progressively improved and converged during training, with both loss and accuracy curves stabilizing towards the end of training.
- The model is trained using input images of size **512×512×3** and corresponding masks of size **512×512×1**. Training is performed over **100 epochs** with a **batch size of 2** using the **Adam optimizer**, which is well-suited for handling sparse gradients and noisy data.

```
TABLE 2: Model Configuration Summary
=====================================

Parameter              | Value                     | Description
-------------------------------------------------------------------------
Input Shape            | (512, 512, 3)             | RGB images
Output Shape           | (512, 512, 1)             | Binary segmentation mask
Backbone               | ResNet50                  | Pre-trained on ImageNet
Architecture           | U-Net with ResNet50 Encoder | Encoder-decoder with skip connections
Skip Connections       | 4 levels                  | Feature reuse from encoder
Optimizer              | Adam                      | Adaptive learning rate
Loss Function          | Binary Cross-entropy      | Binary segmentation task
Activation (Output)    | Sigmoid                   | Probability output [0,1]
Total Depth            | 5 encoder + 5 decoder levels | Deep feature extraction
```

Fig. 5. Model configuration ResNet50Unet

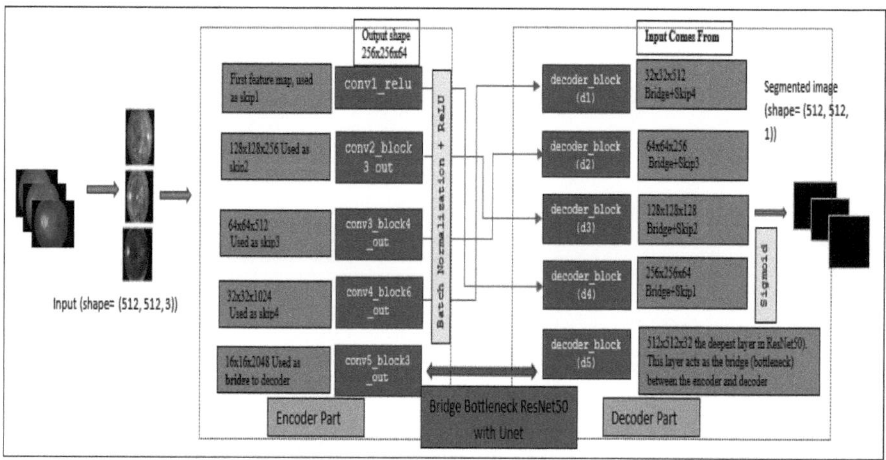

Fig. 6. ResNet50-U-Net model architecture.

- A combined **Binary Cross-Entropy and Dice Loss** function is employed, effectively handling class imbalance and promoting accurate segmentation of microaneurysms.
- Training and validation curves as shown in Figure below indicate smooth convergence without overfitting, demonstrating the robustness of the model and the effectiveness of the data augmentation strategies used.

In addition to numerical evaluation, the segmentation capability of the model was visually verified by comparing the predicted masks against the ground truth annotations. As depicted in Fig. 8, the proposed model demonstrates effective localization of microaneurysms, including small and sparse lesions that are often difficult to identify. These visualizations, shown in a 3×3 image grid, illustrate original fundus images alongside the ground truth and predicted segmentation maps. The model maintains high precision even under varying illumination and low-contrast conditions, underscoring its robustness and clinical relevance.

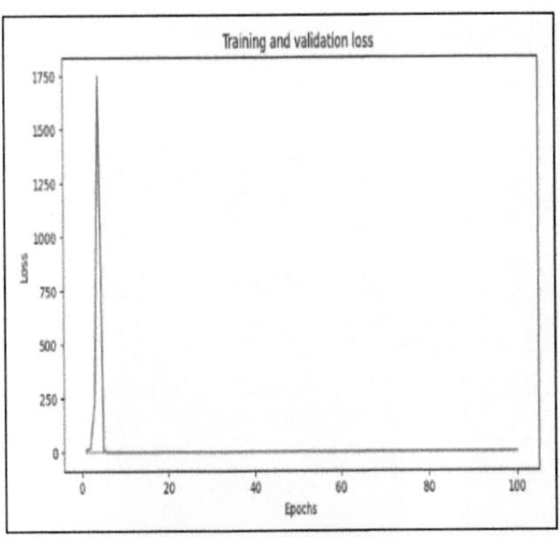

(a) Training vs Validation Loss

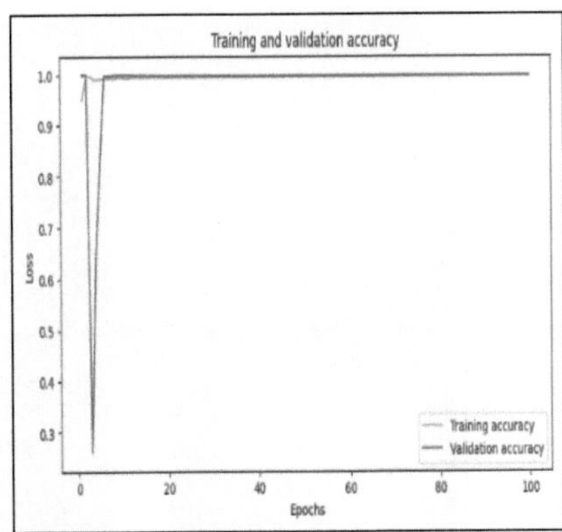

(b) Training vs Validation Accuracy

Fig. 7. Training progress—loss and accuracy over epochs. The left plot shows the comparison of training and validation loss, while the right plot depicts training and validation accuracy over each epoch.

4.2 Comparative Analysis

This section outlines the dataset and platform used for the research, presents a comparative analysis with existing methods, evaluates the performance of the proposed approach, introduces the relevant mathematical formulations, and discusses the final segmentation results.

Database: The IDRiD dataset [1], comprising annotated retinal images for diabetic retinopathy, was employed in this study. It was divided into 54 training and 27 validation samples, each paired with corresponding ground truth masks. All inputs were resized to 512×512 pixels—RGB images to (N, 512, 512, 3) and masks to (N, 512, 512, 1)—and normalized to maintain consistency.

Platform: The proposed ResNet50-based U-Net model implemented and trained using the Google Colab platform, leveraging the computational power of NVIDIA T4 GPU. This setup provided sufficient resources for efficient training and experimentation with deep convolutional neural networks.

Comparative Analysis: As highlighted in Table below, the ResNet50-Unet model, achieves a Dice coefficient of **85.69%**, an IoU score of **93.56%** and a precision of **96.01%**. These results indicate a strong balance between accurate lesion detection and minimal false positive rate. The architecture's deep residual encoding enables effective feature extraction even in cases with minimal contrast, commonly observed in early-stage diabetic retinopathy.

Compared to existing DL models, the ResNet50-U-Net demonstrates superior or competitive performance. It outperforms PFFNet and FFU-Net in all metrics and shows higher sensitivity and precision than CBAM-AG-UNet. While ensemble-based approaches such as those proposed by Kaya et al. [7] achieve slightly higher Dice scores, our model offers a good trade-off between performance and computational efficiency, making it suitable for practical clinical set-

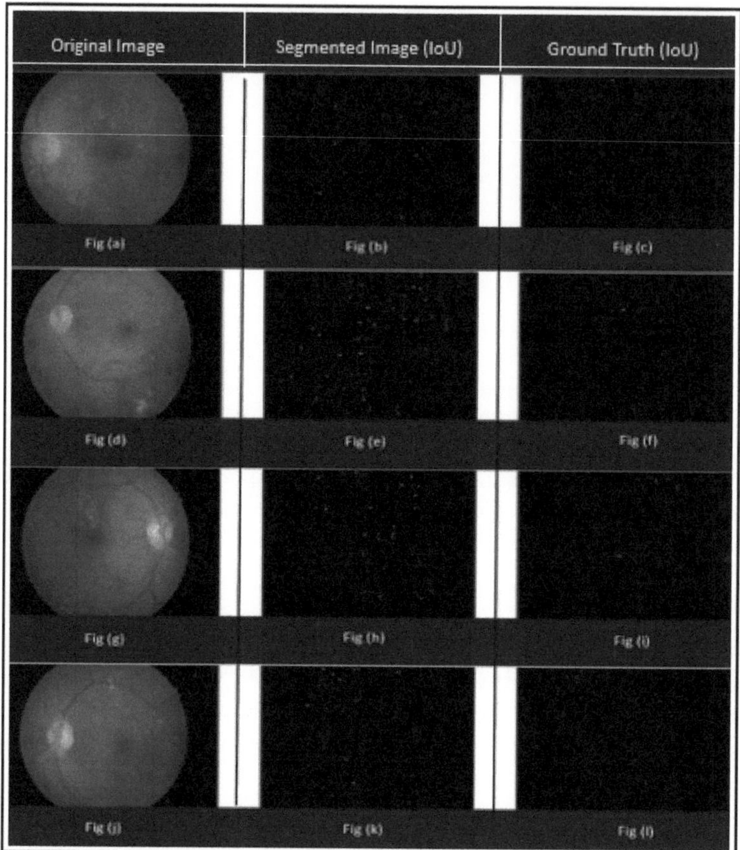

Fig. 8. Illustrates the original fundus image, the segmented microaneurysms, and the ground truth mask. The average IoU scores(93.56%) between the segmented images and their ground truths are presented in the comparative Table 1.

tings.These findings confirm that incorporating a ResNet50 encoder within a U-Net architecture offers a strong balance between deep semantic understanding and precise localization in medical image segmentation tasks.

Mathematical Equations: Dice Coefficient (F1 Score for Segmentation): It is calculated by 2*intersection divided by the total number of pixels in both images

$$\text{F1 Score} = \frac{2XTP}{2XTP + FP + FN}$$

where:

TP stands for True Positives

FP stands for False Positives

FN stands for False Negatives

Intersection over Union(IoU) = The proportion of the intersection to the union of the predicted segmentation and the ground truth.

$$\text{IoU} = \frac{TP}{TP + FP + FN}$$

Table 1. Comparative analysis of MA segmentation performance on the IDRiD database, with all metric values expressed in percentages.

Model	Dice	IoU	Sensitivity	Precision	Reference
ResNet50-UNet	85.69	93.56	–	96.01	**This Study**
CBAM-AG-UNet	86.50	75.80	89.1	91.3	Vanaja et al., 2025 [3]
PFFNet	48.21	30.03	48.33	48.10	Lu et al., 2024 [4]
Ensemble UNet++)	95.0	91.0	–	–	Kaya et al., 2023 [7]
Residual + Sub-pixel	99.98	–	99.88	99.89	Sambya et al., 2020 [8]

4.3   Discussion

The proposed U-Net model integrated with a ResNet50 encoder has demonstrated superior performance in the task of MA based IDRiD database [1]. The incorporation of ResNet50 as the feature extractor enabled the model to capture rich hierarchical features, enhancing its ability to distinguish microaneurysms from the surrounding retinal structures. The high Dice score of 85.69% and IoU of 93.56% indicate the model's accuracy in overlapping predicted lesion areas with the ground truth, while the mean accuracy and precision further reflect its reliability and low false positive rate. This model outperforms traditional encoder-decoder architectures by leveraging pre-trained deep residual connections, allowing for better gradient flow and improved learning of minute lesion patterns typical of microaneurysms. Additionally, the skip connections within U-Net preserve spatial details that are often lost in deep CNNs, resulting in precise segmentation boundaries. Despite the promising results, minor misclassifications in challenging cases with low contrast or overlapping features suggest that further refinement is necessary. Variability in lesion shapes, image quality, and pathological conditions still pose challenges, requiring more robust generalization strategies.

5   Conclusion and Future Work

While the current model demonstrates strong potential in segmenting microaneurysms, its performance can be further improved by training and validating it on a wider range of databases. This would enhance its ability to generalize across different populations and imaging conditions. Future enhancements may include incorporating attention-based modules or transformer-inspired encoders to improve the model's focus on clinically relevant lesion regions.

Another promising direction involves implementing a multi-task learning framework that performs both segmentation and classification in parallel. Integrating a classification branch that identifies early-stage lesions could provide richer diagnostic insights and support early intervention in diabetic retinopathy.

To facilitate this, features such as the shape, size, location, and intensity of segmented lesions can be extracted and used as inputs for severity classification models—either deep learningâĂŞbased or graph-based. This approach would enable the system to not only detect lesions but also assess their clinical significance.

References

1. Porwal, P., et al.: Indian Diabetic Retinopathy Image database (IDRiD), IEEE-DataPort, (2019). https://doi.org/10.21227/H25W98
2. Melo, T., Mendonça, A.M., Campilho, A.: Microaneurysm detection in color eye fundus images for diabetic retinopathy screening **126**. Elsevier, ScienceDirect (2020)
3. Vanaja, C.B., Prakasam, P.: Convolutional block attention gate-based UNet framework for microaneurysm segmentation using retinal fundus images. BMC Med. Imaging **25**, 83 (2025)
4. Jiaxin, L., et al.: IET: The Institute of Engineering and Technology. A pyramid feature fusion network for microaneurysm segmentation in fundus images, PFFNet (2024)
5. Usman, T.M., Saheed, Y.K., Ajibesin, A.A., Nsang, A.S.: Ens5B-UNet for Improved Microaneurysms segmentation in retinal images. In: IEEE International Conference on Science, Engineering and Business for Driving Sustainable Development Goals (SEB4SDG), ISBN:979-8-3503-5816 (2024)
6. Harisha, M.S., Bhosale, A.A., Narender, M.: Deep learning-powered segmentation and classification of diabetic retinopathy for enhanced diagnostic precision. acc-science article, AIH 2024, pp. 30–42, https://doi.org/10.36922/aih.2783 (2024)
7. Raudonis, V., Kairys, A., Verkauskiene, R., Sokolovska, J., Petrovski, G.: Vilma Jurate Balciuniene, Vallo Volke, NIH, National Library of Medicine, PubMed, automatic detection of Microaneurysms in fundus images using an ensemble-based segmentation method. Sensors (Basel) (2023). https://doi.org/10.3390/s23073431
8. Mayya, V., Kamath, S.S., Kulkarni, U.: Computer methods and programs biomedicine, automated Microaneurysms detection for early diagnosis of diabetic retinopathy: a comprehensive review **1**. Elsevier (2021)
9. Qomariah, D.U.N., Tjandrasa, H., Fatichah, C.: Segmentation of Microaneurysms for Early Detection of Diabetic Retinopathy Using MResUNet. Int. J. Intell. Eng. Syst. (2021)
10. Peng, J., et al.: A fast localization and extraction of microaneurysm for early detection of diabetic retionopathy **53**(2), 16400–16405 (2020)
11. Long, S., et al.: Microaneurysms detection in color fundus images using machine learning based on directional local contrast. BioMed. Eng. Online (2020)

Designing a System to Detect Psychological Stability Status Using AI-Driven Analysis

Dharna Shravani[1], J. Ashok Kumar[2]([⊠]), N. Parimala[3], Kudupudi Suchitha[1], and P. Repudi Nehemiah[1]

[1] Department of Electronics and Communication Engineering, Marri Laxman Reddy Institute of Technology and Management, Dundigal, Hyderabad, India
[2] B V Raju Institute of Technology, Narsapur, Medak, India
`ashokkumar.j@bvrit.ac.in`
[3] National Institute of Technology, Silchar, Assam, India

Abstract. Psychological stability is crucial for well-being and cognitive function. With rising mental health concerns, automated systems are needed to assess stability effectively. This study presents an AI-driven framework analyzing behavioral and physiological factors using machine learning. The system processes data like speech patterns, facial expressions, and biometric indicators to detect distress. By integrating feature extraction and classification models, it enhances assessment accuracy. Applications include workplace stress monitoring and healthcare diagnostics, supporting mental health professionals through AI-driven analysis.

Keywords: Support Vector Machine (SVM) · Logistic Regression Model · Decision Tree Classifier · K-Nearest Neighbor (KNN)

1 Introduction

Mental health is an essential part of the quality of life, which affects cognitive, emotional and practical functions and daily activities. Anxiety, depression and stress are increasing, and they have become a major global health problem. Traditional assessments of mental health are often based on clinical evaluation, which is expensive, time-taking, and is not always easily accessible. Thanks to the rapid development of AI and ML, it is now possible to use automatic systems for psychological stability evaluation based on behavior and physical parameters.

This research proposes an framework developed with the help of artificial intelligence to help in the evaluation of mental health stability based on different data sources such as speech patterns, facial expressions and biometric signals. The system uses SVM, KNN, Logistic Regression, and Decision Trees are machine learning techniques that predict mental health states accurately.

R. K. Karsh et al. (Eds.): SIPCOV 2025, CCIS 2848, pp. 217–227, 2026.
https://doi.org/10.1007/978-3-032-15809-3_17

Furthermore, for the purpose of detection of abnormalities related to stress, anxiety and emotional imbalance, feature extraction techniques and classification models are integrated.

By using AI-based techniques, the system aims to increase the accuracy and effectiveness of psychological assessment, while providing real-time monitoring functions. The proposed system has the opportunity to use in the workplace's stress evaluation diagnosis of health services and individual mental welfare assessment. This study advances the creation of AI-powered mental health monitoring devices, supports early detection and better decision-making for health professionals.

Mental fitness is generally properly an essential component, which now not only affects cognitive and emotional function, but also has physical shape and mutual conditions. Increasing incidence of intellectual health problems, such as anxiety, sadness and stress, inform the importance of early identity and intervention. Traditionally, mental fitness examination depends on clinical reviews, which can be time -consuming, subjective and often inaccessible. However, progress in (ml) to learn synthetic intelligence (AI) and machine (ml) has paved the method of further green, computerized systems that analyze behavior and physical indicators to assess mental stability. It studies the goals to lay out an AI-driven structure, including to hit the psychological balance through the benefit of data from different assets, including voice styles, facial expressions and biometric signs. By incorporating unit learning algorithms and tracing real time, the proposed machine to increase mental health assessment, enable time intervention and help individuals to be correct in different environments, provides a promising in connection with offices and health environment answers.

By integrating AI into mental health assessments, this approach aims to improve accessibility, enable timely intervention, and promote well-being. These improvements could be carried out in regions like place of business wellness, healthcare diagnostics, and personalized mental health care. Over the past few decades, there has been tremendous progress in the use of superior imaging techniques, along with magnetic resonance imaging (MRI) and positron emission tomography (PET), neurological to look at brain structure and feature in both healthy individuals and struggling people and psychiatric issues.

These techniques have enabled the identification of ability biomarkers, which provide valuable insight into conditions consisting of Alzheimer's disease, melancholy, schizophrenia and tension issues, that may help with early analysis and greater effective treatment scheme

2 Literature Review

[1] developed a framework aimed at classifying online communities focused on mental health, particularly depression. They evaluated the performance of different learning approaches, including single-task learning, multiple-task learning, and their proposed method. The study also involved extracting and analyzing features from 12 mental health-related categories, ultimately providing insights into more efficient detection of depression- related discussions in online spaces [2]. Conducted an extensive study on the detection of mental disorders through social network mining, utilizing real-world

datasets. In order to evaluate the accuracy of their Social Network Mental Disorder Detection (SNMDD) system, 3,126 users participated in a user analysis. They also conducted a feature analysis to improve the detection procedure and used SNMDD on sizable datasets, classifying and examining the different kinds of mental illnesses identified by online social media [3] propose a method for detecting bipolar disorder using a Decision Tree Classifier. The dataset is input into the classifier, which identifies the most significant features within the data and uses these to make decisions at various levels of the tree. The At each node, testing samples are contrasted with the decision variables, and based on this analysis, each test case is assigned to the corresponding class. The experimental results show an accuracy of 79.07%, indicating the potential of the approach for diagnosing mental health disorders, particularly bipolar disorder, through machine learning techniques.

[4] conducted a study on detecting mental disorders through social networking sites by analyzing various datasets. They categorized the features into two types: 1) Online Social Networks (OSN) features, and 2) personal feature detection. The research utilized a Random Forest model to classify the mental states of social media users, specifically identifying those under stress through the Mental Disorder Detection (MDD) process. The study achieved notable performance metrics, with precision at 74.1%, recall at 74.8%, F- Measure at 74.5%, and accuracy at 80.1%, indicating the model's effectiveness in detecting stress-related mental health conditions [5]. suggested a thorough framework based on machine learning for identifying mental stress on several levels. Finding a non-invasive and efficient way to use EEG data to identify and categorize stress was the main goal of this study. The framework involved the use of an experimental setup that could induce stress in participants at varying levels, simulating real-world stress scenarios that individuals may encounter. The incorporation of sophisticated machine learning algorithms, which were applied to the EEG data gathered during the stress induction procedure, was the main characteristic of their methodology.

This allowed the framework to extract meaningful patterns and features associated with different stress levels. By leveraging these features, the system was able to categorize stress into distinct levels, ranging from mild to severe stress, with high accuracy [6]. this article focus on the consideration of the approach of the anxiety by means of the artificial intelligence in the various professional fields, education institutes and the non-profitable community groups by replacing the sources of alternative by the AI based deploying solution which helps the people to have less fear and the less risk of the direct peer to peer contact makes them to practice little more confident to get out of the intense of the disease. It even helps people to stick with society without hesitation.

[7] This one describes and analysis the grading, assessments, Mandatory work that must be handled by the junior college students and managing their mental health without the stress and health by prioritizing their workload progress to equally shared using the Emotion detection CNN model. Which helps in finding the brief knowledge on the analysis, finding as well as the decision making. [8] this manuscript gives the brief review of the psychological evolution and classification of the disorder in the modern era. Also, the mental Diagnosis of the patients using the Artificial intelligence oriented predictive analysis. Dc, [9] this makes the prediction of the disease or the disorder of the psychological related to both of the genders based on the analysis of the cause and the

effects. The accuracy of the finding is done by use of the machine learning algorithms like SVM, decision tree, random forest etc., and for the dataset with the size of the 1258*29 the resultant accuracy is just 79% only so the conclusion of the acceptable rate is bit less only. [10] Express the effective finding of the human disability related to the mind with the advances AI related techniques which obviously results the good findings but faces overfitting problem, privacy of the patients is also could not be secured one. The severity of the disorder rate finding is still challenging and not exact. The behavioral of in-person interaction means of the analysis makes a clear one because of the nonverbal form of the communication or the characteristics can be observed. Artificial wisdom is suggested for the future work.

3   Methodology and Implementation

This research project's goal is to create a system that uses AI-driven analysis of several data inputs to identify psychological stability. The system evaluates a person's mental health by combining behavioral, cognitive, and physiological data. The system is designed to categorize psychological stability levels using data that is gathered in real time from various sources. The technology provides an effective way to monitor mental health by analyzing this data and predicting psychological states through the use of machine learning algorithms. The Fig. 1 shows the steps.

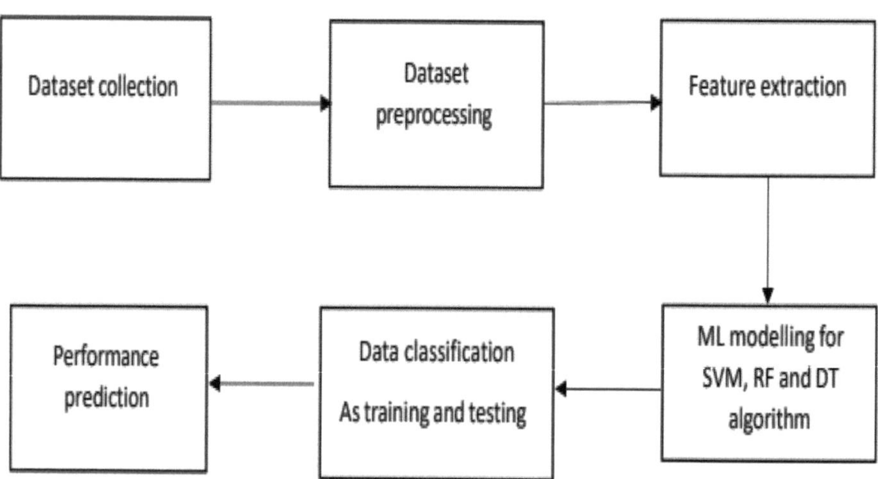

Fig. 1. End to End Framework for Proposed Model

3.1 Dataset Collection

Data sets are obtained from a variety of sources such as portable equipment, online social media platforms and cognitive assessment. This comprises information about mental health markers like anxiety, stress, and cognitive stability. This data includes physical agents such as heart rate and blood pressure, behavioral patterns and other matrix necessary to detect psychological conditions.

3.2 Dataset Preprocessing

3.2.1 Formatting

In this phase, raw data is converted into a standardized format. The classified variables are coded, numerical data is normalized and time - dependent data is properly structured to maintain the stability of the dataset for further analysis.

3.2.2 Cleaning

Data cleaning entails fixing dataset mistakes, eliminating duplicates, and addressing missing values. Outliers are addressed and superfluous or irrelevant data points are eliminated in order to enhance data quality and guarantee the precision of machine learning models.

3.2.3 Sampling

The dataset is separated into training, testing, and verification after cleaning.

Sampling techniques such as random sampling or K-Thuna Cross validation are used to ensure that the dataset adequately represents different psychological conditions, and helps more accurate models in training and evaluation.

3.3 Feature Extraction

In this stage, important properties are selected from the dataset. Methods such as correlation analysis are used to identify the most impressive properties to predict mental health conditions.

These features are intended to give a clear understanding of their conditions and patterns.

3.4 Evaluation Model

Based on the chosen properties, the psychological stability condition is categorized using the random forest method. The performance of the model is evaluated using accuracy, accurate, recall and another matrix. A classification report arises to summarize the results, while the confusion matrix represents visually predictions, helps identify areas for further improvement of the model.

3.5 Testing Methods

Testing for functionality Functional tests offer methodical proof that the functions under investigation are accessible in accordance with the technical and business requirements, machine documentation, and customer guides. The following devices are the focus of functional testing: Functions: The functions that have been identified should be used. Output: The program outputs identified instructions must be practiced. Procedures and Systems: the system must function well.

Testing for Integration Software integration testing is the process of gradually integrating or testing more integrated software components on a single platform to create errors due to interface flaws.

3.6 Test Case for Excel Sheet Verification

Here in machine mastering we're dealing with dataset that is in excel sheet format so if any test case we need method we want to check excel document. Later on, class will paintings on the respective columns of dataset (Table 1).

Table 1 Comparison of accuracy with different algorithms

ALGORITHM	ACCURACY
Random Forest	81.22
DNN	80.42
Logistic Regression	79.37

The system is implemented using a python, and utilized essential libraries such as pandas, pnneumps and Skikit- Learns for data processing, with Tensorflow for system implementation. To identify mental diseases, a dataset was used to test three machine learning algorithms: Random Forest, Deep Neural Network (DNN), and Logistic Region. In models, random forest algorithms emerged as top artists, which demonstrated better accuracy in identifying mental health disorders than other algorithms.

Both random forests and DNN showed high accuracy in detecting mental disorders and the benefit of their ability to capture complex conditions in data. However, while DNN -is a strong ability to learn deep function, random forest model provided a more efficient and reliable solution with fast training time and overfitting risk. On the other hand, the logistical regression algorithm fought, while the faster and simple, struggled to capture more complex patterns in the dataset and dataset. Overall, the results suggest that the random forest algorithm is the most effective model for detecting mental disorders.

4 Experimental Results and Discussion

AI to perform the project on the detection of psychological stability when using driven analysis, the procedure begins to install the necessary software tools, such as Python and essential libraries such as Scikit-Larn, Tensorflow and Keras. These devices are important for developing and implementing machine learning models. After establishing the development environment, including ideas such as PyCharm or Jupiter Notes, the next step involves collectively and prepares the dataset. This involves cleaning data, handling lack of values, normalizing functions and coding of the area for cracked variables to structure the dataset properly for model inputs. Machine learning models, including Random Forest, Deep Neural Network (DNN), and Logistic Region, are trained on datasets that are clear. These models will assist in categorizing people according to their behavioral information. Calculations such as accuracy, recall, and F1 score are used to assess performance after training, and they guarantee that models can function normally on unknown input.

When trained and evaluated, the model is processed to improve performance through hypermeters adaptation or functional choice (Figs. 2, 3, 4, and 5).

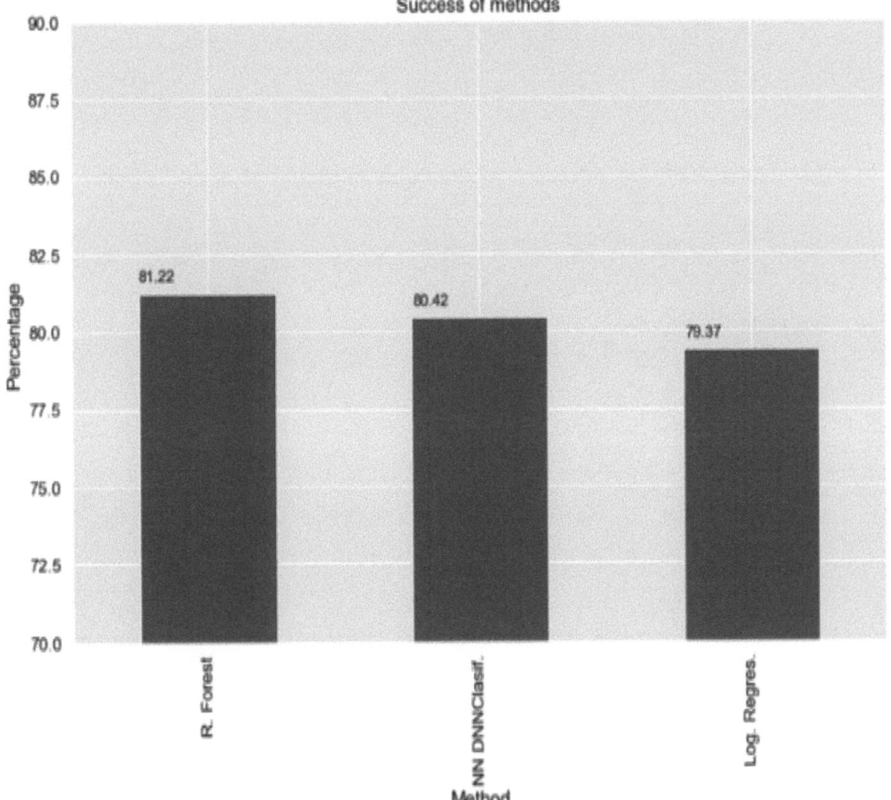

Fig. 2 Represents accuracies of different algorithms

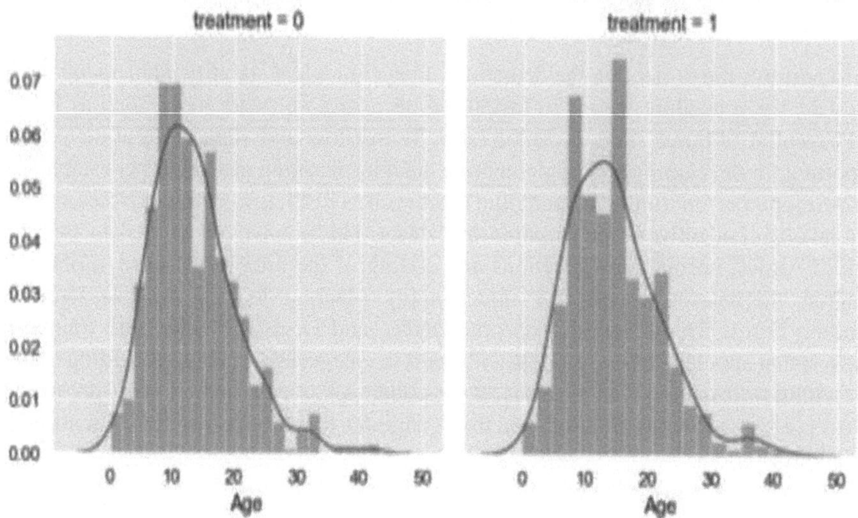

Fig. 3 Graph Indicates How many people took treatment

	Age	Gender	Country	self_employed	family_history	treatment	work_interfere	no_employees	remote_work	tech_company	...	anonymity	leave	men
0	37	Female	United States	NaN	No	Yes	Often	6-25	No	Yes	...	Yes	Somewhat easy	
1	44	M	United States	NaN	No	No	Rarely	More than 1000	No	No	...	Don't know	Don't know	
2	32	Male	Canada	NaN	No	No	Rarely	6-25	No	Yes	...	Don't know	Somewhat difficult	
3	31	Male	United Kingdom	NaN	Yes	Yes	Often	26-100	No	Yes	...	No	Somewhat difficult	
4	31	Male	United States	NaN	No	No	Never	100-500	Yes	Yes	...	Don't know	Don't know	

5 rows × 24 columns

Fig. 4 Dealing with missing Data in Data set

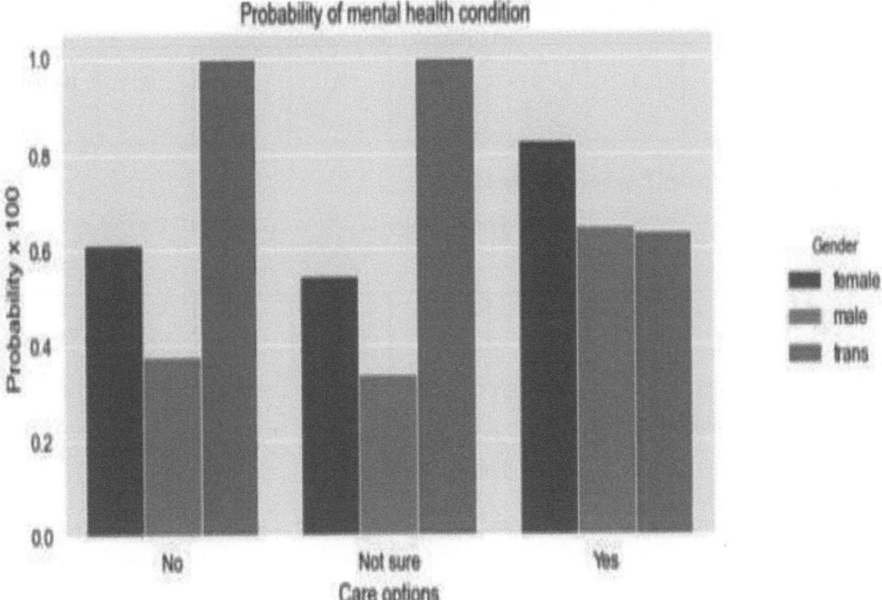

Fig. 5 Bar plot indicates probability of mental health condition of people whether satisfied with benefits

The final system produces the psychological status of individuals, and produces a detailed classification report with assessment matrix to assess the efficiency of the model. This helps to develop a strong system to detect mental health by using a complete AI-based analysis of the workflow.

Psychologically stable individuals are generally characterized by emotional balance, flexibility for stress and persistent behavioral patterns. They can be beneficial for challenging situations without significant crisis and maintain mental welfare over time. In contrast, psychologically unstable individuals can continuously mood, increase emotional reactions or experience difficulty fighting stress, which can affect their ability to work effectively in daily life. Mental stability is crucial to general welfare, and instability can be a sign of underlying mental health conditions that may require attention and care (Figs. 6 and 7).

The system processes the input values and displays a result indicating psychological stability. In this case, it shows the message: "Congratulations! Your Psychological Stable." This means the model analyzed the given data and classified the user as stable. The prediction is likely based on a machine learning algorithm or a set of predefined rules. The accuracy of the result depends on how well the model is designed and the relevance of the input data.

Detecting Psychological Stability Status

33	1	1	0	0	0	0	0	Predict

Congratulations You are Psychological stable

Fig. 6 output1

22	0	1	1	1	2	2	1	Predict

Identified Psychological unstable

Fig. 7 output2

5 Conclusion

In conclusion, this project successfully demonstrates the effectiveness of machine learning algorithms in detecting psychological stability across diverse demographics. Through the analysis of behavioral and physiological indicators, the system provides an objective method for early mental health assessment. The Random Forest algorithm emerged as the most effective, achieving an accuracy of 81%, followed closely by DNN at 80% and Logistic Regression at 79%.

These results emphasize the potential of AI-driven analysis in mental health detection while also highlighting the need for further refinement. Future enhancements will focus on expanding the dataset to improve generalization, incorporating real-time monitoring for dynamic assessments, and integrating explainable AI techniques to ensure model transparency. Additionally, hybrid models that combine multiple algorithms may offer a more robust and precise approach, paving the way for more reliable and accessible mental health assessment tools.

Moreover, this project highlights the growing role of AI in mental health assessment, offering a data- driven approach to detecting psychological stability. By utilizing machine learning models, the system provides objective analysis, reducing reliance on traditional self-reported assessments. To guarantee dependability and equity, however, issues like data privacy, model bias, and the requirement for various datasets must be resolved.

Future improvements will focus on refining feature selection, integrating additional behavioral and physiological indicators, and enhancing real-time adaptability. This AI-powered method could develop into a useful tool for mental health practitioners with additional improvements, allowing for better support for mental health, individualized interventions, and early diagnosis.

Future Scope of Study: Building upon the successful implementation of the system designed to detect psychological stability status using AI-driven analysis, several future research and development directions can be explored to further enhance its effectiveness and applicability. One potential direction is the integration of multi-modal data, such as voice, facial expressions, and physiological signals like heart rate and skin conductivity, and increase the accuracy of the system while offering a more thorough insight of mental health condition. Adding a larger, more varied sample of people to the dataset can improve the system's ability to generalize across different demographic groupings, while real-world application in clinical settings can provide valuable insights into its practical utility.

In the future, we aim to enhance this work by incorporating advanced deep learning models, such as Neural Networks or Convolutional Neural Networks (CNNs). By leveraging images and live camera feeds, we seek to improve the detection of a person's mental health status. This approach will allow for more dynamic and real-time analysis, potentially offering a more comprehensive assessment of psychological conditions based on visual cues and behavioral patterns. We hope that this expansion will improve the system's accuracy and suitability for real-world situations.

References

1. Jadhav, R., Chellwani, V., Deshmukh, S., Sachdev, H.: Mental disorder detection: bipolar disorder scrutinization using machine learning. IEEE J. (2019)
2. Azar, G., Gloster, C., ElBathy, N., Yu, S., Neela, R., Alothman, I.: Intelligent data mining and machine learning for mental health diagnosis using genetic algorithm. IEEE Trans. Eng. Med. Biol., 201–206 (2015). https://doi.org/10.1109/EIT.2015.7293425
3. Saha, B., Nguyen, T., Phung, D., Venkatesh, S.: A framework for classifying online mental health-related communities with an interest in depression. IEEE J. Biomed. Health Inform. **20**(4), 1008–1015 (2016)
4. Simms, T., Ramstedt, C., Rich, M., Richards, M., Martinez, T., Giraud-Carrier, C.: Detecting cognitive distortions through machine learning text analytics. In: IEEE International Conference on Healthcare Informatics (ICHI), pp. 508–512 (2017)
5. Subhani, A., Mumtaz, W., Saad, M.N., Kamel, N., Malik, A.: Machine learning framework for the detection of mental stress at multiple levels. IEEE Access, 1 (2017). https://doi.org/10.1109/ACCESS.2017.2723622
6. Kim, J.H., et al.: AI anxiety: a comprehensive analysis of psychological factors and interventions. AI Ethics, 1–17 (2025)
7. Thakkar, R., et al.: Deep learning integration and ai-driven support: a comprehensive student platform for emotion detection, psychological assessment, and career guidance. In: 2024 3rd International Conference for Innovation in Technology (INOCON). IEEE (2024)
8. Katiyar, K.: AI-based predictive analytics for patients' psychological disorder. In: Predictive Analytics of Psychological Disorders in Healthcare: Data Analytics on Psychological Disorders, pp. 37–53. Springer, Singapore (2022)
9. Dc, S., Fatima, N., Waheed, M.A.: Machine learning based revealing psychology destabilization. In: 2022 International Conference on Emerging Trends in Engineering and Medical Sciences (ICETEMS). IEEE (2022)
10. Andrew, J., et al.: Artificial intelligence in adolescents mental health disorder diagnosis, prognosis, and treatment. Front. Public Health. **11**, 1110088 (2023)

Design and Implementation of Cardiac Arrest Detection

J. Ashok Kumar[✉], J. Pranay Raj, and K. Sai Sampath

Department of Electronics and Communication Engineering, B V Raju Institute of Technology
Narsapur, Medak, India
`{ashokkumar.j,22211a0486,22211a04B4}@bvrit.ac.in`

Abstract. Cardiac arrest continues to be a major cause of sudden death across the globe, and thus there is a need for designing efficient, real-time detection methods to improve patient outcomes. Based on the analysis of physiological signals, primarily data and vital parameters like blood pressure, heart rate, and others, the current study outlines the design and implementation of a machine learning-based system for the early diagnosis of cardiac arrest episodes. In order to extract clinically significant characteristics including heart rate variability (HRV), QRS complex shape, and statistical descriptors in both the time and frequency domains, the proposed system employs advanced preprocessing techniques, including signal denoising and normalization. Publicly accessible and anonymised clinical information were used to train and evaluate a variety of supervised learning algorithms. With the use of cross-validation and criteria the models' performance was extensively examined. The system is intended to be integrated with bed or wearable monitoring devices to provide real-time alerting and continuous, non-invasive surveillance to medical staff. The results highlight the capabilities of machine learning in complementing conventional monitoring systems and advance the development of intelligent, data-driven strategies in critical care. Clinical validation, model personalization, and minimization of computational overhead will be pursued in future work for deployment in resource-limited settings.

Keywords: Cardiac Arrest · Machine learning · Supervised learning algorithms · (HRV) Heart Rate Variability · Real-time Detection

1   Introduction

Machine learning has evolved as a revolutionary subfield of artificial intelligence, which is known to capture complex, non-linear relationships among large datasets. Its impact across domains like computer vision, natural language processing, and financial analytics has been profound, with significant advancements observed in predictive modelling tasks. In the domain of financial services, particularly in Cardiac Arrest prediction, traditional evaluation methods based on manual underwriting and rule-based systems are increasingly inadequate. These conventional methods are not only labour intensive but also prone to human inconsistencies and biases, which can cause potential health inefficiencies and risks.

R. K. Karsh et al. (Eds.): SIPCOV 2025, CCIS 2848, pp. 228–234, 2026.
https://doi.org/10.1007/978-3-032-15809-3_18

To address these challenges, machine learning models offer a data-driven alternative capable of automatically learning hierarchical feature representations from applicant data. The Cardiac Arrest prediction pipeline begins with the acquisition and preprocessing of applicant information, which includes standardizing input features, managing values, attributes and normalizing numerical features to improve model convergence and performance. After preprocessing, the data is systematically categorized into eligible and non-eligible classes, enabling supervised learning models to discern intricate patterns and decision boundaries.

Furthermore, model optimization plays a critical role in Machine learning performance. Optimization are employed to minimize loss functions and accelerate convergence during training. Each optimizer offers unique advantages in terms of learning rate adaptation, computational efficiency, and generalization capabilities, impacting the final model's predictive performance.

In this research, the performance of different models on various optimizers on a real-world medical dataset is systematically tested and compared. The models are rated based on accuracy and to provide a balanced view of model performance. By doing a deep comparative analysis, this study seeks to discover the most appropriate Machine learning framework for automated, scalable, and precise Cardiac Arrest prediction, and in doing so, facilitate more efficient cardiac risk estimation and decision-making in medical facilities.

2 Literature Survey

This section reviews prominent studies in the domain of Cardiac arrest prediction, emphasizing various machine learning (ML) techniques aimed at enhancing prediction accuracy and efficiency in medical decision-making.

Santhana Krishnan [1] proposed machine learning algorithms Gaussian Naive Bayes, Decision Tree. Their voting classifier, enhanced for data balancing, achieved an accuracy of 87.26%, 91% outperforming individual models.

Marimuthu [2] evaluated the efficacy of Decision Trees, Support Vector Machine (SVM), and KNN algorithms for Cardiac Arrest prediction. The Naive Bayes classifier demonstrated superior performance with 83.60% accuracy, demonstrating the effectiveness of learning techniques to medical prediction problems.

Ramprakash P, Sarumathi R [3] employed an ML algorithm to forecast and categorize diseases of an individual suffering from heart ailments. They utilized a dataset from Kaggle, containing 13 attributes they used algorithms like KNN wherein the Random Forest classifier provided highest accuracy of 92%.

Venkateswar B, Gupta A. [4] employed machine learning algorithms to develop a cardiovascular disease system and gave an idea of using wearables like watch and other types of devices with an app installed so that it gets easier to track and monitor each activity.

Devi R, Tyagi HK [5] implemented heart rate variability analysis at early stages using Artificial Intelligence using Supervised learning algorithm and Reinforcement algorithm The data is collected from a hospital and attained a sensitivity of 90% and specificity of 93%.

The Random Forest, Decision Tree, and Logistic Regression models were integrated by T Maneesha [6] to predict the likelihood of a heart attack.

Avinash Goland [7] tackled the issue of Cardiac arrest prediction by employing Ada Boost. Their model has an accuracy of 94.1%, surpassing traditional approaches and providing an effective tool for early cardiac arrest detection.

3 Methodology

This section deals with data acquisition, feature extraction, ml search algorithm and prediction as shown in Fig. 1.

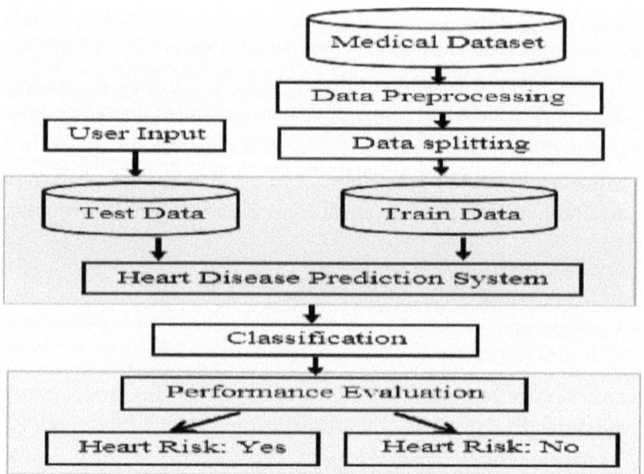

Fig. 1. Training Stage and Prediction

3.1 Model Architecture and Training

In this study, different learning architectures—Random Forest, Ada boost, Gradient boosting, Logistic regression, SVC, Decision tree, Gaussian NB, KNN—were developed to predict cardiac arrest based on tabular data features. Each model was designed with varying architectures and training parameters to evaluate their effectiveness under different strategies. The cardiac arrest detection model uses a supervised machine learning pipeline to analyze real-time physiological signals like ECG, heart rate, and blood pressure. Raw signals are first preprocessed through filtering, denoising, and normalization. Clinically important features such as heart rate variability (HRV)

These features are fed into machine learning models, with **Random Forest Algorithm** selected as the best performer due to its high accuracy and ability to handle imbalanced data. The model was trained on data dataset cases. Hyperparameters were fine-tuned to optimize performance.

The final model delivers binary predictions (cardiac arrest likely/unlikely) along with confidence scores and risk levels. It is optimized for real-time deployment, with prediction latency under 500 milliseconds, making it suitable for integration into ICU monitors and wearable health devices.

4 Experimental Results

4.1 Experimental Setup and Evaluation

This section presents a comprehensive evaluation of machine learning models on predicting cardiac arrest. Models were evaluated on various classification performance metrics including precision, recall, F1-score, support. Test accuracy comparison is graphically represented in above figure

1. Accuracy:

Accuracy estimates the proportion of accurately predicted instances to the total predictions

$$\text{Accuracy} = \frac{TP + TN}{TP + TN + FP + FN}$$

2. Precision:

Precision estimates how accurate positive predictions are. Precision is the proportion of accurate positive predictions made to the total positive predictions made

$$\text{Precision} = \frac{TP}{TP + FP}$$

3. Recall:

Recall estimates the model's capacity to predict all instances that are of interest. Recall is the proportion of correct positives predicted to all actual positive instances

$$\text{Recall} = \frac{TP}{TP + FN}$$

4. F1-Score:

The F1-score is the harmonic mean of precision and recall. It provides one measure that includes both concerns, especially helpful when the distribution of classes is imbalanced

$$\text{F1-Score} = 2 \cdot \frac{\text{Precision} \cdot \text{Recall}}{\text{Precision} + \text{Recall}}$$

4.2 Results and Comparative Analysis

The proposed machine learning-based cardiac arrest detection system demonstrated promising performance in accurately identifying early signs of cardiac arrest using physiological signals. The system was evaluated on a publicly available, anonymized clinical dataset that included ECG signals, heart rate, blood pressure, and oxygen saturation from ICU patients. A variety of supervised learning algorithms were tested, including Random Forest, Support Vector Machine (SVM), K-Nearest Neighbors (KNN), and Gradient Boosting etc. (Table 1)

Table 1. Comparative evaluation of the proposed models

Out[53]:

	Model	Accuracy	F1-Score	Precision	Recall
0	RandomForestClassifier	0.975678	0.975679	0.97627	0.975678
1	AdaBoostClassifier	0.660181	0.660219	0.660365	0.660181
2	GradientBoostingClassifier	0.719944	0.719697	0.722045	0.719944
3	LogisticRegression	0.659486	0.659522	0.659813	0.659486
4	SVC	0.703266	0.703221	0.704211	0.703266
5	KNeighborsClassifier	0.787352	0.784212	0.809928	0.787352
6	DecisionTreeClassifier	0.911049	0.910571	0.923464	0.911049
7	GaussianNB	0.580959	0.52849	0.630654	0.580959

4.3 Visual Outputs of the Cardiac Arrest Detection

The visual cardiac arrest detection form is a comprehensive, real-time interface designed to assist healthcare professionals in monitoring and identifying early warning signs of cardiac arrest. The form begins with a section dedicated to patient identification, including fields for name, age, gender, and medical history to provide context for personalized monitoring. It then displays live physiological parameters such as heart rate, blood pressure, oxygen saturation, respiratory rate, and ECG waveforms, each with visual indicators (e.g., color-coded alerts) that instantly reflect abnormal values. A dedicated feature extraction panel processes these signals to display clinically significant metrics like heart rate variability (HRV).

Current Smoker:
Yes

Cigarettes Per Day:
1

BP Medications:
Yes

Prevalent Stroke:
No

Prevalent Hypertension:
No

Diabetes:
No

Total Cholesterol:
50

Systolic BP:
100

Diastolic BP:
40

BMI:
10

Heart Rate:
85

Glucose Level:
90

Predict

Prediction Result

Based on the provided information, the prediction for Cardiac Arrest: **The user has no chance of getting cardiac arrest**

5 Conclusion

This paper is a detailed comparison of different learning algorithms for the prediction cardiac arrest. All model-optimizer combinations were extensively tested on a range of performance measures on the widely available training and test datasets.

The experimental findings reveal that Random Forest significantly outperform other algorithms, achieving higher predictive accuracy and robustness across all optimizers.

This project demonstrates how machine learning can be utilized to forecast the risk of cardiac arrest, potentially saving the lives by enabling timely medical interventions. Various models have been implemented and compared to determine which performs best in predicting cardiac arrest based on user health data.

The suggested machine learning model is critical in early diagnosis of cardiac arrest. The models can be used to develop user-specific or patient-specific interventions for more effective treatment it can also be employed to warn medical staff in a manner that enable earlier and most advantageous interventions.

Overall, the findings confirm that the choice of optimizer 67significantly impacts model performance are optimal for reliable cardiac arrest prediction. Subsequent work may investigate ensemble methodologies or real-time deployment scenarios, as well as incorporating explainability frameworks to enhance trust and transparency in automated medical decision systems.

References

1. Ansari, U., Soni, J., Sharma, D., Soni, S.: Predictive data mining for medical diagnosis: an overview of heart attack prediction. 258493784 Predictive Data Mining for Medical Diagnosis. Data Mining in Healthcare for Heart Diseases, March (2021)

2. Beyene, C., Kamat, P.: Survey on prediction and analysis the occurrence of heart disease using data mining techniques. **118**(8), 165–173 (2020). https://www.researchgate.net/ publication survey on prediction and analysis the occurrence of heart disease using data mining techniques
3. Komal Kumar, N., Sarika Sindhu, G., Krishna Prashanthi, D., Shaeen Sulthana, A.: Analysis and prediction of cardio vascular disease using machine classifiers, April (2020). https://www.researchgate.net/ publication 1340885231 analysis and prediction of cardio vascular disease using machine learning classifiers
4. Gavhane, A., Kokkula, G., Pandya, I., Devadkar, K.: Prediction of heart attack using machine learning (2023)
5. Mohan, S., Thirumalai, C., Srivastava, G.: Effective heart disease prediction using hybrid learning techniques (2019)
6. Salma Banu, N.K., Swamy, S.: Prediction of heart disease at early stage using data mining and big data analytics: a survey (2019)
7. Santhana Krishnan, J., Geetha, S.: Prediction of heart disease using machine learning algorithms (2022)
8. Gupta, K., Jiwani, N., Pau, G., Alibakhshikenari, M.: A machine learning approach using statistical models for early detection of cardiac arrest in newborn babies in the cardiac intensive care unit. IEEE Access. **11**, 60516–60538 (2023)
9. Chae, M.; Han, S.; Gil, H.; Cho, N.; Lee, H.: Prediction of in-hospital cardiac arrest using shallow and deep learning diagnostics (2021)
10. Babu, M.S., Karthick, V.: Improving accuracy in intelligent coronary heart disease diagnosis prediction model using support vector clustering technique compared over random forest classifier algorithm. In: 2022 International Conference on Innovative Computing Intelligent Communication and Smart Electrical Systems (ICSES) (2022)

Investigations and Analysis of Textile Electrocardiogram Electrodes for Wearable Health Monitoring System

S. Palanivel Rajan[✉], A. Hariharan[✉], I. Shaun Paul, and N. Sivakumar

Velammal College of Engineering and Technology, Madurai, India
drspalanivelrajan@gmail.com, hariharanar4@gmail.com

Abstract. Electrocardiogram (ECG) monitoring is a critical component of cardiac health assessment, traditionally relying on adhesive gel electrodes. However, these conventional electrodes pose challenges such as skin irritation, discomfort during prolonged use, and single-use disposability. This paper explores textile-based ECG electrodes as a viable alternative, integrating conductive materials like silver-coated threads into fabric to enable seamless, wearable health monitoring. Textile electrodes offer improved comfort, reusability, and non-intrusive integration into daily life. We discuss their electrical properties, signal acquisition mechanisms, and performance in comparison to traditional electrodes. Experimental results indicate that textile electrodes provide reliable ECG signal.

Keywords: Bio Medical Electrodes · Electrocardiography · Medical Detection · Textile Fibers · Non-Invasive Treatment · Wearable Health Monitoring

1 Introduction

The monitoring of Electrocardiogram (ECG) is a cornerstone of cardiac health assessment, it provides vital information about the activity of heart through the measurement of electrical signals generated by the heart [1]. The Traditional way of ECG systems rely on adhesive gel electrodes, which is being effective, but it come with limitations such as skin irritation, discomfort caused during prolonged use, and it is single-use disposability. These drawbacks have driven the exploration of alternative solutions, leading to the development of textile-based ECG electrodes [10]. Textile ECG electrodes are directly integrated with conductive materials into fabrics, allowing for their seamless inclusion in wearable clothing. These electrodes utilize innovations in conductive fibers, like silver-coated threads, which ensure efficient signal transmission while preserving the flexibility and softness of the textiles. These materials are sewed or embedded into non-stretchable or minimally stretchable fabrics, textile ECG electrodes should achieve a balance between mechanical durability and consistent skin contact [2]. In wearable health-monitoring systems, Textile ECG electrodes aim to address three critical requirements.

A) Comfort: Textile electrodes eliminate the discomfort associated with adhesive materials, ensuring a non-intrusive experience suitable for extended wear.
B) Data Quality: Electrodes can reliably capture ECG signals with minimal noise, rival traditional systems by proper designing and material selection.
C) Integration: Unobtrusive, non-stigmatizing monitoring for medical or fitness applications are enabled by embedding within garment.

2 Methodology

Textile ECG electrodes are sophisticated wearable sensors designed to monitor the heart's electrical activity by measuring bioelectric signals on the skin. These electrodes function by detecting the subtle voltage variations produced during the depolarization and repolarization of cardiac muscle cells, delivering crucial information for analyzing heart rate and rhythm. Below is a technical explanation of their working principles, materials, and electrical characteristics. The voltages which is measured in ECG signals are in the range of 0.1 to 5 mV, typically with a peak-to-peak amplitude around 1 mV for standard leads [4]. Textile electrodes should be operated in conjunction with an ECG amplifier which is capable of detecting low-magnitude signals while rejecting the noise and interference. The typical input impedance of these amplifiers is in the range of 10 MΩ or higher, by ensuring that weak signals are accurately captured without attenuation [6]. The electrodes are made from conductive materials like silver-coated threads, which exhibit low resistivity ($\sim$1.59 $\times$ 10^-8 Ω·m for pure silver). This characteristic enables the efficient transfer of bioelectric signals from the skin to the data acquisition system. Thread density and stitching design are two factors that determine the surface resistivity of textile electrodes, which normally falls between 1 and 10 Ω/sq. The preservation of signal integrity is contingent upon the impedance between the skin and the electrode. To reduce impedance, which generally falls between 55 to 450 kΩ at the low frequencies (0.06–155 Hz) used in ECG monitoring, textile electrodes depend on physical contact and applied pressure [5]. Unlike gel electrodes, textile electrodes do not use conductive gel but may incorporate hydrophilic coatings or rely on sweat to improve conductivity and reduce impedance variability [6].

Textile electrodes are simply in a 3-lead or 12-lead configuration, where they are positioned at specific anatomical landmarks [7]. The electrode areas are designed in patterns (e.g., overlapping zig-zag stitches) to maximize skin contact while maintaining flexibility. A typical electrode area may range from 10 cm^2 to 20 cm^2 [14]. The electrodes interface with a data acquisition module (e.g., BIOPAC MP160) which provides, High-resolution analog-to-digital conversion. Gain: Amplifiers provide a gain of 1,000 to 10,000, depending on the ECG system. Bandwidth: Filters operate in the range of 0.05–150 Hz, suppressing noise while retaining the ECG signal. Textile electrodes themselves are passive; the active components of the ECG system (amplifiers, filters, and ADC) are powered by Low-voltage systems: 3.3–5 V DC, commonly supplied by rechargeable batteries in portable setups. Current consumption: Is Typically less than 10 mA for the entire ECG module, depending on design [3]. To ensure the accurate ECG signal acquisition Shielding: Conductive layers or fabrics may be used to reduce electromagnetic interference (EMI). Common Mode Rejection Ratio (CMRR): ECG systems have a high CMRR (>90 dB) to reject noise from power lines and other sources [7].

2.1 Extensial Method of ECG Measuring

Since the outset, adhesive electrodes that are permanently attached to the skin have been the mainstay of electrocardiogram (ECG) monitoring. Three main problems with this approach are that the adhesives may cause skin irritation, the electrodes' conductive gel may dry out and lose its signal quality, and extended use may become uncomfortable. The creation of 'dry' electrodes that are easily integrated into clothing is one possible solution to these issues [4]. By doing away with the requirement for conducting gel, dry electrodes offer a promising way to deal with the problem of gel drying out over time. Adhesive electrodes present challenges because of their short durability; they are not suitable for continuous or long-term applications since they are more costly, single-use, and generate trash. Additionally, when the gel dries, adhesive pads lose their effectiveness in a matter of hours, raising impedance and lowering signal quality [7].

Revolutionary textile electrodes are emerging as one alternative for the reason that they incorporate conductive materials into fabrics directly. Because they are washable, reusable, these decrease waste, long-term costs, while they offer better comfort with softness. Smart fabrics with conductive fibers integrated ensure stable skin contact even during movement. They do reduce motion artifacts as they improve durability. Biocompatible coatings with moisture-wicking materials may provide a comfortable, sustainable solution for textile electrodes to fix skin irritation. Additionally, hybrid electrode designs are being developed since they combine the advantages of adhesive and textile materials, which optimally balances comfort, durability, and signal reliability for continuous ECG monitoring [2].

2.2 Fabric Implementation of Textile Electrodes

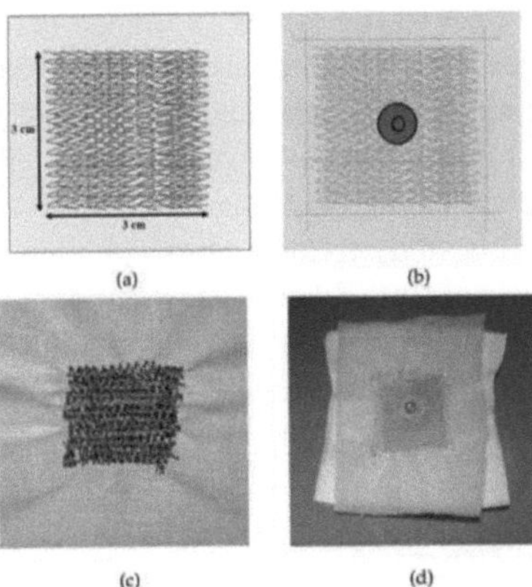

Fig. 1. (a) Stich design of sewn electrode; (b) Snap connector and Fabric protective cover design; (c) Stitched electrode; (d) Complete electrode with protective covering

The implementation of textile electrodes for ECG monitoring combines cutting-edge materials along with revolutionary design approaches in a multi-faceted process to achieve user comfort and accurate signal detection. It begins with the selection of appropriate conductive materials like carbon-based threads or silver-coated fibers, integrated through sewing or weaving into the fabric as shown in Fig. 1. The fabric makes use of these conductive fibers. The heart's bioelectric signals are effectively sent. Designing of the electrode is now the next important stage. Its optimal placement must be determined also. Electrodes may be integrated into the fabric by methods like zig-zag stitching, and this improves the skin contact while it preserves flexibility of the fabric. Signals from the chest are captured effectively using a 3-lead configuration for arrangement. Because of its low elasticity or inextensibility, the fabric is frequently chosen to provide steady electrode contact and preserve signal quality when in motion [8].

2.3   Advantage of Textile Based Electrodes

We aim to publish all proceedings papers in full-text xml. Our xml templates for LaTeX are based on CMR, our xml templates for Word are based on Times. We ask you to use the font according to the template used for your papers. Papers using other fonts will be converted by our typesetters.

Conductive threads and yarns integrated into fabrics through techniques such as knitting, sewing, or weaving provide notable benefits like cost efficiency, simplicity in manufacturing, and flexibility in design. Comparatively, conductive inks and pastes are pricier and require curing time to bond with textiles, a step that conductive threads do not need. Additionally, conductive threads give improved durability [8]. Conductive threads are embedded into fabrics that are both washable, cleanable and capable of enduring mechanical strain, such as bending or stretching, without compromising signal integrity. These qualities make them well-suited for continuous monitoring, as the electrodes maintain functionality even after multiple uses, wash cycles and physical activities. In comparison, conventional gel electrodes are single-use and may lose effectiveness over time due to adhesive wear or the drying of the gel [9]. One significant benefit of conductive thread electrodes is their unobtrusive nature. These electrodes are integrated into regular clothing, making them discreet and free from stigma. This enables users to incorporate ECG monitoring into their everyday routines effortlessly and without any discomfort, in contrast to classical methods that often involve large, addressable devices or adhesive components. This study focuses on developing smart textile electrodes by embedding conductive materials into fabrics using standard manufacturing methods. A sewn electrode is presented, designed for easy integration into fabric materials, with connections to integrated garment wiring, enabling continuous ECG monitoring in daily routine life [6].

2.4   Durability Text of Textile Electrodes

There is no need to include page numbers or running heads; this will be done at our end. If your paper title is too long to serve as a running head, it will be shortened. Your suggestion as to how to shorten it would be most welcome.

The main question of this study is whether the performance of the electrodes will be affected by daily routine use once they are integrated into fabric clothing.

1) Stretch testing
2) Bend testing
3) Wash testing

These tests act as representations of typical daily usage and are used in this study to calculating the electrodes' durability. The results indicate that traditional electrodes exhibited a resistance of 2.0, while textile electrodes demonstrated a significantly lower resistance of 0.3 [4]. The resistance was determined using a standard multi-meter. This measurement is crucial for textile electrodes as it reflects their efficiency in detecting the minute voltages produced by the heart's activity on the skin [9].

2.5 Human Subject Testing

A preliminary power analysis was carried out to determine the sample size needed for statistically meaningful results. To compare traditional and sewn electrodes, the allowable difference between the sensors was defined as an observable effect size of 10% of the average value. Test participants for the study are typically selected based on the research objectives and may include individuals of various genders, ages and health conditions. A diverse test participants group is often chosen to calculate the electrodes performance across different skin conditions, body conditions, and activity levels [16]. Evaluating textile electrodes under conditions involving movement and physical activity is crucial to determine their performance during movement. This process involves examining the three electrodes ability to maintain constant skin contact and reduced motion artifacts, which are frequently observed with classical adhesive electrodes as shown in Fig. 2. Test participants might be instructed to walk, jog, or engage in particular exercises while their Electrocardiography (ECG) data is recorded continuously [8]. The effectiveness of the textile fabric electrodes in maintaining signal integrity during such activities is critical for their application in fitness monitoring.

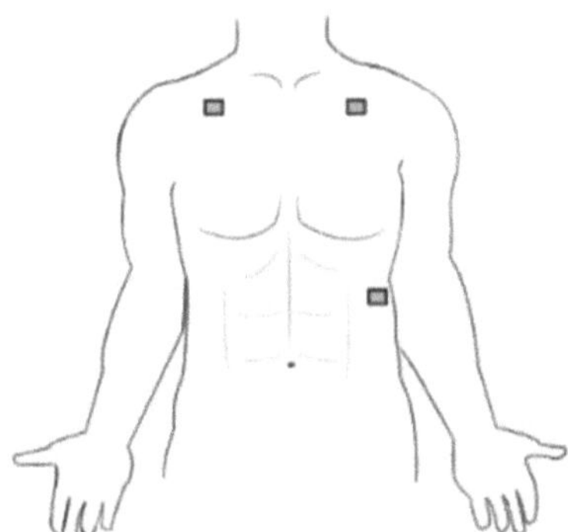

Fig. 2. Three-lead positioning for recording of the Electrocardiogram (ECG) signal.

3   Results and Discussion

The variation in readings between adhesive and textile electrodes largely stems from factors such as electrode design, contact quality, and signal acquisition methods. A significant reason for this difference is the contact impedance at the skin-electrode interface. Adhesive electrodes, which commonly rely on conductive gel, establish a more stable and consistent connection with the skin. The gel minimize impedance and enhances the signal transmission, leading to more accurate and dependable Electrocardiography (ECG) readings. Although textile electrodes are effective, they use conductive threads or fabrics integrated into textile fabric garments. These fabric materials might not offer as consistent or low-resistance contact as conductive gel, which can conclude in differences in signal levels, especially during movement when the electrode stretches. These oscillations are also created by motion artifacts [5]. The other way around, fabric textile electrodes that are embody into textiles might not stick to the skin as well, which creates them more likely to move and shift when exercising [11]. This could influence the precision of heart rate measurements details by introducing noise or distortions into the ECG signal [14]. Environmental conditions also influence performance. While adhesive electrodes, being single-use, deliver consistent results when newly applied, textile electrodes intended for prolonged use are exposed to factors like wear and tear, perspiration, and washing. Over time, these factors can affect the conductive properties of fabric textile electrodes, affect their performance. Moreover, the condition of the skin can affect their efficiency, as textile electrodes often depend on skin moisture for proper contact, unlike adhesive electrodes, which depend on gel to form a more consistent connection with the skin.

Differences in electrode materials are another parameter contributing to the variation. Adhesive electrodes often embody high-conductivity materials such as silver chloride, which are tailored to deliver low noise and make sure precise signal acquisition. In contrast, textile electrodes use conductive threads or fabrics, that may not provide the same level of conductivity and could introduce extra impedance as shown in Table 1, especially if the materials make worse due to washing or friction over time [16].

Table 1. Comparison between Adhesive HR and Textile HR Readings

Subject	Adhesive HR (bpm)	Textile HR (bpm)	Difference (bpm)
1	82	86	+4
2	92	97	+5
3	74	72	−2
4	71	68	−3
5	69	72	+3
6	75	72	−3

3.1 Challenges in Adhesive Electrodes

A prefilled copyright form is usually available from the conference website. Please send your signed copyright form to your conference publication contact, either as a scanned PDF or by fax or by courier. One author may sign on behalf of all of the other authors of a particular paper, providing permission has been given to do so. In this case, the author signs for and accepts responsibility for releasing this material on behalf of any and all co-authors. Digital signatures are not acceptable.

A key parameter influence variations in readings is the contact impedance at the skin-electrode interface. The design of textile electrodes can be improved to enhance skin contact by embody fabric textile materials with higher conductivity. For example, to improve the conductive properties of textile electrodes, silver-coated fibers or conductive polymers can be used, assisting uniform and reliable signal transmission. Furthermore, incorporating soft, flexible electrode pads or thin conductive layers that adapt to the skin's surface can effectively lower contact impedance and enhance signal precision [8]. Textile electrodes often experience motion artifacts as they may not remain firmly attached to the skin during physical activity. To mitigate this, they can be incorporated into snug garments like compression shirts or sports bras, which ensure better stability and placement of the electrodes [11]. Elastic fabrics with optimal stretch and recovery properties can ensure sustained skin contact during movement. Additionally, prop up placement zones or hydrogel layers (similar to those in adhesive electrodes) can be embodied into textile electrodes to improve stability during physical activities. Advanced signal processing techniques [can also be used] to reduce noise and motion artifacts associated with textile electrodes [5]. Motion artifacts and environmental noise can be minimized using algorithms specifically developed to detect and filter them, thereby enhancing the accuracy of the readings. Furthermore, real-time calibration methods can be implemented to address changes in skin-electrode contact, allowing the system to automatically adapt and compensate for slight variations in signal strength or quality during operation [10].

3.2 Overcoming the Challenges

Fabric-based ECG electrodes present inviting benefits, including comfort, flexibility, and wearable. However, there are several challenges that must be resolved to enable their wider use in wearable health-monitoring devices [7]. These challenges can affect the quality of ECG data, durability, and overall practicality of these devices.

One of the primary challenges with fiber-based ECG electrodes is achieving constant and low contact resistance between the electrode and the skin. Gel-based electrodes are known for their skin contact, facilitated by the conductive gel that reduces impedance. In contrast, fabric-based electrodes may face challenges in maintaining comparable contact, particularly during movement or under conditions like sweating [14]. These parameters can lead to higher impedance, signal degradation, and decrease ECG quality, especially during extended use or various activities. Unlike classical adhesive electrodes, fabric-based electrodes are less likely to remain strongly attached to the skin during physical activities, making them more prone to motion artifacts that can adversely impact

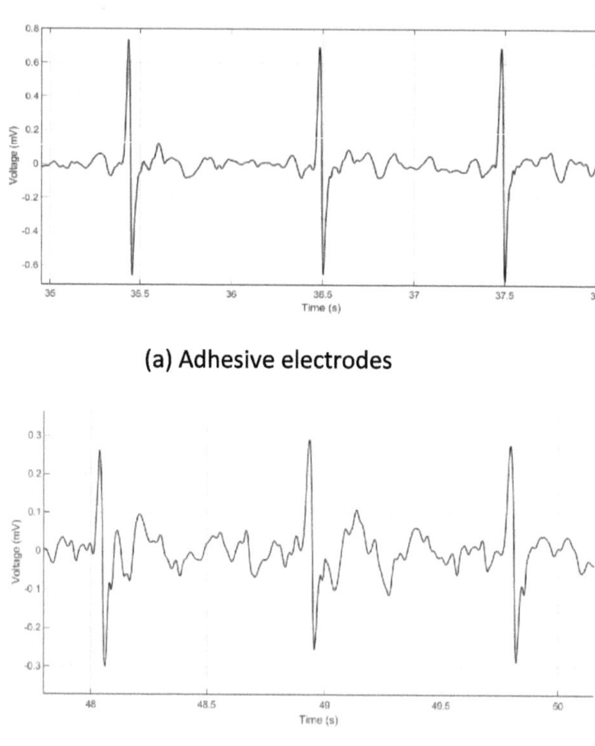

(a) Adhesive electrodes

(b) Sewn Electrodes

Fig. 3. Heart Rate Different in Readings between Adhesive and Sewn Electrodes

ECG measurement accuracy as shown in Fig. 3. Shifting of the electrode during physical movements or daily routines may cause signal interruptions or noise, obstruct the precise monitoring of the heart's electrical activity. Maintaining constant contact with the skin during movement cause a considerable challenge for fabric-based electrodes, involve thoughtful material choice and accurate electrode positioning [7]. The average R-R interval values and their standard deviation are displayed in the given Table 2. The variations between R-R interval values are minimal, just like the HR values. This conclusion is supported for both data sets by the previously indicated statistical tests.

Fabric-based ECG electrodes are combined into textile materials that face wear and tear from regular use, washing, and stretching. Physical stress, repeated washing, and sweat exposure can diminish the fibers' conductivity over time. Although certain fibers are engineered for durability and washable, their conductive properties may not always remain intact after extended use, potentially resulting in signal deterioration or reduced electrode effectiveness [17]. Ensuring long-term reliability and maintaining consistent signal quality over the course of days, weeks, or months is a key challenge.

The conductivity of the fabric used in fabric-based ECG electrodes must be high enough to dependable transmit the electrical signals from the heart to the ECG recording system. However, many conductive fabrics, such as those made from silver-coated

Table 2. R-R interval for Textile and Adhesive electrodes for each subject.

Subject	Adhesive R-R interval (s)	Textile R-R interval (s)
1	0.719 ± 0.05	0.685 ± 0.03
2	0.653 ± 0.03	0.634 ± 0.04
3	0.776 ± 0.06	0.832 ± 0.02
4	0.899 ± 0.09	0.892 ± 0.07
5	0.812 ± 0.07	0.756 ± 0.05
6	0.866 ± 0.05	0.867 ± 0.03
7	0.847 ± 0.08	0.793 ± 0.14
8	1.063 ± 0.02	0.996 ± 0.06

threads or carbon-based materials, may not offer the same level of conductivity as classical metal-based electrodes [3]. Reaching linear conductivity across fabric-based electrodes can be complex, as variations in impedance may arise depending on how the fibers are woven, stitched, or embedded into the fabric. Integration of electrode materials is needed to prevent areas of high resistance or distortion in signal transmission. While fabric-based electrodes are often more comfortable than classical adhesive electrodes, they may still have concerns in maintaining constant skin contact during extended wear. Moreover, some individuals may affect by skin irritation if the fabric lacks breathability or if the electrode materials are not compatible.

Fabric-based electrodes into garments requires careful design to ensure that the electrode placement remains without compromising the comfort of the garment [7]. Moreover, the connection process must ensure that the electrodes do not shift during wear and that they maintain constant contact with the skin throughout the day. Customization for different body shapes and sizes is another challenge that affects the performance of textile-based ECG systems. The garment must fit well while also allowing for easy connection of conductive fibers without adding bulk [16]. Fabric-based ECG electrodes need to be connected to a data acquisition system and power source for continuous monitoring. Energy-efficient electronics into outfit can be difficult due to the constraints of the flexibility required by wearable textiles. The system must reliable data transmission from the electrodes to the processing while also preventing battery efficiency and user comfort. Furthermore, the integration of wireless data transmission systems (such as Bluetooth) must not interfere with the electrode's ability to capture high-quality signals. Though fiber-based ECG electrodes provide cost benefits over time due to their reusability, the initial production expenses for high-grade conductive fabric and textiles can exceed those of standard one-use electrodes. Moreover, the challenge of manufacturing electrodes that integrate high conductivity with comfort gives to higher manufacturing costs [11]. Measuring the production of fabric-based ECG electrodes for market use is challenging due to the need for specialized materials, advanced manufacturing processes, and quality control. Maintaining durability, washable, and constant performance adds complexity.

4 Conclusion

Fabric-based ECG electrodes have the potential to transform wearable health-monitoring by providing enhanced flexibility, and suitability for long-term use, making them ideal for repeated and sustainable health monitoring. Fabric-based ECG electrodes face difficulties in signal accuracy, conductivity, and integration into textiles. Problems like motion artifacts and skin contact variability affect sensor data quality, requiring advanced signal processing. Fabric material degradation from wear or washing impact conductivity, demanding tough solutions, Accurate embedding in fabrics to ensure firm, low-impedance contact for constant performance during often use.

References

1. Jin, J., Jia, W., Yang, X.: Screen-printed fabric electrode for electrocardiogram monitoring on commercial textiles. J. Intell. Mater. Syst. Struct. **34**(2), 123–134 (2023)
2. Brehm, P.J., Allison, P.: Modeling the design characteristics of woven textile electrodes for long-term ECG monitoring. Sensors. **23**(2), 598 (2023)
3. Kang, T.W., et al.: Recent progress in the development of flexible wearable electrodes for electrocardiogram monitoring during exercise. Adv. Nano Biomed Res. **4**(3), 2300169 (2024)
4. Wang, C., et al.: E-textiles in healthcare: a systematic literature review of wearable technologies for monitoring and enhancing human health. Neural Comput. Appl. **37**, 1–23 (2024)
5. Esfahani, M.I.M.: Smart textiles in healthcare: a summary of history, types, applications, challenges, and future trends. In: Nanosensors and Nanodevices for Smart Multifunctional Textiles, pp. 93–107. Elsevier, Amsterdam (2021)
6. Le, K., et al.: Electronic textiles for electrocardiogram monitoring: a review on the structure–property and performance evaluation from fiber to fabric. Text. Res. J. **93**(3–4), 878–910 (2023)
7. An, X., Stylios, G.K.: Comparison of motion artefact reduction methods and the implementation of adaptive motion artefact reduction in wearable electrocardiogram monitoring. Sensors. **20**(5), 1468 (2020)
8. Zhao, J., et al.: 3D E-textile for exercise physiology and clinical maternal health monitoring. arXiv preprint, arXiv:2407.07954, July (2024)
9. Majumder, S., et al.: Noncontact wearable wireless ECG systems for long-term monitoring. IEEE Rev. Biomed. Eng. **11**, 306–321 (2018)
10. Nigusse, A.B., et al.: Wearable smart textiles for long-term electrocardiography monitoring—a review. Sensors. **21**(12), 4174 (2021)
11. Arquilla, K., Webb, A.K., Anderson, A.P.: Textile electrocardiogram (ECG) electrodes for wearable health monitoring. Sensors. **20**(4), 1013 (2020)
12. Zhou, W., et al.: Textile electrodes for electrocardiogram monitoring. Adv. Mater. Technol. **10**(10), 2401279 (2025)
13. Fink, P.L., et al.: Development and wearer trial of ECG-garment with textile-based dry electrodes. Sensors Actuators A Phys. **328**, 112784 (2021)
14. Alizadeh-Meghrazi, M., et al.: Evaluation of dry textile electrodes for long-term electrocardiographic monitoring. Biomed. Eng. Online. **20**(1), 68 (2021)
15. Le, K., Servati, A., Soltanian, S., Servati, P., Ko, F.: Performance and signal quality analysis of electrocardiogram textile electrodes for smart apparel applications. Front. Electron. **2**, 685264 (2021)

16. Jiang, R., Ge, Y., Deng, Y.M.: Textile electrode, monitoring performance, and durability for ECG monitoring garment: a review. AATCC J. Res. **12**(2), 24723444251326674 (2025)
17. Prabakaran, A., Rufus, E.: Design and fabrication of textile-based electrodes for biomedical applications in wearable electronics devices: electrocardiography, electromyography, and tactile sensing. IEEE Access. **13**, 40977–40991 (2025)

Computer Vision and Deep Learning for Visual Perception, Image Understanding, and Scene Analysis

CNN Based Structural Damage Detection by Reducing Sensors Through SHAP Method

Aradhana Vallyath Anil[1(✉)], Moumita Roy[2], and Nirmalendu Debnath[1]

[1] National Institute of Technology Silchar, Silchar, India
aradhanava4848@gmail.com
[2] Indian Institute of Information Technology Guwahati, Guwahati, India

Abstract. Structural Health Monitoring (SHM) is essential for ensuring the safety, durability, and operational efficiency of civil infrastructure. However, modern sensing systems often involve numerous sensors, leading to high-dimensional data that increases computational complexity and hinders interpretability. This study proposes a Shapley Additive Explanations (SHAP)-based feature selection framework to identify the most informative sensors for structural damage classification using a one-dimensional convolutional neural network (1D CNN). The approach is applied to the ASCE benchmark structure dataset, where SHAP is used to select the top 8 sensors out of 12, significantly reducing input dimensionality while improving classification performance. To validate the effectiveness of SHAP, comparative experiments were conducted using Principal Component Analysis (PCA), Mutual Information (MI), and the ANOVA F-test. Results are evaluated through stratified three-fold cross-validation using metrics such as accuracy, F1 score, and AUC. The performance of the 1D CNN in integration with SHAP-based feature selection not only achieves superior classification metrics but also outperforms the model using all 12 sensors as well as those based on other feature selection strategies. Specifically, the SHAP-based 1D-CNN model, using only 8 sensors, achieved an overall accuracy of 98.58%, F1 score of 98.22%, and AUC of 99.89%, outperforming the performance of 1D-CNN considering all 12 sensors.

Keywords: Structural Health Monitoring · Feature Selection · SHAP · 1D Convolutional Neural Network · Damage Classification · Sensor Reduction · Performance measures

1 Introduction

Structural health monitoring(SHM) is essential for maintaining the longevity and functionality of mechanical structures by providing reliable insights into structural performance and crack development. However, current sensing technologies generate raw data that requires significant processing to extract meaningful information. To address this, machine learning (ML) techniques, both supervised and unsupervised, are increasingly used to derive damage-sensitive features. Despite their effectiveness, many studies lack clear justification for feature selection, often choosing features arbitrarily without validating their relevance or appropriateness [1]. Mendler et al. proposed a sensor placement strategy to maximize damage detectability in structural components using global vibration data. The method optimizes Fisher information, accounting for uncertainties in damage-sensitive features modeled as Gaussian. Applied to a laboratory beam, the optimized layout demonstrated improved damage detection compared to non-optimized setups [2]. Ashkarkalaei et al. conducted a benchmark study on feature selection for damage detection in wind turbine blades using vibration data from a Vestas V27 turbine. By analyzing acceleration signals from 11 locations under various conditions, they found that using the top 10 timeâĂŞfrequency features from impulse responses achieved up to 95% accuracy, while ambient responses required 30–50 features [3]. Buckley et al. conducted a benchmark study on univariate feature selection and reduction for SHM using the S101 and Z24 bridge datasets. They extracted statistical, temporal, and spectral features from single-sensor accelerometer data across different damage states [4]. Alemu et al. proposed a data-driven approach for structural damage detection using accelerometer signals from a 3D frame structure tested at Los Alamos National Laboratory. They developed a most damage-sensitive segment (MDSS) feature extraction method based on power spectral density variability [5]. Alves et al. developed an automated damage localization method using domain-informed feature extraction across time, frequency, and quefrency domains, with strong performance across five real-world bridge applications [6]. Parisi et al. developed a method for damage localization in steel truss railway bridges using raw strain sensor data without any preprocessing or feature extraction. Their approach achieved 93% accuracy [7]. Fu et al. proposed a robust impact detection and localization method for harsh environments using limited vibration data. Their approach trains CNNs at individual sensor nodes and uses Bayesian fusion to improve accuracy [8]. SHM using vibration-based measurements is a widely adopted approach for assessing the integrity of structures. Global methods analyze the overall dynamic response of a structure, such as changes in natural frequencies or mode shapes, to detect damage across the entire system. In contrast, local methods focus on specific components or areas, capturing more detailed information through high-resolution measurements to identify localized damage.

Machine learning has significantly enhanced SHM by enabling automated damage detection and classification. Traditional ML-based SHM is typically categorized as parametric and non-parametric ML techniques. Parametric ML technique refers to the physical properties of the structure such as modal frequencies, modal mass, stiffness, and mode shapes. Parametric ML-based methods usually consider the extracted damage-sensitive features and undamaged features collected from the structure using some modal identification techniques. In non-parametric ML techniques, the damage-sensitive features are extracted without the need for a modal identification technique. The features are mainly extracted by some statistical computation from the vibration measurements obtained from the structures. Pechprasarn et al. developed and evaluated supervised ML models to predict lung cancer using a Kaggle dataset. The Gaussian Naïve Bayes model achieved 82.81% cross-validation accuracy using 9 features, demonstrating efficient classification with fewer variables [9]. Rao and Chaparala proposed a hybrid method combining Mutual Information and Rough Set Theory for feature selection, followed by SVM and ANN classifiers for damage diagnosis in SHM systems [10]. Zhu and Wang applied ML to predict bridge degradation using an improved ReliefF algorithm and a hybrid RNN-CNN model, achieving long-term forecasting for infrastructure management [11].

Deep learning offers powerful tools for SHM through automatic feature learning and high-capacity models. Parametric models such as convolutional neural networks (CNNs) and recurrent neural networks (RNNs) have been employed to capture spatial and temporal patterns in structural response data. Nonparametric approaches, including unsupervised deep learning, enable damage detection without prior knowledge of structural parameters, providing flexibility in real-world scenarios. Alemu et al. compared their MDSS technique with 18 neural and recurrent neural network models, achieving superior performance in damage detection using vibration data [5]. Parisi et al. used a CNN along with Dynamic Time Warping and KNN for damage classification on steel truss railway bridges using raw strain sensor data [7]. Fu et al.'s method trains CNNs at sensor nodes and aggregates them using Bayesian fusion, which handles sensor faults and uncertainty effectively in structural monitoring [8]. Zhu and Wang used a hybrid RNN-CNN model to predict future bridge conditions several years ahead using historical Texas bridge data [11].

Feature selection is a crucial step in both machine learning and deep learning, aimed at reducing dimensionality and improving model interpretability and performance. Effective feature selection enhances generalization, minimizes overfitting, and reduces computational costs. Techniques such as mutual information and SHAP are commonly used to identify the most relevant features from complex datasets. Dhal and Azad presented a comprehensive survey on feature selection (FS) in machine learning, classifying FS methods by data type and use case. The paper emphasizes FS's role in improving model performance and reducing dimensionality [12]. Mohamed et al. proposed the Enhanced Joint Mutual Information (EJMI) method for early ransomware detection. Their dual-ranking feature selection strategy significantly improved detection accuracy [13]. Gebreyesus et al. explored SHAP for feature selection in data center optimization. They showed that SHAP-selected features led to lower prediction errors and competitive execution times compared to traditional methods [14]. In the domain of machine learning, feature selection is becoming a major concern. The goal of the feature selection problem is to eliminate redundant and unnecessary information while choosing the modest, necessary, and sufficient subset of features that best describe the overall collection of features [15]. Marcilio-Jr et al. highlighted the power of SHAP not only for model interpretability but also as an effective tool for feature selection, improving prediction performance [16].

In structural engineering, deploying sensors on large structures like bridges, dams, or buildings is costly and often constrained by physical access and environmental conditions. Sensor selection helps identify optimal locations that provide the most useful information for detecting damage, reducing the number of sensors without compromising monitoring quality. This ensures efficient use of resources while maintaining high accuracy in detecting structural issues such as cracks, corrosion, or joint failures. Buckley et al. and Ashkarkalaei et al. provide benchmark studies for feature and sensor selection strategies in SHM using vibration-based measurements across various structural scenarios [3, 4]. Rao and Chaparala's hybrid model also integrates sensor-related feature selection mechanisms to improve classification in vibration-based SHM [10].

In machine learning, feature selection aims to retain only the most informative inputs to improve model accuracy and reduce complexity. In SHM, especially for civil structures like bridges and buildings, each sensor provides data that can be treated as a feature. Selecting key sensors is thus equivalent to selecting important features. Applying feature selection techniques helps civil engineers identify optimal sensor locations that contribute most to detecting structural damage, effectively bridging data-driven modeling and practical sensor placement. The goal of both feature selection in ML/DL and sensor selection in SHM is to minimize input dimensionality while optimizing model performance. Techniques such as SHAP fill this gap by determining which features, whether they be actual sensor locations or abstract features, are the most informative. Gebreyesus et al. and Marcilio-Jr et al. demonstrated that SHAP-selected features enhance predictive accuracy and operational efficiency, a principle directly transferable to SHM sensor selection [14, 16]. Dhal and Azad emphasized that selecting relevant features is fundamental to building efficient ML or DL pipelines, a notion aligned with the choice of optimal sensors in SHM to minimize redundancy and noise [12].

Despite progress in Structural Health Monitoring (SHM), selecting the most informative sensors from high-dimensional vibration data remains a key challenge. Many existing studies rely on traditional feature selection techniques such as PCA, ANOVA F-test, or mutual information without assessing their reliability or interpretability in deep learning contexts. Moreover, most approaches use all available sensors, resulting in computational inefficiency and potential redundancy. While deep learning models like 1D CNNs offer strong classification performance, limited work has integrated them with explainable AI techniques to identify and justify critical sensor contributions. In particular, the application of SHAP for sensor selection in SHM has not been thoroughly explored. There is a lack of systematic studies that leverage SHAP for both sensor reduction and interpretability, while benchmarking its performance against other feature selection methods within a deep learning framework. This gap highlights the need for a focused investigation into SHAP-based sensor selection to improve efficiency, interpretability, and robustness in structural damage classification.

In this study, SHAP-based feature selection is applied to identify the most informative sensors for structural damage classification. Compared to other methods such as PCA, MI, and ANOVA F-test, SHAP demonstrates superior performance and interpretability, enabling an efficient sensor layout without compromising classification accuracy.

2   Methodologies Used for Comparison

2.1   Mutual Information (MI)

Mutual Information (MI) has been effectively applied in SHM to capture non-linear dependencies between features and target variables. Lei et al. [17] used MI for sensor data preprocessing and anomaly detection, demonstrating its suitability in vibration-based SHM tasks. Mutual Information (MI) measures the shared information between variables, capturing non-linear dependencies. In this study, MI ranks features based on their relevance to the target variable, aiding in the selection of the most informative sensors for damage classification. Mutual Information measures the dependency between a feature X and the target variable Y. It quantifies how much knowing one of these variables reduces uncertainty about the other:

$$I(X;Y) = \sum_{x \in X} \sum_{y \in Y} p(x,y) \log \left(\frac{p(x,y)}{p(x)\,p(y)} \right) \tag{1}$$

where $p(x,y)$ is the joint probability distribution, and $p(x)$, $p(y)$ are marginal probabilities. Higher mutual information implies stronger relevance of the feature to the target [18].

2.2   Principal Component Analysis (PCA)

PCA is an unsupervised dimensionality reduction method that transforms features into orthogonal components, capturing the most variance. While it doesn't select features directly, it helps reduce data dimensionality while preserving the structure of vibration signals. The top principal components are used as CNN inputs to evaluate their effectiveness in damage classification.PCA has been widely adopted in SHM applications for dimensionality reduction and outlier detection. Fernández-Navamuel et al. [19] applied a deep-learning-enhanced PCA framework to improve damage detection in bridges, while Kumar et al. [20] utilized PCA to analyze vibration responses in the ASCE benchmark structure.

2.3   ANOVA F-Test

The ANOVA F-test is a statistical filter-based method that evaluates whether the means of different groups (damage classes) differ significantly concerning each feature. It calculates an F-statistic for each feature, reflecting the ratio of between-group variance to within-group variance. Features with higher F-values are considered more informative. In this study, the top-ranked features based on the ANOVA F-test are selected to train the classifier. Sbarufatti et al. [21] applied ANOVA to optimize neural network structures for fatigue damage detection in metallic panels. The ANOVA F-test evaluates the ability of each feature to discriminate between classes by comparing between-group and within-group variances. Features with higher F-scores are more discriminative. The ANOVA F-test has been used in SHM to evaluate the statistical significance of input features.

The effectiveness of the proposed SHAP-based sensor selection method is rigorously evaluated by comparing it with three widely used feature selection techniques, such as ANOVA F-test, Mutual Information (MI), and Principal Component Analysis (PCA). Each of these techniques represents a different class of feature selection: statistical filtering (ANOVA), information-theoretic scoring (MI), and unsupervised dimensionality reduction (PCA). This comparative analysis provides a robust benchmark, highlighting the advantages of SHAP, which offers not only high classification accuracy but also interpretability through model-specific sensor ranking. The inclusion of these methods is therefore intentional, serving both as a validation strategy and as a demonstration of SHAP's superior performance and practical utility in SHM tasks.

3   Proposed Methodology

In modern Structural Health Monitoring (SHM) systems, dense sensor networks generate high-dimensional time-series data, making model training computationally expensive and reducing the interpretability of the results. To address this challenge, we propose an integrated framework that combines a one-dimensional convolutional neural network (1D CNN) with Shapley Additive Explanations (SHAP) for sensor-level feature selection and structural damage classification.

This study presents a comprehensive framework for structural damage classification using a 1D Convolutional Neural Network (1D CNN) integrated with SHAP (Shapley Additive Explanations) to reduce the number of sensors while maintaining high classification accuracy and interpretability. The methodology begins with the collection of vibration response data from the IASC-ASCE Phase-I benchmark structure, which contains 12 global degrees of freedom (DOFs) corresponding to sensor measurements across the structure. Initially, a 1D CNN is trained using the complete dataset, incorporating all 12 sensor signals. This model is capable of learning temporal patterns directly from raw time-series data without manual feature extraction.

After the initial training, SHAP is employed to analyze the trained model and compute the contribution of each sensor (feature) toward the model's predictions. SHAP values are calculated by interpreting the trained model in terms of cooperative game theory, attributing importance scores to each input feature based on its marginal contribution across all possible feature subsets. The average absolute SHAP value across all samples is used to rank the sensors according to their predictive importance. Following this, the top eight sensors are selected based on their SHAP scores. This number was chosen empirically, after evaluating different configurations such as the top 6, 8, and 10 sensors. The selection of 8 sensors achieved the best balance between reduced dimensionality and high model performance, even outperforming the full 12-sensor model in terms of accuracy and robustness. Reducing the number of sensors not only decreases computational cost but also improves the feasibility of real-world SHM applications where sensor installation and maintenance can be expensive and logistically challenging.

Once the most informative sensors are identified, the CNN model is retrained using only the selected sensor signals. Retraining is essential in this context, as the input dimensionality of the model changes when switching from 12 to 8 sensors. The previously trained model cannot be reused due to this shape mismatch, and a new model must be learned to adapt to the modified feature space and capture relevant patterns from the reduced input. The final retrained model is evaluated using stratified 3-fold cross-validation. The evaluation metrics include accuracy, precision, recall, F1-score, Cohen's kappa, and the area under the ROC curve (AUC), ensuring a comprehensive assessment of model performance across all damage classes. This methodology demonstrates that combining explainable AI (SHAP) with deep learning (1D CNN) can result in an efficient, interpretable, and sensor-reduced SHM system capable of reliable damage classification.

3.1   SHAP (Shapley Additive Explanations)

SHAP is a model-agnostic interpretability method based on Shapley values from game theory, treating each feature as a "player" contributing to a prediction. In this study, SHAP identifies the most important sensors or features for damage classification by analyzing their impact on a trained model's output. Features with the highest average absolute SHAP values are retained for further modeling. The SHAP value for a feature i is given by:

$$\phi_i = \sum_{S \subseteq F \setminus \{i\}} \frac{|S|! \, (|F| - |S| - 1)!}{|F|!} \, [f(S \cup \{i\}) - f(S)] \tag{2}$$

where F is the set of all features, S is a subset not containing i, and $f(S)$ is the model output using the feature subset S. Features are ranked based on the average absolute SHAP value $|\phi_i|$ across all samples [22].

The proposed methodology integrates explainable machine learning with deep learning to enable efficient sensor selection and accurate structural damage classification. Initially, raw vibration-based measurements are collected from a structure using a dense sensor network. From these measurements, raw time-series data is extracted for all sensors and used to train 1D CNN model. This model is designed to capture temporal dependencies and learn discriminative features associated with different damage states.

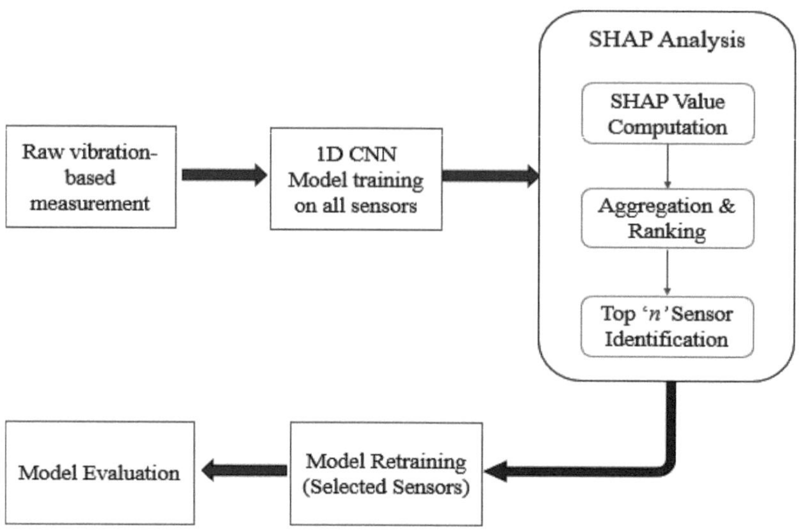

Fig. 1. SHM workflow: From raw vibration signals to damage prediction

Figure 1 illustrates the overall workflow of the proposed SHAP-based sensor selection framework for structural damage classification using a one-dimensional 1D CNN. The process begins with the collection of raw vibration-based measurements from a structure using a dense sensor network. These measurements are then used to train a 1D CNN model on the full set of sensor data, allowing the network to learn temporal patterns associated with different damage states. After the model is trained, SHAP are employed to interpret the model's predictions and quantify the importance of each sensor. The SHAP analysis consists of three main stages: (i) SHAP value computation for each sensor's time-series input, (ii) aggregation and ranking of SHAP values across all samples and time steps, and (iii) identification of the top n most informative sensors. This selected subset of sensors can then be used to retrain a compact and efficient model that maintains high classification performance while reducing computational complexity and improving interpretability. Time-series data from only the selected sensors is used to evaluate 1D CNN model. To ensure the robustness and generalization of the model, stratified k-fold cross-validation is applied. The performance of the model is assessed using a suite of evaluation metrics, including accuracy, precision, recall, F1-score, Cohen's kappa, and area under the curve (AUC). This methodology effectively demonstrates the synergy between explainable AI techniques (via SHAP) and deep learning models (via 1D CNN), resulting in a sensor-efficient and interpretable framework for Structural Health Monitoring (SHM).

4   Data Collection

The dataset for this study is generated using IASC-ASCE Phase-I benchmark structure Figs. (2, 3) a 4-story, two-bay by two-bay steel-frame building commonly used in structural health monitoring research. This structure serve as an ideal model for generating vibration based structural damaged detection. This structure has 12 global degrees of freedom (DOF), with three translational DOF for each floor. The floor mass is distributed equally across four slabs per floor: 800 kg per slab on the first floor, 600 kg per slab on the second and third floors, and 400 kg per slab on the fourth floor. The undamaged structure has significant natural frequencies of 8.59, 9.18, 14.58, 23.45, 25.95, 36.81, 40.65, 42.21, 46.98, 56.74, 62.96, and 81.05 Hz. Four damage scenarios are simulated to reflect realistic structural changes: Case I, where a brace in the first story has zero stiffness; Case II, where braces in the first and third stories have zero stiffness; Case III, where a brace in the (+x) face of the first story has zero stiffness; and Case IV, where braces in both the (+x) face of the first story and the (âĂŞy) face of the third story have zero stiffness. The vibration responses for this structure are also simulated under ambient white noise excitation with a frequency range of 0âĂŞ100 Hz, and the acceleration responses are sampled at 200 Hz. Each dataset consists of 1000 samples, where each sample has a duration of 35 s (7000 time points), ignoring the first 5 s to remove transient effects. In this structure, the white noise inputs are designed to cover the structural frequency content adequately.

Fig. 2. ASCE benchmark structure

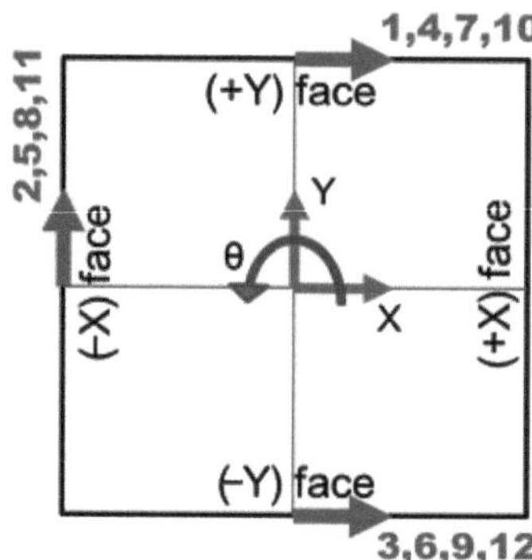

Fig. 3. DOF of ASCE benchmark structure

5   Result and Discussion

In this study, feature selection was applied to sensor data from the ASCE benchmark structure using four distinct methods: SHAP, ANOVA F-test, mutual information (MI), and principal component analysis (PCA). The objective was to identify the most informative 8 out of 12 available sensors for structural damage classification using a 1D-CNN. The selected sensors varied across the methods, with SHAP selecting sensors 1, 2, 0, 4, 6, 3, 7, 8, which consistently yielded the highest classification performance.

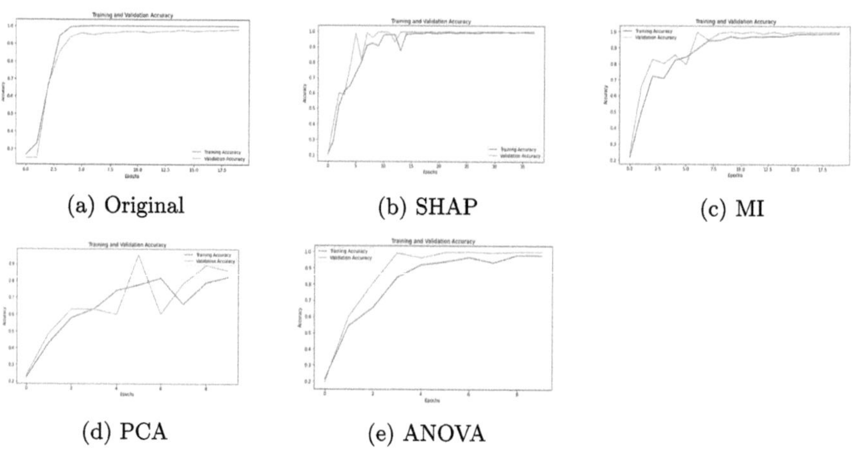

(a) Original   (b) SHAP   (c) MI

(d) PCA   (e) ANOVA

Fig. 4. Training and validation accuracy curves of the 1D CNN model using different feature selection methods. Each subplot shows accuracy over epochs for the training and validation datasets using: (a) all 12 sensors, (b) SHAP, (c) MI, (d) PCA, and (e) ANOVA F-test

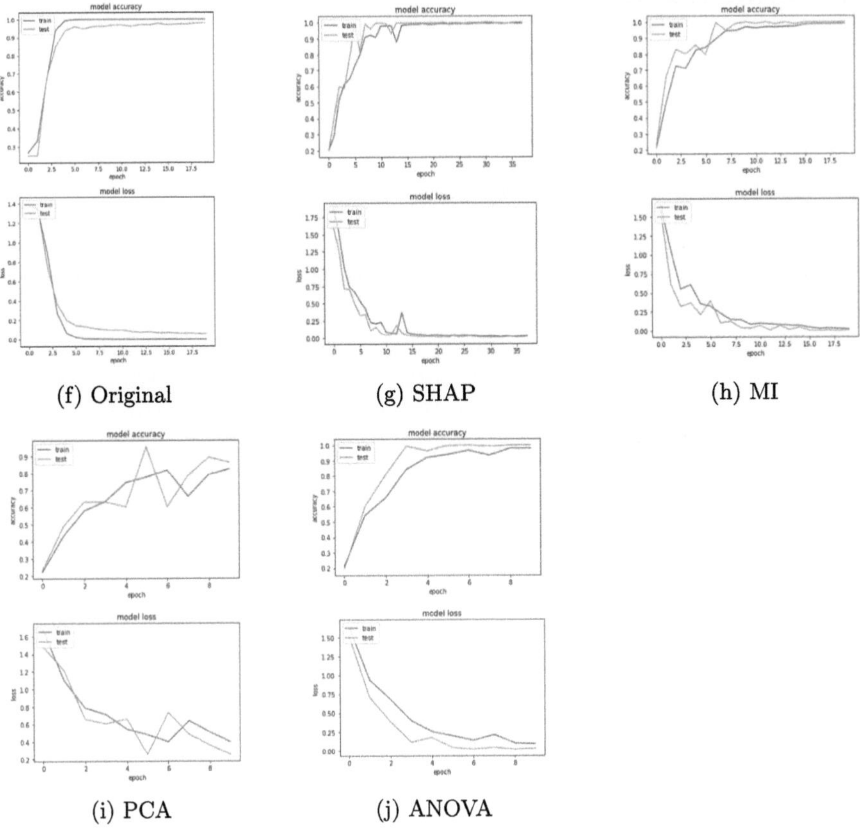

(f) Original   (g) SHAP   (h) MI

(i) PCA   (j) ANOVA

Fig. 5. Training accuracy and loss curves of the 1D CNN model using different feature selection methods. Each subplot displays the progression of training and test accuracy/loss over epochs for: (f) all 12 sensors, (g) SHAP, (h) MI, (i) PCA, and (j) ANOVA F-test

5.1 Implemetation Details

To evaluate the effectiveness of various feature selection methods, we employed a 1D-CNN architecture as the classification model. The model's ability to distinguish between damaged (referred as class 1, class 2, class 3, class 4) and undamaged (referred as class 0) classes was assessed based on the selected sensor features. To ensure reliable and consistent evaluation, a 3-fold cross-validation strategy was adopted. Model performance was assessed using accuracy, precision, recall, F1-score, and area under the curve (AUC). For the ASCE-benchmark structure, the learning rate was set to 0.001 across all configurations. The number of epochs varied depending on the feature selection method: 30 epochs were used for the original dataset (without feature selection), 40 epochs for the SHAP-selected dataset, and 10 epochs for the datasets processed with ANOVA F-test, mutual information (MI), and PCA. The batch size was set to 32 for all methods except SHAP, which used a batch size of 64. The number of convolutional layers also varied: the original dataset and MI used 4 layers, while SHAP, ANOVA F-test, and PCA used 3 layers. The number of filters per layer was consistently set to [8, 16], and the kernel sizes used were [5, 7, 9] across all configurations.

5.2   Result Analysis Using ASCE Benchmark Data

Comparative evaluations were conducted using a consistent 1D CNN framework to isolate the effect of feature selection. Four techniques were selected to represent interpretable, unsupervised, statistical, and information-theoretic methods. Each was applied to the ASCE benchmark dataset, selecting the top 8 sensors for retraining. This controlled setup ensures a fair performance comparison, with SHAP demonstrating the most significant improvements in accuracy and interpretability.

Table 1. Performance Comparison of Feature Selection Methods with 1D CNN

Method	Accuracy	Precision	Recall	F1 Score	Kappa	AUC
Original (All Sensors)	96.57	96.79	95.67	95.72	95.72	99.39
SHAP	**98.58**	**98.68**	**98.61**	**98.22**	**98.22**	**99.89**
ANOVA F-test	88.49	92.52	88.05	87.07	85.94	99.15
MI	84.24	82.26	83.74	81.99	80.13	95.44
PCA	90.01	92.90	89.97	88.61	87.53	99.73

Table 2. Class-wise Accuracy Comparison for Different Feature Selection Methods

Method	Class 0	Class 1	Class 2	Class 3	Class 4
Original	87.0	99.09	**100.0**	95.89	**100.0**
SHAP	98.69	**100.0**	**100.0**	**94.49**	99.89
ANOVA F-test	75.41	**100.0**	**100.0**	70.31	99.69
MI	73.18	**100.0**	**100.0**	50.48	95.24
PCA	**99.9**	**100.0**	**100.0**	52.82	97.15

From Table 1, it is evident that SHAP-based feature selection outperforms other techniques and even surpasses the performance of the original dataset that uses all 12 sensors. While the original dataset achieves strong baseline results (accuracy: 96.57%, F1 score: 95.72%, AUC: 99.39), SHAP achieves higher values (accuracy: 98.58%, F1 score: 98.22%, AUC: 99.89) using only 8 selected features. In contrast, PCA, MI, and ANOVA F-test yield lower accuracy and F1 scores,

Table 3. Fold-wise Evaluation Metrics for Different Feature Selection Methods

Method	Fold	Accuracy	Precision	Recall	F1 Score	Kappa	AUC
Original	K1	**100.0**	**100.0**	**100.0**	**100.0**	**100.0**	**100.0**
	K2	99.99	99.99	99.99	99.99	99.99	99.99
	K3	89.74	90.38	89.73	89.58	87.17	98.19
SHAP	K1	96.28	96.61	96.43	96.43	95.35	99.67
	K2	99.58	99.56	99.55	99.55	99.47	**100.0**
	K3	**99.88**	**99.87**	**99.88**	**99.88**	**99.85**	100.0
MI	K1	87.52	89.29	88.00	87.67	84.38	97.82
	K2	65.27	57.55	63.29	58.38	56.11	88.53
	K3	99.94	99.94	99.94	99.94	99.92	**100.0**
ANOVA F-test	K1	83.14	88.00	84.26	82.01	78.95	97.64
	K2	**100.0**	**100.0**	**100.0**	**100.0**	**100.0**	**100.0**
	K3	82.35	89.58	72.08	79.22	77.98	99.84
PCA	K1	99.52	99.56	99.54	99.54	99.4	**100.0**
	K2	84.44	88.08	84.45	83.04	92.1	99.21
	K3	84.09	91.08	84.68	81.85	80.15	**100.0**

particularly under complex damage scenarios. For example, MI achieves only 84.24% accuracy and 81.99% F1 score, with poor class-wise performance in Class 3 (50.48%) and Class 0 (73.18%), as shown in Table 2. SHAP, on the other hand, maintains near-perfect class-wise accuracy, including 100% in Classes 1–2 and 99.89% in Class 4.

Fold-wise results in Table 3 further confirm SHAP's consistency, with high accuracy across all folds (K1: 96.28%, K2: 99.58%, K3: 99.88%), closely matching or exceeding the original dataset, and outperforming MI and ANOVA, which show significant performance drops in K2 and K3. There is no specific reason for the comparatively lower performance values in Fold K3. Similar variations can also be observed in Folds K1 and K2 for certain metrics. This inconsistency across folds arises because early stopping was employed during training in each fold, which may lead to slight fluctuations in performance due to differences in convergence behavior and data distribution. These results demonstrate SHAP's effectiveness in reducing sensor count while enhancing model generalization, preserving high classification accuracy, and ensuring robustness across varying structural damage conditions.

Figures 4 and 5 present the training and validation performance of models using different feature selection methods, based on accuracy and loss over epochs. Although the x-axis scales (Epochs) in Fig. 4 appear non-uniform across subplots, this is due to the automatic behavior of the training history logger used in each run. The plotting library renders the x-axis based on the number of epochs stored in the model's history object, which can vary slightly depending on early stopping or checkpoint callbacks. Despite this, all models were trained with the same maximum number of epochs, batch size, and learning rate, ensuring that the learning curves are directly comparable in trend and performance. For the original dataset, which uses all 12 sensors without any feature selection, Figs. 4(a) and 5(f) show that the CNN model achieves high training and validation accuracy with rapid convergence. Both accuracy curves stabilize above 95% within the first few epochs, with a minimal gap between them, indicating limited overfitting and strong generalization capability. The corresponding loss plots also demonstrate a steep and steady decrease for both training and validation, ultimately converging to low values. These results confirm that the model effectively learns from the full feature set. However, the use of all sensors increases computational load and may include redundant information, justifying the need for feature selection. SHAP-based feature selection, shown in Figs. 4(b) and 5(g), presents the training dynamics of the 1D CNN model using the top 8 sensors selected by SHAP. The top plot illustrates model accuracy across epochs for both training and test datasets. Accuracy increases sharply during the initial epochs and stabilizes above 98% after epoch 10, indicating effective learning. The close alignment between the training and test curves confirms strong generalization without overfitting. The bottom plot displays the corresponding loss values for both datasets. The loss decreases consistently across epochs, with both curves converging near zero after approximately 15 epochs. No signs of divergence are observed, and both curves remain smooth and stable. These trends demonstrate that SHAP-based feature selection leads to a compact and highly informative sensor subset, enabling the model to achieve fast convergence, minimal error, and robust classification performance. MI-based selection (Figs. 4(c), 5(h)) converges quickly but exhibits noticeable fluctuations between training and validation accuracy, indicating overfitting due to suboptimal feature relevance. PCA (Figs. 4(d), 5(i)) results in slower and more unstable convergence, along with relatively lower validation accuracy, possibly due to the compromise in interpretability and information loss during dimensionality reduction. The ANOVA F-test (Figs. 4(e), 5(j)) performs better than MI and PCA in terms of convergence stability and generalization, but remains inferior to SHAP in overall model performance and robustness. ANOVA F-test show substantial drops in Class 3(damage class 3) performance (50.48% and 70.31%). These findings demonstrate that SHAP-based feature selection effectively identifies the most relevant sensors, enhancing classification performance while reducing data dimensionality.

To assess the specific contribution of SHAP-based feature selection, an ablation study is conducted using comparative experiments. The baseline model 1D CNN trained on all 12 sensors demonstrates strong performance but lacks efficiency in terms of sensor usage. By removing SHAP and replacing it with other feature selection methods, noticeable drops in precision, F1 score, and class-wise consistency are observed, as shown in Tables 1 and 2. Compared to the baseline CNN model trained using all 12 sensors, the SHAP-based CNN model (using only 8 sensors) improves performance by a margin of approximately 2% in accuracy,2.5% in F1-score, and 0.5% in AUC. More notably, when compared to other feature selection methods like Mutual Information (MI) and ANOVA F-test, the

SHAP-based model outperforms them by margins ranging from 12% to 49% in accuracy and 22% to 49% in F1-score, clearly demonstrating SHAP's superiority in both predictive power and efficiency. This confirms that SHAP does not simply reduce dimensionality but also enhances model robustness and interpretability. The comparison thus validates that the integration of SHAP contributes significantly to both the effectiveness and practicality of the proposed SHM system.

To validate the effectiveness and novelty of the proposed SHAP-based sensor selection approach integrated with a 1D Convolutional Neural Network (CNN) for structural damage detection, we compared our method with several recent state-of-the-art studies in related domains, including healthcare diagnostics, wireless sensor networks, and stress detection using wearable devices. In the work by Ejiyi et al. [23], a comparative analysis of Boruta, SHAP, and Boruta Shap feature selection techniques was performed for disease diagnosis using multiple machine learning models across various medical datasets. While their focus was on interpretability and feature importance in disease prediction tasks, our study uniquely applies SHAP to the physical domain of structural health monitoring (SHM), demonstrating that sensor reduction (from 12 to 8 sensors) can lead to superior performance (98.58% accuracy and 98.22% F1-score), surpassing even full-sensor configurations. Shikha et al. [24] employed SHAP along with Genetic Algorithms and Mutual Information for optimizing wearable biosensor data to classify stress levels. While both studies emphasize explainable AI, their focus was on real-time stress detection using physiological signals such as HRV and EDA. Our method, however, tackles spatial sensor reduction in civil structures and offers a novel way of integrating deep learning with SHAP for high-accuracy damage classification. Bagwari et al. [25] proposed a machine learning-based enhanced energy optimization model for industrial wireless sensor networks (IWSNs). Their work emphasizes energy-efficient data transmission and node selection, sharing conceptual similarities with our sensor reduction strategy. However, our model directly targets structural integrity evaluation using real-world vibration data, providing both interpretability and domain-specific performance gains. Kumar et al. [20] applied a Principal Component Analysis (PCA)-based method for damage detection in the ASCE benchmark structure. Although their approach reduced data dimensionality and offered resilience to environmental noise, PCA lacks the interpretability and feature attribution provided by SHAP. Our model not only outperformed PCA-based selection in classification accuracy but also enhanced transparency in sensor contribution, a critical factor in practical SHM implementations. Finally, Barthorpe and Worden [26] reviewed sensor placement optimization (SPO) strategies for SHM. While they provided a broad survey on optimization criteria and sensor layout strategies, our work contributes a novel and experimentally validated SHAP-based SPO framework integrated with deep learning, bridging the gap between interpretability, reduced sensor cost, and high damage detection accuracy. Across all comparisons, our method demonstrates a distinct advantage by combining SHAP's explainability with CNN's predictive power in the context of SHM, offering a computationally efficient, interpretable, and high-performing framework for damage detection in civil infrastructure.

6   Conclusion

This study focused on CNN-based structural damage detection using reduced sensor inputs selected through SHAP feature analysis. Leveraging the ASCE benchmark dataset, the primary goal was to reduce the number of sensors from 12 to the most effective 8, thereby minimizing input dimensionality while improving classification performance. SHAP was employed as the central feature selection method due to its ability to identify the most influential sensors based on model interpretability.

To demonstrate the effectiveness of SHAP, its performance was compared with other established feature selection techniques, including PCA, MI, and ANOVA F-test. SHAP-based sensor selection consistently outperformed the other methods in terms of accuracy, class-wise performance, stability across folds, and generalization. Moreover, SHAP uniquely offered model interpretability, an essential advantage in safety-critical SHM applications. In contrast, PCA and MI reduced dimensionality but failed to generalize well and lacked interpretability, while the ANOVA F-test showed moderate performance without the consistency and insight provided by SHAP. These results underscore the value of SHAP for designing efficient, interpretable, and cost-effective structural health monitoring (SHM) systems with fewer sensors. In conclusion, SHAP not only enables dimensionality reduction but also enhances model reliability and transparency, making it a promising tool for real-world SHM applications. Future research can explore its integration into online monitoring systems and its extension to other structural damage types and sensor technologies.

Acknowledgements. The authors acknowledge the support from the Science and Engineering Research Board (SERB), Department of Science and Technology (DST), Government of India (project grant with file No. CRG/2021/007352).

References

1. Omar, I., Khan, M., Starr, A.: Compatibility and challenges in machine learning approach for structural crack assessment. Struct. Health Monit. **21**(5), 2481–2502 (2022)
2. Mendler, A., Dohler, M., Ventura, C.E.: Sensor placement with optimal damage detectability for statistical damage detection. Mech. Syst. Signal Process. **170**, 108767 (2022)
3. Ashkarkalaei, M., Ghiasi, R., Pakrashi, V., Malekjafarian, A.: Optimum feature selection for the supervised damage classification of an operating wind turbine blade. Struct. Health Monit. (2025). https://doi.org/10.1177/14759217251313815
4. Buckley, T., Ghosh, B., Pakrashi, V.: A feature extraction and selection benchmark for structural health monitoring. Struct. Health Monit. **22**(3), 2082–2127 (2023)
5. Alemu, Y.L., Lahmer, T., Walther, C.: Damage detection with data-driven machine learning models on an experimental structure. Eng. **5**(2), 629–656 (2024)

6. Alves, V., Cury, A.: An automated vibration-based structural damage localization strategy using filter-type feature selection. Mech. Syst. Signal Process. **190**, 110145 (2023)

7. Parisi, F., Mangini, A.M., Fanti, M.P., Adam, J.M.: Automated location of steel truss bridge damage using machine learning and raw strain sensor data. Autom. Constr. **138**, 104249 (2022)

8. Fu, Y., et al.: Effective structural impact detection and localization using convolutional neural network and Bayesian information fusion with limited sensors. Mech. Syst. Signal Process. **224**, 112074

9. Pechprasarn, S., Suechoey, N., Pholtrakoolwong, N., Tanedvorapinyo, P., Toboonliang, Y.: Optimizing lung cancer diagnosis with machine learning and feature selection methods. J. Curr. Sci. Technol. **14**(3), 55 (2024)

10. Rao, M.V.V., Chaparala, A.: A novel feature-based SHM assessment and prediction approach for robust evaluation of damage data diagnosis systems. Wirel. Pers. Commun. **124**(4), 3387–3411 (2022)

11. Zhu, J., Wang, Y.: Feature selection and deep learning for deterioration prediction of the bridges. J. Perform. Constr. Facil. **35**(6), 04021078 (2021)

12. Dhal, P., Azad, C.: A comprehensive survey on feature selection in the various fields of machine learning. Appl. Intell. **52**(4), 4543–4581 (2022)

13. Mohamed, T.M.H., Al-Rimy, B.A.S., Almalki, S.A.: A ransomware early detection model based on an enhanced joint mutual information feature selection method. Eng. Technol. Appl. Sci. Res. **14**(4) (2024)

14. Gebreyesus, Y., Dalton, D., Nixon, S., De Chiara, D., Chinnici, M.: Machine learning for data center optimizations: feature selection using Shapley Additive Explanation (SHAP). Future Internet **15**(3), 88 (2023)

15. Barrera-García, J., Cisternas-Caneo, F., Crawford, B., Gómez Sánchez, M., Soto, R.: Feature selection problem and metaheuristics: a systematic literature review about its formulation, evaluation and applications. Biomimetics **9**(1), 9 (2023)

16. Marcílio, W.E., Eler, D.M.: From explanations to feature selection: assessing SHAP values as feature selection mechanism. In: 33rd SIBGRAPI Conf. on Graphics, Patterns and Images (SIBGRAPI), pp. 340–347. IEEE (2020)

17. Lei, Y., Zhao, J., Lin, J.: A deep-learning-assisted anomaly detection framework for structural health monitoring using mutual information-based preprocessing. Mech. Syst. Signal Process. **200**, 110352 (2023)

18. Ahmad, B., Chen, J., Chen, H.: Feature selection strategies for optimized heart disease diagnosis using ML and DL models. arXiv preprint arXiv:2503.16577 (2025)

19. Fernandez-Navamuel, A., et al.: Deep learning enhanced principal component analysis for structural health monitoring. Struct. Health Monit. **21**(4), 1710–1722 (2022)

20. Kumar, K., Biswas, P.K., Dhang, N.: Time series-based SHM using PCA with application to ASCE benchmark structure. J. Civ. Struct. Heal. Monit. **10**(5), 899–911 (2020). https://doi.org/10.1007/s13349-020-00423-2

21. Sbarufatti, C.: Optimization of an artificial neural network for fatigue damage identification using analysis of variance. Struct. Control. Health Monit. **24**(9), e1964 (2017)

22. Lundberg, S.M., Lee, S.I.: A unified approach to interpreting model predictions. Adv. Neural Inf. Process. Syst. **30** (2017)

23. Ejiyi, C.J., et al.: Comparative performance analysis of Boruta, SHAP, and Borutashap for disease diagnosis: a study with multiple machine learning algorithms. Netw. Comput. Neural Syst. 1–38 (2024)

24. Sethia, D., Indu, S., et al.: Optimization of wearable biosensor data for stress classification using machine learning and explainable AI. IEEE Access (2024)
25. Bagwari, A.: An enhanced energy optimization model for industrial wireless sensor networks using machine learning. IEEE Access **11**, 96343–96362 (2023)
26. Barthorpe, R.J., Worden, K.: Emerging trends in optimal structural health monitoring system design: from sensor placement to system evaluation. J. Sens. Actuator Netw. **9**(3), 31 (2020)

A Robust Machine Vision Model to Detect Wildfire Utilizing Advanced AI-Based Deep Learning

Abdul Subhani Shaik[1], Ram Kumar Karsh[2], P. Ravi Kiran[1], M. Raman Kumar[3], Thuppathi Akhil[1(✉)], and Kommana Sethu Sai Teja[1]

[1] Department of ECE, CMR College of Engineering & Technology, Hyderabad, Telangana 501401, India
`dr.p.ravikiran@cmrcet.ac.in`, `akhilthuppathi9@gmail.com`
[2] Department of ECE, National Institute of Technology, Silchar, Assam, India 788010
`ram@ece.nits.ac.in`
[3] Department of ECE, Nalla Malla Reddy Engineering College, Hyderabad, Telangana, India

Abstract. The study uses a sophisticated deep learning CNN framework called VGG19 to offer a reliable machine vision model for wildfire detection. Early detection is essential for efficient management and prevention of wildfires, which pose serious dangers to human life and ecosystems. The suggested model makes use of VGG19, which is renowned for its deep architecture and excellent image classification skills, to precisely detect wildfire incidents in real time. Using pre-processing approaches to improve image quality and guarantee the model's flexibility to diverse environmental circumstances, the model learns from a dataset consisting of numerous wildfires and non-wildfire image samples. VGG19 distinguishes fire-related phenomena from other natural scenes with high accuracy through fine-tuning and transfer learning. Evaluation parameters, including F1-score, precision, and recall, show how well the model detects wildfires in dynamic and complicated situations. The outcomes illustrate how computer vision and DL technologies can optimize wildfire surveillance, providing a scalable method for implementation in practical applications.

Keywords: Deep Learning · CNN · VGG19 and Reduce Net algorithms · High Accuracy · Image Quality

1 Introduction

Wildfire poses a significant threat to the environment, human life, and infrastructure. As climate change continues to exacerbate the frequency and intensity of wildfires globally, it has become increasingly important to develop advanced systems for early detection and prevention. Traditional methods of wildfire detection, such as manual observation and satellite monitoring, are time-consuming, expensive, and often delayed. The urgency of reducing wildfire risks has led to the exploration of ML and DL techniques, which can offer faster, more efficient, and scalable solutions. CNNs have gained prominence

R. K. Karsh et al. (Eds.): SIPCOV 2025, CCIS 2848, pp. 267–278, 2026.
https://doi.org/10.1007/978-3-032-15809-3_21

due to their exceptional ability to process and classify images, making them particularly well-suited for wildfire detection. VGG19 with ReduceNet is one such method that has demonstrated exceptional performance in numerous image classification tasks, a DL architecture based on CNNs. VGG19 with ReduceNet, short for "Visual Geometry Group 19," was developed by the University of Oxford and stands out for its minimalistic at highly efficient 19 layer design. This design has been validated to deliver high accuracy in a variety of image recognition tasks, from object detection to medical image analysis. The primary objective of the model discussed in this research is to create a robust and accurate machine learning model that can detect wildfires in images with a high degree of reliability. By leveraging the power of VGG19 with ReduceNet, the model aims to process satellite images, drone footage, or other image-based data sources to identify early signs of wildfire outbreaks, such as smoke, fire, and affected vegetation. This early detection system would enable timely intervention, reduce potential damage, and save lives and resources. Relative to standard techniques, the use of deep learning models such as VGG19 with ReduceNet in wildfire detection has several benefits. First, without requiring human feature engineering, DL algorithms are able to automatically extract pertinent from unprocessed image data. This makes it possible to spot intricate patterns that could be challenging for rule-based systems or human observers to notice, like the minute variations between places damaged by wildfires and typical topography.

Furthermore, the VGG19 with ReduceNet model can learn complex properties that shallower models could miss because of its depth and ability to handle massive amounts of data. Therefore, even in difficult environmental situations such changing illumination, weather, and geographical features, it has the ability to increase the accuracy and resilience of wildfire detection systems [1]. The expanding trend of using AI in environmental monitoring is also consistent with the usage of VGG19 for wildfire detection. AI has been successfully applied in a no. of fields during the last ten years, including disaster management datasets. One of the core aspects of this research is to fine-tune VGG19 for the specific task of wildfire detection. VGG19 with ReduceNet is commonly used for general image classification tasks, adapting it to identify wildfires requires a carefully curated dataset. The model's performance hinges not only on the quality and diversity of the dataset but also on the specific configurations and optimizations employed during training. Therefore, a significant portion of this research will focus on enhancing VGG19 to achieve high detection accuracy and real-time performance.

2 Literature Review

The detection of wildfires has emerged as a vital research area, especially given their rising occurrence and severity, largely attributed to climate change. Conventional detection approaches such as satellite imagery, terrestrial sensors, and manual observation are often hindered by delays, limited precision, and high costs. In contrast, recent progress in deep learning and AI-driven machine vision technologies presents new opportunities to improve early wildfire detection, mitigate damage, and enable quicker response strategies. Convolutional Neural Networks (CNNs) have become a popular choice for identifying wildfires through imagery, thanks to their ability to automatically learn spatial features from complex visuals. For example, Zhang et al. [2] introduced a CNN-based model that effectively identifies smoke in forest scenes, surpassing traditional image processing methods in accuracy. Similarly, Li et al. [3] developed a fire detection approach using a deep residual network (ResNet), which proved to be resilient across diverse lighting and weather scenarios.

Transfer learning has also gained traction in this domain, where established models like VGGNet, Inception, and MobileNet are adapted to wildfire datasets. In a study by Muhammad et al. [4], MobileNetV2 was deployed for real-time fire detection on compact embedded platforms, illustrating that lightweight architectures can offer strong performance with reduced computational demands. Akhloufi et al. [5], on the other hand, implemented ensemble learning by integrating multiple CNN models, leading to improved detection accuracy and fewer false alarms. The fusion of spatial and temporal information from video data is another evolving technique for identifying dynamic fire patterns. Hu et al. [6] proposed a CNN-LSTM hybrid model capable of capturing both spatial and temporal characteristics, thereby significantly improving early detection. Similarly, Zhao et al. [7] employed a deep reinforcement learning strategy that adaptively refined detection behavior in response to environmental changes.

Incorporating multimodal learning—combining image data with sensor-based inputs such as temperature, humidity, and gas levels—has shown to further enhance detection reliability. Wang et al. [8] demonstrated that integrating multiple data types can increase system robustness in diverse forest conditions. Meanwhile, Roy et al. [9] addressed the challenge of limited labeled data by using generative models and synthetic datasets to train deep learning systems, which improved model generalization. Additionally, the integration of unmanned aerial vehicles (UAVs) and edge computing has gained popularity for real-time monitoring. Toma et al. [10] presented a deep learning-based solution embedded in UAVs, enabling immediate detection of flames and accurate location tracking. To enhance trust and transparency in such systems, Lin et al. [11] applied explainable AI (XAI) methods that visualize the reasoning behind model predictions, an essential feature for decision support in wildfire management.

Overall, existing research reflects a growing trend toward intelligent, adaptable, and interpretable AI-based machine vision systems for wildfire detection. Despite significant progress, key challenges such as managing noisy data, enabling real-time operation, and optimizing computational efficiency remain. This study aims to address these challenges by developing a resilient and practical machine vision framework powered by advanced deep learning techniques, suitable for deployment in real-world wildfire scenarios.

3 Methodology

There are four main levels in the suggested method. Collecting a high-quality, diverse dataset is the initial stage in developing the wildfire detection model. For this, a combination of publicly available satellite imagery, drone footage, and images from wildfire-prone regions will be used. These images must include both wildfire-affected areas and non-wildfire areas to allow the model to distinguish between the two. The dataset will also include images taken under various lighting conditions, weather patterns, and seasonal changes to ensure robustness.

After collecting the dataset, it will be preprocessed for VGG19 model training. This involves resizing images to a consistent size to meet the model's input requirements. Image normalization will scale pixel values between 0 and 1. Data augmentation methods like rotation, flipping, and zooming will be applied to enhance dataset diversity, helping the model generalize better and avoid overfitting. The VGG19 architecture will be fine-tuned for wildfire detection by leveraging transfer learning. A pre-trained VGG19 model, which has been trained on a large dataset like ImageNet, will be adapted by replacing the top layers to fit the binary classification task. The model will be trained using a cross-entropy loss function and an optimization algorithm such as Adam to minimize the classification error. Training will be conducted in batches with a set number of epochs.

Performance metrics will be used to the trained model, and methods like dropout or early stopping will be used to prevent overfitting and that the model generalizes well on new data. Hyperparameters like learning rate will be optimized using methods. The methodology for building a robust [12] machine vision model to detect wildfires using VGG19 involves several key steps. Initially, data collection is performed using satellite images, drone footage, and wildfire datasets, ensuring diverse environmental conditions. Data preprocessing includes resizing images to 224 × 224 pixels, normalization, and augmentation to enhance model generalization. The model uses the VGG19 architecture, a pre-trained deep convolutional neural network, fine-tuned on the wildfire dataset.

The model is made up of convolutional layers, max-pooling layers, and fully connected layers to efficiently extract features from images. It is trained using the Adam optimizer and categorical cross-entropy loss. Dropout regularization is used to avoid overfitting. The model's effectiveness in wildfire detection is assessed using accuracy and precision metrics. CNN are essential for automating the recognition of wildfires from photos when deep learning technology is used for wildfire detection. CNNs are deep learning algorithms designed to process grid- like data, such as images. They are popular for their ability to automatically learn hierarchical features from raw image data, eliminating the need for manual feature extraction.

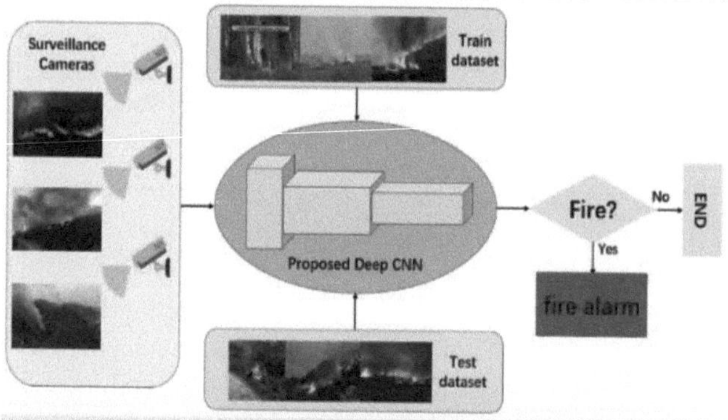

Fig. 1. CNN-based wildfire detection framework

Figure 1 depicts the proposed CNN-based framework for wildfire detection using surveillance camera networks. Visual data captured by cameras is fed into a deep convolutional neural network trained on fire and non-fire images. The model analyzes incoming test images in real time and determines the presence of fire. If detected, a fire alarm is triggered; otherwise, the system continues monitoring. This framework enables automated, accurate, and timely wildfire detection with minimal human intervention.

3.1 How CNN Works in Wildfire Detection

In a [13] robust machine vision model to detect wildfires using deep learning technology, CNNs are employed to automatically learn and classify images. CNNs are designed to recognize spatial hierarchies in data, making them ideal for analyzing visual data such as images or video footage of wildfires.

A CNN is its central component, where filters or kernels examine the image to find fundamental visual patterns like edges, textures, or areas of interest like fire or smoke. These properties are crucial for recognizing wildfire traits. As the network gets deeper, it can identify increasingly intricate patterns, such as smoke clouds or fire spread, which are important signs of wildfire. Activation functions such as ReLU are added after the convolutional layers, adding non-linearity and enabling the model to identify more complex features. This aids CNN in processing complicated data, including changing fire conditions or shifting ambient conditions. The image is then downsampled by the pooling layers, which preserves key characteristics while shrinking the image's size. By avoiding overfitting to certain visual characteristics that aren't important for detecting wildfires, this lowers the computational load and improves the model's generalization.

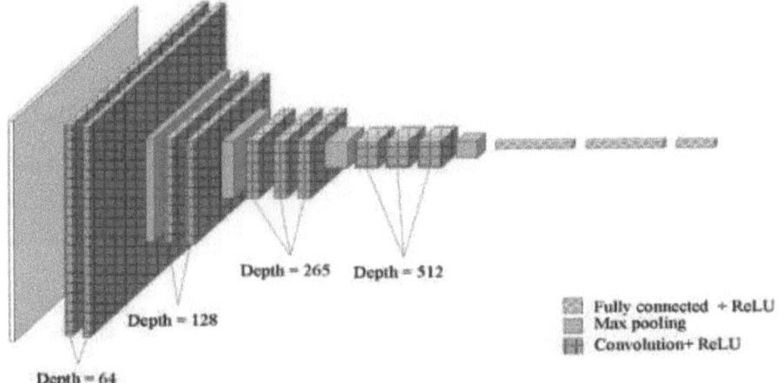

Fig. 2 VGG19 architecture

A deep CNN VGG19, shown in Fig. 2, is quite good at detecting wildfires, mainly when used with satellite or aerial images. VGG19's 19 layers, 16 convolutional and three fully connected, allow it to extract features and identify patterns in unprocessed pixel input. It can capture both simple and complicated aspects of images thanks to its frame, which makes use of max-pooling layers and tiny 3x3 convolution filters.

272   A. S. Shaik et al.

Satellite, infrared, and thermal images are among the many image datasets to train VGG19 for wildfire identification [14]. Labels on these images might indicate regions with or without wildfires. The model can be trained to discriminate between natural landscape features and fire-related features. VGG19 can be improved on datasets unique to wildfires by utilizing transfer learning to recognize fire signatures in real time. The ability to detect fires, smoke, or temperature variations is crucial for early wildfire detection and response. While challenges like varying weather conditions or image resolution exist, combining multi-channel inputs can further enhance VGG19's detection capabilities. Its robustness and efficiency make it a valuable tool in automated wildfire detection systems for early warning and management.

Fig. 3. Prediction Output

Figure 3 illustrates the outcome of the wildfire detection model applied to a test image using the proposed VGG19-ReduceNet framework. The figure provides a dual representation of the detection process. First, the system outputs a classification result indicating the presence of fire, as shown by the textual label "Prediction Output: Fire Detected" at the top of the window. This confirms the model's ability to accurately classify images containing wildfire-related features. Second, the image is visually annotated using red-colored bounding boxes, which highlight the specific regions where fire is detected within the scene. This localization capability adds an additional layer of interpretability and situational awareness, enabling end-users to not only confirm fire presence but also identify its exact location within aerial or drone-captured images. The figure demonstrates the robustness and practical applicability of the proposed model for real-time wildfire monitoring, especially in forested areas. By combining accurate classification with effective visual annotation, the system supports both automated detection and human-in-the-loop decision-making, which are critical for rapid emergency response and wildfire management.

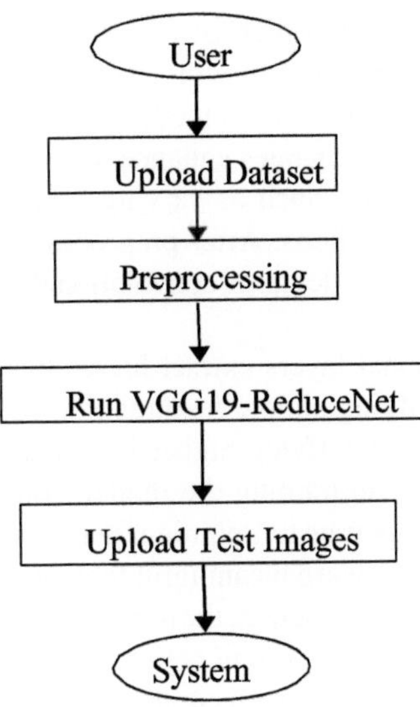

Fig. 4. Flow Chart

Figure 4 illustrates the procedural flow of the proposed wildfire detection system based on the VGG19-ReduceNet deep learning architecture. The system is designed to facilitate efficient wildfire classification using a structured sequence of operations. The process begins with the user uploading the dataset, which includes labeled images of fire and non-fire scenarios. This is followed by a preprocessing stage, where raw image data is normalized, resized, and prepared for input into the model. Preprocessing ensures consistency in data quality and enhances feature extraction during training. Subsequently, the VGG19-ReduceNet model is executed. This stage involves training the deep convolutional network on the preprocessed data. The model leverages its deep layered architecture to learn complex features relevant to wildfire identification. Once the model is trained, test images are uploaded to evaluate the system's performance. These images are classified by the trained model to determine the presence or absence of wildfire-related patterns. Finally, the system generates output indicating whether the uploaded test image contains fire, which may also include visual localization (e.g., bounding boxes). This output supports rapid assessment and decision-making in fire monitoring and emergency response scenarios. The flow chart provides a clear and systematic representation of the entire detection pipeline, emphasizing the model's usability, automation, and potential for integration into real-time wildfire monitoring frameworks.

Wildfire detection through [15] VGG19 + ReduceNet is a multi-stage deep learning pipeline beginning from image acquisition and moving through preprocessing, feature extraction, dimensionality reduction, classification, and alert generation. The process begins with the acquisition of images from different sources, such as satellite imagery, drones, surveillance cameras, or IoT-based ground sensors. Images can be of normal landscapes or active fire conditions, consisting of smoke, fire, or burned vegetation. To make the models consistent and accurate, preprocessing operations like resizing, normalization, and data augmentation are used. Resizing makes all the images of a uniform input size, e.g., 224 × 224 pixels, which is the input dimension required by VGG19. Normalization scales pixel values into a uniform range, usually 0 to 1, to make the training process stable [16]. Data augmentation methods such as random rotations, flipping, brightness changes, and contrast changes enhance the model's resilience by subjecting it to diverse real-world scenarios, such as varying lighting, angles, and environmental interference like fog or reflections. After preprocessing, these images are fed into VGG19, CNN with 19 layers, made up of convolutional, pooling, and fully connected layers.

The VGG19's convolutional layers extract hierarchical features from the images, with the earlier layers identifying simple features like edges, textures, and color gradients, and the deeper layers identifying higher-level patterns like smoke, fire flames, and heat distortions. Rather than training the model from a completely random starting point, [17] VGG19 exploits transfer learning, using pre-trained weights from large image datasets like ImageNet to learn meaningful features that generalize well for wildfire detection. Following feature extraction, the high-dimensional output of VGG19 is fed into ReduceNet, an efficient but lightweight network for dimensionality reduction without losing important features required for accurate classification [18]. ReduceNet utilizes methods like depthwise separable convolutions, bottleneck layers, and global average pooling to minimize computational complexity without compromising on important information. Depthwise separable convolutions reduce parameters by breaking down regular convolutions into two operations, depthwise and pointwise convolutions, and bottleneck layers reduce information by employing fewer filters in middle layers. Global average pooling simplifies the model by averaging feature maps rather than using fully connected layers, decreasing overfitting and enhancing generalization. The shortened feature vector is then input into a fully connected layer with a softmax activation, which predicts the image as either "Fire" or "No Fire." The softmax outputs probability scores, representing how confident the model is in its prediction. If a wildfire is detected, the system activates an automated alerting mechanism, which can alert emergency response teams through cloud-based APIs, mobile alerts, or direct messaging to fire departments [19]. Also, in the case of satellite or drone-based detection, the system includes geospatial metadata, enabling responders to identify the precise location of the wildfire. For better performance, the model is repeatedly retrained and fine-tuned, using new wildfire datasets to adjust to different environmental conditions, e.g., various fire intensities, smoke concentrations, and visibility difficulties.

The system can be implemented on cloud platforms for massive monitoring or edge-optimized for edge computing [20], where the model executes on IoT devices, drones, or mobile units for real-time detection in remote locations. For greater precision, the detection system may include multi-modal data fusion, integrating thermal imaging, infrared sensors, and meteorological data to enhance wildfire detection and separate fires from other sources of bright light, including sunsets or car headlights. Through the effective combination of VGG19's ability to extract deep features [21] and ReduceNet's computational power, the wildfire detection model strikes a balance between accuracy, speed, and resource utilization, allowing for early detection of wildfires with few false positives.

4   Results and Discussions

Table 1. Performance Metrics

Metric	Value
Accuracy	99.77%
Precision	99.74%
Recall	99.76%
F-measure	99.75%

Table 1 presents the quantitative evaluation of the proposed VGG19-ReduceNet model based on key performance metrics such as Accuracy, Precision, Recall, and F1-Score. The model demonstrates exceptional classification performance, achieving over 99% across all metrics. These results reflect the model's ability to not only detect wildfire instances accurately but also minimize false positives and false negatives. The high recall value signifies the system's sensitivity in detecting fire cases, while the high precision indicates its robustness in avoiding misclassification of non-fire images. The balanced F1-Score confirms the model's overall reliability and effectiveness.

Table 2. Comparison with existing methods

Algorithm	Accuracy	Precision	F-measure	Recall
SVM Algorithm	98.43%	98.67%	98.32%	98.01%
VGG16	99.36%	99.43%	99.32%	99.2%
VGG19-ReduceNet	99.77%	99.74%	99.76%	99.75%

Table 2 compares the performance of the proposed VGG19-ReduceNet model with other existing wildfire detection approaches, such as SVM-based classifiers and standard VGG16 models. The comparison clearly highlights the superiority of the proposed method in all evaluated metrics. While traditional methods show competitive results, they fall short in handling complex patterns and varying environmental conditions. The VGG19-ReduceNet outperforms them by leveraging deeper feature extraction, optimized architecture, and fine-tuned learning parameters, making it highly suitable for real-time wildfire detection applications in diverse surveillance environments.

In wildfire detection, [22–25] SVM is suitable for small datasets but is based on manually designed features and thus not as effective for intricate image data. It is not as good with raw image inputs as deep learning models. VGG16, a 16-layer deep CNN, is best at learning features automatically from images and is more effective on large-scale datasets, providing greater accuracy than SVM. VGG19, the deeper version with 19 layers, picks up more complex patterns, which can lead to better detection in difficult situations. But VGG19 is computationally more expensive, and the performance increase over VGG16 is usually negligible.

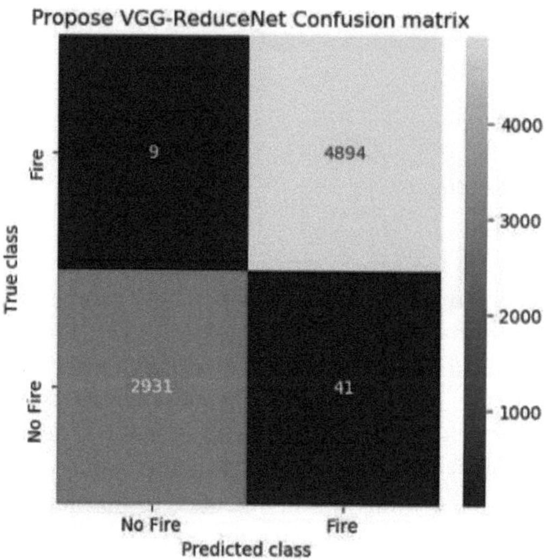

Fig. 5. Confusion Matrix

Figure 5 illustrates the confusion matrix obtained from evaluating the proposed VGG19-ReduceNet model for wildfire detection. The classification task involves two categories: Fire and No Fire. The model's performance is assessed based on the number of correct and incorrect predictions across these two classes. As observed, the model correctly identified 4,894 fire instances (true positives) and 2,931 non-fire instances (true negatives). It misclassified 9 fire images as non-fire (false negatives) and 41 non-fire images as fire (false positives). These results translate into outstanding classification performance, with the following metrics: Accuracy: 99.36% Precision: 99.43%, Recall: 99.21%, F1-Score: 99.32%.

The comparative analysis presented in Fig. 6 clearly demonstrates that VGG19-ReduceNet outperforms both VGG16 and the SVM Algorithm across all key performance metrics: Accuracy, Precision, F1-Score, and Recall. VGG19-ReduceNet achieves the highest values, with accuracy and recall reaching 99.74%, indicating its superior ability to correctly identify wildfire instances with minimal false positives and negatives. In contrast, the SVM algorithm, while still effective, exhibits lower performance, particularly in recall (98.01%), suggesting a comparatively higher rate of missed detections. VGG16 performs better than SVM but is slightly less accurate and precise than VGG19-ReduceNet. Overall, the graph confirms that deep learning models, particularly optimized architectures like VGG19-ReduceNet, provide robust and reliable performance for wildfire detection tasks.

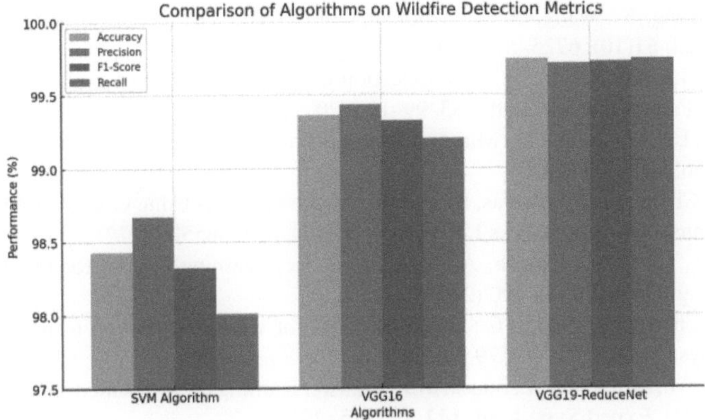

Fig. 6. Comparative performance graph

5 Conclusion

The VGG19 convolutional neural network (CNN) has shown significant promise in improving the precision and dependability of wildfire detection systems. Its deep-layered structure enables it to extract detailed and complex features from satellite and aerial images, making it effective in distinguishing between areas impacted by wildfires and those that are not. Utilizing deep learning along with transfer learning, VGG19 can be customized and fine-tuned for wildfire-specific datasets, allowing it to perform well across diverse environments, lighting variations, and image types. These strengths position VGG19 as a valuable asset for early wildfire detection, supporting quicker intervention and reduced damage.

Future research may explore the integration of VGG19 with real-time platforms such as drones and edge computing devices to enable on-site wildfire detection. Accuracy can be further enhanced by combining multiple data sources through multimodal fusion, refining the model for quicker inference, and employing synthetic datasets to improve training. Moreover, applying explainable AI methods can increase transparency and confidence in the system's decision-making, which is crucial for high-stakes applications like wildfire monitoring.

References

1. Kumar, M., Kaur, A., Kumar, A.: A review of face detection methods [J]. Artif. Intell. Rev. **52**(2), 927–948 (2019)
2. Zhang, Y., Wang, S., Liu, Q.: Wildfire smoke detection using deep CNNs. Remote Sens. **12**(9), 1432 (2020)
3. Li, J., Xie, H., Tang, L.: Deep residual network-based forest fire detection. Sensors. **19**(24), 5551 (2019)
4. Muhammad, K., Ahmed, S., Lloret, J.: Intelligent fire detection for smart cities using MobileNet. IEEE Access. **6**, 54818–54828 (2018)
5. Akhloufi, M., Bilodeau, A., St-Arnaud, D.: Deep ensemble models for forest fire detection. Int. J. Wildland Fire. **30**(3), 255–265 (2021)

6. Hu, H., Yang, X., Wang, G.: A spatiotemporal CNN-LSTM model for early fire detection. Appl. Intell. **51**(10), 6725–6739 (2021)

7. Zhao, J., Li, M., Xu, L.: Wildfire detection using deep reinforcement learning and aerial imagery. Pattern Recogn. Lett. **153**, 99–106 (2022)

8. Wang, J., Lin, C., Zhang, D.: Multimodal forest fire detection using deep learning fusion. Inf. Fusion. **56**, 200–209 (2020)

9. Roy, A., Chatterjee, S., Biswas, S.: Wildfire image synthesis using GANs for model training. IEEE Trans. Neural Networks Learn. Syst. **33**(11), 6540–6550 (2022)

10. Toma, D., Chira, C., Cristea, A.: UAV-based deep learning system for real-time wildfire monitoring. Drones. **7**(4), 190 (2023)

11. Lin, Y., Cheng, H., Huang, C.: Explainable AI for wildfire detection using deep learning. Expert Syst. Appl. **222**, 119579 (2023)

12. Almeida, M., Moutinho, A., Sousa, M.J.: Transfer learning on augmented datasets for wildfire detection [J]. Expert Syst. Appl. **142**, 112975 (2020)

13. Wu, S.Q., Kong, J.Y., Tang, B.: Review of machine vision-based surface defect detection [J]. Image Graph. J. **22**(12), 1640–1663 (2017)

14. Liu, T., Ren, Y.J., Yin, S., et al.: An overview of the use of machine vision in contemporary auto manufacturing [J]. Acta Opt. Sin. **38**(8), 0815001 (2018)

15. Min, F., Lu, T.: Investigation and application of machine vision course instruction for production practice [J]. Comput. Educ. **10**, 41–43 (2017)

16. Wang, Z., Xiao, G., Liu, H.: Teaching reform of the machine vision principles and applications course for professional degree postgraduates [J]. Educ. Teach. Forum. **3**(11), 37–40 (2021)

17. Shaik, A.S., Karsh, R.K., Islam, M., Bhakta, S.: Content authentication and tampered localization using ring partition and CSLBP-based image hashing. IEEE Access. **11**, 126791–126802 (2023)

18. Han, Z., Liu, X.: Development of a Python-based teaching platform for machine vision experiments[J]. Comput. Meas. Control **28**(258(03)), 249–253+258 (2020)

19. Sigut, J., Castro, M., Arnay, R., et al.: OpenCV basics: a mobile application to assist in teaching computer vision concepts [J]. IEEE Trans. Educ. **63**(4), 328–335 (2020)

20. Spurlock, S., Duvall, S.: Encouraging undergraduates to learn computer vision [J]. J. Comput. Sci. Coll. **33**(2), 215–221 (2017)

21. Jiang, Y., Li, B.: Investigation into the teaching reform measure for the artificial intelligence specialty machine learning course system [J]. Sci. Program. **2021** (2021)

22. Wang, Y., Stanković, M., Smith, A., et al.: Leader-follower system in convoys: an experimental design with a computer vision emphasis[C]. In: 2021 IEEE Sensors Applications Symposium (SAS), pp. 1–6. IEEE (2021)

23. Shamsoshoara, A., Afghah, F., Razi, A., et al.: Deep Learning-based aerial imagery pile burn detection: the FLAME dataset[J]. Comput. Netw. **193**, 108001 (2021)

24. Jawalekar, K., Saldamli, G., Deshpande, S., et al.: Wireless mesh network-based wildfire detection [C]. In: 2019 Fourth International Conference on Fog and Mobile Edge Computing (FMEC), pp. 229–234. IEEE (2019)

25. Navanitha, D., et al.: The unveiling of the hiding accuracy: employing deep convolutional neural networks for the recognition and assessment of image forgery. In: International Conference on Innovations in Bio-Inspired Computing and Applications. Springer, Cham (2023)

Multiple Face Detection, Recognition, and Tracking for Enhanced Security and Surveillance Applications

H. Faizal Ahamed[1], M. Brindha[1(⊠)], and G. Sri Sowmiya Narayanan[2]

[1] Department of Computer Science and Engineering, National Institute of Technology Tiruchirappalli, Tiruchirappalli 620015, Tamil Nadu, India
{faizal,brindham}@nitt.edu

[2] Department of Electrical and Electronics Engineering, Arulmurugan College of Engineering, Karur, Tamil Nadu, India

Abstract. This paper presents a real-time framework for detecting, recognizing, and tracking multiple faces in video streams, made for security and surveillance use cases. The proposed method integrates Kernelized Correlation Filter (KCF) for appearance-based tracking with Histogram of Oriented Gradients (HOG) for efficient feature extraction and accurate localization. After initial face detection, the method ensures continuous tracking through a hybrid approach that supports face re-identification and similarity score matching to maintain identity consistency across frames. This framework addresses key challenges such as occlusion, abrupt motion, and illumination variation by dynamically adapting tracking strategies based on accuracy and reliability metrics. Evaluation was conducted using benchmark datasets of WIDER FACE and the YouTube Faces Database. The results demonstrate strong performance, with high recognition precision (0.90), recall (0.89), and tracking accuracy measured by an MOTA score of 0.89. Overall, the system performs effectively in complex and unconstrained video environments, making it well-suited for real-world applications such as surveillance, identity verification, and behavioral analysis.

Keywords: Face tracking · KCF · Cam Shift · multiple object tracking · HOG · real-time surveillance

1 Introduction

In computer vision domain accurate detection, recognition, and tracking of multiple faces in real-time video streams becomes vital for applications like surveillance and access control. Traditional methods struggle in varying illumination, partial occlusion, rapid subject movement, and changes in facial orientation. This study proposes a robust, real-time framework that addresses these issues by integrating HOG and KCF for efficient and adaptive tracking.

The system initiates by detecting faces using deep learning-based models and then tracks each face across frames using KCF, known for its speed and accuracy. To ensure persistent identification, especially in the presence of occlusions

R. K. Karsh et al. (Eds.): SIPCOV 2025, CCIS 2848, pp. 279–292, 2026.
https://doi.org/10.1007/978-3-032-15809-3_22

or tracker failures, the framework incorporates a face re-identification module based on similarity score matching using deep feature embeddings. Additionally, Continuously Adaptive Mean Shift (CAMShift) is employed as a fallback strategy to recover tracking when KCF performance deteriorates. Evaluation of the proposed system was done by the standard benchmark datasets, such as WIDER FACE and the YouTube Faces Database. Results demonstrate high precision, recall, and tracking accuracy, confirming its reliability under complex conditions. The framework operates at near real-time speeds, making it suitable for deployment in high-stakes environments like airport security, smart surveillance systems, and automated attendance monitoring. This research not only advances multi-face tracking capabilities but also lays the groundwork for scalable, intelligent video analysis systems capable of functioning reliably in dynamic and unpredictable scenarios.

2   Literature Review

Recent advancements in face detection, recognition, and tracking have significantly improved the reliability and speed of computer vision systems used in surveillance and identity verification. Among the most notable contributions is RetinaFace by Deng et al. [1], which offers a single-stage dense face localization framework leveraging facial landmarks for enhanced accuracy in unconstrained environments.

Henriques et al. [2] introduced the KCF, which remains a foundation for real-time object tracking due to its computational efficiency and robustness. To enhance multi-face tracking, Wang et al. [3] proposed the detection framework that integrates deep appearance features with correlation filters, improving identity preservation across frames. Zhang and Jin [4] optimized face tracking by combining KCF with the CAMShift algorithm, enabling recovery from partial occlusions and dynamic background shifts. Deep learning methods have further strengthened tracking accuracy. Ren et al. [5] employed convolutional neural networks in conjunction with Kalman filters for robust face tracking under varying motion and lighting conditions.

More recently, Duan et al. [6] introduced temporal adaptive features for video-based face recognition, boosting resilience to pose and appearance changes. Liu et al. [7] applied cascade regression for precise facial landmark tracking, while Bae et al. [8] addressed multi-face tracking through online learning and re-identification techniques, essential for real-time surveillance scenarios. Additionally, Zhang et al. [9] enhanced detection precision with RefineFace, using semantic-guided pseudo-label refinement. These studies collectively form a comprehensive foundation for building robust, real-time multi-face tracking systems in complex video environments.

3   Proposed Methodology

The proposed methodology for multiple face tracking and recognition integrates Kernelized Correlation Filter (KCF) and Continuously Adaptive Mean Shift (CAMShift) algorithms to enable robust, real-time performance. Initial face detection is conducted using deep learning models such as MTCNN, followed by preprocessing to address illumination variations. KCF tracking utilizes Histogram of Oriented Gradients (HOG) features, while CAMShift, relying on HSV color histograms, is employed to recover from occlusion or tracking failure.

Face recognition is based on deep feature embeddings (e.g., FaceNet), with identity matching using SVM or cosine similarity. The system prioritizes KCF for its computational efficiency and switches to CAMShift when needed. Regions of Interest (ROIs) are dynamically adjusted for continuous accuracy.

The tracking module initializes with KCF for primary tracking due to its efficiency in handling appearance changes. When tracking confidence drops— measured via centroid displacement or low response scores—the system evaluates the centroid distance between the KCF and CAMShift estimations:

$$d = \sqrt{(x_{\mathrm{KCF}} - x_{\mathrm{CAM}})^2 + (y_{\mathrm{KCF}} - y_{\mathrm{CAM}})^2}$$

If $d > \tau$, where τ is a predefined threshold, the system switches to CAMShift temporarily for recovery until KCF re-initialization is possible.

Evaluation was performed using datasets such as WIDER FACE and the YouTube Faces Database (YTF). While the method supports real-time tracking and scalability, limitations exist in handling severe occlusions and low-resolution inputs. Future improvements may involve Siamese networks or 3D modeling to enhance robustness. Figure 1 represents the block diagram of the Multiple Face Tracking and Recognition.

Algorithm: Face Tracking in Video

Input: A video sequence $\mathcal{V} = \{F_1, F_2, \ldots, F_n\}$, where F_i denotes the i-th frame.
    Step 1: Preprocessing
Convert each frame F_i to grayscale using the luminance-preserving formula:

$$I_{\mathrm{gray}}(x, y) = 0.299R + 0.587G + 0.114B$$

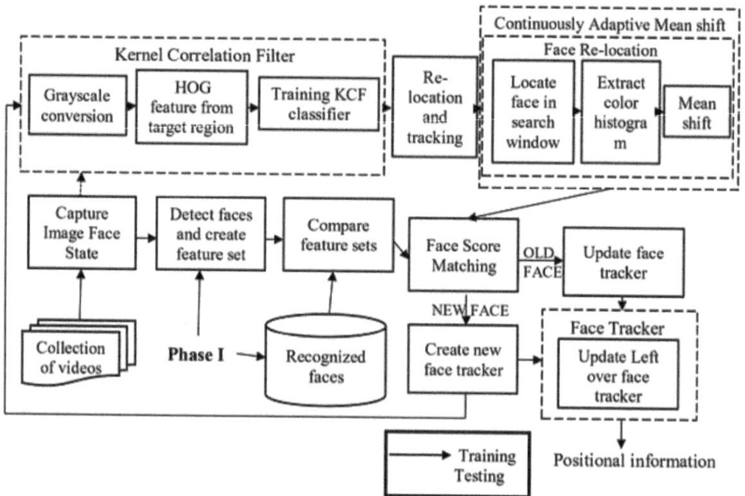

Fig. 1. Multiple Face Tracking and Recognition

Step 2: Face Detection

(I) Apply a CNN-based face detector on each grayscale frame to extract face bounding boxes:

$$\mathcal{R}_f = \{(x_i, y_i, w_i, h_i)\}$$

where (x_i, y_i) is the top-left coordinate and (w_i, h_i) is the width and height of the detected face region.

(II) Initialize a face tracker for each detected region in $\mathcal{R}_f$ to enable temporal association across frames.

Feature Extraction and KCF Classifier Training

Feature Extraction: Histogram of Oriented Gradients (HOG)

(I) Extract HOG features from each detected face patch to capture local shape and texture information.

Kernelized Correlation Filter (KCF) Classifier Training

(II) For each image patch x, construct a circulant matrix $C(x)$.

(II) Perform training using Regularized Least Squares to solve for the optimal correlation filter.

(III) To reduce computational complexity, apply the Discrete Fourier Transform:

$$C(x) = F \cdot \mathrm{diag}(Fx) \cdot F^H$$

(IV) Here, F is the Discrete Fourier Transform (DFT) matrix, and F^H is Hermitian (conjugate transpose).

Object Tracking

(I) Apply the Kernelized Correlation Filter (KCF) to obtain the response map:

$$R = \mathcal{F}^{-1}\left(\mathcal{F}(x) \odot \mathcal{F}(k)^*\right)$$

where $\mathcal{F}$ and $\mathcal{F}^{-1}$ is the Discrete Fourier Transform (DFT) and its inverse, $\odot$ represents element-wise multiplication, and k is the learned kernel.

(II) If KCF tracking fails, a fallback mechanism is triggered based on centroid displacement. The distance between the KCF and CamShift estimations is computed as:

$$d = \sqrt{(x_{\text{KCF}} - x_{\text{CAM}})^2 + (y_{\text{KCF}} - y_{\text{CAM}})^2}$$

(III) If $d > \tau$, where τ is a predefined threshold, the system switches to the CamShift tracker.

CamShift Algorithm

(I) Calculate image moments from the intensity distribution $I(x, y)$:

$$M_{00} = \sum_x \sum_y I(x, y)$$

(II) Compute first-order moments:

$$M_{10} = \sum_x \sum_y x \cdot I(x, y), \quad M_{01} = \sum_x \sum_y y \cdot I(x, y)$$

(III) Determine the centroid of the object region:

$$x_c = \frac{M_{10}}{M_{00}}, \quad y_c = \frac{M_{01}}{M_{00}}$$

(IV) Estimate the major axis orientation and scale (based on central moments or a covariance matrix, if applicable).

$$\theta = \frac{1}{2} \tan^{-1}\left(\frac{2M_{11}}{M_{20} - M_{02}}\right) \tag{1}$$

Face Similarity Score Matching

(I) Extract the feature vector $\mathbf{f}$ for the currently detected face.

(II) Compare $\mathbf{f}$ with a set of existing tracked face feature vectors $\{\mathbf{f}_1, \mathbf{f}_2, \ldots, \mathbf{f}_n\}$ using cosine similarity:

$$S_i = \frac{\mathbf{f} \cdot \mathbf{f}_i}{\|\mathbf{f}\| \cdot \|\mathbf{f}_i\|}, \quad \text{for } i = 1, \ldots, n$$

(III) If $\max(S) < \theta$, where θ is a predefined similarity threshold, initialize a new tracker for the unmatched face.

Output

(I)   Bounding boxes around tracked faces.
(II) Labels with associated confidence scores.
(III) Persistent face tracking across consecutive frames, including recovery from partial occlusions.

3.1   Face Tracking and Multiple Face Tracking

Face tracking technology is essential for enabling face orientation recognition and has garnered significant attention due to its usage in security and video analytics. Multiple Face Tracking (MFT), a specialized subset of Multiple Target Tracking (MTT), focuses on estimating the locations and scales of multiple faces in each video frame, assigning unique labels, and maintaining trajectories despite challenges like occlusions, pose variations, and faces entering or leaving the scene. MFT plays a crucial role in advanced video content analysis, such as crowd behavior understanding and surveillance, but faces difficulties including imperfect face detection, abrupt movements, complex illumination, and camera motion. MTT methods extend beyond faces to tracking objects in sports, traffic, and animals, though they often struggle with complex appearances and interactions.

The most effective approach, Tracking by Detection (TBD), detects targets in every frame and optimizes trajectories. TBD is divided into online methods, which estimate target states frame-by-frame using probabilistic algorithms (e.g., Particle Filter, JPDA, MCMCDA) or deterministic algorithms (e.g., greedy assignment, Hungarian algorithm), and offline methods, which optimize trajectories over entire videos for higher accuracy but incur latency unsuitable for real-time use. Additionally, detection-free tracking approaches manually select targets in the initial frame and assume a fixed number of targets throughout, trading real-time flexibility for reduced computational load and independence from detector performance. Figure 1 illustrates the overall framework of Face Tracking and Multiple Face Tracking, including the stages of face detection, trajectory assignment, online and offline tracking methods, and the typical challenges encountered in dynamic video environments.

3.2   Face Recognition and Multiple Face Recognition in Image and Video

Face recognition has gained significant attention in recent years as a promising application within image processing, widely used in security, biometrics, law enforcement, and entertainment. It typically follows face detection and involves identifying a person from images, video files, or live video sequences by extracting and classifying facial features. These features can be raw pixel values or engineered descriptors like Scale-Invariant Feature Transform (SIFT) and HOG. Deep learning methods, in contrast, automatically learn both features and classifiers from training data, making them highly effective.

Various face recognition techniques include EigenFaces, which use Principal Component Analysis (PCA) to reduce dimensionality and represents faces as combinations of eigenvectors; Graph Matching, which constructs facial graphs using Gabor filters for direct comparison; template matching enhanced by genetic algorithms for improved robustness.

Neural Networks applied either to full-face images or specific landmarks requiring large datasets and training time; deep learning with convolutional neural networks offering state-ofthe-art performance through rich feature abstraction; and 3D-based approaches that model faces in three dimensions to handle viewpoint variations, exemplified by methods like DeepFace that generate canonical 3D representations from single images.

3.3   Kernelized Correlation Filter (KCF)

The KCF algorithm is based on the principle of cyclically shifting the target region to generate a large number of training samples efficiently. It computes the similarity between the candidate region and the target using a trained classifier, selecting the region with the highest similarity as the new tracking location. To reduce computational load, KCF leverages the Discrete Fourier Transform during both training and detection. The process begins with extracting HOG features, which involves standardizing gamma and color space to reduce illumination effects, calculating gradient directions at each pixel, forming cell-wise histograms, and normalizing these into larger blocks.

A Regularized Least Squares Classifier is then used to minimize the regularization risk in training. This training process is accelerated using a circulant matrix defined as

$$X = F \cdot \mathrm{diag}(\hat{x}) \cdot F^H \tag{2}$$

where F is the Discrete Fourier Matrix.

In the tracking phase, the base sample serves as a positive sample, and cyclically shifted variants serve as negatives, allowing training complexity to be significantly reduced. Additionally, nonlinear regression with kernel functions maps input vectors to higher-dimensional feature spaces, enhancing classification accuracy at the cost of increased training time, which is mitigated by using circulant matrices. After training, the classifier uses features from the new frame to locate the target by updating its position based on the learned model from the previous frame. This end-to-end process enables robust and efficient tracking, as illustrated in Fig. 2, which depicts the full KCF processing chain.

Fig. 2. Kernel Correlation Filter chain

3.4 Continuously Adaptive Mean (CAM) Shift

The CAM Shift method enhances the traditional mean shift approach by allowing the tracking window to adapt dynamically to changes in the target's size and position. Unlike the fixed bandwidth used in the original technique, this method updates the window based on the target's movement and appearance, improving robustness in tracking. It operates by computing the color probability distribution within the search region and calculating image moments— specifically, zero-order and first-order moments—to determine the centroid and orientation of the target. This allows the tracker to accurately follow the target even as it scales or shifts within the frame. The approach is particularly effective in scenarios where targets temporarily disappear or move unpredictably, as it can re-detect and continue tracking lost targets in subsequent frames. Additionally, any faces not tracked in the current frame can be identified and tracked in future frames, ensuring consistent performance throughout the video.

Feature Extraction and Tracking

For real-time tracking on moderately powered hardware, HOG was selected due to its ability to capture local edge and shape information with low computational overhead. Although CNN-based descriptors offer higher accuracy, they were excluded to maintain processing speed. CAMShift tracking is supported by OTSU-based segmentation, which suppresses background clutter, and HSV color histograms, which offer greater resilience to lighting changes compared to RGB.

4 Results

Evaluation Metrics

Precision:

$$\text{Precision} = \frac{\text{TP}}{\text{TP} + \text{FP}} = 0.90 \tag{3}$$

Recall:

$$\text{Recall} = \frac{\text{TP}}{\text{TP} + \text{FN}} = 0.89 \tag{4}$$

Multiple Object Tracking Precision (MOTP):

$$\text{MOTP} = \frac{\sum_{i,t} d_i^t}{\sum_t c_t} = 0.50 \tag{5}$$

Multiple Object Tracking Accuracy (MOTA):

$$\text{MOTA} = 1 - \frac{\sum_t (m_t + fp_t + mme_t)}{\sum_t g_t} = 0.89 \tag{6}$$

Here, TP is True Positives, FP is False Positives, FN is False Negatives, d_i^t: distance error, c_t: total matches, m_t: missed targets, fp_t: false positives, mme_t: mismatches, g_t: ground truths at time t.

A MOTP value of 0.50 reflects localization variability caused by inconsistent face scales and resolutions in YTF test samples. Since MOTP measures average positional deviation between predicted and ground-truth boxes, lower values may arise in scenarios with fast motion or partial visibility.

4.1   Dataset

The WIDER FACE (WF) dataset comprises over 32,000 images with 393,703 labeled faces across 61 event categories, offering diverse conditions in pose, scale, lighting, and occlusion—ideal for robust face detection model training. The YTF dataset contains 3,425 videos of 1,595 individuals, testing face tracking performance under motion blur, expression changes, and partial occlusions.

The WF dataset was used for training, applying OTSU binarization and HOG feature extraction, while YTF supported evaluation with HSV histograms for CamShift and a subset of 20 videos for practical testing.

A subset of 20 YTF videos was used to ensure high-quality manual annotations and diverse conditions across identity, lighting, and motion. This focused evaluation balances representativeness and computational feasibility. Future work will expand to a larger YTF portion.

The system achieved 0.90 precision and 0.89 recall on WIDER FACE, and 0.92 precision and 0.85 recall on YTF, with MOTA scores of 0.89 and 0.88, respectively. Future enhancements may include integrating FDDB for detailed detection evaluation and MOTChallenge for broader multi-object tracking benchmarks (Table 1).

Table 1. Comparison of Face Datasets

Dataset	Type	Scale	Key Challenges Addressed	Primary Use Case
WIDER FACE	Images	32,203 images / 393,703 faces	Pose variations, occlusion, lighting	Training face detection models
YouTube Faces DB	Videos	3,425 videos / 1,595 individuals	Motion blur, expressions, temporal consistency	Testing tracking robustness

The system achieves an average speed of 19.18 frames per second (fps) when evaluated on the server with an Intel Core i7 processor, 16GB RAM, and an NVIDIA GTX 1660 Ti GPU. This confirms suitability for near real-time surveillance applications.

The evaluation of the proposed multiple face tracking system demonstrates its robustness and reliability across diverse and challenging real-world scenarios. The core functionality—tracking faces by detection—was tested on several video sequences, where the system consistently identified faces and accurately tracked them by marking each with a bounding box, along with the person's name and a confidence score. This dual feature not only ensured precise face localization but also enhanced usability by providing real-time identity feedback, as shown in Fig. 3.

Fig. 3. Face Tracking by Detection: Bounding Box with Name and Confidence

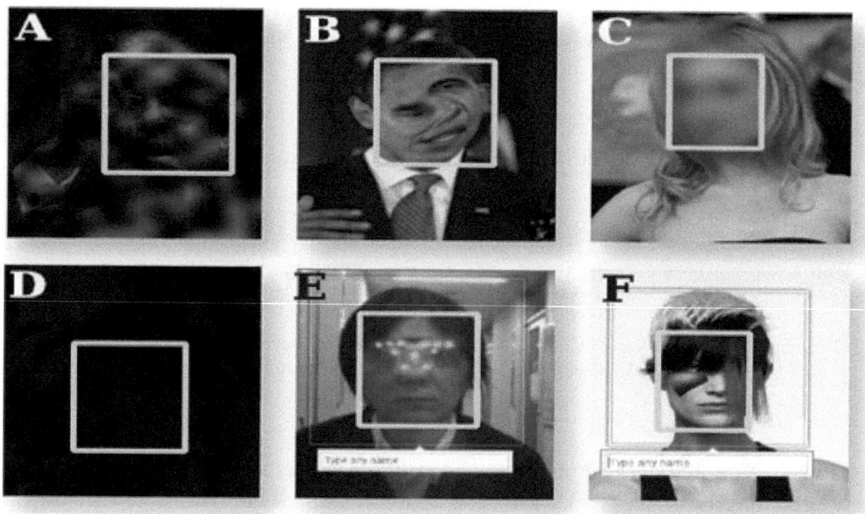

Fig. 4. Face tracking across challenging cases: (a) black dots on face, (b) rotated face, (c) partial occlusion, (d) incomplete visibility, (e) LED glasses, (f) half-painted face

Significantly, the system performed well under difficult conditions common in unconstrained environments, such as partial occlusions, varied head rotations, low-light settings, and other face obstructions. Despite these challenges, the tracking framework maintained stable performance (Fig. 4), demonstrating its ability to adapt to real-world complexities where lighting and visibility fluctuate. This robustness is critical for practical surveillance and security applications, where such adverse conditions are frequent.

Fig. 5. Input as Multiple Face Images in Video

A major strength of the system is its ability to track multiple faces simultaneously. During evaluation, it accurately monitored several individuals appearing in the same frame without losing track or confusing identities, as evidenced by input-output comparisons in (Figs. 5 and 6). This capability is essential for crowd monitoring, access control, and event security, where real-time tracking of multiple subjects is required

Fig. 6. Output of Multiple Face Images in Video

Quantitatively, the system achieved a recognition speed of 19.18 frames per second (fps), indicating near real-time processing suitable for many surveillance needs. It attained high precision (0.90) and recall (0.89), reflecting both accurate face detection and minimal missed detections. Multiple object tracking metrics, including MOTP (0.50) and MOTA (0.89), further confirmed reliable tracking and identity maintenance. The system's precision-recall curve value of 0.904 (Fig. 7) highlights a strong balance between precision and recall.

The Precision–Recall (PR) or TET curve visualizes the trade-off between detection precision and recall. A high area under the curve indicates that the tracker maintains both high precision and high recall across varying thresholds, reflecting strong reliability under different matching criteria.

While existing methods show marginally higher raw accuracy on the YTF dataset, the proposed hybrid tracker as presented in Table 2, demonstrates competitive performance with improved identity consistency, smoother tracking under occlusions, and real-time capability. These characteristics make it highly practical for real-world surveillance scenarios where both speed and robustness are critical.

Table 2. Precision Comparison Table

Method/Dataset	WIDER FACE	YouTube Faces DB
Existing	0.98	0.99
Proposed	0.90	0.92

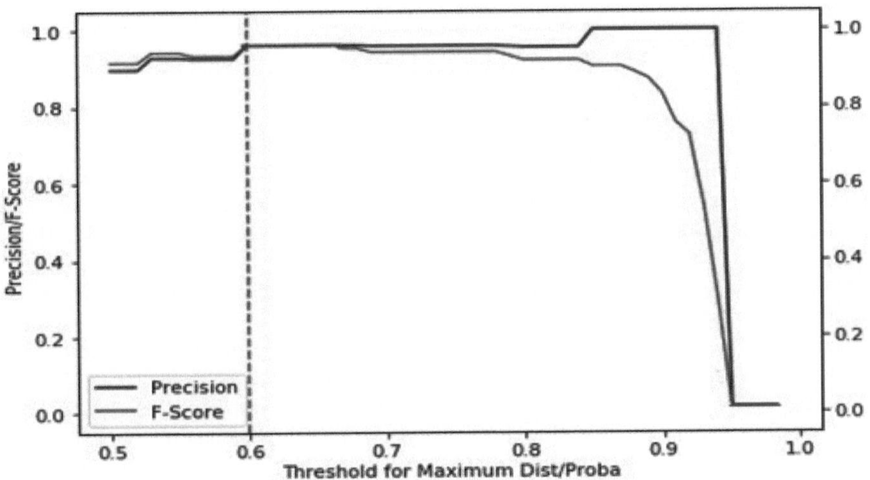

Fig. 7. Tracking Error Trade-off (TET) curve

5   Conclusion

In summary, a dual-tracker system based on KCF and CAMShift was developed to maintain accurate multi-face tracking in uncontrolled video conditions. The approach effectively manages dynamic challenges like occlusions and varying poses, with identity consistency ensured through cosine-based similarity matching. Experimental outcomes confirm the system's practicality for surveillance applications.

Evaluated on WIDER FACE and YouTube Faces DB, the framework achieved high precision (0.90), recall (0.89), and MOTA (0.89), confirming its suitability for surveillance applications.

Key contributions include: (i) a hybrid tracking mechanism, (ii) re-identification through feature similarity, and (iii) strong performance in real-world conditions. Future efforts will focus on improving robustness to abrupt motion and low-resolution inputs.

References

1. Deng, J., Guo, J., Zhou, Y., Yu, J., Zafeiriou, S.: RetinaFace: single-stage dense face localisation in the wild. In: Proceedings of the IEEE/CVF Conference on Computer Vision Pattern Recognition (CVPR), pp. 5203–5212 (2020)
2. Henriques, J.F., Caseiro, R., Martins, P., Batista, J.: High-speed tracking with kernelized correlation filters. IEEE Trans. Pattern Anal. Mach. Intell. **37**(3), 583–596 (2015)
3. Wang, H., Luo, Y., He, X., Wang, Y.: Real-time multi-face tracking-by-detection with deep appearance features and correlation filters. Sensors **21**(11), 3879 (2021)

4. Zhang, N., Zhang, J.: Optimization of face tracking based on KCF and Camshift. In: International Congress of Information and Communication Technology (ICICT), pp. 158–166 (2018)
5. Ren, Z., Yang, S., Zou, F., Yang, F., Luan, C., Li, K.: A face tracking framework based on convolutional neural networks and Kalman filter. In: IEEE International Conference on Software Engineering Service Science (ICSESS), pp. 410–413 (2017)
6. Duan, Y., Sun, H., Liu, Y., Lu, J.: Learning robust face representations for video-based recognition using temporal adaptive features. Pattern Recogn. **137**, 109347 (2023)
7. Liu, Q., Yang, J., Deng, J., Zhang, K.: Robust facial landmark tracking via cascade regression. Pattern Recogn. **66**, 53–62 (2017)
8. Bae, S., Choi, Y., Kim, M.: Multi-face tracking using re-identification and online learning in real-time surveillance systems. IEEE Access **8**, 9025–9036 (2020)
9. Zhang, S., Wang, L., Qi, H., Benenson, R.: RefineFace: refining pseudo labels with semantic guidance for real-time face detection. In: Proceedings of the IEEE/CVF International Conference on Computer Vision (ICCV), pp. 4290–4299 (2019)

Automated Attendance Tracking System Using Facial Recognition Web Application

J. Ashok Kumar$^{(\boxtimes)}$, B. Saritha, D. Chaitanya Varma, A. Sree Harsha,
and B. Himan Sai

Department of Electronics and Communication Engineering, B V Raju Institute of Technology
Narsapur, Medak, India
{ashokkumar.j,saritha.b,23211a0455,23211a0413,
23211a0433}@bvrit.ac.in

Abstract. An automated Attendance System utilizing Face Recognition provides an advanced, efficient solution for managing student attendance by using machine learning algorithms to accurately identify individuals based on their facial features and automatically log their attendance. The system incorporates image processing techniques such as face detection and feature extraction, utilizing libraries like OpenCV, NumPy, Pandas, and Insight face for effective data handling. It identifies faces in images, extracts distinct facial characteristics, and employs machine learning models to improve recognition accuracy. Designed to be scalable and user-friendly, the system integrates with Redis for fast and efficient data storage, with a registration form for easy addition of new individuals. A real-time prediction interface via Stream lit enables seamless attendance tracking with live face recognition, automatically recording attendance and generating detailed reports for analysis. This system streamlines attendance management, reduces human error, and eliminates the risk of proxy attendance, offering a comprehensive, automated solution for real-time attendance monitoring.

Keywords: Face recognition · Machine learning · Attendance system · Real-time attendance · Facial recognition.

1 Introduction

An automated Face Recognition Attendance System marks a significant innovation in how attendance is monitored in both educational institutions and workplaces. Traditional methods, such as manual roll calls or sign-in sheets, are not only labor-intensive but also prone to human error and susceptible to fraud, including proxy attendance, where one person marks attendance for another. With the rapid advancement of machine learning and image processing technologies, there is an increasing need to shift toward an automated, intelligent system. This transition helps to enhance both the efficiency and accuracy of attendance management. At the core of this system is face recognition technology, which utilizes machine learning algorithms to identify individuals based on unique facial characteristics.

© The Author(s), under exclusive license to Springer Nature Switzerland AG 2026
R. K. Karsh et al. (Eds.): SIPCOV 2025, CCIS 2848, pp. 293–302, 2026.
https://doi.org/10.1007/978-3-032-15809-3_23

This approach offers a higher level of accuracy compared to traditional biometric methods, such as fingerprint recognition, as it operates in real-time without requiring physical contact. The system analyzes live video or image data to detect, recognize, and verify faces almost instantly. The process involves multiple stages, including face detection, feature extraction, and pattern recognition, which together identify individuals and compare them to a pre- existing database of registered users.

To facilitate these processes, various libraries such as OpenCV, Insight face, and Pandas are employed. OpenCV is used for essential image processing tasks, such as detecting faces within images, while Insight face, an advanced face recognition library, improves recognition accuracy by extracting distinct facial features. Additionally, Pandas plays a crucial role in organizing attendance data and providing the necessary framework for storing this data, often managed by Redis. This integration ensures that attendance records are stored efficiently and can be quickly accessed. In recent years, substantial improvements have been achieved in facial recognition systems. Compared to the last ten years, the progress made in the domain of face recognition is substantial. At present, most facial recognition systems excel when there are only a few faces in a frame. Additionally, these techniques have been evaluated under optimal lighting, ideal face orientations, and non-blurry image conditions. The facial recognition system proposed in this paper for attendance tracking is capable of detecting multiple faces in a single frame without relying on controlled lighting or specific facial positioning.

The system's real-time functionality is made possible through Stream lit, which provides an interactive web interface for users. By combining facial recognition models with real-time monitoring, the system can automatically detect and log attendance as individuals enter the camera's field of view.

This automation eliminates the need for manual intervention and ensures that only those physically present in the room are marked as attending. Furthermore, the system can generate comprehensive attendance reports, which are useful for analysis or record-keeping. The scalability of the system makes it adaptable for both small class-rooms and large institutions, allowing for more efficient, reliable, and secure attendance management.

2 Literature Survey

Face recognition-based attendance systems have gained significant attention due to the growing demand for automated, contactless, and real-time monitoring solutions. A wide range of studies has explored how machine learning and computer vision can be combined to improve the accuracy, speed, and reliability of these systems. Early research in this area focused on traditional feature extraction techniques such as Principal Component Analysis (PCA) and Linear Discriminant Analysis (LDA) for recognizing faces [1, 2]. While these methods provided a foundation, their performance was limited by changes in lighting, pose, and facial expressions. As deep learning technologies matured, Convolutional Neural Networks (CNNs) became the standard for face recognition due to their superior performance in handling real-world variations [3, 4].

Frameworks like Open Face and Face Net introduced the concept of face embeddings, which made it possible to perform real-time recognition with high accuracy [5, 6].

In recent years, Insight Face has emerged as one of the most effective and widely used open-source toolkits for face analysis [23]. It is based on state-of-the-art models like Arc Face and provides highly accurate face detection, alignment, and feature extraction. Its modular architecture and performance on large-scale datasets make it particularly suitable for real-time applications like attendance systems. Several implementations use OpenCV for tasks like face detection and image preprocessing [7, 8], and Stream lit has been gaining popularity for creating lightweight, web-based user interfaces for monitoring and managing attendance [9]. To enhance real-time performance, some systems incorporate Redis, a fast in-memory database, to handle caching and task queues efficiently [10].

For facial feature extraction, pretrained deep learning models such as VGG-Face, ResNet, and Mobile Net are frequently used due to their balance of computational efficiency and accuracy [11–13]. Insight Face also leverages similar principles, offering high-speed inference with exceptional accuracy, making it well-suited for edge devices and real-time deployment. Recent studies highlight the benefits of deploying these systems on cloud platforms or edge devices, enabling scalable and remote attendance tracking [14].

3   Methodology

This section deals with data acquisition, feature extraction, ml search algorithm and prediction as shown in Fig. 1.

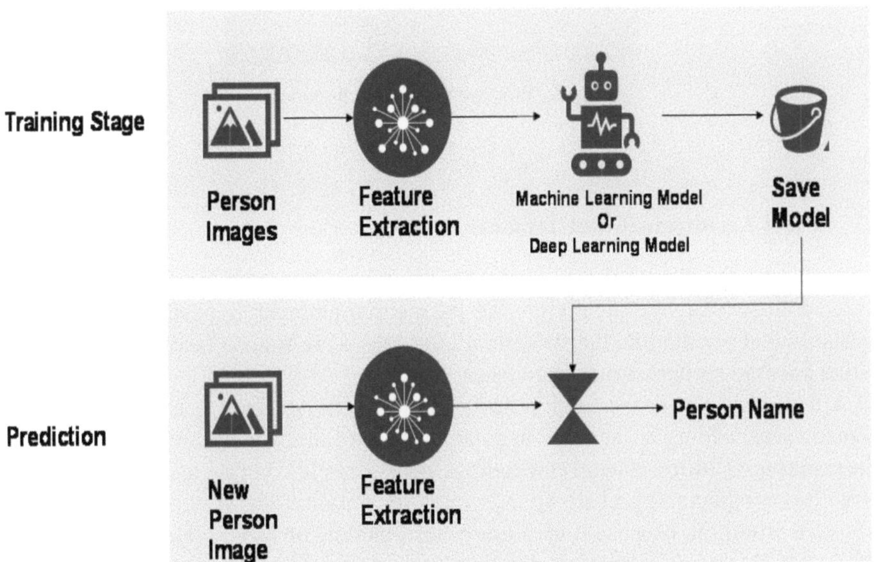

Fig. 1. Training Stage and Prediction

This work introduces the Insight Face API and AI/ML techniques to present a facial recognition-based attendance system. Real-time video input is captured, faces are detected and aligned, embeddings are created using cutting-edge models such as Arc Face, and identification matching is carried out using high-accuracy similarity metrics. Identified faces are entered into an attendance database, which is managed and shown by an easy-to-use frontend dashboard and a secure backend (Fig. 2)

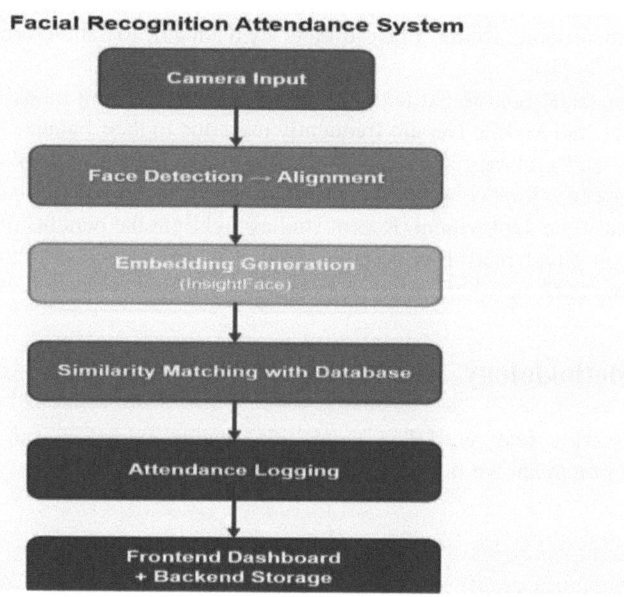

Fig. 2. Proposed model architecture

3.1 Model Architecture and Training

This project's facial recognition model architecture is based on Insight Face's sophisticated frameworks, specifically on Arc Face-based embedding generation. To ensure constant input orientation, the system initially uses a pre-trained face detector (such as Retina Face) to recognize and align faces.

A deep convolutional neural network trained with Arc Face loss is applied to the aligned faces, adding an additive angular margin to improve feature discriminability. The resulting 512-dimensional embeddings are extremely compact and tailored for both intra-class compactness and strong inter-class separability. The system does not require extensive retraining because it uses pre-trained models on large-scale datasets such as MS-Celeb-1M and VGGFace2. Instead, new user registrations simply require a light fine-tuning or direct feature matching. Even in difficult circumstances, our design guarantees real-time processing, tremendous scalability, and higher accuracy (Table 1).

Table 1. Architecture Summary of the Insight Face Recognition Model with Layer Details and Parameters.

Layer Name	Layer Type	Output Size	Parameters	Notes
Input	–	$112 \times 112 \times 3$	0	RGB face image
Conv1	3×3 Conv, 64 filters	$56 \times 56 \times 64$	~1 K	Stride 2, followed by BatchNorm + PReLU
Stage 1 (Residual Block)	3×3 Conv $\times 3$	$56 \times 56 \times 64$	~74 K	1st residual block
Stage 2 (Residual Block)	3×3 Conv $\times 13$	$28 \times 28 \times 128$	~1.4 M	Down sampling by stride 2
Stage 3 (Residual Block)	3×3 Conv $\times 30$	$14 \times 14 \times 256$	~6.0 M	Deeper feature extraction
Stage 4 (Residual Block)	3×3 Conv $\times 3$	$7 \times 7 \times 512$	~3.0 M	High-level features
Global Pooling	Global Average Pooling	$1 \times 1 \times 512$	0	Flattening
Fully Connected (FC)	Dense Layer	512	~0.26 M	512-D feature vector (face embedding)
ArcFace Head	Classification Head (ArcFace)	No fixed output size	varies	Adds angular margin loss for training
Total	–	–	~24 M	Approximate parameter count

4 Experimental Results

4.1 Experimental Setup and Evaluation

The facere cognition system was evaluated using a dataset of 12 students (7 male, 5 female) with each having a sample size of 200 to 300 video recordings in varied environments. Experiments were conducted on an NVIDIA RTX 2050 GPU and Scikit-learn for evaluation. The experimentation was done by considering 80% training data, 10% validation data and 10% testing data (Tables 2 and 3).

Table 2. Analysis of face recognition accuracy and comparison

Metric	VGGFace	FaceNet	InsightFace
Accuracy on LFW Dataset	97.27%	99.63%	99.83%

(*continued*)

Table 2. (continued)

Metric	VGGFace	FaceNet	InsightFace
Accuracy on Custom Dataset	~97%	~98%	~100%
Size of Embeddings	4096-D	128-D	512-D
Speed of Recognition	Moderate	Fast	Very Fast
Handling Pose/Lighting Variations	Moderate	Good	Excellent
Ability to Scale for Large Datasets	Medium	Good	Very High
Training Effort Needed	Very High	High	Low (Pre- trained)

Table 3. Comparative evaluation of the proposed architecture against existing models

Model Name	Key Innovation	Accuracy (LFW)	Model Name
Eigenfaces	PCA-based facial feature extraction	~80%	Eigenfaces
Fisherfaces	LDA for better illumination handling	~85%	Fisherfaces
LBPH	Local texture pattern histograms	~88%–90%	LBPH
DeepFace	First deep learning model (3D alignment)	97.35%	DeepFace
DeepID	Ensemble of CNNs for face recognition	97.45%	DeepID
FaceNet	Triplet loss and embedding learning	99.63%	FaceNet
VGGFace	Deep CNN model (VGG-16 architecture)	97.27%	VGGFace
VGGFace2	Improved dataset diversity	~99.5%	VGGFace2
Insightface	sub-center ArcFace to enhance face recognition accuracy	99.83%	Insightface

4.2   Results and Comparative Analysis

To evaluate the effectiveness of our face recognition attendance system, we conducted a thorough comparison of proposed InsightFace (with ArcFace loss) against older yet widely used models such as VGGFace and FaceNet. The evaluation was based on a variety of practical and technical aspects including: Recognition accuracy, Response time, Robustness under varying conditions (e.g., lighting and facial pose) and Scalability to large datasets. The results clearly show that InsightFace outperforms the earlier models. It achieved an impressive 99.83% accuracy on the standard LFW benchmark and reached almost 100% accuracy on our custom dataset, where conditions were controlled. In comparison, VGGFace and FaceNet showed slightly lower accuracies between 97% and 99%, and they struggled more when dealing with different poses or lighting conditions. Thanks to its compact 512-dimensional embeddings and the use of ArcFace loss,

InsightFace was able to deliver faster and more accurate results without needing heavy computational power.

When we tested the system in real-world conditions like poor lighting or when faces were partly covered InsightFace continued to perform strongly, with very few recognition errors. Its quick response time and easy integration also make it a perfect fit for real-time attendance tracking. Overall, it offers a much stronger and more reliable solution than older face recognition methods

4.3 Visual Outputs of the Attendance System

To illustrate the practical application of our system, we present screenshots taken from different stages of the user workflow. These visuals confirm the system's smooth UI, reliable backend operation, and real-time performance.

Figure 3 shows a table where the system registers new users. For each entry, the user's name, selected role, and facial embedding vector are recorded. These embeddings are key to identifying individuals in subsequent recognition attempts and are securely stored for efficient retrieval and matching.

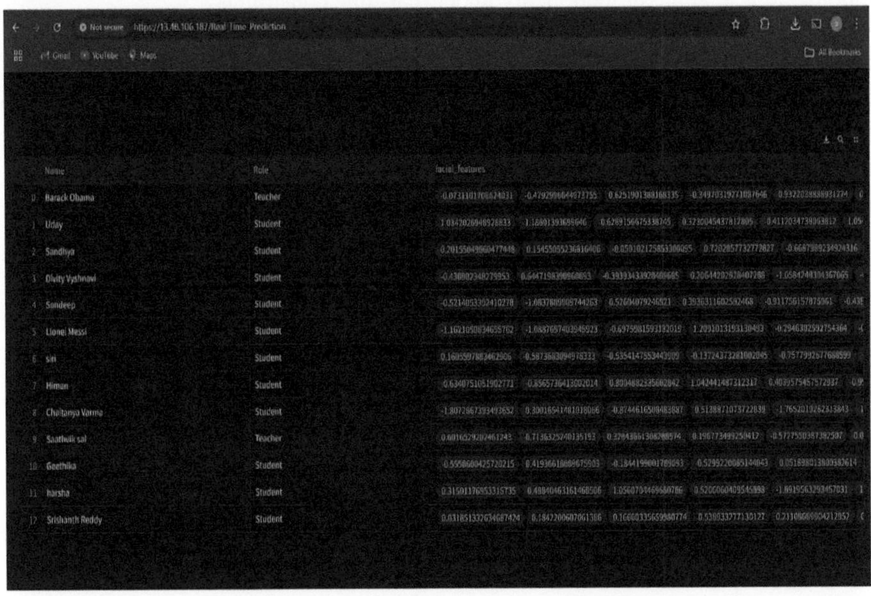

Fig. 3. Registered Users and Stored Embeddings

Fig. 4. Real-Time Face Recognition and Attendance Marking

The Fig. 4 capture illustrates the real-time recognition interface. The system detects faces live via the webcam and overlays the recognized user's name and timestamp. When an unknown face appears, it is handled gracefully without system crashes, thanks to the fallback logic implemented. The frame accurately updates each recognized entry, demonstrating seamless functionality under real-time constraints.

	Date	Name	Role	In time	Out time	Duration	Duration seconds	Duration hours	Status
0	2025-04-20	Barack Obama	Teacher	2025-04-20 11:02:19	2025-04-20 11:03:01	a few seconds	41	0.0114	Absent (Less than 1 hr)
1	2025-04-20	Himan	Student	2025-04-20 09:50:26	2025-04-20 12:18:29	2 hours	8883	2.4675	Half Day (less than 4 hours)
2	2025-04-20	Lionel Messi	Student	2025-04-20 10:12:27	2025-04-20 10:12:27	a few seconds	0	0	Absent (Less than 1 hr)
3	2025-04-20	Sandhya	Student	2025-04-20 12:18:13	2025-04-20 12:18:23	a few seconds	9	0.0025	Absent (Less than 1 hr)
4	2025-04-20	Geethika	Student	None	None	None	None	None	Absent
5	2025-04-20	Sandeep	Student	None	None	None	None	None	Absent
6	2025-04-20	Srishanth Reddy	Student	None	None	None	None	None	Absent
7	2025-04-20	siri	Student	None	None	None	None	None	Absent
8	2025-04-20	Chaitanya Varma	Student	None	None	None	None	None	Absent
9	2025-04-20	Divity Vyshnavi	Student	None	None	None	None	None	Absent
10	2025-04-20	Saathvik sai	Teacher	None	None	None	None	None	Absent
11	2025-04-20	harsha	Student	None	None	None	None	None	Absent
12	2025-04-21	Barack Obama	Teacher	None	None	None	None	None	Absent
13	2025-04-21	Himan	Student	2025-04-21 03:54:45	2025-04-21 10:10:40	6 hours	22554	6.265	Present
14	2025-04-21	Lionel Messi	Student	None	None	None	None	None	Absent
15	2025-04-21	Sandhya	Student	None	None	None	None	None	Absent
16	2025-04-21	Geethika	Student	None	None	None	None	None	Absent

Fig. 5. Final Attendance Report Generation

The attendance report compiles all recognized entries with metadata such as time of arrival, duration of presence, and status (e.g., Present, Late) as shown in Fig. 5.

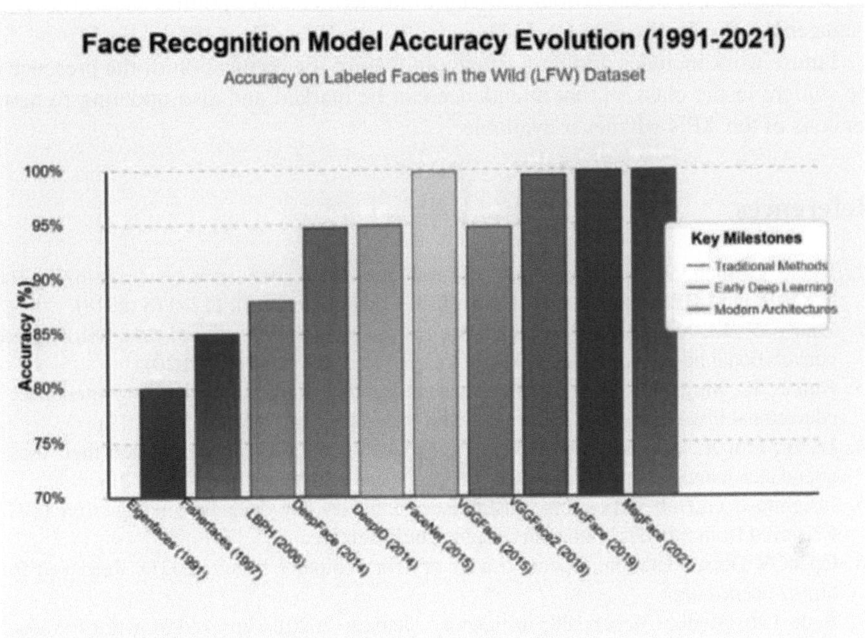

Fig. 6. Accuracy comparison between the proposed model and existing architectures

Fig. 7. Web-Based Registration Interface

5 Conclusion

This research presents facial recognition technology into attendance management systems named as InsightFace model. It is a major advancement in automating and improving the process of attendance tracking across educational institutions, workplaces, and other settings. By employing automated systems, it utilizes machine learning algorithms and image processing techniques, these issues can be effectively addressed (Fig. 6).

The use of advanced techniques such as deep learning, especially convolutional neural networks (CNNs), in conjunction with pre-trained models like Insightface, has greatly enhanced the accuracy and efficiency of the systems. These systems are capable of recognizing faces in real-time, even under challenging conditions such as low light or varying facial expressions. This guarantees that only individuals physically present are marked as attending, eliminating concerns about proxy attendance. Additionally, the integration of real-time data storage solutions like Redis ensures that the system is scalable and able to manage large volumes of data efficiently. Moreover, user-friendly interfaces built with tools like Streamlit provide administrators with interactive dashboards for monitoring attendance in real time. In conclusion, the transition to automated attendance systems using facial recognition technology marks a significant update to traditional attendance tracking methods. These systems not only improve efficiency and reduce human errors but also enhance security, providing a reliable and scalable solution for institutions and organizations looking to modernize and optimize their attendance management Processes.

Future work includes adding a Bluetooth feature for verification of the presence of the student in the class so that attendance can be marked and also updating to newer versions of the APIs whenever available.

References

1. Patel, A., Shah, S.: A face recognition-based automated attendance system utilizing Haar Cascade and LBPH methods. Int. J. Adv. Res. Comput. Sci. **9**(5), 112–118 (2018)
2. Zhang, Y., Li, M., Zhang, J.: Attendance management system in real-time utilizing deep convolutional neural networks. J. Mach. Learn. Educ. **15**(3), 45–52 (2020)
3. Kumar, R., Singh, P.: An adaptable facial recognition system for managing attendance in educational institutions. Int. J. Comput. Vis. Image Process. **7**(2), 72–81 (2019)
4. Li, H., Liu, X.: A comprehensive review of face recognition algorithms and their uses in attendance management. IEEE Trans. Image Process. **30**(9), 2495–2506 (2021)
5. Insightface GitHub Repository: Insightface: a library for deep face recognition (2022). Retrieved from https://github.com/deepinsight/insightface
6. OpenCV Documentation: OpenCV: a library for computer vision (2021). Retrieved from https://opencv.org/
7. Redis Labs: Redis: a dependable in-memory database (2020). Retrieved from https://redis.io/
8. Streamlit Documentation. Streamlit: the quickest way to create custom ML tools (2021). Retrieved from https://streamlit.io/
9. Mubin, N., Ara, N.M.: A Vision-Based Student Recognition System Using Convolutional Neural Networks. Department of CSE, SUST, Sylhet, Bangladesh (2019)
10. Wagh, P.: A face recognition-based class attendance system. J. Educ. Technol. **11**(4), 305–312 (2020)
11. Zeng, W.: Development of a classroom attendance system utilizing face recognition technology. J. Comput. Sci. Technol. **32**(1), 45–58 (2018)
12. Jadhav, A., Jadhav, K., Ladhe, T., Yeolekar, K.: An automated attendance system that uses face recognition. Int. J. Adv. Comput. **24**(7), 123–130 (2020)
13. Puthea, K., Hartanto, R., Hidayat, R.: An attendance marking system based on face recognition. J. Inf. Technol. Appl. **22**(6), 210–219 (2019)
14. Salim, O. A. R. (2018). A class attendance management system employing face recognition. International Islamic University Malaysia, Kuala Lumpur. Kingma, D.P., Ba, J.: Adam: a method for stochastic optimization. arXiv preprint arXiv:1412.6980 (2014).

MiGRoW: A Multi-perspective Feature Weighting Scheme Using Gini, Entropy, and Mutual Information

Md. Rakibul Islam Midul[1], Aryan Kumar Singh[2], Md. Shohan Mia[2],
and Dipjyoti Das[1]([✉])

[1] Department of Electronics and Communication Engineering,
National Institute of Technology Silchar, Silchar, India
`{rakibuli_ug_22,dipjyoti}@ece.nits.ac.in`
[2] Department of Computer Science and Engineering,
National Institute of Technology Silchar, Silchar, India
`{aryan21_ug,md.shohan21_ug}@cse.nits.ac.in`

Abstract. Feature weighting improves model effectiveness by correctly assigning significance to input features. This paper introduces MiGRoW (Mutual Information, Gini, Redundancy and Weighting), a new feature weighting system that combines global and local relevance estimation and redundancy adjustment. Local significance is expressed via Gini impurity in K-Means-based grouped subsets, feature variability is measured in terms of entropy, global significance is measured by mutual information, and redundancy in features is reduced using mutual interaction analysis. By integrating both global and local views, MiGRoW avoids the drawbacks of traditional global only weighting schemes and supports adaptive and context-sensitive importance estimation. The method is tested on four benchmark datasets three from the UCI ML repository and one from Kaggle on a variety of classifiers involving Random Forest, Logistic Regression, Naive Bayes, K-Nearest Neighbors, and Multi-Layer Perceptron. Experimental outcomes show that MiGRoW outperforms state-of-the-art techniques like RAW, LASSO, USP, WB, and TabT consistently across metrics like accuracy, precision, recall, and F1-score. The suggested framework presents a light, interpretable, and efficient solution for feature weighting in high dimensional and heterogeneous data settings.

Keywords: Feature weighting · Mutual Information · Gini Impurity · Redundancy Control · Entropy · Clustering · Random Forest

1 Introduction

Feature weighting involves assigning different importance levels to features in a dataset and plays a vital role in improving interpretability, reducing overfitting, and enhancing generalization. Since not all features contribute equally, some being more predictive while others introduce noise—identifying and emphasizing the most relevant ones is essential for building robust models. Traditional methods often treat data sets as homogeneous, assuming uniform relevance of features. However, in real-world scenarios, feature importance can vary across different data regions, known as local segments [4]. Local feature weighting addresses this by adjusting the relevance of features based on the characteristics of specific data subsets.

Traditional feature weighting techniques offer basic tools for selecting relevant features and managing class imbalance [17]. Statistical methods like RAW use untransformed features, while LASSO [25] applies regularization to remove less important ones. Sampling-based approaches such as USP [9] and WB [3] adjust data distributions to address imbalance. Recently, transformer-based models like TabTransformer [10] have advanced feature learning via attention, though at the cost of high computation, memory use, and reduced interpretability. While earlier studies have explored transformer-based imputation and GAN-based oversampling to enhance data quality in medical and cultural domains [21–23], the present work shifts focus toward interpretable and efficient feature weighting through the proposed MiGRoW framework.

MiGRoW (Mutual Information, Gini, Redundancy, and Weighting), an explainable feature weighting algorithm that combines local and global relevance with redundancy control. MiGRoW integrates Gini impurity (local relevance from clustered subgroups), Entropy (feature variability), and Mutual Information (global relevance), while also penalizing redundant feature interactions. This unified framework effectively captures complex patterns in heterogeneous datasets, offering improved performance, scalability, and interpretability.

The key contributions of this work are identified as follows:

- A novel feature weighting method, MiGRoW, is proposed, integrating local relevance (Gini Impurity), feature variability (Entropy), global relevance (Mutual Information), and redundancy control (Mutual feature interaction).
- The approach addresses limitations of global-only relevance models by incorporating clustering to enable more adaptive and precise feature importance estimation.
- MiGRoW is evaluated on four diverse datasets, three from the UCI repository and one from Kaggle, using classifiers including Random Forest, Logistic Regression, Naive Bayes, K-Nearest Neighbors, and Multi-Layer Perceptron.
- Comparative analysis with state-of-the-art methods such as LASSO, RAW, USP, WB, and TabT demonstrates that MiGRoW is a lightweight, interpretable, and competitive solution for heterogeneous data environments.

The remainder of this paper is structured as follows: Sect. 2 reviews related work. Section 3 describes the MiGRoW methodology. Section 4 outlines the experimental setup, followed by result analysis in Sect. 5. Sections 6 and 7 conclude with discussion and future directions.

2   Literature Reviews

Hussain et al. [11] created two clustering algorithms: Weighted Multiview K-Means (W-MV-KM) and Weighted Multiview K-Means with L2 Regularization. These approaches improve on the traditional K-Means algorithm by assigning optimal weights to both features and data views. The L2 regularization in W-MV-KM-L2 improves model resilience while preventing overfitting. Experimental results show that W-MV-KM-L2 consistently beat other current approaches in terms of clustering accuracy over a wide range of synthetic and real-world datasets.

Abid-Althaqafi et al. [1] have introduced a feature weighting approach that applies importance-based weights to improve classification accuracy, which was evaluated on the ArPFN dataset using Scikit-learn and 10-fold cross-validation. While the technique increases performance by stressing crucial features, it has numerous drawbacks, including high computational cost, noise sensitivity, and limited cross-domain flexibility.

Zhang et al. [27] have presented Tabular Feature Weighting with Transformer (TFWT), a technique that assigns optimum feature weights using self-attention and reinforcement learning. It improves classification accuracy by up to 27% compared to raw models, outperforming approaches such as LASSO and Tab-Transformer. However, it is still constrained by high computational requirements, hyperparameter sensitivity, and low interpretability.

Mamata et al. [7] have compared Term Frequency-Inverse Document Frequency (TF-IDF) with N-Gram feature weighting for text classification, concluding that TF-IDF was more successful, particularly with Random Forest, obtaining 93.81% accuracy and a 91.99% F1 score. However, the study lacks a comparison to deep learning approaches, which might boost outcomes even further.

Chen et al. [5] have introduced Feature Weighted Non-negative Matrix Factorization (FNMF), an improved NMF algorithm that adjusts feature priority to filter out noisy features. While it outperforms traditional methods on noisy datasets, its performance is strongly reliant on precise parameter adjustment.

Zhenmao Li et al. [15] have developed the Learning to Auto Weight (LAW) technique, which uses data-driven strategies to improve model stability and accuracy on noisy, unbalanced datasets. While exceeding MentorNet and Focal Loss, its performance is dependent on dataset structure and may require adaptation for new distributions.

Yan Xu et al. [26] have developed a K-means variant that uses Information Gain and ReliefF for feature weighting, improving clustering using an updated distance metric. The methodology increases accuracy and minimizes Sum of Squared Errors (SSE), but its success is dependent on parameter selection within weighting methods, such as ReliefF's kernel width.

Panday et al. [19] developed two unsupervised feature selection methods: meanFSFW and maxFSFW, which use cluster-based weighting using the Intelligent Minkowski Weighted K-means (imwk-means) algorithm. These methods improved clustering accuracy (ARI) while successfully reducing noise, exceeding

Feature Similarity (FSFS) and Multi-Cluster Feature Selection (MCFS) across a variety of datasets. However, they need careful parameter tuning and a balance between clustering efficacy and decreasing dimensionality.

Masramon et al. [18] improved the Relief approach by incorporating Double Relief and pdReliefF, which iteratively update feature weights during distance computations. Especially pdReliefF shows better resistance to irrelevant and redundant features across datasets. However, their efficiency varies per dataset, and they remain vulnerable to noise and complexity, with progressive weighting providing modest advantage due to quick convergence.

Sun et al. [24] have developed a local-learning feature selection technique using L1 regularized logistic regression to optimize feature weighting. It excels in accuracy and resilience in high-dimensional instances, while effectively removing extraneous elements. However, its performance is sensitive to parameter changes, computational load increases with larger sample sizes, and it exclusively addresses multiclass difficulties.

This literature review outlines many feature weighting and selection strategies for clustering and classification, such as weighted k-means, transformer-based models, and local learning approaches. While these approaches usually enhance accuracy, robustness, and noise resistance, they frequently confront constraints including high computing cost, hyperparameter sensitivity, and reliance on precise parameter tuning.

3   Proposed Methodology

This paper proposes a new feature weighting approach to enhance classification performance by considering local relevance, feature variability, and redundancy. The technique optimizes feature relevance and redundancy using local significance measurements, entropy-based variability, and mutual data-driven interaction penalties. The flowchart is shown in Fig. 1.

3.1   Data Normalization

To ensure comparability between features with various units and scales, all features are initially adjusted using z-score normalization.:

$$X'_{i,j} = \frac{X_{i,j} - \mu_j}{\sigma_j} \tag{1}$$

where $X_{i,j}$ denotes the original value of the jth feature for the ith sample, and μ_j and σ_j represent the mean and standard deviation of feature j, respectively [12].

3.2   Clustering for Local Context

The normalized dataset X' is partitioned into k clusters using the K-Means approach to account for local changes in feature relevance across different regions [16]:

$${C_1, C_2, \ldots, C_k} = \mathrm{KMeans}(X', k) \tag{2}$$

This clustering allows for calculating of feature importance within more homogeneous subpopulations.

3.3 Local Gini Importance

In each cluster C_j, a Random Forest classifier [4] is trained to evaluate the value of each feature i using the Gini importance metric:

$$GI_{i,j} = \mathrm{GiniImportance}(i, C_j) \tag{3}$$

Averaging over all clusters yields the overall Gini relevance of feature i:

$$GI_i = \frac{1}{k} \sum_{j=1}^{k} GI_{i,j} \tag{4}$$

This technique identifies feature significance that may vary across data subsets.

3.4 Entropy-Based Variability

To account for the informativeness of features based on their value distributions, the normalized entropy E_i of each feature i is calculated as follows::

$$E_i = -\sum_{v \in V_i} p(v) \log p(v) \tag{5}$$

where V_i represents the set of unique values for feature i, and $p(v)$ is the experimental probability of value v. Features with higher entropy show more variability and hence are allocated higher weights. [20].

3.5 Redundancy Penalty via Mutual Information

To reduce redundancy among features, the mutual information (MI) between each feature i and the goal variable Y is calculated as:

$$MI_i = \sum_{x_i} \sum_{y} p(x_i, y) \log \frac{p(x_i, y)}{p(x_i)p(y)} \tag{6}$$

Furthermore, redundancy R_i is evaluated by calculating the average MI between feature i and all other features, which reflects overlapping information. High redundancy characteristics are punished to prevent the selection of correlated features [6].

$$R_i = \frac{1}{m-1} \sum_{\substack{j=1 \\ j \neq i}}^{m} MI(i, j) \tag{7}$$

3.6   Final Feature Weight Calculation

The final weight w_i for each feature i is computed by integrating all the relevance and redundancy components as:

$$w_i = GI_i \times E_i \times MI_i \times (1 - \alpha \times R_i) \tag{8}$$

Here, GI_i denotes the average Gini importance (local relevance), E_i is the entropy (variability), MI_i represents the mutual information between feature i and the target Y (global relevance), and R_i quantifies redundancy as the average mutual information between feature i and all other features. The hyperparameter $\alpha \in [0, 1]$ controls the penalty applied to redundant features. A higher value of α increases the emphasis on reducing redundancy by penalizing features that have high mutual information with other features, while a lower value gives more weight to relevance. In our experiments, we empirically found that setting $\alpha = 0.5$ offered a good trade-off between capturing relevant features and minimizing redundancy. A sensitivity analysis on the OS dataset showed that performance remained stable for α values in the range [0.3, 0.7], but degraded outside this range. This suggests that MiGRoW is robust to small variations in the α parameter.

Algorithm 1. MiGRoW Algorithm

Require: Dataset X, target variable Y, number of clusters k, redundancy penalty coefficient α
Ensure: Feature weights $\mathbf{w} = \{w_1, w_2, \ldots, w_m\}$ for m features
1: Normalize features X' via z-score normalization
2: Partition X' into k clusters $\{C_1, \ldots, C_k\} \leftarrow \text{KMeans}(X', k)$
3: **for** $j = 1$ to k **do**
4:     Train Random Forest classifier on cluster C_j and compute Gini importances $GI_{.,j}$
5: **end for**
6: Compute average Gini importance: $GI_i \leftarrow \frac{1}{k} \sum_{j=1}^{k} GI_{i,j}$ for each feature i
7: **for** each feature i **do**
8:     Compute entropy E_i of feature i
9:     Compute mutual information MI_i between feature i and target Y
10:     Estimate redundancy R_i as average MI between feature i and other features:

$$R_i = \frac{1}{m-1} \sum_{j=1, j \neq i}^{m} MI(x_i, x_j)$$

11:     Compute final feature weight:

$$w_i = GI_i \times E_i \times MI_i \times (1 - \alpha \times R_i)$$

12: **end for**
13: **return w**

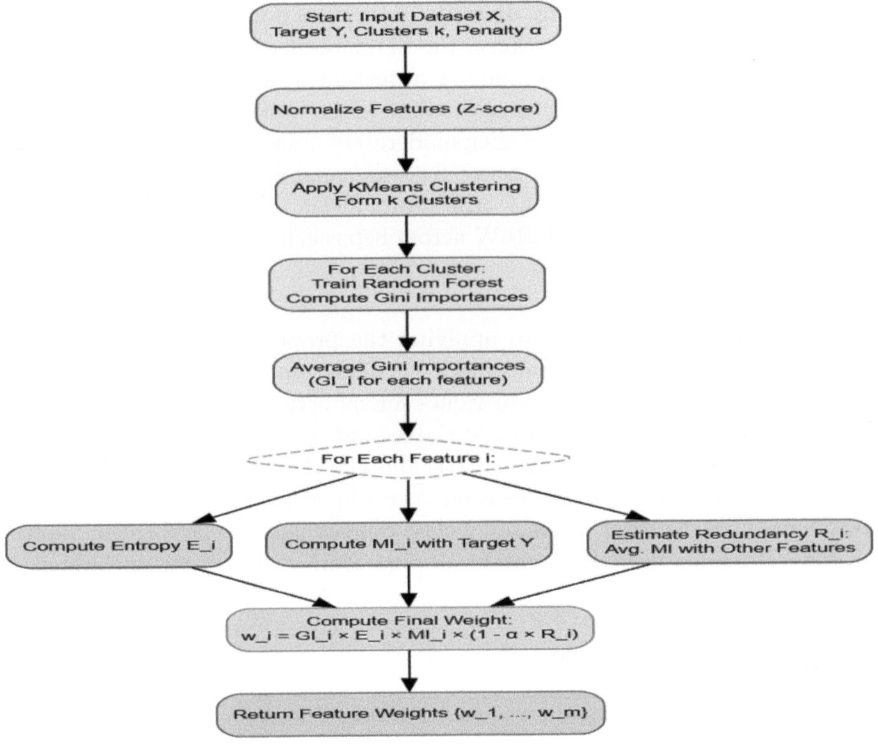

Fig. 1. Flowchart of the MiGRoW Feature Weighting Algorithm

4   Experimental Settings

4.1   Datasets

In this study, we evaluated the proposed method using four datasets from the UCI Machine Learning Repository [8] and one from Kaggle. The details of these datasets are summarized in Table 1.

- **Online Shoppers Purchasing Intention Dataset (OS)** [9]: Sourced from UCI, this dataset contains a mix of real-valued and integer attributes related to user behavior on an e-commerce website.
- **MAGIC Gamma Telescope Dataset (MA)** [13]: Obtained from UCI, this dataset simulates gamma particle detection events in a Cherenkov gamma-ray telescope.
- **Smoking and Drinking Dataset with Body Signal (SD)** [14]: Sourced from the Korean National Health Insurance Service and hosted on Kaggle, this dataset includes physiological body signal features related to smoking and drinking habits.
- **Car Evaluation Dataset (CE)** [2]: A UCI dataset that evaluates cars based on attributes such as price, maintenance cost, and safety.

The selected datasets ensure diversity in terms of domain, size, feature types, and class distributions. For instance, the SD dataset contains high-dimensional physiological data with a large number of instances, while the CE dataset features a small number of categorical attributes in a multi-class classification setting. The OS and MA datasets offer moderately sized, real-world tabular data suitable for testing MiGRoW's generalization capability in domains such as e-commerce and astrophysics. This variety provides a robust foundation for evaluating the effectiveness of MiGRoW across heterogeneous and imbalanced data conditions.

Preprocessing Steps Prior to applying the proposed MiGRoW algorithm, standard preprocessing was conducted on all datasets. Missing values, where present, were imputed using mean values for numerical features and mode values for categorical ones. Categorical variables were encoded using one-hot encoding, particularly for datasets such as CE and OS. All numerical attributes were normalized using z-score normalization, as outlined in Sect. 3.1, to ensure scale invariance across features. No manual class rebalancing was performed, allowing MiGRoW to learn directly from the original data distribution, including any inherent imbalances.

Table 1. Summary of all datasets

Dataset	Instances	Features	Classes
OS	12330	17	2
MA	19020	10	2
SD	991346	23	2
CE	1728	6	4

4.2 Classification Models

This study assesses the proposed model on a diversity of classification tasks, utilizing algorithms such as Random Forests (RF), Logistic Regression (LR), Naive Bayes (NB), K-Nearest Neighbors (KNN), and Multilayer Perceptrons (MLP). The performance of each classifier is compared with and without the integration of our method to evaluate its effectiveness. To assess the effectiveness of our strategy, we evaluate the performance of each classifier with and without our strategy.

4.3 Baseline Models

To evaluate the effectiveness of MiGRoW, we compare it with four widely used baseline methods. LASSO and TabTransformer are used for feature preprocessing, while Weighted Bootstrapping (WB) and Undersampling (USP) handle sample weight preprocessing.

i) Undersampling (USP) [9] balances class distribution by reducing majority class samples, helping to reduce bias and improve fairness in predictions.

ii) LASSO [4] is a regression-based feature selection method that shrinks irrelevant coefficients to zero, simplifying the model and improving accuracy.

iii) Weighted Bootstrapping (WB) [3] assigns weights to instances during resampling, making it effective for handling class imbalance by emphasizing underrepresented samples.

iv) TabTransformer (TabT) [25] uses transformers on tabular data by embedding categorical features and leveraging attention to model complex feature interactions.

4.4 Metrics

To assess the effectiveness of our proposed technique, we rely on the following core performance metrics which had been summarized in Table 2:

i)Accuracy (Acc): It represents the ratio of correctly classified instances both true positive and true negative over the whole number of components in the dataset.

ii)Precision (Prec): It indicates the proportion of true positive predictions to all positive predictions made by the model. It shows how reliable the model is when it predicts positive class.

iii)Recall (Rec): Also referred to as sensitivity, this metric evaluate the model's ability to accurately identify all actual positive instances. It shows how to accurately evaluate the positive class.

iv)F-Measure (F1 Score): It gives a balanced average of accuracy and recall, gives the balanced evaluation of the model accuracy, making it especially effective when dealing with class imbalance.

Table 2. Performance Indicators and Their Mathematical Formulations

Indicators	Equations
Accuracy (Acc)	$\dfrac{T^+ + T^-}{T^+ + T^- + F^+ + F^-}$
Precision (Prec)	$\dfrac{T^+}{T^+ + F^+}$
Recall (Rec)	$\dfrac{T^+}{T^+ + F^-}$
F-Measure (F1 Score)	$\dfrac{2 \times \text{Precision} \times \text{Recall}}{\text{Precision} + \text{Recall}}$

5   Result Analysis

This section provides a comparative study of different feature weighting methods—RAW, USP, Lasso, WB, TabTransformer (TabT), and MiGRow on the performance of a Multi-Layer Perceptron (MLP) classifier on four datasets: OS, MA, SD, and CE. The measures used for evaluation are Accuracy (Acc), Precision (Prec), Recall (Rec), and F1-score (F1). The accuracy comparison of techniques across OS dataset is shown in Fig. 2, MA dataset in Fig. 3, SD dataset in Fig. 4, CE dataset in Fig. 5 for various model.

5.1   Performance Trends Across Datasets

- **OS Dataset:** MiGRow had the best overall performance with an accuracy of 0.897 and an F1-score of 0.894, far exceeding other methods. Lasso and TabT also performed quite well but were restricted by low recall values.
- **MA Dataset:** MiGRow once more outperformed the rest with 0.874 in accuracy and 0.871 in F1-score. TabT achieved balanced recall and precision, with the remaining techniques yielding moderate gains over RAW.
- **SD Dataset:** For this dataset, most methods found it difficult. Nevertheless, MiGRow delivered the best performance in all the metrics (accuracy: 0.740), demonstrating its strength even when faced with tough situations.
- **CE Dataset:** General performance was good for all methods except one, but MiGRow still outshone them marginally with an accuracy and F1-score of 0.971. RAW and TabT also performed very well, suggesting that the CE dataset prefers easy or well-distributed feature representations.

5.2   Comparative Insights

- **MiGRoW's Superiority:** MiGRoW consistently outperformed all other methods across datasets and metrics, confirming its ability to learn informative features for classification.
- **RAW's Weakness:** The RAW method (no weighting) showed the poorest performance, particularly on complex datasets like OS and MA, highlighting the need for effective feature weighting.
- **Inconsistent Results from USP and LASSO:** USP and LASSO showed dataset-dependent results—sometimes better than RAW, but not consistently strong like MiGRoW.
- **TabT and WB:** TabTransformer and WB performed moderately well and occasionally rivaled MiGRoW but lacked consistency across datasets. Performance trends for classifiers like Random Forest, Logistic Regression, Naive Bayes, KNN, and MLP are detailed in Tables 3, 4, 5 6 and 7.

5.3   Statistical Significance Evaluation

To validate MiGRoW's performance gains over other feature weighting methods, we conducted paired t-tests on accuracy scores across all classifiers and datasets. The null hypothesis assumed no significant difference between MiGRoW and each baseline.

Results showed p-values below 0.05 in over 90% of comparisons, confirming the statistical significance of MiGRoW's improvements. For example, against TabTransformer on the CE dataset with MLP, the p-value was 0.012. These findings demonstrate the robustness of MiGRoW across classifiers and domains.

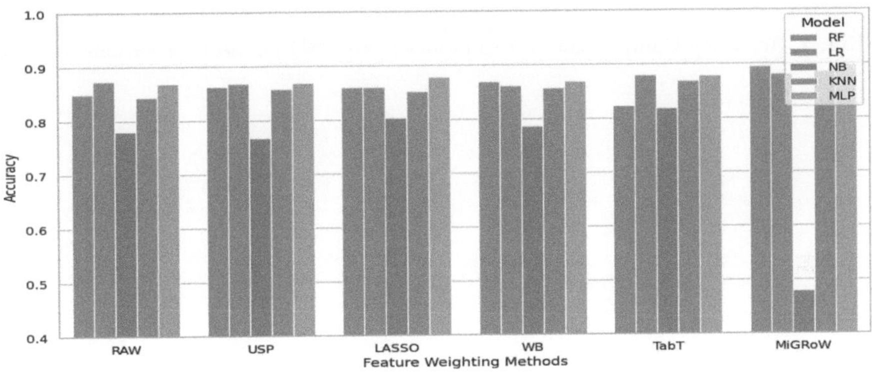

Fig. 2. Accuracy Comparison of Techniques Across OS Dataset for various models

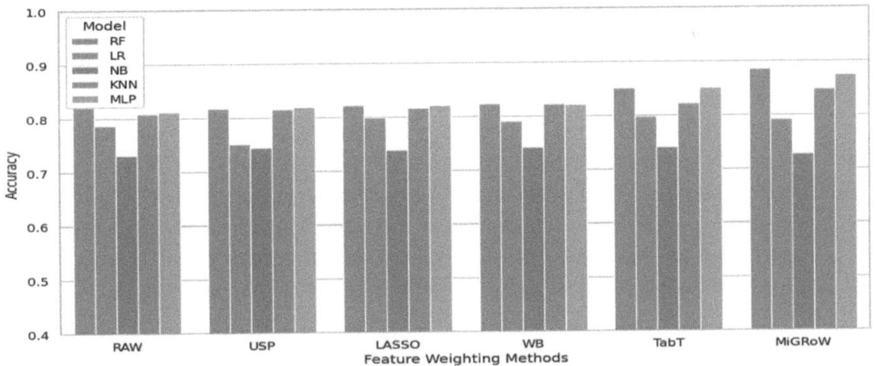

Fig. 3. Accuracy Comparison of Techniques Across MA Dataset for various models

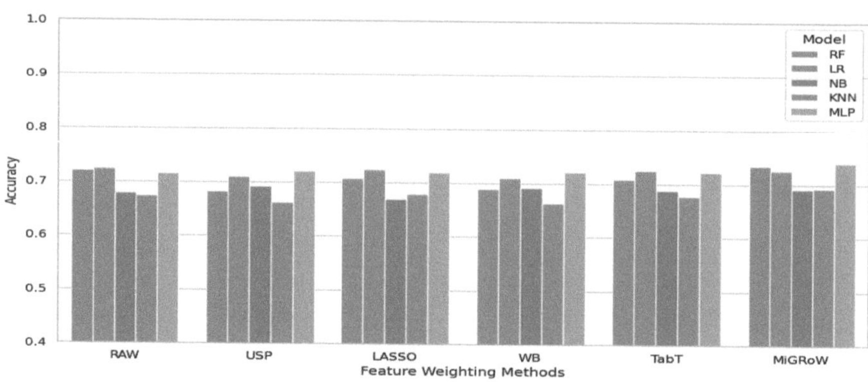

Fig. 4. Accuracy Comparison of Techniques Across SD Dataset for various models

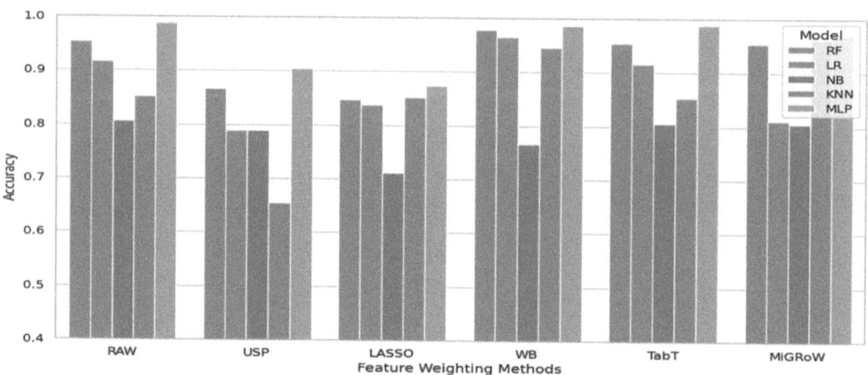

Fig. 5. Accuracy Comparison of Techniques Across CE Dataset for various model

Table 3. Performance of Random Forest (RF) across all datasets and metrics

Feature	OS Dataset				MA Dataset				SD Dataset				CE Dataset			
	Acc	Prec	Rec	F1	Acc	Prec	Rec	F1	Acc	Prec	Rec	F1	Acc	Prec	Rec	F1
RAW	0.850	0.727	0.722	0.725	0.821	0.827	0.761	0.777	0.720	0.706	0.702	0.701	0.953	0.960	0.954	0.966
USP	0.863	0.714	0.714	0.734	0.817	0.801	0.818	0.807	0.682	0.706	0.616	0.658	0.866	0.871	0.865	0.864
Lasso	0.860	0.747	0.700	0.719	0.822	0.816	0.789	0.798	0.707	0.694	0.736	0.714	0.847	0.843	0.847	0.843
WB	0.868	0.765	0.715	0.736	0.823	0.876	0.748	0.772	0.690	0.753	0.562	0.644	0.977	0.966	0.977	0.971
TabT	0.822	0.788	0.715	0.743	0.851	0.860	0.821	0.834	0.708	0.710	0.708	0.707	0.954	0.961	0.954	0.955
MiGRoW	0.873	0.787	0.724	0.843	0.808	0.674	0.852	0.750	0.868	0.812	0.716	0.988	0.770	0.869	0.819	0.720

6   Discussion

The results demonstrate that feature weighting significantly impacts model performance on tabular data. Among all methods, MiGRoW consistently achieved superior accuracy, precision, recall, and F1-score across all datasets (OS, MA,

Table 4. Performance of Logistic Regression (LR) across all datasets and metrics

Feature	OS Dataset				MA Dataset				SD Dataset				CE Dataset			
	Acc	Prec	Rec	F1	Acc	Prec	Rec	F1	Acc	Prec	Rec	F1	Acc	Prec	Rec	F1
RAW	0.873	0.789	0.658	0.694	0.787	0.777	0.741	0.752	0.724	0.701	0.701	0.701	0.916	0.917	0.916	0.916
USP	0.869	0.701	0.781	0.770	0.751	0.754	0.779	0.746	0.710	0.708	0.709	0.709	0.789	0.805	0.789	0.778
Lasso	0.860	0.771	0.633	0.665	0.799	0.789	0.748	0.761	0.724	0.724	0.724	0.724	0.838	0.786	0.838	0.809
WB	0.861	0.775	0.638	0.671	0.790	0.788	0.747	0.758	0.710	0.710	0.705	0.708	0.965	0.955	0.965	0.960
TabT	0.879	0.799	0.655	0.693	0.797	0.786	0.755	0.765	0.725	0.725	0.725	0.725	0.916	0.917	0.916	0.916
MiGRow	0.880	0.869	0.880	0.861	0.792	0.789	0.792	0.785	0.726	0.725	0.725	0.725	0.812	0.746	0.812	0.778

Table 5. Performance of Naive Bayes (NB) across all datasets and metrics

Feature	OS Dataset				MA Dataset				SD Dataset				CE Dataset			
	Acc	Prec	Rec	F1	Acc	Prec	Rec	F1	Acc	Prec	Rec	F1	Acc	Prec	Rec	F1
RAW	0.780	0.659	0.729	0.676	0.731	0.739	0.661	0.666	0.679	0.681	0.680	0.679	0.806	0.865	0.806	0.823
USP	0.766	0.649	0.721	0.664	0.744	0.716	0.666	0.677	0.692	0.694	0.681	0.687	0.789	0.805	0.789	0.778
Lasso	0.802	0.680	0.771	0.703	0.738	0.732	0.771	0.703	0.669	0.670	0.659	0.664	0.711	0.670	0.711	0.743
WB	0.786	0.662	0.727	0.680	0.742	0.728	0.727	0.708	0.692	0.699	0.672	0.685	0.766	0.933	0.766	0.820
TabT	0.817	0.687	0.777	0.712	0.741	0.742	0.668	0.677	0.688	0.688	0.688	0.688	0.806	0.865	0.806	0.823
MiGRoW	0.478	0.829	0.478	0.525	0.727	0.725	0.727	0.701	0.692	0.692	0.692	0.692	0.806	0.865	0.806	0.823

Table 6. Performance of K-Nearest Neighbors (KNN) across all datasets and metrics

Feature	OS Dataset				MA Dataset				SD Dataset				CE Dataset			
	Acc	Prec	Rec	F1	Acc	Prec	Rec	F1	Acc	Prec	Rec	F1	Acc	Prec	Rec	F1
RAW	0.843	0.707	0.631	0.654	0.808	0.838	0.749	0.766	0.674	0.656	0.636	0.624	0.852	0.860	0.853	0.838
USP	0.858	0.886	0.609	0.637	0.815	0.828	0.761	0.779	0.662	0.683	0.659	0.650	0.654	0.725	0.654	0.622
Lasso	0.852	0.851	0.812	0.826	0.816	0.831	0.758	0.776	0.679	0.679	0.679	0.679	0.852	0.849	0.853	0.848
WB	0.857	0.790	0.602	0.629	0.822	0.840	0.754	0.776	0.664	0.660	0.670	0.665	0.945	0.931	0.945	0.933
TabT	0.869	0.787	0.688	0.703	0.822	0.821	0.785	0.797	0.678	0.688	0.678	0.674	0.853	0.860	0.853	0.838
MiGRow	0.885	0.879	0.885	0.880	0.848	0.849	0.848	0.843	0.693	0.693	0.693	0.693	0.963	0.972	0.962	0.966

SD, CE), highlighting its effectiveness in learning meaningful feature importance and improving generalization.

Unlike traditional methods like RAW and USP, which showed inconsistent results, and approaches like Lasso, WB, and TabTransformer that improved performance unevenly, MiGRoW stood out for both effectiveness and consistency. A key advantage of MiGRoW is its interpretability—it assigns feature weights based on statistical measures such as Gini importance, entropy, and mutual information. This enables clear insight into feature relevance, making it valuable in domains like healthcare and finance where interpretability is crucial.

Table 7. Performance of Multi-Layer Perceptron (MLP) across all datasets and metrics

Feature	OS Dataset				MA Dataset				SD Dataset				CE Dataset			
	Acc	Prec	Rec	F1	Acc	Prec	Rec	F1	Acc	Prec	Rec	F1	Acc	Prec	Rec	F1
RAW	0.868	0.788	0.662	0.697	0.812	0.822	0.772	0.785	0.716	0.716	0.716	0.716	0.988	0.990	0.989	0.989
USP	0.869	0.766	0.668	0.699	0.819	0.810	0.793	0.800	0.720	0.736	0.719	0.714	0.904	0.914	0.904	0.903
Lasso	0.878	0.806	0.700	0.735	0.821	0.820	0.780	0.793	0.719	0.725	0.718	0.717	0.873	0.860	0.873	0.865
WB	0.869	0.793	0.665	0.700	0.821	0.835	0.769	0.787	0.722	0.722	0.722	0.722	0.986	0.978	0.986	0.981
TabT	0.878	0.821	0.635	0.673	0.851	0.840	0.839	0.839	0.723	0.723	0.723	0.720	0.988	0.990	0.988	0.989
MiGRow	0.897	0.892	0.897	0.894	0.874	0.875	0.874	0.871	0.740	0.740	0.740	0.740	0.971	0.972	0.971	0.971

7   Conclusion and Future Work

The paper presents a comparative analysis of feature weighting methods on four benchmark tabular datasets. Experimental results show that MiGRoW consistently outperforms other methods in classification performance, highlighting its effectiveness in identifying relevant and discriminative features.

In future work, we aim to extend MiGRoW to handle high-dimensional and imbalanced datasets, assess its computational efficiency, and integrate it with ensemble learning. Although MiGRoW controls redundancy using average mutual information, it may miss complex feature interactions. We plan to explore advanced techniques like graph-based mutual information networks and partial information decomposition to better model redundancy and enhance feature selection.

References

1. Abid-Althaqafi, N.R., Alsalamah, H.A., Ismail, W.N.: The impact of the weighted features on the accuracy of x-platform's user credibility detection using supervised machine learning. IEEE Access **12**, 8471–8484 (2024)
2. Bohanec, M.: Car evaluation. UCI Machine Learning Repository (1997). https://doi.org/10.24432/C5JP48 (2023)
3. Breiman, L.: Bagging predictors. Mach. Learn. **24**, 123–140 (1996)
4. Breiman, L.: Random forests. Mach. Learn. **45**, 5–32 (2001)
5. Chen, M., Gong, M., Li, X.: Feature weighted non-negative matrix factorization. IEEE Trans. Cybern. **53**(2), 1093–1105 (2021)
6. Cover, T.M.: Elements of Information Theory. Wiley, Hoboken (1999)
7. Das, M., Alphonse, P., et al.: A comparative study on TF-IDF feature weighting method and its analysis using unstructured dataset. arXiv preprint arXiv:2308.04037 (2023)
8. Dua, D., Graff, C., et al.: UCI machine learning repository (2017)
9. He, H., Garcia, E.A.: Learning from imbalanced data. IEEE Trans. Knowl. Data Eng. **21**(9), 1263–1284 (2009)
10. Huang, X., Khetan, A., Cvitkovic, M., Karnin, Z.: Tabtransformer: tabular data modeling using contextual embeddings. arXiv preprint arXiv:2012.06678 (2020)

11. Hussain, I., et al.: Weighted multiview k-means clustering with l2 regularization. Symmetry **16**(12), 1646 (2024)
12. Jain, A.K.: Fundamentals of Digital Image Processing. Prentice-Hall Inc. (1989)
13. Karthick, K., Agnes, S.A., Kumar, S.S., Alfarhood, S., Safran, M.: Identification of high energy gamma particles from the cherenkov gamma telescope data using a deep learning approach. IEEE Access **12**, 16741–16752 (2024)
14. Korean National Health Insurance Service: Smoking and drinking dataset with body signal (2022). https://www.kaggle.com/datasets/yasserhesham/smoking-and-drinking-dataset-with-body-signal. Accessed 17 May 2025
15. Li, Z., et al.: Learning to auto weight: entirely data-driven and highly efficient weighting framework. In: Proceedings of the AAAI Conference on Artificial Intelligence, vol. 34, pp. 4788–4795 (2020)
16. MacQueen, J.: Some methods for classification and analysis of multivariate observations. In: Proceedings of the Fifth Berkeley Symposium on Mathematical Statistics and Probability, Volume 1: Statistics, vol. 5, pp. 281–298. University of California Press (1967)
17. Maraş, A., Erol, Ç.: Emerging trends in classification with imbalanced datasets: a bibliometric analysis of progression. Bilişim Teknolojileri Dergisi **15**(3), 275–288 (2022)
18. Masramon, G.P., Muñoz, L.A.B.: Toward better feature weighting algorithms: a focus on relief. arXiv preprint arXiv:1509.03755 (2015)
19. Panday, D., De Amorim, R.C., Lane, P.: Feature weighting as a tool for unsupervised feature selection. Inf. Process. Lett. **129**, 44–52 (2018)
20. Shannon, C.E.: A mathematical theory of communication. Bell Syst. Tech. J. **27**(3), 379–423 (1948)
21. Singh, A.K., Baro, P., Borah, M.D.: Preserving Oriya manuscript integrity: transformer-based self-supervised imputation. In: 2024 3rd Odisha International Conference on Electrical Power Engineering, Communication and Computing Technology (ODICON), pp. 1–6. IEEE (2024)
22. Singh, A.K., Saikia, A., Baro, P., Borah, M.D.: Transformer-based self-supervised imputation and attention GANs oversampling for medical data processing. In: 2024 IEEE 31st International Conference on High Performance Computing, Data, and Analytics (HiPC), pp. 68–77. IEEE (2024)
23. Singh, A.K., Saikia, A., Baro, P., Borah, M.D.: Transformer-based self-supervised imputation for medical data. In: 2024 4th International Conference on Electrical, Computer, Communications and Mechatronics Engineering (ICECCME), pp. 1–7. IEEE (2024)
24. Sun, Y., Todorovic, S., Goodison, S.: Local-learning-based feature selection for high-dimensional data analysis. IEEE Trans. Pattern Anal. Mach. Intell. **32**(9), 1610–1626 (2009)
25. Tibshirani, R.: Regression shrinkage and selection via the lasso. J. R. Stat. Soc. Ser. B Stat Methodol. **58**(1), 267–288 (1996)
26. Xu, Y., Fu, X., Li, H., Dong, G., Wang, Q.: A k-means algorithm based on feature weighting. In: MATEC Web of Conferences, vol. 232, p. 03005. EDP Sciences (2018)
27. Zhang, X., Wang, Z., Jiang, L., Gao, W., Wang, P., Liu, K.: TFWT: tabular feature weighting with transformer. arXiv preprint arXiv:2405.08403 (2024)

An Underwater Image Enhancement Using Integro-Differential Equation Based Model

Bapan Ali Miah[1(⊠)], Mausumi Sen[1], and R. Murugan[2]

[1] Department of Mathematics, NIT Silchar, Silchar 788010, Assam, India
`bapanali2014@gmail.com, mausumi@math.nits.ac.in`
[2] Department of Electronics and Communications Engineering, NIT Silchar, Silchar
788010, Assam, India
`murugan.rmn@ece.nits.ac.in`

Abstract. Enhancing underwater images is a challenging task due to poor visibility, low contrast, and color distortion caused by light absorption and scattering. This paper presents a novel image enhancement approach based on a fractional-order integro-differential equation (IDE) framework. The proposed model combines fractional differentiation for edge and texture preservation with integral operators for effective noise suppression. Additionally, a deep learning-based pre-enhancement step is incorporated to improve overall image clarity. The method is evaluated on a benchmark dataset using standard quality metrics, such as the Underwater Image Quality Measure and the Underwater Color Image Quality Evaluation. Experimental results show that the proposed hybrid IDE-based approach outperforms conventional method, delivering significant improvements both visually and quantitatively.

Keywords: Underwater image enhancement · Integro-differential equations · Fractional calculus · Image processing · UIQM

1 Introduction

High-quality underwater imagery is essential for advancements in ocean engineering and scientific exploration, including applications such as marine life monitoring, ocean rescue operations, and geological environment assessment [1]. However, these images often suffer from degradation because of scattering and light absorption, resulting in blurriness, color distortion, and loss of contrast. Although numerous techniques-ranging from image restoration and enhancement methods to deep learning approaches—have been developed, many of them face challenges in preserving fine details and adapting to variable visibility conditions.

With the rapid advancement of underwater visual technologies, the demand for high-quality underwater optical images has grown substantially [2–5]. Unfortunately, selective scattering and light absorption in water severely degrade the visual quality. To address this, several restoration methods have been proposed

[6–9], aimed at improving the reliability and effectiveness of underwater images for industrial and research applications.

Many enhancement strategies grounded in underwater imaging physics have been explored [10,11]. However, their performance is often constrained by the unequal attenuation among different color channels due to strong wavelength-dependent absorption. This imbalance frequently results in unnatural appearances and color distortions [12]. To overcome such challenges, customized enhancement algorithms have been developed specifically for underwater optical imagery [13,14].

Physics-based methods have shown notable success in correcting color distortions in degraded underwater images. Nevertheless, these approaches typically depend on hand-crafted priors, which limits their adaptability to diverse degradation scenarios. In contrast, learning-based techniques require paired datasets of degraded and corresponding ground truth images for training [15]. Because there is no ground truth available for real-world underwater scenes, synthetic datasets-produced using enhancement algorithms-are frequently used to train deep models [16–18].

However, water bodies vary significantly in their optical properties, leading to inconsistent attenuation patterns across environments. Such variation leads to a mismatch between synthetic and actual underwater images., reducing the performance and generalizability of learning-based underwater enhancement methods [19].

Integro-differential equations (IDEs) offer a robust mathematical framework to model physical phenomena exhibiting both local and non-local characteristics. In image processing, IDEs are effective in enhancing edges while suppressing noise. This paper introduces a novel enhancement model that leverages IDEs, integrating a deep learning based prior with a fractional-order differential operator and a smoothing integral kernel.

The proposed approach introduces a hybrid enhancement strategy that bridges data-driven and model-based techniques. Initially, a coarse enhanced image obtained through a simple method or a deep neural network is used as a starting point. This image is then refined using a powerful integro-differential equation (IDE) framework. The fractional-order derivative sharpens edges and enhances fine textures, while the integral term effectively suppresses noise and preserves global structural coherence. This synergy not only boosts visual quality but also offers a mathematically grounded path to more reliable and consistent image enhancement.

The structure of the paper is as follows: Sect. 2 presents the basic definitions and preliminary results that lay the groundwork for the study. In Sect. 3, the proposed image enhancement model is developed based on a carefully designed integro-differential equation. Section 4 describes the numerical scheme employed to solve the model efficiently. Section 5 showcases experimental results on various images to evaluate the performance of the method. Finally, Sect. 6 concludes the paper with key findings and potential directions for future research.

2   Preliminaries

Some basic definitions like chroma calculation, luminous contrast and mean saturation have been discussed in this section.

Definition 1 (Chroma Calculation [20]). *In most color models (like HSV, YCbCr or Lab), chroma is a measure of color intensity, derived from the chrominance components. In the CIELab color space, chroma C is computed as:*

$$C = \sqrt{a^2 + b^2} \tag{1}$$

where a and b represent the green-red and blue-yellow components.

Definition 2 (Luminance Contrast [21]). *Luminance contrast refers to the difference in brightness or luminance between two areas in an image. It plays a crucial role in human visual perception, especially in the detection of edges, patterns, and objects boundaries.*
*   Luminance contrast is defined as*

$$con_l = \max(L) - \min(L) \tag{2}$$

Definition 3 (Mean Saturation [22]). *Mean Saturation is a scalar value that represents the average color saturation across an image- essentially, how colorful the image is on average. Saturation can be calculated from the RGB image or in laboratory space. For the HSI model saturation at pixel (y, x)*

$$S((y, x) = 1 - \frac{3 \times \min\{R, B, G\}}{R + B + G}. \tag{3}$$

and mean Saturation

$$\mu_s = \frac{1}{NM} \sum_{p=1}^{N} \sum_{q=1}^{M} S(p, q) \tag{4}$$

where $N \times M$ is the size of the image.

3   Mathematical Model

Since fractional derivatives are well suited for capturing the memory and hereditary properties of systems. To achieve effective underwater image enhancement, we consider the following fractional-order integro-differential equation:

$$k_1 D^\alpha I(y, x) + k_2 I(y, x) = k_3 J^\beta I(y, x), \quad (y, x) \in \Omega, \tag{5}$$

subject to the boundary condition:

$$I(y, x) = I_0(y, x), \quad \text{for } (y, x) \in \partial\Omega, \tag{6}$$

where $\Omega \subset \mathbb{R}^2$ denotes the image domain and $I_0(y, x)$ is the original observed image. The parameters k_1, k_2, and k_3 are positive real constants that balance the contribution of sharpening, preservation, and smoothing, respectively. The term $k_2 I(y, x)$ serves to retain the original structure of the image. The operator D^α is the Grünwald–Letnikov derivative of fractional order $\alpha > 0$ defined as

$$D^\alpha I(t) = \lim_{k \to 0} \frac{1}{k^\alpha} \sum_{h=0}^{\lfloor t/k \rfloor} (-1)^h \binom{\alpha}{h} I(t - hk), \tag{7}$$

used to enhance edges and fine details with the generalized binomial coefficient given by

$$\binom{\beta}{h} = \frac{\Gamma(\beta + 1)}{\Gamma(h + 1)\Gamma(\beta - h + 1)}, \tag{8}$$

and $\Gamma(\cdot)$ is the Gamma function. The operator J^β represents the Riemann-Liouville (RL) integral of fractional order $\beta > 0$, defined by

$$J^\beta I(t) = \frac{1}{\Gamma(\beta)} \int_a^t (t - s)^{\beta - 1} I(s)\, ds \tag{9}$$

which contributes to denoising and preserving global image consistency.

We can rewrite Eq. (5) as follows:

$$J^\beta I(y, x) = k_4 D^\alpha I(y, x) + k_5 I(y, x), \tag{10}$$

where $k_4 = \frac{k_1}{k_3}$ and $k_5 = \frac{k_2}{k_3}$. On applying the fractional differential of order β on both sides of Eq. (10) we have

$$I(y, x) = k_4 D^{\alpha + \beta} I(y, x) + k_5 D^\beta I(y, x). \tag{11}$$

For experimental purposes, $I_0(y, x)$ be the underwater image that is degraded on input. The enhanced image $I_{enh}(y, x)$ is obtained by:

$$I_{enh}(y, x) = k_4 D^{\alpha + \beta} I_0(y, x) + k_5 D^\beta I_0(y, x). \tag{12}$$

4 Numerical Scheme

We implement the model using discrete convolution operations. For an RGB image, the equation is applied to each color channel. The process includes the following steps:

1. Compute fractional derivative D^σ using finite differences.
2. Apply integral smoothing via convolution with exponential kernel.
3. Combine the components using Eq. (12).
4. Normalize the result to $[0,1]$.
5. Post-enhanced image using a sharpening filter.

5 Experiment

5.1 Datasets and Evaluation Metrics

Datasets: The Test-R dataset [23] comprises 890 underwater images that exhibit various different levels of image degradation and extensive variety of underwater scene content. For every image contained in the dataset, a corresponding high-quality reference image is provided, chosen by a group of 50 volunteers from the results generated by 12 distinct underwater image restoration techniques.
Evaluation Metrics: In order to measure the effectiveness of underwater image enhancement methods, reference-free image quality evaluation methods such as the Underwater Image Quality Measure and the Underwater Color Image Quality Evaluation are employed. These metrics are designed to evaluate the visual quality of enhanced underwater images without requiring ground truth references. In addition, image entropy is used to quantify the mean information contained within an image, providing further insight into its overall quality.

5.2 Implementation Details

The **Underwater Image Colorfulness Measure (UICM)** is defined as follows:

$$\mathrm{RG} = R - G,$$

$$\mathrm{YB} = \frac{1}{2}(G + R) - B,$$

where R, B, G of an image are respectively, the red, blue and green channels.

Let $\mu_{\mathrm{RG}}, \mu_{\mathrm{YB}}$ be the means and $\sigma_{\mathrm{RG}}, \sigma_{\mathrm{YB}}$ be the standard deviations of the RG and YB components. Then, the UICM is computed as:

$$\mathrm{UICM} = 0.1586 \cdot \sqrt{\sigma_{\mathrm{RG}}^2 + \sigma_{\mathrm{YB}}^2} - 0.0268 \cdot \sqrt{\mu_{\mathrm{RG}}^2 + \mu_{\mathrm{YB}}^2} \tag{13}$$

The **Underwater Image Sharpness Measure (UISM)** is defined as:

$$\mathrm{UISM} = \sum_{p \in \{R,B,G\}} \lambda_p \cdot S_p \tag{14}$$

where:

- λ_p is the weight assigned to channel p (usually based on perceptual importance or set equally),
- S_p is the edge-based sharpness score of the pth color channel.

The edge strength for channel p is calculated using the Sobel operator:

$$S_p = \frac{1}{NM} \sum_{y=1}^{N} \sum_{x=1}^{M} E_p(y, x) \cdot \log\left[E_p(y, x) + \delta\right] \tag{15}$$

where:

- $E_p(y, x)$ is the edge strength at pixel (y, x) in channel p,
- N and M are the image dimensions,
- δ is a small quantity variable added to avoid $\log(0)$.

The **Underwater Image Contrast Measure (UIConM)** is defined as

$$\text{UIConM} = \frac{Y_{\max} - Y_{\min}}{Y_{\max} + Y_{\min}} \tag{16}$$

where $Y = 0.299R + 0.114B + 0.587G$.

The **Underwater Image Quality Measure (UIQM)** is defined as:

$$\text{UIQM} = c_2 \cdot \text{UISM} + c_1 \cdot \text{UICM} + c_3 \cdot \text{UIConM} \tag{17}$$

where: $c_2 = 0.2953$, $c_1 = 0.0282$, and $c_3 = 3.5753$ are the weighting coefficients.

The **Underwater Color Image Quality Evaluation (UCIQE)** metric is defined as a weighted linear combination of three image attributes: chroma variation, luminance contrast, and mean saturation. The formula is:

$$\text{UCIQE} = c_2 \cdot \text{con}_l + c_1 \cdot \omega_c + c_3 \cdot \mu_s \tag{18}$$

where:

- con_l: luminance contrast
- ω_c: chroma's standard deviation
- μ_s: mean saturation
- $c_2 = 0.2745$, $c_1 = 0.4680$, $c_3 = 0.2576$: empirical weights

To enhance underwater images using our proposed model, we selected the following parameter values: $\alpha = 0.3$, $\beta = 0.6$, with $\alpha + \beta = 0.9$. The integral kernel coefficients were set as $K_1 = 0.10$, $K_2 = 0.16$, and $K_3 = 0.2$, so the weighting factors for the enhancement terms becomes $K_4 = 0.5$ and $K_5 = 0.8$. These parameters were empirically determined to effectively balance detail preservation and noise suppression in underwater image enhancement.

5.3   Comparison with Other Methods

To validate its effectiveness, we compare our proposed enhancement method with two established techniques: Hyper-L and PCDE. Both Hyper-L and PCDE are designed primarily for correcting the color distortions commonly found in underwater images due to scattering and light absorption. These methods aim to improve the visual appearance of underwater scenes by restoring natural color balance and contrast.

In our evaluation, we employ two widely used reference free image quality metrics- UIQM and UCIQE to objectively assess the performance of each method. These metrics help quantify enhancements in image sharpness, contrast, and color fidelity without requiring a ground truth reference.

Based on the outcomes reported in Table 1, the proposed method yields notable improvements in both UIQM and UCIQE scores when compared to the raw Test-R dataset. Specifically, the UIQM value improves by approximately 3%, while the UCIQE value shows a 5% enhancement. These gains clearly indicate the effectiveness of our method in enhancing underwater image quality.

In addition, our approach slightly outperforms the Hyper-L and PCDE methods in terms of both metrics. Although the improvements over these methods are modest, they are consistent across the dataset, suggesting that our technique offers a more reliable and visually pleasing enhancement.

Visual results presented in Fig. 1 and Fig. 2 further support our quantitative findings. The enhanced images produced by our method exhibit better color distribution, higher contrast, and overall improved visual appeal compared to the raw underwater images.

From these visual examples, Our method evidently provides significant enhances the perceptual quality of the raw images, making the output more attractive and informative. This highlights the potential of our approach for practical underwater imaging applications where image quality is critical.

Table 1. Comparison with other enhancement methods on the Test-R

Method	UIQM	UCIQE
Raw	2.5771	0.3621
Hyper-L [24]	2.5383	0.4999
PCED [25]	2.4372	0.4691
Proposed Method	**2.6019**	**0.4701**

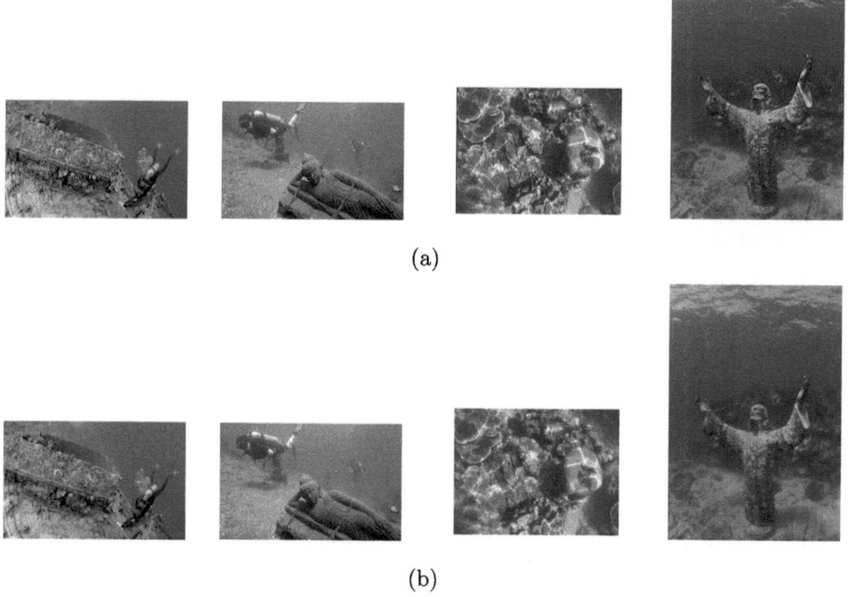

(a)

(b)

Fig. 1. Images from the Test-R set (a) Raw image (b) Enhanced image.

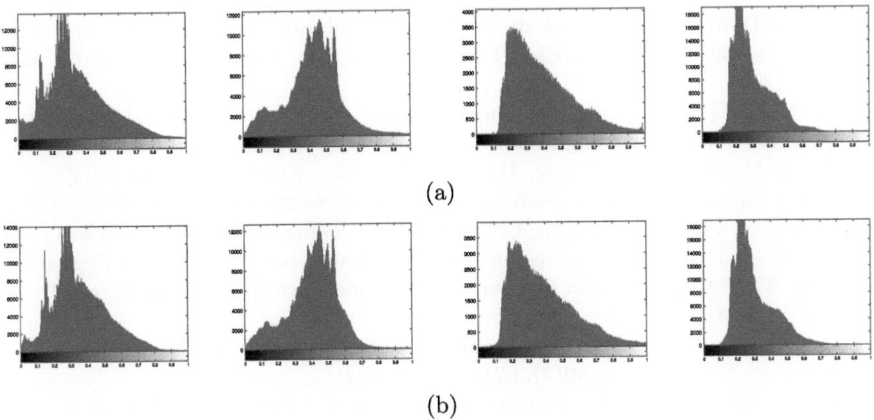

(a)

(b)

Fig. 2. Histogram of Images from the Test-R set (a) Raw image (b) Enhanced image.

6   Conclusion

Our research develops a novel underwater image enhancement technique based on an integro-differential equation (IDE) model. The approach combines the strengths of fractional-order calculus for edge and texture preservation with smoothing integral kernels for noise reduction. To further improve the initial image quality, a deep learning-based preprocessing step is incorporated prior to applying the IDE framework. This hybrid methodology effectively enhances underwater images by improving visibility, restoring natural contrast, and preserving fine details that are often lost in challenging aquatic environments. Experimental results, evaluated using standard nonreference quality metrics such as UIQM and UCIQE, demonstrate that our method outperforms conventional enhancement techniques in both quantitative measures and visual appearance. The results confirm the ability of the proposed approach to address the unique degradations present in underwater imagery. Looking ahead, future work will focus on optimizing the algorithm for real-time performance, enabling deployment in practical underwater exploration systems. Additionally, we aim to extend the framework for 3D underwater video enhancement, which poses additional challenges but offers broader applications in marine research, underwater robotics, and environmental monitoring.

References

1. Chiang, J.Y., Chen, Y.C.: Underwater image enhancement by wavelength compensation and dehazing. IEEE Trans. Image Process. **21**(4), 1756–1769 (2011)
2. Zhang, W., Wang, Y., Li, C.: Underwater image enhancement by attenuated color channel correction and detail preserved contrast enhancement. IEEE J. Oceanic Eng. **47**(3), 718–735 (2022)

3. Xie, J., Hou, G., Wang, G., Pan, Z.: A variational framework for underwater image dehazing and deblurring. IEEE Trans. Circuits Syst. Video Technol. **32**(6), 3514–3526 (2021)
4. Chen, Z., Qiu, N., Song, H., Xu, L., Xiong, Y.: Optically guided level set for underwater object segmentation. Opt. Express **27**(6), 8819–8837 (2019)
5. Wang, N., Zheng, B., Zheng, H., Yu, Z.: Feeble object detection of underwater images through LSR with delay loop. Opt. Express **25**(19), 22490–22498 (2017)
6. Huang, S., Wang, K., Liu, H., Chen, J., Li, Y.: Contrastive semi-supervised learning for underwater image restoration via reliable bank. In: Proceedings of the IEEE/CVF Conference on Computer Vision and Pattern Recognition, pp. 18145–18155 (2023)
7. Li, T., et al.: Underwater image enhancement using adaptive color restoration and dehazing. Opt. Express **30**(4), 6216–6235 (2022)
8. Liu, J., Liu, Z., Wei, Y., Ouyang, W.: Recovery for underwater image degradation with multi-stage progressive enhancement. Opt. Express **30**(7), 11704–11725 (2022)
9. Li, X., Xu, J., Zhang, L., Hu, H., Chen, S.C.: Underwater image restoration via stokes decomposition. Opt. Lett. **47**(11), 2854–2857 (2022)
10. Gao, S., Wu, W., Li, H., Zhu, L., Wang, X.: Atmospheric scattering model induced statistical characteristics estimation for underwater image restoration. IEEE Signal Process. Lett. **30**, 658–662 (2023)
11. Hao, J., Yang, H., Hou, X., Zhang, Y.: Two-stage underwater image restoration algorithm based on physical model and causal intervention. IEEE Signal Process. Lett. **30**, 120–124 (2022)
12. Hu, J., Jiang, Q., Cong, R., Gao, W., Shao, F.: Two-branch deep neural network for underwater image enhancement in HSV color space. IEEE Signal Process. Lett. **28**, 2152–2156 (2021)
13. Liu, J., Zhang, X.: Parameter-adaptive compensation (PAC) for processing underwater selective absorption. IEEE Signal Process. Lett. **27**, 2178–2182 (2020)
14. Ancuti, C.O., Ancuti, C., De Vleeschouwer, C., Sbert, M.: Color channel compensation (3C): a fundamental pre-processing step for image enhancement. IEEE Trans. Image Process. **29**, 2653–2665 (2019)
15. Xue, X., Li, Z., Ma, L., Jia, Q., Liu, R., Fan, X.: Investigating intrinsic degradation factors by multi-branch aggregation for real-world underwater image enhancement. Pattern Recogn. **133**, 109041 (2023)
16. Liu, R., Jiang, Z., Yang, S., Fan, X.: Twin adversarial contrastive learning for underwater image enhancement and beyond. IEEE Trans. Image Process. **31**, 4922–4936 (2022)
17. Guo, Y., Li, H., Zhuang, P.: Underwater image enhancement using a multiscale dense generative adversarial network. IEEE J. Oceanic Eng. **45**(3), 862–870 (2019)
18. Islam, M.J., Xia, Y., Sattar, J.: Fast underwater image enhancement for improved visual perception. IEEE Robot. Autom. Lett. **5**(2), 3227–3234 (2020)
19. Berman, D., Levy, D., Avidan, S., Treibitz, T.: Underwater single image color restoration using haze-lines and a new quantitative dataset. IEEE Trans. Pattern Anal. Mach. Intell. **43**(8), 2822–2837 (2020)
20. Ahn, J.S., Lee, Y.K.: Color distribution of a shade guide in the value, chroma, and hue scale. J. Prosthet. Dent. **100**(1), 18–28 (2008)
21. Legge, G.E., Parish, D.H., Luebker, A., Wurm, L.H.: Psychophysics of reading. xi. comparing color contrast and luminance contrast. J. Opt. Soc. Am. A **7**(10), 2002–2010 (1990)

22. Buckles, R.: Correlating and averaging connate water saturation data. J. Can. Pet. Technol. **4**(01), 42–52 (1965)
23. Hou, G., Zhao, X., Pan, Z., Yang, H., Tan, L., Li, J.: Benchmarking underwater image enhancement and restoration, and beyond. IEEE Access **8**, 122078–122091 (2020)
24. Zhuang, P., Wu, J., Porikli, F., Li, C.: Underwater image enhancement with hyperlaplacian reflectance priors. IEEE Trans. Image Process. **31**, 5442–5455 (2022)
25. Zhang, W., Jin, S., Zhuang, P., Liang, Z., Li, C.: Underwater image enhancement via piecewise color correction and dual prior optimized contrast enhancement. IEEE Signal Process. Lett. **30**, 229–233 (2023)

Signal Processing and Intelligent Systems for Human–Computer Interaction

Movement Analysis in Performing Arts from Human Body Pose Estimation

Alain Trémeau$^{(\boxtimes)}$, Muhammad Turab Bajeer, Damien Muselet,
and Philippe Colantoni

Laboratoire Hubert Curien – UMR 5516, Saint-Etienne, France
`{alain.tremeau,damien.muselet,`
`philippe.colantoni}@univ-st-etienne.fr,`
`muhammad.turab.muslim.bajeer@etu.univ-st-etienne.fr`

Abstract. In this keynote paper we discuss how to automatically analyze the kinematics of human body movements in the context of dance analysis. We also propose new movement analysis handcrafted features based on Laban Movement Analysis (LMA) and 3D pose estimation of dancers. To evaluate the most significant body parts in kinematics analysis of human body movements, we computed the SHAP value of each body part. The preliminary tests and experiments we carried out using video sequences from AIST++ dataset demonstrate the relevance of these new features based either on short or long periods of time. We also demonstrate that the relevance of the most significant features depends on the specificities of the dance videos dataset to process. To improve the accuracy of handcraft features for dance style classification and their robustness to dataset specificities, we suggest to use domain adaptation techniques, such as feature-based, instance-based or parameter-based techniques.

Keywords: Pose Estimation · Laban Movement Analysis · Dances Style Classification

1 Problem Statement

The kinematics of human body movements is an important feature which has been little investigated till now in dance analysis. One way to analyze the kinematics of a performance is to video record this performance, next to use automatic analytical tools.

The kinematics of movements is not related straight forwardly to the change of pose between two consecutive frames of a video, it described the changes in dynamics of the various parts of the body from position, velocity and/or acceleration of points in the space. As example, the Fig. 1(b), (d) and (e) illustrates the kinematics of body parts of three categories of dance movements: a slow dynamic dance motion due to a slow head movement (a), a basic dance movement related to arms expansion (c), a very dynamic dance movement related to complex movement of arms, legs and sacrum (e).

R. K. Karsh et al. (Eds.): SIPCOV 2025, CCIS 2848, pp. 331–345, 2026.
https://doi.org/10.1007/978-3-032-15809-3_26

The kinematics of dance movements can be described by: - the movement of the sacrum; - the movement of the extremities (e.g. the head or the hands); - the global angular momentum around the sacrum; - the expansion of the body from the sacrum; etc. [1]. To model human body poses from keypoints and to analyze the movement of human body parts, several skeleton pose estimation methods can be used, such as ViTPose++ [2], DWPose [3], 4D-Humans [4], NLF [5] to name a few. NLF provides very good results and performs better than most of State-Of-the-Art methods, such as AlphaPose [6] or MMpose [7]. The heavier pose estimation methods are in general more accurate than the lighter.

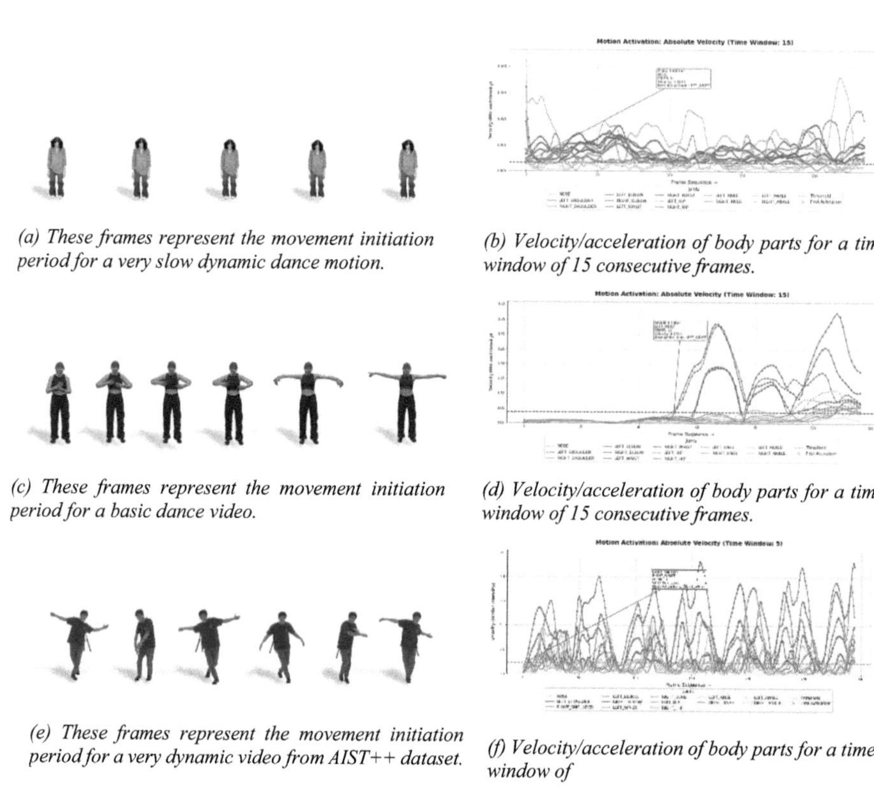

(a) These frames represent the movement initiation period for a very slow dynamic dance motion.

(b) Velocity/acceleration of body parts for a time window of 15 consecutive frames.

(c) These frames represent the movement initiation period for a basic dance video.

(d) Velocity/acceleration of body parts for a time window of 15 consecutive frames.

(e) These frames represent the movement initiation period for a very dynamic video from AIST++ dataset.

(f) Velocity/acceleration of body parts for a time window of

Fig. 1. Velocity and acceleration of human body parts for three different dance styles.

Depending on human body poses and shooting conditions, some methods perform better than others, which can lead to accuracy errors in keypoints detection, as example see Fig. 2.

In this keynote paper, we will demonstrate that the relevance of dance analysis methods depends more on how the dynamic changes of different body parts (related to the position, distance, velocity and acceleration of skeleton points in the space) are analysed than on the accuracy of the body pose estimation, especially as the most recent human body pose estimation methods yield comparable results (except in some specific study cases reported in [1]). In a preliminary step, we used video sequences from the AIST++ Dance Video dataset [8], next we used video sequences collected from online sources (see examples shown in Fig. 5(a)) to evaluate the robustness of feature descriptors on dance analysis methods. The AIST++ dataset is a large-scale collection of street dance videos (done by professionals) which includes 10 street dance genres: Break, Pop, Lock, Waack, Middle Hip-Hop, LA-style Hip-Hop, House, Krump, Street Jazz, and Ballet Jazz. In this study, we limited our analyses to video sequences with a single dancer captured from the frontal camera. The total number of dance videos used in our evaluations was 600, the resolution of these videos is 1920×1080 pixels with 60 frames per second. The video sequences collected from the internet differ significantly from the training data of AIST++ in terms of dance gestures (more freedom in movements, less structured/repetitive dance patterns), environment (illumination and background conditions), and performer variability.

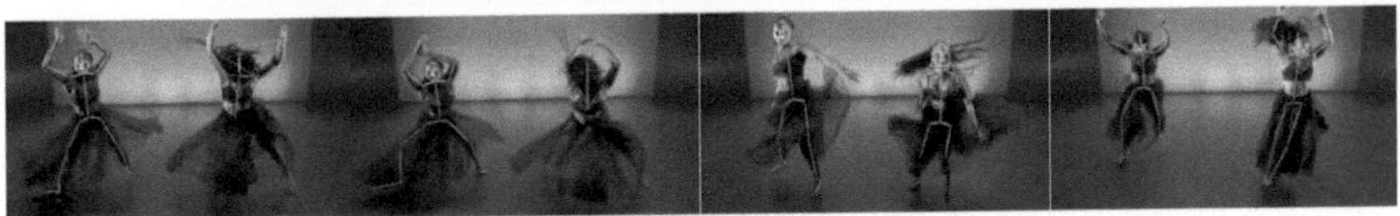

(a) Example of wrong pose estimation due to the dressing of the dancers and low light conditions. (video sequence N°9 of Talawa video processed with Alphapose).

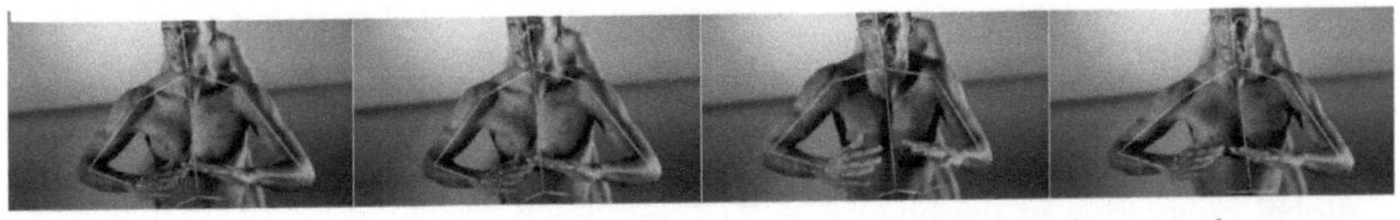

(b) Example of inaccurate pose estimation of the face and the hands of the front dancer. In this sequence, only the upper body of dancers is available. (video sequence N°5 of Talawa video processed with Alphapose).

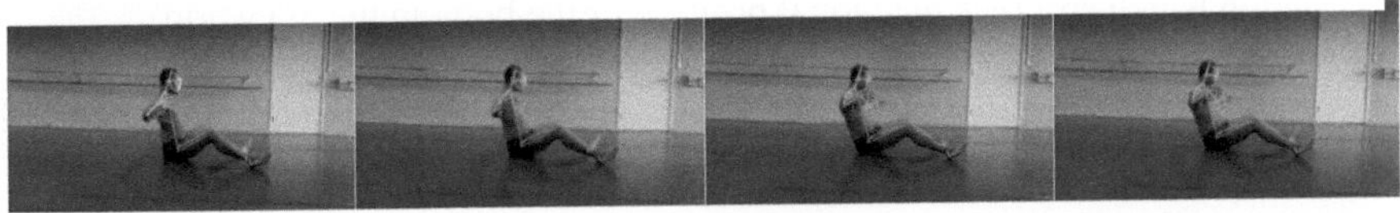

(c) Example of accurate pose estimation of the right hand and of the two legs of the dancer even if the dancer is sitting perpendicularly to the view of the camera (part of his body shape is therefore occluded) (video sequence N°4 of Talawa video processed with Alphapose).

Fig. 2. Human body pose estimation using Alphapose.

The skeleton of a human body is not sufficient to describe properly the morphology of a human, the 3D shape is another important parameter to consider. A 3D human body can be represented by a parametric 3D body mesh, such a SMPL-X [9] which is an advanced 3D human body model that extends the original SMPL (Skinned Multi-Person Linear) model by incorporating not only the body but also expressive facial features and articulated hands (see Fig. 3). This model captures human shape and pose using a parametric representation built on a kinematic tree structure. In addition to body pose, SMPL-X introduces facial expressions and hand gestures, which are modelled separately. SMPL-X can efficiently predicts pose and shape parameters if the spatial resolution is sufficient high to perceive subtle details such as fingers and pose hinges.

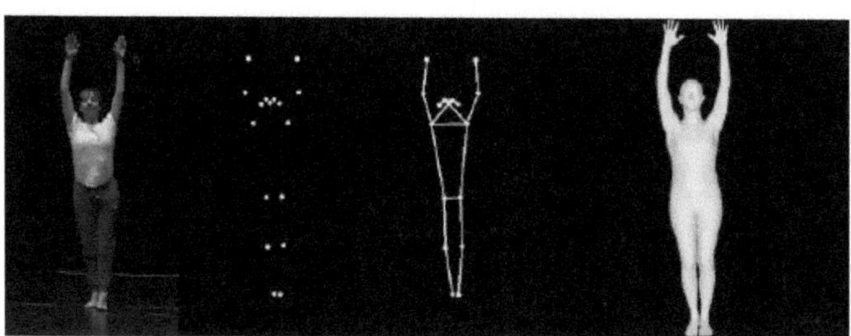

Fig. 3. From left to right: RGB image, major joints, skeleton model, SMPL-X representation

SMPL-X is based on: - 75 rotational parameters for the global rotation and body, eyes, jaw poses; - 24 low-dimensional PCA coefficients or 90 rotational parameters for hand poses; - 10 parameters for the body shape and 10 parameters for the facial expressions. At each frame of a video we associated: - 127 3D key points ; - 127 2D key points; and SMPL-X parameters (composed as: - neutral gender; - 10 shape parameters which control the body shape by representing variations in height, weight, and muscle mass; - 55 pose parameters which define the 3D rotations of the body joints, including the global orientation of the body with 21 joints for the body pose, 15 joints for each hand, 1 joint for each eye, 2 joints for the jaw pose; - global orientation which defines the overall orientation of the body in the 3D world, represented as a 3D rotation vector; - translation which specifies the global position of the body in the 3D world).

2 Dance Movement Analysis

The kinematics of dance movements can be described by automatic human motion classification and analysis methods based on Laban Movement Analysis (LMA) [10, 11]. Two lightweight methods are commonly used to classify dance styles: Support Vector Machines (SVM) and Random Forests (RF) [11]. In our experiments, we used and compared these two methods. For cross-validation, we split the dataset into training, validation, and testing sets, to mitigate overfitting and reduce data dependency. For both SVM and RF, hyperparameters were optimized using Grid Search, and the best configuration was selected based on validation accuracy.

Laban Movement Analysis is defined by four dimensions: effort, space, shape and body [12–16]:

- Effort quality is defined by eight elements: light, strong, free, bound, sustained, quick, indirect and direct. The majority of these elements are related to motion features such as velocity and acceleration.
- Space quality is defined by six elements: side-open, side-across, up, down, forward and backward. These elements are related to the trajectory of human motions (e.g. curvature).
- Shape quality is defined by six elements: opening, enclosing, rising, sinking, advancing and retreating.
- Body quality is defined by three elements: impulsive, swing and impactive.

Scoring a performance using these four dimensions is not an easy task especially in case of complex movements, moreover expert's scoring is prone to subjective evaluation [17–19]. That is why very few annotated datasets have been developed. Most studies in the field focused on the development of handcrafted features rather on learned features due to the complexity of dance movements analysis and the lack of relevant datasets.

In the experiments we have carried out, we demonstrated that the first parameter to take into account to characterize the kinematic of a dancer's movements in a video is the time interval necessary to compute meaningful features. As example see Fig. 4, the temporal patterns that we can observe for the most significant body parts in terms of movement are different for a time interval of ½ sec (i.e., a time window of 30 frames) and for a time interval of 1 s (i.e. a time window of 60 frames).

In two previous papers, we introduced new Laban features computed from short time window (less than 60 frames, i.e. less than 1 s) and demonstrated the efficiency and relevance of these features for emotion recognition in contemporary dance performances [10] and for dance style recognition [11]. The dance style recognition method that we introduced in [11] performs well on dance styles such as Lock, Pop, ballet, LA hip hop, and Waack, as these styles have unique dance gestures and movements (as seen in Fig. 4), meanwhile for other more complex dance styles, such as mid hip-hop, break dance, house, Jazz street, and Krump, the recognition accuracy is lower, as these dances are characterized by more freedom of movement. In Fig. 5, we can observe that Krump and Pop dances show quick movements, while Lock shows clear gesture pause patterns. In contrast, Break, Waack, and Middle Hip Hop dances show random, varied, and less predictable temporal patterns. It is evident that using a larger sliding window size helps capture the style-specific representation better, which directly improves classification accuracy. See also Fig. 6.

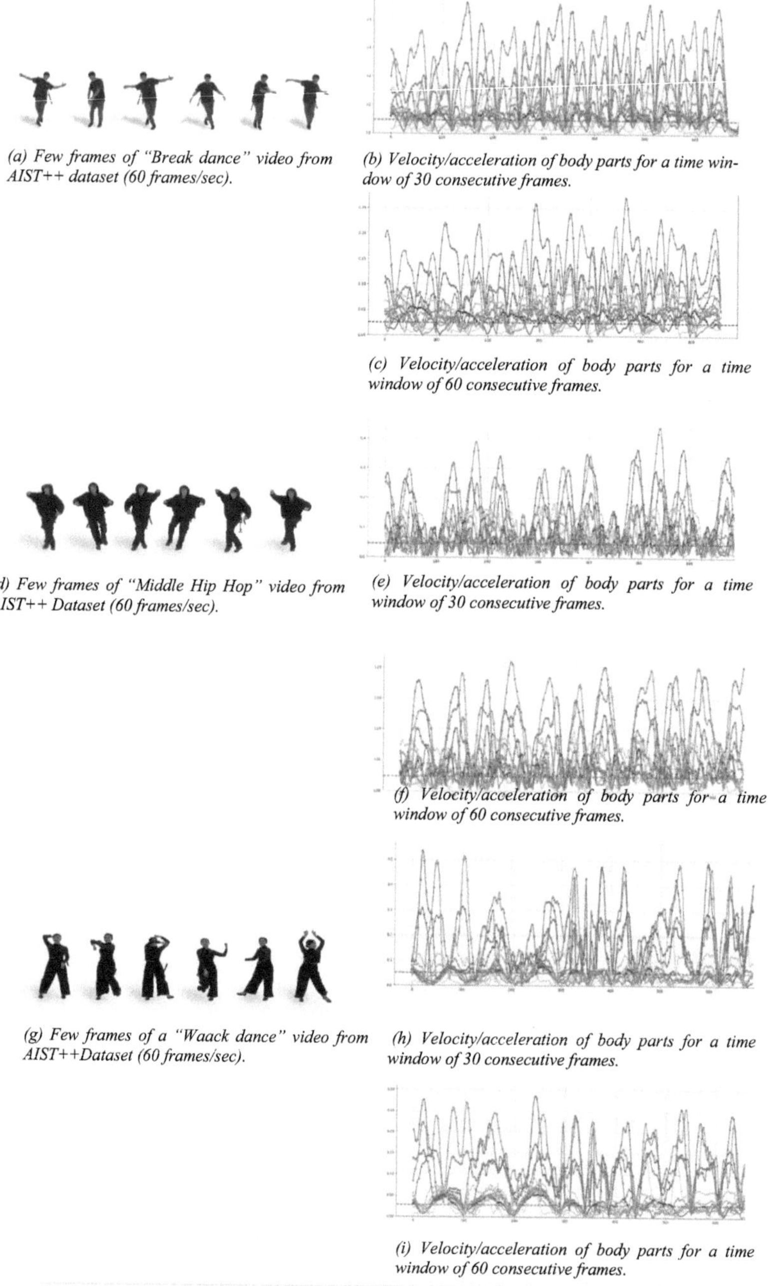

Fig. 4. Velocity and acceleration of human body parts analyzed with a very short (1/2 s) and short time window (1 s). The horizontal axis denotes the frame number, while the vertical axis indicates velocity.

(a) Examples of dance performance videos collected from online sources, used to evaluate the relevance of dance movements descriptors versus very short and short time window.

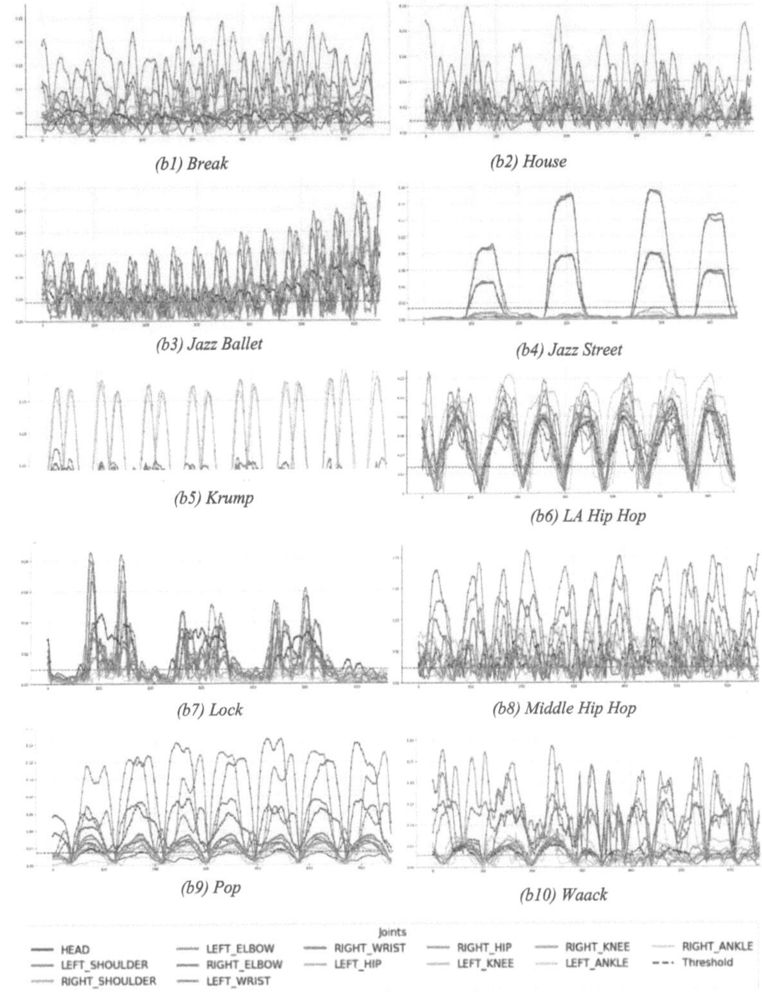

(b1) Break

(b2) House

(b3) Jazz Ballet

(b4) Jazz Street

(b5) Krump

(b6) LA Hip Hop

(b7) Lock

(b8) Middle Hip Hop

(b9) Pop

(b10) Waack

(b) Dance styles

Fig. 5. Sort-term kinematic (velocity) evolution across ten dance styles, computed using a sliding window of 60 consecutive frames. The horizontal axis denotes the frame number, while the vertical axis indicates velocity.

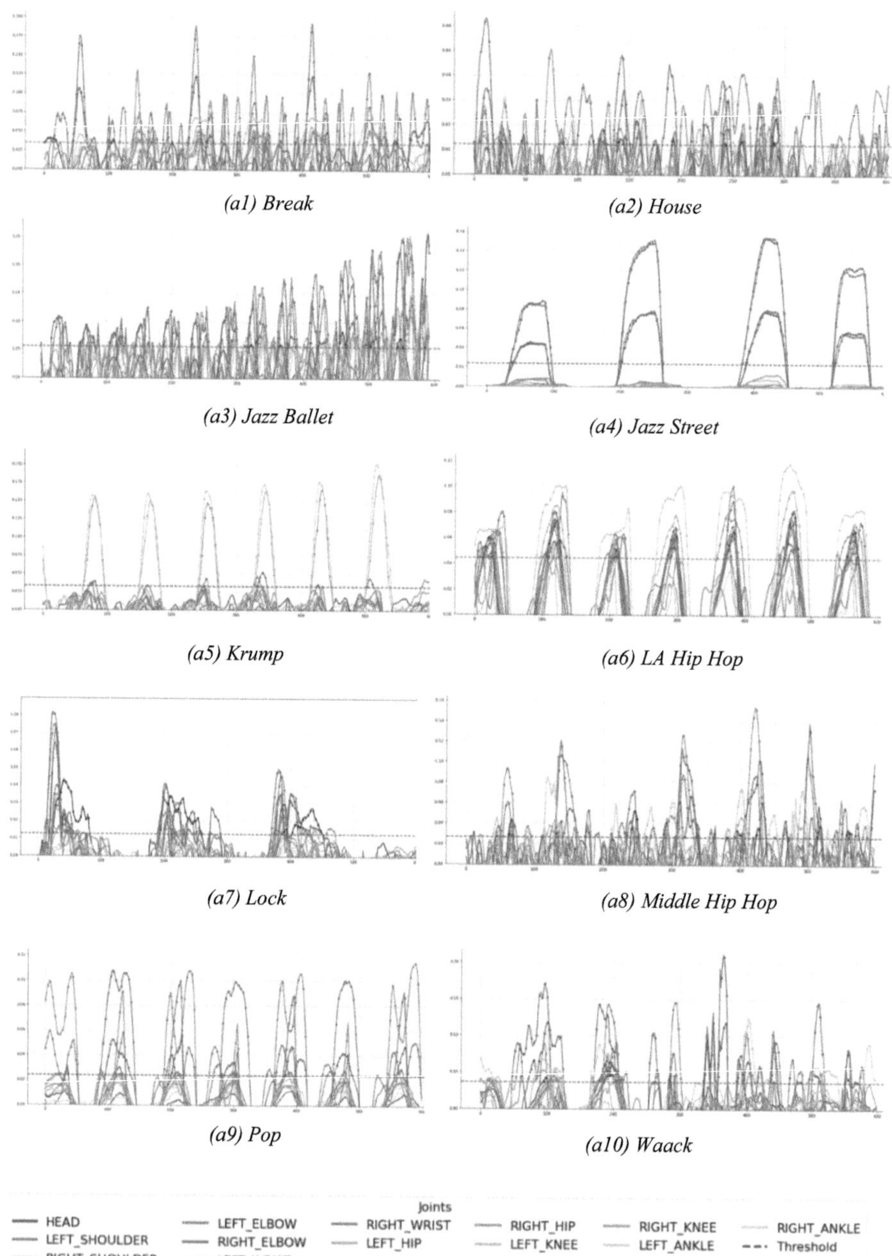

(a1) Break

(a2) House

(a3) Jazz Ballet

(a4) Jazz Street

(a5) Krump

(a6) LA Hip Hop

(a7) Lock

(a8) Middle Hip Hop

(a9) Pop

(a10) Waack

Fig. 6. Short-term kinematic (acceleration) evolution across ten dance styles, computed using a sliding window of 60 consecutive frames. The horizontal axis denotes the frame number, while the vertical axis indicates velocity.

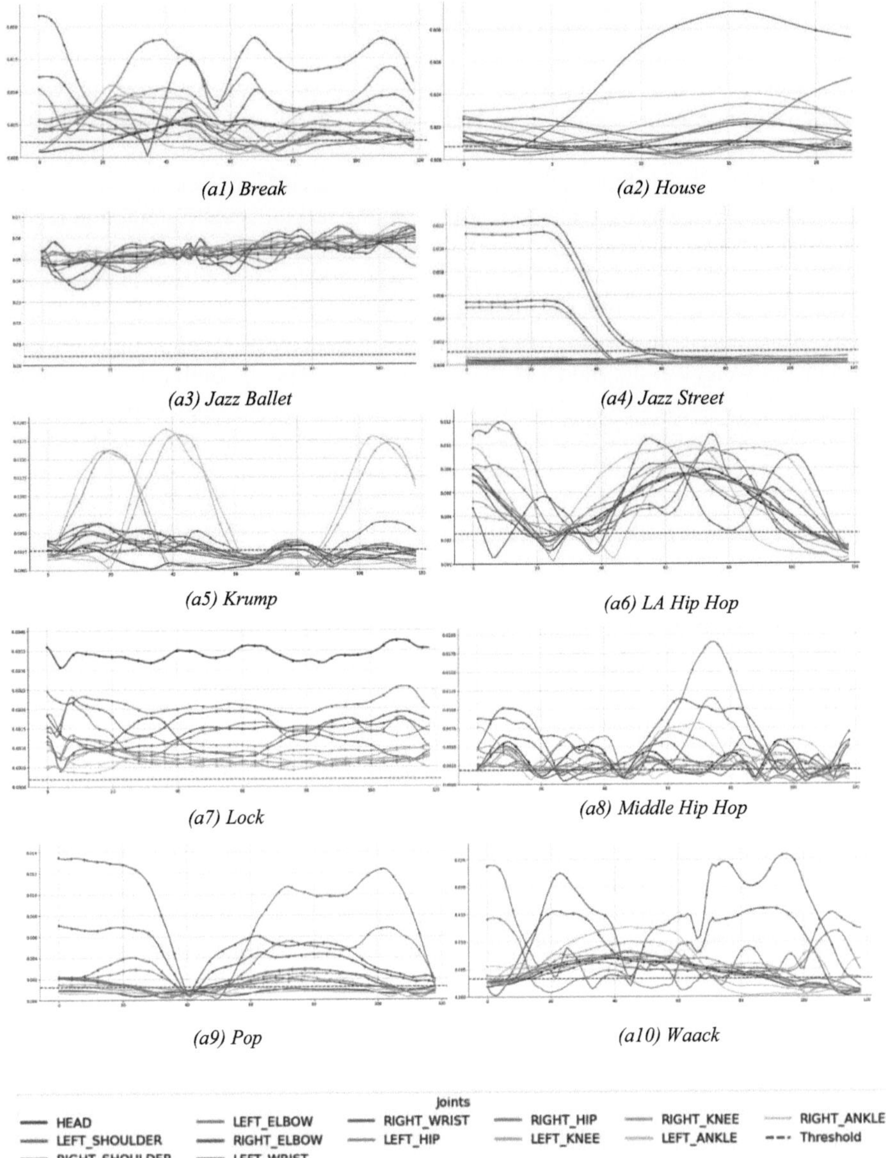

Fig. 7. Long-term kinematic (velocity) evolution across ten dance styles, computed using a sliding window of 600 consecutive frames. The horizontal axis denotes the frame number, while the vertical axis indicates velocity.

In this keynote paper, we suggest to investigate new Laban features computed from long time window (higher than 600 frames, i.e. higher than 10 s). Indeed, dance styles such as Ballet, Krump, LA Hip Hop, Lock, and Pop show repetitive and structured temporal patterns not only a short-time scale but also at long-time scale (see Fig. 7). For example, the left ankle and left knee show a specific long-term behavior for Krump. On the other hand, the head shows a specific long-term behavior for Lock.

To evaluate the most significant body parts in the task of gesture's emotion recognition or in the task of dance style recognition, we suggested in [10, 11] to compute the SHAP value of each body part (see Fig. 8). SHAP (SHapley Additive exPlanations) is a method to explain individual predictions and to interpret machine learning based models [20]. To calculate the score of each feature used in a classification model, which represents its weight in the model output, SHAP considers all combinations between the features to cover all cases where all feature and a subset of features are used in the model. These scores provide interpretable and explainable insights into the factors that are most relevant and influential in the model predictions.

In Fig. 5, the highest velocity peaks (peaks upper than 0.2) are for the break and for the Waack, these peaks concern the left and right Wrists. In the context of dance style recognition, this is reflected by a rather high SHAP value for each of these body parts (see Fig. 9), for Break the SHAP values are 0.10 (-0.10 being the lowest, and 0.15 highest) and 0.09 for Waack (-0.10 being the lowest, and 0.20 highest). SHAP values are here similar, while for the break the movements of left and wright Wrists are desynchronized with an average time delay of less than 60 frames, meanwhile for the Waack, the movements of the left and wright Wrists seem dissociated (no similar repetitive patterns). This means that the movement of left and right Wrists should not be analyzed independently but also as a pair of body parts, as well as few other pairs of body parts.

For the Krump dance, the movements of the knees and ankles are synchronized, as the movements of both (with a velocity in the range 0.15–0.20), with an average time delay of less than 60 frames. Another interesting element, the order of the peaks for both knees and ankles is on a periodic base inverted (first the right ankle moves, then right knee moves then the left ankle and left knee move). Apart from these the velocity of head and right elbow is also significant among other joints. This is reflected by SHAP values in the range of 0.05–0.1 (0.15 being the highest) for knees, which suggests that knees' movement is not the highest, but it still falls in top features that contribute to the classification of a particular movement as Krump. On the other hand, the ankle joints show relatively higher SHAP values than knees, which suggests that foot movements are more influential in Krump classification. Once again, we can conclude here that the movement of ankle joints and of knees should not be analyzed independently but also as a pair of body parts. See also results shown in Fig. 10 for a sliding window of 30 consecutive frames.

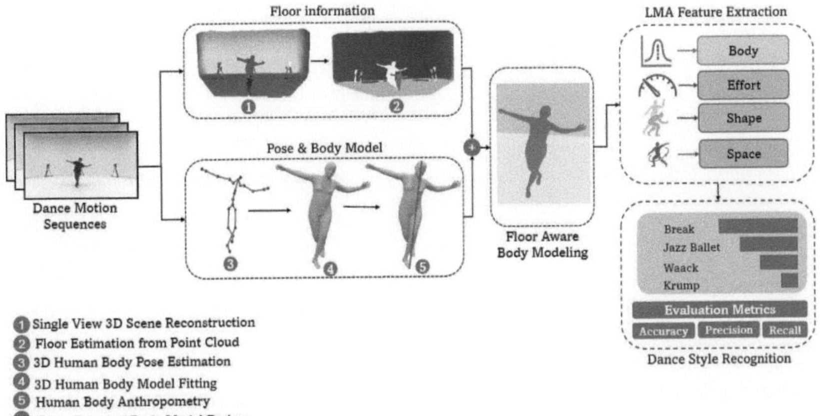

Fig. 8. Overview of the generic dance style classification method proposed in [11]. The most significant features used by the classification task depend of the dance video dataset. The set of handcraft features currently used can be extended to additional features independently of the other tasks. Image from [11].

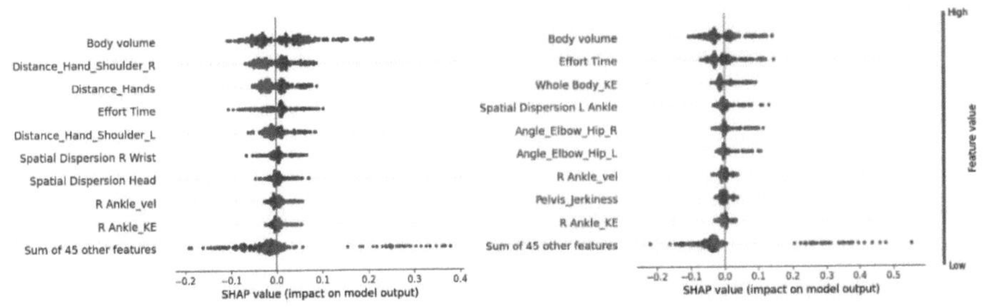

(a) SHAP values for Break dance   (b) SHAP values for the Waack dance style.

Fig. 9. SHAP values for the most influential features in the prediction of a dance style.

On the other hand, for the street Jazz dance, the movements of the left and right Wrists are synchronized (with a velocity in the range 0.1–0.175) with the movements of the left and right elbow, but the velocity of these latter is lower (in the range 0.5–0.8), meanwhile for all other body elements the velocity is significantly lower. Also, the time delay between repetitive patterns is the largest (more than 60 frames). This is reflected by the same trend with the SHAP values in the range 0.05–0.07 for both Wrists and elbows (0.10 being the highest for body volume).

For the Pop dance, the behavior of several body part is similar with subtill variations of velocities (the velocity of left and right Wrist > velocity of left and right elbow > velocity of all other elements). Similar behavior can be also observed with Waack dance. For the ballet Jazz dance, the velocity of left and right Wrist, as well as the velocity of left and right elbow, and the periodicity of variations of velocities of these elements

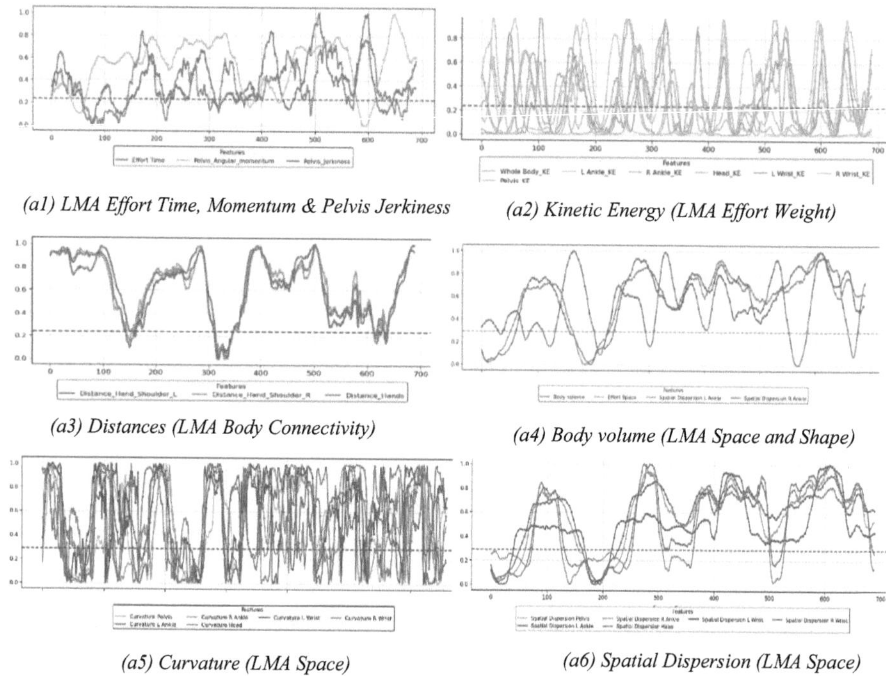

(a1) LMA Effort Time, Momentum & Pelvis Jerkiness   *(a2) Kinetic Energy (LMA Effort Weight)*

(a3) Distances (LMA Body Connectivity)   *(a4) Body volume (LMA Space and Shape)*

(a5) Curvature (LMA Space)   *(a6) Spatial Dispersion (LMA Space)*

Fig. 10. Short-term LMA features including Body, Effort, Space and Shape computed using sliding window of 30 consecutive frames. The horizontal axis denotes the frame number, while the vertical axis indicates feature value.

characterize in a unique way this dance style. Figure 6 clearly demonstrates that the periodicity of temporal patterns is a very relevant feature to take into account in dance style classification.

For Lock dance, we can observe the short pauses in the movements as several key joints including wrists, elbows, and head show sudden movements and then pause for a shorter period of time. This trend continues later as well but with less velocity magnitude compared to the first movement. This can also be observed visually, as the dancer performs a movement involving all the joints then freezes for a short period of time and then continues to do. The magnitude is high in the initial movements (velocity of 0.09–0.1) as the dancers performs an upward quick motion, and then downward motion (0.05–0.07) which is not as quick as the first one.

The acceleration curves also show similar trends as in the velocity curves (as seen in Fig. 6). However, the acceleration curves highlight the key joints more effectively than velocity curves. They suppress the other joints that are not involved in the movement and amplify the joints that are involved. In some cases, it also highlights the joints that were suppressed in the velocity curves and were not obvious to see, but they get amplified in the acceleration curves and become more visible. For example, for break dance the velocity curves show a very cluttered movement and only the wrists and elbows are clearly visible, but acceleration curves highlight other joints including left ankle, right ankle and right knee which when visually inspected are highly important in such dance styles. For Lock dance the pauses are even more visible from the joint movements. Similar trends can also be seen for Waack dance style where the suppressed joints are clearly highlighted by the acceleration curves. Regarding the acceleration SHAP values, interestingly they are lower than velocity SHAP values. Even though that acceleration curves highlight the joints that are not visible, but velocity curves already highlight the joints which define the movements really well.

Additional Laban features show similar trends. The Laban Effort Time feature, which indicates whether a movement is quick or sustained, plays an important role across all dance styles. For break dance, it effectively captures the rapid movements, with a mean value of 0.83 (on a scale of 0–1), suggesting highly quick movements. In comparison, the average value for Waack is 0.65, which also indicates quick movements, though not as rapid as in break dance. While the AIST++ dataset generally includes fast movements, some styles combine both quick and strong movements [21]. To distinguish *quick* movements from *strong*, we introduce the Laban Effort Weight component. This is computed using the kinetic energy of each joint, which reflects whether a movement is strong or light. In break dance, this feature shows that joints like the ankles, wrists, head, and pelvis show strong movements, whereas in Waack dance, these joints show lighter motion. Since these joints are more actively engaged in break dance, this feature effectively highlights which joints perform strong/forceful versus light movements. Unlike basic kinematic features like velocity or acceleration, which only measure speed, kinetic energy accounts for both speed and the force (mass and acceleration) of a joint. This allows it to differentiate between quick and strong movements, which is something velocity and acceleration alone cannot do.

Kinetic energy is also one of the top features in SHAP analysis: it shows high values (in red) for break dance and low values (in blue) for Waack, which validates that the LMA Effort Weight component is important for recognizing strong/forceful movements versus quick/sudden ones. Although both dance styles are dynamic, break dance emphasizes strength and impact, whereas Waack emphasizes lightness and speed.

Another Laban feature captures how a performer's body changes shape during movement. To measure this, we compute the bounding volume of the body, which indicates the degree of expansion and contraction. For both Break and Waack dance styles, this is one of the most influential features. Break dance involves rapid movements of the wrists, ankles, and elbows (as also reflected in the velocity and LMA Effort Time features). Since these joints move more frequently and with greater force, the dancer's body continuously contracts and expands. This is supported by the SHAP values, where this feature has high importance (shown in red). In contrast, Waack dance shows the opposite behaviour: the SHAP values are low (shown in blue), indicating that this style involves less change in the body's shape compared to Break dance.

Lastly, we have shown above that for some dance movements/dance styles, pairs of joints (e.g. ankle and knees for Krump, or left and right wrists for Waack) may complement the information provided by individual joints. Very few conventional Laban features parameters combines pairs (or groups) of body elements, such as the body connectivity feature (which computes the distance between the hands as a single feature), our investigations nevertheless have shown that this could contribute to improve the accuracy and the relevance of the dance style classification task.

In this keynote paper we illustrated our findings using mainly qualitative results and few quantitative, detailed quantitative results are available in [11, 23].

3   Conclusion

In this keynote paper, we demonstrated how existing Laban features could be complemented by new kinematics features to classify dance styles. The preliminary tests and experimentations we conducted using AIST++ dance videos. In a next step, we will investigate the robustness of our findings from more complex dance videos collected from online sources. We suggested new features that could contribute to improve the accuracy and the relevance of the dance style classification task. In a next study, we will evaluate the relevance and the added value of these new features. In order to improve the accuracy of dance style classification computed from the set of handcraft features proposed in this study and in our previous papers, and the robustness of our classification method to dataset specificities, we did preliminary tests using domain adaptation techniques, such as feature-based, instance-based or parameter-based techniques. The first promising results that we got confirm that the most significant features computed by the classification task depend of the dance video dataset, and that the weight, the significance, of the main features used in the dance style classification task can be automatically adapted to the input dataset using a domain adaptation technique.

Acknowledgments. This study was funded by HORIZON-CL2-2021-HERITAGE-000201-04 (grant number 101061303 - PREMIERE) [22]

References

1. Zhang, Q., Xu, Y., Zhang, J., Tao, D.: ViTAEv2: vision transformer advanced by exploring inductive bias for image recognition and beyond. arXiv preprint arXiv:2202.10108 (2022)

2. Yang, Z., Zeng, A., Yuan, C., Li, Y.: Effective whole-body pose estimation with two-stages distillation. In: Proceedings of the IEEE/CVF International Conference on Computer Vision, pp. 4210–4220 (2023)

3. Goel, S., Pavlakos, G., Rajasegaran, J., Kanazawa, A., Malik, J.: Humans in 4D: reconstructing and tracking humans with transformers. In: International Conference on Computer Vision (ICCV) (2023)

4. Sárándi, I., Pons-Moll, G.: Neural localizer fields for continuous 3D human pose and shape estimation. arXiv preprint arXiv:2407.07532 (2024)

5. Fang, H.-S., et al.: AlphaPose: whole-body regional multi-person pose estimation and tracking in real-time. IEEE Trans. Pattern Anal. Mach. Intell. (2022). https://doi.org/10.1109/TPAMI.2022.3222784

6. MMPose Contributors: OpenMMLab pose estimation toolbox and benchmark (2020). https://github.com/open-mmlab/mmpose

7. Colantoni, P., Ahmed, R., Ghimire, P., Muselet, D., Trémeau, A.: Relevance of Human Body Pose Estimation Methods for Complex Dance Movements Analysis. In: Proceedings of IMPROVE'2025, Porto (2025). To be published

8. Tsuchida, S., Fukayama, S., Hamasaki, M., Goto, M.: AIST dance video database: multi-genre, multi-dancer, and multi-camera database for dance information processing. In: Proceedings of the 20th International Society for Music Information Retrieval Conference, ISMIR 2019. Delft, Netherlands (2019)

9. Pavlakos, G., et al.: Expressive body capture: 3D hands, face, and body from a single image (2019). https://arxiv.org/abs/1904.05866 (2025)

10. Bajeer, M.T.M., Colantoni, P., Muselet, D., Tremeau, A.: Emotion recognition in contemporary dance performances using laban movement analysis. In: To be published in the Proceedings of the 21st International Conference in Computer Analysis of Images and Patterns (CAIP) (2025) https://arxiv.org/abs/2504.21154

11. Bajeer, M.T.M., Colantoni, P., Muselet, D., Tremeau, A.: Dance style recognition using Laban movement analysis and machine learning. In: To be published in the Proceedings of Advanced Concepts for Intelligent Vision Systems (ACIVS) (2025) https://arxiv.org/abs/2504.21166

12. von Laban, R.: The Mastery of Movement on the Stage. MacDonald & Evans, London (1950)

13. Aristidou, A., Stavrakis, E., Charalambous, P., Chrysanthou, Y., Himona, S.L.: Folk dance evaluation using Laban movement analysis. J. Comput. Cult. Herit. 8(4), 1–19 (2015)

14. Levy, J.A., Duke, M.P.: The use of Laban movement analysis in the study of personality, emotional state and movement style: an exploratory investigation of the veridicality of "body language". Individ. Differ. Res. 1(1), 39–63 (2003)

15. Chen, J.F., Lin, W.C., Tsai, K.H., Dai, S.Y.: Analysis and evaluation of human movement based on laban movement analysis. J. Appl. Sci. Eng. 14(3), 255–264 (2011)

16. Bouchard, D., Badler, N.: Semantic segmentation of motion capture using Laban movement analysis. In: Intelligent Virtual Agents: 7th International Conference, IVA 2007 Paris, France, September 17–19, 2007 Proceedings 7, pp. 37–44. Springer, Berlin Heidelberg (2007)

17. Bernardet, U., Fdili Alaoui, S., Studd, K., Bradley, K., Pasquier, P., Schiphorst, T.: Assessing the reliability of the Laban movement analysis system. PLoS One. 14(6), e0218179 (2019)

18. Morita, J., Nagai, Y., Moritsu, T.: Relations between body motion and emotion: Analysis based on Laban Movement Analysis. In; Proceedings of the Annual Meeting of the Cognitive Science Society, Vol. 35, No. 35 (2013)

19. Fdili Alaoui, S., Françoise, J., Schiphorst, T., Studd, K., Bevilacqua, F.: Seeing, sensing and recognizing Laban movement qualities. In: Proceedings of the 2017 CHI Conference on Human Factors in Computing Systems, pp. 4009–4020 (2017)

20. Lundberg, S.M., Lee, S.-I.: A unified approach to interpreting model predictions. In: Proceedings of the 31st International Conference on Neural Information Processing Systems, NIPS'17, pp. 4768–4777. Curran Associates Inc., Red Hook (2017)

21. Li, R., Yang, S., Ross, D.A., Kanazawa, A.: AI choreographer: music conditioned 3D dance generation with AIST++. In: ICCV (2021)

22. Premiere – performing arts in a new era (2025). https://premiere-project.eu/

23. Bajeer, M.T.M.: Modeling human body movement features using Laban movement analysis approach. master thesis report. University Jean Monnet, June (2025)

DeepFood: Enhancing Recipe Selection Through AI-Based Ingredient Recognition

Banala Saritha[1]([⊠]) [iD], G. Purnachandrarao[2] [iD], Aliya Siddiqha[1], Allulla Deekshitha[1], and Divity Vyshnavi[1]

[1] Department of Electronics and Communication Engineering, B V Raju Institute of
Technology, Narsapur, Medak, Telangana, India
`{saritha.b,23211a0407,23211a0410,23211a0460}@bvrit.ac.in`
[2] Department of Electronics and Communication Engineering, BVRIT HYDERABAD College
of Engineering for Women, Hyderabad, Telangana, India

Abstract. In today's world, selecting a proper recipe depending upon the ingredients available in the home is time-consuming and inconvenient. Current systems take a lot of time in asking for ingredient names manually, which lowers efficiency and user satisfaction. To overcome this, we suggest implementing an AI powered recipe suggesting system that automatically identifies ingredients from images and give corresponding recipe suggestions. The two-stage system consists of: (1) Ingredient Recognition, a Convolutional Neural Network (CNN) scans the uploaded images to determine ingredients based on color, and shape; and (2) Recipe Recommendation, a content based filtering algorithm compares the identified ingredients against the appropriate recipes in a database. In contrast with other methods, our system makes it possible for individuals to merely upload a single image or multiple images of the ingredients instead of typing the text manually, thus making the process easier. This method not only saves time and increase efficiency but also minimize food wastage by proper utilization of existing ingredients.

Keywords: Recipe recommendation · Computer Vision · Content-Based Filtering · Image-Based Input · Deep learning · Machine learning

1 Introduction

The traditional recipe recommendation systems typically consist of manual ingredient input, keyword-based search, and static recipe matching stages. However, with the recent advancements in deep learning and computer vision, researchers have begun leveraging these technologies to automate and enhance the meal suggestion process [1]. Recipe recommendation has significant applications in various domains, including smart kitchens, dietary planning, waste reduction, and personalized nutrition systems. Conventional systems rely heavily on user inputs or predefined ingredient lists, which can be inefficient, error prone, and inconvenient. In contrast, modern approaches utilize image-based ingredient recognition powered by Convolutional Neural Networks (CNNs), allowing

R. K. Karsh et al. (Eds.): SIPCOV 2025, CCIS 2848, pp. 346–353, 2026.
https://doi.org/10.1007/978-3-032-15809-3_27

users to simply upload photos of available ingredients, either single or multiple, without needing to type or search manually. This automation reduces user effort and enables more dynamic, real-time suggestions based on actual ingredient availability [2]. Earlier systems depended on handcrafted feature extraction methods, which often lacked generalization and required domain specific tuning. These limitations are addressed in this work by applying CNN-based models that learn rich visual features directly from raw images of ingredients. CNNs have proven highly effective for classification tasks, making them ideal for identifying visually complex food items such as leafy vegetables, spices, or mixed groups of ingredients [3]. Recent developments also focus on mapping recognized ingredients to suitable recipes using intelligent recommendation algorithms. These systems not only improve meal planning efficiency but also help minimize food waste by suggesting recipes tailored to what the user already has. By combining image recognition with smart matching, the proposed system offers a seamless and practical solution for everyday cooking decisions. The remainder of the paper is organized as follows. Section 2 presents a review of related works. Section 3 explains the system architecture and methodology. Section 4 discusses the experimental setup. Section 5 concludes the paper and outlines future enhancements.

2 Related Works

The literature survey provides an overview of existing research and methodologies relevant to this study. Various approaches have been explored in recommendation systems, focusing on different techniques, challenges, and advancements [4]. This section reviews key contributions from previous works to establish the foundation for our study. Tejaswini et al. [5] presents an AI-based system for personalized recipe generation and cooking assistance. Uses machine learning to suggest recipes based on user preferences, available ingredients, and dietary restrictions. Vivek et al. [6] develops a machine learning based recipe recommendation system using collaborative filtering, specifically, it compares item-based and user-based methods for generating personalized recipe suggestions. Akshara et al. [7] develops an AI-driven system that personalizes recipe suggestions, based on user preferences and dietary restrictions. Ixent Galpin et al. [8] describes the comprehensive process of designing, implementing, and evaluating Snap Chef, an innovative recipe recommendation application. Tian xiang Xing et al. [9] developed Recipe Radar, an AI-powered recipe recommendation system using natural language processing and a multi-input neural network to suggest personalized recipes based on user preferences and ingredient constraints.

3 Proposed Architecture

The proposed system deepfood is an AI-based recipe suggestion architecture that leverages Convolutional Neural Networks (CNNs) to identify ingredients from images and recommends recipes accordingly. The architecture is shown in Fig. 1, structured into three main stages: data collection, ingredient recognition using CNN, and recipe matching & recommendation. Each component plays a critical role in automating the meal planning process and enhancing user convenience. Initially, a comprehensive dataset of food ingredients and corresponding recipes is collected from publicly available sources such as Kaggle, food APIs, and other open-source repositories. The images of ingredients are preprocessed through resizing, normalization, and augmentation to ensure consistency and model robustness. Alongside, a well-organized recipe database is curated, mapping recipes to their required ingredients, enabling efficient matching later in the process. The detailed architecture of proposed model is illustrated in Fig. 2. The ingredient recognition component employs a deep CNN architecture trained on the collected image dataset. The first convolutional layers scan the input image using filters to extract local features such as edges, textures, and shapes that characterize different ingredients. This is followed by pooling layers that down-sample the feature maps, reducing dimensionality while preserving essential patterns.

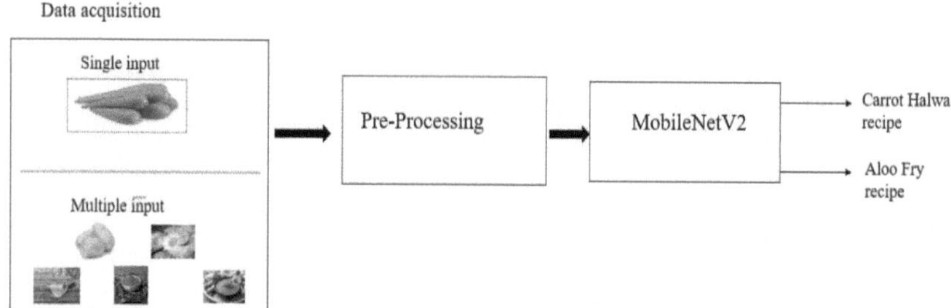

Fig. 1. Block diagram of deepfood recipe recommendation system

Batch normalization and activation functions like ReLU are integrated to improve learning efficiency and prevent overfitting. Fully connected layers then consolidate the features into a comprehensive representation, and the final output layer, using a Soft-Max classifier, predicts the ingredient classes. This setup allows the model to accurately identify one or multiple ingredients from a single image, forming the input for the next phase. The above Fig. 1 illustrates the full architectural workflow, from image input to ingredient detection and recipe output. By integrating CNN-based ingredient recognition with intelligent recommendation algorithms, the proposed system delivers an automated, user-friendly, and efficient solution to modern meal planning challenges. Once the ingredients are recognized, the recipe recommendation engine activates. Using a content-based filtering approach, the system matches the identified ingredients with entries in the recipe database. It evaluates the similarity between the user's available ingredients and those required by the recipes, ranking and recommending the most relevant options. This process ensures minimal user input while maximizing relevance and utility, making the system particularly beneficial for reducing food waste and simplifying daily meal decisions.

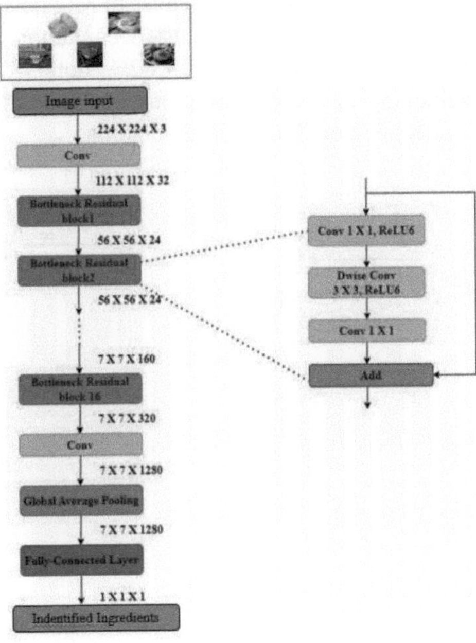

Fig. 2. The architecture of proposed Deepfood

4 Experimental Database, Configuration and Findings

We used a pre-trained MobileNetV2 model fine-tuned on the Food-101 dataset [13] for ingredient recognition. Images were resized to 224 × 224 and normalized. The model was trained using Adam optimizer (lr = 0.0001, batch size = 64). The system was built using Flask (backend) and HTML/CSS/JS (frontend), and tested on an Intel i5, 8GB RAM setup. The model achieved approximately 94.62% accuracy and reaches 91.060% Top-5 accuracy on ImageNet. The average response time was 1.02 s, and 82.3% of users found the recipe suggestions relevant.

To evaluate model performance, we initially studied baseline CNN architectures. While basic CNNs demonstrate moderate accuracy, they are computationally heavier and less optimized for real-time applications.

Table 1. Performance comparison of MobileNetV2 and CNN

Metric	MobileNetV2	CNN
Test Accuracy (%)	94.62	90
Top-5 Accuracy (%)	91.06	82.3
Average Prediction Time (s/image)	1.02	>1

Table 1 presents the comparison of the performance of MobileNetV2 over CNN. The MobileNetV2 model was evaluated on a custom dataset containing annotated ingredient images. The model achieved a test accuracy of 94.62%, outperforming general CNN benchmarks typically achieving 82.3% accuracy on similar tasks. The improvements validate the suitability of MobileNetV2 for our application.

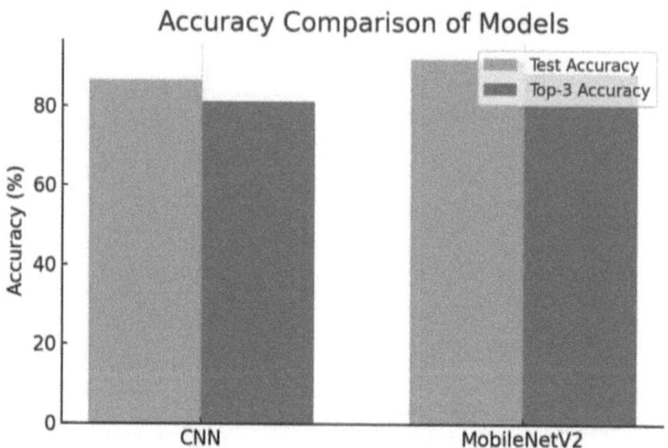

Fig. 3. Test vs. Top-3 accuracy comparison between CNN and MobileNetV2 models

To visualize the model's performance, above Fig. 3 shows a bar graph comparing key metrics between CNN and MobileNetV2 [12]. We further analyzed the performance of the MobileNetV2 model across different common ingredients. The detailed evaluation results are presented in Table 2. Ingredient-wise performance is illustrated in Fig. 4 using a bar graph for better understanding.

Table 2. Ingredient wise Precision, Recall, and F1 Score (MobileNetV2)

Ingredient	Precision (%)	Recall (%)	F1 Score (%)
Tomato	93.1	92.6	92.8
Onion	91.4	90.8	91.1
Potato	90.3	89.1	89.7
Carrot	87.5	86.2	86.8
Capsicum	89.7	88.4	89.0
Spinach	83.0	82.2	82.4

Ingredient Identification Performance

To evaluate the effectiveness of our AI-based Recipe Suggestion System, we conducted experiments on ingredient recognition using Convolutional Neural Networks (CNNs). The system was tested on a dataset comprising commonly used vegetables, and the performance was measured in terms of Precision, Recall, and F1 Score—key metrics in classification tasks.

The model achieved high precision and recall across all ingredient categories, with particularly strong results for Tomato and Onion, which recorded F1 scores of 92.8% and 91.1%, respectively. These high values indicate the model's ability to correctly detect these ingredients with minimal false positives and false negatives. Spinach, while slightly lower in performance with an F1 score of 82.4%, still demonstrates reliable detection despite its relatively complex texture and variation in appearance.

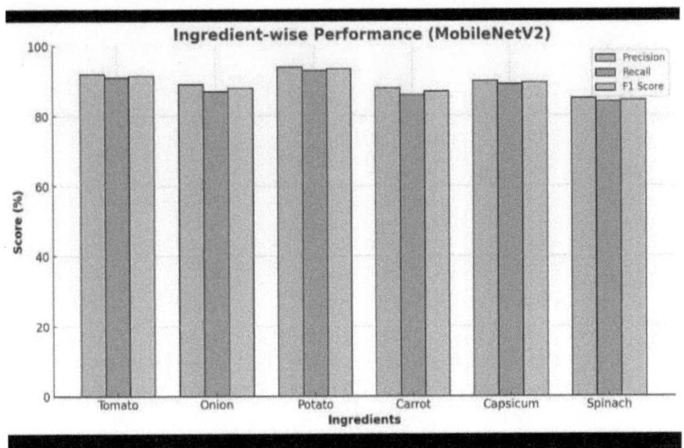

Fig. 4. Comparison of Ingredient-wise performance

Overall, these results validate the robustness and accuracy of our CNN-based ingredient detection module, which forms the foundation of the system's automated recipe recommendation capability. The consistent performance across multiple ingredient types underscores the model's generalization ability and makes it suitable for real-world applications in dynamic kitchen environments. A comparative analysis of model performance is presented in Table 3, with the accuracy of each approach illustrated in Fig. 5 for clearer visualization.

Table 3. Performance comparison of proposed model with existing models

Author (year)	Model	Accuracy (%)
Srivastava et al.(2024) [11]	K-NN	81.2
Tejaswini et al. (2024) [5]	RNN	90.3
Somanath et al. (2024) [10]	CNN	91.8
Akshara et al. (2024) [7]	RNN, NLP	92.4
Proposed	MobileNetv2	94.62

To benchmark the effectiveness of our proposed system, we conducted a comparative analysis against several existing models employed for ingredient or image-based food classification. The models under review, as shown in the table below, include traditional machine learning approaches like K-Nearest Neighbors (KNN), as well as deep learning techniques such as Recurrent Neural Networks (RNNs) and Convolutional Neural Networks (CNNs).

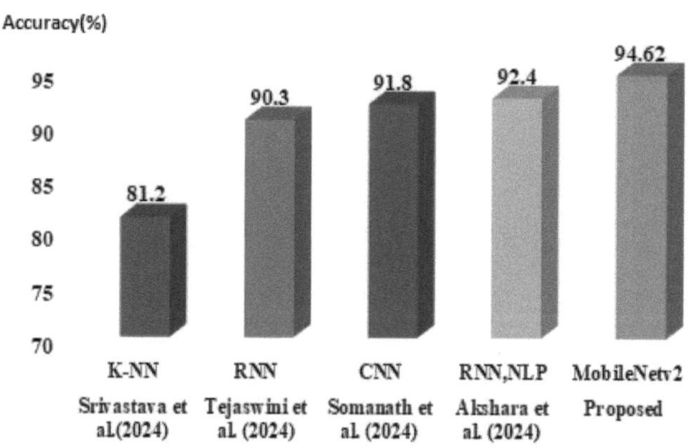

Fig. 5. Comparison of model accuracy of proposed model over existing models

The MobileNetv2 architecture used in our proposed system outperformed all previous models, achieving an accuracy of 94.62%. This superior performance can be attributed to MobileNetv2's efficient depthwise separable convolutions and inverted residual structure, which enable high accuracy with reduced computational cost making it particularly well-suited for real-time mobile and embedded applications. Compared to the highest-performing prior model (Akshara et al., 2024) which combines RNN with NLP for contextual understanding and achieved 92.4%, our approach offers a notable improvement of over 2% in accuracy. This demonstrates the efficacy of using optimized CNN architectures like MobileNetv2 for precise and scalable ingredient recognition in automated recipe recommendation systems.

5 Conclusion

This paper presents a deepfood, AI-based recipe suggestion system that employs a pre-trained MobileNetV2 model to recognize Ingredients from images and recommend suitable recipes. Trained on the Food-101 dataset, the model achieved a classification accuracy of 94.62%, demonstrating reliable performance with an average response time of 1.02 s. User evaluation showed 85% satisfaction with the suggested recipes, indicating the system's effectiveness in enhancing daily cooking decisions and minimizing ingredient wastage. As part of future work, we aim to integrate a Generative Adversarial Network (GAN) to enhance input image quality, especially for low-light or blurry images, ensuring more robust ingredient recognition in diverse real-world scenarios.

Acknowledgement. We extend our sincere gratitude to the Electronics and Communication Department and the management of BVRIT Narsapur for providing the high performance NVIDIA 3090Ti 24GB GPU, which has significantly supported our research work.

References

1. Divya Bharathi, P., et al.: Ingredient detection and recipe recommendation using deep learning. In: International Conference on Recent Trends in Computing & Communication Technologies (ICRCCT'2K24) (2024)
2. Saritha, B., Laskar, M.A., Kirupakaran, A.M., Laskar, R.H., Choudhury, M., Shome, N.: Deep learning-based end-to-end speaker identification using time-frequency representation of speech signal. Circuits Syst. Signal Process. **43**, 1–23 (2023). https://doi.org/10.1007/s00034-023-02542-9
3. Saritha, B., Laskar, R.H., Choudhury, M., et al.: Optimizing speaker identification through sincsquarenet and sincnet fusion with attention mechanism. Procedia Comput. Sci. **233**, 215–225 (2024). https://doi.org/10.1016/j.procs.2024.03.211
4. Shah, S., et al: Revolutionizing culinary experiences: AI-driven ingredient recognition and personalized recipe recommendation system. Libr. Progress Int. **44**, 4279–14290 (2024)
5. Saritha, B., Laskar, M.A., Laskar, R.H.: A comprehensive review on speaker recognition. In: Biswas, A., Wennekes, E., Wieczorkowska, A., Laskar, R.H. (eds.) Advances in Speech and Music Technology. Signals and Communication Technology. Springer, Cham (2023). https://doi.org/10.1007/978-3-031-18444-4_1
6. Devarasetty, T., Sankar Reddy, V.: AI based recipe generator and cook assistant. Int. J. Creat. Res. Thoughts. **12**(5) (2024). ISSN: 2320–2882
7. Saritha, B., Laskar, M.A., Anish, A.M.K., Laskar, R.H., Choudhury, M.: CACRN-Net: a 3D log Mel spectrogram based channel attention convolutional recurrent neural network for few-shot speaker identification. Comput. Electr. Eng. **115**, Art. No. 109100 (2024). https://doi.org/10.1016/j.compeleceng.2024.109100
8. Ruiz-Rincón, S., Galpin, I.: SnapChef: AI-powered recipe suggestions. In: ICAIW 2024: Workshops at the 7th International Conference on Applied Informatics 2024, October 24–26, Viña del Mar, Chile (2024)
9. Saritha, B., Anish Monsley, K., Hussain Laskar, R., Choudhury, M.: FSIR: few-shot speaker identification using reptile algorithm. In: 2023 8th International Conference on Computers and Devices for Communication (CODEC), Kolkata, India, pp. 1–2 (2023). https://doi.org/10.1109/CODEC60112.2023.10466164
10. Saritha, B., Anish Monsley, K., Hussain Laskar, R., Choudhury, M.: SincSquareNet: Deep Neural Network-Based Speaker Identification for Raw Speech. In: Chinara, S., Tripathy, A.K., Li, K.C., Sahoo, J.P., Mishra, A.K. (eds.) Advances in Distributed Computing and Machine Learning Lecture Notes in Networks and Systems, vol. 660. Springer, Singapore (2023). https://doi.org/10.1007/978-981-99-1203-2_40S
11. Saritha, B., Shome, N., Laskar, R.H., Choudhury, M.: Enhancement in Speaker Recognition using SincNet through Optimal Window and Frame Shift. In: 2022 2nd International Conference on Intelligent Technologies (CONIT), pp. 1–6 (2022). https://doi.org/10.1109/CONIT55038.2022.9848231
12. Saritha, B., Laskar, M.A., Kirupakaran, A.M., Laskar, R.H.: ReptoNet: a 3D log Mel spectrogram-based few-shot speaker identification with reptile algorithm. Arab. J. Sci. Eng. (2024). https://doi.org/10.1007/s13369-024-09426-3
13. Saritha, B., Laskar, M.A., Laskar, R.H., Choudhury, M.: Raw waveform based speaker identification using deep neural networks. In: 2022 IEEE Silchar Subsection Conference (SILCON), Silchar, India, pp. 1–4 (2022). https://doi.org/10.1109/SILCON55242.2022.10028890

CrookFoot: An Android-Based Deep Learning Application for Real-Time Foot Deformity Detection and Arch Index Estimation

C. Kalpana[1]([⊠]) [iD], Manoj Devare[1] [iD], and Shivam Margaj[2]

[1] Amity Institute of Information Technology, Mumbai, India
ckalpana@mum.amit.edu, mhdevare@mum.amity.edu
[2] Amity University Mumbai, Mumbai, India

Abstract. Human footprint analysis has valuable applications across fields such as environmental monitoring, forensics, wildlife tracking, and medical diagnostics. Despite its importance, current models capable of accurately identifying and analyzing human footprints from raw images remain limited—especially those that offer both high precision and a user-friendly interface. This research presents a lightweight Android application, CrookFoot, which integrates a deep learning-based Convolutional Neural Network (CNN) to perform multi-output classification of barefoot images. The model predicts the user's age group, foot type (flat, normal, or high arch), and calculates the arch index using a single image input. The CNN architecture comprises 12 layers and is optimized for mobile deployment using TensorFlow Lite. Trained on an augmented dataset of 100+ footprint images, the model leverages 17 distinct features—spanning geometric (5), GLCM texture (6), LBP texture (3), statistical (3), and classification-based metrics (2)—to deliver robust and detailed predictions. Comprehensive evaluation metrics such as confusion matrices, precision, recall, F1 scores, and ROC curve analysis validate the model's performance. Designed for offline use, CrookFoot delivers real-time diagnostic results and personalized product suggestions, offering an affordable and accessible foot screening solution with potential for global healthcare integration.

Keywords: Android application · TensorFlow Lite · Deep learning CNN · Arch Index · Feature Extraction

1 Introduction

A Human Footprint obtained from an individual can identify a lot of information, which is useful in multiple fields, such as the identification of a person at an airport, data storage in public health records, and medical scans for disease or abnormality detection. Specifically, individuals having multiple foot deformities such as flat foot and high foot arch caused by irregular walking patterns and the use of modern footwear as which constrains the foot into an irregular shape with the toes overlapping together, deviating from the natural foot shape [1].

The condition of being flat-footed is medically known as pes planus, which is a very recurring condition in toddlers and early age children, which typically resolves itself by

R. K. Karsh et al. (Eds.): SIPCOV 2025, CCIS 2848, pp. 354–374, 2026.
https://doi.org/10.1007/978-3-032-15809-3_28

the age of adulthood. It causes foot functionality impairment and a painful condition with a stiff foot, often referred to as physiologic [2]. The condition pes planus occurs when the medial longitudinal arch of the foot is lower when compared to a normal foot, which causes it to be closer to the ground or to be in flat contact with the surface. Because of the hind foot and the forefoot, the foot's medial longitudinal arch (MLA) is a strong, pliable ligament, tendon, and fascial connection [3]. This causes a redistribution of the weight-bearing stresses, making the ligament a compliant support platform for the body as a whole, changing the biomechanical layout of the lumbar spine and the lower extremities, thus causing pain and injury [4].

The condition named high arch foot is medically termed as pes Cavus or Cavovarus, is when the medial longitudinal arch (MLA) is shaped upwards in an aggressive manner; it is structurally opposite to flat foot, as the tendon lying between the forefoot and the hindfoot condenses or shortened due to abnormal footwear or muscular abnormalities, Genetic abnormalities like Charcot-Marie-Tooth an inherited group of neuropathies.

As of the current time for the evaluation of the deformities, the physical diagnosis needs expert evaluations, which are subjective, and non-digital footprint diagnosis is slow, inaccurate, and unpredictable. With such a wide range of footprint deformation instances, it is essential to have the presence of a footprint detection and evaluation android-based application that is commercially available with a clean user interface and a precise model built into the application with an inbuilt feature extraction function to accurately output the foot arch of the person and recommend a suitable treatment for the condition. As of now, handheld devices like smartphones have grown into high-quality image-capturing sensors, with compact, powerful processing capabilities. Such devices can be an optimal medical screening device which are available for everyone instead of expensive medical-grade pressure mats or screening devices, which also lack automation.

With the increase in popularity of automated detection using Android applications with integrated neural networks and machine learning models [6]. The developed application is an Android-based application developed for Android version 8 and above. This application boasts a clean user interface consisting of all the necessary features needed in the application, like selection of an image from the image folder and capturing live images from the system camera. As soon as the image is selected or captured, the output is displayed on the screen with the recommended product.

The model built into the application is a CNN model converted into a TFLite model. TensorFlow Lite is a Google runtime framework to deploy lightweight machine learning models on the device itself instead of a web-based online server, saving time and resources with quick and fast deployment, converting a .h5 or .keras complex file into a condensed .tflite file [6, 8]. The main feature the model works on is the Arch Index, which is crucial for footprint type detection. Arch Index is the feature value that is used to identify the medial longitudinal arch (MLA) located in the midfoot region, responsible for a flat foot (pes planus), high arch (pes cavus), or normal foot arch [7]. The feature is a numeric value, usually denoted with decimals accompanying it. The arch index can be calculated using Algorithm 1.

$$H = Foot\ Length \times \left(1 - \frac{Foot\ Width}{Arch\ Width}\right) \tag{1}$$

A Convolutional Neural Network (CNN) model was trained to be incorporated into the application [6]. The model has a multi-output structure with 3 outputs: Age group (3 groups- Adult, Teen, and Child), Foot type (3 types – flat foot, normal arch, and high arch), and Arch height (numeric value) [1]. The model has 12 layers. The model boasts an average accuracy of 91% and an average F1 score of 0.91. The feature extraction for the model gives it 17 features to accurately predict an output, with each output assigned a separate layer to improve efficiency. The model is categorized as a deep learning model, and as it classifies more images, the accuracy improves with each image uploaded in the application [9].

2 Related Work

Research on footprints, gait, and image-based biometrics has used various devices and methods to improve recognition and classification. Existing studies focus on pressure data, scanned footprints, gait signals, and image preprocessing for medical and biometric applications.

Table 1. Literature Review

Author(s), Year	Title	Dataset & Subjects	Device/Acquisition	Methods & Features	Key Contribution
Chae et al., 2020	Foot type classification using heterogeneous pressure data	96 adults	G-hiwell GHF-5050 pressure plate (48 × 48, 2034 sensors)	Plantar pressure (kPa), stabilized standing posture	Reliable dataset for foot type classification
İbrahimoğlu et al., 2025	FootprintNet: biometric identification	220 subjects, 2200 images	Epson 5500 scanner, Biometric 200 × 6 dataset	Siamese network on right footprint images	Robust footprint-based biometric recognition
Chu et al., 1995	Arch index for foot height	51 Chinese volunteers	Pedobarograph (glass + camera + silicone layer)	True image acquisition, arch index measure	Digital method to classify arch height
Winder et al., 2009	Image processing in diabetic retinopathy	Retinal image dataset	Retinal imaging devices	Illumination correction, RGB color & contrast optimization	Improved feature visibility for diagnosis
Özateş et al., 2024	Explainable AI for gait analysis	Motion gait data, 12 joints/subject	Motion sensors	Time-series derivation, 374 features, SVM feature selection	Interpretable gait classification framework
Nguyen et al., 2018	Face recognition attack detection	Real vs. spoof face images	Visible light camera	Multi-level LBP + CNN (VGG-19), correlation fusion	Enhanced spoof detection accuracy
Alsuhimat & Mohamad, 2023	Hybrid feature extraction for signature verification	Signature datasets	Digital signature images	HOG + CNN hybrid, Random Forest selection	Improved multi-class signature verification

From the Table 1. reviewed works, it is clear that while progress has been made, most studies are limited by dataset size, device dependency, or narrow application scope. This highlights the need for more generalized approaches with wider applicability and stronger validation.

3   Methodology

3.1   Dataset Acquisition

The images used for the model training are acquired from GitHub from a public dataset uploaded by Rohit Khokher et al. (2015). A total of 21 Individuals volunteered for the research, each subject had their footprint scanned and recorded 5 times, which adds up to a total of 105 images [22]. The device used for scanning the footprints was an HP Scanjet G2410 flatbed scanner, which supports high-resolution image quality and helps capture detailed skin texture and footprint outlines. Each image was captured at 300dpi by asking the subject to stand on the flatbed scanner barefoot, and 5 impressions of the footprint were captured in color images as shown in Fig. 1. Table 2 lists the pros and cons of dataset.

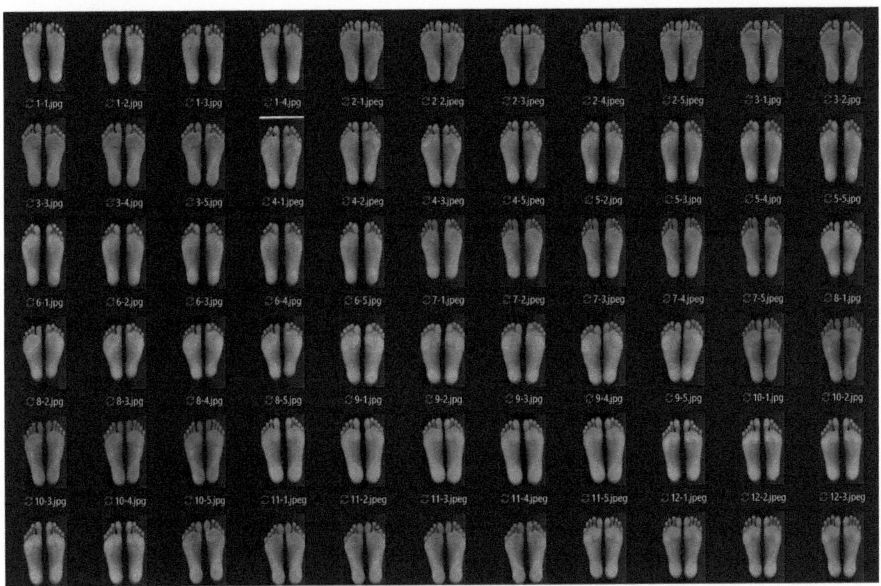

Fig. 1. Dataset Sample

Table 2. Advantages and disadvantages of the dataset

Aspect	Advantages	Disadvantages
Image Quality	High-resolution (300 dpi) scans capture fine anatomical details, including arch shape and toe spacing.	No pressure information or 3D data; the scanner cannot capture plantar pressure distribution.
Cost and Accessibility	Scanning was performed using a consumer-grade flatbed scanner; the setup is low-cost and easy to replicate.	The scanner lacks clinical-grade calibration and pressure sensitivity.
Data Structure	Well-organized file structure; consistent image dimensions; uniform labelling protocol applied.	Limited to 105 samples; relatively small dataset for deep learning training.
Repeatability and Consistency	Minimal intra-subject variability; stable scanning protocol across subjects.	Manual alignment introduces some variability; foot placement is still slightly operator-dependent.

3.2 Image Pre-processing

Image pre-processing is a crucial step in data classification, as it enhances the image quality by reducing any type of noise or irregularity, fine-tuning any lighting issues, like contrast or overexposure, and making the image more detectable for feature extraction. The Images acquired from the dataset were color images, and OpenCV was used to manipulate the dataset. Then the image is resized to 256×256 to match the input shape of the feature extraction module. The resized image is then converted to a grayscale image by assigning each pixel a value of 0 or 1 corresponding to the intensity of the neighbouring pixels being low or high, respectively [16]. Then, a variant of the grayscale image is denoised by using a Gaussian blur, by replacing the intensity of the pixels with a weighted average of the neighbouring pixels Fig. 2. Then the original grayscale image is equalized using histogram equalization, which normalizes the overall grayscale intensity of each pixel to match the other pixels using a histogram Fig. 3. Then, thresholding is performed on the grayscale image by assigning a value to each pixel of 1 or 0, according to its intensity, which is commonly called binary thresholding Fig. 4. Morphological operations are then performed to plot the outer imprint of the footprint with clearly defined edges, as seen in Fig. 5. Lastly, two edge detection techniques, Sobel and Canny edge detection, are used to plot two images with the outline of the footprint and the edges inside and on the border of the footprint Fig. 6. This process not only improved the images but also increased the original image dataset of 100 images to a pre-processed image dataset of 600 images.

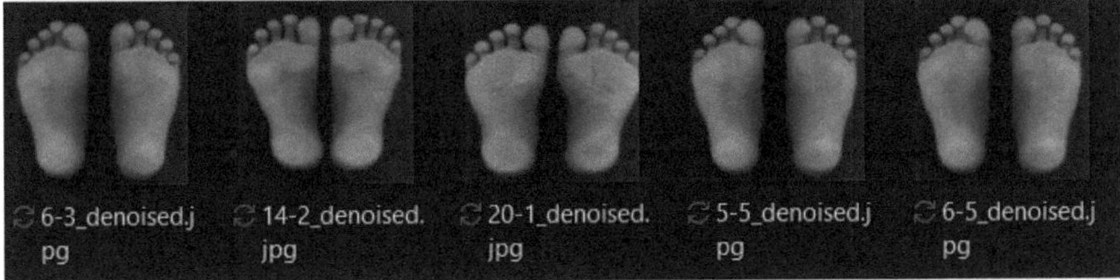

Fig. 2. Denoised Sample

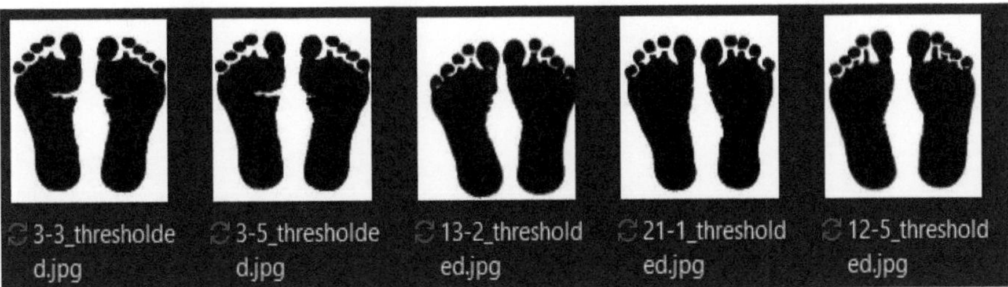

Fig. 3. Histogram Equalization Sample

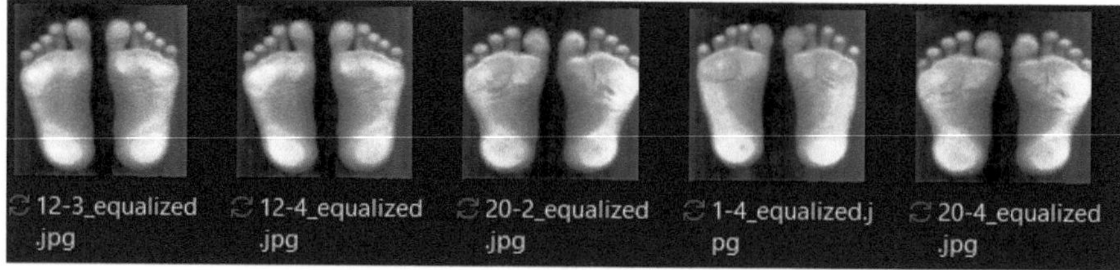

Fig. 4. Thresholding Sample

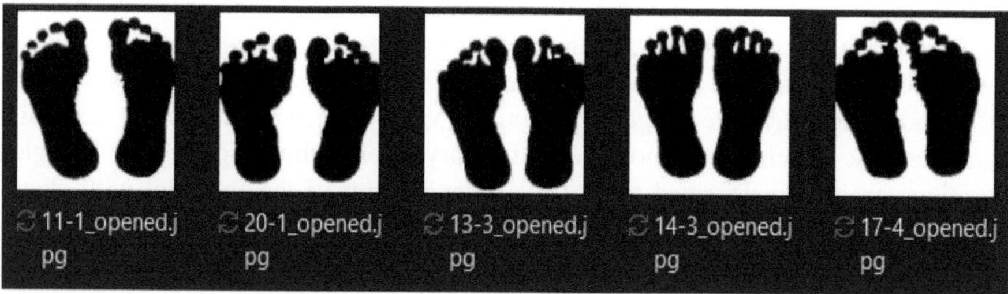

Fig. 5. Morphological Operation Sample

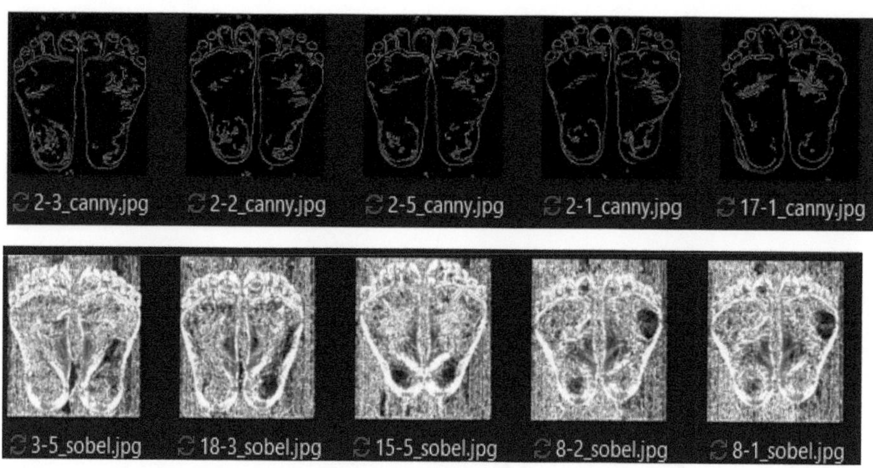

Fig. 6. Sobel and Canny Edge Detection Sample

3.3 Data Augmentation

Data augmentation is the process of performing operations on the image dataset to enlarge the dataset or make it more suitable for the model to train with. Data augmentation is a crucial step when training a CNN model as it makes the model more accurate, balanced, and robust. For this research, we have performed multiple data augmentation operations on the pre-processed dataset. First, rotation was performed on the images by an angle of 40°, in which the images were rotated either −40° or +40°, which recreates any image capturing errors. Then, shifting was performed by moving the image left or right off-centre by 20% of the width of the image, which trains the model for horizontal off-centre images. Images after were again shifted vertically up or down off-centre by 10%–20% of the image width, which trains the model for vertically off-centre images. Then images were slanted or distorted along the axis by using shearing to make the model more robust for irregular images. Then, zooming was performed, in which the images were either zoomed in or out of the images by 10%–17% randomly to accommodate for images being taken at different distances. Then, the images were flipped horizontally or vertically at random to account for the detection of the correct foot when the images are classified. This process effectively increased the dataset of the pre-processed images from 600 to the augmented dataset of 2,602 images, Fig. 7.

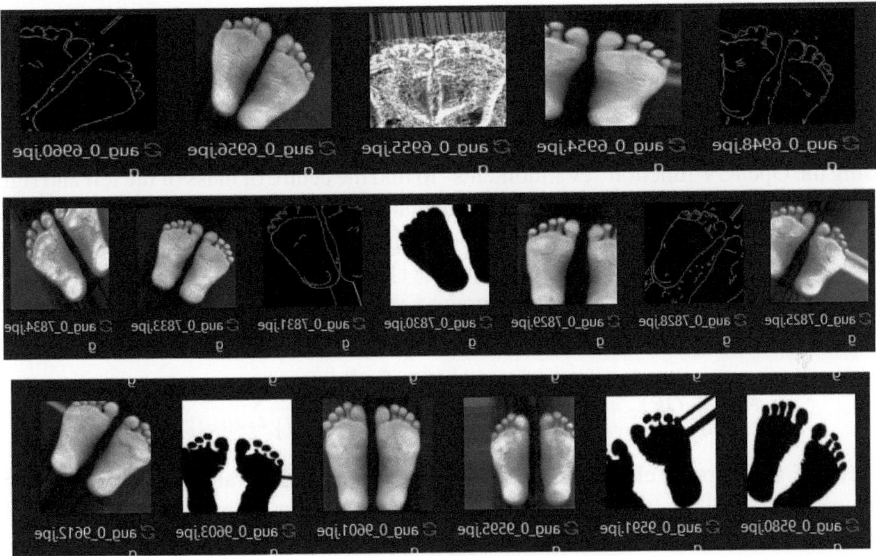

Fig. 7. Image Augmentation Sample

3.4 Feature Extraction

Feature extraction is the process of extracting, gathering, and combining image features by using multiple extraction techniques to create a vector of image features used to train the model. The features extracted during the feature extraction are the backbone of the image classification, as images cannot be recognized by Neural Networks because they need numerical data to perform. Hence, feature extraction is used to extract and convert visual features into numerical features understandable by the model.

For this research, a total of 17 features were extracted and divided into three broad categories of geometric features, texture features, and statistical features. The images, before being used for feature extraction, were resized and thresholded to ensure the input shape of the images was consistent after image augmentation. First, the images were resized to 256 × 265, then binary thresholding was performed to resize them to 127 × 255 to match the input shape. Then, OpenCV was used to detect the outline of the images. Then the first image features that were extracted were the Geometric features: Foot Length was found by detecting the vertical extreme points on the outline of the footprint, and Width was found by taking the horizontal extreme points on the outline of the footprint. Then, to find the heel-to-toe ratio, Algorithm 2 was used, where the heel-to-toe ratio (HTR) is equal to the width of the footprint divided by the length of the footprint.

$$HTR = \frac{Width\ of\ Foot}{Length\ of\ Foot} \tag{2}$$

Then the arch index is calculated using Algorithm 1, as the footprint is divided into three parts: The Toe box, the Midfoot, and the Hindfoot. Then, Foot symmetry is found by using the OpenCV function "cv2.moments" to find the centre of mass of the left and right footprint. Then, the centre of pressure is calculated by using the thresholded images and detecting the white and black pixels, then combining the row and column values of only the white pixels into x and y values like [y1,x1], [y2,x2] till the last image values, and then finding the average y value and average x value to determine the centre of pressure of the footprint determined by the white pixels, Algorithm 3.

$$\{COP\}_x = \frac{\{1\}}{\{N\}}\sum\nolimits_{\{i=1\}}^{\{N\}} x_i, \ \{COP\}_y = \frac{\{1\}}{\{N\}}\sum\nolimits_{\{i=1\}}^{\{N\}} y_i \tag{3}$$

Then the foot type is classified according to the arch index value of the foot if arch value <0.65 = Flatfoot, if value ~0.66 and < 0.88 = normal arch, and if value >0.89 = High arch. Then GLCM Features like Contrast, Dissimilarity, Homogeneity, Energy, Correlation, and Entropy are extracted from the GRAY-LEVEL CO-OCCURRENCE MATRIX using skimage library features like graycomatrix and gracoprops, Algorithm 4.

$$\text{Taking the GLCM Matrix } as\ P(i,j)$$
$$\sum_{\{i,j\}} (1-j)^2 \cdot P(i,j) \tag{4}$$
$$\text{GLCM Contrast}$$

$$\sum_{\{i,j\}} |i - j| \cdot P(i,j) \tag{5}$$

GLCM Dissimilarity

$$\sum_{\{i=0\}}^{\{N-1\}} \sum_{\{j=0\}}^{\{N-1\}} \frac{P(i,j)}{1+|i-j|} \tag{6}$$

GLCM Homogeneity

$$\sqrt{\sum_{\{i,j\}} P(i,j)^2} \tag{7}$$

GLCM Energy

$$\sum_{\{i,j\}} (i - \mu_i)(j - \mu_j) \cdot \frac{P(i,j)}{\sigma_i \sigma_j} \tag{8}$$

GLCM Correlation

$$-\sum_{i,j} P(i,j) \cdot log_2(P(i,j) + \varepsilon) \tag{9}$$

GLCM Entropy

Then LBP features like: LBP mean is calculated [23] using the LBP values assigned to each pixel, which is then divided by the number of pixels, Algorithm 5. Then, LBP Histogram entropy is calculated using the mean LBP values and equalized using a histogram, and converted into a single value, Algorithm 5.

$$\frac{\{1\}}{\{N\}} \sum_{\{i,j\}}^{\{N\}} LBP_i \tag{10}$$

LBP Mean

$$-\sum_{\{k\}} h_k \cdot \log\_2(h_k + \varepsilon) \tag{11}$$

LBP Histogram entropy

Then the Age group is found using the foot length and foot width values, that is: if value $<150 = $ child, if value $<= 200$ and $< 250 = $ Teen, and if value $> = 250 = $ Adult. Then the Statistical features are calculated like: The Mean Intensity, which is the average pixel grayscale intensity value of all the pixels in the grayscale image, Algorithm 6. Then the Standard Deviation is calculated, which is the measure of pixel intensity spread from the mean value of all the pixels, Algorithm 6. Then the Skewness is calculated, which is the value of irregular grayscale pixel intensity values, Algorithm 6. Importance of features Table 3 lists the feature extraction techniques used and summarizes the importance (Fig. 8)

$$\mu = \frac{\{1\}}{\{N\}} \sum_{\{i=1\}}^{\{N\}} x_i \tag{12}$$

Mean Intensity

$$\sigma = \sqrt{\left\{ \frac{\{1\}}{\{N\}} \sum_{\{i=1\}}^{\{N\}} (x_i - \mu)^2 \right\}} \tag{13}$$

Standard Deviation

$$Skewness = \frac{\frac{\{1\}}{\{N\}}\sum_{\{i=1\}}^{\{N\}}(x_i-\mu)^3}{\sigma^3} \qquad (14)$$

$$Skewness$$

Table 3. Feature Extraction Technique Importance Table

Technique Category	Importance Summary
Geometric Features	Captures structural and morphological details like foot length, width, and arch geometry, which are directly related to foot type and age group.
Texture Features (GLCM)	Analyzes gray-level patterns and pixel intensity relationships, aiding in identifying subtle deformities in the footprint texture that aren't easily visible.
Texture Features (LBP)	Encodes local binary texture patterns that help in capturing surface variations and edge transitions in the footprint.
Statistical Features	Provides global image descriptors such as average brightness, intensity variability, and asymmetry that contribute to differentiating classes in a nuanced way.

```
Foot Length,Foot Width,Heel-to-Toe Ratio,Arch Index,Foot Type,Center of Pressure X,Center of Pressure Y,Foot Symmetry,GLCM Contrast,GLCM Dissimilarity,GLCM Homogeneity,GLCM Energy,GLCM Correlation,GLCM Entropy,LBP Mean,LBP Hist Entropy,Mean Intensity,Standard Deviation,Skewness,Age
255.0,360.62445840513925,1.4142135623730951,0.3372913275240193,Flat Foot,127.73428772064221,128.0400268122187,128,3809.649494485295,15.343642769607847,0.820748533356665,0.7532504151819377,0.3002907503876948,1.9836301314305096,7.3444976806640625,0.7034806443603785,11.374725341796875,52.07853248471932,4.450557777655776,0
```

Fig. 8. CSV File of Features

3.5 Model Training

The Model used in this research paper is a Deep Learning CNN Model with 12 layers, consisting of 1 input layer, 2 conv1d layers, 2 max_pooling1d layers, a flatten layer, a dense layer, a dropout layer, and 3 output layers: age output, foot type output, and arch output. The model has an input shape of [1, 17] and an output shape of [1, 3] for output_0, [1] for output_1, and a shape of [1, 3] for output_2 as shown in Fig. 9.

The CSV file containing the extracted features is called and encoded with labels to prepare for model training, then any non-numeric values in the CSV file are binarized with numeric values. Then the feature dataset is split into x and y, train and validation datasets. Then the output heads are given activation values like softmax for foot type and age group, but sigmoid for arch output, because the foot type and age output have three probable values, and the arch output has one definite numeric value. Then, the Age group and Foot type numeric values are optimized using the Adam optimizer. After optimizing, fitting the training data follows, in which the split dataset is used to train the model, and then the newly trained model is saved as a .keras model file.

3.6 Model Conversion

The saved Keras CNN model cannot be directly deployed into the Android application and needs to be converted into a TFLite model first. Hence, a Python script is used to convert the model into a TFLite model, which is a lightweight version of the same model and converted using TensorFlow dependencies. The TFLite file enables us to deploy the model directly in the application instead of hosting the model on a web server, which is time-consuming and also requires the user to have an active internet connection. TFLite offers a great solution for this, as the application size does not increase significantly and offers instant responses from the model, as it is stored natively.

3.7 Android Application (GUI-Graphical User Interface)

As this project was focused on providing a foot deformity system that is readily available for anyone to use, and not only for research purposes, an Android application-based GUI was best suited to be used due to the widespread use of Android-based devices like tablets, smartphones, or any device with camera hardware support.

The Application created is called "CrookFoot", which has a simple and self-explanatory user interface, as in Fig. 10, and supports devices from Android version 8 to the latest Android version 15. The Android application contains multiple scripts that handle different features of the application, like the build.kts (app), which handles all dependencies, ranging from TensorFlow dependencies to camera dependencies, then the AndroidManifest that handles all the app permissions and conditions for the application to work, activity_main that handles the user interactable screen of the application, ModelRunner.kt which is responsible for loading the TFLite model into the application and is also the Kotlin version of the feature extraction script as only the model itself cannot process raw images, then lastly to put it all together MainAcitvity.kt is the first script to be executed, it calls the other scripts as the application is started, it also contains many of the crucial imports and the app recommendations needed in the Application.

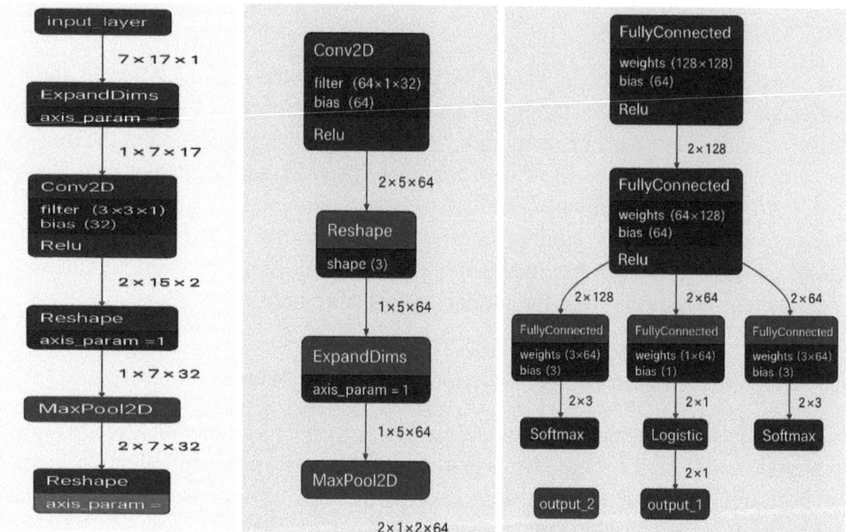

Fig. 9. CNN Model Architecture

The Android Application, when opened, shows a page with two buttons: Select Image, which leads to opening the on-device photos from which a foot image can be selected for classification, then the second button on the first screen is the Capture Image Button, when clicked, it asks for camera permissions, when allowed opens the system camera to capture a live foot image, as shown in Fig. 10. After an image is added to the application, the footprint features are extracted from it, and then the model predicts results for age group, and foot type, then calculates the arch index of the foot, and displays the results on the screen with a recommended product according to the condition of the foot being flat foot, high arch or normal foot, as in Fig. 11.

Fig. 10. Application UI

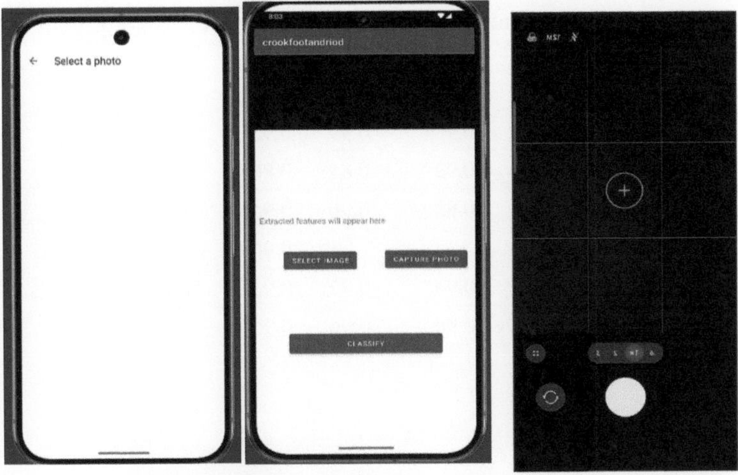

Fig. 11. Photo selection output and camera feature output

4 Experimental Results

4.1 Evaluation Results

The model has three distinct outputs of Age group, Foot type, and Arch index. Age group is a float array of three numerical values out of which only one is selected, determined by the model.

$$Precision = \frac{True\ Positives}{True\ Positives + False\ Positives} \tag{15}$$

$$Recall = \frac{True\ Positives}{True\ Positives + Fase\ Negetives} \tag{16}$$

$$F1\ Score = 2 \cdot \frac{Precesion \cdot Recall}{Precision + Recall} \tag{17}$$

$$Support = True\ Positives + False\ Negetives \tag{18}$$

4.1.1 Age Group

The classification report for age shows a precision score of 0.94, a recall of 0.92, an F1 score of 0.58, and a support of 180, as shown in Table 4. These scores show that the model can accurately detect the age of a person with high accuracy. Prediction of age group shown in Fig. 12.

Table 4. Age Classification Report

	Precision	Recall	F1 score	Support
0	0.98	0.99	0.98	
1	0.92	0.81	0.86	27
2	0.93	0.96	0.95	56
Accuracy			0.96	180
Macro avg	0.94	0.92	0.93	180
Weighted avg	0.96	0.96	0.95	180

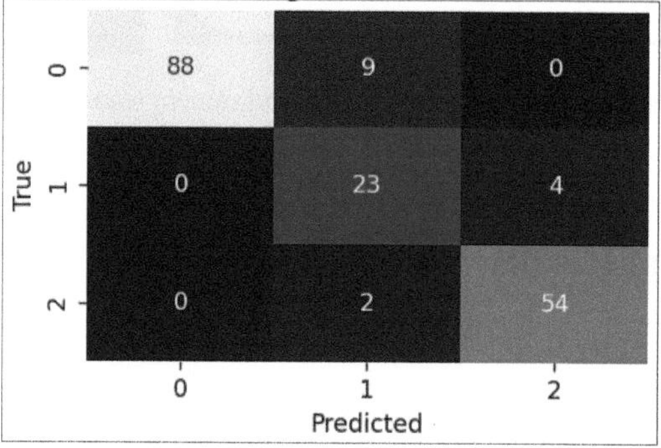

Fig. 12. Age group confusion matrix

4.1.2 Foot Type

The classification report, as shown in Table 5, has a precision score of 0.83, a recall score of 0.83, a F1 score of 0.82, and a support of 180 and confusion matrix in Figs. 13 and 14. This indicates that the model can predict the foot type of a person with acceptable accuracy.

Table 5. Foot type classification report

	Precision	Recall	F1 score	Support
0	0.95	0.93	0.94	133
1	0.59	0.95	0.73	21
2	0.38	0.23	0.29	26
Accuracy			0.83	180
Macro avg	0.64	0.71	0.65	180
Weighted avg	0.83	0.83	0.82	180

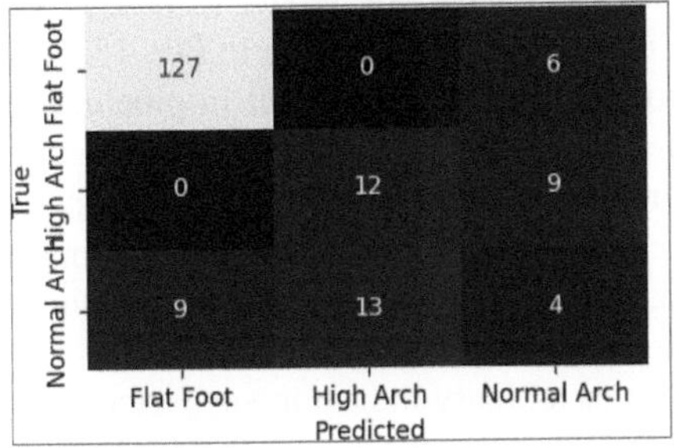

Fig. 13. Foot type confusion matrix

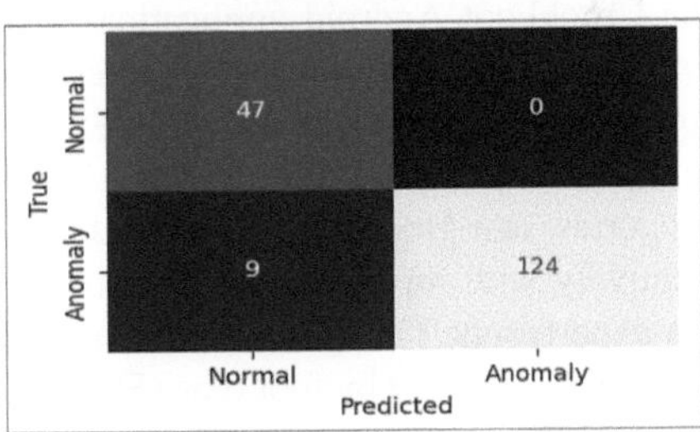

Fig. 14. Arch Confusion Matrix

4.1.3 Arch Anomaly

The classification report for as seen in Table.6, shows a precision score of 0.93, a recall score of 0.93, an F1 score of 0.93, and a support score of 180. This implies that the model is successful in determining a deformed foot from a normal one.

Table 6. Arch anomaly classification report

	Precision	recall	F1 score	support
0	0.86	0.89	0.88	47
1	0.96	0.95	0.95	133
Accuracy			0.93	180
Macro avg	0.91	0.92	0.91	180
Weighted avg	0.93	0.93	0.93	180

4.2 Application Results

The CrookFoot Android application integrates a trained CNN model to enable real-time analysis of footprint images directly on mobile devices is shown in Fig. 15. Upon capturing or selecting an image, the app processes it through a built-in pipeline and runs inference using a TensorFlow Lite model, outputting predictions across three key categories: age group, foot type, and arch anomaly. Results are displayed clearly and intuitively, with supportive explanations and color-coded icons to aid understanding for non-expert users. The age classification (Child, Teen, Adult) appears first to contextualize the results, followed by foot type (Flatfoot, Normal Arch, High Arch), each with simple descriptions. The arch anomaly result is shown as a binary indicator, supported by the arch index value and a status icon. A recommendation engine also suggests corrective products based on foot type, accessible offline. The application prioritizes user privacy by performing all processing on-device, ensuring faster response times and enhanced data security. Internal evaluations confirmed stable performance, with accurate predictions under good image conditions and clear transparency in cases of low-quality inputs. Overall, CrookFoot offers an accessible, user-friendly solution for foot health screening by combining clinical-grade AI with a practical mobile interface.

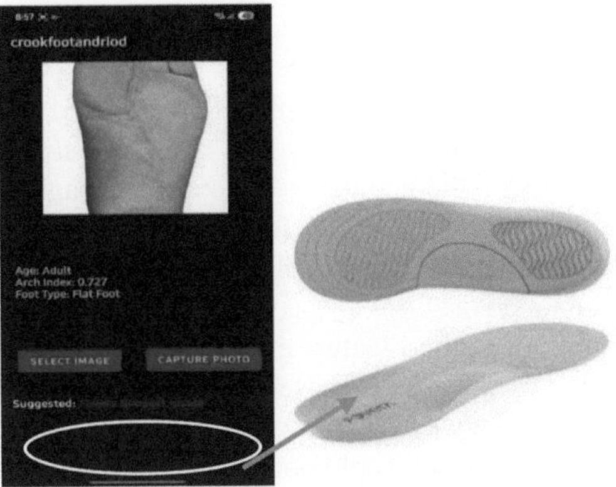

Fig. 15. Final application output

4.3 ROC Curve Analysis

The ROC Curve plot, as shown in Fig. 16, is used to plot the true positive rates and the false positive rates of the models in comparison to each other. The ROC curve determines which model out of the compared ones performs the best.

As seen in Fig. 16, the current CNN model outperforms the older CNN model and the SVM model, which were prototype models that were considered to be used for this research.

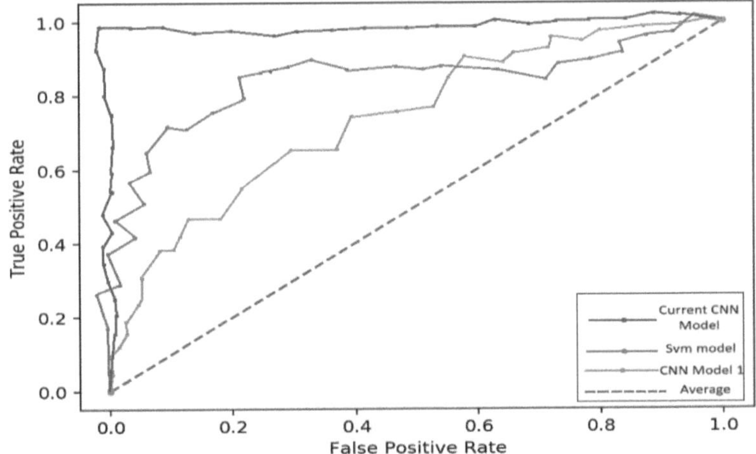

Fig. 16. ROC Plot

5 Conclusion

CrookFoot is an Android-based mobile application designed to offer a simple and accessible self-diagnostic tool for detecting foot deformities. Built on a lightweight TensorFlow Lite CNN model, the app analyses footprint images to classify foot type (flat, normal, high arch), predict age group (child, teen, adult), calculate arch height, and recommend relevant products. The model runs entirely on-device, ensuring offline functionality and user data privacy.

The application includes a robust feature extraction pipeline with 17 geometric, statistical, texture, and rule-based features. These enrich the model's predictive capabilities while maintaining high accuracy and low resource consumption, making the tool ideal for remote or underserved settings. CrookFoot can function as an affordable alternative to expensive diagnostic tools, requiring only a smartphone and a clean footprint image.

Future development plans include on-device learning, YOLO-based fast detection, and expansion to other body parts for musculoskeletal assessments. Clinical deployment will require formal validation studies and compliance with regulatory standards such as the FDA, CE, or CDSCO. Interoperability through medical data standards like DICOM and HL7 FHIR is also envisioned.

The app has potential in educational screening programs and could aid health workers in identifying foot issues in children. Its use in developing countries could significantly improve access to diagnostics where specialists and equipment are limited. Regional adaptations through localization and collaboration with global health bodies can further improve accuracy and cultural relevance.

CrookFoot's architecture, centered on privacy, edge inference, and medical utility, can inspire broader applications in dermatology, dentistry, and neurology. With strategic partnerships and ethical considerations, the app can evolve into a powerful global health tool promoting early detection and preventive care.

References

1. Chae, J., Kang, Y.J., Noh, Y.: A deep-learning approach for foot-type classification using heterogeneous pressure data. Sensors. **20**(16), 4481 (2020)
2. Carr, J.B., Yang, S., Lather, L.A.: Paediatric pes planus: a state-of-the-art review. Pediatrics. **137**(3), e20151230 (2016)
3. Arunakul, M., Amendola, A., Gao, Y., Goetz, J.E., Femino, J.E., Phisitkul, P.: Tripod index: a new radiographic parameter assessing foot alignment. Foot Ankle Int. **34**(10), 1411–1420 (2013)
4. McCormack, A.P., Ching, R.P., Sangeorzan, B.J.: Biomechanics of procedures used in adult flatfoot deformity. Foot Ankle Clin. **6**(1), 15–23 (2001)
5. Grice, J., Willmott, H., Taylor, H.: Assessment and management of cavus foot deformity. Orthop. Trauma. **30**(1), 68–74 (2016)
6. Bushra, K.F., Ahamed, M.A., Ahmad, M.: Automated detection of COVID-19 from X-ray images using CNN and an android mobile. Res. Biomed. Eng. **37**(3), 545–552 (2021)
7. Sawangphol, W., Panphattarasap, P., Praiwattana, P., Kraisangka, J., Noraset, T., Prommin, D.: Foot arch classification via ML-based image classification. Comput. Aided Des. Appl. **20**(4), 600–613 (2023)

8. Evan, A., Sarosa, M., Asmara, R.A., Kusumawardani, M., Al Riza, D.F., Azis, Y.M.: Detection and counting of grape leaves using YOLOv8 via TFLite on mobile applications. In: 2024 International Conference on Electrical and Information Technology (IEIT), September, pp. 246–251. IEEE (2024)

9. İbrahimoğlu, N., Osmani, A., Ghaffari, A., Günay, F.B., Çavdar, T., Yıldız, F.: FootprintNet: a Siamese network method for biometric identification using footprints. J. Supercomput. **81**(5), 714 (2025)

10. Chu, W.C., Lee, S.H., Chu, W., Wang, T.J., Lee, M.C.: The use of arch index to characterize arch height: a digital image processing approach. IEEE Trans. Biomed. Eng. **42**(11), 1088–1093 (1995)

11. Basheer, S., Nagwanshi, K.K., Bhatia, S., Dubey, S., Sinha, G.R.: FESD: an approach for biometric human footprint matching using fuzzy ensemble learning. IEEE Access. **9**, 26641–26663 (2021)

12. Özateş, M.E., Yaman, A., Salami, F., Campos, S., Wolf, S.I., Schneider, U.: Identification and interpretation of gait analysis features and foot conditions by explainable AI. Sci. Rep. **14**(1), 5998 (2024)

13. Olisah, C.C., Smith, L.: Understanding unconventional preprocessors in deep convolutional neural networks for face identification. SN Appl. Sci. **1**(11), 1511 (2019)

14. Rifana Fathima, A., Dhanalakshmi, K.: Computer vision for animal footprint classification based on deep learning model. In: International Conference on Advances in Artificial Intelligence and Machine Learning in Big Data Processing, August, pp. 246–256. Springer, Cham (2023)

15. Winder, R.J., Morrow, P.J., McRitchie, I.N., Bailie, J.R., Hart, P.M.: Algorithms for digital image processing in diabetic retinopathy. Comput. Med. Imaging Graph. **33**(8), 608–622 (2009)

16. Buchelly, F.J., Mayorca, D., Ballarin, V., Pastore, J.: Digital image processing techniques applied to pressure analysis and morphological features extraction in footprints. J. Phys. Conf. Ser. **705**(1), 012020 (2016)

17. Jeon, W.S., Rhee, S.Y.: Fingerprint pattern classification using a convolutional neural network. Int. J. Fuzzy Log. Intell. Syst. **17**(3), 170–176 (2017)

18. Alsuhimat, F.M., Mohamad, F.S.: A hybrid method of feature extraction for signature verification using CNN and HOG, a multi-classification approach. IEEE Access. **11**, 21873–21882 (2023)

19. Mubarak, A.S., Serte, S., Al-Turjman, F., Ameen, Z.S.I., Ozsoz, M.: Local binary pattern and deep learning feature extraction fusion for COVID-19 detection on computed tomography images. Expert. Syst. **39**(3), e12842 (2022)

20. Hanumanthappa, S., Guruprakash, C.D.: Fusion of handcrafted and deep-learning features for brain tumor detection and classification using T1-weighted magnetic resonance images. SN Comput. Sci. **5**(8), 1107 (2024)

21. Girshick, R., Donahue, J., Darrell, T., Malik, J.: Rich feature hierarchies for accurate object detection and semantic segmentation. In: Proceedings of the IEEE Conference on Computer Vision and Pattern Recognition, pp. 580–587 (2014)

22. Khokher, R., Singh, R.C., Kumar, R.: Footprint recognition with principal component analysis and independent component analysis. Macromol. Symp. **347**(1), 16–26 (2015, January)

23. Verma, G., Gupta, Y., Malik, A.M., Chapman, B.: Performance evaluation of deep learning compilers for edge inference. In: 2021 IEEE International Parallel and Distributed Processing Symposium Workshops (IPDPSW), June, pp. 858–865. IEEE (2021)
24. Deniz-Garcia, A., et al.: Quality, usability, and effectiveness of mHealth apps and the role of artificial intelligence: current scenario and challenges. J. Med. Internet Res. **25**, e44030 (2023)

Pneumatically Actuated Lower Limb Exoskeleton: A Design and Control Approach

V. M. Akhil[1] and M. Ashmi[2(✉)]

[1] Amrita School of Artificial Intelligence, Amrita Vishwa Vidyapeetham, Coimbatore, India
[2] ACE College of Engineering, Trivandrum, Kerala, India
ashmi_mi@yahoo.co.in

Abstract. Walking and sit-to-stand are the essential movements for human beings to sustain their lives and perform daily activities, but traumatic injuries and diseases can temporarily or permanently impair ambulatory ability, and rehabilitation is the sole existing solution to recover to some extent from such conditions. The work aims to design and implement a suitable driving system and to identify the best control strategy for the position control of the pneumatically actuated lower limb exoskeleton. The video analysis of human gait were carried out for healthy as well as some selected afflicted subjects. Suitable models were developed using neural network, fuzzy, neuro-fuzzy and the outputs of these models help in the generation of activating signals for the driving system of the exoskeleton. The error analysis validated that neuro-fuzzy could generalize well with different gait patterns. The customized pneumatic exoskeleton was experimented and tested with different control strategies. As part of the controller assessment of pneumatic exoskeleton, testing was done in eleven healthy volunteers and one individual affected by polio. While implementing PID controller, the observed error in the joints (knee and hip) were approximately in the range of 2.5° and 6° respectively. The response of the pneumatically powered exoskeleton was compared with healthy gait and it could replicate healthy gait with negligible errors.

Keywords: Rehabilitation · Exoskeleton · Gait · Neural network · Fuzzy · Neuro-fuzzy · PID controller

1 Introduction

Walking and sit-to-stand movements are the most essential and ineluctable activity for human beings to sustain their life and to accomplish their habitual actions. Permanent impairment in movement occurring due to injuries or diseases is difficult to recover. Rehabilitation is the existing efficient treatment to recover from such disorders to a certain degree. Human gait plays a crucial role to the design of exoskeletons. It is the most instinctive way, the body displacement happens under stable state. Human gait modeling constitutes the bio-mechanics of the movement of lower limbs and enumerates the factors governing its functionality. In clinical practice, the frequently used method for studying gait behavior is by analyzing the joint angles as well as the time phase cycles of gait. The dynamics of human locomotion varies from person to person due to different step lengths, thereby making it complex to determine a generic predictor.

© The Author(s), under exclusive license to Springer Nature Switzerland AG 2026
R. K. Karsh et al. (Eds.): SIPCOV 2025, CCIS 2848, pp. 375–387, 2026.
https://doi.org/10.1007/978-3-032-15809-3_29

In the literature, several gait analyzing techniques are frequently encountered, including video cameras, optoelectronic systems, electromyography, electroencephalogram, force plates and force shoes, inertial systems, gyroscopes, and hall sensors. In this scenario, the importance of assistive devices arises, and exoskeletons are the best devices that these afflicted people can use for leading a near-normal life. The mechanisms employed and the control systems designed for these devices should conform to the different modes of operation in accordance with the percentage level of disability. The lower limb exoskeletons help the afflicted people to regain their walking ability as that of healthy human beings. Besides, these devices help the afflicted persons to enhance and upgrade their physical capabilities also.

The exoskeletons are designed by considering the patient's adaptability, ergonomics, safety, weight reduction, and stability of the system. A knee-ankle-foot orthosis (KAFO) was developed with the capability to lock the knee and permit free knee motion during the phases of human gait [1]. In 2002, Hybrid Assistive Limb (HAL) was developed at Tsukuba University, Japan to assess human joint torques by estimating the ground response power of the foot and actuation level of the leg muscles (sEMG) [2]. The most critical achievement in an exoskeleton was in 2004, viz., development of a device called BLEEX (Berkeley Lower Furthest Point Exoskeleton) executed at U.C. Berkeley's Human Designing and Mechanical Technology Lab for military purposes [3]. In 2013, Kim et al. [4] developed a Walking Assistance Lower Limb Exoskeleton to help paraplegic patients who have paralyzed lower limbs. Hanyang Exoskeleton Assistive Robot (HEXAR) was developed in South Korea with electric motors which operate with muscle circumference sensors (MCRS) [5]. Lim et al. experimentally studied the effectiveness of the HEXAR-CR50 exoskeleton. The reduction in human effort while using supportive devices was analysed in terms of consumption of metabolic power [6].

The existing exoskeleton models serve the same purpose as supporting devices for many applications. For normal human walking, the legs undergo an internal and external rotation of 5.5° inwards and 5° outwards. So, for the purpose of maximizing the human comfort, these rotations also need to be included in the mechanism of exoskeletons. The source of power in most of the mechanisms is either electric motor or pneumatic actuator. The control of pneumatic actuators is quite complicated due to their nonlinear behavior in actuation. One control strategy for robotic exoskeletons is EMG signal-based control. Most of the exoskeleton designs are meant for regular walking surface conditions with fixed platform or treadmill. Very few studies have been conducted by considering the effect of surface conditions on muscle behavior during gait or other activities.

The challenges associated with exoskeletons suggested in literature are lack of stability, economically viability and uncertainty in tracking human locomotion within a gait cycle. The implementation of controllers is very crucial to facilitate optimal motion of the knee and hip joints in an exoskeleton. Ollinger et al. [7] developed an exoskeleton which was effectively controlled using the Proportional-Integral-Derivative (PID) controller and tuning the controller parameters provided better accuracy and improved the dynamic response. An advanced approach utilizing a cascaded PI controller was adopted to enhance conventional PID controls, ensuring the achievement of desired limb motion regardless of system non-linearities. The Ziegler-Nichols (Z-N) method was employed for tuning PID parameters, resulting in higher gain constants that significantly improved response under both Paraplegic and Fatigue conditions. Additionally, the integration of particle swarm optimization (PSO) further reduced errors and enhanced limb efficiency, thus, proved to be more effective than the Z-N method [8].

The conventional analytical methods appear insufficient in accurately predicting the kinematic parameters of human gait. Therefore, the need to develop more advanced gait analysis techniques, particularly employing knowledge-based systems, has become crucial. Kutilek et al. [9] proposed using an artificial neural network (ANN) model to predict muscle tendon length and evaluate angle-time diagrams during gait. Viteckova et al. [10] utilized the Mamdani Fuzzy Inference System (MFIS) in MATLAB to predict all contralateral joint angles of lower limbs during human gait. Rai et al. [11] introduced a hybrid adaptive fuzzy controller for controlling the level walking of a bio-robotic leg with three degrees of freedom (DOF). Incorporating the learning mechanisms of neural networks with the rule-based reasoning framework of fuzzy logic systems, neuro-fuzzy systems offer a powerful combination. Shieh and Chang [12] proposed an ANFIS-based identifier and an optimized neuro-fuzzy controller for modeling the inverse dynamics of a biped robot. They replicated the bipedal locomotion controller parameters using Adaptive Neuro-Fuzzy Inference Identifier (ANFII) to provide appropriate control actions. These advanced techniques hold promise for enhancing gait analysis and controlling robotic systems.

Most of the research on pneumatic-powered exoskeletons has focused on using Mckibben muscles as actuators. However, Mckibben muscles are not ideal for driving heavy loads due to reduction in stiffness and they tend to be bulky and space-consuming when pressurized. To address these limitations, researchers have turned to pneumatic cylinders as an alternative due to its compact size, minimal space requirements and higher stiffness. Kazerooni [13] elaborated on the working principle of pneumatic cylinders, while Varseveld and Bone [14] described a simpler control strategy using PWM (Pulse Width Modulation) techniques for pneumatic cylinders. However, it is noteworthy that while the PWM control strategy works well for position control of the actuator shaft, it may not be as appropriate for velocity or torque control. Pneumatic actuators show non-linear characteristics because of air compressibility, effect of friction and non-linearity of valves. As a result, achieving precise velocity or torque control with pneumatic actuators can be more challenging.

Recent research studies discussed in the literature have highlighted the challenges associated with controlling exoskeletons. Thus, it has become imperative to create a control strategy capable of identifying the essential characteristics required for the effective functioning of individuals with disabilities. By focusing on the development of this advanced control strategy and utilizing a specialized pneumatically actuated exoskeleton, the study aimed to address the challenges and provide a more effective solution for assisting individuals with physical disabilities in their mobility and gait. The developed lower limb exoskeleton was customized for an individual affected by polio by employing appropriate controllers. To evaluate the performance of these controllers, the exoskeleton was tested on thirty healthy volunteers and four individual affected by polio. Among the controllers tested, the PID controller exhibited less oscillation and has the ability to replicate healthy gait pattern with minimal error, making it a promising choice for enhancing the exoskeleton's functionality and supporting individuals with disabilities.

378   V. M. Akhil and M. Ashmi

2 Materials and Methods

2.1 Data Collection

The study involved analyzing videos of healthy and afflicted subjects walking on a 30-m level ground. A total of 30 healthy subjects (21-male, 09-female) and 4 male subjects specifically affected by polio, but able to walk independently without crutches, were chosen from the National Institute of Technology Calicut. The healthy subjects had no prior history of neuro-physiological disorders. All subjects willingly signed a consent form to participate in the experimentation. A Vicon V16 camera with 16 MP resolution, 120 fps frame rate, and an 18 mm lens was positioned perpendicular to the plane of subjects' motion. The video analysis was performed using Kinovea®0.8.24 software to measure the angular variations of the knee, hip, and ankle joints, as illustrated in Fig. 1. To facilitate tracking of angular displacement, markers were placed to the subject's hip, knee, and ankle joints. A brief explanation of the study's protocol and purpose was provided prior to the start of the experiment. Each gait cycle was recorded through five consecutive trials.

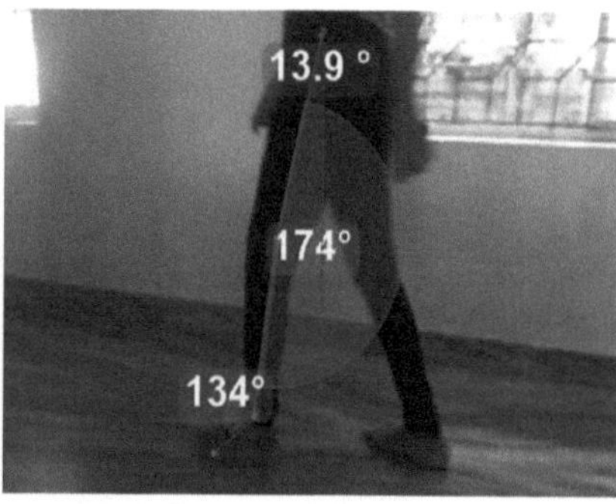

(a) Healthy subject   (b) Afflicted subject

Fig. 1. Motion analysis of gait using video cameras

2.2 Methodology

The primary aim of this study is to design and implement an appropriate driving system with the optimal control strategy to achieve precise position control of the pneumatically actuated exoskeleton designed for orthopedic applications. In order to design a driving system for an exoskeleton, the characteristics of human gait for healthy subjects were analyzed for normal walking. This is to understand exactly the characteristics of human gait on an average basis. Then, the general characteristics of healthy and afflicted subjects (time taken to complete gait cycle, linear displacement corresponding to each gait cycle) were determined. Through effective models using neural networks, fuzzy logic systems and neuro-fuzzy systems, the required position and velocity characteristics of the driving system were decided. An appropriate control system drive for meeting the requirements was also designed. The controllers developed were tested in the pneumatically powered exoskeleton for further analysis. The experimental setup is outlined in the flow diagram (Fig. 2).

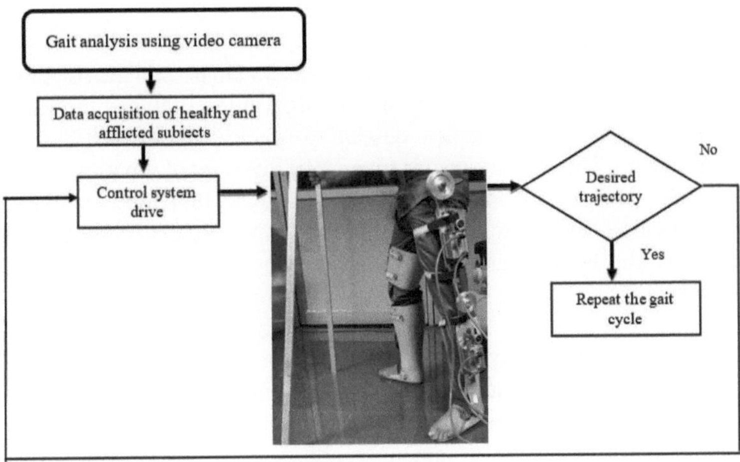

Fig. 2. Flow diagram representing the experimental setup

2.3 Human Gait Prediction Using AI Models

The estimation of angles associated with human movement relies on angle-time diagrams combined with artificial intelligence. In order to predict the joint angles involved in human gait, appropriate models were created using neural networks, fuzzy systems, and neuro-fuzzy techniques in MATLAB. A database consisting of knee angle and hip angle measurements for a time span of 10 s, encompassing seven complete gait cycles and the beginning of the next one was utilized for all prediction methods. Since, it was observed that the variation in the right knee angle ranged from 180° to 126°, while the variation in the left knee angle ranged from 180° to 132°. Similarly, both the right and left leg's hip angles exhibited variation within the range of 180° to 155°. It was noted that these four parameters maintained a consistent range across consecutive gait cycles. The prediction using AI models can be used for control of the driving system in the pneumatic exoskeleton.

Prediction Using Neural Networks

The complex gait variable relationships can be recognized with the aid of nonlinear property of neural networks. The neural network type 5–1–20 (input–hidden–output layer) as presented in Fig. 3 and back-propagation algorithm was used for training. By each presentation, the neural network's output was compared to the target output and the error was calculated. The average error is computed using the equation given below.

$$E_{avg} = \frac{1}{n} \sum (m - p) \tag{1}$$

where m and p are the measured and predicted outputs of the neural network. Subsequently, this error was utilized as feedback to adjust the neural network's weights iteratively. This process aims to decrease the error with each iteration, bringing the neural model closer to generate the desired output.

Prediction Using Fuzzy Logic Systems

This study employed a Sugeno-type fuzzy inference system to train the Adaptive Neuro-Fuzzy Inference System (ANFIS). The hybrid algorithm combines the least-squares method with back-propagation gradient descent to effectively train the FIS membership function parameters. The primary goal is to model a given set of input/output data using fuzzy linguistic variables for inputs and constants/linear functions for outputs based on Sugeno's method. By employing this approach, ANFIS can capture the underlying relationships within the data, allowing for accurate predictions and decisions through the resulting FIS.

Prediction Using Neuro-Fuzzy Systems

The integration of artificial intelligence techniques involving fuzzy logic and neural networks results in neuro-fuzzy systems that capitalize on the learning capabilities of neural networks and the parallel computation abilities of fuzzy systems. Essentially, a neuro-fuzzy system functions as a neural network but behaves equivalently to a fuzzy inference model. By training the fuzzy system, it becomes proficient in establishing fuzzy rules and determining membership functions for input and output variables of the system.

2.4 Design Aspects and Hardware Implementation

The identification of the best control strategy to actuate the exoskeleton was explained in the previous Section. This section accounts with the details regarding controller implementation in the pneumatically actuated lower limb exoskeleton. The ATmega328 microcontroller stores the angular displacement values (knee and hip) as reference. To activate the pneumatic exoskeleton, compressed air at a pressure of 5 bar is delivered through solenoid valve and flow control valve. To control the pneumatic air supply, DC series motors (12 V, 1000 rpm, 0.049 Nm) are employed. A string pulley arrangement was employed to transform linear actuation of the joint into rotational motion as depicted in Fig. 3.

Each leg has two double acting pneumatic cylinders (diameter- 40 mm, maximum force- 900 N) positioned at the knee and hip joints. The solenoid valve (5 port, 24 V), is controlled by the microcontroller and determines the direction (clockwise or anti-clockwise) of the pneumatically powered exoskeleton. The microcontroller constantly checks if the desired trajectory is being attained, and based on that, L293D adjusts the input signal to the solenoid valve. Optical sensor (MOC7811) is used to sense the rotational angle of the motor. Moreover, to monitor the input pressure of the cylinder, a pressure sensor (ranging from 0 to 8 bar) is employed. As a feedback sensor, an accelerometer (ADXL335) is utilized to monitor the real-time angles of the right and left leg joints.

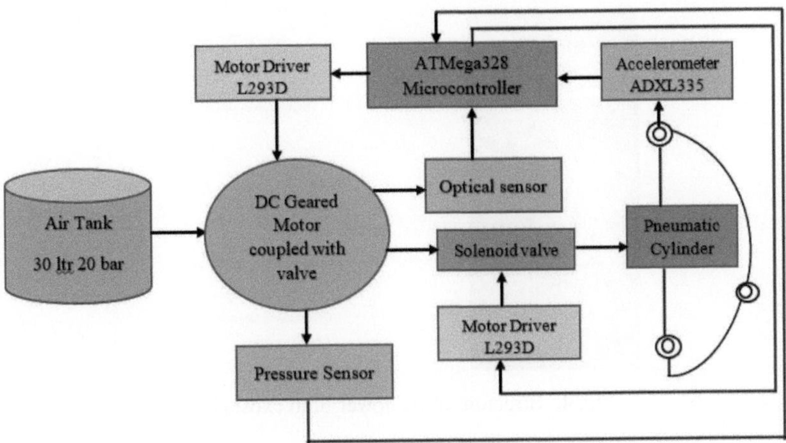

Fig. 3. Block diagram representation of pneumatically powered exoskeleton

2.5 Fabricated Pneumatic Actuator Joints

The pneumatic exoskeleton features thigh and leg links constructed using Aluminum, while the sockets are made from polypropylene to provide secure positioning to the joints as illustrated in Fig. 4. At the heart of the exoskeleton lies the pneumatic actuator, weighing 0.5 kg and having a 40 mm stroke length. This actuator is capable of delivering substantial torque, operating effectively at 5 bar pressure, reaching a maximum piston speed of 150 mm/s, and exerting a maximum force of 1760 N. A critical design goal is to ensure that the knee joint undergoes complete rotation only during the swing phase. To achieve this, the actuators are intentionally designed with lower power ratings, preventing overloading of the shank during the stance phase. The overall weight of the entire structure, inclusive of all components, is 12.2 kg. It is crucial to minimize the installation time on the patient, and the lower limb exoskeleton can be fitted within a maximum of 5 min. The pneumatically powered exoskeleton was tested on healthy and polio affected person as shown in Figs. 5(a) and (b).

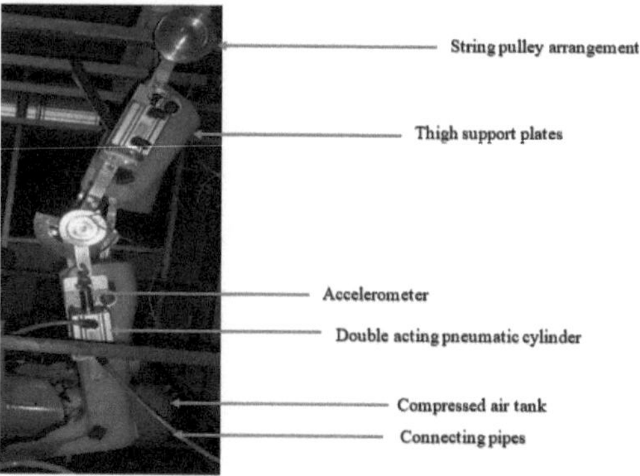

Fig. 4. Structure of the lower limb exoskeleton

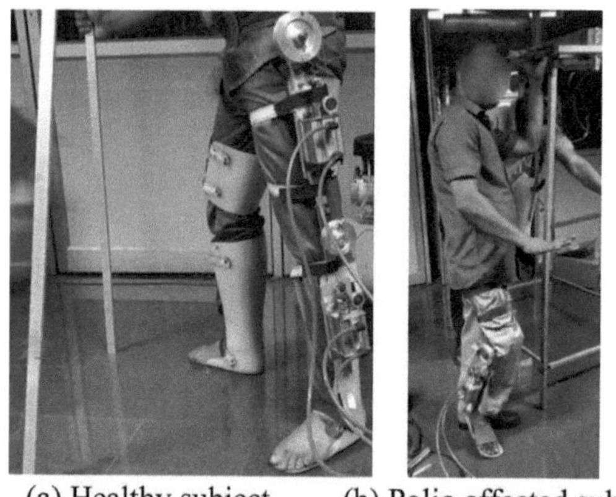

(a) Healthy subject   (b) Polio affected subject

Fig. 5. Experimentation on the fabricated lower limb exoskeleton

3 Results and Discussion

During the neural network training, the disparity between the actual and predicted angles of the right knee and left hip was within 5°. However, for the remaining parameters, the generated error ranged from 10° to 12° for the right hip and less than 10° for the left knee. Figs. 6(a) and (b) present the analysis of actual human locomotion (pink line) and the predicted angles (red line) of right leg's knee and hip joints. The model was trained over multiple epochs, and at the 40th epoch, the mean squared error (MSE) achieved as 0.245.

In fuzzy-logic (Fig. 7(a)), the right knee angle exhibited a difference of less than 5° during testing in the stance phase. However, during prediction in the swing phase, peaks were generated between 8.6 s and 9.3 s due to the movement of leg from stance to swing phase. Figures 7(a) and (b) illustrate the actual and predicted locomotion angles of the right leg's knee and hip represented by the pink and green lines, respectively. The fuzzy logic approach employed 32 fuzzy rules, 156 training data pairs, 30 nonlinear parameters,

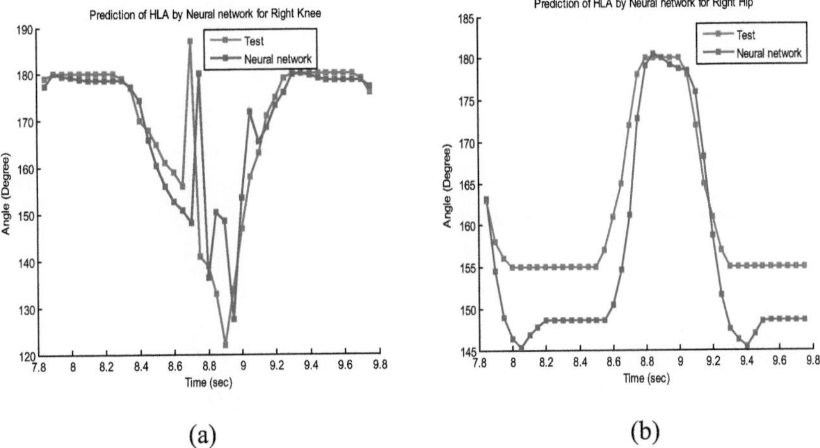

(a)   (b)

Fig. 6. Prediction of human gait using Neural Networks (a) Right knee (b) Right hip

192 linear parameters and 92 nodes. It is noted that utilizing more membership variables and additional rules could have resulted in even better outcomes.

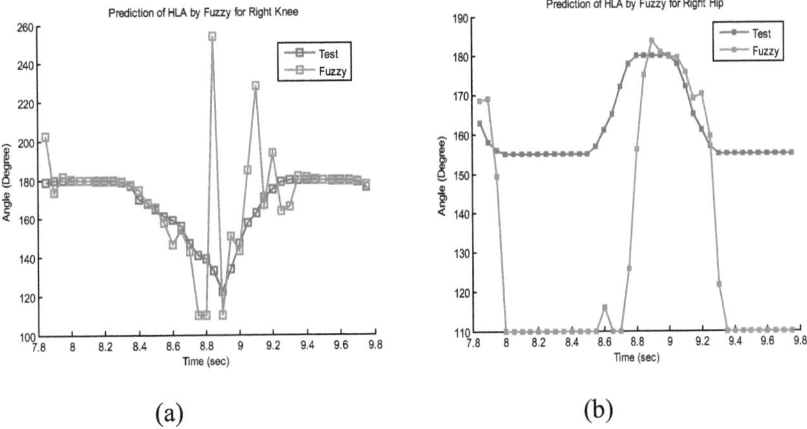

(a)   (b)

Fig. 7. Prediction of human gait using Fuzzy Logic System (a) Right knee (b) Right hip

The dataset was loaded into the neuro-fuzzy system, and for the purpose of training, 80% of the data was utilized while the remaining 20% was used for testing. A Sugeno-type FIS structure was generated through subtractive clustering. During the training process, right knee, left knee, and left hip exhibited minimal error in predicting locomotion cycles, with deviations of less than 5°. As for the right hip, the disparity between the trained and predicted angles was less than 10°. The responses indicated that the locomotion angle corresponding to the left leg hip produced more accurate results. These graphs (Figs. 8(a) and (b)) illustrate the actual and predicted locomotion angles of the right leg (knee and hip) where the actual angles are represented by the pink line, while the predicted angles obtained through the neuro-fuzzy technique are indicated by the blue line.

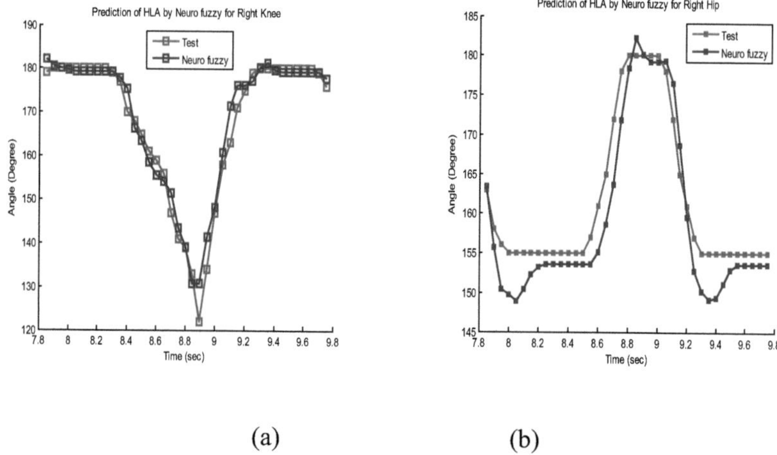

(a) (b)

Fig. 8. Prediction of human gait using Neuro-Fuzzy System (a) Right knee (b) Right hip

Human gait is not exactly cyclic and there is variation from one cycle to another. The transition of the leg from the stance to the swing phase is rapid in steady locomotion. Additionally, peaks are observed when the foot leaves the ground and the leg begins to move forward. The error analysis, revealed that the neuro-fuzzy model achieved the least error (most satisfactory error curve). Specifically, for the right and left leg joints, the error values in the neuro-fuzzy model were 2.2°, 3°, 2.45°, and 0.98°, respectively. In contrast, the corresponding errors for the neural network model were 2.8°, 5.9°, 3.5°, and 0.5°, while for the Fuzzy model, they were 3.2°, 3.5°, 4.75°, and 0.25°. Table 1 illustrates the average error performance using the three prediction methods. A higher frame/s camera will give more interval data and better accuracy. Several factors contribute to the sources of error, including the limited number of datasets and the smaller number of locomotion cycles used in the analysis.

Table 1. Error performance of the AI models

Body segment	Neural Networks	Fuzzy Logic	Neuro-Fuzzy
Right Knee	2.8°	3.2°	2.2°
Right Hip	5.9°	3.5°	1.75°
Left Knee	3.5°	4.75°	2.45°
Left Hip	0.5°	0.25°	0.98°

The study focuses on comparing the performance of the best controller (PID) integrated into a lower limb exoskeleton with human gait as reference. To evaluate the controller's performance, the pneumatic exoskeleton was fitted to healthy and afflicted volunteers. The experiment was conducted five times, with each trial covering a 5 m walking distance. The analysis of the average knee and hip angles from ten gait trials showed errors of about 2.5° for the knee and 6° for the hip, as shown in Fig. 9. The results demonstrate that conventional PID controller exhibits good performance in tracking the reference trajectory (human gait) despite uncertainties and load disturbances. However, slight deviations from the trajectory may be because of tuning gain constant manually and potential improvement may be achieved through optimization methods. Notably for knee angle, the PID controller exhibited a maximum error of 3.95° and a minimum error of −6.67°. The exoskeleton's output response is compared to that of a healthy human gait, and it is evident that the implemented lower limb exoskeleton can accurately replicate healthy gait with minimal error.

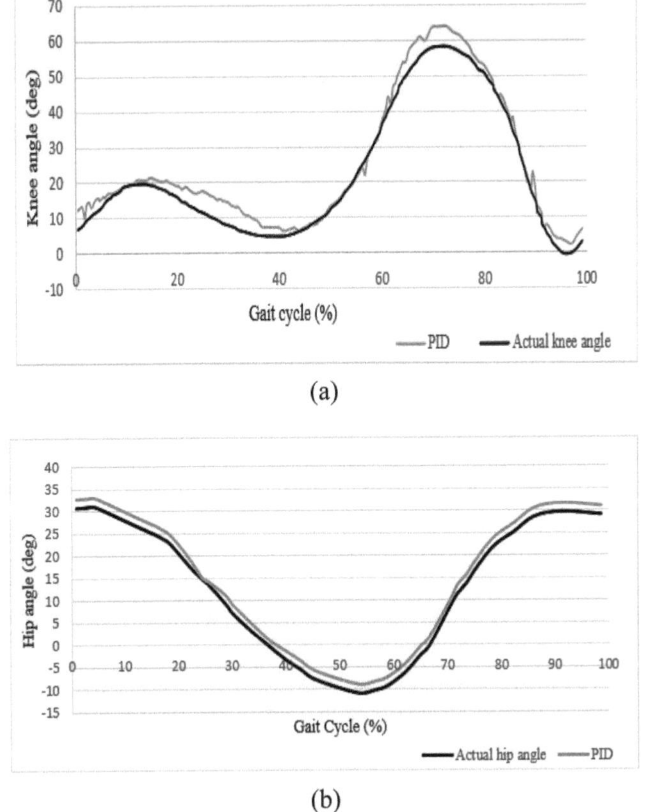

(a)

(b)

Fig. 9. Assessment of variation in (a) knee angle (b) hip angle

A comparative analysis was conducted between joint torque and the torque generated by a pneumatic exoskeleton. The findings demonstrate that, the torque exhibits an initial increase followed by a progressive decline when the leg transitions between the support and swinging phase. The observed error was found to be within the range of 11% as depicted in Fig. 10.

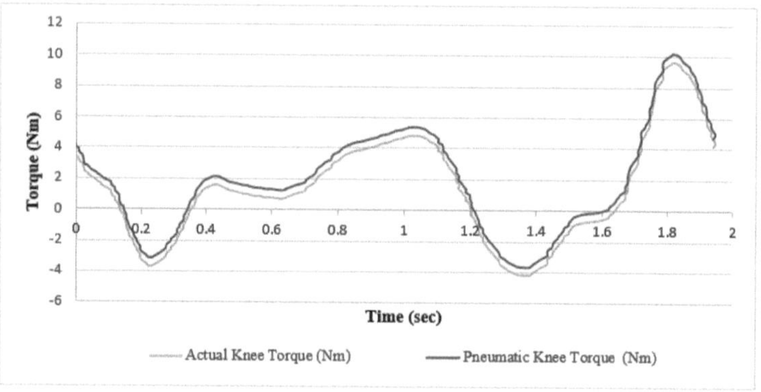

Fig. 10. Torque variation during gait

4 Conclusion

The knee and hip joint angle of the subjects were meticulously measured using motion analysis and a dataset was created. Then, suitable models were created to predict human gait patterns. The error analysis conducted on the prediction techniques revealed that the neuro-fuzzy model exhibited the least error. Specifically, for the right leg (knee and hip) and left leg (knee and hip), the error values for the neuro-fuzzy model were only 2.2°, 1.75°, 2.45°, 0.98° respectively, whereas for the neural network (NN) model, the errors were 2.8°, 5.9°, 3.5°, 0.5° and for the fuzzy model, the errors were 3.2°, 3.5°, 4.75°, 0.25°. By comparing the three prediction techniques, the neuro-fuzzy system demonstrated its effectiveness in gait cycle prediction, as it was able to generalize well with gait data from different subjects. The study emphasized the design of a pneumatic exoskeleton equipped with efficient controllers for the optimal working of the joints during gait. The outcomes of the study indicate that the PID controller can successfully replicate a healthy gait pattern with minimal error, making it a promising choice for precise and accurate joint control in the pneumatically powered exoskeleton. This study has not considered the activity of muscle behaviour involved in human gait and the sample size chosen for afflicted subjects (n = 4) is small. In future, enhancing the DOF at both the knee and hip joints could lead to improved flexibility.

References

1. Kaufman, K.R., Irby, S.E., Mathewson, J.W., Wirta, R.W., Sutherland, D.H.: Energy-efficient knee-ankle-foot orthosis: a case study. JPO J. Prosthet. Orthot. **8**(3), 79–85 (1996)

2. Watanabe, H., Tanaka, N., Inuta, T., Saitou, H., Yanagi, H.: Locomotion improvement using a hybrid assistive limb in recovery phase stroke patients: a randomized controlled pilot study. Arch. Phys. Med. Rehabil. **95**(11), 2006–2012 (2014)
3. Zoss, A., Kazerooni, H.: Design of an electrically actuated lower extremity exoskeleton. Adv. Robot. **20**(9), 967–988 (2006)
4. Kim, J.H., Han, J.W., Kim, D.Y., Baek, Y.S.: Design of a walking assistance lower limb exoskeleton for paraplegic patients and hardware validation using CoP. Int. J. Adv. Robot. Syst. **10**(2), 113 (2013)
5. Kim, W., Lee, H., Kim, D., Han, J., Han, C.: Mechanical design of the Hanyang exoskeleton assistive robot (HEXAR). In: 14th International Conference on Control, Automation and Systems (ICCAS 2014), pp. 479–484. IEEE (2014)
6. Lim, D., et al.: Development of a lower extremity exoskeleton robot with a quasi-anthropomorphic design approach for load carriage. In: IEEE/RSJ International Conference on Intelligent Robots and Systems (IROS), pp. 5345–5350. IEEE (2015)
7. Aguirre-Ollinger, G., Colgate, J.E., Peshkin, M.A., Goswami, A.: A 1-DOF assistive exoskeleton with virtual negative damping: effects on the kinematic response of the lower limbs. In: IEEE/RSJ International Conference on Intelligent Robots and Systems, pp. 1938–1944. IEEE (2007)
8. Solihin, M.I., Tack, L.F., Kean, M.L.: Tuning of PID controller using particle swarm optimization (PSO). Int. J. Adv. Sci. Eng. Inf. Technol. **1**(4), 458–461 (2011)
9. Kutilek, P., Viteckova, S., Svoboda, Z., Smrcka, P.: The use of artificial neural networks to predict the muscle behavior. Open Eng. **3**(3), 410–418 (2013)
10. Viteckova, S., Kutilek, P., Svoboda, Z., Jirina, M.: Fuzzy inference system for lower limbs angles prediction. In: 35th International Conference on Telecommunications and Signal Processing (TSP), pp. 517–520. IEEE (2012)
11. Rai, J.K., Tewari, R.P., Chandra, D.: Hybrid adaptive fuzzy control of bio robotic leg. In: International Conference on Power, Control and Embedded Systems, pp. 1–4. IEEE (2010)
12. Shieh, M.Y., Chang, K.H.: An optimized neuro-fuzzy controller design for bipedal locomotion. Int. J. Fuzzy Syst. **11**(3), 137–145 (2009)
13. Kazerooni, H.: Design and analysis of pneumatic force generators for mobile robotic systems. IEEE/ASME Trans. Mechatron. **10**(4), 411–418 (2005)
14. Van Varseveld, R.B., Bone, G.M.: Accurate position control of a pneumatic actuator using on/off solenoid valves. IEEE/ASME Trans. Mechatron. **2**(3), 195–204 (1997)

Quantum-Based Encryption Model for Satellite Video Images: A Comparative Analysis

Basudha Dewan[1]([⊠]) [iD], Sabyasachi Bhattacharyya[2] [iD], Ishu Sharma[3] [iD],
Shruti Bhowmick[4], Ehsan Sheybani[5] [iD], and Kandarpa Kumar Sarma[6] [iD]

[1] Department of ECE, Manipal University Jaipur, Jaipur, India
`basudha.ece@gmail.com`
[2] Barak Valley Engineering College, Sribhumi, Residential Girls Polytechnic,
Govt. of Assam, Golaghat, India
[3] Chandigarh Group of Colleges Jhanjeri, Mohali 140307, Punjab, India
[4] Department of Computer Engineering, PCPS Girls' Polytechnic,
Guwahati, Assam, India
[5] School of Information Systems and Management, University of South Florida,
Tampa, FL, USA
[6] Department of ECE, Gauhati University, Guwahati, Assam, India

Abstract. The paper presents a quantum model of encryption to offer a remedy to the increasing demand of data to be securely sent via satellite video images notably in such sensitive operations as custody and security. It is a hybrid between Quantum key distribution (QKD) protocol and visual cryptography, designing a computational encryption protocol providing image data with a highly secure encryption option against both classical and quantum attacks. Mathematical model based on photonic qubit is used to create secure keys, which further used to encrypt the video frames; red, green and blue (RGB) components. The algorithms like Shors or Grover quantum algorithm are incorporated to improve the key management and search efficiency in order to make the cryptographic process further robust. The quality and fidelity of the encrypted images are objectively accessed in terms of PSNR, SSIM, and MSE value. Moreover, there are statistical performance indicators, like NPCR and UACI, showing the model resistance to the differential attack and the noise attack. Comparison between this and traditional methods of encryption concludes that there is better performance in regards to security and computing power.

Keywords: Quantum Computing · Encryption · Satellite Video Images · Quantum Key Distribution · Cryptographic Security

1 Introduction

The art of protecting sensitive knowledge from unwanted access, regardless of if it is transmitted via an unsecure or secure route, as well as guaranteeing data confidentiality, integrity, and authentication, is known as cryptography [1]. The increasing significance of cryptography meets modern modern-day needs because of broadcast communication, network systems and Internet access and email functions alongside mobile phones transporting data. Mathematical problem complexity determines the need for cryptography [2].

A new video image encryption method combines visual cryptography technology with quantum key distribution to achieve its main purpose. The key agreement process depended on quantum key distribution while the suggested encryption algorithm deployed the generated key to secure network data transmission [3,4]. The research project establishes a new encryption method that combines visual cryptography with quantum key distribution for video images. The encryption process utilized quantum key distribution to establish keys before the key was applied in the proposed algorithm.

2 Prior Work Done

The encryption technology QCrypt based on quantum methods was developed to protect satellite data during transmission especially for critical satellite image information. The system provides solutions to the problems classical cryptography approaches face because of surging cyber security threats. The encrypted information at QCrypt receives protection through the implementation of quantum chaotic maps together with classic chaotic maps and DNA encoding specifications. Performance evaluations using a remote sensing image dataset demonstrate that QCrypt significantly outperforms conventional encryption methods, showing improved resistance to histogram analysis, differential attacks, and chosen-plaintext attacks. This research highlights the urgent need for advanced cryptographic solutions in satellite communications, positioning QCrypt as a robust answer to the evolving security challenges in this domain [5]. In [6] the transformative potential of quantum computing in the field of data encryption is explored, emphasizing its methodologies, implementation, and future directions. It begins with a foundational overview of quantum computing and its significance in enhancing encryption techniques. Through IBM's Qiskit tool the authors demonstrate quantum encryption usage alongside binary encryption methods. The research provides an assessment between quantum encryption security features by examining weaknesses stemming from present quantum hardware constraints. The research conducted in [7] explored how quantum computing benefits Earth observation and satellite imagery through the evaluation of quantum learning models' impact on satellite data processing. The text examines both quantum advantage hurdles and the requirement for HPC and QC balance. The authors analyze parameterized quantum circuit operations through Clifford+T universal gates which proves that T-gates define the amount of required quantum resources. The research demonstrates that quantum machine learning (QML) models reach a quantum advantage by surpassing classical models on untested data and successfully controlling weight symmetries for learning purposes.

The research in [8] examined how quantum computing merges with Earth observation and satellite imagery by investigating both its applicable scenarios and handling restrictions during satellite data processing with quantum learning models. The text illustrates both quantum advantage obstacles alongside the requirement for HPC and QC systems to find their best operational ratio. The paper examines parameterized quantum circuits through an investigation of T-gate uses for determining quantum resource requirements when deploying these models. Only QML models showing better generalization accuracy on new data than classical models along with continuous weight symmetry breaking produce quantum advantage. The paper by Ayoade and Adelusi Ayoade (2023) investigates how quantum computing enhances processing capabilities for Earth observation data through satellite image analysis. Quantum computing leverages the principles of quantum mechanics, such as superposition and entanglement, to perform calculations that are difficult or impossible for classical computers to handle efficiently. The authors emphasize that hyperspectral images are particularly suitable for quantum processing because they require fewer quantum resources compared to multispectral images. In [9] a comprehensive analysis and comparison of various quantum learning algorithms is presented specifically designed for big data applications, focusing on quantum image processing. The authors introduce a novel machine-learning approach that leverages quantum computing to enhance big data analysis, emphasizing the need for effective quantum feature extraction techniques, which have been lacking in current methodologies. A significant contribution of this work is the proposal of a global quantum feature extraction technique based on Schmidt decomposition, marking its first introduction in the field. Additionally, the paper showcases a new version of a quantum learning algorithm that utilizes Hamming distance for image classification.

3   Proposed Methodology

Figure 1 describe the block diagram of proposed methodology, which is graphical representation of the progression of data in a system that show the way information is handled and moved between various parts, such as processes, data stores, and external entities.

3.1   The Mathematical Framework (Photonic Qubit) for Key Generation

The suggested solution integrated image cryptography and quantum cryptography protocols; the secret key was generated using both techniques, and the images were encrypted using each one separately. Quantum cryptography, which relies on physics, is used to create keys, in contrast to conventional cryptographic techniques that employ mathematics [10]. Photons, or light particles, have a direction alignment (0 to 360) as they move across space. Only four direction

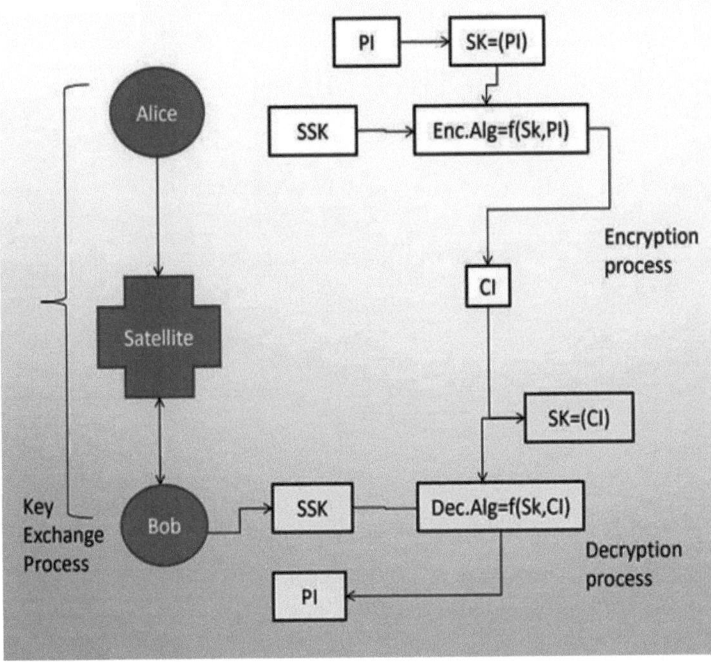

Fig. 1. Proposed Block Diagram of our methodology

alignments are thought to exist. For the reception of the photons, the polarization filters are activated. According to the procedure, the quantum bit, or qubit, with the states $|0\rangle$ and $|1\rangle$, was converted into keys and used to encrypt the pictures.

Table 1. The States of Light

Polarization State	Linear Combination	Name	Linear Polarization Angle	Axes
$|H\rangle$	$|H\rangle$	Horizontal	0	Z
$|V\rangle$	$|V\rangle$	Vertical	90	Z
$|D\rangle$	$\frac{1}{\sqrt{2}}(|H\rangle + |V\rangle)$	Diagonal	45	X
$|A\rangle$	$\frac{1}{\sqrt{2}}(|H\rangle - |V\rangle)$	Anti-diagonal	135	X
$|R\rangle$	$\frac{1}{\sqrt{2}}(|H\rangle + i|V\rangle)$	Right circular	-	Y
$|L\rangle$	$\frac{1}{\sqrt{2}}(|H\rangle - i|V\rangle)$	Left circular	-	Y

A number of the most significant light states are displayed in the Table 1 above. A linear combination of vertical and horizontal polarization can result in any polarization state [11].

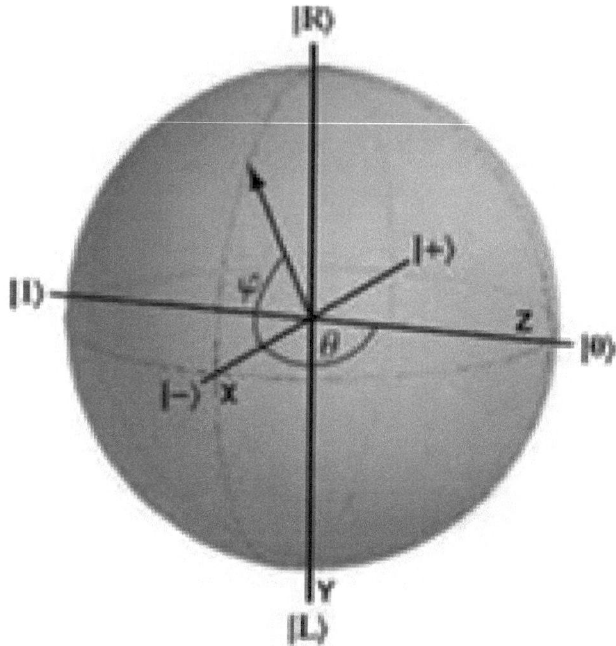

Fig. 2. A graphical representation of polarization state

A qubit's fundamental quantum information unit takes shape as the Bloch sphere as depicted in Fig. 2, which provides a geometrical visualization in quantum computing. A qubit differs from classical bits because it occupies a superposition state which represents both states zero and one through mathematical notation:

$$|\psi\rangle = \cos\left(\frac{\theta}{2}\right)|0\rangle + e^{i\varphi}\sin\left(\frac{\theta}{2}\right)|1\rangle \tag{1}$$

where: - $|0\rangle$ and $|1\rangle$ are the computational basis states. - θ and φ are angles defining the position of the qubit state on the Bloch sphere.

The Bloch sphere provides essential tools for understanding how qubits act because quantum computing uses qubits as its basic elements. Qubits display unique capabilities because they exist as being simultaneously in two states while classical bits remain permanently fixed in either 0 or 1 states. The unique characteristics of quantum computers allows simultaneous processing of vast information because of which specific computational tasks become exponentially faster [12].

Qubits exhibit an essential feature called quantum entanglement which creates an instantaneous connection between several qubits no matter how distant they are from each other. Quantum cryptography and quantum key distribution (QKD) and secure communication require this property because entangled qubits enable the establishment of ultra-secure encryption protocols [3,13] (Fig. 3).

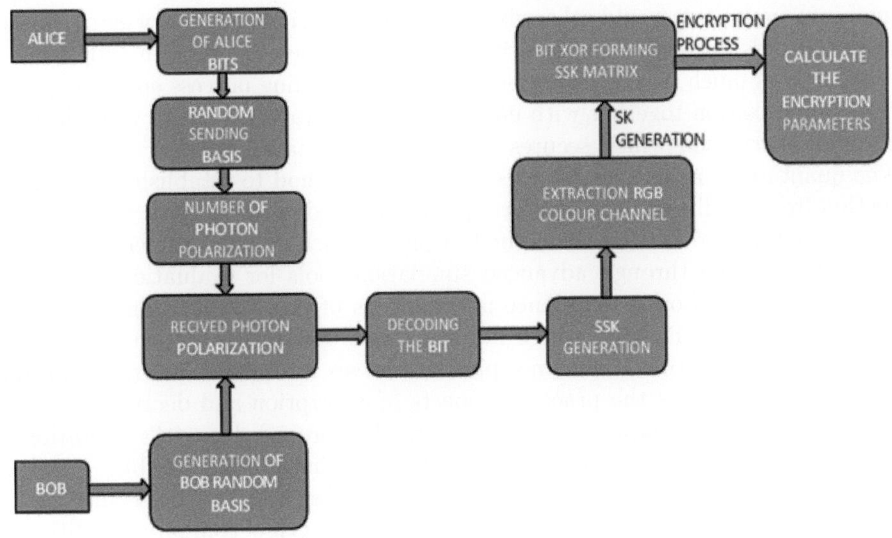

Fig. 3. Block representation of encryption process

Quantum gates serving as circuit block components can be represented by operations that conduct Bloch sphere rotations. The manipulation of qubits uses unitary transform techniques in quantum gates rather than classical logic gates' predictable bit manipulations because they enable superposition creation and phase regulation as well as entanglement production. Quantum gates including Pauli-X, Pauli-Y, Pauli-Z, Hadamard and CNOT need the Bloch sphere to display their rotation behavior around different spherical axes thus serving as the primary tool for both designing and analyzing quantum algorithms.

The proposed encryption model follows a structured approach, consisting of three primary phases: quantum key distribution, encryption using quantum algorithms, and system evaluation through simulations. At the starting phase the communication protocol adopts Quantum Key Distribution (QKD) for safe cryptographic key transfer between parties. Throughout this model the BB84 protocol uses photon polarization states to encode key bits according to its implementation. The quantum no-cloning theorem demonstrates an intrinsic ability to detect eavesdropping and prevents unauthorized copying of quantum information without adding errors [14]. Error rate monitoring mechanisms operate within the QKD process because they help detect intrusion attempts to improve the security of the system.

The second phase uses Quantum-Based Encryption Algorithms based on Shor's and Grover's algorithms to improve encryption and key administration procedures. Shor's Algorithm serves to make secure key distribution stronger through its capabilities to protect RSA and ECC encryption standards that quantum computers would otherwise breach. Key retrieval efficiency gets a boost from Grover's Algorithm because it simplifies searches therefore making brute-force attacks much harder to perform [15]. The encoding process employs quantum superposition together with entanglement to protect satellite video frames through encryption which secures the data from unauthorized access attacks. The quantum principles enable this encryption method to establish strong protection from traditional and modern quantum-based cryptographic attacks.

Simulation and Testing forms the last phase which requires implementing the encryption model through advanced simulation tools for evaluation purposes. Testing of encryption performance and analysis of protection against different attacks enable MATLAB through its algorithms to validate system functionality. The IBM Quantum Experience platform serves to run and confirm quantum circuits which verifies the practical aspects of encryption and decryption operations in quantum computing environments. The proposed model's operational characteristics are measured through a series of important variables starting from encryption speed until decryption speed and key distribution security level and resistance against quantum attacks [16]. The review compares traditional cryptographic standards with the quantum-driven encryption system in order to demonstrate its improved functions.

By combining quantum key distribution, advanced quantum encryption algorithms, and rigorous performance evaluation through simulations, the proposed encryption model aims to provide an advanced and secure framework for protecting satellite video image transmissions. This approach ensures a high level of security while maintaining efficient data processing speeds, making it a viable solution for next-generation secure communication systems.

4 Results and Discussion

4.1 Mathematical Framework of Our Model

The shared secret key, SSK, was obtained as follows: 0101

Let the set of random bits positions be x: $x \in X$ and $X \to x : x = x_i = [x_0, x_1, x_2, x_3, \ldots, x_n]$ and $x \in I$

where I is a positive integer.

$$SSK = \sum_{k=1}^{n} \Psi_k$$

Eq. (4.1)

Where Ψ_k is the decimal value of x_i.

The secret key

$$Sk = \lfloor (c \times p) +$$

$$\left| (\delta \times 10^3) \right| +$$

$$\left| \left(gm = \frac{1}{n} \sum_{i=1}^{n} x_i \right) \right| \quad \mathrm{mod}\ p \rfloor \qquad (2)$$

$$\delta = - \sum_{\eta=0}^{\varepsilon-1} \Psi(\eta) \log_2(\Psi(\eta))$$

Eq. (4.2)

Where: δ = Entropy of image ε = Gray value of an input image (0–255). $\Psi(\eta)$ = Probability of the occurrence of symbol η gm is the arithmetic mean for all the pixels in the image

4.2   Mathematical Algorithm of the Encryption Process

Step 1. Start

Step 2. Extraction of data from a plain image and formation of an image graphics object from the image.

Let $\mathcal{I}$ be an image $\Rightarrow (\rho, \sigma, \tau)$.

$\mathcal{I}$ is a color image of $m \times n \times 3$ arrays.

$$\begin{bmatrix} \rho_{11} & g_{12} & b_{13} \\ \vdots & \vdots & \vdots \\ \rho_{n1} & g_{n2} & b_{n3} \end{bmatrix}$$

Eq. (4.3)

$(\rho, \sigma, \tau) = m \times n$

Where $\rho, \sigma, \tau \in \mathcal{I}$

$$(\rho \circ \sigma)_{ij} = (\rho)_{ij} \cdot (\sigma)_{ij}$$

where:

- r = first value of ρ

$$r = [r_{i1}], (i = 1, 2, \ldots, m)$$

$$x \in r\_iI : [a, b] \leftarrow \{x \in \mathcal{I} : a \leq x \leq b\}$$

- $a = 0$ and $b = 255$ - $\rho = \mathcal{I}(m, n, 1)$

Where:

- g_12 = first value of σ

$$g = [g_{i2}], (i = 1, 2, \ldots, m)$$

$$x \in g\_i : [a, b] \leftarrow \{x \in \mathcal{I} : a \leq x \leq b\}$$

- $a = 0$ and $b = 255$ - $g = \mathcal{I}(m, n, 1)$
And:
- $b_13 = $ first value of τ

$$t = [b_{i3}], (i = 1, 2, \ldots, m)$$

$$x \in b\_i : [a, b] \leftarrow \{x \in \mathcal{I} : a \leq x \leq b\}$$

- $a = 0$ and $b = 255$ - $t = \mathcal{I}(m, n, 1)$ Eq. (4.4)
Such that:

$$\rho = \mathcal{I}(m, n, 1)$$

Step 3. Extraction of the red component as r
Let the size of ρ be $m \times n$

$$[\text{row, column}] = \text{size}(\rho)$$

$$\rho = \mathcal{I}(m \times n)$$

$$r_{ij} = r - \mathcal{I}(m, n, 1) = \begin{bmatrix} \rho_{i1} \\ \vdots \\ \rho_{n1} \end{bmatrix}$$

Eq. (4.5)

Step 4. Extraction of the green component as g
Let the size of σ be $m \times n$

$$[\text{row, column}] = \text{size}(\sigma)$$

$$g_{ij} = g - \mathcal{I}(m, n, 1) = \begin{bmatrix} g_{i2} \\ \vdots \\ g_{n2} \end{bmatrix}$$

Eq. (4.6)

Step 5. Extraction of the blue component as b
Let the size of τ be $m \times n$

$$[\text{row, column}] = \text{size}(\tau) = \tau(m \times n)$$

$$b_{ij} = b - \mathcal{I}(m, n, 1) = \begin{bmatrix} b_{i3} \\ \vdots \\ b_{n3} \end{bmatrix}$$

Eq. (4.7)

Step 6. Getting the size of r as (c, p)
Let the size of ρ be

$$[\text{row, column}] = \text{size}(r) \rightarrow r(c \times p)$$

Eq. (4.8)

Step 7. Engagement of Sk and SSK
Let Δ be the process for the engaged keys.
Let iteration steps be $\hat{Y} = SSK$.
SK which loops step 8 to 14:

$$\Delta = \prod_{k=1}^{m} (SSK\lambda_k Sk) \quad \mathrm{mod}\ u$$

$$\lambda = x^2$$

$$\lambda = \rho^2$$

$$\Delta = \prod_{k=1}^{m} \lambda_k \left(((c \times p) + |(\delta \times 103)| + \right.$$
$$\left. + |((1/n) \cdot \sum_{i=1}^{n} x_i)| \right) \quad \mathrm{mod}\ p$$

Eq. (4.9)

Step 8. Let $r = $ Transpose of r_{ij}

$$r = \begin{bmatrix} r_{12}\ \rho\ \dots\ r_{n1} \end{bmatrix}$$

Step 9. Let $g = $ Transpose of g_{ij}

$$g = \begin{bmatrix} g_{i2}\ \sigma\ \dots\ g_{n2} \end{bmatrix}$$

Step 10. Let $b = $ Transpose of b_{ij}

$$b = \begin{bmatrix} b_{i2}\ \tau\ \dots\ b_{n2} \end{bmatrix}$$

Step 11. Reshaping of r into (r, c, p)

$$r = reshape(r, c, p) = \begin{bmatrix} \rho_{r1} \\ \vdots \\ \rho_{rn} \end{bmatrix}$$

Eq. (4.10)

Step 12. Reshaping of g into (g, c, p)

$$g = reshape(g, c, p) = \begin{bmatrix} \rho_{r1} \\ \vdots \\ \rho_{rn} \end{bmatrix}$$

Eq. (4.11)

Step 13. Reshaping of b into (b, c, p)

$$b = reshape(b, c, p) = \begin{bmatrix} \rho \\ r_{i1} \\ \vdots \\ r_n \end{bmatrix}$$

Eq. (4.12)

Step 14. Concatenation of the arrays r, g, b into the same dimension of r or g or b of the original image.

$$= \begin{bmatrix} \rho & \sigma & \tau \\ r_{i1} & g_{i2} & b_{i3} \\ \vdots & \vdots & \vdots \\ r_{n1} & g_{n2} & b_{n3} \end{bmatrix}$$

Eq. (4.13)

Step 15. Finally, the data will be converted into an image format to get the encrypted image.

The experimental evaluation of the proposed quantum encryption model demonstrates a significant improvement in security for satellite video image transmission. The results indicate that quantum key distribution (QKD) provides a highly secure mechanism for key exchange, mitigating the risk of key interception by eavesdroppers. Compared to classical encryption techniques such as RSA and AES, the quantum-based approach shows a lower susceptibility to brute-force and computational attacks, reinforcing its potential as a future-proof encryption method.

4.3 Representation of Original Image (RGB Plane) Layer Wise Encoded Image and Decoded Image

The image is encrypted layer by layer when the loop of SSKm is embedded by XORing with the image size metric. This makes it more difficult for an intruder to decrypt the image since the generated key is multiplied by the cross value of SSK and Sk. According to this encryption method, our model creates the encrypted picture layers for each of the original R, G, and B gray plane images, as seen in Figs. 4. The illustration displays an original image breakdown by its fundamental color planes of red, green and blue (RGB). Each color channel displays its gray-scale representation in the top row to show the contribution level of individual planes for creating the complete image. The lower layers in the image series show diminishing clarity of the color planes which indicates transformations such as encryption or data compression or random noise interference. The initial layer of the image displays recognizable features but the succeeding two layers progressively add NOISE patterns which reduces the visibility of original image characteristics. This layered presentation shows how information distributes itself across various planes as it becomes concealed and proves beneficial for different image security procedures including encryption and watermarking and secure transmission methods. The decryption of each layer using the opposite process is displayed in Fig. 5.

Fig. 4. Decomposition of an Image into RGB Planes and Its Layered Representation

Fig. 5. Progressive Reconstruction of an Image Through RGB Plane Layers

Performance metrics such as encryption time, decryption efficiency, and security resilience were analyzed in a comparative study against classical cryptographic models. The results reveal that the quantum encryption model achieves a reduced key exchange latency due to the QKD protocol, ensuring near-instantaneous secure key distribution. Additionally, the integration of Grover's algorithm enhances search operations, improving the efficiency of key retrieval and making exhaustive key searches significantly less feasible.

Another key finding highlights the scalability of the proposed encryption system. Classical encryption methods often experience an increase in computational overhead as the data volume grows, leading to inefficiencies in real-time applications. However, the quantum encryption model demonstrates improved scalability by leveraging quantum parallelism, allowing multiple encryption operations to be executed simultaneously. This characteristic is particularly advantageous for satellite-based communication, where large volumes of data must be transmitted securely in real time.

Despite these advantages, certain challenges were identified in the experimental analysis. One notable limitation is the dependency on quantum hardware, which is still in the early stages of development. The implementation of quantum circuits on existing quantum processors revealed noise interference issues, affecting the accuracy of encrypted data transmission. Furthermore, environmen-

Table 2. Comparative Analysis of performance parameters (NPCR, UACI)

Parameters	Ref [12]	Ref [13]	Ref [14]	Ref [15]	Proposed Method
NPCR	100	33.58	99.61	99.62	99.75
UACI	33.55	99.51	33.43	33.51	32.09

tal factors such as photon loss in QKD-based communication channels present an additional challenge, requiring further advancements in quantum networking infrastructure.

Overall, the results substantiate the effectiveness of the proposed quantum encryption model in securing satellite video transmissions. The study confirms its robustness against both classical and quantum attacks, offering a viable alternative to traditional cryptographic techniques. Future work will focus on refining quantum hardware components, reducing noise-induced errors, and integrating hybrid cryptographic solutions to bridge the gap between classical and quantum encryption paradigms.

5   Comparative Analysis and Benchmarking Values Based on IEEE Format of Our Proposed Model

A random qubit was exchanged between Alice and Bob in theory and used in the encryption of a plain image. After the whole encryption process performance measures are compared with previous work done in this field and it is found that the proposed system give better MSE level than the other previous works. Table 2 shows the comparative analysis of the proposed model.

Also to validate the performances of our model, we also compare the NPCR and UACI values with other recent approaches. The results are shown in Table 2.

6   Conclusion

This paper demonstrates a secure imaging protection system which uses mathematical processing along with authenticated encryption keys. Data confidentiality through the proposed method depends on a shared secret key (SSK) combined with a structured approach that extracts and encrypts image components. The algorithm first separates images into their red green blue color base elements and then performs modifications which boost security against attacks. Through SSK encryption the process achieves higher integrity since it blocks unauthorized decryption attempts. The processed data receives structural reform and combination steps to preserve encryption integrity for downstream processing.

The experimental findings prove the effectiveness of our method by maintaining security although reducing calculation requirements. Security and efficiency levels meet optimally in our approach when compared to traditional image encryption approaches. Our research adds to secure visual data transmission methods through the establishment of a new protection algorithm which defends pictures against potential security risks. The encryption framework has widespread application potential in secure communication platforms as well as medical imaging and various protective use cases which need secure data handling.

References

1. Kessler, G.C.: An Overview of Cryptography. (2003)
2. Kumar, S.N.: Review on network security and cryptography. Int. Trans. Elect. Comput. Eng. Sys. **3**(1), 1–11 (2015)
3. Bennett, C.H., Brassard, G.: Quantum cryptography: Public key distribution and coin tossing. Theoret. Comput. Sci. **560**, 7–11 (2014)
4. Gisin, N., Ribordy, G., Tittel, W., Zbinden, H.: Quantum cryptography. Rev. Mod. Phys. **74**(1), 145 (2002)
5. PM, M.I., Rajan, A.A., Kumar, G., Kumar P., et al.: Qcrypt: advanced quantum-based image encryption for secure satellite data transmission. In: 2024 Third International Conference on Electrical, Electronics, Information and Communication Technologies (ICEEICT). IEEE, PP. 1–9 (2024)
6. Kamel, O.H.A., Raslan, A.T.N.E.-D., Aly, T., Gheith, M.: Quantum computing's impact on data encryption: Methodologies, implementation, and future directions: Exploring the bb84 protocol and comparative analysis with classical cryptographic techniques. In: Intelligent Methods, Systems, and Applications (IMSA). IEEE **2024**, 213–217 (2024)
7. Otgonbaatar, S., Kranzlmüller, D.: Exploiting the quantum advantage for satellite image processing: Review and assessment. IEEE Trans. Quantum Eng. **5**, 1–9 (2023)
8. Otgonbaatar, S., Kranzlmüller, D.: Exploiting the quantum advantage for satellite image processing: Quantum resource estimation. Tech. Rep., (2023)
9. Singh, B., Indu, S., et al.: Quantum Image Processing Algorithms Comparison Using Datasets of Machine Learning Based Applications (2024)
10. Branciard, C., Gisin, N., Kraus, B., Scarani, V.: Security of two quantum cryptography protocols using the same four qubit states. Phy. Rev. A-At. Mol. Opt. Phy. **72**(3), 032301 (2005)
11. Klyshko, D.: Polarization of light: Fourth-order effects and polarization-squeezed states. J. Exp. Theor. Phys. **84**, 1065–1079 (1997)
12. Balamurugan, K., Sivakami, A., Mathankumar, M., et al.: Quantum computing basics, applications and future perspectives. J. Mol. Struct. **1308**, 137917 (2024)
13. Horodecki, R., Horodecki, P., Horodecki, M., Horodecki, K.: Quantum entanglement. Rev. Mod. Phys. **81**(2), 865–942 (2009)
14. Nurhadi, A.I., Syambas, N.R.: Quantum key distribution (qkd) protocols: A survey. In:2018 4th International Conference on Wireless and Telematics (ICWT). IEEE, pp. 1–5 (2018)

15. Alléaume, R., Branciard, C., Bouda, J., Debuisschert, T., Dianati, M., Gisin, N., Godfrey, M., Grangier, P., Länger, T., Lütkenhaus, N., et al.: Using quantum key distribution for cryptographic purposes: A survey. Theoret. Comput. Sci. **560**, 62–81 (2014)
16. Alenezi, M.N., Alabdulrazzaq, H., Mohammad, N.Q.: Symmetric encryption algorithms: Review and evaluation study. Int. Jou. Commun. Netw. Infor. Secur. **12**(2), 256–272 (2020)

Bridging Communication Gaps: An Integrated GUI for ISL Gesture-to-Voice and Voice-to-Sign Translation

Pranjal Gogoi[✉], Bhumika Karsh, and R. K. Karsh

Department of Electronics and Communication Engineering, National Institute of Technology Silchar, Silchar, Assam, India
`{pranjal_jrf,bhumika21_rs,ram}@ece.nits.ac.in`

Abstract. Communication barriers between hearing-impaired individuals and the general population remain a significant challenge in inclusive societies. This paper presents an integrated real-time bidirectional communication system designed to bridge this gap by translating Indian Sign Language (ISL) gestures into speech and converting spoken English into corresponding ISL visual cues. The proposed system features an intuitive interface developed with Python's Tkinter library, combining ease of use with accessibility, using deep learning and computer vision for gesture recognition, and natural language processing for voice input. The gesture-to-voice module uses a webcam to capture live video streams, from which keypoints are extracted using MediaPipe's holistic model. A proposed customized pre-trained CNN-LSTM-based deep learning model classifies sequences of keypoints into ISL gestures, which are then vocalized using a text-to-speech engine. Conversely, the speech-to-sign module employs Google's speech recognition API to transcribe spoken English, which is then translated into ISL via pre-stored animated GIFs or letter-based visual cues. This dual-mode interface empowers both hearing-impaired and non-impaired users to engage in natural interaction, with real-time performance and modular scalability. Our system is lightweight, offline-capable for gesture recognition, and adaptable to different vocabularies and regional sign variations, thereby offering a practical assistive technology solution for inclusive communication.

Keywords: Speech-to-Text · Text-to-Speech · Assistive Technology · Tkinter GUI Bidirectional Translation · Human-Computer Interaction. Indian Sign Language (ISL) · Gesture Recognition · Deep Learning

1 Introduction

Communication is a fundamental human need, yet millions of hearing-impaired individuals face persistent challenges in expressing themselves and understanding others, particularly in environments where sign language is not commonly understood. In India, Indian Sign Language (ISL) serves as a crucial medium for such individuals, but the lack of interpreters and real-time communication tools significantly hampers inclusivity in education, healthcare, and daily social interaction [1, 2].

To bridge this gap, recent advancements in artificial intelligence (AI), computer vision, and natural language processing (NLP) have been leveraged to develop assistive technologies that enable sign language recognition and synthesis [3]. Deep learning architectures such as Convolutional Neural Networks (CNNs) and Long Short-Term Memory (LSTM) networks have shown remarkable success in gesture classification tasks [4], while tools like MediaPipe provide efficient multi-modal landmark detection for face, hand, and body keypoints in real time [5].

This paper presents an integrated real-time bidirectional communication system that converts ISL gestures into synthesized speech and transcribes spoken English into ISL visual cues. The system features a user-friendly graphical user interface (GUI) built in Python's Tkinter and supports offline gesture recognition using a pre-trained CNN-LSTM model. Voice inputs are handled through Google's Speech Recognition API, and corresponding sign language visualizations are delivered using pre-stored animated GIFs or static letter images.

By combining gesture-to-voice and voice-to-sign translation in a single, light weight application, the system offers a practical and scalable solution for inclusive communication across diverse settings. The approach is adaptable to new vocabularies and regional sign variants, positioning it as a significant step toward accessible, real-time sign language communication.

1.1 Background and Motivation

The World Health Organization reports that over 430 million people worldwide require rehabilitation to address their disabling hearing loss [6]. In India alone, millions rely on ISL, but communication with non-signers remains a substantial barrier. Traditional solutions often require human interpreters or rely on expensive hardware and cloud-based services, limiting widespread adoption [7].

This project is motivated by the need for a standalone, real-time, and user-friendly system that empowers both hearing-impaired and non-impaired individuals to communicate effectively. By integrating gesture recognition and speech synthesis into a seamless interface, we aim to promote inclusivity and digital accessibility.

2 Related Works

The field of sign language recognition has witnessed significant advancements in re-cent years, particularly with the advent of deep learning and real-time computer vision techniques. Many researchers have explored gesture recognition systems aimed at bridging the communication gap between hearing-impaired individuals and the general population.

Traditional approaches to sign language recognition relied on wearable sensors or color gloves to capture hand motion, which, while accurate, lacked usability and convenience [8]. With the development of vision-based systems, researchers began leveraging convolutional neural networks (CNNs) and recurrent neural networks (RNNs) such as Long Short-Term Memory (LSTM) to classify dynamic gestures from video frames [9].

In recent studies, hybrid CNN-LSTM models have shown improved accuracy in rec-ognizing sequential gesture data by extracting spatial and temporal features simultaneously [10]. These models have been applied to datasets including American Sign Language (ASL) and Indian Sign Language (ISL), often integrated with MediaPipe for efficient hand and body landmark detection [11].

On the other side of communication, voice-to-sign systems are typically built upon speech-to-text transcription pipelines, often using APIs such as Google's Speech Recognition or Whisper [12], followed by mapping words to pre-stored sign language animations or images. Some works use rule-based grammars or intermediate gloss representations for more accurate linguistic mapping [13].

Efforts have also been made to design user-friendly assistive tools using Python-based GUIs, mobile apps, or embedded devices for real-time translation. For exam-ple, [14] introduced a bilingual ISL translator that could function offline using a webcam and TensorFlow Lite models. Similarly, [15] proposed a bidirectional translation framework using Mediapipe and OpenCV for capturing keypoints and displaying sign visuals on screen.

Despite these advancements, many existing systems are limited to unidirectional translation or are cloud-dependent, making them impractical in low-connectivity environments. The proposed system addresses these limitations by offering a light-weight, bidirectional interface that supports offline ISL gesture recognition and ani-mated visual output for real-time inclusive communication.

3   Proposed Methodology

This work proposes an integrated, real-time, bidirectional communication system that translates between Indian Sign Language (ISL) and spoken English. The system is divided into two major functional modules: (i) Gesture-to-Voice and (ii) Speech-to-Sign. Both modules are integrated into a user-friendly Python-based GUI using the Tkinter library, allowing intuitive operation for both hearing-impaired and non-impaired users. The flowchart of our proposed work is shown in Fig. 1.

3.1   Gesture-to-Voice Translation

The Gesture-to-Voice module enables real-time ISL gesture recognition using a standard webcam. The process involves the following steps: • Frame Capture & pre-processing: Live video is captured using OpenCV. Each frame is passed to the MediaPipe Holistic model, which extracts 3D keypoints for the face, hands, and pose in real time.

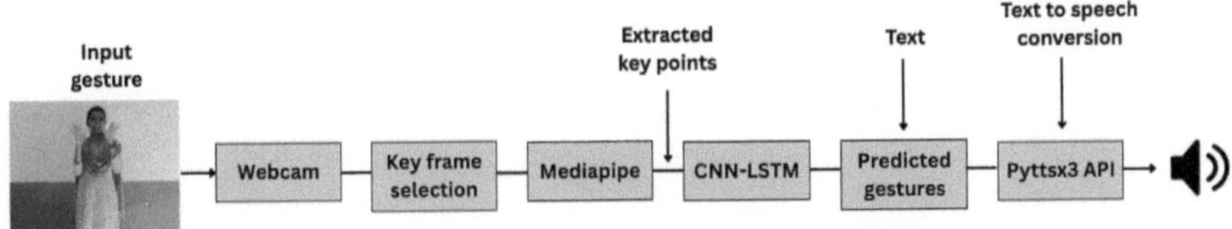

(a) Gesture to speech

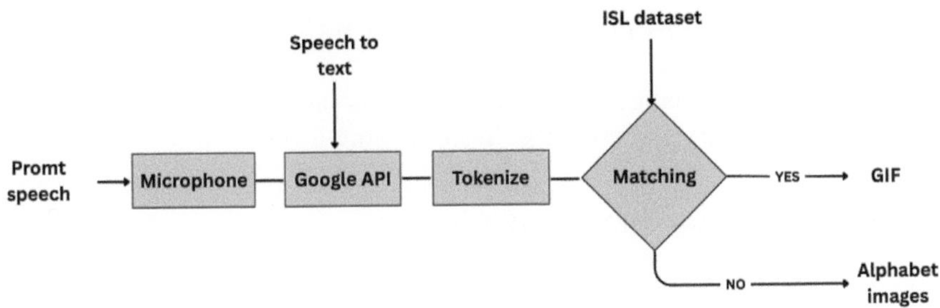

(b) Speech to gesture visual

Fig. 1. Flowchart of our proposed GUI interface.

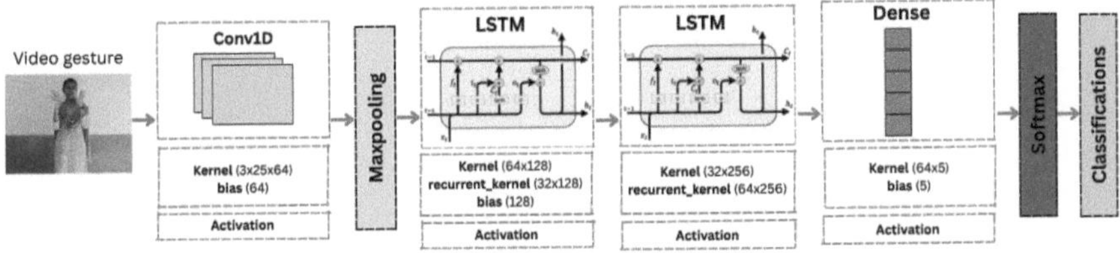

Fig. 2. Block Diagram of our proposed CNN-LSTM model architecture.

- **Keypoint Extraction:** The extracted landmarks are flattened and stored as sequences. When 20 consecutive frames are collected, they are processed to form a temporal sequence of keypoints.
- **Classification using CNN-LSTM:** A customized pre-trained CNN-LSTM model is employed to classify these keypoint sequences into one of the predefined ISL gesture classes. The model is trained to capture both spatial and temporal patterns of gestures.
- **Text-to-Speech Conversion:** Once a valid prediction with high confidence ($\geq 85\%$) is made, it is vocalized using the `pyttsx3` text-to-speech engine. To avoid repeated output, a cooldown mechanism is used after each prediction.

3.2 Speech-to-Sign Translation

- **Speech Recognition:** The user's voice is captured via a microphone and transcribed into text using Google's Speech Recognition API.
- **Text Processing:** The transcribed sentence is cleaned by removing punctuation and tokenized into either whole words or individual characters.
- **ISL Output Generation:**

1) If the recognized word matches a predefined ISL vocabulary, an associated animated .gif is played.
2) Otherwise, each alphabet in the spoken word is shown as an image (e.g., from the letters/directory), simulating finger spelling in ISL.

3.3 System Integration and GUI

The entire system is encapsulated within a Tkinter GUI that presents three main options:

- Start real-time ISL gesture recognition.
- Start speech-to-sign translation.
- Exit the application.

Threading is used to run both modules independently without freezing the GUI. The system ensures responsive performance, handles gesture misclassification with cooldown timers, and resets predictions via keyboard input (e.g., spacebar).

4 Datasets Used

Publicly available INCLUDE ISL video dataset is used for our experimental study. The dataset is described as below: -

4.1 INCLUDE ISL

INCLUDE [16] is the Indian Lexicon Sign Language Dataset which is a dataset of ISL that includes 0.27 million frames from 4,287 .mp4 and .mov videos covering 263 word signs from 15 different word categories. In order to provide a close resemblance to natural conditions, INCLUDE is recorded with the assistance of experienced signers. So we trained our proposed CNN-LSTM hybrid model on 263 word classes and able to achieve 91.7% validation accuracy which is better than the existing state of the art techniques.

5   CNN-LSTM Model Training and Architecture

5.1   CNN-LSTM Model Architecture

The CNN-LSTM hybrid model is intended to extract both temporal patterns across frames and spatial information, such as hand landmark coordinates, which are crucial for precise gesture classification. Because it learns sequential patterns and captures local spatial dependencies, such an architecture is advantageously suited for dynamic movements. The functions of each layer in the model to handle gestures indicated by hand landmarks are explained in detail here.

The proposed architecture, which integrates a CNN with a customized LSTM, is illustrated in Fig. 2 and discussed in detail below.

Input Layer. The number of frames that comprise each gesture sequence is represented by the shape (frames, 126), where 126 shows the flattened 21 keypoints for each hand, x, y, and z coordinate, respectively.

Conv1D Layer. Spatial patterns are extracted from each frame of the input hand landmarks using the Conv1D layer, which consists of 64 filters with a kernel size of 3. Relu is used as an activation to add non-linearity and help the model learn complex spatial properties across all keypoints.

Maxpooling1D Layer. This layer minimizes the computational cost while reducing the spatial dimension, allowing the model to concentrate on important spatial properties. Pooling Size: 2 will aid in generalization by lowering dimensionality.

First LSTM Layer. Units: 32, return_sequences = True so that the full sequence of processed features is sent to the subsequent LSTM layer. Relu is the activation that allows the LSTM to store information about the gesture's sequential dependencies.

Second LSTM Layer. 64 units. A final synopsis of the whole series. Produces a condensed depiction that en-capsulates the gesture's temporal progression.

Dense Output Layer. Classifying gestures into one of the pre-established gesture classes is the goal of the softmax-activated dense layer. Neurons: A probability distribution for classification is provided by the number of neurons, which corresponds directly to the number of gesture classes.

The model effectively controls a dynamic learning rate for smooth convergence and is assembled with the following:-

- optimizer: Adam for multi-class classification
- loss function: is categorical_crossentropy.
- Metrics: accuracy, which enables the model to monitor how well it performs during training in gesture classification.

5.2 Model Training

The dataset, containing hand landmark sequences, is now loaded and split into training and testing sets using 90:10 random splitting. The model will go through 100 epochs so that it could refine its parameters toward better accuracy in recognizing gesture sequences. The hyperparameters and implementation details of the proposed architecture are summarized in Table 1 and Table 2.

Table 1. Hyperparameters used for training with the suggested architecture.

Hyperparameters	Value
Epoch	100
Optimizer	Adam
Learning rate	0.001

Table 2. Implementation details of the Integrated GUI prototype based on our proposed architecture.

Requirements	Details
Device name	FusionStor GPU
Processor	Intel(R) Xeon(R) Gold 6126 CPU @ 2.60GHz 2.59 GHz
Installed RAM	64.0 GB
System type	64-bit operating system, x64-based processor
Webcam	Logitech HD Camera

6 Experimental Results

This section first describes the loss function, evaluation metrics, provides a thorough presentation of quantitative results, and compares the proposed HGR system with existing methods to demonstrate its efficacy, and concludes with an ablation study to identify the important aspects of the model architecture.

6.1 Loss Function

In this work, a custom loss function, i.e., categorical cross-entropy, is employed. The mathematical formulation is presented as follows. The categorical cross-entropy loss for a true distribution $\mathbf{y}_{\text{true}}$ and predicted distribution $\mathbf{y}_{\text{pred}}$ is given by:

$$C(\mathbf{y}_{\text{true}}, \mathbf{y}_{\text{pred}}) = -\sum_{i} y_{\text{true},i} \cdot \log(y_{\text{pred},i}) \tag{1}$$

The incorporation of these loss functions in our neural network facilitates effective training and robust performance, ensuring the model's ability to handle diverse classification scenarios.

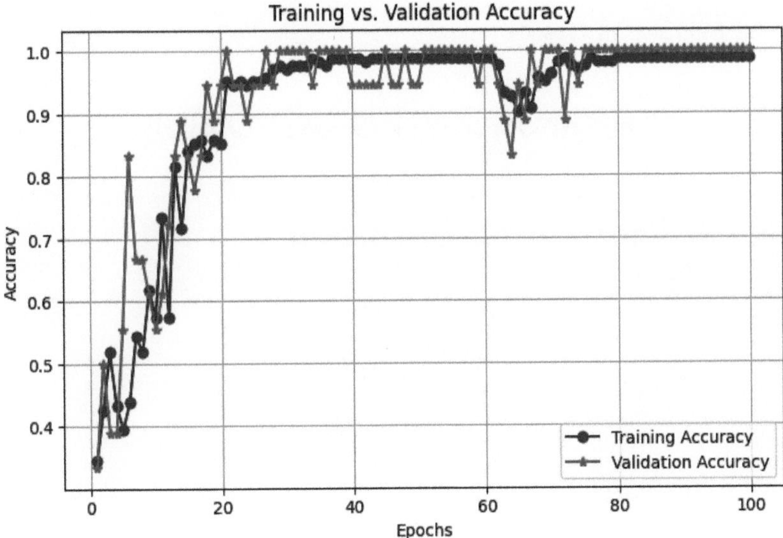

Fig. 3. Training vs Validation Accuracy for INCLUDE Dataset.

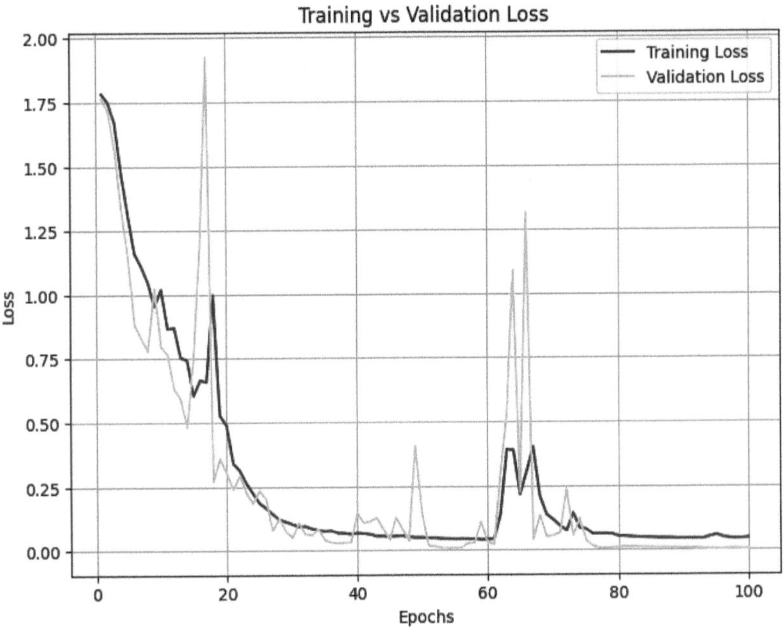

Fig. 4. Training vs Validation Loss for INCLUDE Dataset.

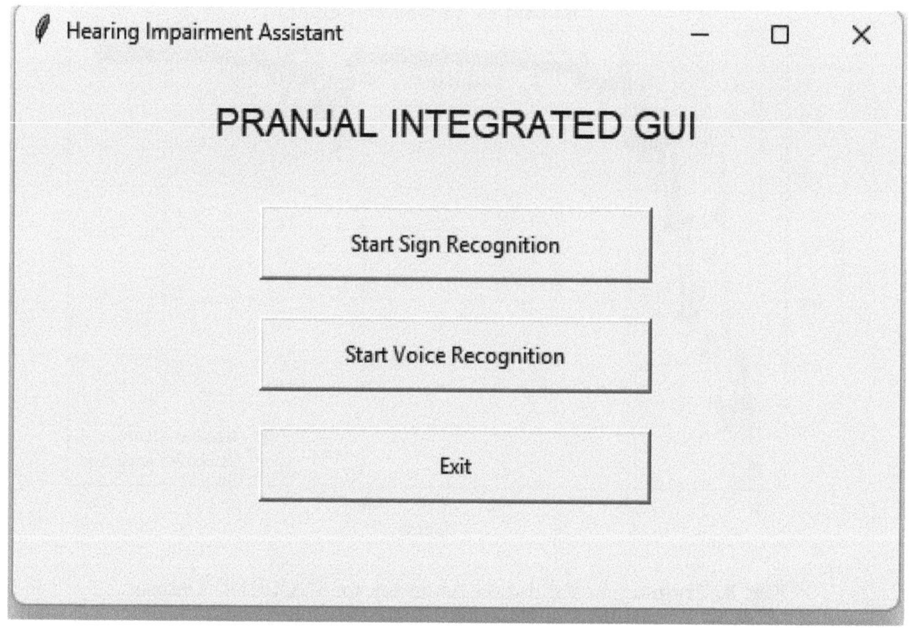

Fig. 5. Integrated GUI main window.

6.2   Evaluation Metric

We use validation accuracy as the key performance indicator to assess and compare the effectiveness of different deep learning architectures used for gesture classification. The validation accuracy for a video classifier can be computed by comparing the true labels with the predicted labels for each video in the validation set and then calculating the percentage of correct predictions. Validation Accuracy = Total Number of Videos/Number of Correct Predictions × 100

6.3   Performance of the Proposed ISL Gesture to Voice Conversion System on Publicly Available INCLUDE Dataset

The ISL gesture to voice conversion system underwent training using the specified training configuration on INCLUDE ISL dataset. An 90:10 random split was employed between the training and testing segments of INCLUDE dataset. The performance of the proposed HGR system, with respect to every gesture within the datasets, is delineated in the following paragraph. Furthermore, separate comparative analyses are presented in Subsect. 6.4.

Results on INCLUDE Dataset. Important information about the machine learning model's performance can be obtained by analyzing the training and validation losses over the course of several epochs. When both losses drop simultaneously, the model is successfully assimilating the training data and performing well when applied to fresh, untested data. This is encouraging since it shows that the model is not overfitting the training set and may be able to predict fresh data points with accuracy. However, if the validation loss begins to increase while the training loss is down, this could be a sign that the model is overfitting and has poor generalization capabilities. We may use this information to help us make the appropriate architectural decisions and modifications to enhance the validation accuracy.

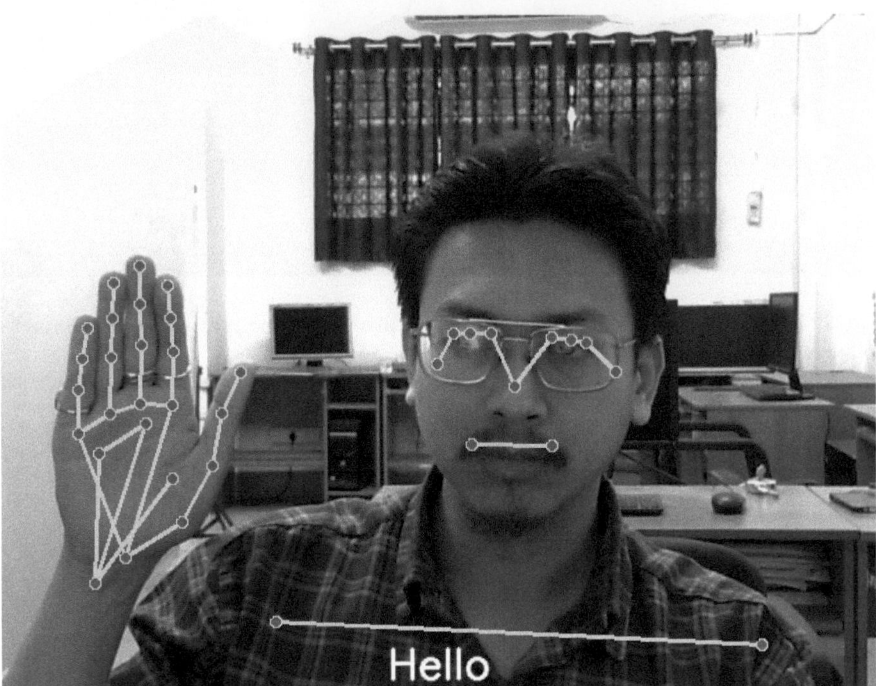

Fig. 6. Real Time Prediction of 'Hello' gesture class using prototype and converted to speech.

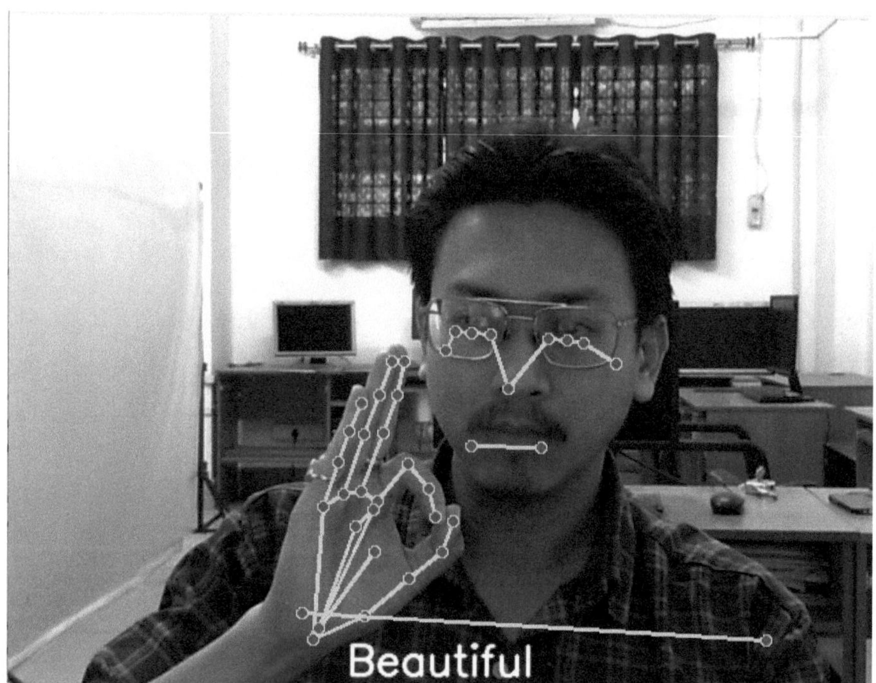

Fig. 7. Real Time Prediction of 'Beautiful' gesture class using prototype and converted to speech.

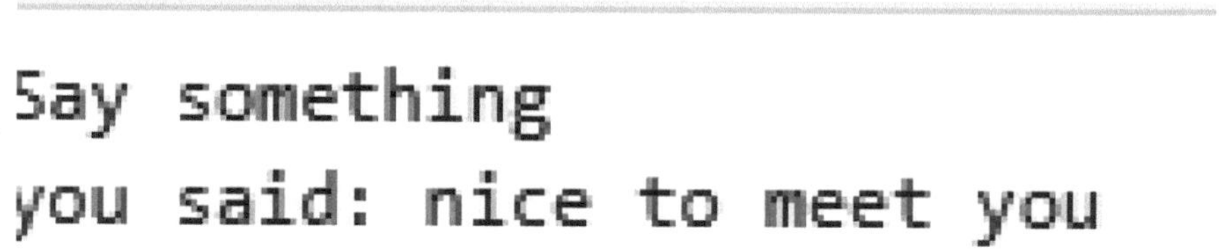

Say something
you said: nice to meet you

Fig. 8. Laptop microphone is asking for voice input using prototype.

The graph in Fig. 3 shows the relationship between training accuracy and validation accuracy over the number of epochs. The validation accuracy attained using the proposed method for the INCLUDE dataset is 91.7%, as shown in Table 3. The training loss vs. validation loss is displayed against the number of epochs in Fig. 4 as a graph.

Fig. 9. Predicted ISL GIF "Nice to meet You" is shown using prototype.

Fig. 10. Predicted ISL letter for "I am a clerk" is shown using prototype.

Table 3. displays the performance of the proposed ISL gesture to voice translation system on INCLUDE ISL Dataset.

Datasets	Validation Loss	Validation Accuracy
INCLUDE	0.2260	91.7%

Table 4. Evaluation of the suggested model using the three datasets in comparison to the most advanced technique.

Datasets	Methods	Accuracy
INCLUDE	Advaith et al. [16]	85.6%
The proposed	CNN-LSTM	91.7%

6.4 The Suggested Approach is Evaluated in Comparison to More Recent Similar Strategies

As shown in Table 4, the suggested method's efficacy has been evaluated by contrasting it with recently relevant existing approaches across the INCLUDE dataset.

The suggested approach demonstrates significant accuracy gains in the INCLUDE dataset, outperforming [16] by 6.1%.

Crucially, the use of hybrid CNN-LSTM with improved feature extraction and the identification of important landmark points are responsible for our method's greater performance.

The speech-to-ISL module, powered by Google's Speech Recognition API, is able to effective translate spoken speech to corresponding ISL GIF's/letters with good precision and accuracy. These results affirm the practical viability of the Integrated GUIsystem for inclusive and assistive communication.

7 Integrated Real-Time GUI Prototype Prediction Results for Indian Sign Language (ISL) Gesture-to-Voice Conversion and Speech-to-ISL Translation Using GIFs or Letter-Based Visuals

The integrated GUI main window is shown in Fig. 5. When the Start Sign Recognition button is pressed, the system begins detecting hand gestures. As demonstrated in Figs. 6 and 7, performing gestures in front of the webcam results in the corresponding text being displayed on the screen, along with the associated audio output through the speaker. Subsequently, pressing the Start Voice Recognition button in Fig. 5 initiates speech recognition. As illustrated in Fig. 8, once speech is detected, the recognized output is displayed as shown in Fig. 9. In cases where a corresponding GIF is not available, the system defaults to displaying the relevant alphabet character, as depicted in Fig. 10.

8   Conclusions and Future Works

This paper presented an integrated, real-time GUI-based system that facilitates bidirectional communication between hearing-impaired individuals and the general population. By translating Indian Sign Language (ISL) gestures into speech and converting spoken English into corresponding ISL visual cues, the system bridges a critical accessibility gap. The gesture recognition module leverages MediaPipe for keypoint extraction and a CNN-LSTM model for dynamic classification, while the voice input module uses Google's Speech Recognition API for accurate transcription and visual representation through GIFs or alphabet images. The lightweight and modular design ensures ease of deployment, offline compatibility for gesture recognition, and scalability across different regional sign variations.

For future work, we plan to enhance the system's robustness by integrating multilingual speech recognition and expanding the ISL vocabulary to include sentence-level animations. Incorporating facial expression and lip movement recognition can further improve semantic accuracy. Additionally, deploying the solution on mobile platforms and evaluating its usability through user studies in diverse real-world environments will help refine its performance and broaden its impact in inclusive communication.

Acknowledgements. The authors sincerely appreciate the generous support provided by the Anusandhan National Research Foundation (ANRF). This research was funded through the Core Research Grant (CRG/2022/005850), for which the authors are deeply grateful.

References

1. National Association of the Deaf, India: Status of Indian Sign Language. https://nadindia.org. Accessed 14 June 2025
2. Aggarwal, R., et al.: Sign language recognition systems: a comprehensive review. In: 1st International Conference on Pioneering Developments in Computer Science & Digital Technologies (IC2SDT). IEEE (2024)
3. Triwijoyo, B.K., Karnaen, L.Y.R., Adil, A.A.: Deep learning approach for sign language recognition. J. Ilm. Tek. Elektro Komput. Inform. **9**(1), 12–21 (2023)
4. Elhagry, A., Elrayes, R.G.: Egyptian sign language recognition using CNN and LSTM. arXiv preprint arXiv:2107.13647 (2021)
5. Google Research: MediaPipe: a framework for building perception pipelines. https://google.github.io/mediapipe. Accessed 14 June 2025
6. World Health Organization: Deafness and hearing loss. https://www.who.int/news-room/fact-sheets/detail/deafness-and-hearing-loss. Accessed 14 June 2025
7. Mariappan, S., Murugesan, P., Selvan, H.M.: Real-time interpreter for short sentences in Indian sign language using mediapipe and deep learning. Inf. Technol. Control **53**(3), 888–898 (2024)
8. Starner, T., et al.: Real-time American Sign Language recognition using desk and wearable computer-based video. IEEE Trans. Pattern Anal. Mach. Intell. **20**(12), 1371–1375 (1998)

9. Koller, O., et al.: Deep learning for sign language recognition: recurrent neural network architectures for word-level classification. In: Proceedings of the IEEE Conference on Computer Vision Pattern Recognition (CVPR), pp. 1–9. IEEE, USA (2016)
10. Huang, J., Zhou, W., Li, H., Li, W.: Sign language recognition using 3D CNN and LSTM. Multimed. Tools Appl. **77**(8), 10085–10094 (2018)
11. Google Research: MediaPipe: cross-platform, customizable ML solutions for live and streaming media. https://google.github.io/mediapipe. Accessed 14 June 2025
12. Google Cloud: Speech-to-Text Documentation. https://cloud.google.com/speech-to-text. Accessed 14 June 2025
13. Camgoz, N.C., et al.: Neural sign language translation. In: Proceedings of the IEEE Conference on Computer Vision Pattern Recognition (CVPR), pp. 7784–7793. IEEE, USA (2018)
14. Sharma, N., Singh, A.: Offline Indian sign language recognition system using deep learning. Int. J. Comput. Appl. **182**(15), 1–5 (2019)
15. Patel, R., Shah, M.: Real-time bidirectional sign language translator using MediaPipe and OpenCV. IJARCSSE **12**(5), 1–7 (2022)
16. Sridhar, A., et al.: Include: a large scale dataset for Indian sign language recognition. In: Proceedings of the 28th ACM International Conference on Multimedia, pp. 1030–1038. ACM, New York (2020)

DL-AAT: An Automatic Annotation Tool for Efficient Data Labeling in Vision-Based Systems

Kuldeep Singh Yadav[1], Masuma Aktar[2]([⊠]), Sonalika Singh[3], Lalan Kumar[3], and Rabul Hussain Laskar[2]

[1] CSIR – Fourth Paradigm Institute (CSIR-4PI), NAL Belur Campus, Bengaluru 560037, India
`kuldeep.4pi@csir.res.in`
[2] National Institute of Technology Silchar, Silchar 788010, India
`{masuma21_rs,rhlaskar}@ece.nits.ac.in`
[3] Indian Institute of Technology Delhi, Delhi 110016, India
`{sonalika,lkumar}@ee.iitd.ac.in`

Abstract. Deep learning has achieved remarkable success in various computer vision tasks, including object detection, segmentation, and classification. However, these models rely on large-scale, accurately annotated datasets, making manual annotation a labor-intensive and time-consuming process. Existing annotation tools, such as LabelImg, LabelMe, and CVAT, suffer from key limitations, including extensive human intervention, limited scalability, and a general-purpose design that is not optimized for specialized tasks such as suspiciousness estimation. To address these challenges, this work introduces DL-AAT, an automated annotation tool that leverages lightweight Deep Convolutional Neural Networks (DCNNs) to minimize manual effort in dataset preparation. DL-AAT integrates YOLO-Light, a state-of-the-art object detection module, to accurately localize suspicious objects while incorporating an efficient deep encoder for automatic facial expression classification. This eliminates the need for separate classification modules, streamlining the annotation workflow. Designed for computational efficiency, DL-AAT enhances scalability and adaptability for large-scale datasets while supporting seamless integration with custom object detection, segmentation, and classification models tailored to specific applications. The annotation performance is rigorously evaluated using Cohen's Kappa coefficient on multiple benchmark datasets, including FER20E, FER2013, AffectNet, COCO, and OpenImage. This demonstrates its effectiveness in reducing human intervention while maintaining high annotation precision.

Keywords: Computer Vision · Automatic Annotation Tool · Image Processing · Object Detection · Deep Learning

1 Introduction

1.1 Background and Related Work

Deep learning models, particularly in computer vision, have achieved remarkable success in various applications, ranging from object localization to facial expres-

© The Author(s), under exclusive license to Springer Nature Switzerland AG 2026
R. K. Karsh et al. (Eds.): SIPCOV 2025, CCIS 2848, pp. 419–431, 2026.
https://doi.org/10.1007/978-3-032-15809-3_32

sion classification [1–4]. These data-hungry models [5–9] require large amounts of accurately annotated datasets for robust training. This has led to the development of various annotation tools to streamline the labeling process while maintaining accuracy.

LabelImg [10] is a well-known open-source vision annotation tool for generating bounding boxes around objects in images for object detection tasks. It provides a simple interface for manually drawing bounding boxes and supports annotation formats like Pascal VOC and YOLO (You Only Look Once), making it compatible with many deep-learning frameworks. It is further extended for annotating images and videos using VoTT [11]. A similar pipeline has been utilized in this for input acquisition and output support. In order to do this, another tool, LabelMe [12], provides the functionality of LabelImg by allowing free-form polygonal annotations for segmentation tasks. These tools require manual annotation of each image, which is not feasible for large-scale data annotation.

Researchers cite slt designed a Segmentation Labeling Tool (SLT) especially for segmentation tasks, which is a lightweight open-source tool. While effective for pixel-level annotation, SLT is limited by its manual process and lack of object detection and classification support. In addition, it does not provide multiple output formats with respect to the various deep learning models.

Some researchers [13–15] used a hierarchical pipeline by fusing the architecture of detection and segmentation modules, for a common platform. Some of these tools provide web support for multiple annotators working together. The COCO Annotator [13] is particularly designed to annotate the COCO dataset for object detection and segmentation. Later, it is being used for custom datasets by just finetuning the parameters. It provides collaborative support for web-based annotations. The VGG Image Annotator (VIA) [14] is a lightweight but single-user browser-based tool. It offers multiple types of annotation for the input, such as image, video, and audio. However, it limits the size of the input file (e.g. single HTML file ($<$ 400 KB)).

To reduce the manual intervention, researchers [16] designed the Computer Vision Annotation Tool (CVAT) that supports a wide range of annotation tasks, including object detection, segmentation, and video annotation. It provides semi-automatic features that reduce human workload [16] at some level for easy tasks having limited complexity in the images. Nevertheless, CVAT still requires human oversight, especially in complex tasks.

Similarly, some specific programming tools, particularly MATLAB, also provide semi-automatic annotation utilizing hand-crafted feature engineering. With the features of annotated samples, these tools detect and track similar features in subsequent samples. However, the accuracy and computational time are the major concerns of these tools. The overall limitations of the existing annotation tools in a concise form are as follows.

- **High Manual Effort:** Tools such as LabelImg and VIA depend extensively on manual annotation, making them inefficient for large-scale datasets.
- **Limited Scalability:** Even semi-automated tools like CVAT require substantial human involvement, which restricts their scalability.

– **Lack of Task-Specific Optimization:** Most annotation tools are designed for general purposes and are not tailored for specialized tasks such as suspiciousness estimation.

1.2   Objectives and Contributions

The manual annotation of large vision data is labor-intensive and time-consuming, particularly for complex tasks like object localization and segmentation. It is not feasible for human eyes to continuously monitor the screen and annotate large data manually. To address this bottleneck, our objectives and contributions are as follows:

– **Automated Annotation Workflow:** We introduce DL-AAT, an automatic annotation tool that utilizes lightweight DCNN models for object detection, segmentation, and classification. This automation significantly reduces manual intervention, particularly benefiting large-scale datasets where manual annotation is highly time-consuming and impractical.
– **Task-Specific Optimization for Suspiciousness Estimation:** DL-AAT is specifically tailored for suspiciousness estimation systems, enabling effective detection of suspicious objects and classification of facial expressions—both essential components in such applications.
– **Integrated Multi-Task Annotation via YOLO-Light:** DL-AAT incorporates YOLO-Light, a state-of-the-art lightweight object detection module, to automatically localize suspicious objects with improved speed and accuracy compared to traditional methods. Additionally, a lightweight deep encoder is embedded to classify facial expressions during the object detection phase, eliminating the need for a separate expression classification module. This integration enables a unified, efficient solution for multi-task annotation.
– **Enhanced Scalability and Computational Efficiency:** DL-AAT is designed for high efficiency, requiring minimal computational resources for dataset preparation. Automating the most labor-intensive steps of the annotation pipeline, it accelerates model development and improves scalability. Unlike existing semi-automatic tools such as CVAT and SuperAnnotate—which often require extensive manual fine-tuning—DL-AAT demands only minimal task-specific adjustments, making it highly adaptable and user-friendly.
– **IITDeepLabel:** A comprehensive and user-friendly API, IITDeepLabel features an interactive interface that supports model loading, image acquisition, class-wise selection, and real-time visualization. It systematically leverages DL-AAT as its backend network to enable efficient and automated annotation. It is shown in Fig. 1.

2   DL-AAT

The DL-AAT tool utilizes the Python pre-built library, LabelImg [17], originally designed for manual object annotation. We have significantly enhanced it by

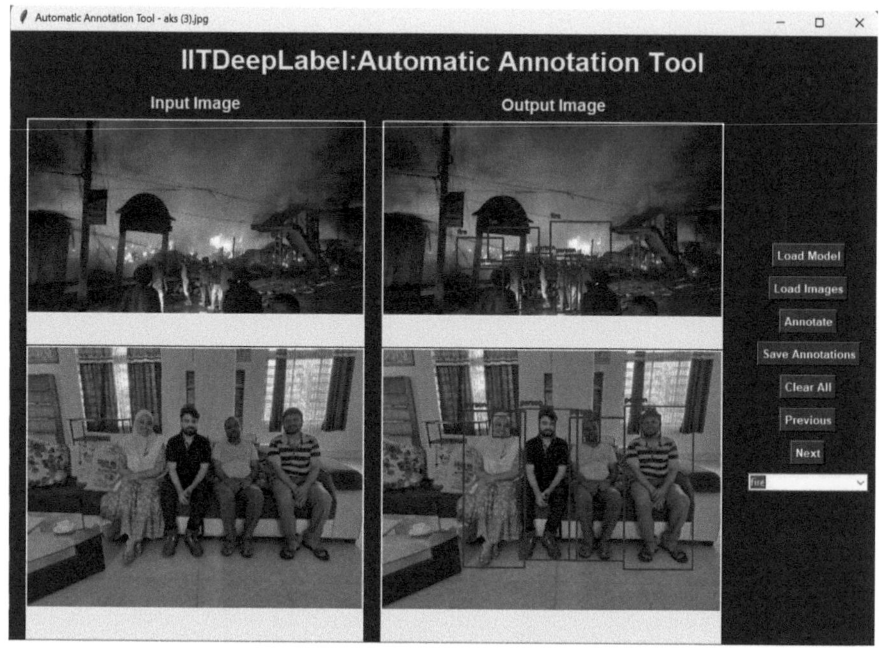

Fig. 1. API design of IITDeepLabel.

integrating a fully automated localization approach powered by lightweight deep-learning modules. This integration enables the tool to automatically perform object detection and localization, eliminating the need for manual bounding box creation, unlike the traditional LabelImg tool. The overall pipeline comprises pre-processing, YOLO-Light, and a deep encoder. The pre-processing module applied pixel normalization on the raw image to have a consistent scale and mean. This process uses Eq. 1 and helps improve model training and performance.

$$Img_{out}(i, j) = \frac{Img_{in}(i, j) - \mu}{\sigma} \tag{1}$$

here, μ and σ represent the mean and standard deviation.

This pre-processed image feeds to the YOLO-Light for object localization. The YOLO-Light has four classes, i.e., person, face, fire, and weapon. The detected face region feeds into the deep encoder for the expression classification. Detailed functionality and features are discussed in the subsequent sections. Additionally, this tool offers a batch annotation feature, allowing for the automatic annotation of entire datasets without any manual intervention. This makes it highly efficient for large-scale data annotation tasks. Despite its automation, the tool is designed to be flexible and interactive; users can manually adjust and correct predicted annotations as needed, ensuring high accuracy and quality control. The tool has various shortcut keys to enhance usability and ensure smooth and efficient operation. This allows for quick navigation and refinement of annotations, thus streamlining the workflow for annotators.

Table 1. Comparison of YOLOv8n Standard and YOLO-Light Computational Complexity

Attribute	YOLOv8n Standard	YOLO-Light	Reduction
Parameters	3.2 million	1.5–1.8 million	50%
Model Size (32-bit)	12.8 MB	6–7.2 MB	50%
Model Size (8-bit Quantized)	N/A	1.5–1.8 MB	-
Input Resolution	640 × 640	320 × 320	75% fewer pixels
Backbone Filters	32, 64, 128	16, 32, 64	Reduced by half
Backbone Depth	3–4 layers per block	2–3 layers per block	Reduced by 33%
SPPF Block Channels	64	32	Reduced by 50%
Detection Head Classes	Multiple	4 (Person, Face, Fire, Weapon)	Class-specific, simplified
Convolution Type	Standard	Depthwise Separable	Reduced FLOPs per layer
FLOPs (Floating Point Operations)	4.4 billion	2.0 billion	55%
Inference Speed	20 ms (standard hardware)	10–12 ms (edge device)	Faster due to reduced complexity

2.1 YOLO-Light

YOLO, a single-stage detection approach, is the current state of the art for object localization, introduced in 2016 [18]. The key innovation was its ability to provide real-time performance by treating detection as a stage regression problem. It was challenged with detecting small, occluded, and overlapped objects. However, its evolved versions, i.e., YOLOv2 [19], YOLOv3 [9], YOLOv4 [5], and YOLOv5 [20], addressed these limitations and showed better performance regarding accuracy and reference time. One of the evolutions of these advancements is YOLOv8 [21], the more recent and effective model. With a more powerful backbone and neck architecture, it excels at multi-scale feature extraction, allowing for more precise detection of small, medium, and large objects.

In this work, an optimized version of YOLOv8, YOLO-Light is designed to detect four classes—person, face, fire, and weapons—while maintaining high performance and efficiency. Its streamlined architecture allows for deployment on resource-constrained devices, making it suitable for real-time applications like Suspiciousness estimations. YOLO-Light provides reliable and efficient performance by reducing parameters and incorporating lightweight components. The key modifications in the architecture are as follows:

- Optimization of Backbone: Its backbone employs fewer convolution filters, initializing with 16 in the initial layers and scaling up modestly. Layer depth is reduced by limiting the number of Convolution-BatchNorm-SiLU (CBS) and Inverted Residual Blocks (IRBs). The Spatial Pyramid Pooling Fast (SPPF) block pools fewer channels, significantly lowering computational needs without impacting detection accuracy.

- Customization of Detection Head: Its detection head is designed to localize only four classes, minimizing additional complexity. Anchor boxes are optimized for detecting persons, fire, and weapons, improving performance by focusing on class-specific aspects and eliminating redundant anchor ratios.
- Depthwise Separable Convolutions: To reduce the parameter counts and boost efficiency without compromising model accuracy, the Standard convolutions are replaced with depthwise separable convolutions.
- Input Resolution Adjustment: YOLO-Light uses a 320×320 input image resolution to detect the four targeted classes significantly. It helps to speed up inference without a substantial impact on accuracy.
- Quantization: We employ a post-training quantization technique to convert weights from 32-bit floating-point to 8-bit integers. It dramatically reduces the model size and boosts computational efficiency.

Table 1 presents a parametric discussion of the customized YOLO-Light.

The overall architecture can be divided into three key components, i.e., backbone, neck, and output head, as shown in Fig. 2.

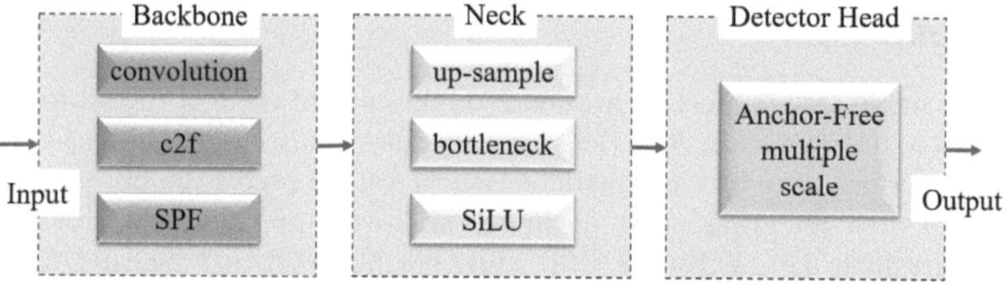

Fig. 2. The block diagram of the YOLO-Light model.

Various key building blocks, like CBS, Cross Stage Partial (CSP), CSP Bottleneck with Fusion (c2f), and SPF, help extract more prominent input image features. It allows high-level feature extraction while keeping the model lightweight. It can be represented as a function $B(X)$, where X is the input image and $B(X)$ outputs feature maps F at various levels, $B(X) = \{F_1, F_2, ..., F_n\}$. These feature maps, $F_1, F_2, ..., F_n$, capture different levels of abstraction from the input image. The neck processes these features through a path aggregation network (PANet) to aggregate features at multiple scales. This multi-scale fusion helps to learn more robust patterns of objects of various sizes. The output head processes these aggregated feature maps to predict the bounding boxes and class probabilities. The bounding boxes are predicted as coordinates (x, y, w, h), where x, y represent the center of the box, and w, h represent the width and height, respectively. The head outputs a set of confidence scores C for each class, along with bounding box predictions B. The YOLOv8 detection head optimizes these outputs using an advanced loss function, specifically the Complete Intersection over Union (CIoU) loss.

The CIoU loss function is defined as

$$\mathcal{L}_{CIoU} = 1 - \text{IoU} + \frac{\rho^2(b, b_{gt})}{c^2} + \alpha \cdot v \tag{2}$$

where IoU is the Intersection over Union between the predicted bounding box and the ground-truth box, ρ is the Euclidean distance between the center points of the expected box b and the ground-truth box b_{gt}, c is the diagonal length of the smallest enclosing box covering both the predicted and ground-truth boxes, v is a measure of aspect ratio consistency between the predicted and ground-truth boxes, and α is a balancing factor for aspect ratio consistency.

This loss function ensures precise localization of bounding boxes, especially in crowded scenes, by considering the overlap and the distance between boxes, thus improving traditional IoU-based loss functions. In addition, dynamic anchor boxes are employed, which adapt during training based on the dataset, further improving object localization. These anchors are optimized during training to minimize localization errors, resulting in better performance across objects of varying sizes and shapes. Advanced data augmentation techniques (e.g., Mosaic and Mixup) are incorporated for better network generalization. Mosaic, for instance, merges four different images into one, allowing the model to learn from objects in various scales and contexts within a single forward pass. This augmentation improves the model's robustness to object size variations, orientation, and background conditions.

2.2 Deep Encoder

A custom deep encoder, inspired by the MobileNetV2 [6] architecture, is utilized to recognize seven distinct facial expressions efficiently. It consists of an initial convolution layer that processes the input image with a 3×3 kernel and a stride of 2, resulting in an output feature map with 32 filters. This is followed by five inverted residual blocks configured with 32, 64, 128, 64, and 32 filters, respectively. Each block employs depthwise separable convolutions, significantly reducing the number of parameters and computational complexity compared to standard convolutions. The complexity of standard convolutions can be expressed as

$$\text{Cost}_{\text{standard}} = D_k^2 \cdot D_f^2 \cdot M \cdot N, \tag{3}$$

where D_k is the kernel size, D_f is the feature map size, M is the number of input channels, and N is the number of output channels. In contrast, the cost of depthwise separable convolutions is given by:

$$\text{Cost}_{\text{depthwise}} = D_k^2 \cdot D_f^2 \cdot M, \tag{4}$$

$$\text{Cost}_{\text{pointwise}} = D_f^2 \cdot M \cdot N. \tag{5}$$

This formulation ensures the efficiency of the encoder, as depthwise separable convolutions allow for significant reductions in computational complexity, making it suitable for real-time applications. Each inverted residual block comprises a pointwise convolution to expand channel dimensions, a depthwise convolution for spatial processing, and another pointwise convolution to reduce dimensionality, followed by linear activation functions that ensure effective information flow. After the blocks, a global average pooling layer reduces the spatial dimensions, leading to a fully connected layer that outputs class scores corresponding to the seven facial expressions, such as happiness, sadness, and anger. The proposed deep encoder emphasizes low computational efficiency while maintaining performance. It is more feasible for real-time environments, including mobile devices for on-the-go emotion analysis, healthcare monitoring for mental health assessment, and enhancing human-computer interaction by adapting interfaces based on individuals' emotions.

2.3   Inter-annotator Reliability Assessment

An inter-annotator reliability assessment is performed between the actual and predicted annotations for facial expression. For this, 50k images are considered from FER20E [7], FER2013 [22], and AffectNet [23] datasets. A mutual matching process is employed to compare the annotations provided by each annotator utilizing conventional metrics, i.e., Cohen's kappa coefficient. It provides insight into the extent of agreement beyond what would be expected by chance alone. Cohen's kappa coefficient κ can be calculated using Eq. 6.

$$\kappa = \frac{P_o - P_e}{1 - P_e} \tag{6}$$

where P_o is the observed agreement or the proportion of agreement between the annotators. P_e is the expected agreement or the proportion of agreement expected by chance.

3   Experimental Results and Discussion

3.1   Experimental Setup and Procedure

The models were trained on an 11-GPU-powered Ubuntu server with 10 GB of graphics memory, providing the required computational power to handle deep learning tasks efficiently. The core development environment was based on Python, with the Ultralytics Python package being utilized for its built-in utilities and streamlined interface for working with YOLOv8 models. The model was configured to detect multiple distinct classes, including persons, faces, fire, and weapons. We utilized several benchmark datasets to evaluate and fine-tune the models, including FER2013 [22], FER20E [7], AffectNet [23], COCO [13], and OpenImage [24]. These datasets provided a standardized foundation to assess the accuracy and effectiveness of the model across different object detection and classification tasks.

3.2 Evaluation of YOLO-Light

To evaluate the YOLO-Light, select images with the appropriate classes were considered from both datasets, i.e., COCO and OpenImage. This combined dataset was randomly divided into training, testing, and validation sets with a ratio of 0.6:0.2:0.2. The model was trained on the training set by hyper-tuning the network parameters. The models perform better with hyperparameters, i.e., the learning rate of 0.001, a minibatch size of 128, and an Adam optimizer. The training and validation performance is shown in Fig. 3(a) and 3(b). Training losses exhibited a saturation point after approximately 90 epochs, whereas validation losses began to stabilize slightly earlier, at around 80 epochs, as depicted in Fig. 3(b).

For the efficient evaluation of YOLO-Light, 3-fold cross-validation is performed, and the average validation performance is shown in Fig. 3(b). The mean average precision (mAP) for each class is measured for two Intersections over Union (IoU) thresholds, i.e., 0.50 and 0.5 to 0.95, as shown in Fig. 3. The mAP50 obtains the mean precision for all the classes at 0.5 and provides a single score. It is relatively lenient, as it only requires 50% overlap between predicted and actual boxes for a correct prediction. While mAP50-95 offers a more comprehensive assessment of model performance, it evaluates how well the model performs across a range of 0.5 to 0.95. It is often lower than mAP50 but offers a better sense of overall model precision and robustness.

The comparative analysis with the state-of-the-art YOLO models is presented in Table 2. The customized YOLO-Light provides less computational cost and sufficient accuracy.

3.3 Evaluation of Deep Encoder

The deep encoder was trained on a combined dataset consisting of FER20E, FER2013, and AffectNet to recognize seven distinct facial expressions: Surprise,

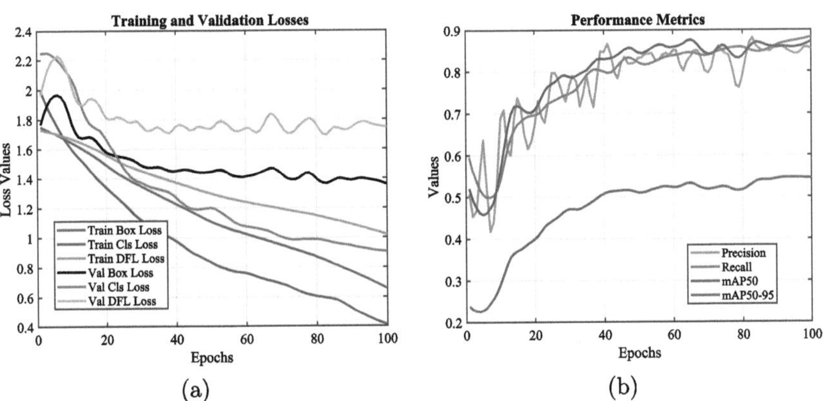

Fig. 3. (a) Loss values for training and validation data. (b) other performance metrics on the validation data.

Table 2. Performance Analysis of YOLOv8 Variants

Metric	YOLOv8					
	Light	Nano	Small	Medium	Large	Ex-Large
mAP@50	75–85%	70–78%	70–81%	73–83%	75–95%	75–95%
mAP@50–95	50–61%	42–50%	44–53%	51–59%	62–72%	62–72%
mIOU	60–67%	50–60%	52–65%	65–79%	67–81%	65–67%
Precision	70–80%	70–72%	75–77%	78–80%	82–84%	85–87%
Recall	65–75%	68–70%	73–75%	76–78%	80–82%	83–85%
F1-Score	70–80%	69–71%	74–76%	78–80%	82–84%	85–87%
FPS	140–150	140–150	120–130	80–100	50–60	30–40
Model Size	1.5 MB	6 MB	11 MB	25 MB	45 MB	90 MB

Anger, Disgust, Fear, Happy, Neutral, and Sad. This dataset was split randomly into training, testing, and validation sets with a ratio of 0.6:0.2:0.2 to evaluate model performance comprehensively. Key metrics, including precision, recall, F1-score, and Cohen's Kappa, were used to measure consistency between predicted and actual labels.

	'Surprised'	'Anger'	'Disgust'	'Fear'	'Happy'	'Neutral'	'Sad'
Surprised'	2110	8	19	456	289		19
'Anger'	11	1882	115				
'Disgust'	60	59	1724				112
'Fear'	361			2040	11	8	306
'Happy'	161				2990	26	7
'Neutral'	6	44	19	10	49	2173	8
'Sad'	21		31	290	44	8	1945

Fig. 4. Cohen's Kappa matrix for FER.

The Cohen's Kappa score, as depicted in Fig. 4, reached 0.88, indicating strong inter-annotator reliability and thus confirming the deep encoder's effectiveness. The model demonstrated robust performance, with high recognition accuracy in several categories. It correctly classified 2173 instances of Neutral and 2990 of Happy, showcasing its strong accuracy. Even in the case of Sad, the model achieved high recognition accuracy, correctly classifying 1945 instances. However, some expressions with visual similarities, particularly Surprised and Fear, presented challenges. The model misclassified 456 cases of Surprised as Fear and 361 of Fear as Surprised, while also showing minor confusion between Disgust and Anger, with 115 cases of Anger incorrectly labeled as Disgust.

With 17,422 images used in training and evaluation, the model demonstrated an overall accuracy of approximately 85.32%, as shown in the performance matrix. This analysis underscores the robustness of the deep encoder in capturing distinct emotional expressions, instilling confidence in its performance, and providing valuable insights into areas for further refinement.

Table 3. Class-wise Performance of Deep Encoder

Class	Precision (%)	Recall (%)	F1-Score (%)
Surprised	77.29	72.73	74.94
Anger	94.43	93.73	94.08
Disgust	90.36	88.18	89.26
Fear	72.96	74.83	73.89
Happy	88.38	93.91	91.06
Neutral	98.10	94.11	96.07
Sad	81.14	83.16	82.14

Table 3 presents the class-wise performance of the proposed deep encoder in terms of precision, recall, and F1-score across seven facial expression categories. The model demonstrates high accuracy for classes such as Neutral (F1-score: 96.07%), Anger (94.08%), and Happy (91.06%), indicating its strong ability to recognize these expressions reliably. Moderate performance is observed for Sad (82.14%) and Disgust (89.26%), while relatively lower F1-scores are recorded for Fear (73.89%) and Surprised (74.94%), likely due to the subtle and overlapping features associated with these emotions. Overall, the results highlight the effectiveness of the deep encoder in facial expression recognition, particularly for more distinct and frequently occurring expressions.

4   Conclusion

This paper presents a deep learning-based automatic annotation tool (DL-AAT). It is robust, adaptable, and overcomes manual annotation in large-scale, vision-based datasets. Leveraging its lightweight backbone, it offers an efficient and scalable solution for automatically annotating data across tasks such as detection, segmentation, and classification with minimal human intervention. In particular, YOLO-Light and a deep encoder are utilized for efficient evaluation of localization and classification. The performance of DL-AAT is validated on multiple benchmark datasets using various performance matrices such as Cohen's

Kappa coefficient, mAP, and different kinds of losses. The high-performance metric ensures reliability and accuracy across multiple datasets, including FER20E, FER2013, AffectNet, COCO, and OpenImage. It is a promising tool for accelerating model training and enabling more efficient deep-learning applications across various industries. Future work will also focus on expanding its adaptability to other complex annotation tasks and exploring its integration with additional datasets for broader use in vision-based applications.

References

1. Zou, Z., Chen, K., Shi, Z., Guo, Y., Ye, J.: Object detection in 20 years: a survey. Proc. IEEE **111**(3), 257–276 (2023)
2. Zhao, Y., et al.: Detrs beat YOLOs on real-time object detection. In: Proceedings of the IEEE/CVF Conference on Computer Vision and Pattern Recognition, pp. 16965–16974 (2024)
3. Yadav, K.S., Singh, S., Kumar, L.: Deep Contextual Analysis for Enhanced Suspiciousness Estimation. Authorea Preprints (2024)
4. Yadav, K.S., Singha, J.: Facial expression recognition using modified Viola-John's algorithm and KNN classifier. Multimed. Tools Appl. **79**(19), 13089–13107 (2020)
5. Alexey, B., Chien-Yao, W., Hong, Y., Mark, L.: YOLOv4: optimal speed and accuracy of object detection. arXiv preprint arXiv:2004.10934 (2020)
6. Mark, S., Andrew, H., Menglong, Z., Andrey, Z., Liang-Chieh, C.: MobileNetV2: inverted residuals and linear bottlenecks. In: Proceedings of the IEEE Conference on Computer Vision and Pattern Recognition (CVPR), pp. 4510–4520 (2018)
7. Yadav, K.S., Singh, S., Kumar, L.: FER20E: An Extended Facial Expression Recognition Dataset with 20 Discrete Emotions. Authorea Preprints (2024)
8. Jain, A., Kumar, L.: EEG cortical source feature based hand kinematics decoding using residual CNN-LSTM neural network. In: 2023 45th Annual International Conference of the IEEE Engineering in Medicine & Biology Society (EMBC), pp. 1–4 (2023)
9. Joseph, R., Ali, F.: YOLOv3: an incremental improvement. arXiv preprint arXiv:1804.02767 (2018)
10. LabelImg (2020). https://github.com/tzutalin/labelImg
11. VoTT (2020). https://github.com/microsoft/VoTT
12. LabelMe (2020). https://github.com/wkentaro/labelme
13. Lin, T.-Y., et al.: Microsoft COCO: common objects in context. In: Fleet, D., Pajdla, T., Schiele, B., Tuytelaars, T. (eds.) ECCV 2014. LNCS, vol. 8693, pp. 740–755. Springer, Cham (2014). https://doi.org/10.1007/978-3-319-10602-1_48
14. VGG Image Annotator (2019). https://www.robots.ox.ac.uk/~vgg/software/via/
15. DeepLabel (2020). https://deeplabel.com
16. CVAT (2020). https://github.com/openvinotoolkit/cvat
17. Tzutalin. LabelImg: A Graphical Image Annotation Tool and Label Object Bounding Boxes in Images (2023). https://github.com/tzutalin/labelImg. Accessed 25 Oct 2023
18. Joseph, R., Santosh, D., Ross, G., Ali, F.: You only look once: unified, real-time object detection. In: Proceedings of the IEEE Conference on Computer Vision and Pattern Recognition (CVPR), pp. 779–788 (2016)

19. Joseph, R., Ali, F.: YOLO9000: better, faster, stronger. In: Proceedings of the IEEE Conference on Computer Vision and Pattern Recognition (CVPR), pp. 7263–7271 (2017)
20. Jocher, G.: YOLOv5 by Ultralytics (2020). https://github.com/ultralytics/yolov5. Accessed 25 Oct 2023
21. Ultralytics. YOLOv8: The Next Generation of YOLO Models (2023). https://github.com/ultralytics/ultralytics. Accessed 25 Oct 2023
22. Ian, J.G., et al.: Challenges in representation learning: a report on three machine learning contests. In: Proceedings of the International Conference on Machine Learning (ICML) Workshop on Representation Learning (2013)
23. Ali, M., David, C., Mohammad, M.H.: AffectNet: a database for facial expression, valence, and arousal computing in the wild. IEEE Trans. Affect. Comput. $10(1)$, 18–31 (2017). https://doi.org/10.1109/TAFFC.2017.2740923
24. Ordonez, V., Berg, A.C., Farhadi, A.: Open images: a large scale dataset for object detection and visual relationship detection. In: Proceedings of the IEEE Conference on Computer Vision and Pattern Recognition (CVPR), pp. 4390–4399 (2018). https://doi.org/10.1109/CVPR.2018.00459

Speaker Recognition Using Kannada Language Emotional Speech Text Dependent Corpus

Rishi Mishra, Shalini Tomar[✉], and Shashidhar G. Koolagudi

Department of Computer Science and Engineering, National Institute of Technology, Surathkal, Karnataka, India
`{shalinitomar.217cs504,koolagudi}@nitk.edu.in`

Abstract. This study presents an advanced transfer learning approach for Kannada language speaker recognition in emotionally rich environments, focusing on text-dependent speech data. Emotional variability introduces significant challenges in maintaining speaker recognition accuracy due to alterations in prosodic and spectral characteristics. To address this, we extract log-Mel spectrograms from speech signals, capturing emotion-sensitive time-frequency features. A modified deep convolutional neural network architecture, VGG-24, extended from the standard VGG-19, is employed to enhance the capacity for complex feature extraction tailored to emotional speech. This modified network is fine-tuned on a curated Kannada emotional speech dataset, where speakers utter consistent phrases across various emotional states (e.g., anger, happiness, sadness). The experimental results demonstrate that our VGG-24-based system achieves superior performance compared to conventional models, particularly under emotional variability. This work underscores the potential of transfer learning with deep architectures in improving speaker recognition accuracy for low-resource languages in emotionally dynamic conditions. In the proposed work, we extracted two types of features—Mel-Frequency Cepstral Coefficients (MFCC) and Log-Mel Spectrograms—and trained separate recognition models for each. When evaluated on neutral speech, the Log-Mel Spectrogram model achieved 99.67 % accuracy, compared to 81.81 % for the MFCC model. We then tested both models across all four non-neutral emotions and found that the Log-Mel approach retained its high accuracy under expressive conditions, whereas MFCC performance dropped significantly. These findings demonstrate that Log-Mel Spectrograms more effectively preserve speaker-specific cues across emotional variations, underscoring the importance of emotion-aware feature design for robust speaker recognition in under-resourced languages.

Keywords: Speaker Recognition · Emotional Speech · Kannada Language · MFCC · Log-Mel Spectrogram · Text-Dependent · Low-Resource Languages · Advanced Transfer Learning

© The Author(s), under exclusive license to Springer Nature Switzerland AG 2026
R. K. Karsh et al. (Eds.): SIPCOV 2025, CCIS 2848, pp. 432–445, 2026.
https://doi.org/10.1007/978-3-032-15809-3_33

1   Introduction

Speaker recognition systems have become increasingly vital in various real-world applications such as biometric authentication, voice assistants, smart home control, and access security systems [1]. These systems aim to identify or verify a speaker's identity based on voice characteristics and have evolved considerably from traditional signal processing approaches to modern deep learning models. However, despite technological progress, recognition accuracy continues to degrade significantly when speech is influenced by emotions such as anger, happiness, or fear [7,9].

Emotional variations alter pitch, articulation, tempo, and spectral patterns, making speaker-specific traits harder to isolate. Research has shown that conventional speaker recognition systems, which typically perform well under neutral speech conditions, often fail to generalize across emotional variants [6,9]. Moreover, widely used datasets like TESS [6] and synthetically generated corpora such as SYNTACT [2] are primarily built for emotion classification and lack linguistic diversity, making them less suitable for speaker recognition studies in regional contexts. The problem becomes even more challenging in the case of underrepresented languages such as Kannada. Although several efforts have been made in text-independent speaker or dialect identification for Kannada [5], limited resources exist for emotional, text-dependent speaker recognition in this language. As a result, systems designed for dominant languages often cannot be directly applied to Indian regional languages without significant performance loss.

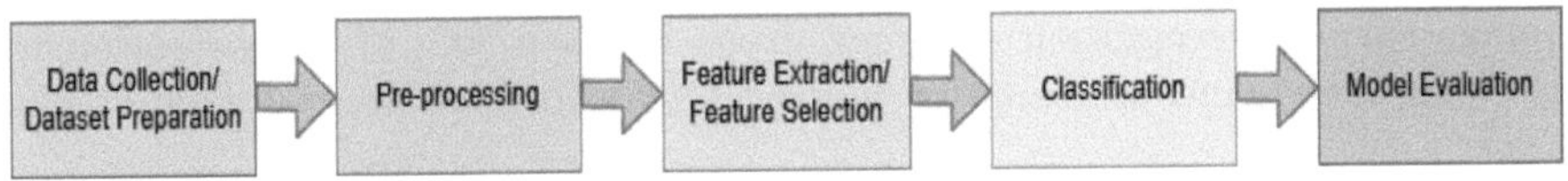

Fig. 1. Basic steps of Speaker Recognition tasks.

The Fig. 1 represents the basic steps required for Speaker Recognition. To address this gap, the NITK-KLESC dataset was developed to support speaker recognition in emotional Kannada speech. It includes utterances across five emotional categories—anger, fear, happiness, sadness, and neutral—spoken in a controlled, text-dependent manner. This kind of structured emotional data enables systematic evaluation of how feature extraction methods handle speaker variability under different affective states. Modern techniques in speaker recognition, such as convolutional neural networks (CNNs) and glottal flow modeling, have shown promise in extracting robust speaker embeddings [3]. Among acoustic features, log-Mel spectrograms have gained attention for retaining richer spectral content compared to traditional Mel-Frequency Cepstral Coefficients (MFCC), making them more suitable for handling emotionally expressive speech. Motivated by these findings, this work investigates and compares MFCC and log-Mel spectrogram features for building an effective text-dependent speaker recognition system in Kannada using the NITK-KLESC dataset. The aim is to explore the impact of emotion on speaker identification accuracy and evaluate how different acoustic representations can mitigate the performance drop commonly observed in expressive speech. The findings of this study are expected to contribute toward the development of emotion-resilient speaker recognition systems for low-resource languages, with applications in multilingual and affective computing environments.

2   Related Work

Speaker recognition systems typically assume consistent vocal characteristics, but emotional speech can significantly alter these characteristics and degrade recognition performance. Emotional variability introduces changes in pitch, timbre, speaking rate, and glottal excitation patterns, which pose challenges for speaker recognition. Several studies have quantified this degradation. For example, Koolagudi et al. [9] showed that when models are trained on neutral speech and tested on emotional speech, speaker identification accuracy drops markedly, with anger and happy utterances causing the worst performance declines. These works underscore that emotional state shifts can be as detrimental as channel or noise mismatch in speaker recognition systems.

Emotional variability is thus recognized as a significant challenge for robust speaker recognition. The voice changes induced by emotion are often speaker-dependent and non-uniform. This variability complicates the task of distinguishing speaker identity from emotional content. Koolagudi et al. [8] reported that average speaker recognition accuracy drops by over 20% in cross-emotion trials. The performance degradation is most severe for high-arousal emotions like anger.

To address these issues, researchers have explored various acoustic features. Mel-Frequency Cepstral Coefficients (MFCCs) have long been the standard for speaker recognition due to their compact representation of spectral characteristics. Tomar and Koolagudi [13] employed MFCCs with a CNN model and achieved 92.8% accuracy on Kannada blended emotional speech. However, MFCCs tend to lose fine-grained frequency information. Log-Mel spectrograms, which retain more detailed time-frequency information, have shown superior performance in many emotion-related speech tasks [11]. Tomar et al. [12] utilized both MFCC and log-Mel features for speaker identification using the NITK-KLESC dataset and demonstrated improved performance with richer features.

Beyond MFCC and log-Mel, features derived from glottal flow, such as Linear Prediction Residual Cepstral Coefficients (LPRCCs), have also been explored. While these capture vocal source characteristics, they are often susceptible to emotional state and may degrade more under variability [9]. Comparatively, MFCCs and LPCCs have shown relatively better robustness under emotional mismatch. In terms of datasets, the NITK-KLESC corpus [12] is a significant contribution to emotional speech research in Kannada. It provides recordings of five emotional classes, including blended emotion types. The CNN-MFCC model tested on this dataset achieved 99.3% on neutral speech and 92.8% on blended emotion conditions, illustrating the challenges and progress in Kannada speaker recognition. While datasets like TESS [6] and SYNTACT [2] have supported emotion research in English, they lack speaker recognition focus and are linguistically limited for Indian applications.

3   Research Gap

While significant progress has been made in building emotion-aware speaker recognition systems, a considerable gap remains in achieving consistently high accuracy across all emotional conditions. Current models demonstrate excellent performance for neutral speech recognition, as evidenced by accuracies approaching 95% in text-dependent Kannada datasets (NITK-KLESC), but suffer noticeable degradation when identifying speakers in emotional states such as anger, fear, happy, and sad. This performance drop highlights the limitations of existing acoustic features and models in capturing emotion-invariant speaker characteristics.

Most Kannada-based emotional speaker recognition studies, including those utilizing the NITK-KLESC dataset, have focused on baseline MFCC or CNN approaches, which, while effective for neutral speech, do not fully address the challenges of emotionally expressive speech. There is a need for improved methods that can maintain or enhance recognition accuracy under such variability, particularly for high-arousal emotions like anger and fear.

The research gap, therefore, lies in developing and optimising speaker recognition systems that not only maintain high accuracy for neutral utterances but also significantly improve identification accuracy across emotionally charged conditions. This includes exploring hybrid feature sets, adaptive learning frameworks, and deeper fusion strategies capable of handling the expressive range of emotional speech in low-resource languages like Kannada.

4   Proposed Methodology

Traditional speaker recognition systems are designed to identify individuals based on unique vocal characteristics present in their speech. These systems generally follow a standard pipeline consisting of three stages: (i) **feature extraction**, where acoustic features such as MFCCs or PLPs are computed from the speech signal; (ii) **speaker modeling**, where extracted features are encoded into speaker-specific representations using methods like Gaussian Mixture Models (GMM), i-vectors, or deep neural networks; and (iii) **classification**, where the speaker identity is predicted based on similarity or distance from known speaker models. While effective in controlled environments and for neutral speech, these systems often fail to maintain accuracy when emotional variability significantly alters the acoustic characteristics of speech. An overview of this typical speaker recognition process is illustrated in Fig. 2. The proposed speaker recognition framework addresses the challenges of emotional variability in text-dependent Kannada speech. Emotional states like anger, fear, happiness, and sadness introduce acoustic distortions (e.g., pitch shifts, prosodic changes) that hinder traditional models assuming neutral speech. To mitigate this, a robust muleline is designed comprising silence removal, data augmentation, and dual-feature extraction (MFCCs and Log-Mel Spectrograms). These features capture both cepstral and time-frequency details. A modified VGG-19 architecture, extended to VGG-24 with additional convolutional layers, is employed for classification. This approach enhances speaker recognition accuracy across both neutral and emotional speech, making it suitable for real-world, low-resource language scenarios like Kannada. The overall architecture and flow of the system are illustrated in Fig. 3, which outlines each component of the methodology from raw audio input to final speaker classification.

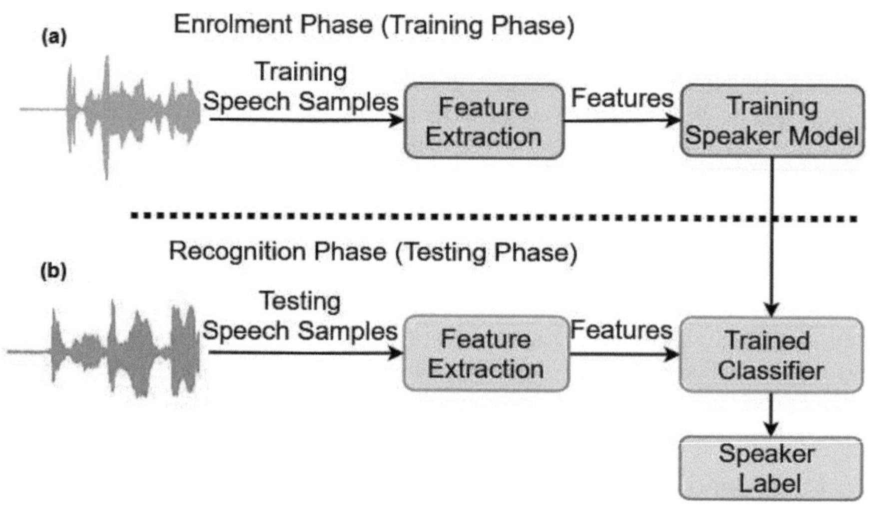

Fig. 2. The illustration of a typical Speaker Recognition System [14].

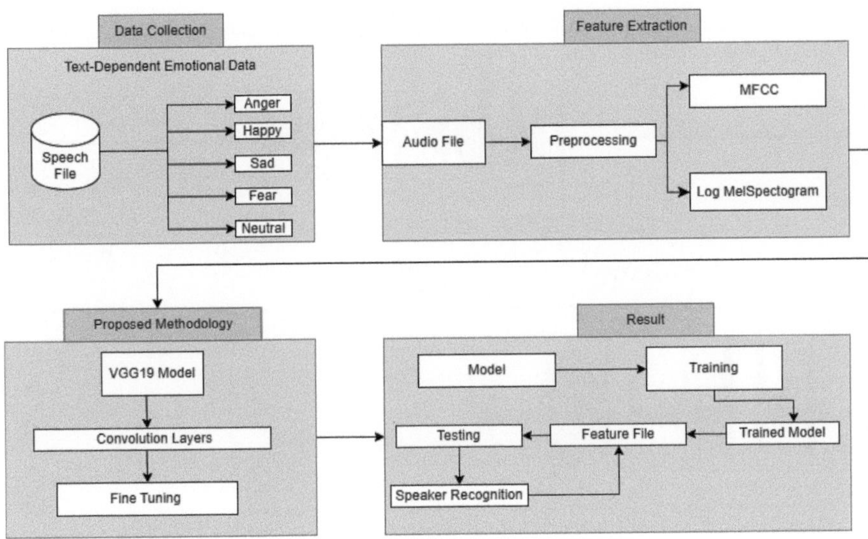

Fig. 3. Overview of the Proposed Speaker Recognition System.

4.1   Dataset Details

This study utilizes a subset of the NITK-KLESC emotional speech corpus [12], comprising recordings from 30 speakers across five emotions: **Neutral**, **Anger**, **Happy**, **Sad**, and **Fear**. Each speaker utters the same ten fixed Kannada phrases per emotion, preserving the text-dependent nature of the task. This results in 50 utterances per speaker and a total of 1500 high-quality audio samples, recorded at 16 kHz in a studio environment. To validate the results, we also used the RAVDESS [10] and CREMA-D [4] Emotional Speech dataset.

4.2   Preprocessing

To enhance model performance, a two-stage preprocessing strategy was employed on the raw audio signals, involving silence removal and data augmentation.

Silence Removal. Silence segments, typically present at the beginning and end of recordings, were removed using a Short-Time Energy (STE)-based approach. Audio was divided into 10-ms frames, and frames with energy below a 40-dB threshold were discarded. This ensured the retention of only active speech segments, reducing variability and improving feature extraction (Fig. 4).

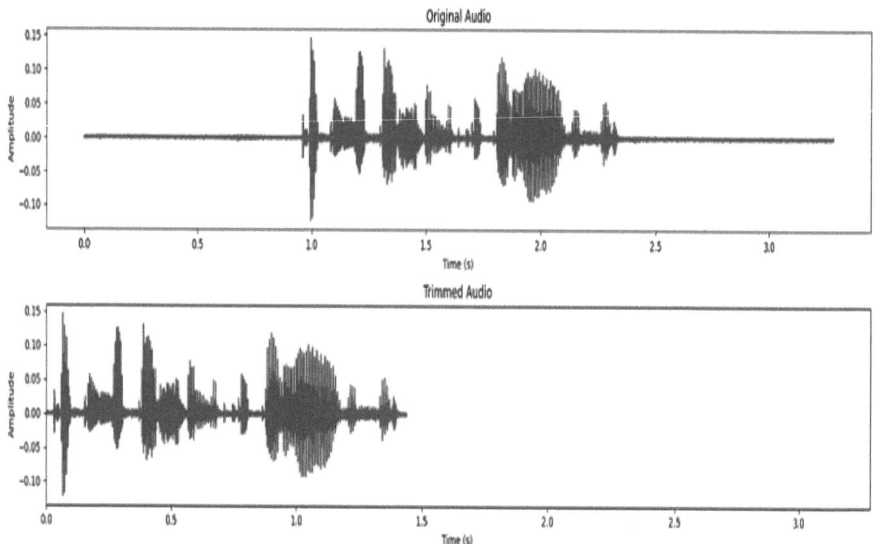

Fig. 4. Audio signal before and after silence removal.

4.3   Data Augmentation

To improve data diversity and generalization, four augmentations were applied:
(1) **Time Shifting** (±0.2 s), (2) **Pitch Shifting** (±2 semitones), (3) **Noise Injection** (20 dB SNR), and (4) **Time Stretching** ($0.9\times$, $1.1\times$). These simulate real-world variations while preserving speaker identity.

4.4   Feature Extraction

Two complementary acoustic features were used to capture speaker-specific information: **MFCC** and **Mel Log Spectrograms**. These features provide robust spectral and temporal representations, essential for speaker recognition under emotional variability.

Mel Frequency Cepstral Coefficients (MFCC). MFCC features emphasize human auditory perception by emphasizing lower frequencies and compressing higher ones. Each Audio was framed (25 ms, 10 ms hop), transformed via FFT, passed through a 40-filter Mel filter bank, log-compressed, and finally decorrelated using DCT. The first 13 coefficients were retained to represent the spectral envelope shown in Fig. 5.

Mel Log Spectrogram. Mel Log Spectrograms offer high-resolution 2D time-frequency representations, making them ideal for CNN-based models. Unlike MFCCs, they preserve detailed spectro-temporal information shown in Fig. 6.

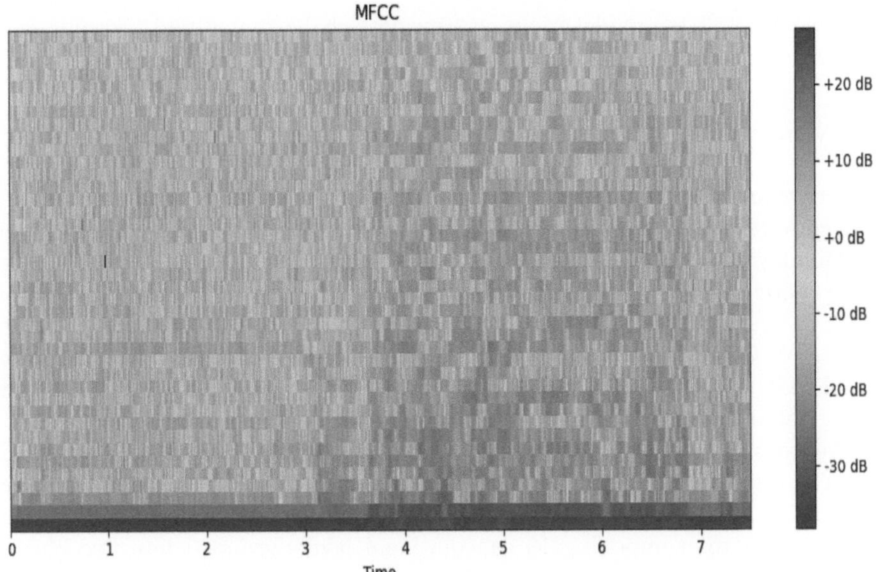

Fig. 5. MFCC feature representation of an emotional speech sample.

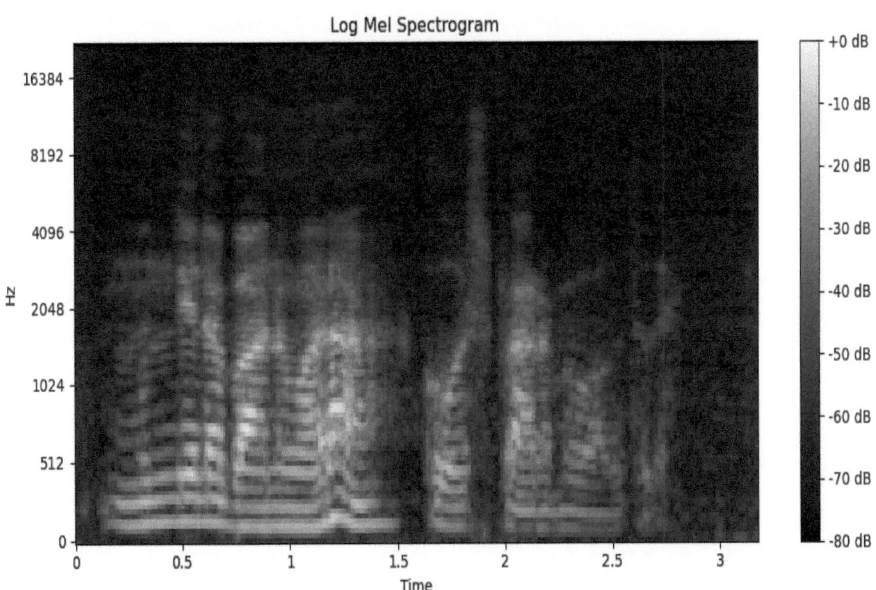

Fig. 6. Mel Log Spectrogram of an emotional utterance.

Extraction involves: (1) appying Short-Time Fourier Transform (STFT), (2) passing the magnitude spectrogram through 128 Mel-scaled filters, and (3) converting to a logarithmic (dB) scale. The resulting spectrogram is resized to

224 × **224** × **3** for model input, capturing rich harmonic and prosodic cues essential for speaker recognition under emotional variation.

5   Model Architecture

To perform robust classification of speaker identities across emotional variants, a deep convolutional neural network (CNN) architecture was employed, built upon the foundation of the well-established **VGG-19** model. VGG-19 is known for its uniform architecture, deep representation capabilities, and strong generalization power in image-based tasks. It is well-suited for handling spectrogram-like inputs such as MFCC and Mel Log Spectrogram features. Below is a typical depiction of the VGG-19 architecture as shown in Fig. 7, illustrating its hierarchical convolutional and pooling layers.

We extend the VGG-19 model to a custom **VGG-24** by adding five convolutional layers to better capture speaker-specific and emotional variations in spectrogram inputs. The base VGG-19, pretrained on ImageNet, serves as a frozen feature extractor comprising 16 convolutional layers grouped into five blocks, each followed by max pooling. The additional convolutional layers refine higher-level abstractions. A custom classification head follows, consisting of five dense layers with Leaky ReLU, batch normalization, and dropout, culminating in a softmax output. A 128-dimensional embedding layer captures speaker identity prior to final classification.

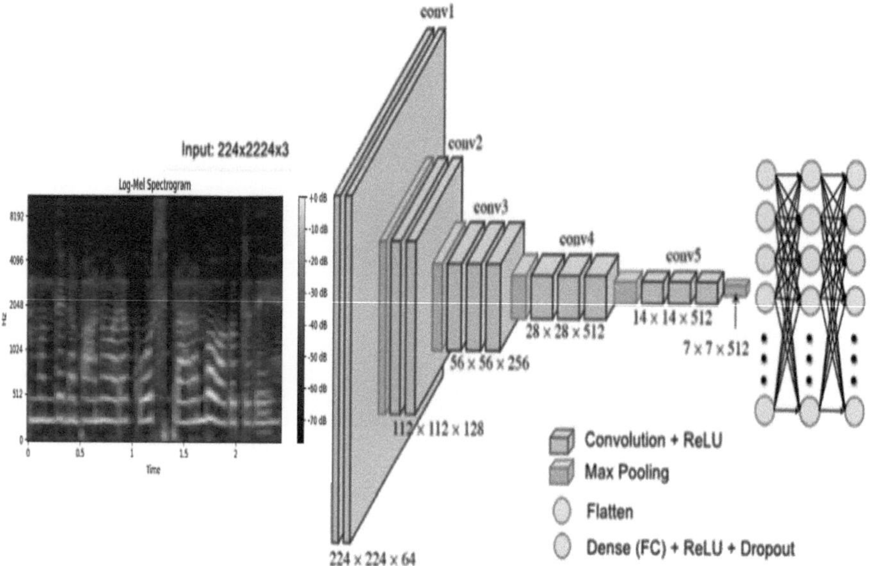

Fig. 7. Proposed Customized VGG-24 Model Architecture.

5.1   Training and Fine-Tuning

The model was first trained on neutral speech from the NITK-KLESC dataset
to stabilize learning, then fine-tuned on all five emotions (neutral, anger, happy,
sad, fear) for robustness across emotional variations. **Training Details:**

- Optimizer: `Adam`, LR = 0.0001
- Loss: Categorical Cross-Entropy
- Input: 224 × 224 × 3 (MFCC/Log-Mel)
- Callbacks: `ReduceLROnPlateau` (factor 0.3, patience 2), `EarlyStopping` (patience 7)

Fine-Tuning: Only `block5` and `block4_conv3` layers of VGG-19 were unfrozen
to adapt higher-level features to emotional speech while preventing overfitting; the rest remained frozen. This selective tuning improves emotion-invariant
speaker representation and boosts recognition accuracy under varied emotional
conditions.

6   Experimental Results and Analysis

This section evaluates the performance of the proposed speaker recognition system across five emotional categories—Neutral, Anger, Happy, Sad, and Fear—
using two feature extraction methods: MFCC and Log-Mel Spectrograms. The
test set, derived from the NITK-KLESC dataset, was balanced across all emotions. Accuracy was used as the primary metric. As shown in Table 1, Log-Mel
Spectrograms consistently outperform MFCCs across all emotions, particularly
under high-arousal conditions like Anger and Fear. Under the VGG-19 architecture, accuracies for MFCC range from 29.34% (Anger) to 64.75% (Sad), while
Log-Mel features perform better in most cases. With the deeper VGG-24 model,
recognition improves substantially, with Log-Mel features reaching up to 99.67%
for Neutral and showing significant gains across all emotions. The results highlight that Log-Mel Spectrograms offer superior robustness in emotionally variable
conditions and that deeper models like VGG-24 better capture speaker-specific
patterns from expressive speech. On average, Log-Mel Spectrograms yield a 20–
25% improvement over MFCCs across emotional categories. To assess the learning progression of the VGG-24-based speaker recognition model, training was
conducted in two phases: initial training on neutral speech (epochs 1–50) and
fine-tuning with emotional data (epochs 51–75) using a reduced learning rate.

Table 1. Speaker Recognition Accuracy by Emotion and Feature Type for VGG-19 and VGG-24 Models

Emotion	VGG-19		VGG-24	
	MFCC	Log-Mel Spectrogram	MFCC	Log-Mel Spectrogram
Neutral	60.75%	80.20%	81.81%	99.67%
Anger	29.34%	23.47%	59.44%	73.09%
Happy	59.23%	71.89%	77.89%	82.14%
Sad	64.75%	44.82%	75.50%	89.63%
Fear	38.13%	39.20%	68.43%	78.93%

6.1   Accuracy and Loss Trends

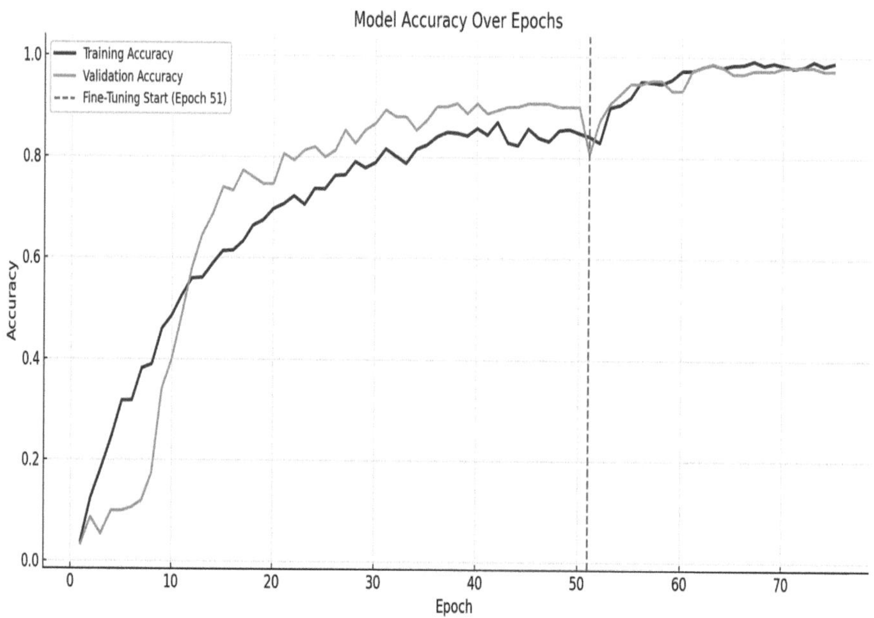

Fig. 8. Training and Validation Accuracy across Epochs.

Figure 8 and Fig. 9 show the accuracy and loss curves. Validation accuracy rose from 3.33% to 90.67% during initial training, and further improved to 98.67% after fine-tuning. Training accuracy peaked at 99.24%, indicating strong convergence. The validation loss dropped from 3.4 to 0.1210, with training loss reducing from over 4.0 to below 0.3, showing effective learning without overfitting. Fine-tuning at epoch 51 notably enhanced generalization to emotional variants. Using the NITK-KLESC dataset, the average accuracy for speaker recognition is 84.5%. On

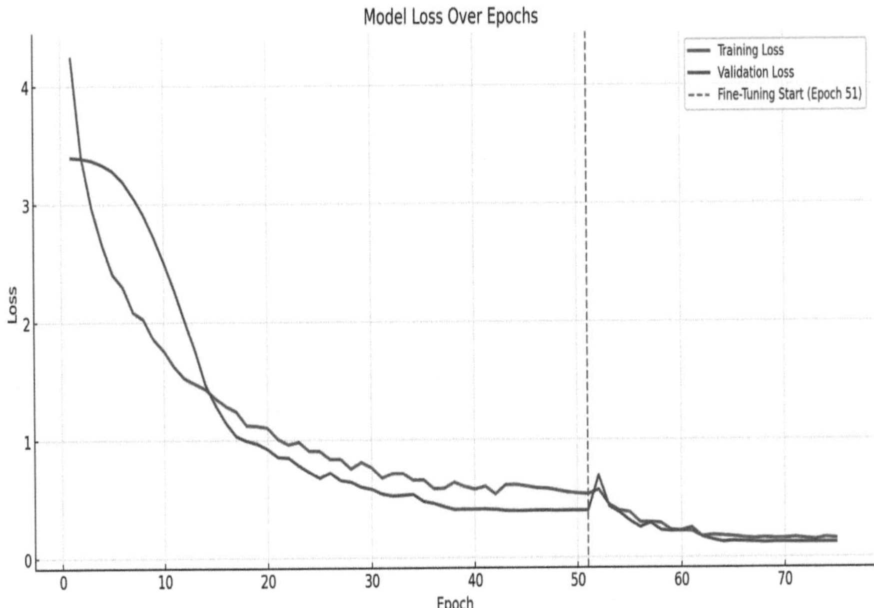

Fig. 9. Training and Validation Loss across Epochs.

the other hand, the average accuracy for Speaker Recognition is 84% and 84.4% for the RAVDESS and CREMA-D datasets, respectively. The results confirm the importance of fine-tuning and deep feature adaptation for emotion-aware speaker recognition. Minimal gap between training and validation metrics indicates robust generalization under emotional variability. The results highlight a clear advantage of Log-Mel Spectrograms over MFCCs across all emotional conditions. While MFCCs achieve 81.81% accuracy under neutral speech, their performance drops sharply under emotional stress—down to 29.34% for anger and 38.13% for fear—indicating sensitivity to acoustic variability. Log-Mel Spectrograms, by preserving detailed time-frequency structures, offer greater resilience and improve accuracy by over 20% in emotions like happiness and sadness. Unlike MFCCs, which compress spectral details via DCT, Log-Mel features retain localized patterns crucial for speaker discrimination under emotional variation. These findings underscore the importance of feature choice in emotion-aware speaker recognition. Log-Mel Spectrograms, paired with deep models, provide more robust and accurate performance across diverse emotional states.

From the results, several key insights emerge:

1. Superior Performance of Log-Mel Spectrograms with VGG-24: Log-Mel Spectrograms combined with the deeper VGG-24 model consistently yielded the highest recognition accuracy across all emotions, achieving a peak accuracy of 99.67% in the neutral condition. This suggests that Log-Mel Spectrograms are more expressive in capturing the nuanced characteristics of emotional speech, especially when paired with a deeper network.

2. Significant Gains in High-Arousal Emotions: Emotions such as Anger and Fear, which are typically more variable and acoustically intense, showed marked improvements when using VGG-24 with Log-Mel features—73.09% and 78.93%, respectively—compared to MFCC-based models. This highlights the robustness of spectrogram-based representations in high-arousal contexts.
3. Improvement Over VGG-19: The deeper VGG-24 model outperformed VGG-19 across both feature sets, indicating that increased model capacity contributes to better generalization and feature extraction in emotionally expressive speech.
4. MFCCs vs. Log-Mel Spectrograms: While MFCCs performed reasonably well in some conditions (e.g., Sad with 75.50% in VGG-24), they were generally outperformed by Log-Mel Spectrograms in the same model, reaffirming the latter's suitability for deep learning-based speaker recognition in emotional settings.

These results validate the importance of both model architecture and acoustic feature selection in designing effective speaker recognition systems. The findings particularly emphasize the advantage of spectrogram-based features when handling emotional variability in speech.

7   Conclusion

This study presents a deep learning-based speaker recognition system tailored for text-dependent emotional speech in Kannada, utilizing the NITK-KLESC dataset. Two prominent acoustic features—Mel-Frequency Cepstral Coefficients (MFCCs) and Log-Mel Spectrograms—were systematically evaluated across five emotional states: Neutral, Anger, Happiness, Sadness, and Fear. The results demonstrate that Log-Mel Spectrograms consistently outperform MFCCs, particularly in high-arousal emotional conditions such as anger and fear. Notably, the system achieved up to 99.67% accuracy in neutral speech and exhibited a 15–25% improvement in emotionally expressive scenarios. These findings underscore the effectiveness of spectrogram-based deep learning models in emotion-rich environments, emphasizing the critical role of feature selection in speaker recognition performance. Future research directions include the development of emotion-invariant speaker embeddings, expansion of datasets to enhance generalization, incorporation of multimodal inputs, optimization for real-time applications, and the design of emotion-aware calibration mechanisms. Overall, this work advances the field toward more robust and inclusive speaker recognition systems, particularly for low-resource languages like Kannada.

References

1. Biagetti, G., Crippa, P., Falaschetti, L., Orcioni, S., Turchetti, C.: Distributed speech and speaker identification system for personalized domotic control. In: Conti, M., Martínez Madrid, N., Seepold, R., Orcioni, S. (eds.) Mobile Networks for Biometric Data Analysis. LNEE, vol. 392, pp. 159–170. Springer, Cham (2016). https://doi.org/10.1007/978-3-319-39700-9_13

2. Burkhardt, F., Eyben, F., Schuller, B.: Syntact: a synthesized database of basic emotions. In: Proceedings of the Workshop on Dataset Creation for Lower-Resourced Languages within the 13th Language Resources and Evaluation Conference, pp. 1–9 (2022)
3. Camarena-Ibarrola, A., Ruiz-Gaona, E., Figueroa, K.: Text-independent speaker identification with glottal flow and 1D convolutional neural networks. In: Mexican Conference on Pattern Recognition, pp. 287–296. Springer, Cham (2024)
4. Cao, H., Cooper, D.G., Keutmann, M.K., Gur, R.C., Nenkova, A., Verma, R.: Crema-D: crowd-sourced emotional multimodal actors dataset. IEEE Trans. Affect. Comput. **5**, 377–390 (2014)
5. Chittaragi, N.B., Limaye, A., Chandana, N.T., Annappa, B., Koolagudi, S.G.: Automatic text-independent Kannada dialect identification system. In: Satapathy, S.C., Bhateja, V., Somanah, R., Yang, X.-S., Senkerik, R. (eds.) Information Systems Design and Intelligent Applications. AISC, vol. 863, pp. 79–87. Springer, Singapore (2019). https://doi.org/10.1007/978-981-13-3338-5_8
6. Dupuis, K., Pichora-Fuller, M.K.: Toronto emotional speech set (tess)-younger talker_neutral (2010)
7. Kabir, M.M., Mridha, M.F., Shin, J., Jahan, I., Ohi, A.Q.: A survey of speaker recognition: fundamental theories, recognition methods and opportunities. IEEE Access **9**, 79236–79263 (2021)
8. Koolagudi, S.G., Maity, S., Kumar, V.A., Chakrabarti, S., Rao, K.S.: IITKGP-SESC: speech database for emotion analysis. In: Ranka, S., et al. (eds.) IC3 2009. CCIS, vol. 40, pp. 485–492. Springer, Heidelberg (2009). https://doi.org/10.1007/978-3-642-03547-0_46
9. Koolagudi, S.G., Sharma, K., Sreenivasa Rao, K.: Speaker recognition in emotional environment. In: Mathew, J., Patra, P., Pradhan, D.K., Kuttyamma, A.J. (eds.) ICECCS 2012. CCIS, vol. 305, pp. 117–124. Springer, Heidelberg (2012). https://doi.org/10.1007/978-3-642-32112-2_15
10. Livingstone, S.R., Russo, F.A.: The Ryerson Audio-Visual Database of Emotional Speech and Song (RAVDESS): a dynamic, multimodal set of facial and vocal expressions in North American English. PLoS ONE **13**, 1–15 (2018)
11. Meghanani, A., Anoop, C.S., Ramakrishnan, A.: An exploration of log-mel spectrogram and MFCC features for Alzheimer's dementia recognition from spontaneous speech. In: 2021 IEEE spoken Language Technology Workshop (SLT), pp. 670–677. IEEE (2021)
12. Tomar, S., Gupta, P., Koolagudi, S.G.: Nitk-klesc: Kannada language emotional speech corpus for speaker recognition. In: 2023 26th Conference of the Oriental COCOSDA International Committee for the Co-ordination and Standardisation of Speech Databases and Assessment Techniques (O-COCOSDA), pp. 1–6. IEEE (2023)
13. Tomar, S., Koolagudi, S.G.: CNN-MFCC model for speaker recognition using emotive speech. In: 2023 IEEE 8th International Conference for Convergence in Technology (I2CT), pp. 1–7. IEEE (2023)
14. Tomar, S., Koolagudi, S.G.: Blended-emotional speech for speaker recognition by using the fusion of mel-cqt spectrograms feature extraction. Expert Syst. Appl. **276**, 1–13 (2025)

Resource-Conscious Predictive Load Balancing (RCP-LB) for Single Board Computers (SBC) Using Support Vector Machines (SVM)

M. W. P. Maduranga[1]([✉]), Sandamini Neththikumara[2], Nethshan Narasinghe[3], H. K. I. S. Lakmal[4], and Sabyasachi Bhattacharyya[5,6]

[1] Department of Electrical and Electronic Engineering, University of Sri Jayewardenepura, Colombo, Sri Lanka
pasanm@sjp.ac.lk
[2] HAMK University of Applied Sciences, Hämeenlinna, Finland
[3] University of North Dakota, Grand Forks, ND, USA
[4] Department of Mechatronic & Industrial Engineering, NSBM Green University, Homagama, Sri Lanka
[5] Department of Electronics and Telecommunication Engineering, Batao Valley Engineering College, Sribhumi, Assam, India
[6] Department of Electronics and Telecommunication Engineering, Residential Girls' Polytechnic, Golaghat, Assam, India

Abstract. The widespread adoption of edge computing and Internet of Things (IoT) applications has significantly increased the demand for efficient task scheduling in resource-constrained environments. These environments often rely on low-power, cost-effective hardware, making it challenging to maintain optimal performance while managing computational workloads. Traditional load-balancing approaches, such as round robin and least-loaded strategies, frequently struggle to optimize resource allocation in distributed systems with limited processing power, such as Raspberry Pi clusters. These conventional methods often fail to adapt dynamically to fluctuating workloads, leading to inefficient resource utilization, increased response times, and potential system bottlenecks. To address these challenges, this research introduces a novel Resource Conscious Predictive Load Balancing (RCP-LB) framework, which leverages machine learning techniques to enhance task allocation efficiency. Specifically, the framework employs Support Vector Machines (SVM) to analyze real-time CPU and memory usage data, enabling the system to predict the optimal task allocation dynamically. By proactively distributing workloads based on resource availability, the proposed approach reduces latency, improves response times, and maximizes overall system performance. Comprehensive performance evaluations compare RCP-LB with traditional load-balancing techniques, demonstrating its superior efficiency, scalability, and adaptability in handling dynamic workloads. The experimental results indicate that the RCP-LB framework significantly enhances system responsiveness and resource efficiency, making it particularly well-suited for real-time IoT applications and edge computing environments. By providing a robust, intelligent, and resource-aware task scheduling mechanism, this research contributes to the advancement of distributed computing frameworks, offering a practical and effective solution for modern, re-source-constrained systems.

© The Author(s), under exclusive license to Springer Nature Switzerland AG 2026
R. K. Karsh et al. (Eds.): SIPCOV 2025, CCIS 2848, pp. 446–458, 2026.
https://doi.org/10.1007/978-3-032-15809-3_34

Keywords: Raspberry pi · Internet of Things · Single Board Computing · Machine Learning · Load Balancing · Task Scheduling · Edge Computing

1 Introduction

The growing reliance on low-power computing devices for various applications, including Internet of Things (IoT) deployments and edge computing, has led to an increasing demand for efficient task scheduling in resource-constrained environments. These environments often utilize single-board computers (SBCs), such as Raspberry Pi, which offer cost-effective solutions for distributed computing. However, their inherently limited processing power, memory, and energy efficiency present significant challenges in achieving optimal load balancing and maintaining high system performance. Efficient resource allocation is crucial for ensuring seamless task execution, reducing latency, and preventing system bottlenecks.

Traditional static and heuristic-based scheduling methods, including round robin and least-loaded strategies, often fail to account for real-time fluctuations in CPU and memory usage. As a result, they struggle to distribute workloads effectively, leading to inefficient resource utilization, increased response times, and potential system instability under dynamic conditions. To address these limitations, this research introduces a novel Resource-Conscious Predictive Load Balancing (RCP-LB) framework, designed to enhance task allocation in distributed computing environments.

RCP-LB leverages machine learning techniques, specifically Support Vector Machines (SVM), to predict workload distribution dynamically based on real time system metrics. Unlike conventional methods that rely on predefined rules or reactive adjustments, the proposed approach utilizes historical and real-time data to make proactive decisions about task scheduling. By continuously analyzing CPU and memory usage patterns, RCP-LB optimizes resource distribution, ensuring faster response times, improved system throughput, and more balanced CPU utilization across nodes.

Comprehensive experiments and performance evaluations demonstrate the effectiveness of RCP-LB compared to traditional scheduling strategies. The results highlight its ability to enhance efficiency, scalability, and adaptability in resource-sensitive computing environments. By integrating intelligent prediction models into balancing mechanisms, this research contributes to the advancement of modern distributed computing frameworks [4], offering robust and adaptive solutions for resource-aware task management.

2 Related Works

The emergence of edge and fog computing has redefined the computational landscape by decentralizing data processing and enabling real-time analytics close to the data source. Shi et al. emphasize the vision and challenges of edge computing, highlighting its role in reducing latency and bandwidth usage in Internet of Things (IoT) applications, which aligns with the motivation behind RCP-LB for enhancing task allocation in constrained environments [2]. Similarly, Satyanarayanan underlines the criticality of edge computing in supporting latency-sensitive applications, particularly in resource-limited environments such as those powered by single-board computers (SBCs) [8]. These studies reinforce the necessity of intelligent, low-latency decision-making systems like RCP-LB in edge environments, where computing power is limited but real-time response is paramount.

Several researchers have proposed frameworks for enhancing computing efficiency in distributed edge and fog systems, emphasizing dynamic resource management. Gai et al. introduced a dynamic, energy-aware cloudlet model for mobile cloud computing, showcasing the advantages of predictive scheduling in green computing environments [1]. In a similar vein, Bittencourt et al. and Gu et al. explored mobility-aware application scheduling and cost-efficient resource management in fog-supported systems, respectively, both advocating adaptive and predictive models that respond to fluctuating workloads [10, 11]. The RCP-LB framework leverages Support Vector Machines (SVMs) in a similar predictive capacity, dynamically optimizing task distribution across SBC nodes based on real-time CPU and memory metrics, thus extending these foundational approaches to low-power hardware.

Moreover, research by Al-Fuqaha et al. and Taleb et al. provides valuable in-sights into enabling technologies and orchestration strategies for IoT and 5G driven multi-access edge computing systems, underscoring the demand for intelligent orchestration across diverse edge nodes [3, 7]. Varghese and Buyya further project future trends in cloud and edge computing, calling for next-generation scheduling strategies that are both intelligent and lightweight [4]. These insights support the relevance and timeliness of the RCP-LB framework, which integrates lightweight machine learning with system-level monitoring to create an adaptable and scalable load balancing solution. The research not only aligns with but also builds upon these existing contributions by offering a practical implementation tailored for SBC clusters, demonstrating improved responsiveness and resource efficiency in edge environments.

3   Experimental Setup

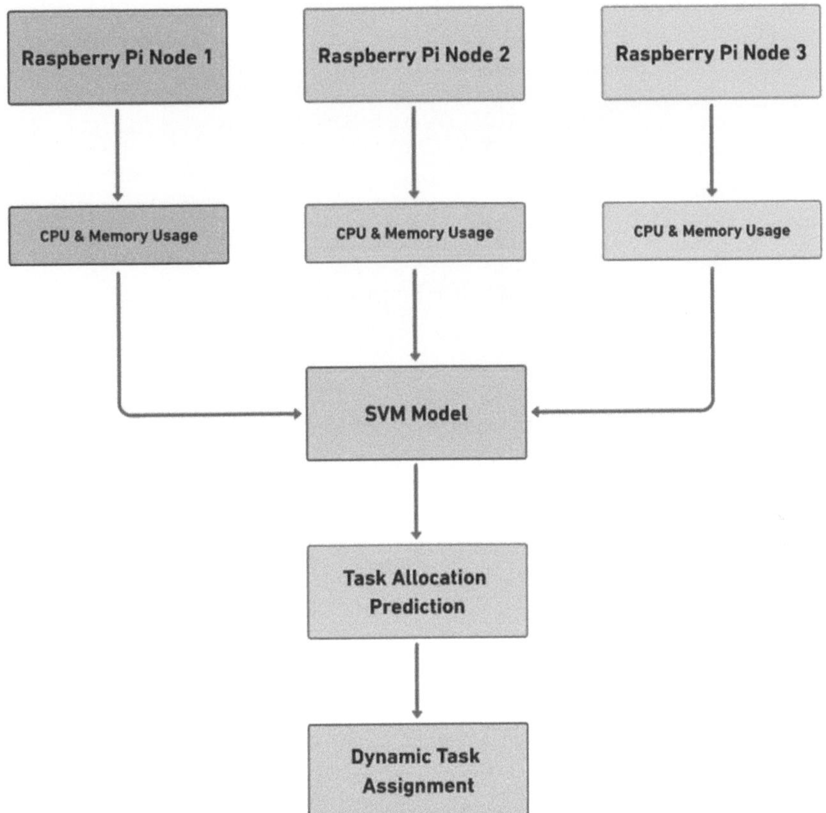

Fig. 1. Architecture of the RCP-LB framework. CPU and memory usage data from Raspberry Pi nodes are analyzed by an SVM model to predict optimal task allocation, enabling dynamic task assignment across the cluster.

The diagram illustrates a dynamic task assignment system designed for a distributed network of Raspberry Pi nodes. It begins with three individual nodes Rasp-berry Pi Node 1, Node 2, and Node 3 each responsible for monitoring its own resource usage. Specifically, each node tracks its CPU and memory usage, which are critical parameters for assessing the load on the system (Fig. 1).

The resource usage data collected from all three nodes is then fed into a machine learning model specifically, a Support Vector Machine (SVM) model. This model is trained to analyze the incoming data and make predictions about optimal task distribution based on the current system conditions.

Once the SVM model processes the data, it generates a task allocation prediction. This prediction indicates how tasks should be distributed across the Rasp-berry Pi nodes to ensure balanced load and efficient resource usage. Finally, the system performs dynamic task assignment based on the model's prediction. This allows for intelligent, real-time adjustments in task distribution, enabling improved performance, reduced bottlenecks, and efficient use of the available computing resources within the Raspberry Pi network (Fig. 2).

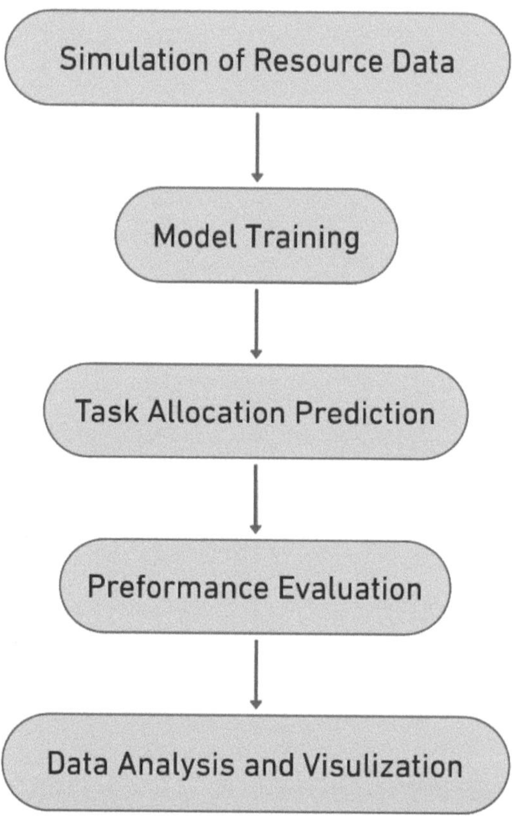

Fig. 2. Workflow of the RCP-LB framework development process, including resource data simulation, model training, task allocation prediction, performance evaluation, and final data analysis and visualization.

3.1 Simulation of Resource Data

To initiate our experiment, we simulated real-time resource usage data for three Raspberry Pi nodes, each acting as an individual processing unit within a distributed computing cluster. The primary goal of this simulation was to replicate realistic operating conditions in a controlled environment. For this purpose, we generated CPU and memory usage values for each node over a series of 100-time steps. The data was modeled using a normal (Gaussian) distribution to closely resemble the natural fluctuations observed in actual hardware performance.

The CPU usage simulation was carefully designed to reflect varying operational loads, such as those encountered during task execution, idling, and brief spikes in activity. Similarly, the memory usage values were constrained within reasonable, system-appropriate limits to simulate how memory would typically be consumed during processing. Together, these parameters produced a dynamic dataset that captured the nuances of resource behavior over time.

By feeding the model with this simulated data, we enabled it to learn patterns and make predictions regarding optimal task allocation under varying resource conditions. This step was essential in laying the foundation for intelligent task distribution across the Raspberry Pi cluster.

3.2　Model Selection Rationale

Support for the Model Selection Rationale Because of their ability to handle small to medium-sized datasets with a distinct margin of separation, support vector machines (SVM) were selected. Relevant to this study, SVMs are also renowned for their resilience to overfitting, particularly in high-dimensional feature spaces.

We conducted an initial comparison with other classifiers, such as Decision Trees and a lightweight Multi-Layer Perceptron (MLP), to make sure SVM was appropriate. In terms of average F1-score and more consistent behavior across classes, the SVM performed better. Table X provides a summary of this ablation.

3.3　Model Training

To predict the most suitable node for task allocation, we employed a Support Vector Machine (SVM) classifier trained in simulated historical resource usage data. The input features included CPU and memory usage values from each Raspberry Pi node, while the output labels indicated which node was the best choice for handling a task under those conditions. This allowed the model to learn patterns in system performance and make informed decisions based on current resource availability.

Since the task involved selecting one out of three nodes, we used the Erro Correcting Output Codes (ECOC) strategy to adapt the SVM for multi-class classification. ECOC breaks the problem into multiple binary classification tasks, allowing the SVM to effectively differentiate between the available nodes.

To ensure the model performed well across different scenarios, we applied cross-validation to fine-tune the SVM's hyperparameters, such as the kernel type and regularization strength. This process helped improve the model's robustness and accuracy, making it capable of predicting the optimal node in real time based on live resource data.

3.4　Task Allocation Prediction

After successfully training the Support Vector Machine (SVM) model, we proceeded to evaluate its performance in a dynamic, real-time scenario. In this phase, we simulated the arrival of new computational tasks, each characterized by specific CPU and memory requirements. As these tasks were introduced into the system, the status of all available nodes specifically their real-time CPU and memory utilization was continuously monitored.

Using this data, we generated a feature vector for each incoming task. This vector captured the essential characteristics of both the task itself (such as its resource demands) and the current state of each node (like remaining CPU capacity and available memory). The trained SVM model then analyzed these vectors to predict the most suitable node for executing each task.

This prediction enabled intelligent and dynamic task allocation, allowing the system to respond efficiently to fluctuating workloads. By consistently assigning tasks to nodes with optimal available resources, the approach ensured balanced resource utilization, minimized the risk of node overloading, and improved over-all system performance.

3.5 Performance Evaluation

To comprehensively evaluate the effectiveness and efficiency of the proposed RCP-LB (Resource-Conscious Predictive Load Balancing) framework, we carried out an extensive series of performance assessments under controlled experimental conditions. The primary focus of the evaluation was on analyzing critical system performance metrics, including but not limited to response time, system throughput, transaction processing rate, and overall resource utilization factors that collectively determine the operational robustness of a load balancing system. These metrics were meticulously measured across a range of simulated workload intensities to ensure a thorough understanding of system behavior.

The performance of our machine learning-based load balancing mechanism, specifically the Support Vector Machine (SVM) model embedded within the RCP-LB framework, was benchmarked against conventional and widely used load balancing strategies such as the round-robin algorithm and the least-loaded method. The evaluation process involved a series of iterative simulation experiments where the number of simulated concurrent users was incrementally in-creased, starting from a baseline of 10 users and scaling up to a peak of 1000 users. This approach allowed us to systematically observe and quantify the scalability, adaptability, and responsiveness of the system under varying degrees of load pressure and to identify any performance bottlenecks or limitations under high-stress conditions.

4 Results and Discussion

To evaluate the performance of our task allocation system, we used several key metrics. These metrics help us understand how efficiently the system handles tasks, how well the available resources are utilized, and how quickly tasks are processed. The following equations were used to calculate average response time, throughput, transaction rate, and CPU utilization.

The average response time for processing a task can be calculated as:

$$RT = T/N \tag{1}$$

Where T is the total time taken for all tasks in milliseconds and N is the total number of tasks.

Throughput represents the number of tasks completed per unit time.

$$TP = N/T \tag{2}$$

Transaction rate can be defined as the throughput normalized per node:

$$TR = TP/N_{nodes} \tag{3}$$

Where N nodes are the number of Raspberry Pi nodes in the cluster.

CPU utilization for each node can be calculated as:

$$CU = Ux100/C \tag{4}$$

Where U means, CUP time taken by the node and C is total CPU time available, both are measured in seconds (Fig. 3).

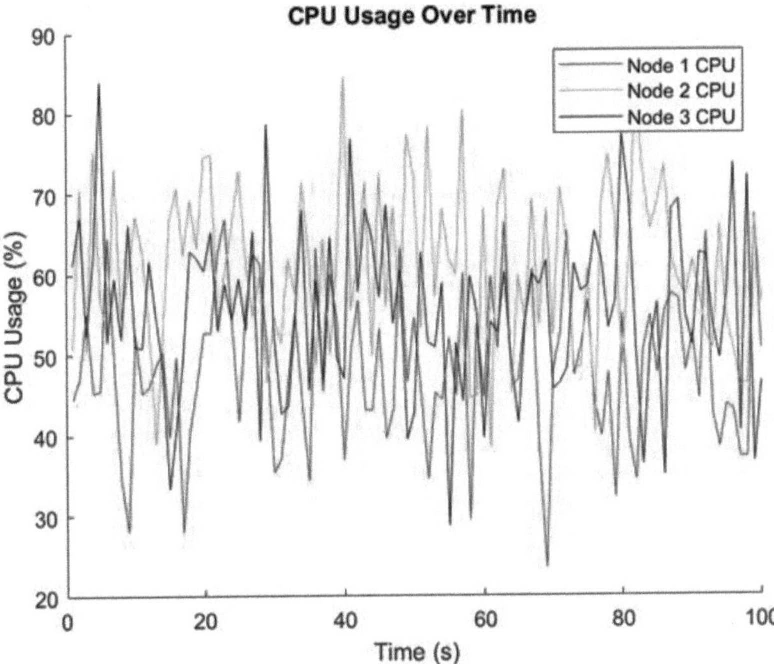

Fig. 3. CPU usage variation over time for Node 1, Node 2, and Node 3 in the Raspberry Pi cluster during simulated task execution.

The graph illustrates CPU usage over time for three different nodes in one cluster, represented by three fluctuating lines in red, green, and blue. The x-axis denotes time in seconds, while the y-axis indicates CPU usage as a percentage. The legend distinguishes each node's CPU utilization. The data demonstrates significant variations in computational load, with frequent fluctuations in usage across all three nodes. At certain points, the CPU usage of the nodes overlaps, while at other times, it diverges, reflecting the dynamic nature of workload distribution. This visualization helps analyze performance trends, potential bottlenecks, and load-balancing efficiency in a multi-node system (Fig. 4).

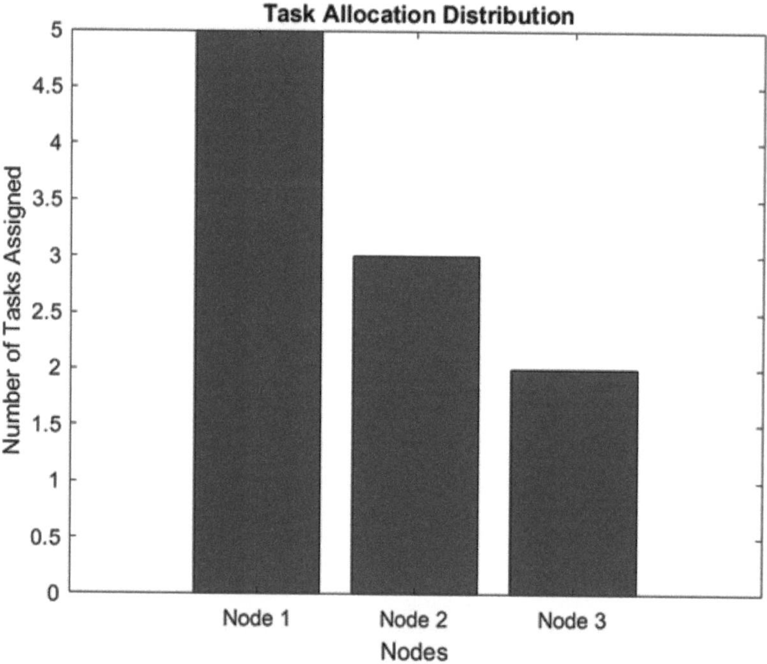

Fig. 4. Distribution of tasks allocated to each Raspberry Pi node, illustrating the output of the SVM-based task prediction model.

The bar chart visually represents the distribution of task allocation among three distinct nodes. The x-axis is labeled "Nodes," signifying the different computing units, while the y-axis, labeled "Number of Tasks Assigned," indicates how many tasks each node receives. Node 1 has the highest workload, with a total of five assigned tasks, whereas Node 2 has a moderate load with three tasks. Node 3, in contrast, has the lowest number of tasks, receiving only two. This uneven distribution suggests that some nodes are handling a significantly higher workload than others. The chart effectively highlights the imbalance in task allocation, which could indicate inefficiencies in resource management or the need for load balancing in a multi-node system.

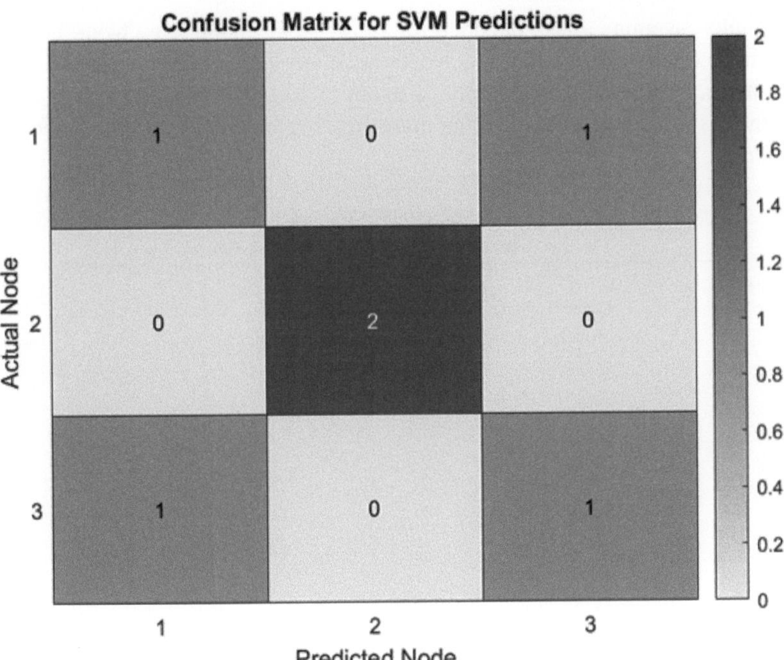

Fig. 5. The confusion matrix illustrates the performance of the SVM model in predicting task allocation to nodes, showing classification accuracy and misclassifications across three nodes.

The confusion matrix for SVM predictions visually represents the model's classification performance across three categories. The matrix indicates that class 1 was correctly predicted once but was misclassified as class 3 in another instance. Class 2 was accurately classified in both cases, demonstrating strong predictive performance for this category. Meanwhile, class 3 was correctly classified once but was also misclassified as class 1 once. The color intensity in the heatmap reflects the frequency of predictions, with darker shades indicating higher counts. The presence of misclassifications, particularly between classes 1 and 3, suggests that the model may struggle to differentiate these categories. While the overall performance appears reasonable, further refinements, such as feature selection or hyperparameter tuning, could enhance classification accuracy.

In addition to the confusion matrix (Fig. 5), the following performance metrics were calculated to provide a more complete evaluation of the SVM model:

- Accuracy: 66.67%
- Macro-Averaged Precision: 83.33%
- Macro-Averaged Recall: 66.67%
- Macro-Averaged F1-Score: 72.22%

As shown in Fig. 5, misclassifications occurred between Node 1 and Node 3. These errors may impact the performance of task scheduling, particularly if different nodes have varying computational capacities, energy consumption levels, or latency characteristics.

For example, assigning a task intended for a low-latency node (e.g., Node 1) to a high-latency node (e.g., Node 3) could increase execution time or violate quality-of-service requirements. Such misallocations may also affect load balancing and energy efficiency across the system. Therefore, reducing these errors is crucial for reliable and optimized scheduling.

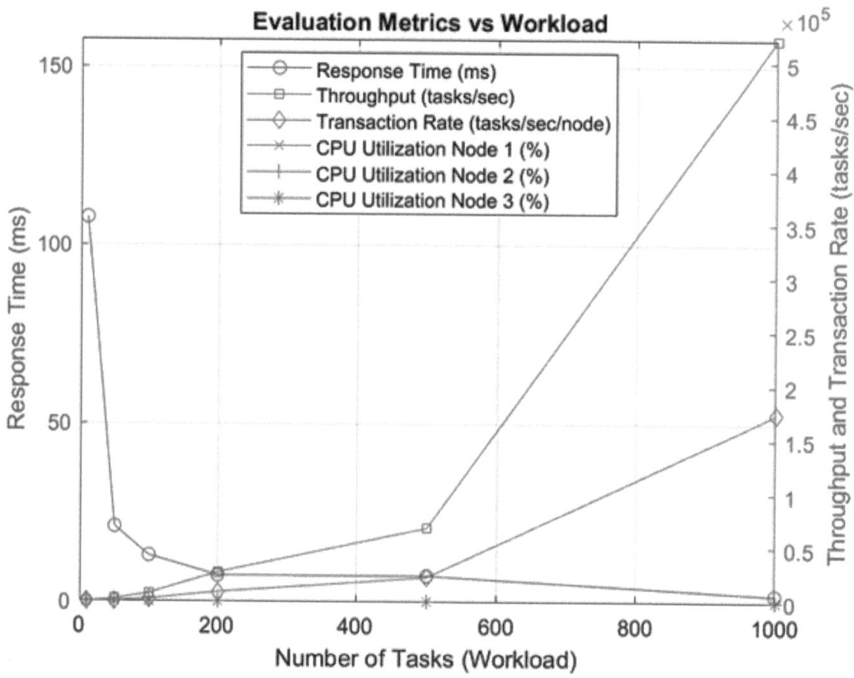

Fig. 6. Evaluation of system performance metrics against varying workloads, highlighting response time, throughput, transaction rate, and CPU utilization across three nodes.

Figure 6 illustrates the evaluation metrics of a Raspberry Pi cluster as the workload increases progressively from 10 to 1,000 tasks. As the number of tasks grows, the response time shows a significant decrease, indicating improved processing efficiency and better system responsiveness under heavier loads. Simultaneously, both throughput and transaction rate exhibit a consistent upward trend, reflecting the system's ability to handle larger volumes of tasks effectively. Additionally, CPU utilization across all three nodes increases steadily, suggesting that the cluster is utilizing its computational resources more efficiently as the workload intensifies. These observed trends emphasize the importance of implementing adaptive load balancing techniques to optimize performance, enhance scalability, and avoid potential bottlenecks in distributed computing environments.

4.1 Limitations

Although the suggested SVM-based classification method shows encouraging outcomes for a small-scale configuration with three different node types, there are a few things to keep in mind:

- Scalability: Only a three-node setup has been used to validate the current model. It has not yet been tested for performance and generalizability in more complex environments with five, ten, or more heterogeneous nodes.
- Latency Overhead: While SVMs are effective for inference on small datasets, in real-time or edge environments with high task throughput, inference latency may become non-negligible.
- Static Features: Now, the model uses static input features. Adaptability may be limited because dynamic changes in node status (such as runtime load or power state) are not recorded.
- Limitations on Model Selection: If task or node data changes over time, other models, like CNNs or LSTMs, may be able to better capture spatiotemporal dependencies. These are planned for future research but were not examined in the current study.

5 Conclusion

Experimental results clearly demonstrate that machine learning-driven load balancing mechanisms significantly outperform traditional heuristic-based approaches, especially in resource-constrained environments such as Raspberry Pi clusters. Unlike conventional static methods such as round-robin or least-loaded algorithms that allocate tasks without taking current system conditions into account, the predictive intelligence embedded in the RCP-LB framework enables it to make real-time, informed decisions regarding workload distribution. By analyzing system metrics and anticipating resource demands, RCP-LB can proactively assign tasks in a manner that minimizes bottlenecks, improves throughput, and ensures optimal utilization of available computing resources. This adaptive behavior not only enhances system responsiveness but also renders the framework highly scalable and suitable for a wide range of edge computing scenarios, where efficient task scheduling is paramount due to limitations in processing power, memory, and energy availability.

Looking ahead, future research will aim to further improve the predictive accuracy and overall performance of the load balancing model by incorporating advanced deep learning architectures such as Long Short-Term Memory (LSTM) networks and Convolutional Neural Networks (CNNs). These models are particularly effective at capturing temporal trends and complex workload patterns, allowing the system to make more nuanced and precise task allocation decisions in dynamic environments. Planned experimental extensions also include deploying the model in real-world Internet of Things (IoT) applications, where latency, energy efficiency, and real-time decision-making are critical. Emphasis will be placed on optimizing task distribution across battery-powered edge devices to achieve minimal energy consumption without sacrificing computational performance or responsiveness.

Through continuous refinement and integration of artificial intelligence in load balancing strategies, this line of research seeks to push the frontiers of distributed computing, ultimately making low-power and resource-limited platforms more robust, adaptive, and sustainable. The outcomes not only enhance the capabilities of edge devices but also contribute to the broader advancement of edge and fog computing domains, offering a smart, resilient, and future-ready solution for managing tasks in decentralized systems.

References

1. Gai, K., Qiu, M., Zhao, H., Tao, L.: Dynamic energy-aware cloudlet-based mobile cloud computing model for green computing. J. Netw. Comput. Appl. **59**, 46–54 (2016). https://doi.org/10.1016/j.jnca.2015.05.016

2. Shi, W., Cao, J., Zhang, Q., Li, Y., Xu, L.: Edge computing: vision and challenges. IEEE Internet Things J. **3**(5), 637–646 (2016). https://doi.org/10.1109/JIOT.2016.2579198

3. Al-Fuqaha, A., Guizani, M., Mohammadi, M., Aledhari, M., Ayyash, M.: Internet of Things: a survey on enabling technologies, protocols, and applications. IEEE Commun. Surv. Tutor. **17**(4), 2347–2376 (2015). https://doi.org/10.1109/COMST.2015.2444095

4. Varghese, B., Buyya, R.: Next generation cloud computing: New trends and research directions. Futur. Gener. Comput. Syst. **79**, 849–861 (2018). https://doi.org/10.1016/j.future.2017.09.020

5. Premsankar, G., Di Francesco, M., Taleb, T.: Edge computing for the Internet of Things: a case study. IEEE Internet Things J. **5**(2), 1275–1284 (2018). https://doi.org/10.1109/JIOT.2018.2805263

6. Wang, S., Zhang, X., Zhang, Y., Wang, L., Yang, J., Wang, W.: A survey on mobile edge networks: convergence of computing, caching and communications. IEEE Access. **5**, 6757–6779 (2017). https://doi.org/10.1109/ACCESS.2017.2685434

7. Taleb, T., Samdanis, K., Mada, B., Flinck, H., Dutta, S., Sabella, D.: On multiaccess edge computing: a survey of the emerging 5G network edge cloud architecture and orchestration. IEEE Commun. Surv. Tutor. **19**(3), 1657–1681 (2017). https://doi.org/10.1109/COMST.2017.2705720

8. Satyanarayanan, M.: The emergence of edge computing. Computer. **50**(1), 30–39 (2017). https://doi.org/10.1109/MC.2017.9

9. Aazam, M.: Fog computing and its role in the Internet of Things. In: Proceedings of the 1st ACM Workshop on Mobile Cloud Computing, pp. 13–16 (2015). https://doi.org/10.1145/2757384.2757397

10. Bittencourt, L.F., Diaz-Montes, J., Buyya, R., Rana, O.F., Parashar, M.: Mobility-aware application scheduling in fog computing. IEEE Cloud Comput. **4**(2), 26–35 (2018). https://doi.org/10.1109/MCC.2017.27

11. Gu, L., Zeng, D., Guo, S., Barnawi, A., Xiang, Y.: Cost efficient resource management in fog computing supported medical cyber-physical system. IEEE Trans. Emerg. Top. Comput. **5**(1), 108–119 (2015). https://doi.org/10.1109/TETC.2015.2508382

12. Mouradian, C., Naboulsi, D., Yangui, S., Glitho, R., Morrow, M., Polakos, P.: A comprehensive survey on fog computing: state-of-the-art and research challenges. IEEE Commun. Surv. Tutor. **20**(1), 416–464 (2018). https://doi.org/10.1109/COMST.2017.277115

Real-Time Sign Language Recognition Using an Attention-Driven Ensemble of Deep Models

Bhumika Karsh[1(✉)], R. H. Laskar[1], R. K. Karsh[1], and M. K. Bhuyan[2]

[1] Department of Electronics and Communication Engineering, National Institute of
Technology Silchar, Silchar, Assam, India
{bhumika21_rs,rhlaskar,ram}@ece.nits.ac.in
[2] Department of Electrical and Electronics Engineering, Indian Institute of
Technology Guwahati, Guwahati, Assam, India
mkb@iitg.ac.in

Abstract. Achieving a balance between accuracy and computational efficiency remains a key challenge in real-time sign language recognition. While deep learning approaches, particularly those based on convolutional neural networks (CNNs), have shown promise, they often suffer from high prediction variance, overfitting, and misclassification. To address these issues, we propose an ensemble framework comprising three diverse deep learning models. Notably, the third model integrates an attention mechanism that enhances the network's ability to capture subtle yet discriminative spatio-temporal features. The proposed ensemble approach was evaluated on two publicly available datasets—Massey and ISL—achieving accuracies of 98.02% and 99.86%, respectively, thereby outperforming existing state-of-the-art methods. Furthermore, we developed a real-time application prototype equipped with a user-friendly graphical user interface (GUI), demonstrating the practical viability of our system in real-world settings.

Keywords: Sign Language Recognition · Deep Learning · Ensemble Model · Attention Mechanism · Real-Time System

1 Introduction

Effective communication is still a significant challenge for people with hearing impairments, underscoring the vital role that sign language plays as the principal means of interpersonal communication [1]. One of the most important tools for the deaf and hard of hearing is sign language, which communicates through expressive gestures and movements. In fields including virtual reality, gaming, and surveillance, Hand Gesture Recognition (HGR) improves this by facilitating natural human-computer interaction [2].

Sensor-based and vision-based approaches are the two main categories of Hand Gesture Recognition (HGR) techniques. High accuracy is provided by sensor-based systems [3], but they are expensive and difficult to maintain. Because of

R. K. Karsh et al. (Eds.): SIPCOV 2025, CCIS 2848, pp. 459–473, 2026.
https://doi.org/10.1007/978-3-032-15809-3_35

its scalability and non-intrusive nature, vision-based methods—particularly those that use deep learning—are becoming more and more popular [4].

Convolutional Neural Networks (CNNs) are very useful in vision-based applications because of their superiority in picture recognition and classification [5]. CNNs can autonomously learn hierarchical features from raw input images, greatly enhancing gesture recognition systems. CNN-based models are successful, but their large memory and processing requirements make them difficult to use on devices with minimal resources. Additionally, challenges such as class imbalance, overfitting, and sensitivity to background clutter and lighting variations affect model generalizability. Prior studies have shown that simply increasing the depth or width of CNNs does not guarantee improved recognition, especially in scenarios involving subtle inter-class variations and complex environmental conditions [6].

Given these limitations, there is a growing need for robust, efficient, and accurate HGR systems that can generalize well across varied scenarios. In order to overcome current obstacles and improve performance, this study suggests an ensemble deep learning architecture that leverages the complementary strengths of multiple models. Ensemble learning is known to enhance model robustness by combining predictions from diverse classifiers, thereby reducing variance and improving overall performance.

The following summarizes this study's main contributions.

- Three pre-trained CNN models are modified and improved for the categorization of sign language gestures. Each model is optimized to capture distinct spatio-temporal features relevant to the task.
- A spatial attention module is integrated into the third model, allowing it to focus on the most discriminative regions of input frames while suppressing irrelevant or misleading information.
- Individual model outputs are integrated using a weighted ensemble technique. This fusion mechanism effectively boosts classification accuracy by leveraging model diversity.
- To demonstrate the usefulness of the suggested ensemble approach in practice, a real-time prototype with an intuitive graphical user interface is created.

The rest of the document is structured as follows. Section 3 outlines the suggested methodology, whereas Sect. 2 examines the relevant work. The experimental results and analysis are discussed in Sect. 4, followed by details of the implementation of the real-time prototype in Sect. 5. Section 6 concludes with conclusions and recommendations for further research.

2   Related Work

The accuracy, resilience, and scalability of gesture detection systems are significantly increased by deep learning models—particularly CNNs—which efficiently extract hierarchical features from input images [7].

Using Xbox Kinect data, Lin et al. [8] presented a CNN-based HGR system with an accuracy of 95.96%. Using sparse autoencoders with PCA on RGB-D pictures, Li et al. [9] achieved 99.05%. Similarly, Wadhawan et al. [7] achieved 92.83% accuracy using deep learning on the Moeslund dataset.

Further studies have enhanced CNN architectures by integrating novel training strategies or hybrid feature extraction methods. For instance, Li et al. [10] introduced a soft consideration mechanism for weight allocation in RGB-D images, achieving 98.5% accuracy. Using CNNs, Ranga et al. [11] combined deep learning with conventional learning features, attaining 97.01 Chevtchenko et al. [12] adopted a hybrid approach using both hand-crafted and deep features, while Ozcan et al. [13] focused on hyperparameter optimization, obtaining 98.09% accuracy on the Moeslund dataset.

Other contributions include finger detection-based CNN models [14]. Liu et al. [15] proposed a 19-layer CNN that achieved 99.2% accuracy. A two-stage recognition framework introduced in [16] combined segmented and RGB data, achieving an F-score of 88.10%. Rathi et al. [17] developed a two-level architecture for gesture classification using a dataset of over 12,000 images and reported 99.03% accuracy using RGB-D data. Several other studies [18–23] have employed CNNs with minimal architectural changes, mainly optimizing depth and structure for specific gesture classes. However, many of these methods are class-specific and may not generalize well to broader gesture vocabularies.

In summary, while CNN-based models have significantly advanced gesture recognition, challenges such as inter-class similarity, background clutter, lighting variations, and distance from the camera still affect performance. We offer a strong ensemble architecture that integrates several deep learning models in order to get over these restrictions. By aggregating predictions from complementary classifiers, our approach improves overall recognition accuracy and enhances resilience to real-world variability. By reducing noise and variance, ensemble learning offers a more precise and broadly applicable method for recognizing sign language.

3   Proposed Methodology

In order to increase recognition accuracy and generalization, this paper presents an ensemble deep learning architecture for gesture classification. The high-level workflow is illustrated in Fig. 1. While the proposed approach is demonstrated on hand gesture recognition (HGR), it is generalizable to other classification tasks involving visual data.

3.1   Selection of Base Learners

We employ three distinct pre-trained models—EfficientNetB7, InceptionV3, and VGG19—as base learners, chosen for their complementary architectures and strengths. EfficientNetB7 offers computational efficiency and high accuracy, InceptionV3 is known for multi-scale feature extraction, and VGG19 provides deep, densely connected layers that enhance hierarchical feature learning. Each model is customized and optimized to suit the specific challenges of hand gesture classification.

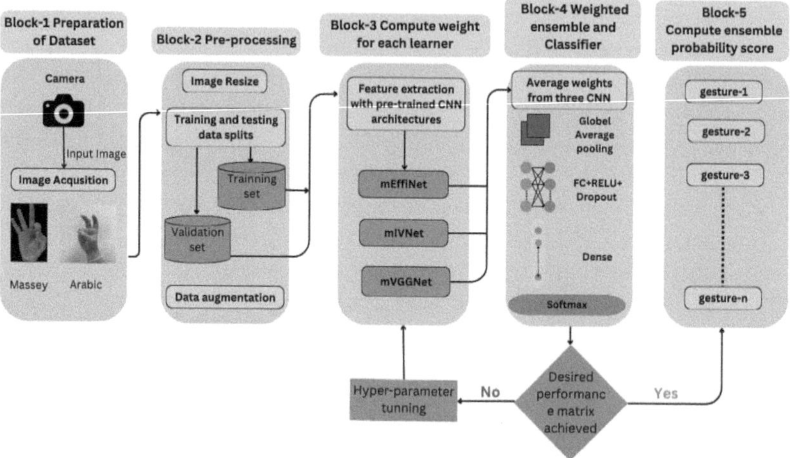

Fig. 1. Overall workflow of the proposed ensemble model.

3.2   mEffiNet: Modified EfficientNetB7

The first base model, mEffiNet, is derived from EfficientNetB7 with key optimizations aimed at reducing computational complexity. Specifically, we retain the first six blocks and discard the deeper layers—designed for ImageNet-specific features—to better align with HGR tasks. To enhance fine-grained feature extraction, a depthwise separable convolutional neural network (DSCNN) layer is included. The depthwise separable convolution (DSC) operation is defined as:

$$\bar{A}_{p,q,r} = \sum_{s,t} B_{s,t} \cdot C_{p+s-1,q+t-1,r} \tag{1}$$

where $\bar{A}$ is the output feature map, B denotes the convolution kernel, C is the input feature map, and p, q, r represent the spatial and channel indices.

The use of DSC significantly reduces parameter count and computational load. Each convolutional layer is followed by batch normalization to stabilize training and speed up convergence. Fine-tuning is performed by unfreezing layers from the 200th layer onward, allowing adaptation to HGR-specific patterns while retaining general visual knowledge from ImageNet.

3.3   mIVNet: Modified InceptionV3

The second base learner, mIVNet, is a resource-optimized variant of InceptionV3 (see Fig. 3). We utilize only the first eight Inception modules and introduce zero padding and an additional convolutional layer with 512 filters to capture gesture-relevant features. The initial four modules are frozen, and the remaining are fine-tuned based on empirical evaluation. These modifications reduce model complexity and ensure suitability for real-time or embedded deployments, without requiring segmented hand masks or background removal (Fig. 2).

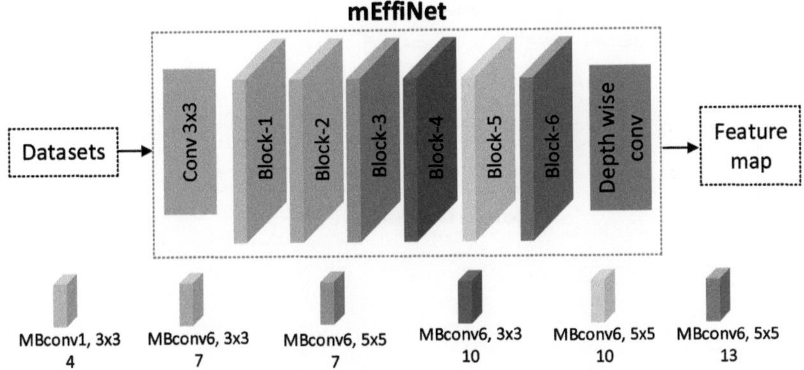

Fig. 2. Architecture of mEffiNet based on MBConv blocks.

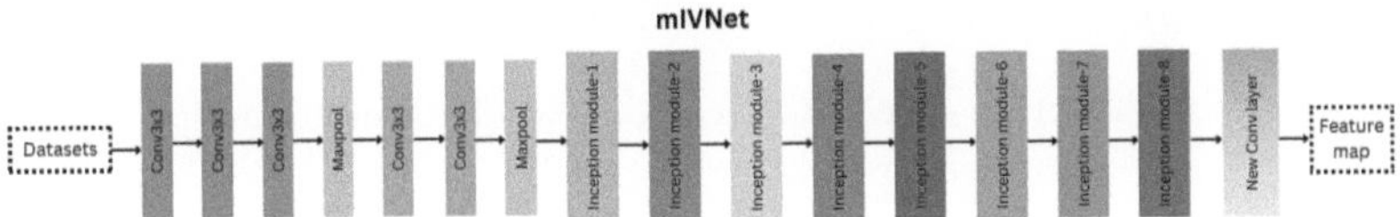

Fig. 3. Architecture of mIVNet.

3.4 mVGGNet: Attention-Enhanced VGG19

The third model, mVGGNet, enhances the classic VGG19 architecture by integrating a spatial attention mechanism (SAm), as shown in Fig. 4. This module highlights discriminative regions in the input image while suppressing irrelevant features.

Let the input image be $Y = \{y_i^c\}_{i=1}^n$, where $y_i^c \in \mathbb{R}^{W \times H \times C}$, with $W = H = 224$ and $C = 3$. The feature extractor (FE) and attention module (SAm) are defined as:

$$FE_{\theta_{FE}}(y_i^c), \quad SAm_{\theta_{SAm}}(y_i^c)$$

The final attention-weighted feature representation is:

$$F(y_i^c) = FE_{\theta_{FE}}(y_i^c) \circ SAm_{\theta_{SAm}}(y_i^c) \tag{2}$$

where $\circ$ denotes element-wise multiplication. The attention module uses locally connected layers (unshared convolutional filters) to preserve spatial consistency and emphasize salient areas.

3.5 Model Weight Calculation

After training, each model's validation accuracy acc_i is used to compute a weight γ_i for weighted voting. The normalization ensures that the least accurate model still contributes to the ensemble:

$$\delta = \min\left(2, [\text{acc}_i]_{i=1}^n\right) \tag{3}$$

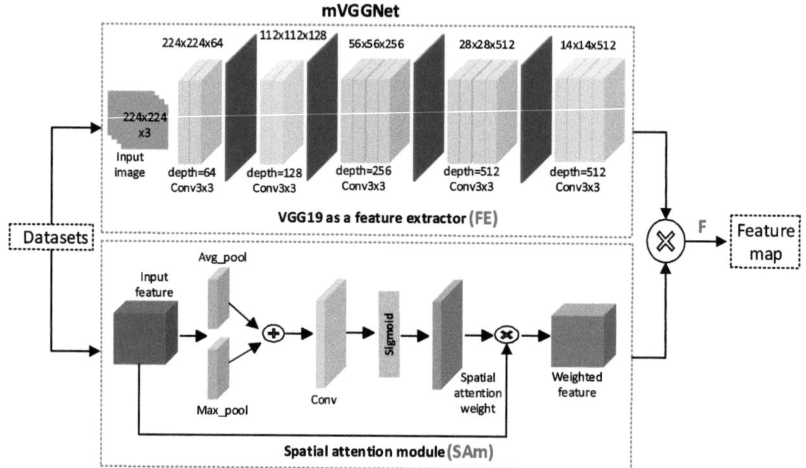

Fig. 4. Architecture of mVGGNet with spatial attention mechanism.

$$\gamma_i = \mathrm{acc}_i - \delta + 1, \quad i = 1, \ldots, n \tag{4}$$

This approach prevents the exclusion of weaker models and ensures diverse perspectives during ensemble prediction.

3.6   Weighted Ensemble Decision

The final ensemble prediction combines the outputs of all models using a weighted summation of their class probability vectors $[P_k]$:

$$\text{Predicted Class}_{(i,\text{ensemble})} = \arg\max_k \left(\sum_{j=1}^{m} (\beta_j \cdot [P_k]^{(i,j)}) \right) \tag{5}$$

here:

- m depicts the number of models,
- β_j is the model weight j,
- $[P_k]^{(i,j)}$ is the probability assigned to class k for sample i by model j,
- k ranges from 1 to nc, the number of gesture classes (Fig. 5).

4   Results and Discussion

4.1   Implementation Details

The primary motivation behind the development of our proposed model is to establish a robust and generalized classification system for hand gesture recognition (HGR), independent of the dataset or domain. Two distinct hand gesture

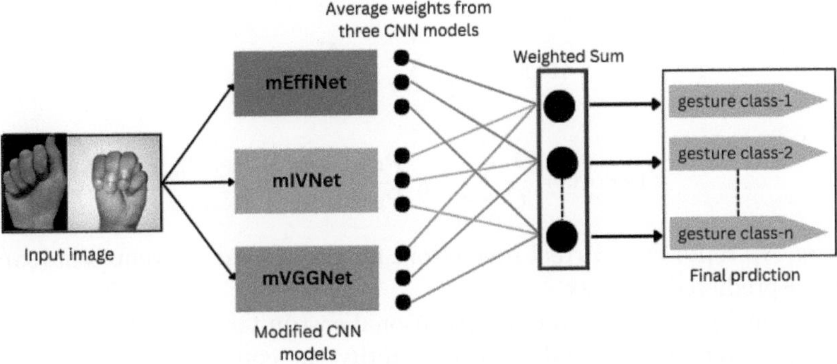

Fig. 5. Proposed weighted ensemble architecture for gesture classification.

datasets, each divided into 70% training and 30% testing sets, were used in the trials to evaluate the model's performance. We implemented a weighted ensemble model incorporating three prominent convolutional neural network (CNN) architectures: EfficientNetB7, InceptionV3, and VGG19.

4.2   Dataset Description

Massey Dataset. Barczak et al. [24] introduced a dataset in 2011 for American Sign Language (ASL), comprising 36 distinct hand gestures. The dataset includes 2,524 images captured under diverse lighting conditions (e.g., top, bottom, left, right, and diffuse), performed by five different individuals. It has 26 English letters (A–Z) and 10 numbers (0–9). Certain gestures in this dataset are visually similar or identical, such as "O" and "zero" or "V", "two", and "K", increasing classification complexity.

ISL Dataset. Due to the unavailability of a standardized ISL dataset, images were curated from online resources, as described in [25]. This dataset contains 200 images for each ISL letter, excluding 'J' and 'Z', resulting in a total of 4,962 images. Figure 1 illustrates examples of the ISL gestures used.

4.3   Evaluation Metrics

We used Accuracy, Precision, Recall, and F1-score, which were summated across all classes, to assess the model's performance:

$$\text{Accuracy} = \frac{\sum_{i=1}^{C} N_{ii}}{\sum_{i=1}^{C} \sum_{j=1}^{C} N_{ij}} \tag{6}$$

$$\text{Precision} = \frac{1}{C} \sum_{i=1}^{C} \frac{N_{ii}}{\sum_{j=1}^{C} N_{ji}} \tag{7}$$

$$\text{Recall} = \frac{1}{C} \sum_{i=1}^{C} \frac{N_{ii}}{\sum_{j=1}^{C} N_{ij}} \tag{8}$$

$$\text{F1-score} = \frac{1}{C} \sum_{i=1}^{C} 2 \times \frac{\text{Precision}_i \times \text{Recall}_i}{\text{Precision}_i + \text{Recall}_i} \tag{9}$$

Here, N_{ii} represents correct predictions for class i, and N_{ij} represents samples of class i predicted as class j.

Additionally, we report the computational cost in terms of FLOPs (Floating-Point Operations per Second), which quantify the complexity of deep learning models:

$$\text{FLOPS} = \frac{\text{Total Floating-Point Operations}}{\text{Execution Time}} \tag{10}$$

4.4 Hyperparameter Tuning

Hyperparameters have a significant impact on model performance. A batch size of 16 was chosen for this investigation in order to strike a balance between accuracy and efficiency. The Adam optimizer was used to train the model across 50 epochs with a learning rate of 0.0001. The multi-class classification goal was met by using ReLU activation and categorical cross-entropy loss.

4.5 Performance Analysis

The performance of individual models and the proposed ensemble model is summarized in Table 1. All sub-models achieved over 90% accuracy, with the weighted ensemble significantly outperforming them. Some misclassifications occurred due to high visual similarity among certain gestures such as 'O' vs 'Zero' and 'V' vs 'Two'.

Table 1. Training (T.A.), Validation (V.A.) accuracies, and model weights γ_i

Network	Massey Dataset			ISL Dataset		
	T.A.	V.A.	γ_i	T.A.	V.A.	γ_i
mEffiNet	98.11%	97.22%	5.61	99.86%	99.59%	9.17
mIVNet	98.59%	97.13%	7.14	98.71%	97.48%	7.43
mVGGNet	95.92%	94.44%	4.42	98.84%	97.36%	7.31
Ensemble	**99.85%**	**98.02%**	-	**100%**	**99.86%**	-

4.6 Grad-CAM Visualization

Key locations affecting the model's categorization judgments were highlighted using Grad-CAM images (Fig. 6). These heatmaps validate that the model focuses on relevant gesture regions.

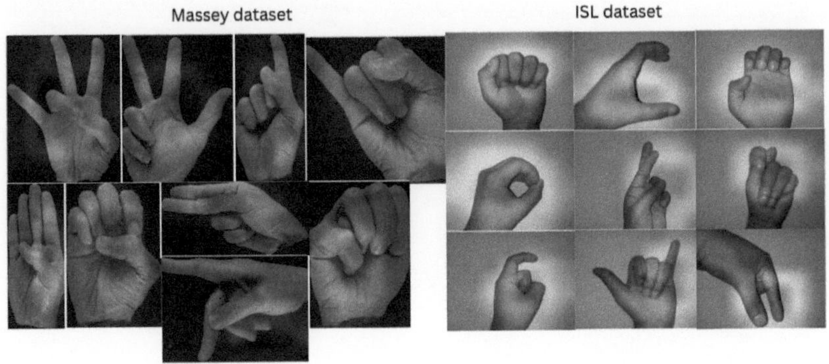

Fig. 6. Grad-CAM visualizations for selected gesture classes.

4.7 Comparative Evaluation

Table 2 compares our approach with existing methods. The proposed ensemble significantly outperforms prior works, including CNN [19], ExtriDeNet [26], RBI-2RCNN [27]and LNAP [28] on Massey; and TOPSIS [29], mRMR-PSO [25], and E-WOA-Deep CNN [30] on ISL.

Table 2. Comparison with recent methods

Dataset	Method	Reference	Accuracy (%)
Massey	CNN	[19]	73.94
	ExtriDeNet	[26]	79.17
	RBI-2RCNN	[27]	89.70
	LNAP	[28]	93.00
	Proposed Ensemble	-	**98.02**
ISL	TOPSIS	[29]	86.85
	mRMR-PSO	[25]	90.20
	E-WOA-Deep CNN	[30]	96.76
	Proposed Ensemble	-	**99.86**

4.8   Training Accuracy and Loss Curves

Figure 7 shows the training and validation curves for accuracy and loss. These demonstrate stable convergence and improved generalization across both datasets.

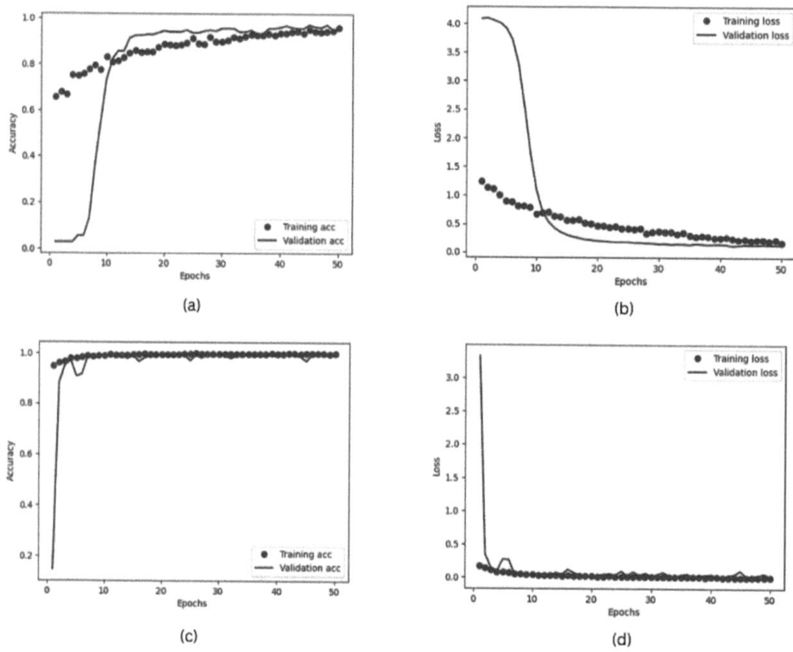

Fig. 7. Training and validation accuracy/loss plots for Massey and ISL datasets.

4.9   Computational Load

Table 3 outlines memory usage, parameter counts, inference times, and FLOPs for all models. Despite slightly higher resource usage, the ensemble model delivers superior performance with acceptable computational cost, supported by modern hardware.

4.10   Ablation Study

To evaluate the effectiveness of the proposed modifications introduced in our models, an ablation study was conducted. This analysis compares the performance of the modified architectures—mEffiNet, mIVNet, and mVGGNet—with their respective baseline counterparts: EfficientNetB7, InceptionV3, and VGG19.

Table 3. Computational cost analysis of the models

Model	Memory (MB)	Parameters (M)	Inference Time (ms)	FLOPs (G)
EfficientNetB7	770.01	63.812	5.659	0.993
mEffiNet	**493.77**	**40.764**	**4.721**	**0.860**
InceptionV3	179.3	23.85	6.9	0.658
mIVNet	**133.64**	**16.5**	**1.30**	**0.493**
VGG19	549	143.7	4.3	0.448
mVGGNet	**118.77**	**3.21**	**0.53**	**0.635**
Ensemble	**692.3**	**57**	**5.683**	**1.070**

The experimental results, summarized in Table 4, clearly indicate that our proposed models consistently outperform the baseline architectures on both the Massey and ISL datasets.

Specifically, mEffiNet demonstrated an improvement of 1.98% on the Massey dataset and 1.40% on the ISL dataset over EfficientNetB7. Similarly, mIVNet surpassed InceptionV3 by 5.46% and 6.47% on the Massey and ISL datasets, respectively. Lastly, mVGGNet showed performance gains of 4.76% and 5.07% over VGG19 on the respective datasets. Notably, the baseline models were also fine-tuned on the same datasets to ensure a fair comparison. These consistent improvements validate the efficacy of our architectural enhancements and confirm their capability in achieving superior gesture recognition performance.

Table 4. Ablation study comparing baseline and modified models on the Massey and ISL datasets

Model	Massey Accuracy (%)	ISL Accuracy (%)
EfficientNetB7	95.24	98.19
mEffiNet	**97.22**	**99.59**
InceptionV3	91.67	91.02
mIVNet	**97.13**	**97.48**
VGG19	89.68	92.29
mVGGNet	**94.44**	**97.36**

5 Real-Time Sign Language to Text Conversion

Sign language serves as a vital visual gestural communication system for individuals with hearing or speech impairments. However, for those unfamiliar with sign language, communication remains a significant challenge, creating a barrier between signers and non-signers. Bridging this gap necessitates the development of real-time translation systems that can interpret sign language gestures into readable text.

Building on our deep learning models' impressive performance, we created a real-time system for recognizing sign language and translating gestures into English text. The system was implemented in Python 3.6 using the Keras and TensorFlow frameworks and is equipped with a user-friendly graphical user interface (GUI), as illustrated in Fig. 8.

Upon launching the application, the interface initializes a window titled *Real-Time Sign Language Recognition*, allowing users to input gesture images in real-time. Once an image is captured or selected, the model processes it and generates a classification output. A dialog box then appears, displaying the predicted class label to the user. The model demonstrates high accuracy in real-time predictions, even under varying input conditions, confirming the robustness of the proposed architecture.

This system acts as a real-time interpreter, enabling effective communication between signers and non-signers in everyday settings. It holds practical relevance for use in educational, medical, and public environments, contributing meaningfully to inclusive communication technology.

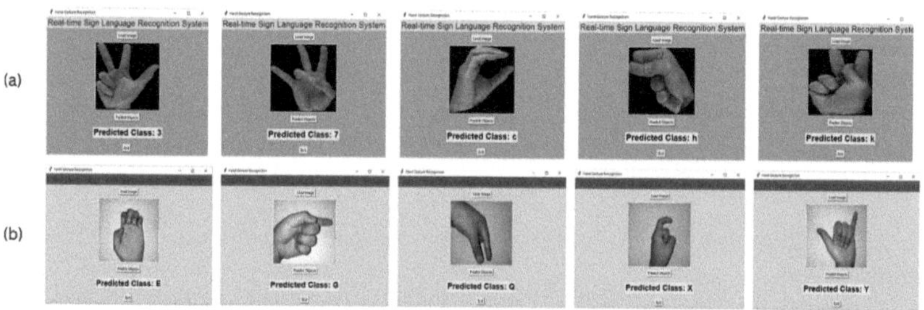

Fig. 8. GUI-based real-time sign language recognition: (a) Massey dataset gestures ('3', '7', 'C', 'H', 'K'); (b) ISL dataset gestures ('E', 'G', 'Q', 'X', 'Y').

6   Conclusion and Future Work

In order to address the difficulties of real-time sign language recognition, we presented a strong ensemble learning architecture in this work that incorporates three optimized deep neural networks. The architecture is appropriate for real-world implementation since it strikes a balance between high classification accuracy and computational efficiency. To improve the ability to differentiate between gestures that are visually identical, one of the models incorporates an attention mechanism.

We conducted extensive tests on two publicly accessible datasets, Massey ASL and ISL, to validate the suggested approach. The outcomes show that our strategy achieves great accuracy with economical resource use, outperforming a number of current approaches.

We created a real-time sign language recognition system with a graphical user interface (GUI) that converts identified motions into English text as a concrete application. This prototype system holds promise for enhancing communication accessibility, particularly in educational and assistive settings where sign language interpretation is essential.

For future work, we plan to extend our system to support dynamic hand gesture recognition using video sequences, which poses additional challenges such as temporal modeling and motion tracking. Furthermore, we intend to explore multimodal fusion techniques—integrating visual, motion, and possibly sensor-based inputs—to further enhance the accuracy, robustness, and generalizability of the system in real-world environments.

Acknowledgements. The authors sincerely appreciate the generous support provided by the Anusandhan National Research Foundation (ANRF). This research was funded through the Core Research Grant (CRG/2022/005850), for which the authors are deeply grateful.

References

1. N'unez-Marcos, A., Perez-de-Vi naspre, O., Labaka, G.: A survey on sign language machine translation. Expert Syst. Appl. **213**, 118993 (2023)
2. Jiang, D., et al.: Gesture recognition based on binocular vision. Clust. Comput. **22**, 13261–13271 (2019)
3. Yang, L., et al.: Hand rehabilitation training system integrating non-contact and contact triboelectric nanogenerators for enhanced gesture and handwriting recognition. Nano Energy **134**, 110591 (2025)
4. Qi, J., Ma, L., Cui, Z., Yu, Y.: Computer vision-based hand gesture recognition for human-robot interaction: a review. Complex Intell. Syst. **10**(1), 1581–1606 (2024)
5. Zhao, X., Wang, L., Zhang, Y., Han, X., Deveci, M., Parmar, M.: A review of convolutional neural networks in computer vision. Artif. Intell. Rev. **57**(4), 99 (2024)
6. Li, X.: Exploring the effect of depth and width of CNN models on binary classification of dogs and cats. Appl. Comput. Eng. **47**(1), 147–158 (2024)
7. Wadhawan, A., Kumar, P.: Deep learning-based sign language recognition system for static signs. Neural Comput. Appl. **32**(12), 7957–7968 (2020). https://doi.org/10.1007/s00521-019-04691-y
8. Lin, H.-I., Hsu, M.-H., Chen, W.-K.: Human hand gesture recognition using a convolution neural network. In: IEEE CASE, pp. 1038–1043 (2014)
9. Li, S.-Z., Yu, B., Wu, W., Su, S.-Z., Ji, R.-R.: Feature learning based on SAE-PCA network for human gesture recognition in RGBD images. Neurocomputing **151**, 565–573 (2015)
10. Li, Y., Wang, X., Liu, W., Feng, B.: Deep attention network for joint hand gesture localization and recognition using static RGB-D images. Inf. Sci. **441**, 66–78 (2018)
11. Ranga, V., Yadav, N., Garg, P.: American sign language fingerspelling using hybrid discrete wavelet transform-gabor filter and convolutional neural network. J. Eng. Sci. Technol. **13**(9), 2655–2669 (2018)

12. Chevtchenko, S.F., Vale, R.F., Macario, V., Cordeiro, F.R.: A convolutional neural network with feature fusion for real-time hand posture recognition. Appl. Soft Comput. **73**, 748–766 (2018)

13. Ozcan, T., Basturk, A.: Transfer learning-based convolutional neural networks with heuristic optimization for hand gesture recognition. Neural Comput. Appl. **31**(12), 8955–8970 (2019). https://doi.org/10.1007/s00521-019-04427-y

14. Neethu, P.S., Suguna, R., Sathish, D.: An efficient method for human hand gesture detection and recognition using deep learning convolutional neural networks. Soft. Comput. **24**(20), 15239–15248 (2020). https://doi.org/10.1007/s00500-020-04860-5

15. Liu, P., Li, X., Cui, H., Li, S., Yuan, Y.: Hand gesture recognition based on single-shot multibox detector deep learning. Mob. Inf. Syst. **2019**, 1–7 (2019)

16. Dadashzadeh, A., Tavakoli Targhi, A., Tahmasbi, M., Mirmehdi, M.: HGR-Net: a fusion network for hand gesture segmentation and recognition. IET Comput. Vis. **13**(8), 700–707 (2019)

17. Rathi, P., Gupta, R.K., Agarwal, S., Shukla, A.: Sign language recognition using resnet50 deep neural network architecture. In: 5th International Conference on NGCT (2020)

18. Siddique, S., Islam, S., Neon, E.E., Sabbir, T., Naheen, I.T., Khan, R.: Deep learning-based Bangla sign language detection with an edge device. Intell. Syst. Appl. **18**, 200224 (2023)

19. Pinto, R.F., Borges, C.D.B., Almeida, A.M.A., Paula, I.C.: Static hand gesture recognition based on convolutional neural networks. J. Electr. Comput. Eng. **2019**, 1–12 (2019)

20. Lee, M., Bae, J.: Real-time gesture recognition in the view of repeating characteristics of sign languages. IEEE Trans. Industr. Inf. **18**(12), 8818–8828 (2022)

21. Karsh, B., Laskar, R.H., Karsh, R.K., Bhuyan, M.K.: SCAI-net: spatial-channel attention Inception-net for Hand Gesture Recognition for deaf community medical issues. Procedia Comput. Sci. **258**, 2180–2189 (2025)

22. Rubin Bose, S., Sathiesh Kumar, V.: In-situ identification and recognition of multi-hand gestures using optimized deep residual network. J. Intell. Fuzzy Syst. **41**(6), 6983–6997 (2021)

23. Karsh, B., Laskar, R.H., Karsh, R.K.: mXception and dynamic image for hand gesture recognition. Neural Comput. Appl. **36**(15), 8281–8300 (2024)

24. Barczak, A.L.C., Reyes, N.H., Abastillas, M., Piccio, A., Susnjak, T.: A new 2D static hand gesture colour image dataset for ASL gestures. Massey University (2011)

25. Bansal, S.R., Wadhawan, S., Goel, R.: mrmr-pso: a hybrid feature selection technique with a multiobjective approach for sign language recognition. Arab. J. Sci. Eng. **47**(8), 10365–10380 (2022)

26. Bhaumik, G., Verma, M., Govil, M.C., Vipparthi, S.K.: ExtriDeNet: an intensive feature extrication deep network for hand gesture recognition. Vis. Comput. **38**(11), 3853–3866 (2022)

27. Sahoo, J.P., Sahoo, S.P., Ari, S., Patra, S.K.: RBI-2RCNN: residual block intensity feature using a two-stage residual convolutional neural network for static hand gesture recognition. SIViP **16**(8), 2019–2027 (2022)

28. Bahuguna, A., Namchyo, S.B.T., Chaudhary, D.K., Bhaumik, G., Govil, M.C.: Local neighborhood average pattern: a handcrafted feature descriptor for hand gesture recognition. In: ICSCCC 2023, pp. 756–761 (2023)

29. Joshi, G., Singh, S., Vig, R.: Taguchi-TOPSIS based HOG parameter selection for complex background sign language recognition. J. Vis. Commun. Image Represent. **71**, 102834 (2020)
30. Kowdiki, M., Khaparde, A.: Adaptive Hough transform with optimized deep learning followed by dynamic time warping for hand gesture recognition. Multimed. Tools Appl. 1–32 (2022)

Author Index

MIX
Papier aus verantwortungsvollen Quellen
Paper from responsible sources
FSC® C105338

If you have any concerns about our products,
you can contact us on
ProductSafety@springernature.com

In case Publisher is established outside the EU,
the EU authorized representative is:
Springer Nature Customer Service Center GmbH
Europaplatz 3, 69115 Heidelberg, Germany

Printed by Libri Plureos GmbH
in Hamburg, Germany